To Bill,

On your Birthday,

Wishing you every blessing

with love and best

Wishes

Joan and Anthony

July 1976.

Psalm 91.

'A ship in Harbour is safe,
But that is not what
Ships are designed for.'

Never loose your zeal, your
vision, your love of the lord
Bill, continue to strive in
His service — Be a flag-ship.
Bill, and encourage others
to serve our lord!
Hold fast to The Word and
the principles we grew to
love — and You'll see Great
Things happen. Bless His Name
Your Brother in Christ
TONY.

C. H. SPURGEON AUTOBIOGRAPHY

C. H. SPURGEON AUTOBIOGRAPHY

Volume 1: The Early Years

1834–1859

A revised edition,
originally compiled by Susannah Spurgeon
and Joseph Harrald

THE BANNER OF TRUTH TRUST

THE BANNER OF TRUTH TRUST
3 *Murrayfield Road, Edinburgh* EH12 6 EL
78b *Chiltern Street, London* WIM IPS
P.O. Box 652, *Carlisle, Pa* 17013, *U.S.A.*

*

*Autobiography first published
in four volumes,* 1897-1900

*This revised edition published by
the Banner of Truth Trust in two volumes*

Volume 1 *first published* 1962
Reprinted 1973

© *The Banner of Truth Trust*

ISBN 0 85151 076 0

This book is set in 11 *on* 12 *Garamond and printed in
Great Britain by Billing &* Sons Limited, Guildford and London*

"*We want again Luthers, Calvins, Bunyans, Whitefields, men fit to mark eras, whose names breathe terror in our foemen's ears. We have dire need of such. Whence will they come to us? They are the gifts of Jesus Christ to the Church, and will come in due time. He has power to give us back again a golden age of preachers, a time as fertile of great divines and mighty ministers as was the Puritan age, and when the good old truth is once more preached by men whose lips are touched as with a live coal from off the altar, this shall be the instrument in the hand of the Spirit for bringing about a great and thorough revival of religion in the land.*

"*I do not look for any other means of converting men beyond the simple preaching of the gospel and the opening of men's ears to hear it. The moment the Church of God shall despise the pulpit, God will despise her. It has been through the ministry that the Lord has always been pleased to revive and bless His Churches.*"

C. H. S.

ACKNOWLEDGMENT

The Publishers acknowledge with gratitude the kind permission given by the Principal of Spurgeon's College, Dr. G. R. Beasley-Murray, for access to Spurgeon's own albums of family photographs and letters, which have provided the illustrations in this volume.

CONTENTS

ILLUSTRATIONS

xi

PREFACE

It is not easy to explain why C. H. Spurgeon's Autobiography, first published during the years 1897–1900, has fallen into such long neglect. Publishers have passed by it, and the majority of evangelical Christians have probably not even been aware of its existence. Biographers have indeed quarried some of the riches from the mines of this classic and included them in the popular lives of C. H. Spurgeon which have appeared during this century, but a good deal was left untouched and in consequence there are aspects of Spurgeon which are little known to the present generation. Moreover, even the passages which have been extracted and retold can at best be poor substitutes for the original, for who would want to see a copy of a Rembrandt or a Constable if he could admire the master's own work? There is a tone in the Autobiography (an unction, to give it its spiritual name) and there are depths and shades, lights and colours, which no hand but the author's could have imparted to the record of his life. Nevertheless, the fact remains that the Autobiography has not been reprinted; it has found no place among popular evangelical literature, and it has been little read for many years.

One reason for the neglect of the Autobiography undoubtedly lies in the cumbrous bulk of that first edition which appeared in four large quarto volumes. As a work of publishing art it could be admired at leisure amidst the spacious days of Victoria, but it is not the format that any publisher would choose to meet the wishes of the present age. As everyone knows, large books, like long sermons, are decidedly out of fashion and so the monumental size of the original, far from being an attraction to the grandchildren of Victorians, has proved an effective deterrent in the way of its republication.

A consciousness of the timeliness of a reprint of the Autobiography, to strengthen the hands and inspire the hearts of Christians at this critical period in our nation's spiritual history, led the present publishers to examine the original to see if there was any alternative to a major abridgment. We felt that rather than undertake the latter the Autobiography would be better left alone.

It was soon evident that the four volumes naturally fall into two parts, the second volume terminating at 1859 with the close of Spurgeon's historic ministry at the Surrey Gardens Music Hall. This section covering the epoch of his early years could thus be reprinted on its own without dislocating the record of his life. The remainder (consisting of Volumes III and IV of the original) would commence at the natural starting point of his ministry in the Metropolitan Tabernacle, and it is hoped that this may also be reprinted at a later date.

Confining our attention, therefore, to the two volumes it was then found that some chapters could be omitted without loss to the autobiographical sequence. To explain how this was possible, it is necessary to state how the Autobiography was originally compiled. The work was not published in Spurgeon's lifetime, indeed it was far from complete by the time of the preacher's death in 1892. In the rare moments of his leisure—mainly, says his wife, "in the bright sunshine at Mentone"—he would write down some portions of his life and conclude with the exclamation, "There's another chapter for my Autobiography!" But this work of pleasure was never given priority over the constant literary burden that was expressed in his weekly printed sermons, his monthly magazine and his various other writings. For him the Word of God was always supreme and it was characteristic of the man that when he died at Mentone at the age of fifty-seven he was occupied with a commentary on the Gospel of Matthew. The completion of the Autobiography therefore fell to his wife and private secretary. In bringing the work to its final shape they made a number of additions to Spurgeon's own chapters and added further chapters. It is this which has enabled us to shorten the work by omitting some of the editors' material while retaining, practically in full, what Spurgeon wrote.

The present reprint is therefore far from being a general abridgment; it includes virtually all the biographical material of the first half of the original. The only biographical chapter omitted is the one entitled "First Visit to Scotland", which is partially covered by Mrs. Spurgeon in the chapter on "Love, Courtship and Marriage". The non-biographical material omitted consists of such things as sermon outlines, newspaper opinions, a youthful essay by Spurgeon on "Popery", and some letters.

Owing to the unsystematic way in which Spurgeon wrote his Autobiography, and the irregular times he had for doing it, there is a certain lack of continuity between its various sections. The present editors have tried to remedy this by rearranging the material in some parts and inserting new prefaces to several chapters; they have also occasionally supplied additional information by footnotes which are marked "P". In several instances short chapters have been incorporated into larger ones and two or more chapters of the original have been combined under a new heading. Except where entire chapters are compiled by his wife and private secretary, material which was added by them has been put into square brackets. There may well be other reasons, beyond publishing difficulties, which have contributed to the disappearance of this work, but what is certain is that these pages bear glorious testimony to the converting power of the Gospel and to the blessing of a life lived in fellowship with the Father and the Son. What is more needed today than a recovery of faith in these two realities? This volume is sent out with the prayer that the Holy Spirit will use these pages to that end.

The Publishers,
78b Chiltern Street, W.1.
18th September, 1962.

PEDIGREE OF THE SPURGEON (SPURGEN, SPURGIN,

The Spurgeon family was seated within a radius of five miles of the village of Halstead as early as 1465 (5 Edw
of Halstead, wherein the names of John and Thomas Spirjon appear as witnesses to a conveyance of land in that plac
Bourchier's College to William Parr, Marquis of Northampton, dated June 24, 1551, we find these words: " Rent of
From the earliest Court Roll of the Manor of Dynes in the parish of Great Maplestead, dated May 19, 1575, we learn

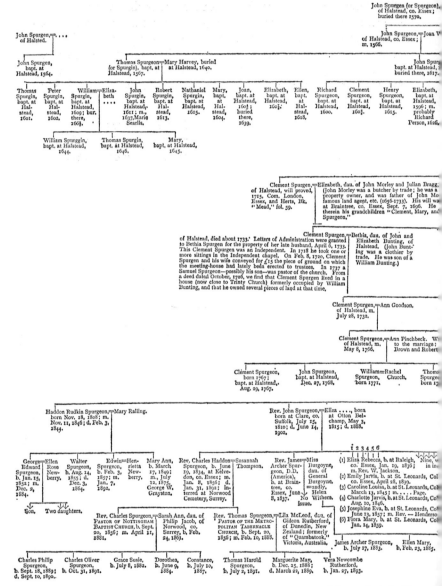

This is a photo-litho reproduction of the genealogical table appea

7.), as is proved from a deed dated December 2 of that year at Great Maplestead, three and a half miles north-east lst from the Patent Roll of 5 Edward VI. (now in the Public Record Office), being the grant of the Chantry called nement and parcel of land, parcel of Fitzjohes aforesaid in the tenure of Richard Spurgeon " (yearly 33s. 4d.). he Thomas Spurgeon was the tenant of the manor. Of this family was undoubtedly—

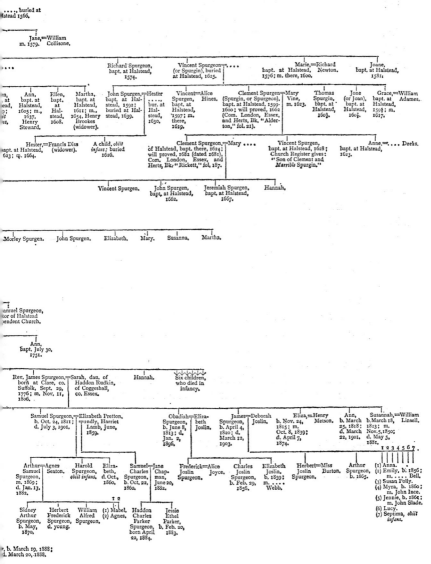

he Spurgeon Family by W. Miller Higgs (London, 1906).

B

CHRONOLOGICAL SUMMARY

1834	June 19	Born at Kelvedon, Essex.
1835		Parents move to Colchester.
		Goes to live with grandparents at Stambourne.
1840		Returns home to Colchester.
1848		Goes to St. Augustine's College, Maidstone.
1849	August 17	Becomes pupil-assistant at Newmarket, Cambridgeshire.
	September 10	First public speech—missionary meeting.
1850	January 6	Converted at Colchester.
	May 3	Baptized at Isleham Village, Cambridgeshire.
	August	Removes to Mr. Leeding's School, Cambridge.
		Begins preaching—Teversham.
1851	October	Becomes pastor of Waterbeach Baptist Chapel.
1853		Publication of Waterbeach Tracts.
	December 18	Preaches at New Park Street Chapel, London.
1854	April 28	Accepts pastorate of New Park Street.
1855	January	First sermon in "New Park Street Pulpit" published.
	January	Earliest attack in the Press appears.
	February 11	First preaches at Exeter Hall, London.
	July	First visit to Scotland.
1856	January 8	Marries Susannah Thompson.
	June	Metropolitan Tabernacle Building Committee formed.
	September 20	Twin sons born.
	October 19	Surrey Gardens Music Hall disaster.
	November 23	Recommences services in Music Hall.
1857	October 7	Preaches at the Crystal Palace.
1858	August	First visit to Ireland.
1859	August 16	Foundation stone of Metropolitan Tabernacle laid.
	December 11	Last service in Surrey Gardens Music Hall.

C. H. SPURGEON
The Early Years

Charles Haddon Spurgeon was born on June 19, 1834, in the little Essex village of Kelvedon. He had no memories of the place, for he was but ten months old when the family moved to Colchester, and four months later the little boy was taken to live with his grandparents in the heart of the countryside at Stambourne—a few miles west of the road between Halstead and Haverhill. There he remained until he was about five and thus his earliest recollections are of the place where his grandfather, James Spurgeon (1776–1864), had ministered since 1810.

Although the human reason why Spurgeon's infancy was spent with his grandparents is obscure, the Divine purpose is not. The old pastor of Stambourne "seemed to live as one of the last representatives of the Old Dissent. In all his tastes, manners, and aspirations, the veteran belonged to a generation which had long since passed away." The old divinity preached in Commonwealth days when Essex was a Puritan stronghold was still loved in Stambourne when Queen Victoria ascended the throne, for the congregation there "was a rare instance of Puritan fervour burning on through two centuries." It was as though God had preserved the seventeenth-century manse and "Meeting House" at Stambourne until the witness they had faithfully preserved was passed on to one who was appointed to declare it again to the nation.

Of the many stories told of these early days at Stambourne it is not always clear whether the incidents occurred during that first stay of five years, or in some of the long holidays which the young lad subsequently spent there.

Chapter 1

Childhood at Stambourne

A DRAWING of the old manse at Stambourne[1] has far more charms for me than for any of my readers, but I hope that their generous kindness to the writer will cause them to be interested in it. Here my venerable grandfather lived for more than fifty years, and reared his rather numerous family. In its earlier days it must have been a very remarkable abode for a dissenting teacher; a clear evidence that either he had an estate of his own, or that those about him had large hearts and pockets. It was in all respects a gentleman's mansion of the olden times. The house has been supplanted by one which, I doubt not, is most acceptable to the excellent minister who occupies it, but to me it can never be one-half so dear as the revered old home in which I spent some of my earliest years. It is true the old parsonage had developed devotional tendencies, and seemed inclined to prostrate its venerable form, and therefore it might have fallen down of itself if it had not been removed by the builder; but, somehow, I wish it had kept up for ever and ever. I could have cried, "Builders, spare that home. Touch not a single tile, or bit of plaster," but its hour was come, and so the earthly house was happily dissolved, to be succeeded by a more enduring fabric.

It was a very noble parsonage, with its eight windows in front, although at least three, and I think four, of these were plastered up, and painted black, and then marked out in lines to imitate glass. They were not such very bad counterfeits, or the photograph would betray this. Some of us can remember the window tax, which seemed to regard light as a Latin commodity—*lux*, and therefore a luxury, and as such to be taxed. So much was paid on each aperture for the admission of light, but the minister's small income forced economy upon him, and so room after room of the manse was left in darkness, to be regarded by my childish mind with reverent awe. Over other windows were put up boards marked DAIRY, or CHEESE-ROOM, because by being labelled with these names they would escape the tribute. What a queer mind must his have been who first invented taxing the light of the sun! It was, no doubt, meant to be a fair way of estimating the size of a house, and thus getting at the wealth of the inhabitant; but, incidentally, it led occupiers of large

[1] See Plate 2. The drawing is evidently a copy of an early photograph.—P.

3

houses to shut out the light for which they were too poor to pay.

*   *   *

Let us enter by the front door. We step into a spacious hall, innocent of carpet. There is a great fireplace, and over it a painting of David, and the Philistines, and Giant Goliath. The hall-floor was of brick, and carefully sprinkled with fresh sand. We see this in the country still, but not often in the minister's house. In the hall stood "the child's" rocking-horse. It was a grey horse, and could be ridden astride or side-saddle. When I visited Stambourne, in the year 1889, a man claimed to have rocked me upon it. I remembered the horse, but not the man —so sadly do we forget the better, and remember the baser. This was the only horse that I ever enjoyed riding. Living animals are too eccentric in their movements, and the law of gravitation usually draws me from my seat upon them to a lower level; therefore I am not an inveterate lover of horseback. I can, however, testify of my Stambourne steed, that it was a horse on which even a member of Parliament might have retained his seat.

How I used to delight to stand in the hall, with the door open, and watch the rain run off the top of the door into a wash-tub! How much better to catch the overflow of the rain in a tub than to have a gutter to carry it off! So I thought; but do not now think. What bliss to float cotton-reels in the miniature sea! How fresh and sweet that rain seemed to be! The fragrance of the water which poured down in a thunder-shower comes over me now.

Where the window is open on the right, was the best parlour. Roses generally grew about it, and bloomed *in the room* if they could find means to insert their buds between the wall and the window-frame. They generally found ample space, for nothing was quite on the square. There had evidently been a cleaning up just before my photograph was taken, for there are no roses creeping up from below. What vandals people are when they set about clearing up either the outsides or the insides of houses! On the sacred walls of this "best parlour" hung portraits of my grandparents and uncles, and on a piece of furniture stood the fine large basin which grandfather used for what he called "baptisms". In my heart of hearts, I believe it was originally intended for a punch-bowl, but, in any case, it was a work of art, worthy of the use to which it was dedicated.

An Apple in a Bottle

I remember well, in my early days, seeing upon my grandmother's mantel-shelf an apple contained in a phial. This was a great wonder to me, and I tried to investigate it. My question was, "How came the apple to get inside so small a bottle?" The apple was quite as big round as the phial; by what means was it placed within it? Though it was treason to touch the treasures on the mantel-piece, I took down the bottle, and convinced my youthful mind that the apple never passed through its neck, and by means of an attempt to unscrew the bottom, I became equally certain that the apple did not enter from below. I held to the notion that by some occult means the bottle had been made in two pieces, and afterwards united in so careful a manner that no trace of the join remained. I was hardly satisfied with the theory, but as no philosopher was at hand to suggest any other hypothesis, I let the matter rest. One day, the next summer, I chanced to see upon a bough another phial, the first cousin of my old friend, within which was growing a little apple which had been passed through the neck of the bottle while it was extremely small. "Nature well known, no prodigies remain." The grand secret was out. I did not cry, "*Eureka! Eureka!*" but I might have done so if I had then been versed in the Greek tongue.

This discovery of my juvenile days shall serve for an illustration at the present moment. Let us get the apples into the bottle while they are little: which, being translated, signifies, let us bring the young ones into the house of God by means of the Sabbath-school, in the hope that, in after days, they will love the place where His honour dwelleth, and there seek and find eternal life. By our making the Sabbath dreary, many young minds may be prejudiced against religion: we would do the reverse. Sermons should not be so long and dull as to weary the young folk, or mischief will come of them, but with interesting preaching to secure attention, and loving teachers to press home the truth upon the youthful heart, we shall not have to complain of the next generation that they have "forgotten their resting-places."

*   *   *

In this best parlour grandfather would usually sit on Sunday mornings, and prepare himself for preaching. I was put into the room with him that I might be quiet, and, as a rule, *The Evangelical Magazine* was given me. This contained a portrait of a reverend divine, and one picture of a mission-station. Grandfather often requested me to be quiet, and always gave as a reason that I "had the magazine." I did not at the time perceive the full force of the argument to be derived from that fact, but no doubt my venerable relative knew more about the sedative effect of the magazine than I did. I cannot support his opinion from personal experience. Another means of stilling "the child" was much more effectual. I was warned that perhaps grandpa would not be able to preach if I distracted him, and then—ah! then, what would happen, if poor people did not learn the way to Heaven? This made me look at the portrait and the missionary-station once more. Little did I dream that some other child would one day see my face in that wonderful Evangelical portrait-gallery.

*   *   *

When I was a very small boy, I was allowed to read the Scriptures at family prayer.[1] Once upon a time, when reading the passage in Revelation which mentions the bottomless pit, I paused, and said, "Grandpa, what can this mean?" The answer was kind, but unsatisfactory, "Pooh, pooh, child, go on." The child, however, intended to have an explanation, and therefore selected the same chapter morning after morning, and always halted at the same verse to repeat the enquiry, hoping that by repetition he would importune the good old gentleman into a reply. The process was successful, for it is by no means the most edifying thing in the world to hear the history of the Mother of Harlots, and the beast with seven heads, every morning in the week, Sunday included, with no sort of alternation either of Psalm or Gospel; the venerable patriarch of the household therefore capitulated at discretion, with, "Well, dear, what is it that puzzles you?" Now "the child" had often seen baskets with but very frail bottoms, which in course of wear became bottomless, and allowed the fruit placed therein to drop upon the ground; here, then, was the puzzle—if the pit aforesaid had no bottom, where would all those people fall to who dropped out at its lower end?—a puzzle which rather startled the propriety of family worship, and had to be laid aside for explanation at some more convenient season. Queries of the like simple but rather unusual stamp would frequently break up into paragraphs of a miscellaneous length the Bible-reading of the assembled family, and had there not been a world of love and licence allowed to the inquisitive reader, he would very soon have been

---

[1] "Even at six years old, when some children have advanced no farther in spelling than words of one syllable, he could read out with a point and emphasis really marvellous in one so young." *The Life and Work of C. H. Spurgeon* by G. H. Pike, Vol. I, p. 20.—P.

deposed from his office. As it was, the Scriptures were not very badly rendered, and were probably quite as interesting as if they had not been interspersed with original and curious enquiries.

I can remember the horror of my mind when my dear grandfather told me what his idea of "the bottomless pit" was. There is a deep pit, and the soul is falling down—oh, how fast it is falling! There! the last ray of light at the top has disappeared, and it falls on—on—on, and so it goes on falling—on—on—on for a thousand years! "Is it not getting near the bottom yet? Won't it stop?" No, no, the cry is, "On—on—on." "I have been falling a million years; am I not near the bottom yet?" No, you are no nearer the bottom yet; it is "the *bottomless* pit." It is on—on—on, and so the soul goes on falling perpetually into a deeper depth still, falling for ever into "the bottomless pit"—on—on—on—into the pit that has no bottom! Woe, without termination, without hope of its coming to a conclusion!

*   *   *

In my grandfather's garden there was a fine old hedge of yew, of considerable length, which was clipped and trimmed till it made quite a wall of verdure. Behind it was a wide grass walk, which looked upon the fields; the grass was kept mown, so as to make pleasant walking. Here, ever since the old Puritanic chapel was built, godly divines had walked, and prayed, and meditated. My grandfather was wont to use it as his study. Up and down it he would walk when preparing his sermons, and always on Sabbath-days when it was fair, he had half-an-hour there before preaching. To me, it seemed to be a perfect paradise; and being forbidden to stay there when grandfather was meditating, I viewed it with no small degree of awe. I love to think of the green and quiet walk at this moment, but I was once shocked and even horrified by hearing a farming man remark concerning this *sanctum sanctorum*, "It 'ud grow a many 'taturs if it wor ploughed up." What cared he for holy memories? What were meditation and contemplation to him? Is it not the chief end of man to grow potatoes, and eat them? Such, on a larger scale, would be an unconverted man's estimate of joys so elevated and refined as those of Heaven. Alphonse Karr tells a story of a servant-man who asked his master to be allowed to leave his cottage, and sleep over the stable. What was the matter with his cottage? "Why, sir, the nightingales all around the cottage make such a 'jug, jug, jug,' at night that I cannot bear them." A man with a musical ear would be charmed with the nightingales' song, but here was a man without a musical soul who found the sweetest notes a nuisance. This is a feeble image of the incapacity of unregenerate man for the enjoyments of the world to come, and as he is incapable of enjoying them, so is he incapable of longing for them.

*　　　*　　　*

While my grandfather was preacher at the meeting-house, Mr. James Hopkins was Rector at the church. They preached the same gospel, and without surrendering their principles, were great friends. The Bible Society held its meetings alternately in connection with the church and the meeting-house. At times, the leading resident went to church in the morning, and to chapel in the afternoon; and, when I was a boy, I have, on Monday, gone to the Squire's to tea, with Mr. Hopkins and my grandfather. The glory of that tea-party was that we four, the three old gentlemen, and the little boy, *all ate sugared bread and butter together for a treat*. The sugar was very brown, but the young boy was very pleased, and the old boys were merry also. Yes, Stambourne had its choice pleasures!

It is pleasant to read of the harmony between these two men of God: they increased in mutual esteem as they increased in years. As Mr. Hopkins had more of the meat, and Mr. Spurgeon more of the mouths, the Rector did not forget to help his friend in divers quiet ways; such as a five-pound note for a sick daughter to go to the sea-side, and presents of comforts in illness. On one occasion, it is said that, having a joint of beef on the Rectory table, the clergyman cut it in halves, and sent his man on horseback with one half of it to the Independent Parsonage, while it was yet hot—a kind of joke not often practised between established and dissenting ministers.

*　　　*　　　*

In the front of the house, towards the left, nearly hidden by a shrub, is a very important window, for it let light into the room wherein were the oven, the mangle, and, best of all, the kneading-trough. How often have I gone to that kneading-trough, for it had a little shelf in it, and there would be placed *"something for the child!"* A bit of pastry, which was called by me, according to its size, a pig or a rabbit, which had little ears, and two currants for eyes, was carefully placed in that sacred shrine, like the manna in the ark. Dear grandmother, how much you laboured to spoil that "child"! Yet your memory is more dear to him than that of wiser folks, who did not spoil "the child". Do you now look down from your mansion above upon your petted grandson? Do you feel as if he would have been better if you had been sour and hard? Not a bit of it. Aunt

Ann,[1] who had a finger in it all, would spoil "the child" again if she had a chance.

The dairy at the back of the house was by no means a bad place for a cheese-cake, or for a drink of cool milk. It makes one think of the hymn—

"I have been there; and still would go."

The cupboard under the stairs, where they kept the sand for the floors, would be a real Old Curiosity Shop nowadays, but there it was, and great was the use of it to the cottagers around.

There was a sitting-room at the back of the house, where the family met for meals. In that which looks like a blank side in our picture there certainly was a window looking out upon the garden; perhaps it was a little further back than the picture goes. A very pleasant outlook there was from that window down the green garden paths, and over the hedge into the road. When I last saw the "keeping-room", a bit of ivy had forced its way through the lath and plaster, and had been trained along the inside of the room, but in my childish days we were not so verdant. I remember a mark on the paper which had been made by the finger of one of my uncles, so they told me, when one year the flour was so bad that it turned into a paste, or pudding, inside the loaf, and could not be properly made into bread. History has before this been learned from handwritings on the wall. The times of the old Napoleon wars, and of the Corn Laws, must often have brought straitness of bread into the household, and a failure in the yield of the little farm made itself felt in the family.

There was a mysterious jack over the fire-place, and with that fire-place itself I was very familiar; for candles were never used extravagantly in grandfather's house, and if anyone went out of the room, and took the candle with him, it was just a little darker, not very much; and if one wished to read, the fire-light was the only resort. There were mould candles now and then in the best room, but that was only on very high days and holidays. My opinion, derived from personal observation, was that all every-day candles were made of rushes and tallow.

Our young readers in London and other large towns have probably never seen a pair of snuffers, much less the flint and steel with which a light had to be painfully obtained by the help of a tinder-box and a brimstone match. What a job on a cold raw morning to strike, and

[1] This was an unmarried sister of his father who resided with her parents at Stambourne. It is said that she lavished on her baby nephew that wealth of affection maiden aunts are so often seen to bestow.—P.

strike, and see the sparks die out because the tinder was damp! We are indeed living in an age of light when we compare our incandescent gas-burners and electric lights with the rushlights of our childhood. And yet the change is not all one way; for if we have more light, we have also more fog and smoke, at least in London. Our "keeping-room" was a very nice, large, comfortable dining-room, and it had a large store-closet at one end. You should have seen the best china! It only came out on state occasions, but it was very marvellous in "the child's" eyes.

A quaint old winding stair led to the upper chambers. The last time I occupied the best bedroom, the floor appeared anxious to go out of the window, at least, it inclined that way. There seemed to be a chirping of birds very near my pillow in the morning, and I discovered that swallows had built outside the plaster, and sparrows had found a hole which admitted them inside of it, that there they might lay their young. It is not always that one can lie in bed and study ornithology. I confess that I liked all this rural life, and the old chintz bed-furniture, and the paper round the looking-glass cut in the form of horse-chestnut leaves and dahlias, and the tottery old mansion altogether.

The Boy among the Books

I am afraid I am amusing myself rather than my reader, and so I will not weary him with more than this one bit more of rigmarole just now. But there was one place upstairs which I cannot omit, even at the risk of being wearisome. Opening out of one of the bedrooms, there was a little chamber of which the window had been blocked up through that wretched window-duty. When the original founder of Stambourne Meeting quitted the Church of England, to form a separate congregation, he would seem to have been in possession of a fair estate, and the house was quite a noble one for those times.[1] Before the light-excluding tax had come into operation, that little room was the minister's study and closet for prayer; and a very nice cosy room, too. In my time, it was a dark den—but *it contained books,*

---

[1] The reference here is to the Ejectment of 1662 when, along with nearly 2,000 of his fellow ministers, Henry Havers, the Puritan Rector of Stambourne, resigned his living rather than comply with the Act of Uniformity. "Being a man of property he purchased a farm in the parish where many came to him for spiritual instruction. After some time he purchased the plot of ground on which the Parsonage house and the chapel now stand, on which he erected a large timber-built house called his mansion, and a chapel which, with galleries on three sides, would hold about two hundred persons." *Memories of Stambourne*, C. H. Spurgeon and B. Beddow (London 1891), pp. 33 ff. The old Meeting House and Manse were subsequently pulled down and rebuilt during Spurgeon's lifetime, but the graveyard, the manse garden with its old yew hedge, and the surrounding countryside are still much as they were in Spurgeon's childhood.—P.

and this made it a gold mine to me.[1] Therein was fulfilled the promise, "I will give thee the treasures of darkness." Some of these were enormous folios, such as a boy could hardly lift. Here I first struck up acquaintance with the martyrs, and specially with "Old Bonner," who burned them; next, with Bunyan and his "Pilgrim"; and further on, with the great masters of Scriptural theology, with whom no moderns are worthy to be named in the same day. Even the old editions of their works, with their margins and old-fashioned notes, are precious to me. It is easy to tell a real Puritan book even by its shape and by the appearance of the type. I confess that I harbour a prejudice against nearly all new editions, and cultivate a preference for the originals, even though they wander about in sheepskins and goatskins, or are shut up in the hardest of boards. It made my eyes water, a short time ago, to see a number of these old books in the new Manse: I wonder whether some other boy will love them, and live to revive that grand old divinity which will yet be to England her balm and benison.

Out of that darkened room I fetched those old authors when I was yet a youth, and never was I happier than when in their company. Out of the present contempt into which Puritanism has fallen, many brave hearts and true will fetch it, by the help of God, ere many years have passed. Those who have daubed up the windows will yet be surprised to see Heaven's light beaming on the old truth, and then breaking forth from it to their own confusion.

*   *   *

[The following incident in Spurgeon's childhood's days is here given as it was related by his "Aunt Ann" on the occasion when he visited Stambourne in the summer of 1887.

One of the members of the church at Stambourne, named Roads, was in the habit of frequenting the public-house to have his "drop of beer", and smoke his pipe, greatly to the grief of his godly pastor, who often heaved a sigh at the thought of his unhappy member's inconsistent conduct. Little Charles had doubtless noticed his grandfather's grief on this account, and laid it to heart. One day he suddenly exclaimed, in the hearing of the good old gentleman, "I'll kill old Roads, that I will!" "Hush, hush! my dear," said the good pastor, "you mustn't talk so; it's very wrong, you know, and you'll get taken up by the police, if you do anything wrong." "I shall not do anything bad; but I'll kill him though, that I will." Well, the good grandfather

---

[1] It is remarkable that this library which had been in the property of Henry Havers had been preserved till the middle of the nineteenth century.—P.

was puzzled, but yet perfectly sure that the child would not do any-thing which he knew to be wrong, so he let it pass with some half-mental remark about "that strange child." Shortly after, however, the above conversation was brought to his mind by the child coming in and saying, "I've killed old Roads; he'll never grieve my dear grandpa any more." "My dear child," said the good man, "what have you done? Where have you been?" "I haven't been doing any harm, grandpa," said the child; "I've been about the Lord's work, that's all."

Nothing more could be elicited from little Charles, but, before long, the mystery was cleared up. "Old Roads" called to see his pastor, and, with downcast looks and evident sorrow of heart, narrated the story of how he had been killed, somewhat in this fashion: "I'm very sorry indeed, my dear pastor, to have caused you such grief and trouble. It was very wrong, I know; but I always loved you, and wouldn't have done it if I'd only thought." Encouraged by the good pastor's kindly Christian words, he went on with his story. "I was a-sitting in the public just having my pipe and mug of beer, when that child comes in—to think an old man like me should be took to task, and reproved by a bit of a child like that! Well, he points at me with his finger, just so, and says, 'What doest thou here, Elijah? sitting with the ungodly; and you a member of a church, and breaking your pastor's heart. I'm ashamed of you! I wouldn't break my pastor's heart, I'm sure.' And then he walks away. Well, I did feel angry, but I knew it was all true, and I was guilty; so I put down my pipe, and did not touch my beer, but hurried away to a lonely spot, and cast myself down before the Lord, confessing my sin and begging for forgiveness. And I do know and believe the Lord in mercy pardoned me; and now I've come to ask you to forgive me, and I'll never grieve you any more, my dear pastor." It need not be said that the penitent was freely forgiven, and owned a brother in the Lord, and the Lord was praised for the wonderful way in which it had all come about.

The genuineness of the backslider's restoration is evident from the testimony of Mr. J. C. Houchin, the minister at Stambourne who succeeded Spurgeon's grandfather, and who has also ascertained from official records the correct way of spelling "Old Roads' " name. Houchin writes:

"Thomas Roads was one of the old men of the table-pew—an active, lively, little man, but quite illiterate—not much above a labourer, but he kept a pony and cart, and did a little buying and selling on his own account. . . . I found him an earnest and zealous Christian, striving to be useful in every way possible to him; especially in the prayer-meetings and among the young people, opening his house for Christian conversation and prayer. He only lived about four years of my time, and was sustained with a cheerful confidence to the end. When near death, on my taking up the Bible to read and pray with him, he said, 'I have counted the leaves, sir.' I said, 'Why! what did you do that for?' and he replied, 'I never could read a word of it, and thought I would know how many leaves there were.' This was very pathetic, and revealed much. We had a good hope of him, and missed him greatly."]

"I have photographed upon my heart just now, the portrait of one very, very dear to me, and I think I may venture to produce a rough sketch of him, as no mean example of how honourable it is to endure to the end. This man began while yet a youth to preach the Word. Sprung of ancestors who had loved the Lord and served his Church, he felt the glow of holy enthusiasm. Having proved his capabilities, he entered college, and after the close of its course, settled in a spot where for more than fifty years he continued his labours. In his early days, his sober earnestness and sound doctrine were owned of God in many conversions both at home and abroad. Assailed by slander and abuse, it was his privilege to live it all down. He outlived his enemies, and though he had buried a generation of his friends, yet he found many warm hearts clustering round him to the last. Visiting his flock, preaching in his own pulpit, and making very many journeys to other Churches, years followed one another so rapidly, that he found himself the head of a large tribe of children and grand-children, most of them walking in the truth. At the age of four-score years, he preached on still, until laden with infirmities, but yet as joyful and as cheerful as in the heyday of his youth, his time had come to die. He was able to say truthfully, when last he spake to me, 'I do not know that my testimony for God has ever altered, as to the fundamental doctrines; I have grown in experience, but from the first day until now, I have had no new doctrines to teach my hearers. I have had to make no confessions of error on vital points, but have been held fast to the doctrines of grace, and can now say that I love them better than ever.' Such an one was he, as Paul the aged, longing to preach so long as his tottering knees could bear him to the pulpit. I am thankful that I had such a grandsire. He fell asleep in Christ but a few hours ago, and on his dying bed talked as cheerfully as men can do in the full vigour of their health."—C. H. S. in Sermon on Matthew x.22 preached February 14, 1864.

Chapter 2

Stambourne Meeting-house

It was a rare old chapel. I wish it could have remained for ever as I used to know it: let me see if I can sketch it with my pen. When I was a boy of twelve, I made a drawing of the back of the old meeting-house. I have been welcomed at a farmer's table on the promise of making a picture of his house. I am rather glad that the pencil memorial was preserved by my dear Aunt Ann; but I must now, forty-five years after, use the pen on the same subject.

The pulpit was glorious as "the tower of the flock". Over it hung a huge sounding-board: I used to speculate as to what would become of grandfather if it ever dropped down upon him. I thought of my Jack-in-the-box, and hoped that my dear grandpapa would never be shut down and shut up in such a fashion. At the back of the pulpit was a peg to hold the minister's hat: inside, there was room for two, for I have sat there with grandfather when quite a little boy; but I guess that two grown-up people would have found it "quite too small enough", as my Dutch friend puts it.

Just below, and in front of the pulpit, was the table-pew, wherein sat the elders of the congregation, the men of gracious "light and leading". There Uncle Haddon generally stood, and gave out the hymns and the notices; and from that semi-sacred region was raised the block of wood by which to the singers upstairs the metre of the hymn was made known—Common, Long, or Short. There were big tomb-stones forming the bottom of this large pew, which took its name from containing *the table*, on which were spread the bread and wine on days *when they had the ordinance*: I think that was the correct phrase when our good folks intended "the communion". I don't remember hearing them style infant baptism "the ordinance", but I suppose they thought it to be one. A few had qualms upon the question, and were baptized quietly at some Baptist Chapel.

The pews in the middle were mostly square in form, and roomy. Those on either side were aristocratic, and lined with green baize, for the most part very faded. In some cases, brass rods carried up little curtains, which made the family pew quite private, and shut out all sights but that of the grave and reverend senior who dispensed to us the Word of Life. There were flaps inside the pew so as not to lose the space where the door opened, and flaps for the poor to sit upon

15

in the aisle outside of these pews; and when the time came to go home, there was such a lifting up and letting down of flaps, and flap-seats, within the pew, and without the pew, as one never does see in these degenerate days. A little boy on a hassock on the floor of one of these holy loose-boxes ought to have been good, and no doubt was as good there as anywhere, especially if he had a peppermint to suck, and nobody to play with.

I cannot forget the big clock which had a face outside the chapel as well as one inside. When his long body had been newly grained, he seemed a very suitable piece of furniture for a nice, clean, old-fashioned Puritan meeting-house. If I am rightly informed, the veteran time-keeper was bought by the miller, and is now upon one of his sheds. To what strange uses we may come at last!

The people were mainly real Essex: they talked of places down in "the Shires" as if they were quite foreign parts, and young fellows who went down into "the Hundreds" were explorers of a respectable order of hardihood. They loved a good sermon, and would say, "Mr. Spurgeon, I *heard* you well this morning." I thought the good man had *preached* well, but their idea was not so much to his credit; they judged that they had *heard* him well, and there's something in the different way of putting it; at any rate, it takes from the preacher all ground of glorying in what he has done. They were a people who could and would hear the gospel, but I don't think they would have put up with anything else. They were as apt at criticism as here and there one: some of them were very wise in their remarks, and some were otherwise. Well do I remember an occasion upon which the preacher had treated "the tares" after the manner of the East, and was altogether right in so doing, but they said, "He wouldn't know a tare if he saw one. It was painful to hear a man talk so ignorant. To say that you couldn't tell wheat from tares when they were a-growing was ridiculous." The rustic critics were wrong for once, but on matters of doctrine or experience, you would have found them quite a match for you.

I do not think our folks were anything like so superstitious and weak as the peasants I came to know ten years after in Cambridge-shire. Tales of white wizards and witches were unknown to my juvenile mind, though I heard enough of them when my age was between sixteen and twenty. Then one of my best workers told me that a witch had dragged a cat down his naked back by its tail: he did not show me the marks, but he fully believed in the feline operation. We cannot forget that in the village of Hedingham, which is not more than five miles from Stambourne, a murder was committed so late as

1865, which grew out of popular belief in witchcraft. The old men I talked with, as a little child, were, I am sure, far above all such nonsense, and upon many a Biblical, or political, or ecclesiastical, or moral subject, they would have uttered great and weighty thoughts in their own savoury Essex dialect.

There were, no doubt, in Stambourne a few rough fellows who did not go to any place of worship, but those who came to the meeting-house were the great majority,[1] and the plain, practical, common-sense sermons which they heard had lifted them out of that dense superstition which still benumbs the brains of too many of the East Anglian peasantry.

The Singing at Stambourne Meeting-house

The prayer-meetings during the week were always kept up, but at certain seasons of the year grandfather and a few old women were all that could be relied upon. It occurred to me, in riper years, to ask my venerated relative how the singing was maintained. "Why, grandfather," said I, "we always sang, and yet you don't know any tunes, and certainly the old ladies didn't." "Why, child," said he, "there's one Common metre tune which is all, 'Hum Ha, Hum Ha,' and I could manage that very well." "But how if it happened to be a Long or Short metre hymn?" "Why, then, I either put in more Hum Ha's, or else I left some out; but we managed to praise the Lord." Ah, shade of my dear old grandsire! your grandson is by no means more gifted as to crotchets and quavers than you were, and to this day the only solo he has ever ventured to sing is that same universally useful tune![2] Even that he has abandoned; for audiences are growing either more intelligent or less tolerant than they used to be.

My grandfather once ventured upon publishing a volume of hymns. I never heard anyone speak in their favour, or argue that they ought to have been sung in the congregation. In that volume he promised a second, if the first should prove acceptable. We forgive him the first collection because he did not inflict another. The meaning was good, but the dear old man paid no attention to the mere triviality of rhyme. We dare not quote even a verse. It may be among the joys of Heaven for my venerated grandsire, that he can now compose and sing new songs unto the Lord. When we say we dare not quote, we do not refer to the meaning or the doctrine: in that respect,

---

[1] The chapel accommodated some 600 people, and on Sunday afternoons it was generally well filled. (See *James Archer Spurgeon* by G. Holden Pike (1894), p. 12).—P.

[2] An allusion to the solo sung by Spurgeon on the occasion of his address on "Old Fugal Tunes" in the Metropolitan Tabernacle, June 4, 1889.—P.

we could quote every line before the Westminster Assembly, and never fear that a solitary objection would or could be raised.

The Stambourne style of singing led me into trouble when I returned to my home. The notion had somehow entered my little head that the last line of the hymn must always be repeated, and grandfather had instilled into me as a safe rule that I must never be afraid to do what I believed to be right; so, when I went to the chapel where my parents attended, I repeated the last line whether the congregation did so or not. It required a great deal of punishment to convince me that a little boy must do what his parents think to be right; and though my grandfather made a mistake in that particular instance, I have always been grateful to him for teaching me to act according to my belief whatever the consequences might be.

*   *   *

Outside the meeting-house near the long side, which was really the front, there stood a horsing-block. Ladies went up the steps, and found themselves on a platform of the same height as their horse's back. It was a commendable invention: how often have I wished for something of the sort when I have had to climb my Rosinante! To me, this horsing-block was dear for quite another reason. The grand old lime trees shed their leaves in profusion, and when these were swept up, the old chapel-keeper would ram a large quantity of them under the horsing-block. When I had pulled out about as many as fitted my size, I could creep in, and there lie hidden beyond fear of discovery. My friend, Mr. Manton Smith, has written a book called *Stray Leaves*, and another which he has entitled *More Stray Leaves*; I entered into his work before he was born. So good was the hiding-place, that it remained a marvel where "the child" could be. The child would get alone, but where he went to, his guardian angels knew, but none on earth could tell. Only a little while ago, my dear old Aunt Ann said, "But, Charles, where did you get to when you were such a little child? We used to look everywhere for you, but we never found you till you came walking in all by yourself." The horsing-block was the usual haunt when there were leaves, and an old tomb would serve at other times. No, I did not get into the grave, but it had a sort of altar tomb above it, and one of the side stones would move easily, so that I could get inside, and then by setting the slab of stone back again I was enclosed in a sort of large box where nobody would dream of looking for me. I went to the aforesaid tomb to show my aunt my hiding-place, but the raised altar was gone, and the top of it, with the name of the deceased thereon, was laid flat on the ground. Some of the side-stones, which formerly held up the memorial, were used to make door-steps when the buildings were put into their present state of repair, and the top stone was made to occupy the same space, only it lay flat upon the ground, instead of being raised some two feet above it.

Still, I remembered well the place, and what the tomb had formerly been. How often have I listened to the good people calling me by my name! I heard their feet close to my den, but I was wicked enough still to be "lost", though the time for meals was gone. Dreaming of days to come befell me every now and then as a child, and to be quite alone was my boyish heaven. Yet, there was a seventh heaven above that: let me but hear the foxhounds, and see the red coats of their pursuers, and I had seen the climax of delight. When the huntsmen did come down by Stambourne woods, it was a season of delirious excitement to others besides "the child". At other times, all the women and children were solemnly working at straw-plait, but what they did when the fox went by I will not venture upon guessing, for I don't remember what I did myself. The woods at the back of the chapel had a charming mystery about them to my little soul, for who could tell but a fox was there? As a child, when asked what I would be, I usually said I was going to be a huntsman. A fine profession, truly! Many young men have the same idea of being parsons as I had of being a huntsman—a mere childish notion that they would like the coat and the horn-blowing; the honour, the respect, the ease—and they are probably even fools enough to think—the riches of the ministry. (Ignorant beings they must be if they look for wealth in connection with the Baptist ministry.) The fascination of the preacher's office is very great to weak minds, and hence I earnestly caution all young men not to mistake whim for inspiration, and a childish preference for a call of the Holy Spirit.

I once learnt a lesson, while thus fox-hunting, which has been very useful to me as a preacher of the gospel. Ever since the day I was sent to shop with a basket, and purchased a pound of tea, a quarter-of-a-pound of mustard, and three pounds of rice, and on my way home saw a pack of hounds, and felt it necessary to follow them over hedge and ditch (as I always did when I was a boy), and found, when I reached home, that all the goods were amalgamated—tea, mustard, and rice—into one awful mess, I have understood the necessity of packing up my subjects in good stout parcels, bound round with the thread of my discourse; and this makes me keep to firstly, secondly, and thirdly, however unfashionable that method may now be. People will not drink mustard tea, nor will they enjoy muddled-up sermons, in which they cannot tell head from tail, because they have neither, but are like Mr. Bright's Skye terrier, whose head and tail were both alike.

*   *   *

Somehow, I don't think our Sunday-school came to so very, very much. It was a great day when every child brought his own mug, and there was real cake, and tea, or milk and water, and an address; but that high festival came but once a year. Having been on one occasion pressed into the service when I was still a boy, but was in Stambourne on a vist, I felt myself a failure, and I fancied that some around me were not brilliant successes, Still, in those early times, teaching children to read, and to repeat verses of hymns, and to say the Catechism by heart, were a good beginning. Dr. Watts's Catechism, which I learned myself, is so simple, so interesting, so suggestive, that a better condensation of Scriptural knowledge will never be written; and the marvel is that such a little miracle of instruction should have been laid aside by teachers. While I am writing, one question and answer come to me with special freshness:

"Who was Isaiah?"

"He was that prophet who spake more of Jesus Christ than all the rest."

At the distance of fifty-three years, I remember a little book which was read to me about a pious child at Colchester; I recollect Janeway's *Token for Children*, and I recall the bad conduct of some juveniles of my own age, who not only kicked up a dust, but literally kicked the teachers. Memory makes a selection as she goes along, and in my case, the choice of things retained is so miscellaneous, that I cannot discover my own character by their guidance.

The week-day school for the very juveniles was kept by old Mrs. Burleigh, and to that fane of useful knowledge I was sent. The only thing that I remember was that I heard a good deal of her son Gabriel, and therefore asked, as a great favour, that when he came home from the town where he lived, he might come and see me. I had my desire; but after all these years, I have not got over my disappointment. To see Gabriel! I don't think I had absolutely reckoned upon the largest kind of wings; but wings certainly, or something otherwise angelic. To see only a young man, a youth in trousers, with no trace of cherubim or seraphim about him, was too much of a come-down. "What's in a name?" was a question not yet known to me; but no one will ever need to ask me now. Names are mere labels, and by no means proofs that the things are there.

To come back to the old chapel, the best point about it was the blessing which rested on the ministry carried on within. The dew of the Spirit from on high never left the ministry. Wherever my grandfather went, souls were saved under his sermons. When I first of all became a preacher, there were persons who said, "I heard your grandfather, and I would run my shoes off my feet any day to hear a Spurgeon." This was encouraging. Another told me that, to hear my grandfather once, made his wing-feathers grow a foot. He could mount as eagles, after being fed with such Heavenly food. "He was always so experimental," was the summing-up of one of the most devout of working-men. "You felt as if he had been inside of a man." Buildings may perish, and new shrines may succeed them, but no earthly house will accommodate a sounder or more useful ministry than that of my grandfather.[1]

*   *   *

I recollect, when first I left my grandfather, how grieved I was to part from him; it was the great sorrow of my little life. Grandfather seemed very sorry, too, and we had a cry together; he did not quite know what to say to me, but he said, "Now child, to-night, when the moon shines at Colchester, and you look at it, don't forget that it is the same moon your grandfather will be looking at from Stambourne;" and for years, as a child, I used to love the moon because I thought that my grandfather's eyes and my own somehow met there on the moon.

[1] Rev. James Spurgeon's ministry at the little Essex chapel lasted for fifty-four years and he continued preaching with power and success up to the time of his death at the age of 88, in 1864.—P.

Spurgeon's father, John Spurgeon (1810–1902), was the second son of the pastor of Stambourne and he faithfully continued the witness which had been in the family as far back as the seventeenth century. "The faith I hold bears upon it marks of the blood of my ancestors," Spurgeon would say, and he had in mind men like Job Spurgeon of Dedham who endured hard imprisonment for his Nonconformity in the days of Charles II.

John Spurgeon married Eliza Jarvis (born at Otton Belchamp in 1815) and their first home at Kelvedon still stands. Whatever the reason of the separation from his parents in his infancy, Charles was happy to come to the new home on Hythe Hill, Colchester, and in after years he affirmed that the two reasons by which he accounted for the position God had given him were, "My mother, and the truth of my message." Perhaps he did not see a great deal of his father, for besides a pastorate nine miles away at Tollesbury he was in charge of the accounts in a coal merchant's office. But it was far from a lonely childhood; two sisters and a brother were born by the time Charles was five, and whether addressing them from a hayrick "pulpit" or leading them in their games, he was their natural leader. One day, as he was playing with toy ships with his brother, they proposed naming the boats. "I shall call mine *The Thunderer*," exclaimed Charles, "for a vessel to gain the victory must bear a worthy name." In later years his family name was to inspire him in a different realm, "I dare say our fathers were poor weavers, but I had far rather be descended from one who suffered for the faith than bear the blood of all the emperors within my veins."

Not a trace now remains of the home where the Spurgeons lived for sixteen years close to St. Leonard's Church, on the opposite side of the road. It was pulled down a few years after the Second World War. John Spurgeon, after further pastorates at Cranbrook and Islington died at the age of ninety-one, having survived his eldest son by ten years.

Chapter 3

Childhood Incidents

No man can write the whole of his own biography. I suppose, if the history of a man's thoughts and words could be written, scarce the world itself would contain the books, so wonderful is the tale that might be told. Of my life at home and at school, I can only give a few incidents as I am able to recall them after the lapse of forty or fifty years. One of the earliest, and one that impressed itself very deeply upon my childish mind, relates to—

My First and Last Debt

When I was a very small boy, in pinafores, and went to a woman's school, it so happened that I wanted a stick of slate pencil, and had no money to buy it with. I was afraid of being scolded for losing my pencils so often, for I was a real careless little fellow, and so did not dare to ask at home; what then was I to do? There was a little shop in the place, where nuts, and tops, and cakes, and balls were sold by old Mrs. Pearson, and sometimes I had seen boys and girls get trusted by the old lady. I argued with myself that Christmas was coming, and that somebody or other would be sure to give me a penny then, and perhaps even a whole silver sixpence. I would, therefore, go into debt for a stick of slate pencil, and be sure to pay at Christmas. I did not feel easy about it, but still I screwed my courage up, and went into the shop. One farthing was the amount, and as I had never owed anything before, and my credit was good, the pencil was handed over by the kind dame, and *I was in debt*. It did not please me much, and I felt as if I had done wrong, but I little knew how soon I should smart for it.

How my father came to hear of this little stroke of business, I never knew, but some little bird or other whistled it to him, and he was very soon down upon me in right earnest. God bless him for it; he was a sensible man, and none of your children-spoilers; he did not intend to bring up his children to speculate, and play at what big rogues call financing, and therefore he knocked my getting into debt on the head at once, and no mistake. He gave me a very powerful lecture upon getting into debt, and how like it was to stealing, and upon the way in which people were ruined by it, and how a boy who would owe a farthing, might one day owe a hundred pounds, and get into prison, and bring his family into disgrace. It was a lecture, indeed; I think I can hear it now, and can feel my ears tingling at the recollection of it. Then I was marched off to the shop, like a deserter marched into barracks, crying bitterly all down the street, and feeling dreadfully ashamed, because I thought everybody knew I was in debt. The farthing was paid amid many solemn warnings, and the poor debtor was set free, like a bird let out of a cage. How sweet it felt to be out of debt! How did my little heart vow and declare that nothing should ever tempt me into debt again! It was a fine lesson, and I have never forgotten it. If all boys were inoculated with the same doctrine when they were young, it would be as good as a fortune to them, and save them waggon-loads of trouble in after life. God bless my father, say I, and send a breed of such fathers into old England to save her from being eaten up with villainy, for what with companies, and schemes, and paper-money, the nation is getting to be as rotten as touch-wood! Ever since that early sickening, I have hated debt as Luther hated the Pope.

Another occurrence of those early days is rather more to my credit. Long after my own sons had grown to manhood, I recalled to my father's recollection an experience of which, until then, he had never had an explanation. My brother, as a child, suffered from weak ankles, and in consequence frequently fell down, and so got into trouble at home. At last, hoping to cure him of what father thought was only carelessness, he was threatened that he should be whipped every time he came back showing any signs of having fallen down. When I reminded my father of this regulation, he said quite triumphantly, "Yes, it was so, and he was completely cured from that time." "Ah!" I answered, "so you thought, yet it was not so, for he had many a tumble afterwards, but I always managed to wash his knees, and to brush his clothes, so as to remove all traces of his falls."

ILLUSTRATIONS FROM CHILDHOOD'S DAYS

I recollect, when a child, seeing on the mantel-piece a stone apple—wonderfully like an apple, too, and very well coloured. I saw that apple years after, but it was no riper. It had been in favourable circumstances for softening and sweetening, if it ever would have become mellow, but I do not think, if the sun of the Equator had shone on it, or if the dews of Hermon had fallen on it, it would ever have been fit to be brought to table. Its hard marble substance would have broken a giant's teeth. It was a hypocritical professor, a hard-hearted mocker of little children, a mere mimic of God's fruits. There are church-members who used to be unkind, covetous, censorious, bad-tempered, egotistical, everything that was hard and stony; are they so now? Have they not mellowed with the lapse of years? No, they are worse, if anything, very dogs in the house for snapping and snarling, rending and devouring; great men at hewing down the carved work of the sanctuary with their axes, or at filling up wells, and marring good pieces of land with stones. When the devil wants a stone to fling at a minister, he is sure to use one of them.

When we were small children, we had a little plot of garden-ground, and we put our seeds into it. I well recollect how, the day after I had put in my seed, I went and scraped the soil away to see if it was not growing, as I expected it would have been after a day or so at the very longest, and I thought the time amazingly long before the seed would be able to make its appearance above the ground. "That was childish," you say. I know it was, but I wish you were as childish with regard to your prayers, that you would, when you have put them in the ground, go and see if they have sprung up; and if not at once—be not childish in refusing to wait till the appointed time comes—always go back and see if they have begun to sprout. If you believe in prayer at all, expect God to hear you. If you do not expect, you will not have. God will not hear you unless you believe He will hear you; but if you believe He will, He will be as good as your faith. He will never allow you to think better of Him than He is; He will come up to the mark of your thoughts, and according to your faith so shall it be done unto you.

When we used to go to school, we would draw houses, and horses, and trees on our slates, and I remember how we used to write "house" under the house, and "horse" under the horse, for some persons might have thought the horse was a house. So there are some people who need to wear a label round their necks to show that they are Christians at all, or else we might mistake them for sinners, their actions are so like those of the ungodly.

I remember once, when a lad, having a dog, which I very much prized, and some man in the street asked me to give him the dog; I thought it was pretty impudent, and I said as much. A gentleman, however, to whom I told it, said, "Now suppose the Duke of So-and-so"—who was a great man in the neighbourhood—"asked you for the dog, would you give it to him?" I answered, "I think I would." So the gentleman said, "Then you are just like all the world; you would give to those who do not need".

I can never forget the rushlight, which dimly illuminated the sitting-room of the old house; nor the dips, which were pretty fair when there were not too many of them to the pound; nor the mould candles, which came out only when there was a party, or some special personage was expected. Short sixes were very respectable specimens of household lights. Composites have never seemed to me to be so good as the old sort, made of pure tallow, but I daresay I may be wrong. Nevertheless, I have no liking for composites in theology, but prefer the genuine article without compromise.

A night-light is a delightful invention for the sick. It has supplanted the rushlight, which would frequently be set in a huge sort of tower, which, to me, as a sick child at night, used to suggest dreadful things. With its light shining through the round holes at the side, like so many ghostly eyes, it looked at me staringly; and with its round ring on the ceiling, it made me think of Nebuchadnezzar's burning fiery furnace.

Once, I thoughtlessly hung a pound of tallow candles on a clothes-horse. This construction was moved near the fire, and the result was a mass of fat on the floor, and the cottons of the candles almost divested of tallow—a lesson to us all not to expose certain things to a great heat, lest we dissolve them. I fear that many a man's good resolutions only need the ordinary fire of daily life to make them melt away. So, too, with fine professions, and the boastings of perfection which abound in this age of shams.

*   *   *

During one of my many holidays at Stambourne, I had a varied experience which I am not likely to forget. My grandfather was very fond of Dr. Watts's hymns, and my grandmother, wishing to get me to learn them, promised me a penny for each one that I should say to her perfectly. I found it an easy and pleasant method of earning money, and learned them so fast that grandmother said she must reduce the price to a halfpenny each, and afterwards to a farthing, if she did not mean to be quite ruined by her extravagance. There is no telling how low the amount per hymn might have sunk, but grandfather said that he was getting overrun with rats, and offered me a shilling a dozen for all I could kill. I found, at the time, that the occupation of rat-catching paid me better than learning hymns, but I know which employment has been the more permanently profitable to me. No matter on what topic I am preaching, I can even now, in the middle of any sermon, quote some verse of a hymn in harmony with the subject; the hymns have remained with me, while those old rats for years have passed away, and the shillings I earned by killing them have been spent long ago.

RICHARD KNILL'S VISIT TO STAMBOURNE

The story of Richard Knill's prophesying that I should preach the gospel in Rowland Hill's Chapel, and to the largest congregations in the world, has been regarded by many as a legend, but it was strictly true. Mr. Knill took the county of Essex in the year 1844, and traversed the region from town to town, as a deputation for the London Missionary Society.[1] In the course of that journey, he spent a little time at Stambourne Parsonage. In his heart burned the true missionary spirit, for he sought the souls of young and old, whenever they came in his way. He was a great soul-winner, and he soon spied out the boy. He said to me, "Where do you sleep? for I want to call you up in the morning." I showed him my little room, and he took good note of it. At six o'clock he called me up. There stood in my grandfather's garden two arbours made of yew trees, cut into sugar-loaf fashion. Though the old manse has given way to a new one, and the old chapel has gone also, yet the yew trees flourish as aforetime. We went into the right-hand arbour, and there, in the sweetest way, he told me of the love of Jesus, and of the blessedness of trusting in Him and loving Him in our childhood. With many a story he preached Christ to me, and told me how good God had been to him, and then he prayed that I might know the Lord and serve Him. He knelt down in that arbour, and prayed for me with his arms about my neck. He did not seem content unless I kept with him in the interval between the services. He heard my childish talk with patient love, and repaid it with gracious instruction. On three successive days he taught me, and prayed with me; and before he had to leave, my grandfather had come back from the place where he had gone to preach, and all the family were gathered to morning prayer. Then, in the presence of them all, Mr. Knill took me on his knee, and said, "This child will one day preach the gospel, and he will preach it to great multitudes. I am persuaded that he will preach in the chapel of Rowland Hill, where (I think he said) I am now the minister." He spoke very

[1] Richard Knill's connection with the London Missionary Society dated back to 1816 when he had been accepted as a missionary for India. Ill health prevented him from remaining in that country more than three years and St. Petersburg became for the next thirteen years his field of labour. After returning to England in 1833 he carried on most successful deputation work for the Society throughout the United Kingdom until 1842 when, worn out by incessant labours, he settled as minister at Wotton-under-Edge. The last years of his life were spent as pastor of a church in Chester where he died in 1857 at the age of 70. It was estimated that up to the time of his death fourteen million of his tracts had been put into circulation in England and America.—P.

solemnly, and called upon all present to witness what he said. Then he gave me sixpence as a reward if I would learn the hymn—

"God moves in a mysterious way
His wonders to perform."

I was made to promise that, when I preached in Rowland Hill's Chapel, that hymn should be sung. Think of that as a promise from a child! Would it ever be other than an idle dream? Years flew by. After I had begun for some little time to preach in London, Dr. Alexander Fletcher was engaged to deliver the annual sermon to children in Surrey Chapel; but as he was taken ill, I was asked in a hurry to preach to the children in his stead. "Yes," I replied, "I will, if you will allow the children to sing, 'God moves in a mysterious way.' I have made a promise, long ago, that so that hymn should be sung." And so it was: I preached in Rowland Hill's Chapel, and the hymn was sung. My emotions on that occasion I cannot describe, for the word of the Lord's servant was fulfilled. Still, I fancy that Surrey was not the chapel which Richard Knill intended. How was I to go to the country chapel? All unsought by me, the minister at Wotton-under-Edge, which was Rowland Hill's summer residence,[1] invited me to preach there. I went on the condition that the congregation should sing, "God moves in a mysterious way"—which was also done. To me it was a very wonderful thing, and I no more understood at that time how it came to pass than I understand to-day why the Lord should be so gracious to me.

Did the words of Mr. Knill help to bring about their own fulfilment? I think so. I believed them, and looked forward to the time when I should preach the Word: I felt very powerfully that no unconverted person might dare to enter the ministry; this made me, I doubt not, all the more intent upon seeking salvation, and more hopeful of it, and when by grace enabled to cast myself upon the Saviour's love, it was not long before my mouth began to speak of His redemption. How came that sober-minded minister to speak thus of one into whose future God alone could see? How came it that he lived to rejoice with his young brother in the truth of all that he had spoken? We think *we* know the answer but each reader has a right to his own: so let it rest, but not till we have marked one practical

[1] Although ordained a deacon in the Church of England, Rowland Hill (1744–1833) was, on account of his irregular preaching, refused priest's orders. Nevertheless he continued to preach wherever he could find hearers and a chapel was built for him at Wotton-under-Edge in Gloucestershire. When Surrey Chapel, London, was erected in 1783 it became henceforth the usual scene of his labours; yet he officiated for a part of every year at Wotton.—P.

lesson. Would to God that we were all as wise as Richard Knill, and habitually sowed beside all waters! On the day of his death, in his eighty-seventh year, John Eliot, "the apostle of the Indians", was occupied in teaching the alphabet to an Indian child at his bedside. A friend said, "Why not rest from your labours now?" "Because," replied the man of God, "I have prayed God to render me useful in my sphere, and He has heard my prayers; for now that I am unable to preach, He leaves me strength enough to teach this poor child his letters." To despise no opportunity of usefulness, is a leading rule with those who are wise to win souls. Mr. Knill might very naturally have left the minister's little grandson on the plea that he had other duties of more importance than praying with children, and yet who shall say that he did not effect as much by that act of humble ministry as by dozens of sermons addressed to crowded audiences? At any rate, *to me* his tenderness in considering the little one was fraught with everlasting consequences, and I must ever feel that his time was well laid out. May we do good everywhere as we have opportunity, and results will not be wanting!

*   *   *

The following letter from Mr. Knill to my grandfather is very interesting, as showing how the good man thought of the matter:

"Chester, 17th April, 1855.

Revd. Mr. Spurgeon,
Dear Sir,
Perhaps you have forgotten me: but I have not forgotten my visit to you and your ancient chapel, and the fine trees which surround it, and your garden with the box and yew trees, and your dear grandson with whom I conversed, and on whose head I placed my hand, when I prayed with him in the arbour.

Two years ago, he wrote to me, reminding me of these things, and of his warm feelings on the occasion.

Last week I was at Leamington, and dined with a young artist, who had come from London to see his parents. His conversation was much about a popular young minister from the country, whom he had heard preach at Exeter Hall, whose name was Spurgeon. I said I knew him. 'How is it possible?' said the gentleman. I told him of my visit, and of your grandson's letter to me, and of his preaching to John Berridge's people at Waterbeach, near Cambridge. Oh, it was a fine season of interest and rejoicing! I hardly slept the following night for joy.

A day or two afterwards I dined near Warwick with a party of friends. Their conversation was also about your grandson, not knowing that I had heard of him. Two of the party had been his hearers in London, and were very full of the subject. One of them said, 'He mentioned your praying with him at his relative's in the garden.' I have prayed much *for* him and *about* him, that God may keep him at the foot of the cross, that popularity may not puff him up.

Will you please give me his address, as I should like to write to him? Forgive me for this intrusion. I feel much about this dear youth, very much. I have four or five of our ministers in London, and my heart goes out much after them. I have been settled in this city upwards of seven years, and have received more than four hundred members into the church. Matthew Henry's Chapel is still standing, but is in the possession of the Unitarians. Ours is an off-shoot from some of Matthew's old members, who would have orthodox preaching.

The Lord bless you and all your family! I have a distant recollection of seeing some of them at your house.

Yours very truly,

RICHARD KNILL."

After that, I went to preach for Mr. Knill himself, who was then at Chester. What a meeting we had! He was preaching in the theatre, and consequently I had to take his place at the footlights. His preaching in a theatre took away from me all fear about preaching in buildings of doubtful use, and set me free for the campaigns in Exeter Hall and the Surrey Music Hall. How much this had to do with other theatre services many know.

> "God moves in a mysterious way,
> His wonders to perform."

After more than forty years of the Lord's lovingkindness, I sat again in that arbour in the year 1887. No doubt it is a mere trifle for outsiders to hear about, but to me it was an overwhelming moment. In July of the year 1887, I went down to Stambourne, and walked about the place like one in a dream. The present minister of Stambourne Meeting-house, and the members of his family, including his son and his grandchildren, were in the garden, and I could not help calling them together around that arbour, while I praised the Lord for His goodness to me. One irresistible impulse was upon me: it was to pray God to bless those lads that stood around me. Memory begat prayer. He who had blessed me, would bless others also. I wanted the lads to remember, when they grew up, my testimony of God's goodness to me. God has blessed me all my life long, and redeemed me from all evil, and I pray that He may be the God of all the young people who read this story.

As already recorded, Spurgeon began his schooling at "Old Mrs. Burleigh's" in Stambourne. On returning to Colchester he went to a school run by a Mrs. Cook until he was ten when he entered Stockwell House School—which provided a good middle-class education. It was here that the gifted teacher of classics and mathematics, Mr. Leeding—who appears again at a later stage of the story—began to exercise a far-reaching influence on his eager pupil. Later Spurgeon's schoolboy contemporaries remembered him not only by his attainments in Latin and Euclid but also by the diversion he often gave them in the lunch hour. Spurgeon and some of the other boys were too far from home to return for dinner so they brought lunch with them and while eating together "it was his usual custom to be turning over the pages of a joke or riddle or anecdote book. Many were the laughs we had, and many the half-chokings in trying to feed and read and laugh all at once. The playground was never Spurgeon's forte; play of the intellect was his delight."

In 1848 Spurgeon and his brother James were sent to a college at Maidstone. Little information exists on this period of his childhood but sometimes illustrations he used in later years illuminate some of his own childhood feelings. Preaching once on John xvii. 24, "Father, I will that they also, whom thou hast given me, be with me where I am; that they may behold my glory," he said, "A child may be happy at school, but he longs for the holidays. Is it merely to escape his lessons? Ah, no! Ask him, and he will tell you, 'I want to go home to see my father.'"

Chapter 4

Memories of Schooldays

MANY memories were awakened, one day, when I opened my copy of White's *Natural History of Selborne*, and read the following inscription:

STOCKWELL SCHOOL, COLCHESTER.
Adjudged to
MASTER C. SPURGEON,
as the First Class English Prize,
at the Half-yearly Examination,
December 11th, 1844.
T. W. DAVIDS, *Examiner.*

After I had once succeeded in gaining my position at the top of the class, I was careful to retain it, except at one particular period, when I made up my mind to get right down to the bottom. My teacher could not understand my unusual stupidity, until it suddenly occurred to him that I had purposely worked my way from the head of the class, which was opposite a draughty door, down to the foot, which was next to the stove. He therefore reversed the position of the scholars, and it was not long before I had again climbed to the place of honour, where I had also the enjoyment of the heat from the fire.

*   *   *

I was about the age of fourteen when I was sent to a Church of England school—now called St. Augustine's College, Maidstone. We had three clergymen who came by turns to teach us their doctrines; but, somehow or other, the pupils did not seem to get on much, for when one of them was asked by a clergyman how many sacraments there were, he said, "Seven," and when that was denied, he said, "Oh, sir, there is one that they take at the *h*altar!" upon which I could not help saying, "That's hanging, I should think," which suggestion made even the reverend gentleman smile, although, of course, I was bidden not to be so rude as to interrupt again. I am sure many of the sons of the gentry in that establishment were more ignorant of Scripture than the boys in some of our Ragged Schools.

One of the clergy was, I believe, a good man, and it is to him I owe that ray of light which sufficed to show me believers' baptism. I was usually at the head of the class, and on one occasion, when the Church of England Catechism was to be repeated, something like the following conversation took place:

Clergyman.—What is your name?

Spurgeon.—Spurgeon, sir.

C.—No, no; what is your name?

S.—Charles Spurgeon, sir.

C.—No, you should not behave so, for you know I only want your Christian name.

S.—If you please, sit, I am afraid I haven't got one.

C.—Why, how is that?

S.—Because I do not think I am a Christian.

C.—What are you, then—a heathen?

S.—No, sir; but we may not be heathens, and yet be without the grace of God, and so not be truly Christians.

C.—Well, well, never mind; what is your first name?

S.—Charles.

C.—Who gave you that name?

S.—I am sure I don't know, sir; I know no godfathers ever did anything for me, for I never had any. Likely enough, my mother and father did.

C.—Now, you should not set these boys a-laughing. Of course I do not wish you to say the usual answer.

He seemed always to have a respect for me, aud gave me *The Christian Year*, in calf, as a reward for my great proficiency in religious knowledge. Proceeding with the Catechism, he suddenly turned to me, and said—

Spurgeon, you were never properly baptized.

S.—Oh, yes, sir, I was; my grandfather baptized me in the little parlour, and he is a minister, so I know he did it right!

C.—Ah, but you had neither faith nor repentance, and therefore ought not to have received baptism!

S.—Why, sir, that has nothing to do with it! All infants ought to be baptized.

C.—How do you know that? Does not the Prayer Book say that faith and repentance are necessary before baptism? And this is so Scriptural a doctrine, that no one ought to deny it. (Here he went on to show that all the persons spoken of in the Bible as being baptized were believers; which, of course, was an easy task.) Now, Charles, I shall give you till next week to find out whether the Bible does not declare faith and repentance to be necessary qualifications before baptism.

I felt sure enough of victory; for I thought that a ceremony my grandfather and father both practised in their ministry must be right; but I could not find it—I was beaten—and made up my mind as to the course I would take.

C.—Well, Charles, what do you think now?

S.—Why, sir, I think you are right, but then it applies to you as well as to me!

C.—I wanted to show you this; for this is the reason why we appoint sponsors. It is that, without faith, I had no more right than you to holy baptism, but the promise of my sponsors was accepted by the Church as an equivalent. You have no doubt seen your father, when he has no money, give a note-of-hand for it, and this is regarded as an earnest of payment, because, as an honest man, we have reason to expect he will honour the note he has given. Now, sponsors are generally good people, and in charity we accept their promise on behalf of the child. As the child cannot at the time have faith, we accept the bond that he will; which promise he fulfils at confirmation, when he takes the bond into his own hands.

S.—Well, sir, I think it is a very bad note-of-hand.

C.—I have no time to argue that, but I believe it to be good. I will only ask you this: which seems to have the greater regard to Scripture —I, as a Churchman, or your grandfather as a Dissenter? He baptizes in the very teeth of Scripture; and I do not, in my opinion, do so, for I require a promise, which I look upon as an equivalent of repentance and faith, to be rendered in future years.

S.—Really, sir, I think you are more like right; but since it seems to be the truth that only believers should be baptized, I think you are both wrong, though you seem to treat the Bible with the greater politeness.

C.—Well, then, you confess that you were not properly baptized; and you would think it your duty, if in your power, to join with us, and have sponsors to promise on your behalf.

S.—Oh, no! I have been baptized once, before I ought; I will wait next time till I am fit for it.

C.—(Smiling.) Ah, you are wrong, but I like to see you keep to the Word of God! Seek from Him a new heart and Divine direction, and you will see on truth after another, and very probably there will be a great change in those opinions which now seem so deeply rooted in you.

I resolved, from that moment, that if ever Divine grace should work a change in me, I would be baptized, since, as I afterwards told my friend the clergyman, "I never ought to be blamed for improper baptism, as I had nothing to do with it; the error, if any, rested with my parents and grandparents."

*   *   *

It was while I was at Maidstone that I had the opportunity of attending the services of the Established Church, and therefore was able, long afterwards, to say to the students of the Pastors' College: "There is an ecclesiastical twang which is much admired in the Establishment, a sort of steeple-in-the-throat grandeur, an aristocratic, theologic, parsonic, supernatural, infra-human mouthing of language and rolling over of words. It may be illustrated by the following specimen—'He that hath yaws to yaw, let him yaw,' which is a remarkable, if not impressive, rendering of a Scripture text. Who does not know the hallowed way of pronouncing—'Dearly-beloved brethren, the Scripture moveth us in divers places'? It rolls in my ears now like Big Ben, coupled with boyish memories of monotonous peals of 'The Prince Albert, Albert Prince of Wales, and all the Royal Family. . . . Amen.' Now, if a man who talks so unnaturally does *not* get bronchitis, or some other disease, I can only say that throat diseases must be very sovereignly dispensed. At the Nonconformist hobbies of utterance I have already struck a blow, and I believe it is by them that larynx and lungs become delicate, and good men succumb to silence and the grave."

I had a variety of experiences while at that Church school. One piece of mischief I remember to this day. There was a large jar of ammonia in a certain cupboard, and I used to lead the new boys to it, and tell them to take a good sniff, the usual result being that they would be quite overpowered. Once, when a boy fell down in a dead faint, I was really frightened, and I did not want to play the same trick on anyone else. Perhaps I took the more liberty as the master (Mr. David Walker) was my uncle; at any rate, I was a great favourite with my aunt, and that fact helped me out of many a difficulty.

Mr. Walker's usual plan of punishing his pupils was to make the sentence bear as much resemblance as possible to the offence they had committed. For instance, the boys had gone one night, and borrowed a boat from the river; so, the next night, they were roused from their slumbers, and made to go at once to return it to its proper place. They would probably be all the more careful not to repeat their wrong-doing when they found how much discomfort it brought to themselves.

It often happened that, when corporal punishment was to be administered, my uncle would send me out to find a cane for him. It

was not a very pleasant task, and I noticed that I never once succeeded in selecting a stick which was liked by the boy who had to
feel it. Either it was too thin, or too thick; and, in consequence, I was
threatened by the sufferers with condign punishment if I did not do
better next time. I learned from that experience never to expect God's
children to like the particular rod with which they are chastened.

I greatly offended my uncle, on one occasion, by pointing out an
error in an arithmetical problem he was working on the blackboard.
He said that it was derogatory to his dignity to be corrected before his
pupils, but I maintained that it was not right for me to let the mistake
pass without mentioning it after I had detected the blunder. I think,
after that incident, he judged that I could employ my time to the
greatest advantage by taking my books, and studying by myself
beneath an old oak-tree by the river Medway; at all events, he showed
his appreciation of my mathematical progress by allowing me to
make the calculations which are, I believe, still used by a certain Life
Insurance Society in London.

*   *   *

[In the month of July, 1889, Spurgeon paid a short visit to the town
of Maidstone. On the Sabbath evening after his drive into Kent, he
preached at the Metropolitan Tabernacle a sermon upon Psalm lxxv.
17, in which he said:

I went down, last week, to Maidstone, in Kent. It is as near as
possible to the day, forty years ago, when I left the school called a
"College" there. I thought that I must go down and look at the spot,
and specially at a tree which stands by the river Medway. Under that
tree I spent many hours, and many days, and even many weeks, reading all day long. "In school-time?" say you. Yes, my master thought
that I should do better under that tree than in the class; and he was a
wise man. He gave me my book, and left me to myself; and as I stood
last week under that tree, with the smoothly-flowing river at my feet,
I could thank God for His mercy to me for all these forty years, and
I could say, "O God, Thou hast taught me from my youth: and
hitherto have I declared Thy wondrous works." There may be some
young people here to-night, just come back from school, boys and
girls who are just finishing their school days. I would to God that
they would spend some time in holy, quiet thought about their future,
about whom they will serve, who shall be their Teacher, for whom
they will become teachers, and how the life which has now become
more public than before shall be spent.

As I stood there, last week, I could not help praising God that, not long after I left that school, He led me to faith in Christ, and to rest in Him, and find eternal life; and I could not but thank God that I went to that school for twelve months. It was a Church of England school. I had never seen anything of Church of Englandism till that time, but there was a turning in my life, through being there, to which I owe my being here. The Church of England Catechism has in it, as some of you may remember, this question, "What is required of persons to be baptized?" and the answer I was taught to give, and did give, was, "Repentance, whereby they forsake sin, and faith, whereby they steadfastly believe the promises of God made to them in that sacrament." I looked that answer up in the Bible, and I found it to be strictly correct as far as repentance and faith are concerned, and of course, when I afterwards became a Christian, I also became a Baptist; and here I am, and it is due to the Church of England Catechism that I am a Baptist. Having been brought up among Congregationalists, I had never looked at the matter in my life. I had thought myself to have been baptized as an infant; and so, when I was confronted with the question, "What is required of persons to be baptized?" and I found that repentance and faith were required, I said to myself, "Then I have not been baptized; that infant sprinkling of mine was a mistake; and please God that I ever have repentance and faith, I will be properly baptized." I did not know that there was one other person in the world who held the same opinion; for so little do Baptists make any show, or so little did they do so then, that I did not know of their existence. So I feel grateful to the Church school, and grateful to the Church Catechism, for what I learnt at Maidstone. I do not know that I have any vivid gratitude for any other question in the Catechism, but I am very thankful for that particular one, for it led me where it was never intended to lead me by those who wrote it. It led me, however, as I believe, to follow the Scriptural teaching that repentance and faith are required before there can be any true baptism.]

The Young Usher's Teacher in Theology

The first lessons I ever had in theology were from an old cook in the school at Newmarket where I was an usher.[1] She was a good old soul, and used to read *The Gospel Standard*.[2] She liked something very

[1] Spurgeon came to Newmarket, Cambridgeshire, from Maidstone in August, 1849. The principal of this school was John Swindell.—P.
[2] A magazine founded in 1835 which under the Editorship of J. C. Philpot (1802–1869), who seceded from the Church of England in 1835, rose to a monthly circulation of over 17,000. Philpot's aim was to "cut down natural religion and to demolish some of those mighty castles of letter-religion which Satan everywhere builds up." After his death, Spurgeon wrote: "We have read Mr. Philpot's sermons with much profit; he was

sweet indeed, good strong Calvinistic doctrine, but she lived strongly as well as fed strongly. Many a time we have gone over the covenant of grace together, and talked of the personal election of the saints, their union to Christ, their final perseverance, and what vital godliness meant; and I do believe that I learnt more from her than I should have learned from any six doctors of divinity of the sort we have now-adays. There are some Christian people who taste, and see, and enjoy religion in their own souls, and who get at a deeper knowledge of it than books can ever give them, though they should search all their days. The cook at Newmarket was a godly experienced woman, from whom I learned far more than I did from the minister of the chapel we attended. I asked her once, "Why do you go to such a place?" She replied, "Well, there is no other place of worship to which I can go." I said, "But it must be better to stay at home than to hear such stuff." "Perhaps so," she answered; "but I like to go out to worship even if I get nothing by going. You see a hen sometimes scratching all over a heap of rubbish to try to find some corn; she does not get any, but it shows that she is looking for it, and using the means to get it, and then, too, the exercise warms her." So the old lady said that scratching over the poor sermons she heard was a blessing to her because it exercised her spiritual faculties and warmed her spirit. On another occasion I told her that I had not found a crumb in the whole sermon, and asked how she had fared. "Oh!" she answered, "I got on better to-night, for to all the preacher said, I just put in a *not*, and that turned his talk into real gospel."

*   *   *

[After Spurgeon was "called home", Professor J. D. Everett, F.R.S., of Queen's College, Belfast, wrote to *The Christian World*: "In the summer of 1849, when I was not quite eighteen, I went to Newmarket to assist in a school kept by a Mr. Swindell. There were two other assistants, but not long after my arrival they went off, and I was left for a week or so as the sole assistant. I was then relieved of part of my duty by a lad of fifteen, who came as an articled pupil. This was Charles H. Spurgeon, and for the next three months we shared the work between us. We boarded in the house, occupied the same bedroom, took our walks together, discussed our common griev-ances, and were the best of friends.

"He was rather small and delicate, with pale but plump face, dark brown eyes and hair, and a bright, lively manner, with a never-failing

incomparable on his one theme." *The Sword and Trowel*, 1870, p. 332. Cf. *The Seceders* 3 vols., edited by J. H. Philpot and S. F. Paul.—P.

flow of conversation. He was rather deficient in muscle, did not care for cricket or other athletic games, and was timid at meeting cattle on the roads.

"He had been well brought up in a family with strong Puritanical tendencies, and was proficient in the subjects taught in the middle-class schools of those days. He knew a little Greek, enough Latin to gather the general sense of Virgil's 'Æneid' without a dictionary, and was fond of algebra. He had a big book of equation problems (by Bland, I think), and could do all the problems in it, except some two or three, which I was proud to be able to do for him. He was a smart, clever boy at all kinds of book learning; and, judging from the accounts he gave me of his experiences in his father's counting-house, he was also a smart man of business. He was a keen observer of men and manners, and very shrewd in his judgments. He enjoyed a joke, but was earnest, hard-working, and strictly conscientious.

"He had a wonderful memory for passages of oratory which he admired, and used to pour forth to me with great gusto, in our walks, long screeds from open-air addresses of a very rousing description, which he had heard delivered at Colchester Fair, by the Congregational minister, Mr. Davids. His imagination had evidently been greatly impressed by these services, at which, by-the-by, his father was selected to give out the hymns on account of the loudness of his voice—a quality which would appear to have run in the family, but which had not at that time shown itself in my young friend. I have also heard him recite long passages from Bunyan's *Grace Abounding*. He was a delightful companion, cheerful and sympathetic; a good listener as well as a good talker.[1] And he was not cast in a common conventional mould, but had a strong character of his own.

"As to the early history of his theological views, I can add something to what has been already published. In Mr. Swindell's household there was a faithful old servant—a big, sturdy woman, who was well known to me and all the inmates as 'cook'.[2] She was a woman of strong religious feelings, and a devout Calvinist. Spurgeon, when under deep religious conviction, had conversed with her, and been deeply impressed with her views of Divine truth. He explained this

[1] Everett also records in his diary that on Monday afternoon, September 10, 1849 the boys had a missionary meeting in the school room, at which Spurgeon was chairman and spoke fluently. It was possibly his first speech.—P.

[2] The cook's name was Mary King. "From her," Spurgeon wrote in his first published book (*The Saint and his Saviour*, 1857) "I got all the theology I ever needed." In her closing years Spurgeon had the pleasure of supplying the financial needs of this gracious woman.—P.

to me, and told me, in his own terse fashion, that it was 'cook' who had taught him his theology. I hope I am not violating his confidence in mentioning this fact. It is no discredit to the memory of a great man that he was willing to learn from the humblest sources."]

"It would not be easy for some of us to recall the hour when we first heard the name of Jesus. In very infancy that sweet sound was as familiar to our ear as the hush of lullaby. Our earliest recollections are associated with the house of God, the family altar, the Holy Bible, the sacred song, and the fervent prayer. Like young Samuels, we were lighted to our rest by the lamps of the sanctuary, and were awakened by the sound of the morning hymn. Many a time has the man of God, whom a parent's hospitality has entertained, implored a blessing on our head, desiring in all sincerity that we might early call the Redeemer blessed; and to his petition a mother's earnest "Amen" has solemnly responded. Perhaps the first song we learned to sing was concerning the children's best Friend. The first book that we began to read contained His sweet name, and many were the times when we were pressed by godly ones to think of Jesus, and to give our young hearts to Him."—C. H. S.

Chapter 5

Early Religious Impressions

I WAS privileged with godly parents, watched with jealous eyes, scarcely ever permitted to mingle with questionable associates, warned not to listen to anything profane or licentious, and taught the way of God from my youth up. There came a time when the solemnities of eternity pressed upon me for a decision, and when a mother's tears and a father's supplications were offered to Heaven on my behalf. At such a time, had I not been helped by the grace of God, but had I been left alone to do violence to conscience, and to struggle against conviction, I might perhaps have been at this moment dead, buried, and doomed, having through a course of vice brought myself to my grave, or I might have been as earnest a ringleader amongst the ungodly as I now desire to be an eager champion for Christ and His truth.

I do speak of myself with many deep regrets of heart. I hid as it were my face from Him, and I let the years run round—not without twinges of conscience, not without rebukes, when I knew how much I needed a Saviour; not without the warnings which came from others whom I saw happy and rejoicing in Christ, while I had no share in His salvation. Still, I put it off, as others are doing, from day to day, and month to month, and thought that Christ might come in some odd hour, and when I had nothing else to do, I might think of Him whose blood could cleanse me. O my soul, I could fain smite thee now! Truly, I could lay this rod about my own heart to think that weeks and months should have rolled over my head, and I should have hid as it were my face from Christ in wilful neglect of my dear Lord whose heart had bled for me.

Children are often very reticent to their parents. Often and often have I spoken with young lads about their souls, and they have told me they could not talk to their fathers upon such matters. I know it was so with me. When I was under concern of soul, the last persons I should have elected to speak to upon religion would have been my parents—not through want of love to them, nor absence of love on their part; but so it was. A strange feeling of diffidence pervades a seeking soul, and drives it from its friends. Yet I cannot tell how much I owe to the solemn words of my good mother. It was the custom on Sunday evenings, while we were yet little children, for her to stay at home with us, and then we sat round the table, and read verse by verse, and she explained the Scripture to us. After that was done, then came the time of pleading; there was a little piece of Alleine's *Alarm*, or of Baxter's *Call to the Unconverted*, and this was read with pointed observations made to each of us as we sat round the table; and the question was asked, how long it would be before we would think about our state, how long before we would seek the Lord. Then came a mother's prayer, and some of the words of that prayer we shall never forget, even when our hair is grey. I remember, on one occasion, her praying thus: "Now, Lord, if my children go on in their sins, it will not be from ignorance that they perish, and my soul must bear a swift witness against them at the day of judgment if they lay not hold of Christ." That thought of a mother's bearing swift witness against me, pierced my conscience, and stirred my heart. When I was a child, if I had done anything wrong, I did not need anybody to tell me of it; I told myself of it, and I have cried myself to sleep many a time with the consciousness that I had done wrong; and when I came to know the Lord, I felt very grateful to Him because He had given me a tender conscience.

Fathers and mothers are the most natural agents for God to use in the salvation of their children. I am sure that, in my early youth, no teaching ever made such an impression upon my mind as the instruction of my mother; neither can I conceive that, to any child, there can be one who will have such influence over the young heart as the mother who has so tenderly cared for her offspring. A man with a soul so dead as not to be moved by the sacred name of "mother" is creation's blot. Never could it be possible for any man to estimate what he owes to a godly mother. Certainly I have not the powers of speech with which to set forth my valuation of the choice blessing which the Lord bestowed on me in making me the son of one who prayed *for* me, and prayed *with* me. How can I ever forget her tearful eye when she warned me to escape from the wrath to come? I thought her lips right eloquent; others might not think so, but they certainly were eloquent to me. How can I ever forget when she bowed her knee, and with her arms about my neck, prayed, "Oh, that my son might live before Thee!" Nor can her frown be effaced from my memory—that solemn, loving frown, when she rebuked my budding iniquities; and her smiles have never faded from my recollections— the beaming of her countenance when she rejoiced to see some good thing in me towards the Lord God of Israel.

Well do I remember hearing my father speak of an incident that greatly impressed him. He used to be frequently away from home preaching, and at one time, as he was on his way to a service, he feared that he was neglecting his own family while caring for the souls of others. He therefore turned back, and went to his home. On arriving there, he was surprised to find no one in the lower rooms of the house but, on ascending the stairs, he heard a sound as of someone engaged in prayer. On listening at the bedroom door, he discovered that it was my mother, pleading most earnestly for the salvation of all her children, and specially praying for Charles, her first-born and strong-willed son. My father felt that he might safely go about his Master's business while his dear wife was caring so well for the spiritual interests of the boys and girls at home, so he did not disturb her, but proceeded at once to fulfil his preaching engagement.

My mother said to me, one day, "Ah, Charles! I often prayed the Lord to make you a Christian, but I never asked that you might become a Baptist." I could not resist the temptation to reply, "Ah, mother! the Lord has answered your prayer with His usual bounty, and given you exceeding abundantly above what you asked or thought."

Up to the age of fourteen, I had not even heard of people called Baptists, and when I did hear of them, it was not at all a favourable report that was given to me concerning them. I do not suppose my parents meant me to believe that Baptists were bad people, but I certainly did think so; and I cannot help feeling that, somewhere or other, I must have heard some calumnies against them, or else how should I have had that opinion?

I remember seeing a baby sprinkled within less than an hour of its death, and I seem to hear even now the comfort which a certain good man gave to the bereaved parents—"What a mercy the child was baptized! What a consolation it must be!" This was in an Independent family, and the words were spoken by an Independent minister.

I knew an instance of an aged minister, of the same persuasion, who sprinkled a little boy, although the father was averse to it. The child was running about in the hall of the minister's house, and his mother was looking on. He was caught up, and the pious man exclaimed, "Come along, Mrs. S——, the poor child shall not live like a heathen any longer." So the conjuration was performed, and the little boy was put into the Pædo-Baptist covenant. He was not only suffered to come, but forced to come, and, doubtless, went on his way rejoicing to think it was over.

It is said by some that children cannot understand the great mysteries of religion. We even know some Sunday-school teachers who cautiously avoid mentioning the great doctrines of the gospel because they think the children are not prepared to receive them. Alas! the same mistake has crept into the pulpit; for it is currently believed, among a certain class of preachers, that many of the doctrines of the Word of God, although true, are not fit to be taught to the people, since they would pervert them to their own destruction. Away with such priestcraft! Whatever God has revealed ought to be preached. Whatever HE has revealed, if I am not capable of understanding it, I will still believe and preach it. I do hold that there is no doctrine of the Word of God which a child, if he be capable of salvation, is not capable of receiving. I would have children taught all the great doctrines of truth without a solitary exception, that they may in their after days hold fast by them.

I can bear witness that children *can* understand the Scriptures; for I am sure that, when but a child, I could have discussed many a knotty point of controversial theology, having heard both sides of the question freely stated among my father's circle of friends. In fact, children are capable of understanding some things in early life, which we hardly understand afterwards. Children have eminently a simplicity of faith, and simplicity of faith is akin to the highest knowledge; indeed, I know not that there is much distinction between the simplicity of a child and the genius of the profoundest mind. He who receives things simply, as a child, will often have ideas which the man who is prone to make a syllogism of everything will never attain unto. If you wish to know whether children can be taught, I point you to many in our churches, and in pious families—not prodigies, but such as we frequently see—Timothys and Samuels, and little girls, too, who have early come to know a Saviour's love. As soon as a child is capable of being lost, it is capable of being saved. As soon as a child can sin, that child can, if God's grace assist it, believe and receive the Word of God. As soon as children can learn evil, be assured that they are competent, under the teaching of the Holy Spirit, to learn good.

In the household in which I was trained, no cooking was ever done on the Sabbath, and if in the winter time something hot was brought on the table, it was a pudding prepared on the Saturday, or a few potatoes, which took but little trouble to warm. Is not this far better, far more Christian-like, than preparing a great Sunday feast, and compelling servants to slave in the kitchen? If the horse was taken out because the distance to the meeting-house was too great, or the weather too rough for walking, Christians of the good old school always gave the animal its Sabbath on the Saturday or the Monday; and as to the coachman, when they employed one, they always took care to give him time to put up the horse, that he might come in and

1. *Spurgeon remained but ten months in his birthplace, Kelvedon, Essex. The house, occupied as an inn when this picture was taken, still stands*

2. *The old Manse and Meeting House, Stambourne, where James Spurgeon ministered for more than 50 years. Here his young grandson first made acquaintance with that Puritan theology which he was later to preach so powerfully and defend so courageously*

Home Juvenile Society

Vol 1

No 2

April 1846

Colchester. C. Spurgeon

1 Pin per line is the cost for notices not of the societies

Juvenile Magazine

3 for one ½ penny

Contributions have been received from Eliza, Spurgeon

Sunday 19th

Praymeeting very good, carry it on & let me say that on 26th there is another.

Blessings come through prayer

Sunday 26

No prayermeeting what a decline imitate the page before.

Certainly this morning there is an excuse but only one in a month is shameful

4. *Spurgeon's father, John Spurgeon, who ministered for sixteen years to the Independent congregation at Tollesbury near Colchester. He enjoyed a long and useful life, dying at the age of ninety-one*

3. [opposite] *Pages from the "Juvenile Magazine" which Spurgeon at the age of eleven produced for the benefit of his brother and sisters reveal the literary bent of his young mind. The top half of the plate shows the front and back outside cover of the "magazine"*

My dear friends Mr & Mrs B.

I am very ill, but I had rather
a better night the last, freer from
the pains in hands then I have
felt for some nights past, and
feel a little better this morn g.

I do hope the Lord by my affliction
is preparing me for a better state.
I have been preaching almost
60 Years, and I'm not ashamed
to say, that I have not done one act
In & of myself, that I could rest upon for eternity.
all my support is, and thro' Christ

His covenant engagement I can
rest upon with pleasure, for
those he loves once, he will
never leave nor forsake. My
Dear friend, seek him now while
he is to be found, call upon him

while he is near, if you seek him
He will be found of you, but if you
forsake him he will cast you off
for ever. We need encouragement
and stirring up we are so apt
to forget him, who only can
can save us. I hope Mrs B,
is better then when you wrote
My sight begins to fail me. I
can hardly see what I write
You shall hear from me again
soon if I stand. Love to you
all.   H Spurgeon Sen

Mamborne 29 April 63

Newmarket
May 1st 1850

My Dear Mother,

Many, very many,
happy returns of this your
Birthday. In this instance
my wish will certainly be
realized, for in heaven you
are sure to have an eternity
of happy days. May you in
your coming years live beneath
the sweet smiles of the God of
peace; may joy and singing
attend your footsteps, to a blissful haven of rest & tranquility.
Your birthday will now be
doubly memorable, for on the
third of May, the boy for whom
you have so often prayed, the
boy of hopes and fears, your
firstborn, will join the visi-

church of the Redeemed on earth, and will bind himself doubly to the Lord his God, by open profession. You my mother, have been the great means in God's hand, of rendering me what I hope I am. Your kind warning Sabbath evening addresses were too deeply settled on my heart to be forgotten. You by God's blessing prepared the way for the preached word, & for that Holy Book the Rise & Progress. If I have any courage if I feel prepared to follow my Saviour not only into the water but should he call me, even into the fire; I love you as the preacher to my heart of such courage, as my praying, watching mother. Impossible I think it is that I should ever cease to love you, or you to love me,

7. *The interior of Artillery Street Methodist Chapel into which Spurgeon turned on the snowy morning of 6th January 1850. The commemoration plaque on the left marks the spot near where he sat*

8. *The river Lark at Isleham Ferry, Cambridgeshire, the spot to which Spurgeon walked eight miles to be baptized on May 3, 1850*

worship with the family, and they were content to wait till he could come round for them after service, for they did not want him to lose even the Benediction.

*　　　*　　　*

I recollect, when I was a boy, hearing a minister preach from this text, "Who can find a virtuous woman? for her price is far above rubies." The opening of that memorable discourse was somewhat in this fashion: " 'Who can find a virtuous woman?' Why, anyone who chooses to look for her; and the only reason why Solomon could not find her was because he looked in the wrong place. Virtuous women kept clear of a king who had such a multitude of wives. But," said the preacher, "if Solomon were here now, and were made truly wise, he would not long ask, 'Who can find a virtuous woman?' He would join the church, and find himself at once among a band of holy women, whose adornment is a meek and quiet spirit. If he were permitted to look in upon the Dorcas meeting, he would see many of the sort of whom he once said, 'She stretcheth out her hand to the poor; yea, she reacheth forth her hands to the needy.' If he would adjourn to the Sunday-school, he would there meet with others of whom he would say, 'She openeth her mouth with wisdom; and in her tongue is the law of kindness.' We, who serve the Lord Jesus, meet many a time with virtuous women, of each of whom we could say with the wise king, 'Her price is far above rubies.' "

The preacher of whom I have spoken, interested me by the remark, "Why 'above *rubies*'? Why not above *diamonds*? My brethren, the diamond is but a pale and sickly stone, which needs the glare of candle-light or gas to set it off; but the ruby is a ruddy, healthy gem, which is beautiful by daylight. Lovely is the woman whose face is full of the glow of activity in domestic life. That is the kind of woman who makes the housewife in whom the heart of her husband safely trusteth."

Whatever one may think of the correctness of the exposition, the sentiment of the preacher was sound and practical.

I have not all pleasant reminiscences of the preachers of my boyhood. I used to hear a divine who had a habit, after he had uttered about a dozen sentences, of saying, "As I have already observed," or, "I repeat what I before remarked." Well, good soul, as there was nothing particular in what he had said, the repetition only revealed the more clearly the nakedness of the land. If it was very good, and you said it forcibly, why go over it again? And if it was a feeble affair, why exhibit it a second time? Occasionally, of course, the repetition

E

of a few sentences may be very telling; anything may be good occasionally, and yet be very vicious as a habit. Who wonders that people do not listen the first time when they know it is all to come over again? I once heard a most esteemed minister, who mumbled sadly, compared to "a bumble bee in a pitcher"—a vulgar metaphor, no doubt, but so exactly descriptive, that it brings to my mind the droning sound at this instant most distinctly, and reminds me of the parody upon Gray's *Elegy*:

> "Now fades the glimmering subject from the sight,
>   And all the air a sleepy stillness holds,
>   Save where the parson hums his droning flight,
>   And drowsy tinklings lull the slumb'ring folds."

What a pity that a man who from his heart delivered doctrines of undoubted value, in language the most appropriate, should commit ministerial suicide by harping on one string, when the Lord had given him an instrument of many strings to play upon! Alas! alas! for that dreary voice, it hummed and hummed, like a mill-wheel, to the same unmusical tune, whether its owner spake of Heaven or hell, eternal life or everlasting wrath. It might be, by accident, a little louder or softer, according to the length of the sentence, but its tone was still the same, a dreary waste of sound, a howling wilderness of speech in which there was no possible relief, no variety, no music, nothing but horrible sameness. When the wind blows through the Æolian harp, it swells through all the chords, but the Heavenly wind, passing through some men, spends itself upon one string, and that, for the most part, the most out of tune of the whole. Grace alone could enable hearers to edify under the drum—drum—drum of some divines. I think an impartial jury would bring in a verdict of justifiable slumbering in many cases where the sound emanating from the preacher lulls to sleep by its reiterated note.

I have a very lively, or rather a deadly, recollection of a certain series of discourses on the Hebrews, which made a deep impression on my mind of the most undesirable kind. I wished frequently that the Hebrews had kept the Epistle to themselves, for it sadly bored one poor Gentile lad. By the time the seventh or eighth discourse had been delivered, only the very good people could stand it: these, of course, declared that they never heard more valuable expositions, but to those of a more carnal judgment it appeared that each sermon increased in dulness. Paul, in that Epistle, exhorts us to *suffer* the word of exhortation, and we did so. I also recollect hearing in my younger days long passages out of Daniel, which might have been exceedingly instructive to me if I had obtained the remotest conception of what they meant. I remember hearing a sermon from these words, "Who passing through the valley of Baca make it a well." Certainly, the preacher did not make his sermon a well, for it was as dry as a stick, and not worth hearing. There was nothing like cheerfulness in it, but all the way through a flood of declamation against hopeful Christians, against people going to Heaven who are not always grumbling, and murmuring, and doubting; fumbling for their evidences amidst the exercises of their own hearts, ever reading and striving to rival Job and Jeremiah in grief, taking the Lamentations as the fit expression of their own lips, troubling their poor brains, and vexing their poor hearts, and smarting, and crying, and wearying themselves with the perpetual habit of complaining against God, saying, "My stroke is heavier than my groaning."

I used to hear a minister whose preaching was, as far as I could make it out, "Do this, and do that, and do the other, and you will be saved." According to his theory, to pray was a very easy thing; to make yourself a new heart, was a thing of a few instants, and could be done at almost any time; and I really thought that I could turn to Christ when I pleased, and that therefore I could put it off to the last part of my life, when it might be conveniently done upon a sick bed. But when the Lord gave my soul its first shakings in conviction, I soon knew better. I went to pray. I did pray, God knoweth, but it seemed to me that I did not. What, *I* approach the throne? Such a wretch as *I* lay hold on the promise? *I* venture to hope that God could look on me? It seemed impossible. A tear, a groan, and sometimes not so much as that, an "Ah!" a "Would that!" a "But"—the lip could not utter more. It was prayer, but it did not seem so then. Oh, how hard is prevailing prayer to a poor God-provoking sinner! Where was the power to lay hold on God's strength, or wrestle with the angel? Certainly not in me, for I was weak as water, and sometimes hard as the nether millstone.

Once, under a powerful sermon, my heart shook within me, and was dissolved in the midst of my bowels; I thought I would seek the Lord, and I bowed my knee, and wrestled, and poured out my heart before Him. Again I ventured within His sanctuary to hear His Word, hoping that in some favoured hour He would send a precious promise to my consolation; but, ah! that wretched afternoon, I heard a sermon wherein Christ was not; I had no longer any hope. I would have sipped at that fountain, but I was driven away; I felt that I would have believed in Christ, and I longed and sighed for Him. But, ah! that dreadful sermon, and those terrible things that were uttered! My poor soul knew not what was truth, or what was error; but I thought the man was surely preaching the truth, and I was driven back. I dared not go, I could not believe, I could not lay hold on Christ; I was shut out, if no one else was.

"Hardly a glimmer of the humbling truth of our natural depravity dawns on the dull apprehension of the worldly-wise, though souls taught from above know it and are appalled by it. In divers ways the discovery comes to those whom the Lord ordains to save. . . .

"There is a vital connection between soul-distress and sound doctrine. Sovereign grace is dear to those who have groaned deeply because they see what grievous sinners they are. Witness Joseph Hart and John Newton, whose hymns you have often sung, or David Brainerd and Jonathan Edwards, whose biographies many of you have read. You seldom hear much of God's everlasting covenant in these modern times, for few men feel that thorough conviction of sin which comes directly from the teaching of the Holy Spirit. In the economy of redemption the effectual operation of the Spirit in enlightening the heart concerning its own sinfulness is sure evidence of the Father's personal love to His chosen people, and of the special atonement that the Son of God made for their transgressions."—C. H. S.

Chapter 6

"Through much Tribulation"

MY heart was fallow, and covered with weeds; but, on a certain day, the great Husbandman came, and began to plough my soul. Ten black horses were His team, and it was a sharp ploughshare that He used, and the ploughers made deep furrows. The ten commandments were those black horses, and the justice of God, like a ploughshare, tore my spirit. I was condemned, undone, destroyed—lost, helpless, hopeless—I thought hell was before me. Then there came a cross-ploughing, for when I went to hear the gospel, it did not comfort me; it made me wish I had a part in it, but I feared that such a boon was out of the question. The choicest promises of God frowned upon me, and His threatenings thundered at me. I prayed, but found no answer of peace. It was long with me thus.

The abundant benefit which we now reap from the deep ploughing of our heart is enough of itself to reconcile us to the severity of the process. Precious is that wine which is pressed in the winefat of conviction; pure is that gold which is dug from the mines of repentance; and bright are those pearls which are found in the caverns of deep distress. We might never have known such deep humility if the Lord had not humbled us. We had never been so separated from fleshly trusting had He not, by His rod, revealed the corruption and disease of our heart. We had never learned to comfort the feeble-minded, and confirm the weak, had He not made us ready to halt, and caused our sinew to shrink. If we have any power to console the weary, it is the result of our remembrance of what we once suffered—for here lies our power to sympathize. If we can now look down with scorn upon the boastings of vain, self-conceited man, it is because our own vaunted strength has utterly failed us, and made us contemptible in our own eyes. If we can now plead with ardent desire for the souls of our fellow-men, and especially if we feel a more than common passion for the salvation of sinners, we must attribute it in no small degree to the fact that we have been smitten for sin, and therefore, knowing the terror of the Lord, are constrained to persuade men. The laborious pastor, the fervent minister, the ardent evangelist, the faithful teacher, the powerful intercessor, can all trace the birth of their zeal to the sufferings they endured through sin, and the knowledge they thereby attained of its evil nature. We have ever drawn the sharpest arrows from the quiver of our own experience. We find no sword-blades so true in metal as those which have been forged in the furnace of soul-trouble.

A spiritual experience which is thoroughly flavoured with a deep and bitter sense of sin is of great value to him that hath had it. It is terrible in the drinking, but it is most wholesome in the bowels, and in the whole of the after-life. Possibly, much of the flimsy piety of the present day arises from the ease with which men attain to peace and joy in these evangelistic days. We would not judge modern converts, but we certainly prefer that form of spiritual exercise which leads the soul by the way of Weeping-cross, and makes it see its blackness before assuring it that it is "clean every whit". Too many think lightly of sin, and therefore think lightly of the Saviour. He who has stood before his God, convicted and condemned, with the rope about his neck, is the man to weep for joy when he is pardoned, to hate the evil which has been forgiven him, and to live to the honour of the Redeemer by whose blood he has been cleansed.

*   *   *

Our own experience recalls us to the period when we panted for the Lord, even for Him, our only want. Vain to us were the mere ordinances—vain as bottles scorched by the Simoom, and drained of their waters. Vain were ceremonies—vain as empty wells to the thirsty Arab. Vain were the delights of the flesh—bitter as the waters of Marah, which even the parched lips of Israel refused to drink. Vain were the directions of the legal preacher—useless as the howling of the wind to the benighted wanderer. Vain, worse than vain, were our refuges of lies, which fell about our ears like Dagon's temple on the heads of the worshippers. One only hope we had, one sole refuge for our misery. Save where that ark floated—North, South, East, and West was one broad expanse of troubled waters. Save where that star burned, the sky was one vast field of unmitigated darkness. Jesus, *Jesus*, JESUS! He alone, He without another, had become the solitary hiding-place against the storm. As the wounded soldier, lying on the battle-field, with wounds which, like fires, consume his moisture, utters only one monotonous cry of thrilling importunity, "Water, water, water!" so did we perpetually send our prayer to Heaven, "Jesus, Thou Son of David, have mercy on me! O Jesus, come to me!"

We have, we hope, many a time enjoyed nearness to the throne of grace in prayer, but, perhaps, never did such a prayer escape our lips as that which we offered in the bitterness of our spirit when seeking the Saviour. We have often poured out our hearts with greater freedom, with more delight, with stronger faith, in more eloquent language, but never, never have we cried with more vehemence of unquenchable desire, or more burning heat of insatiable longing. There was then no sleepiness or sluggishness in our devotion; we did not then need the whip of command to drive us to labours of prayer, but our soul could not be content unless with sighs and lamentations, with strong crying and tears, it gave vent to our bursting heart. Then we had no need to be dragged to our closets like oxen to the slaughter, but we flew to them like doves to their windows; and when there, we needed no pumping up of desires, but they gushed forth like a fountain of waters, although at times we felt we could scarcely find them a channel.

* * *

I remember the first time I ever sincerely prayed. I do not recollect the words I used; surely, there were few enough words in that petition. I had often repeated a form; I had been in the habit of continually repeating it. At last, I came really to pray, and then I saw myself standing before God, in the immediate presence of the heart-searching Jehovah, and I said within myself, "I have heard of Thee by the hearing of the ear, but now mine eye seeth Thee; wherefore I abhor myself, and repent in dust and ashes." I felt like Esther when she stood before the king, faint and overcome with dread. I was full of penitence of heart, because of His majesty and my sinfulness. I think the only words I could utter were something like these, "Oh!— Ah!" And the only complete sentence was, "God be merciful to me, a sinner!" The overwhelming splendour of His majesty, the greatness of His power, the severity of His justice, the immaculate character of His holiness, and all His dreadful grandeur—these things over-powered my soul, and I fell down in utter prostration of spirit, but there was in that prayer a true and real drawing near to God.

I have not many relations in Heaven, but I have one whom I dearly love, who, I doubt not, often prayed for me, for she nursed me when I was a child, and brought me up during part of my infancy, and now she sits before the throne in glory—suddenly called home. I fancy she looked upon her darling grandson, and as she saw him in the ways of sin, waywardness, and folly, she could not look with sorrow, for there are no tears in the eyes of glorified ones; she could not look with regret, because they cannot know such a feeling before the throne of God; but, ah! that moment when, by sovereign grace, I was constrained to pray, when all alone I bent my knee and wrestled, methinks I see her as she said, "Behold, he prayeth; behold, he prayeth." Oh!

I can picture her countenance. She seemed to have two Heavens for a moment—a double bliss, a Heaven in me as well as in herself—when she could say, "Behold, he prayeth."

I have known some who have suspended prayer through the idea that the petitions of the wicked are an abomination to the Lord, and that therefore it was but committing sin to attempt to offer their supplications. Well can I remember, when coming to Jesus myself, that for years I sought pardon, and found it not. Often, in the deep anguish of my spirit, did I stay my petitions, because I thought them hopeless; and when again the Holy Spirit drew me to the mercy-seat, a deep horror rested on me at the recollection of my repeated, but unanswered cries. I knew myself to be unworthy, and therefore I conceived that Divine justice would not allow an answer to come to me. I thought that the heavens were brass above me, and that if I cried never so earnestly, the Lord would shut out my prayer. I durst not pray, I was too guilty; and when I did dare to pray, 'twas hardly prayer, for I had no hope of being heard. "No," I said, "it is presumption; I must not plead with Him;" and when, at times, I would have prayed, I could not; something choked all utterance, and the spirit could only lament, and long, and pant, and sigh to be able to pray.

Yet I recollect, even as a child, God hearing my prayer. I cannot tell what it was about, it may have been concerning a mere trifle, but to me, as a child, it was as important as the greatest prayer that Solomon ever offered for himself, and God heard that prayer, and it was thus early established in my mind that the Lord was God. And afterwards, when I came really to know Him—for, like the child Samuel, I did not then know the Lord, I only felt after Him in prayer—afterwards, when I came to cry to Him intelligently, I had this prayer answered, and that petition granted, and many a time since then—I am only telling what any who know the Lord could also say—many a time since then He has answered our requests. I cannot tell all about this matter, for there is many a secret between us and our dear Lord. It would not be prudent, proper, or even possible, to mention all the answers to prayer which we have received, for there are love-passages between Christ and the soul, which never must be told, unless it be in choice company, and on rare occasions. Some of our communings with the Lord Jesus are too sacred, too spiritual, too heavenly, ever to be spoken of this side the gates of pearl, but the bulk of the Lord's replies to our petitions are such as might be written athwart the skies, that every eye might read them. It is beginning to be questioned, in many quarters, whether there is any real effect produced by prayer, except that "it excites certain pious emotions in the breasts of those who pray." This is a pretty statement! We ought to be extremely obliged to those superior persons who allow that even so much may result from our visits to the throne of grace! I wonder they did not assert that prayer was ridiculous, or hypocritical, or immoral! Their moderation puts us under obligations! And yet I do not know: when I look again at their admission, I thank them for nothing, for they as good as call us fools. Do they think that we perform a useless exercise merely for the sake of exciting pious emotions? We must be grievous idiots if we can receive benefit from a senseless function. We are not willing to whistle to the wind for the sake of the exercise. We should not be content to go on praying to a god who could be proved to be both deaf and dumb. We have still some little common sense left, despite what our judicious friends consider to be fanaticism. We are sure that we obtain answers to prayer. Of this fact I am as certain as that I am a living man, and that I preach in the Tabernacle. I solemnly declare that I have received of the Lord that which I have asked at His hands, and I am not alone in such testimony, for I am associated with multitudes of men and women who bear witness to the same fact, and declare that they also sought the Lord by prayer and supplication, and He heard them, and delivered them out of their distresses.

* * *

Neither in the Church militant nor in the host triumphant is there one who received a new heart, and was reclaimed from sin without a wound from Jesus. The pain may have been but slight, and the healing may have been speedy, but in each case there has been a real bruise, which required a Heavenly Physician to heal. With some of us, this wounding commenced in early life, for, as soon as infancy gave place to childhood, the rod was exercised upon us. We can remember early convictions of sin, and apprehensions of the wrath of God on its account. An awakened conscience in our most tender years drove us to the throne of mercy. Though we knew not the hand which chastened our spirit, yet did we "bear the yoke in our youth". How many were "the tender buds of hope" which we then put forth, alas! too soon to be withered by youthful lusts; how often were we scared with visions and terrified with dreams, while the reproof of a parent, the death of a playfellow, or a solemn sermon made our hearts melt within us! Truly, our goodness was but "as the morning cloud and the early dew"; but who can tell how much each of these separate woundings contributed toward that killing by the law, which proved to be the effectual work of God? In each of these arousings we discover a gracious purpose; we trace every one of these awakenings to His hand who watched over our path, determined to deliver us from our sins. The small end of that wedge, which has since been driven home, was inserted during these youthful hours of inward strife.

Let none despise the strivings of the Spirit in the hearts of the young; let not boyish anxieties and juvenile repentances be lightly regarded. He incurs a fearful amount of guilt who in the least promotes the aim of the evil one by trampling upon a tender conscience in a child. No one can guess at what age children become capable of conversion. I, at least, can bear my personal testimony to the fact that grace operates on some minds at a period almost too early for recollection. When but young in years, I felt with much sorrow the evil of sin. My bones waxed old with my roaring all the day long. Day and night God's hand was heavy upon me. I hungered for deliverance, for my soul fainted within me. I feared lest the very skies should fall upon me, and crush my guilty soul. God's law had laid hold upon me, and was showing me my sins. If I slept at night, I dreamed of the bottomless pit, and when I awoke, I seemed to feel the misery I had dreamed. Up to God's house I went; my song was but a sigh. To my chamber I retired, and there, with tears and groans, I offered up my prayer, without a hope and without a refuge, for God's law was flogging me with its ten-thonged whip, and then rubbing me with brine afterwards, so that I did shake and quiver with pain and anguish, and my soul chose strangling rather than life, for I was exceeding sorrowful.

That misery was sent for this reason, that I might then be made to cry to Jesus. Our Heavenly Father does not usually cause us to seek the Saviour till He has whipped us clean out of all our confidence; He cannot make us in earnest after Heaven till He has made us feel something of the intolerable tortures of an aching conscience, which is a foretaste of hell. I remember, when I used to awake in the morning, the first thing I took up was Alleine's *Alarm*, or Baxter's *Call to the Unconverted*. Oh, those books, those books! I read and devoured them when under a sense of guilt, but it was like sitting at the foot of Sinai. For five years, as a child, there was nothing before my eyes but my guilt, and though I do not hesitate to say that those who observed my life would not have seen any extraordinary sin, yet as I looked upon myself, there was not a day in which I did not commit such gross, such outrageous sins against God, that often and often have I wished I had never been born. Sickness is a terrible thing, more especially when it is accompanied with pain, when the poor body is racked to an extreme, so that the spirit fails within us, and we are dried up like a potsherd, but I bear witness that sickness, however agonizing, is nothing like the discovery of the evil of sin. I had rather pass through seven years of the most wearisome pain, and the most languishing sickness, than I would ever again pass through the terrible discovery of the evil of sin. It was my sad lot, at that time, to feel the greatness of my sin, without a discovery of the greatness of God's mercy. I had to walk through this world with more than a world upon my shoulders, and sustain a grief that as far exceeds all other griefs as a mountain exceeds a mole-hill, and I often wonder, to this day, how it was that my hand was kept from rending my own body in pieces through the awful agony which I felt when I discovered the greatness of my transgression. Yet, I had not been, openly and publicly, a greater sinner than others, but heart sins were laid bare, sins of lip and tongue were discovered, and then I knew—oh, that I may never have to learn over again in such a dreadful school this terrible lesson!—"the iniquity of Judah and of Israel is exceeding great". Before I thought upon my soul's salvation, I dreamed that my sins were very few. All my sins were dead, as I imagined, and buried in the graveyard of forgetfulness. But that trumpet of conviction, which aroused my soul to think of eternal things, sounded a resurrection-note to all my sins; and, oh, how they rose up in multitudes more countless than the sands of the sea! Now, I saw that my very thoughts were enough to damn me, that my words would sink me lower than the lowest hell, and as for my acts of sin, they now began to be a stench in my nostrils so that I could not bear them. I thought I had rather have been a frog or a toad than have been made a man. I reckoned that the most defiled creature, the most loathsome and contemptible, was a better thing than myself, for I had so grossly and grievously sinned against Almighty God.

*　　　　*　　　　*

Through the Lord's restraining grace, and the holy influence of my early home-life, both at my father's and my grandfather's, I was kept from certain outward forms of sin in which others indulged; and, sometimes, when I began to take stock of myself, I really thought I was quite a respectable lad, and might have been half inclined to boast that I was not like other boys—untruthful, dishonest, disobedient, swearing, Sabbath-breaking, and so on. But, all of a sudden, I met Moses, carrying in his hand the law of God, and as he looked at me, he seemed to search me through and through with his eyes of fire. He bade me read "God's Ten Words"—the ten commandments —and as I read them, they all seemed to join in accusing and condemning me in the sight of the thrice-holy Jehovah. Then, like Daniel, "my comeliness was turned in me into corruption, and I retained no strength;" and I understood what Paul meant when he wrote, "Now we know that what things soever the law saith, it saith to them who are under the law: that every mouth may be stopped, and all the world may become guilty before God." When I saw myself in this condition, I could say nothing in self-defence, or by way of excuse or extenuation. I confessed my transgression in solemn silence unto the Lord, but I could speak no word of self-justification, or apology, for I felt that I was verily guilty of grievous sins against the Holy One of Israel. At that time, a dreadful silence reigned within my spirit; even if I had tried to say a word in my own favour, I should have been self-condemned as a liar. I felt that Job's words might be applied to me, "If I wash myself with snow water, and make my hands never so clean; yet shalt Thou plunge me in the ditch, and mine own clothes shall abhor me. For He is not a man, as I am, that I should answer Him."

Then there came into my startled conscience the remembrance of the universality of law. I thought of what was said of the old Roman empire that, under the rule of Cæsar, if a man once broke the law of Rome, the whole world was one vast prison to him, for he could not get out of the reach of the imperial power. So did it come to be in my aroused conscience. Wherever I went, the law had a demand upon my thoughts, upon my words, upon my rising, upon my resting. What I did, and what I did not do, all came under the cognizance of the law; and then I found that this law so surrounded me that I was always running against it, I was always breaking it. I seemed as if I was a sinner, and nothing else but a sinner. If I opened my mouth, I spoke amiss. If I sat still, there was sin in my silence. I remember that when the Spirit of God was thus dealing with me, I used to feel myself to be a sinner even when I was in the house of God. I thought that when I sang, I was mocking the Lord with a solemn sound upon a false tongue; and if I prayed, I feared that I was sinning in my prayers, insulting Him by uttering confessions which I did not feel, and asking for mercies with a faith that was not true at all, but only another form of unbelief. At the very mention of that word conviction, I seem to hear my chains rattling anew. Was there ever a bond-slave who had more bitterness of soul than I, five years a captive in the dungeons of the law, till my youth seemed as if it would turn into premature old age, and all the buoyancy of my spirit had vanished? O God of the spirits of all men, most of all ought I to hate sin, for surely most of all have I smarted beneath the lash of Thy law!

While I was in the custody of the law, I did not take any pleasure in evil. Alas! I did sin, but my sense of the law of God kept me back from many forms of iniquity. I have thanked God a thousand times in my life that, before my conversion, when I had ill desires, I had no opportunities of sinning, and, on the other hand, when I had the opportunities, I had no desires towards evil. When desires and opportunities come together, like the flint and the steel, they make the spark that kindles the fire, but neither the one nor the other, though they may both be dangerous, can bring about any very great amount of evil so long as they are kept apart. I could not, as others did, plunge into profligacy, or indulge in any of the grosser vices, for that law had me well in hand. I sinned enough without acting like that. Oh, I used to tremble to put one foot before another, for fear I should do wrong! I felt that my old sins seemed to be so many, that it were well to die rather than commit any more. I could not rest while in the grip of the law. If I wanted to sleep a while, or to be a little indifferent and careless, some one or other of those ten commandments roughly aroused me, and looking on me with a frowning face, said, "You have broken me." I thought that I would do some good works, but, somehow, the law always broke my good works in the making. I fancied that, if my tears flowed freely, I might make some recompense for my wrong-doing, but the law held up the looking-glass, and I soon saw my face all smeared and made more unhandsome by my tears.

The law seemed also to blight all my hopes with its stern sentence, "Cursed is every one that continueth not in all things which are written in the book of the law to do them." Only too well did I know that I had not continued in all those things, so I saw myself accursed, turn which way I might. If I had not committed one sin, that made no difference if I had committed another; I was under the curse. What if I had never blasphemed God with my tongue? Yet, if I had coveted, I had broken the law. He who breaks a chain might say, 'I did not break that link, and the other link.' No, but if you break one link, you have broken the chain. Ah, me, how I seemed shut up then! I had offended against the justice of God; I was impure and polluted, and I used to say, "If God does not send me to hell, He ought to do it." I sat in judgment upon myself, and pronounced the sentence that I felt would be just. I could not have gone to Heaven with my sin unpardoned, even if I had had the offer to do it, for I knew that it would not be right that I should do so, and I justified God in my own conscience while I condemned myself. The law would not even let me despair. If I thought I would give up all desire to do right, and just go and drown my conscience in sin, the law said, "No, you cannot do that; there is no rest for you in sinning. You know the law too well to be able to sin in the blindness of a seared conscience." So the law worried and troubled me at all points; it shut me up as in an iron cage, and every way of escape was effectually blocked up.

One of the things that shut me up dreadfully was, when I knew the spirituality of the law. If the law said, "Thou shalt not commit adultery," I said to myself, "Well, I have never committed adultery." Then the law, as interpreted by Christ, said, "Whosoever looketh on a woman to lust after her hath committed adultery with her already in his heart." The law said, "Thou shalt not steal," and I said, "Well, I never stole anything;" but then I found that even the desire to possess what was not my own, was guilt. The spirituality of the law astounded me; what hope could I have of eluding such a law as this which every way surrounded me with an atmosphere from which I could not possibly escape?

Then I remembered that, even if I kept the law perfectly, and kept it for ten, twenty, or thirty years, without a fault, yet if, at the end of that time, I should break it, I must suffer its dread penalty. Those words spoken by the Lord to the prophet Ezekiel came to my mind: "If he trust to his own righteousness, and commit iniquity, all his righteousnesses shall not be remembered; but for his iniquity that he hath committed, he shall die for it." So I saw that I was, indeed, "kept under the law, shut up." I had hoped to escape this way, or that way, or some other way. Was I not "christened" when I was a child? Had I not been taken to a place of worship? Had I not been brought up to say my prayers regularly? Had I not been an honest, upright, moral youth? Was all this nothing? "Nothing," said the law, as it drew its sword of fire: "Cursed is every one that continueth not in all things which are written in the book of the law to do them." So there was no rest for my spirit, nay, not even for a moment. What was I to do? I was in the hands of one who showed no mercy whatever, for Moses never said, "Mercy." The law has nothing to do with mercy. That comes from another mouth, and under another dispensation. But before faith came, I was "kept under the law, shut up unto the faith which should afterwards be revealed."

I am bold to say that, if a man be destitute of the grace of God, his works are only works of slavery; he feels forced to do them. I know, before I came into the liberty of the children of God, if I went to God's house, I went because I thought I must do it; if I prayed, it was because I feared some misfortune would happen in the day if I did not; if I ever thanked God for a mercy, it was because I thought I should not get another if I were not thankful; if I performed a righteous deed, it was with the hope that very likely God would reward me at last, and I should be winning a crown in Heaven. I was a poor slave, a mere Gibeonite, hewing wood and drawing water! If I could have left off doing it, I should have loved to do so. If I could have had my will, there would have been no chapel-going for me, no religion for me—I would have lived in the world, and followed the ways of Satan, if I could have done as I pleased. As for righteousness, it was slavery; sin would have been my liberty. Yet, truth to tell, of all bondage and slavery in this world, there is none more horrible than the bondage of sin. Tell me of Israel in Egypt, unsupplied with straw, yet preparing the full tale of bricks; tell me of the negro beneath the lash of his cruel task-master, and I confess it is a bondage fearful to be borne; but there is one far worse—the bondage of a convinced sinner when he is brought to feel the burden of his guilt; the bondage of a man when once his sins are baying him, like hounds about a weary stag; the bondage of a man when the burden of sin is on his shoulder—a burden too heavy for his soul to bear—a burden which will sink him in the depths of everlasting torment, unless he doth escape from it. Methinks I see such a person. He hath ne'er a smile upon his face; dark clouds have gathered on his brow; solemn and serious he stands; his very words are sighs; his songs are groans, his smiles are tears; and when he seems most happy, hot drops of grief roll in burning showers, scalding furrows on his cheek. Ask him *what he is*, and he tells you he is "a wretch undone". Ask him *how he is*, and he confesses that he is "misery incarnate". Ask him *what he shall be*, and he says, "I shall be lost in hell for ever; there is no hope for me." Such is the poor convinced sinner under bondage. Such have I been in my days, and I declare that, of all bondage, this is the most painful—the bondage of the law, the bondage of corruption.

My impression is, that this is the history of all the people of God, more or less. We are not all alike in every respect. We differ greatly in certain particulars, yet the main features of all the children of God will be found to be the same, and their Christian experience will resemble that of the other members of the Lord's family. I do not say that all have felt the apprehension of coming judgment as I did, but this is how it came to me. I knew that I was guilty, I knew that I had offended God, I knew that I had transgressed against light and knowledge, and I did not know when God might call me to account, but I did know this, when I awoke in the morning, the first thought I had was that I had to deal with a justly-angry God, who might suddenly require my soul of me. Often, during the day, when I had a little time for quiet meditation, a great depression of spirit would

F

come upon me because I felt that sin—*sin*—SIN had outlawed me from my God. I wondered that the earth bore up such a sinner as I was, and that the heavens did not fall and crush me, and the stars in their courses did not fight against such a wretch as I felt myself to be. Then, indeed, did I seem as if I should go down to the pit, and I had perpetually to endure the tortures of the never-dying worm of conscience that was gnawing at my heart. I went to the house of God, and heard what I supposed was the gospel, but it was no gospel to me. My soul abhorred all manner of meat; I could not lay hold upon a promise, or indulge a well-grounded hope of salvation. If anyone had asked me what would become of me, I must have answered, "I am going down to the pit." If anyone had entreated me to hope that mercy might come to me, I should have refused to entertain such a hope. I used to feel that I was in the condemned cell. In that dungeon, the man writes bitter things against himself; he feels absolutely sure that the wrath of God abideth on him; he wonders the stones beneath his feet do not open a grave to swallow him up; he is astonished that the walls of the prison do not compress and crush him into nothingness; he marvels that he has his breath, or that the blood in his veins does not turn into rivers of flame. His spirit is in a dreadful state; he not only feels that he shall be lost, but he thinks it is going to happen now. The condemned cell in Newgate, I am told, is just in such a corner that the criminal can hear the putting-up of the scaffold. Well do I remember hearing my scaffold built, and the sound of the hammer of the law as piece after piece was put together! It appeared as if I heard the noise of the crowd of men and devils who would witness my eternal execution, all of them howling and yelling out their accursed things against my spirit. Then there was a big bell that tolled out the hours, and I thought that very soon the last moment would arrive, and I must mount the fatal scaffold to be cast away for ever. Oh, that condemned cell! Next to Tophet, there can be no state more wretched than that of a man who is brought there!

When I was for many a month in this state, I used to read the Bible through, and the threatenings were all printed in capitals, but the promises were in such small type I could not for a long time make them out; and when I did read them, I did not believe they were mine; but the threatenings were all my own. "There," said I, "when it says, 'He that believeth not shall be damned,' that means me!" But when it said, "He is able also to save them to the uttermost that come unto God by Him," then I thought I was shut out. When I read, "He found no place of repentance, though he sought it carefully with tears;" I thought, "Ah! that is myself again." And when I read, "That which beareth thorns and briers is rejected, and is nigh unto cursing; whose end is to be burned;" "Ah!" I said, "that describes me to the very letter." And when I heard the Master say, "Cut it down; why cumbereth it the ground?" "Ah!" thought I, "that is my text; He will have me down before long, and not let me cumber the ground any more." But when I read, "Ho! every one that thirsteth; come ye to the waters;" I said, "That does not belong to me, I am sure." And when I read, "Come unto Me, all ye that labour and are heavy laden, and I will give you rest," I said, "That belongs to my brother, to my sister," or those I knew round about me; for they were all "heavy laden", I thought, but I was not; and though, God knoweth, I would weep, and cry, and lament till my heart was breaking within me, if any man had asked me whether I sorrowed for sin, I should have told him, "No, I never had any true sorrow for sin." "Well, do you not feel the burden of sin?" "No!" "But you really are a convinced sinner?" "No," I should have said, "I am not." Is it not strange that poor sinners, when they are coming to Christ, are so much in the dark that they cannot see their own hands? They are so blind that they cannot see themselves; and though the Holy Spirit has been pleased to work in them, and give them godly fear and a tender conscience, they will stand up, and declare that they have not those blessings, and that in them there is not any good thing, and that God has not looked on them nor loved them.

*   *   *

I speak what I do know, and not what I have learned by report, when I say that there is a chamber in the experience of some men where the temptations of the devil exceed all belief. Read John Bunyan's *Grace Abounding*, if you would understand what I mean. The devil tempted him, he says, to doubt the existence of God, the truth of Scripture, the manhood of Christ, then His Deity; and once, he says, he tempted him to say things which he will never write, lest he should pollute others. Ah! I recollect a dark hour with myself when I, who do not remember to have even heard a blasphemy in my youth, much less to have uttered one, found rushing through my mind an almost infinite number of curses and blasphemies against the Most High God. I specially recall a certain narrow and crooked lane, in a country town, along which I was walking one day, while I was seeking the Saviour. On a sudden, it seemed as if the floodgates of hell had been opened; my head became a very pandemonium; ten thousand evil spirits seemed to be holding carnival within my brain, and I held my mouth lest I should give utterance to the words of blasphemy that were poured into my ears. Things I had never heard or thought of before came rushing impetuously into my mind, and I could scarcely withstand their influence. It was the devil throwing me down and tearing me. These things sorely beset me; for half-an-hour together, the most fearful imprecations would dash through my brain. Oh, how I groaned and cried before God! That temptation passed away, but ere many days, it was renewed again, and when I was in prayer, or when I was reading the Bible, these blasphemous thoughts would pour in upon me more than at any other time. I consulted with an aged godly man about it. He said to me, "Oh, all this many of the people of God have proved before you! But," he asked, "do you hate these thoughts?" "I do," I truly answered. "Then," said he, "they are not yours; serve them as the old parish officers used to do with vagrants, whip them, and send them on to their own parish. So," said he, "do with those evil thoughts. Groan over them, repent of them, and send them on to the devil, the father of them, to whom they belong, for they are not yours."

I have never been thoroughly an unbeliever but once, and that was not before I knew the need of a Saviour, but after it. It was just when I wanted Christ, and panted after Him, that, on a sudden, the thought crossed my mind—which I abhorred but could not conquer—that there was no God, no Christ, no Heaven, no hell, that all my prayers were but a farce, and that I might as well have whistled to the winds or spoken to the howling waves. Ah! I remember how my ship drifted along through that sea of fire, loosened from the anchor of my faith which I had received from my fathers. I no longer moored myself hard by the coasts of Revelation; I said to reason, "Be thou my captain;" I said to my own brain, "Be thou my rudder;" and I started on my mad voyage. Thank God, it is all over now, but I will tell you its brief history. It was one hurried sailing over the tempestuous ocean of free thought. I went on, and as I went, the skies began to darken, but to make up for that deficiency, the waters were gleaming with coruscations of brilliancy. I saw sparks flying upwards that pleased me, and I felt, "If this be free thought, it is a happy thing." My thoughts seemed gems, and I scattered stars with both my hands; but anon, instead of these coruscations of glory, I saw grim fiends, fierce and horrible, start up from the waters; and as I dashed on, they gnashed their teeth, and grinned upon me; they seized the prow of my ship, and dragged me on, while I, in part, gloried at the rapidity of my motion, but yet shuddered at the terrific rate with which I passed the old landmarks of my faith. I went to the very verge of the dreary realms of unbelief. I went to the very bottom of the sea of infidelity. As I hurried forward at an awful speed, I began to doubt if there was a world. I doubted everything, until at last the devil defeated himself by making me doubt my own existence. I thought I was an idea floating in the nothingness of vacuity; then, startled with that thought, and feeling that I was substantial flesh and blood after all, I saw that God was, and Christ was, and Heaven was, and hell was, and that all these things were absolute truths. The very extravagance of the doubt proved its absurdity, and there came a voice which said, "And can this doubt be true?" Then I awoke from that death-dream, which, God knows, might have damned my soul, and ruined my body, if I had not awoke. When I arose, faith took the helm; from that moment, I doubted not. Faith steered me back; faith cried, "Away, away!" I cast my anchor on Calvary; I lifted my eye to God; and here I am alive, and out of hell. Therefore, I speak what I do know. I have sailed that perilous voyage; I have come safe to land. Ask me again to be an infidel! No; I have tried it; it was sweet at first, but bitter afterwards. Now, lashed to God's gospel more firmly than ever, standing as on a rock of adamant, I defy the arguments of hell to move me, for "I know whom I have believed, and am persuaded that He is able to keep that which I have committed unto Him." I should not be astonished if many others, who now believe, have also been upon the very borders of atheism, and have doubted almost everything. It is when Satan finds the heart tender that he tries to stamp his own impress of infidelity upon the soul, but, blessed be God, he never accomplishes it in the sinner who is truly coming to Christ! Now, whenever I hear the sceptic's stale attacks upon the Word of God, I smile within myself, and think, "Why, you simpleton! how can you urge such trifling objections? I have felt, in the contentions of my own unbelief, ten times greater difficulties." We who have contended with horses are not to be wearied by footmen. Gordon Cumming and other lion-killers are not to be scared by wild cats, nor will those who have stood foot to foot with Satan resign the field to pretentious sceptics, or any other of the evil one's inferior servants.

I do think it often proves a great blessing to a man that he had a terrible conflict, a desperate encounter, a hard-fought engagement in passing from the empire of Satan into the kingdom of God's dear Son. Sooner or later, each saved man will have his hand-to-hand fight with the prince of darkness, and, as a general rule, it is a great mercy to have it over at the outset of one's career, and to be able afterwards to feel, "Whatever comes upon me, I never can suffer as I suffered when I was seeking Christ. Whatever staggering doubt, or hideous blasphemy, or ghastly insinuations, even of suicide itself, may assail my feeble heart, they cannot outdo the horror of great darkness through which my spirit passed when I was struggling after a Saviour." I do not say that it is desirable that we should have this painful ordeal, much less that we should seek it as an evidence of regeneration, but when we have passed through it victoriously, we may so use it that it may be a perpetual armoury to us. If we can now defy all doubts and fears that come, because they cannot be so potent as those which already, in the name of Jesus Christ our Saviour, we have overthrown, shall we not use that fact for ourselves, and can we not equally well use it for others? Full often have I found it good, when I have talked with a young convert in deep distress about his sin, to tell him something more of his anxious plight than he knew how to express; and he has wondered where I found it, though he would not have wondered if he had known where I had been, and how much deeper in the mire than he. When he has talked about some horrible thought that he has had, with regard to the impossibility of his own salvation, I have said, "Why, I have thought that a thousand times, and yet have overcome it through the help of God's Spirit!" I know that a man's own experience is one of the very best weapons he can use in fighting with evil in other men's hearts. Often, their misery and despondency, aggravated, as it commonly is, by a feeling of solitariness, will be greatly relieved before it is effectually driven out when they find that a brother has suffered the same, and yet has been able to overcome. Do I show him how precious the Saviour is to my soul? He glorifies God in me. Right soon will he look into the same dear face and be lightened, and then he will magnify the Lord with me, and we shall exalt His name together.

*   *   *

Multitudes of persons are sailing in what they think to be the good ship of self-righteousness: they are expecting that they shall get to Heaven in her. But she never did carry a soul safely into the fair Haven yet, and she never will. Self-righteousness is as rapid a road to ruin as outward sin itself. We may as certainly destroy ourselves by opposing the righteousness of Christ as by transgressing the law of God. Self-righteousness is as much an insult to God as blasphemy is, and God will never accept it, neither shall any soul enter Heaven by it. Yet this vessel manages to keep on her way against all the opposition of Scripture; for, often, men have a soft South wind blowing, and things go easily with them, and they believe that through their own doings they shall assuredly find the Port of Peace. I am glad, therefore, when some terrible tempest overtakes this vessel, and when men's hopes through their own doings and their own feelings are utterly wrecked.

I rejoice when the old ship parts timber from timber, when she goes aground and breaks to pieces, and men find safety in some other way, for whatever seeming safety they may have to-day will only delude them. It must end in destruction, and it is therefore a thousand mercies when they find it out soon enough to get a better hope of being saved than this, which will certainly deceive them. I recollect very well when that terrific Euroclydon blew on my vessel. It was as good a ship as any others have, although I have no doubt they would vindicate their own. Her sails needed mending, and here and there she wanted a little touch of paint; but, for all that, she was sea-worthy, and fit to be registered "A1 at Lloyd's", and entered in the first class—at least, so I thought. The storm blew over her, and she went to pieces, and I bless God that she did, for I should have been kept on board to this very minute if I had not been washed off. I tried to cling to the old hulk to the last plank, but I was obliged to give it up, and look somewhere else for help and safety.

Before I came to Christ, I said to myself, "It surely cannot be that, if I believe in Jesus, just as I am, I shall be saved? I must feel something; I must do something." I could pour scorn upon myself to think of some of the good resolutions I made! I blew them up, like children with their pipes and their soap, and fine bubbles they were, reflecting all the colours of the rainbow! But a touch, and they dissolved. They were good for nothing—poor stuff to build eternal hopes upon. Oh, that working for salvation! What slavery it was, but what small results it produced! I was a spinner and weaver of the poorest sort, yet I dreamed that I should be able by my own spinning to make a garment to cover myself withal. This was the trade of father Adam and mother Eve when they first lost their innocence; "they sewed fig leaves together, and made themselves aprons." It is a very laborious business, and has worn out the lives of many with bitter bondage, but its worst feature is that the Lord has declared concerning all who follow this self-righteous craft, "Their webs shall not become garments, neither shall they cover themselves with their works."

Oh, the many times that I have wished the preacher would tell me something to *do* that I might be saved! Gladly would I have done it, if it had been possible. If he had said, "Take off your shoes and stockings, and run to John o' Groat's," I would not even have gone home first, but would have started off that very night, that I might win salvation. How often have I thought that, if he had said, "Bare your back to the scourge, and take fifty lashes;" I would have said, "Here I am! Come along with your whip, and beat as hard as you please, so long as I can obtain peace and rest, and get rid of my sin." Yet that simplest of all matters—believing in Christ crucified, accepting His finished salvation, being nothing, and letting Him be everything, doing nothing but trusting to what He has done—I could not get a hold of it. Once I thought there was salvation in good works, and I laboured hard, and strove diligently to preserve a character for integrity and uprightness; but when the Spirit of God came into my heart, "sin revived, and I died." That which I thought had been good, proved to be evil; wherein I fancied I had been holy, I found myself to be unholy. I discovered that my very best actions were sinful, that my tears needed to be wept over, and that my prayers needed God's forgiveness. I discovered that I was seeking after salvation by the works of the law, that I was doing all my good works from a selfish motive, namely, to save myself, and therefore they could not be acceptable to God. I found out that I could not be saved by good works for two very good reasons; first, I had not got any, and secondly, if I had any, they could not save me. After that, I thought, surely salvation might be obtained, partly by reformation, and partly by trusting in Christ, so I laboured hard again, and thought, if I added a few prayers here and there, a few tears of penitence, and a few vows of improvement, all would be well. But after fagging on for many a weary day, like a poor blind horse toiling round the mill, I found I had gone no farther, for there was still the curse of God hanging over me, and there was still an aching void in my heart, which the world could never fill—a void of distress and care, for I was sorely troubled because I could not attain unto the rest which my soul desired.

What a struggle that was which my young heart waged against sin! When God the Holy Ghost first quickened me, little did I know of the precious blood which has put my sins away, and drowned them in the depths for ever. But I did know this, that I could not remain as I was; that I could not rest happy unless I became something better, something purer than I was; and, oh, how my spirit cried to God with groanings—I say it without any exaggeration—groanings that could not be uttered! and, oh, how I sought, in my poor dark way, to overcome first one sin and then another, and so to do battle, in God's strength, against the enemies that assailed me, and not, thank God, altogether without success, though still the battle had been lost unless He had come who is the Overcomer of sin and the Deliverer of His people, and had put the hosts to flight. I tried a long time to improve myself, but I never did make much of it; I found I had a devil within me when I began, and I had ten devils when I left off. Instead of becoming better, I became worse; I had now got the devil of self-righteousness, of self-trust, and self-conceit, and many others that had come and taken up their lodging within my heart. While I was busy sweeping my house, and garnishing it, behold, the one I sought to get rid of, who had only gone for a little season, returned, and brought with him seven other spirits more wicked than himself, and they entered in and dwelt there. Then I laboured to believe. It is a strange way of putting it, yet so it was. When I wished to believe, I found I could not. It seemed to me that the way to Heaven by Christ's righteousness was as difficult as by my own, and that I could as soon get to Heaven by Sinai as by Calvary. I could do nothing, I could neither repent nor believe. I fainted with despair, feeling as if I must be lost despite the gospel, and be for ever driven from Jehovah's presence, even though Christ had died.

I must confess that I never would have been saved if I could have helped it. As long as ever I could, I rebelled, and revolted, and struggled against God. When He would have me pray, I would not pray: when He would have me listen to the sound of the ministry, I would not. And when I heard, and the tear rolled down my cheek, I wiped it away, and defied Him to melt my heart. There came an election sermon, but that did not please me. There came a law sermon, showing me my powerlessness, but I did not believe it. I thought it was the whim of some old experimental Christian, some dogma of ancient times that would not suit men now. Then there came another sermon, concerning death and sin, but I did not believe I was dead, for I thought I was alive enough, and could repent and make myself right by-and-by. Then there came a strong exhortation sermon, but I felt I could set my house in order when I liked, as well as I could do it at once. So did I continually trust in my self-sufficiency. When my heart was a little touched, I tried to divert it with sinful pleasures, and would not then have been saved, until God gave me the effectual blow, and I was obliged to submit to that irresistible effort of His grace. It conquered my depraved will, and made me bow myself before His gracious sceptre. When the Lord really brought me to myself, He sent one great shot which shivered me to pieces; and, lo, I found myself utterly defenceless. I thought I was more mighty than the angels, and could accomplish all things; but I found myself less than nothing.

Jesus said to Zacchæus, "Make haste, and *come down*." Can I not remember when He also told me to come down? One of the first steps I had to take was to go right down from my good works; and, oh, what a fall was that! Then I stood upon my own self-sufficiency, and Christ said, "Come down! I have pulled you down from your good works, and now I will pull you down from your self-sufficiency." So I had another fall, and I felt sure I had gained the bottom, but again Christ said, "Come down!" and He made me come down till I fell on some point at which I felt I was yet salvable. But still the command was, "Down, sir! come down further yet." And down I came until, in despair, I had to let go every bough of the tree of my hopes, and then I said, "I can do nothing; I am ruined." The waters were wrapped round my head, and I was shut out from the light of day, and thought myself a stranger from the commonwealth of Israel. But Christ said, "Come down lower yet, sir! thou hast too much pride to be saved." Then I was brought down to see my corruption, my wickedness, my filthiness, for God always humbles the sinner whom He means to save. While I was in this state, trying to make myself believe, a voice whispered, "Vain man, vain man, if thou wouldst believe, come and see!" Then the Holy Spirit led me by the hand to a solitary place, and while I stood there, suddenly there appeared before me One upon His cross. I looked up; I had then no faith. I saw His eyes suffused with tears, and the blood still flowing; I saw His enemies about Him, hunting Him to His grave; I marked His miseries unutterable; I heard the groaning which cannot be described; and as I looked up, He opened His eyes, and said to me, "The Son of man is come to seek and to save that which was lost." Yet I needed more than that gracious word. The general call of the gospel is like the sheet lightning we sometimes see on a summer's evening—beautiful, grand—but who ever heard of anything being struck by it? But the special call is the forked flash from heaven; it strikes somewhere. It is the arrow shot in between the joints of the harness. The call which saves is like that of Jesus, when He said, "Mary," and she said unto Him, "Rabboni." Can I not recollect the hour when He whispered my name, when He said in mine ear, "Come unto Me"! That was an effectual call; there was no resisting it. I know I laughed at religion; I despised, I abhorred it; but oh, that call! I would not come. But Christ said, "Thou shalt come. 'All that the Father giveth Me shall come to Me.' " "Lord, I will not." "But thou shalt," said Jesus. I have gone up to God's house, sometimes, almost with a resolution that I would not listen, but listen I must. Oh, how the Word came into my soul! Was there any power of resistance remaining in me? No; I was thrown down; each bone seemed to be broken. I began to think there never would be a trace of anything built up in my heart. What a trench was dug in my soul! Out went my supposed merits! What a heap of rubbish! Out went my knowledge, my good resolves, and my self-sufficiency! By-and-by, out went all my strength. When this digging-out was completed, the ditch was so deep that, as I went down into it, it seemed like my grave.

Such a grief it was for me to know my own sinfulness, that it did not seem possible that this could help my upbuilding in comfort and salvation. Yet, so it is, that if the Lord means to build high, He always digs deep; and if He means to give great grace, He gives deep consciousness of need of it. Long before I began with Christ, He had begun with me; but when I began with Him, it was, as the law-writers say, "*In formâ pauperis*," after the style of a wretched mendicant—a pauper who had nothing of his own, and looked to Christ for everything. I know, when I first cast my eye to His dear cross, and rested in Him, I had not any merit of my own, it was all demerit. I was not deserving, except that I felt I was hell-deserving: I had not even a shade of virtue that I could confide in. It was all over with me. I had come to an extremity. I could not have found a farthing's worth of goodness in myself if I had been melted down. I seemed to be all rottenness, a dunghill of corruption, nothing better, but something a great deal worse. I could truly join with Paul at that time, and say that my own righteousnesses were dung; he used a strong expression, but I do not suppose he felt it to be strong enough: "I count them but dung, that I may win Christ, and be found in Him."

*   *   *

I do not know what may be the peculiarity of my constitution, but I have always loved safe things. I have not, that I know of, one grain of speculation in my nature. Safe things—things that I can see to be made of rock, and that will bear the test of time—I lay hold of with avidity. I was reasoning thus in my boyish spirit: Scripture tells me that he that believeth in Christ shall never perish. Then, if I believe in Jesus, I shall be safe for time and for eternity, too. There will be no fear of my ever being in hell; I shall run no risk as to my eternal state, that will be secure for ever. I shall have the certainty that, when my eyes are closed in death, I shall see the face of Christ, and behold Him in glory. Whenever I heard the doctrine of the final preservation of the saints preached, my mouth used to water to be a child of God. When I used to hear the old saints sing that hymn of Toplady's, which begins—

> "A debtor to mercy alone,
>   Of covenant mercy I sing;
> Nor fear, with Thy righteousness on,
>   My person and off'rings to bring;—"

I thought I should never be able to sing it myself, it was too high doctrine, too sweet, too consoling, but when they came to the climax, in the last verse—

> "My name from the palms of His hands
>   Eternity will not erase;
> Impress'd on His heart it remains
>   In marks of indelible grace;
> Yes, I to the end shall endure,
>   As sure as the earnest is giv'n;
> More happy, but not more secure,
>   The glorified spirits in Heav'n"—

my heart was as if it would leap out of my body, and I would cry to God, "Oh, that I had a part and lot in such a salvation as that!" I distinctly remember having a meditation something like this: "Now I should not like to be a thief, or a murderer, or an unclean person." I had such a training that I had an abhorrence of sin of every sort. "And yet," I thought to myself, "I may even be hanged; there is no reason why I should not turn out a thief;" because I recollected there were some of my schoolfellows, older than I was, who had already become proficient in dishonesty; and I thought, "Why may not I?" No one can tell the rapture of my spirit, when I thought I saw in my Bible the doctrine that, if I gave my heart to Christ, He would keep me from sin, and preserve me as long as I lived. I was not quite certain whether that truth was revealed in the Bible, though I thought so; but I remember, when I heard the minister of some small "Hyper" chapel utter the same doctrine, my heart was full of rapture; I panted after that kind of gospel. "Oh!" I thought, "if God would but love me, if I might but know myself to be His!" For the enchanting part of it was that, if I were so loved, He would keep me to the end. That made me so in love with the gospel that, boy as I was, knowing nothing savingly about the truth, I was all the more earnest in desiring to be saved, because, if saved, God would never turn me out of doors. That made the gospel very precious to me; so that, when the Holy Spirit showed me my guilt, and led me to seek the Saviour, that doctrine was like a bright star to my spirit. The Bible seemed to me to be full of this truth, "If you trust Christ, He will save you from all evil; He will keep you in a life of integrity and holiness while here, and He will bring you safe to Heaven at the last." I felt that I could not trust man, for I had seen some of the very best wandering far from the truth; if I trusted Christ, it was not a chance as to whether I should get to Heaven, but a certainty, and I learned that, if I rested all my weight upon Him, He would keep me, for I found it written, "The righteous shall hold on his way, and he that hath clean hands shall wax stronger and stronger." I found the apostle saying, "He which hath begun a good work in you will perform it," and such-like expressions. "Why," I reasoned, "I have found an Insurance Office, and a good one, too; I will insure my soul in it; I will go to Jesus as I am, for He bids me do so; I will trust myself with Him." If I had listened to the Arminian theory, I should never have been converted, for it never had any charms for me. A Saviour who casts away His people, a God who leaves His children to perish, is not worthy of my worship, and a salvation which does not save outright is neither worth preaching nor worth listening to.

I recollect the time when I was afraid that Jesus would never save me, but I used to feel in my heart that, even if He did not, I must love Him for what He had done for other poor sinners. It seemed to me, as I read the wondrous story of His life and death, that if He refused me, I would still lie at His feet, and say, "Thou mayest spurn me, but Thou art a blessed Christ for all that; and if Thou dost curse me, yet I can only say to Thee that I well deserve it at Thy hands. Do what Thou wilt with me; but Thou didst save the dying thief, and Thou didst save her out of whom Thou didst cast seven devils, and if Thou dost not deign to save me, yet Thou art a blessed Christ, and I cannot rail at Thee, or find fault with Thee, but I lie down at Thy feet, and worship Thee." I could not help saying, once, that, even if He damned me, I would love God because He was so gracious to others. One text of Scripture especially cheered me; I lived upon it for months. I felt the weight of sin, and I did not know the Saviour; I feared God would blast me with His wrath, and smite me with His hot displeasure! From chapel to chapel I went to hear the Word preached, but never a gospel sentence did I hear, but this one text preserved me from what I believe I should have been driven to—the commission of suicide through grief and sorrow. It was this sweet word, "Whosoever shall call upon the name of the Lord shall be saved." Well, I thought, I cannot believe on Christ as I could wish, I cannot find pardon, but I know I call upon His name, I know I pray, ay, and pray with groans, and tears, and sighs, day and night; and if I am ever lost, I will plead that promise, "O God, Thou saidst, Whosoever shall call upon My name shall be saved! I did call; wilt Thou cast me away? I did plead Thy promise; I did lift up my heart in prayer; canst Thou be just, and yet condemn the sinner who did really call upon Thy name?"

My heart was greatly impressed by something which I heard my mother say. I had been some years seeking Christ, and I could not believe that He would save me. She said she had heard many people swear and blaspheme God, but one thing she had never known—she had never heard a man say he had sought Christ, and Christ had rejected him. "And," she added, "I do not believe that God would permit any man to live to say that." I thought that I could say it; I thought I had sought Him, and He had cast me away, and I determined that I would say it; even if it destroyed my soul, I would speak what I thought was the truth. But I said to myself, "I will try once more;" and I went to the Master, with nothing of my own, casting myself simply on His mercy; and I believed that He died for me, and now, blessed be His holy name, I never shall be able to say that He has cast me away! As the result of personal experience, I can add my own testimony to that of my mother. I have heard many wicked things in my life—I also have heard men swear and blaspheme God, till I have trembled; but there is one thing I never did hear a man say yet, and I think God would scarcely permit any man to utter such a lie; I never knew even a drunken man say, "I sincerely sought God with full purpose of heart, yet He has not heard me, and will not answer me, but has cast me away." I scarcely think it possible, although I know that men can be almost infinitely wicked, that any man could utter such an abominable falsehood as that. At any rate, I can say I have never heard it.

An outbreak of fever in the school at Newmarket brought Spurgeon's first term to an end before the appointed time and he returned home for the winter holidays. Christmas passed and when the first Sunday of the New Year dawned it was cold and snowing. The day was January 6, 1850. Prevented by the weather from accompanying his father on the nine mile journey to Tollesbury and from walking into the town, Spurgeon was led to the place of his conversion, a Primitive Methodist Chapel in Artillery Street close to their home on Hythe Hill.

The Chapel was built in 1839 and though it was partially rebuilt in 1897 it structurally remains much as it was when Spurgeon knew it. In recent years the building, like so many others, fell into disuse and was given up as a place of worship. It is, however, rented at the present time (1962) by some young Christians who use it for evangelistic meetings. Preaching in this Chapel on October 11, 1864, Spurgeon pointed to a seat on the left of the building under the gallery and said, "I was sitting in that pew when I was converted." To the end of his life he constantly used the suddenness of his own conversion as an illustration of the fact that in a single moment our relationship to God may be changed for all eternity—"the saved soul is as near and dear to God the first moment he believes as he ever will be; a true heir of all things in Christ, and as truly so as even when he shall mount to heaven to be glorified and to be like his Lord."

Chapter 7

The Great Change—Conversion

LET our lips crowd sonnets within the compass of a word; let our voice distil hours of melody into a single syllable; let our tongue utter in one letter the essence of the harmony of ages; for we write of an hour which as far excelleth all other days of our life as gold exceedeth dross. As the night of Israel's passover was a night to be remembered, a theme for bards, and an incessant fountain of grateful song, even so is the time of which we now tell, the never-to-be-forgotten hour of our emancipation from guilt, and our justification in Jesus. Other days have mingled with their fellows till, like coins worn in circulation, their image and superscription are entirely obliterated, but this day remaineth new, fresh, bright, as distinct in all its parts as if it were but yesterday struck from the mint of time. Memory shall drop from the palsied hand full many a memento which now she cherishes, but she shall never, even when she tottereth to the grave, unbind from her heart the token of the thrice-happy hour of the redemption of our spirit. The emancipated galley-slave may forget the day which heard his broken fetters rattle on the ground; the pardoned traitor may fail to remember the moment when the axe of the headsman was averted by a pardon; and the long-despairing mariner may not recollect the moment when a friendly hand snatched him from the hungry deep; but O hour of forgiven sin, moment of perfect pardon, our soul shall never forget thee while within her life and being find an immortality! Each day of our life hath had its attendant angel, but on this day, like Jacob at Mahanaim, hosts of angels met us. The sun hath risen every morning, but on that eventful morn he had the light of seven days. As the days of Heaven upon earth, as the years of immortality, as the ages of glory, as the bliss of Heaven, so were the hours of that thrice-happy day. Rapture divine, and ecstasy inexpressible, filled our soul. Fear, distress, and grief, with all their train of woes, fled hastily away; and in their place joys came without number.

*   *   *

When I was in the hand of the Holy Spirit, under conviction of sin, I had a clear and sharp sense of the justice of God. Sin, whatever it might be to other people, became to me an intolerable burden. It was not so much that I feared hell, as that I feared sin; and all the while, I had upon my mind a deep concern for the honour of God's name, and the integrity of His moral government. I felt that it would not satisfy my conscience if I could be forgiven unjustly. But then there came the question—"How could God be just, and yet justify me who had been so guilty?" I was worried and wearied with this question; neither could I see any answer to it. Certainly, I could never have invented an answer which would have satisfied my conscience. The doctrine of the atonement is to my mind one of the surest proofs of the Divine inspiration of Holy Scripture. Who would or could have thought of the just Ruler dying for the unjust rebel? This is no teaching of human mythology, or dream of poetical imagination. This method of expiation is only known among men because it is a fact: fiction could not have devised it. God Himself ordained it; it is not a matter which could have been imagined.

I had heard of the plan of salvation by the sacrifice of Jesus from my youth up; but I did not know any more about it in my innermost soul than if I had been born and bred a Hottentot. The light was there, but I was blind: it was of necessity that the Lord Himself should make the matter plain to me. It came to me as a new revelation, as fresh as if I had never read in Scripture that Jesus was declared to be the propitiation for sins that God might be just. I believe it will have to come as a revelation to every new-born child of God whenever he sees it; I mean that glorious doctrine of the substitution of the Lord Jesus. I came to understand that salvation was possible through vicarious sacrifice; and that provision had been made in the first constitution and arrangement of things for such a substitution. I was made to see that He who is the Son of God, co-equal, and co-eternal with the Father, had of old been made the covenant Head of a chosen people, that He might in that capacity suffer for them and save them. Inasmuch as our fall was not at the first a personal one, for we fell in our federal representative, the first Adam, it became possible for us to be recovered by a second Representative, even by Him who has undertaken to be the covenant Head of His people, so as to be their second Adam. I saw that, ere I actually sinned, I had fallen by my first father's sin, and I rejoiced that, therefore, it became possible in point of law for me to rise by a second Head and Representative. The fall by Adam left a loophole of escape; another Adam could undo the ruin wrought by the first.

When I was anxious about the possibility of a just God pardoning me, I understood and saw by faith that He who is the Son of God became man, and in His own blessed person bore my sin in His own body on the tree. I saw that the chastisement of my peace was laid on Him, and that with His stripes I was healed. It was because the Son of

God, supremely glorious in His matchless person, undertook to vindicate the law by bearing the sentence due to me, that therefore God was able to pass by my sin. My sole hope for Heaven lies in the full atonement made upon Calvary's cross for the ungodly. On that I firmly rely. I have not the shadow of a hope anywhere else. Personally, I could never have overcome my own sinfulness. I tried and failed. My evil propensities were too many for me, till, in the belief that Christ died for me, I cast my guilty soul on Him, and then I received a conquering principle by which I overcame my sinful self. The doctrine of the cross can be used to slay sin, even as the old warriors used their huge two-handed swords, and mowed down their foes at every stroke. There is nothing like faith in the sinners' Friend: it overcomes all evil. If Christ has died for me, ungodly as I am, without strength as I am, then I cannot live in sin any longer, but must arouse myself to love and serve Him who hath redeemed me. I cannot trifle with the evil which slew my best Friend. I must be holy for His sake. How can I live in sin when He has died to save me from it?

There was a day, as I took my walks abroad, when I came hard by a spot for ever engraven upon my memory, for there I saw this Friend, my best, my only Friend, murdered. I stooped down in sad affright, and looked at Him. I saw that His hands had been pierced with rough iron nails, and His feet had been rent in the same way. There was misery in His dead countenance so terrible that I scarcely dared to look upon it. His body was emaciated with hunger, His back was red with bloody scourges, and His brow had a circle of wounds about it: clearly could one see that these had been pierced by thorns. I shuddered, for I had known this Friend full well. He never had a fault; He was the purest of the pure, the holiest of the holy. Who could have injured Him? For He never injured any man: all His life long He "went about doing good;" He had healed the sick, He had fed the hungry, He had raised the dead: for which of these works did they kill Him? He had never breathed out anything else but love; and as I looked into the poor sorrowful face, so full of agony, and yet so full of love, I wondered who could have been a wretch so vile as to pierce hands like His. I said within myself, "Where can these traitors live? Who are these that could have smitten such an One as this?" Had they murdered an oppressor, we might have forgiven them; had they slain one who had indulged in vice or villainy, it might have been his desert; had it been a murderer and a rebel, or one who had committed sedition, we would have said, "Bury his corpse: justice has at last given him his due." But when Thou wast slain, my best, my only-beloved, where lodged the traitors? Let me seize them, and they shall be put to death. If there be torments that I can devise, surely they shall endure them all. Oh! what jealousy, what revenge I felt! If I might but find these murderers, what would I not do with them! And as I looked upon that corpse, I heard a footstep, and wondered where it was. I listened, and I clearly perceived that the murderer was close at hand. It was dark, and I groped about to find him. I found that, somehow or other, wherever I put out my hand, I could not meet with him, for he was nearer to me than my hand would go. At last I put my hand upon my breast. "I have thee now," said I; for lo! he was in my own heart; the murderer was hiding within my own bosom, dwelling in the recesses of my inmost soul. Ah! then I wept indeed, that I, in the very presence of my murdered Master, should be harbouring the murderer, and I felt myself most guilty while I bowed over His corpse, and sang that plaintive hymn—

> " 'Twas you, my sins, my cruel sins,
>   His chief tormentors were;
>   Each of my crimes became a nail,
>   And unbelief the spear."

Amid the rabble rout which hounded the Redeemer to His doom, there were some gracious souls whose bitter anguish sought vent in wailing and lamentations—fit music to accompany that march of woe. When my soul can, in imagination, see the Saviour bearing His cross to Calvary, she joins the godly women, and weeps with them; for, indeed, there is true cause for grief—cause lying deeper than those mourning women thought. They bewailed innocence maltreated, goodness persecuted, love bleeding, meekness about to die; but my heart has a deeper and more bitter cause to mourn. My sins were the scourges which lacerated those blessed shoulders, and crowned with thorns those bleeding brows: my sins cried, "Crucify Him! Crucify Him!" and laid the cross upon His gracious shoulders. His being led forth to die is sorrow enough for one eternity; but my having been His murderer, is more, infinitely more grief than one poor fountain of tears can express.

Why those women loved and wept, it were not hard to guess; but they could not have had greater reasons for love and grief than my heart has. Nain's widow saw her son restored; but I myself have been raised to newness of life. Peter's wife's mother was cured of the fever; but I of the greater plague of sin. Out of Magdalene seven devils were cast; but a whole legion out of me. Mary and Martha were favoured with visits from Him; but He dwells with me. His mother bare His body; but He is formed in me, "the hope of glory." In nothing behind the holy women in debt, let me not be behind them in gratitude or sorrow.

> "Love and grief my heart dividing,
>   With my tears His feet I'll lave;
> Constant still in heart abiding,
>   Weep for Him who died to save."

William Huntington says, in his autobiography, that one of the sharpest sensations of pain that he felt, after he had been quickened by Divine grace, was this, "He felt such pity for God." I do not know that I ever met with the expression elsewhere, but it is a very striking one, although I might prefer to say that I have sympathy with God, and grief that He should be treated so ill. Ah, there are many men that are forgotten, that are despised, and that are trampled on by their fellows, but there never was a man who was so despised as the ever-lasting God has been! Many a man has been slandered and abused, but never was man abused as God has been. Many have been treated cruelly and ungratefully, but never was one treated as our God has been. I, too, once despised Him. He knocked at the door of my heart, and I refused to open it. He came to me, times without number, morning by morning, and night by night; He checked me in my conscience, and spoke to me by His Spirit, and when, at last, the thunders of the law prevailed in my conscience, I thought that Christ was cruel and unkind. Oh, I can never forgive myself that I should have thought so ill of Him! But what a loving reception did I have when I went to Him! I thought He would smite me, but His hand was not clenched in anger, but opened wide in mercy. I thought full sure that His eyes would dart lightning-flashes of wrath upon me; but, instead thereof, they were full of tears. He fell upon my neck, and kissed me; He took off my rags, and did clothe me with His righteousness, and caused my soul to sing aloud for joy; while in the house of my heart, and in the house of His Church, there was music and dancing, because His son that He had lost was found, and he that had been dead was made alive again.

*   *   *

There is a power in God's gospel beyond all description. Once I, like Mazeppa, lashed to the wild horse of my lust, bound hand and foot, incapable of resistance, was galloping on with hell's wolves behind me, howling for my body and my soul as their just and lawful prey. There came a mighty hand which stopped that wild horse, cut my bands, set me down, and brought me into liberty. Is there power in the gospel? Ay, there is, and he who has felt it must acknowledge it. There was a time when I lived in the strong old castle of my sins, and rested in my own works. There came a trumpeter to the door, and bade me open it. I with anger chid him from the porch, and said he ne'er should enter. Then there came a goodly Personage, with loving countenance; His hands were marked with scars where nails had been driven, and His feet had nail-prints, too. He lifted up His cross, using it as a hammer; at the first blow, the gate of my prejudice shook; at the second, it trembled more; at the third, down it fell, and in He came; and He said, "Arise, and stand upon thy feet, for I have loved thee with an everlasting love." The gospel a thing of power! Ah! that it is. It always wears the dew of its youth; it glitters with morning's freshness, its strength and its glory abide for ever. I have felt its power in my own heart; I have the witness of the Spirit within my spirit, and I know it is a thing of might, because it has conquered me, and bowed me down.

> "His free grace alone, from the first to the last,
> Hath won my affections, and bound my soul fast."

In my conversion, the very point lay in making the discovery that I had nothing to do but to look to Christ, and I should be saved. I believe that I had been a very good, attentive hearer; my own impression about myself was that nobody ever listened much better than I did. For years, as a child, I tried to learn the way of salvation, and either I did not hear it set forth, which I think cannot quite have been the case, or else I was spiritually blind and deaf, and could not see it and could not hear it; but the good news that I was, as a sinner, to look away from myself to Christ, as much startled me, and came as fresh to me, as any news I ever heard in my life. Had I never read my Bible? Yes, and read it earnestly. Had I never been taught by Christian people? Yes, I had, by mother, and father, and others. Had I not heard the gospel? Yes, I think I had; and yet, somehow, it was like a new revelation to me that I was to "believe and live." I confess to have been tutored in piety, put into my cradle by prayerful hands, and lulled to sleep by songs concerning Jesus, but after having heard the gospel continually, with line upon line, precept upon precept, here much and there much, yet, when the Word of the Lord came to me with power, it was as new as if I had lived among the unvisited tribes of Central Africa, and had never heard the tidings of the cleansing fountain filled with blood, drawn from the Saviour's veins.

When, for the first time, I received the gospel to my soul's salvation,

I thought that I had never really heard it before, and I began to think that the preachers to whom I had listened had not truly preached it. But, on looking back, I am inclined to believe that I had heard the gospel fully preached many hundreds of times before, and that this was the difference—that I then heard it as though I heard it not; and when I did hear it, the message may not have been any more clear in itself than it had been at former times, but the power of the Holy Spirit was present to open my ear, and to guide the message to my heart. I have no doubt that I heard, scores of times, such texts as these —"He that believeth and is baptized shall be saved;" "Look unto Me, and be ye saved, all the ends of the earth;" "As Moses lifted up the serpent in the wilderness, even so must the Son of man be lifted up: that whosoever believeth in Him should not perish, but have everlasting life;" yet I had no intelligent idea of what faith meant. When I first discovered what faith really was, and exercised it—for with me these two things came together, I believed as soon as ever I knew what believing meant—then I thought I had never before heard that truth preached. But, now, I am persuaded that the light often shone on my eyes, but I was blind, and therefore I thought that the light had never come there. The light was shining all the while, but there was no power to receive it; the eyeball of the soul was not sensitive to the Divine beams.

I could not believe that it was possible that *my* sins could be forgiven. I do not know why, but I seemed to be the odd person in the world. When the catalogue was made out, it appeared to me that, for some reason, I must have been left out. If God had saved me, and not the world, I should have wondered indeed; but if He had saved all the world except me, that would have seemed to me to be but right. And now, being saved by grace, I cannot help saying, "I am indeed a brand plucked out of the fire!" I believe that some of us who were kept by God a long while before we found Him, love Him better perhaps than we should have done if we had received Him directly; and we can preach better to others, we can speak more of His loving-kindness and tender mercy. John Bunyan could not have written as he did if he had not been dragged about by the devil for many years. I love that picture of dear old Christian. I know, when I first read *The Pilgrim's Progress*, and saw in it the woodcut of Christian carrying the burden on his back, I felt so interested in the poor fellow, that I thought I should jump with joy when, after he had carried his heavy load so long, he at last got rid of it; and that was how I felt when the burden of guilt, which I had borne so long, was for ever rolled away from my shoulders and my heart.

Once, God preached to me by a similitude in the depth of winter. The earth had been black, and there was scarcely a green thing or a flower to be seen. As I looked across the fields, there was nothing but barrenness—bare hedges and leafless trees, and black, black earth, wherever I gazed. On a sudden, God spake, and unlocked the treasures of the snow, and white flakes descended until there was no blackness to be seen, and all was one sheet of dazzling whiteness. It was at the time that I was seeking the Saviour, and not long before I found Him, and I remember well that sermon which I saw before me in the snow: "Come now, and let us reason together, saith the Lord: though your sins be as scarlet, they shall be as white as snow; though they be red like crimson, they shall be as wool."

*   *   *

Personally, I have to bless God for many good books; I thank Him for Dr. Doddridge's *Rise and Progress of Religion in the Soul*; for Baxter's *Call to the Unconverted*; for Alleine's *Alarm to Unconverted Sinners*; and for James' *Anxious Enquirer*, but my gratitude most of all is due to God, not for books, but for the preached Word—and that too addressed to me by a poor, uneducated man, a man who had never received any training for the ministry, and probably will never be heard of in this life, a man engaged in business, no doubt of a humble kind, during the week, but who had just enough of grace to say on the Sabbath, "Look unto Me, and be ye saved, all the ends of the earth." The books were good, but the man was better. The revealed Word awakened me, but it was the preached Word that saved me; and I must ever attach peculiar value to the *hearing of the truth*, for by it I received the joy and peace in which my soul delights. While under concern of soul, I resolved that I would attend all the places of worship in the town where I lived, in order that I might find out the way of salvation. I was willing to do anything, and be anything, if God would only forgive my sin. I set off, determined to go round to all the chapels, and I did go to every place of worship; but for a long time I went in vain. I do not, however, blame the ministers. One man preached Divine Sovereignty; I could hear him with pleasure, but what was that sublime truth to a poor sinner who wished to know what he must do to be saved? There was another admirable man who always preached about the law, but what was the use of ploughing up ground that needed to be sown? Another was a practical preacher. I heard him, but it was very much like a commanding officer teaching the manœuvres of war to a set of men without feet. What could I do? All his exhortations were lost on me. I knew it was said, "Believe on the

Lord Jesus Christ, and thou shalt be saved," but I did not know what it was to believe on Christ. These good men all preached truths suited to many in their congregations who were spiritually-minded people, but what I wanted to know was, "How can I get my sins forgiven?"— and they never told me that. I desired to hear how a poor sinner, under a sense of sin, might find peace with God, and when I went, I heard a sermon on, "Be not deceived, God is not mocked," which cut me up still worse, but did not bring me into rest. I went again, another day, and the text was something about the glories of the righteous; nothing for poor me! I was like a dog under the table, not allowed to eat of the children's food. I went after time, and I can honestly say that I do not know that I ever went without prayer to God, and I am sure there was not a more attentive hearer than myself in all the place, for I panted and longed to understand how I might be saved.

I sometimes think I might have been in darkness and despair until now had it not been for the goodness of God in sending a snowstorm, one Sunday morning, while I was going to a certain place of worship. When I could go no further, I turned down a side street, and came to a little Primitive Methodist Chapel. In that chapel there may have been a dozen or fifteen people. I had heard of the Primitive Methodists, how they sang so loudly that they made people's heads ache; but that did not matter to me. I wanted to know how I might be saved, and if they could tell me that, I did not care how much they made my head ache. The minister did not come that morning; he was snowed up, I suppose. At last, a very thin-looking man,[1] a shoemaker, or tailor, or something of that sort, went up into the pulpit to preach. Now, it is well that preachers should be instructed, but this man was really stupid. He was obliged to stick to his text, for the simple reason that he had little else to say. The text was—

"LOOK UNTO ME, AND BE YE SAVED, ALL THE ENDS OF THE EARTH."

He did not even pronounce the words rightly, but that did not matter. There was, I thought, a glimpse of hope for me in that text. The preacher began thus: "My dear friends, this is a very simple text indeed. It says, 'Look.' Now lookin' don't take a deal of pain. It ain't liftin' your foot or your finger; it is just, 'Look.' Well, a man needn't go to College to learn to look. You may be the biggest fool, and yet you can look. A man needn't be worth a thousand a year to be able to look. Anyone can look; even a child can look. But then the text says,

---

[1] It is remarkable that no fewer than three persons claimed to have been the preacher on this occasion, but Spurgeon did not recognize any one of them as the man to whom he then listened.

'Look unto *Me*.' Ay!" said he, in broad Essex, "many on ye are lookin'
to yourselves, but it's no use lookin' there. You'll never find any
comfort in yourselves. Some look to God the Father. No, look to
Him by-and-by. Jesus Christ says, 'Look unto *Me*.' Some on ye say,
'We must wait for the Spirit's workin'.' You have no business with
that just now. Look to *Christ*. The text says, 'Look unto *Me*.' "

    Then the good man followed up his text in this way: "Look unto
Me; I am sweatin' great drops of blood. Look unto Me; I am hangin'
on the cross. Look unto Me; I am dead and buried. Look unto Me;
I rise again. Look unto Me; I ascend to Heaven. Look unto Me; I
am sittin' at the Father's right hand. O poor sinner, look unto Me!
look unto Me!"

    When he had gone to about that length, and managed to spin out
ten minutes or so, he was at the end of his tether. Then he looked at
me under the gallery, and I daresay, with so few present, he knew me
to be a stranger. Just fixing his eyes on me, as if he knew all my
heart, he said, "Young man, you look very miserable." Well, I did,
but I had not been accustomed to have remarks made from the
pulpit on my personal appearance before. However, it was a good
blow, struck right home. He continued, "and you always will be
miserable—miserable in life, and miserable in death—if you don't
obey my text; but if you obey now, this moment, you will be saved."
Then, lifting up his hands, he shouted, as only a Primitive Methodist
could do, "Young man, look to Jesus Christ. Look! Look! Look!
You have nothin' to do but to look and live." I saw at once the way
of salvation. I know not what else he said—I did not take much
notice of it—I was so possessed with that one thought. Like as when
the brazen serpent was lifted up, the people only looked and were
healed, so it was with me. I had been waiting to do fifty things, but
when I heard that word, "Look!" what a charming word it seemed to
me! Oh! I looked until I could almost have looked my eyes away.
There and then the cloud was gone, the darkness had rolled away,
and that moment I saw the sun; and I could have risen that instant,
and sung with the most enthusiastic of them, of the precious blood of
Christ, and the simple faith which looks alone to Him. Oh, that
somebody had told me this before, "Trust Christ, and you shall be
saved." Yet it was, no doubt, all wisely ordered, and now I can say—

> "E'er since by faith I saw the stream
>   Thy flowing wounds supply,
> Redeeming love has been my theme,
>   And shall be till I die."

I do from my soul confess that I never was satisfied till I came to Christ; when I was yet a child, I had far more wretchedness than ever I have now; I will even add, more weariness, more care, more heart-ache than I know at this day. I may be singular in this confession, but I make it, and know it to be the truth. Since that dear hour when my soul cast itself on Jesus, I have found solid joy and peace; but before that, all those supposed gaieties of early youth, all the imagined ease and joy of boyhood, were but vanity and vexation of spirit to me. That happy day, when I found the Saviour, and learned to cling to His dear feet, was a day never to be forgotten by me. An obscure child, unknown, unheard of, I listened to the Word of God; and that precious text led me to the cross of Christ. I can testify that the joy of that day was utterly indescribable. I could have leaped, I could have danced; there was no expression, however fanatical, which would have been out of keeping with the joy of my spirit at that hour. Many days of Christian experience have passed since then, but there has never been one which has had the full exhilaration, the sparkling delight which that first day had. I thought I could have sprung from the seat on which I sat, and have called out with the wildest of those Methodist brethren who were present, "I am forgiven! I am forgiven! A monument of grace! A sinner saved by blood!" My spirit saw its chains broken to pieces, I felt that I was an emancipated soul, an heir of heaven, a forgiven one, accepted in Christ Jesus, plucked out of the miry clay and out of the horrible pit, with my feet set upon a rock, and my goings established. I thought I could dance all the way home. I could understand what John Bunyan meant, when he declared he wanted to tell the crows on the ploughed land all about his conversion. He was too full to hold, he felt he must tell some-body.

It is not everyone who can remember the very day and hour of his deliverance; but, as Richard Knill said, "At such a time of the day, clang went every harp in heaven, for Richard Knill was born again," it was e'en so with me.[1] The clock of mercy struck in heaven the hour and moment of my emancipation, for the time had come. Between half-past ten o'clock, when I entered that chapel, and half-past twelve o'clock, when I was back again at home, what a change had taken place in me! I had passed from darkness into marvellous light, from death to life. Simply by looking to Jesus, I had been delivered from despair, and I was brought into such a joyous state of mind that, when

---

[1] It is definitely known that the date of Spurgeon's conversion was January 6, 1850, for preaching at New Park Street Chapel, on Lord's-day morning, January 6, 1856, from Isaiah xlv. 22, he said that, six years before, that very day, and at that very hour, he had been led to look to Christ, by a sermon from that text.

they saw me at home, they said to me, "Something wonderful has happened to you," and I was eager to tell them all about it. Oh! there was joy in the household that day, when all heard that the eldest son had found the Saviour, and knew himself to be forgiven—bliss compared with which all earth's joys are less than nothing, and vanity. Yes, I had looked to Jesus as I was, and found in Him my Saviour. Thus had the eternal purpose of Jehovah decreed it; and as, the moment before, there was none more wretched than I was, so, within that second, there was none more joyous. It took no longer time than does the lightning-flash; it was done, and never has it been undone. I looked, and lived, and leaped in joyful liberty as I beheld my sin punished upon the great Substitute, and put away for ever. I looked unto Him, as He bled upon that tree; His eyes darted a glance of love unutterable into my spirit, and in a moment, I was saved. Looking unto Him, the bruises that my soul had suffered were healed, the gaping wounds were cured, the broken bones rejoiced, the rags that had covered me were all removed, my spirit was white as the spotless snows of the far-off North; I had melody within my spirit, for I was saved, washed, cleansed, forgiven, through Him that did hang upon the tree. My Master, I cannot understand how Thou couldst stoop Thine awful head to such a death as the death of the cross—how Thou couldst take from Thy brow the coronet of stars which from old eternity had shone resplendent there; but how Thou shouldst permit the thorn-crown to gird Thy temples, astonishes me far more. That Thou shouldst cast away the mantle of Thy glory, the azure of Thine everlasting empire, I cannot comprehend; but how Thou shouldst have become veiled in the ignominious purple for a while, and then be mocked by impious men, who bowed to Thee as a pretended king; and how Thou shouldst be stripped naked to Thy shame, without a single covering, and die a felon's death—this is still more incomprehensible. But the marvel is that Thou shouldst have suffered all this for *me*! Truly, Thy love to me is wonderful, passing the love of women! Was ever grief like Thine? Was ever love like Thine, that could open the flood-gates of such grief? Was ever love so mighty as to become the fount from which such an ocean of grief could come rolling down?

There was never anything so true to me as those bleeding hands, and that thorn-crowned head. Home, friends, health, wealth, comforts—all lost their lustre that day when He appeared, just as stars are hidden by the light of the sun. He was the only Lord and Giver of life's best bliss, the one well of living water springing up unto everlasting life. As I saw Jesus on His cross before me, and as I mused upon His sufferings and death, methought I saw Him cast a look of love upon me; and then I looked at Him, and cried —

> "Jesu, lover of my soul,
> Let me to Thy bosom fly."

He said, "Come," and I flew to Him, and clasped Him; and when He let me go again, I wondered where my burden was. It was gone! There, in the sepulchre, it lay, and I felt light as air; like a winged sylph, I could fly over mountains of trouble and despair, and oh! what liberty and joy I had! I could leap with ecstasy, for I had much forgiven, and I was freed from sin. With the spouse in the Canticles, I could say, "*I found Him;*" I, a lad, found the Lord of glory; I, a slave to sin, found the great Deliverer; I, the child of darkness, found the Light of life; I, the uttermost of the lost, found my Saviour and my God; I, widowed and desolate, found my Friend, my Beloved, my Husband. Oh, how I wondered that *I* should be pardoned! It was not the pardon that I wondered at so much; the wonder was that it should come to *me*. I marvelled that He should be able to pardon such sins as mine, such crimes, so numerous and so black, and that, after such an accusing conscience, He should have power to still every wave within my spirit, and make my soul like the surface of a river, undisturbed, quiet, and at ease. It mattered not to me whether the day itself was gloomy or bright, I had found Christ; that was enough for me. He was my Saviour, He was my all; and I can heartily say, that one day of pardoned sin was a sufficient recompense for the whole five years of conviction. I have to bless God for every terror that ever scared me by night, and for every foreboding that alarmed me by day. It has made me happier ever since, for now, if there be a trouble weighing upon my soul, I thank God it is not such a burden as that which bowed me to the very earth, and made me creep upon the ground like a beast, by reason of heavy distress and affliction. I know I never can again suffer what I have suffered; I never can, except I be sent to hell, know more of agony than I have known; and now, that ease, that joy and peace in believing, that "no condemnation" which belongs to me as a child of God, is made doubly sweet and inexpressibly precious, by the recollection of my past days of sorrow and grief. Blessed be Thou, O God, for ever, who by those black days, like a dreary winter, hast made these summer days all the fairer and the sweeter! I need not walk through the earth fearful of every shadow, and afraid of every man I meet, for sin is washed away; my spirit is no more guilty; it is pure, it is holy. The frown of God no longer resteth upon me; but my Father smiles, I see His eyes—they are glancing love; I hear His voice—it is full of sweetness. I am forgiven, I am forgiven, I am forgiven!

When I look back upon it, I can see one reason why the Word was blessed to me as I heard it preached in that Primitive Methodist Chapel at Colchester; I had been up betimes crying to God for the blessing. As a lad, when I was seeking the Saviour, I used to rise with the sun, that I might get time to read gracious books, and to seek the Lord. I can recall the kind of pleas I used when I took my arguments, and came before the throne of grace: "Lord, save me; it will glorify Thy grace to save such a sinner as I am! Lord, save me, else I am lost to all eternity; do not let me perish, Lord! Save me, O Lord, for Jesus died! By His agony and bloody sweat, by His cross and passion, save me!" I often proved that the early morning was the best part of the day; I liked those prayers of which the psalmist said, "In the morning shall my prayer prevent Thee."

*   *   *

The Holy Spirit, who enabled me to believe, gave me peace through believing. I felt as sure that I was forgiven as before I felt sure of condemnation. I had been certain of my condemnation because the Word of God declared it, and my conscience bore witness to it, but when the Lord justified me, I was made equally certain by the same witnesses. The Word of the Lord in the Scripture saith, "He that believeth on Him is not condemned," and my conscience bore witness that I believed, and that God in pardoning me was just. Thus I had the witness of the Holy Spirit and also of my own conscience, and these two agreed in one. That great and excellent man, Dr. Johnson, used to hold the opinion that no man ever could know that he was pardoned —that there was no such thing as assurance of faith. Perhaps, if Dr. Johnson had studied his Bible a little more, and had had a little more of the enlightenment of the Spirit, he, too, might have come to know his own pardon. Certainly, he was no very reliable judge of theology, any more than he was of porcelain, which he once attempted to make, and never succeeded. I think both in theology and porcelain his opinion is of very little value.

How can a man know that he is pardoned? There is a text which says, "Believe on the Lord Jesus Christ, and thou shalt be saved." I believe on the Lord Jesus Christ; is it irrational to believe that I am saved? "He that believeth on the Son hath everlasting life," saith Christ, in John's Gospel. I believe on Christ; am I absurd in believing that I have eternal life? I find the apostle Paul speaking by the Holy Ghost, and saying, "There is therefore now no condemnation to them that are in Christ Jesus. Being justified by faith, we have peace with God." If I know that my trust is fixed on Jesus only, and that I have faith in Him, were it not ten thousand times more absurd for me not to be at peace, than for me to be filled with joy unspeakable? It is but taking God at His Word, when the soul knows, as a necessary consequence of its faith, that it is saved. I took Jesus as my Saviour, and I was saved; and I can tell the reason why I took Him for my Saviour. To my own humiliation, I must confess that I did it because I could not help it; I was shut up to it. That stern law-work had hammered me into such a condition that, if there had been fifty other saviours, I could not have thought of them—I was driven to this One. I wanted a Divine Saviour, I wanted One who was made a curse for me, to expiate my guilt. I wanted One who had died, for I deserved to die. I wanted One who had risen again, who was able by His life to make me live. I wanted the exact Saviour that stood before me in the Word, revealed to my heart; and I could not help having Him. I could realize then the language of Rutherford when, being full of love to Christ, once upon a time, in the dungeon of Aberdeen, he said, "O my Lord, if there were a broad hell betwixt me and Thee, if I could not get at Thee except by wading through it, I would not think twice, but I would go through it all, if I might but embrace Thee, and call Thee mine!" Oh, how I loved Him! Passing all loves except His own, was that love which I felt for Him then. If, beside the door of the place in which I met with Him, there had been a stake of blazing faggots, I would have stood upon them without chains, glad to give my flesh, and blood, and bones, to be ashes that should testify my love to Him. Had He asked me then to give all my substance to the poor, I would have given all, and thought myself to be amazingly rich in having beggared myself for His name's sake. Had He commanded me then to preach in the midst of all His foes, I could have said—

> "There's not a lamb in all Thy flock
> I would disdain to feed,
> There's not a foe, before whose face
> I'd fear Thy cause to plead."

Has Jesus saved *me*? I dare not speak with any hesitation here; I *know* He has. His Word is true, therefore I *am* saved. My evidence that I am saved does not lie in the fact that I preach, or that I do this or that. All my hope lies in this, that Jesus Christ came to save sinners. I am a sinner, I trust Him, then He came to save me, and I am saved; I live habitually in the enjoyment of this blessed fact, and it is long since I have doubted the truth of it, for I have His own Word to sustain my faith. It is a very surprising thing—a thing to be marvelled at most of all by those who enjoy it. I know that it is to me even to this day the greatest wonder that I ever heard of, that God should ever justify *me*. I feel myself to be a lump of unworthiness, a mass of corruption, and a heap of sin, apart from His almighty love; yet I know, by a full assurance, that I am justified by faith which is in Christ Jesus, and treated as if I had been perfectly just, and made an heir of God and a joint-heir with Christ; though by nature I must take my place among the most sinful. I, who am altogether undeserving, am treated as if I had been deserving. I am loved with as much love as if I had always been godly, whereas aforetime I was ungodly.

I have always considered, with Luther and Calvin, that the sum and substance of the gospel lies in that word *Substitution*—Christ standing in the stead of man. If I understand the gospel, it is this: I deserve to be lost for ever; the only reason why I should not be damned is, that Christ was punished in my stead, and there is no need to execute a sentence twice for sin. On the other hand, I know I cannot enter Heaven unless I have a perfect righteousness; I am absolutely certain I shall never have one of my own, for I find I sin every day, but then Christ had a perfect righteousness, and He said, "There, poor sinner, take My garment, and put it on; you shall stand before God as if you were Christ, and I will stand before God as if I had been the sinner; I will suffer in the sinner's stead, and you shall be rewarded for works which you did not do, but which I did for you." I find it very convenient every day to come to Christ as a sinner, as I came at the first. "You are no saint," says the devil. Well, if I am not, I am a sinner, and Jesus Christ came into the world to save sinners. Sink or swim, I go to Him; other hope I have none. By looking to Him, I received all the faith which inspired me with confidence in His grace; and the word that first drew my soul—"Look unto Me"—still rings its clarion note in my ears. There I once found conversion, and there I shall ever find refreshing and renewal.

Let me bear my personal testimony of what I have seen, what my own ears have heard, and my own heart has tasted. First, Christ is the only-begotten of the Father. He is Divine to me, if He be human to all the world besides. He has done that for me which none but a God could do. He has subdued my stubborn will, melted a heart of adamant, broken a chain of steel, opened the gates of brass, and snapped the bars of iron. He hath turned for me my mourning into laughter, and my desolation into joy; He hath led my captivity captive, and made my heart rejoice with joy unspeakable, and full of glory. Let others think as they will of Him, to me He must ever be the only-begotten of the Father; blessed be His holy name!

> "Oh, that I could now adore Him,
> Like the Heavenly host above,
> Who for ever bow before Him,
> And unceasing sing His love!
> Happy songsters!
> When shall I your chorus join?"

Again, I bear my testimony that He is full of grace. Ah, had He not been, I should never have beheld His glory. I was full of sin to over-flowing. I was condemned already, because I believed not upon Him. He drew me when I wanted not to come, and though I struggled hard, He continued still to draw; and when at last I came to His mercy-seat, all trembling like a condemned culprit, He said, "Thy sins, which are many, are all forgiven thee: be of good cheer." Let others despise Him; but I bear witness that He is full of grace.

Finally, I bear my witness that He is full of truth. True have His promises been; not one has failed. I have often doubted Him, for that I blush; He has never failed me, in this I must rejoice. His promises have been yea and Amen. I do but speak the testimony of every believer in Christ, though I put it thus personally to make it the more forcible. I bear witness that never servant had such a Master as I have; never brother had such a Kinsman as He has been to me; never spouse had such a Husband as Christ has been to my soul; never sinner a better Saviour; never soldier a better Captain; never mourner a better Comforter than Christ hath been to my spirit. I want none beside Him. In life, He is my life; and in death, He shall be the death of death; in poverty, Christ is my riches; in sickness, He makes my bed; in darkness, He is my Star; and in brightness, He is my Sun. By faith I understand that the blessed Son of God redeemed my soul with His own heart's blood; and by sweet experience I know that He raised me up from the pit of dark despair, and set my feet on the rock. He died for me. This is the root of every satisfaction I have. He put all my transgressions away. He cleansed me with His precious blood; He covered me with His perfect righteousness; He wrapped me up in His own virtues. He has promised to keep me, while I abide in this world, from its temptations and snares; and when I depart from this world, He has already prepared for me a mansion in the Heaven of unfading bliss, and a crown of everlasting joy that shall never, never fade away. To me, then, the days or years of my mortal sojourn on this earth are of little moment. Nor is the manner of my

H

decease of much consequence. Should foemen sentence me to martyrdom, or physicians declare that I must soon depart this life, it is all alike—

> "A few more rolling suns at most
> Shall land me on fair Canaan's coast."

What more can I wish than that, while my brief term on earth shall last, I should be the servant of Him who became the Servant of servants for me? I can say, concerning Christ's religion, if I had to die like a dog, and had no hope whatever of immortality, if I wanted to lead a happy life, let me serve my God with all my heart; let me be a follower of Jesus, and walk in His footsteps. If there were no here-after, I would still prefer to be a Christian, and the humblest Christian minister, to being a king or an emperor, for I am persuaded there are more delights in Christ, yea, more joy in one glimpse of His face than is to be found in all the praises of this harlot-world, and in all the delights which it can yield to us in its sunniest and brightest days. And I am persuaded that what He has been till now, He will be to the end, and where He hath begun a good work, He will carry it on. In the religion of Jesus Christ, there are clusters even on earth too heavy for one man to carry; there are fruits that have been found so rich that even angel lips have never been sweetened with more luscious wine; there are joys to be had here so fair that even cates ambrosial and the nectared wine of Paradise can scarcely excel the sweets of satisfaction that are to be found in the earthly banquets of the Lord. I have seen hundreds and thousands who have given their hearts to Jesus, but I never did see one who said he was disappointed with Him, I never met with one who said Jesus Christ was less than He was declared to be. When first my eyes beheld Him, when the burden slipped from off my heavy-laden shoulders, and I was free from condemnation, I thought that all the preachers I had ever heard had not half preached, they had not told half the beauty of my Lord and Master. So good! so generous! so gracious! so willing to for-give! It seemed to me as if they had almost slandered Him; they painted His likeness, doubtless, as well as they could, but it was a mere smudge compared with the matchless beauties of His face. All who have ever seen Him will say the same. I go back to my home, many a time, mourning that I cannot preach my Master even as I myself know Him, and what I know of Him is very little compared with the matchlessness of His grace. Would that I knew more of Him, and that I could tell it out better!

"Our faith at times has to fight for its very existence. The old Adam within us rages mightily, and the new spirit within us, like a young lion, disdains to be vanquished; and so these two strong ones contend, till our spirit is full of agony. Some of us know what it is to be tempted with blasphemies we should not dare to repeat, to be vexed with horrid temptations which we have grappled with and overcome, but which have almost cost us resistance unto blood. In such inward conflicts, saints must be alone. They cannot tell their feelings to others, they would not dare; and if they did, their own brethren would despise or upbraid them, for the most of professors would not even know what they meant. Even those who have trodden other fiery ways would not be able to sympathize in all, but would answer the poor troubled soul, "These are points in which we cannot go with you." Christ alone was tempted in all points like as we are, though without sin. No one man is tempted in all points exactly like another man, and each one has certain trials in which he must stand alone amid the rage of war, with not even a book to help him, or a biography to assist him, no man ever having gone that way before except that one Man whose trail reveals a nail-pierced foot. He alone knows all the devious paths of sorrow. Yet, even in such byways, the Lord is with us, helping us, sustaining us, and giving us grace to conquer at the close."—C. H. S.

Chapter 8

Experiences after Conversion

WHEN my eyes first looked to Christ, He was a very real Christ to me; and when my burden of sin rolled from off my back, it was a real pardon and a real release from sin to me; and when that day I said for the first time, "Jesus Christ is mine," it was a real possession of Christ to me. When I went up to the sanctuary in that early dawn of youthful piety, every song was really a psalm, and when there was a prayer, oh, how I followed every word! It was prayer indeed! And so was it, too, in silent quietude, when I drew near to God, it was no mockery, no routine, no matter of mere duty; it was a real talking with my Father who is in Heaven. And oh, how I loved my Saviour Christ then! I would have given all I had for Him! How I felt towards sinners that day! Lad that I was, I wanted to preach, and—

> "Tell to sinners round,
> What a dear Saviour I had found."

One of the greatest sorrows I had, when first I knew the Lord, was to think about certain persons with whom I knew right well that I had held ungodly conversations, and sundry others whom I had tempted to sin; and one of the prayers that I always offered, when I prayed for myself, was that such an one might not be lost through sins to which I had tempted him. This was the case also with George Whitefield, who never forgot those with whom, before his conversion, he used to play cards, and he had the joy of leading every one of them to the Saviour.

I think about five days after I first found Christ, when my joy had been such that I could have danced for very mirth at the thought that Christ was mine, on a sudden I fell into a sad fit of despondency. I can tell now why it was so with me. When I first believed in Christ, I am not sure that I thought the devil was dead, but certainly I had a kind of notion that he was so mortally wounded that he could not disturb me. And then I also fancied that the corruption of my nature had received its death-blow. I read what Cowper said—

> "Since the dear hour that brought me to Thy foot,
> And cut up all my follies by the root;"

and I really thought that the poet knew what he was saying; whereas, never did anyone blunder so terribly as Cowper did when he said that, for no man, I think, has all his follies thus cut up by the roots. However, I fondly dreamed that mine were, I felt persuaded they would never sprout again. I was going to be perfect—I fully calculated upon it—and lo, I found an intruder I had not reckoned upon, an evil heart of unbelief in departing from the living God. So I went to that same Primitive Methodist Chapel where I first received peace with God, through the simple preaching of the Word. The text happened to be, "O wretched man that I am: who shall deliver me from the body of this death?" "There," I thought, "that's the text for me." I had just got as far as that in the week. I knew that I had put my trust in Christ, and I knew that, when I sat in that house of prayer, my faith was simply and solely fixed on the atonement of the Redeemer. But I had a weight on my mind, because I could not be as holy as I wanted to be. I could not live without sin. When I rose in the morning, I thought I would abstain from every hard word, from every evil thought and look; and I came up to that chapel groaning because, "when I would do good, evil was present with me." The minister began by saying, "Paul was not a believer when he said this." Well now, I knew I was a believer, and it seemed to me from the context that Paul must have been a believer, too. (Now, I am sure he was.) The man went on to say that no child of God ever did feel any conflict within. So I took up my hat, and left the chapel, and I have very seldom attended such places since. They are very good for people who are unconverted to go to, but of very little use for children of God. That is my notion of Methodism. It is a noble thing to bring in strangers; but a terrible thing for those that are brought in to sit and feed there. It is like the parish pound, it is a good place to put sheep in when they have strayed, but there is no food inside; they had better be let out as soon as possible to find some grass. I saw that that minister understood nothing of experimental divinity, or of practical heart theology, or else he would not have talked as he did. A good man he was, I do not doubt, but utterly incompetent to the task of dealing with a case like mine.

Oh, what a horror I have had of sin ever since the day when I felt its power over my soul! O sin, *sin*, I have had enough of thee! Thou didst never bring me more than a moment's seeming joy, and with it there came a deep and awful bitterness which burns within me to this day! Well do I recollect when I was the subject of excessive tenderness—some people called it "morbid sensibility". How I shuddered and shivered at the very thought of sin, which then appeared exceedingly sinful! The first week after I was converted to God, I felt afraid to put one foot before the other for fear I should do wrong. When I thought over the day, if there had been a failure in my temper, or if there had been a frothy word spoken, or something done amiss, I did chasten myself sorely. Had I, at that time, known anything to be my Lord's will, I think I should not have hesitated to do it; to me it would not have mattered whether it was a fashionable thing or an unfashionable thing, if it was according to His Word. Oh, to do His will! to follow Him whithersoever He would have me go! It seemed then as though I should never, never, never be slack in keeping His commandments.

* * *

I do not know whether the experience of others agrees with mine; but I can say this, that the worst difficulty I ever met with, or I think I can ever meet with, happened a little time after my conversion to God. When I first knew the weight of sin, it was as a burden, as a labour, as a trouble, but when, the second time,

> "I asked the Lord that I might grow,
> In faith, and love, and every grace;
> Might more of His salvation know,
> And seek more earnestly His face;"

and when He answered me by letting all my sins loose upon me, they appeared more frightful than before. I thought the Egyptians in Egypt were not half so bad as the Egyptians out of Egypt; I thought the sins I knew before, though they were cruel task-masters, were not half so much to be dreaded as those soldier-sins, armed with spears and axes, riding in iron chariots with scythes upon their axles, hastening to assault me. It is true, they did not come so near to me as heretofore; nevertheless, they occasioned me more fright even than when I was their slave. The Israelites went up harnessed, marching in their ranks, and, I doubt not, singing as they went, because they were delivered from the daily task and from the cruel bondage; but suddenly they turned their heads while they were marching, for they heard a dreadful noise behind them, a noise of chariots and of men shouting for battle; and at last, when they could really see the Egyptians, and the thick cloud of dust rising behind them, then they said that they should be destroyed, they should now fall by the hand of the enemy. I remember, after my conversion (it may not have happened to all, but it did to me), there came a time when the enemy said, "I will pursue, I will overtake, I will divide the spoil; my lust shall be satisfied upon them; I will draw my sword, my hand shall destroy them." So Satan, loth to leave a soul, pursues it hot-foot. He will have it back if he can; and often, soon after conversion, there comes a time of dreadful conflict, when the soul seems as if it could not live. "Was it because there were no graves in Egypt that the Lord brought us into this condition of temporary freedom, that we might be all the more distressed by our adversaries?" So said unbelief; but God brought His people right out by one final stroke. Miriam knew it when she took her timbrel, and went forth with the women, and answered them in the jubilant song, "Sing ye to the Lord, for He hath triumphed gloriously; the horse and his rider hath He thrown into the sea." I love best of all that note in the song of Moses where he says, "The depths have covered them." "There remained not so much as one of them." What gladness must have been in the hearts of the children of Israel when they knew that their enemies were all gone! I am sure it was so with me, for, after my conversion, being again attacked by sin, I saw the mighty stream of redeeming love roll over all my sins, and this was my song, "The depths have covered them." "Who shall lay anything to the charge of God's elect? It is God that justifieth. Who is he that condemneth? It is Christ that died, yea, rather, that is risen again, who is even at the right hand of God, who also maketh intercession for us."

I was brought up, as a child, with such care that I knew but very little of foul or profane language, having scarcely ever heard a man swear. Yet do I remember times, in my earliest Christian days, when there came into my mind thoughts so evil that I clapped my hand to my mouth for fear I should be led to give utterance to them. This is one way in which Satan tortures those whom God has delivered out of his hand. Many of the choicest saints have been thus molested. Once, when I had been grievously assailed by the tempter, I went to see my dear old grandfather. I told him about my terrible experience, and then I wound up by saying, "Grandfather, I am sure I cannot be a child of God, or else I should never have such evil thoughts as these." "Nonsense, Charles," answered the good old man; "it is just because you are a Christian that you are thus tempted. These blasphemies are no children of yours; they are the devil's brats, which he delights to lay at the door of a Christian. Don't you own them as yours, give them neither house-room nor heart-room." I felt greatly comforted by what my grandfather said, especially as it confirmed what another old saint had told me when I was tempted in a similar manner while I was seeking the Saviour. A great many people make fun of that verse—

> " 'Tis a point I long to know,
>   Oft it causes anxious thought,
> Do I love the Lord, or no?
> Am I His, or am I not?"

If they ever find themselves where some of us have been, they will not do so any more. I believe it is a shallow experience that makes people always confident of what they are, and where they are, for there are times of terrible trouble, that make even the most confident child of God hardly know whether he is on his head or on his heels. It is the mariner who has done business on great waters who, in times of unusual stress and storm, reels to and fro, and staggers like a drunken man, and is at his wits' end. At such a time, if Jesus whispers that I am His, then the question is answered once for all, and my soul has received a token which it waves in the face of Satan, so that he disappears, and I can go on my way rejoicing.

*   *   *

I have found, in my own spiritual life, that the more rules I lay down for myself, the more sins I commit. The habit of regular morning and evening prayer is one which is indispensable to a believer's life, but the prescribing of the length of prayer, and the constrained remembrance of so many persons and subjects, may gender unto bondage, and strangle prayer rather than assist it. To say I will humble myself at such a time, and rejoice at such another season, is nearly as much an affectation as when the preacher wrote in the margin of his sermon, "Cry here," "Smile here." Why, if the man preached from his heart, he would be sure to cry in the right place, and to smile at a suitable moment; and when the spiritual life is sound, it produces prayer at the right time, and humiliation of soul and sacred joy spring forth spontaneously, apart from rules and vows. The kind of religion which makes itself to order by the Almanack, and turns out its emotions like bricks from a machine, weeping on Good Friday, and rejoicing two days afterwards, measuring its motions by the moon, is too artificial to be worthy of my imitation.

Self-examination is a very great blessing, but I have known self-examination carried on in a most unbelieving, legal, and self-righteous manner; in fact, I have so carried it on myself. Time was when I used to think a vast deal more of marks, and signs, and evidences, for my own comfort, than I do now, for I find that I cannot be a match for the devil when I begin dealing in these things. I am obliged to go day by day with this cry—

"I, the chief of sinners am,
But Jesus died for me."

While I can believe the promise of God, because it is His promise, and because He is my God, and while I can trust my Saviour because He is God, and therefore mighty to save, all goes well with me, but I do find, when I begin questioning myself about this and that perplexity, thus taking my eye off Christ, that all the virtue of my life seems oozing out at every pore. Any practice that detracts from faith is an evil practice, but especially that kind of self-examination which would take us away from the cross-foot, proceeds in a wrong direction.

I used, when I first knew the Saviour, to try myself in a certain manner, and often did I throw stumbling-blocks in my path through it, and therefore I can warn any who are doing the same. Sometimes I would go up into my chamber, and by way of self-examination, I used to ask myself this question—"*Am I afraid to die?* If I should drop down dead in my room, can I say that I should joyfully close my eyes?" Well, it often happened that I could not honestly say so. I used to feel that death would be a very solemn thing. "Ah, then!" I said, "I have never believed in Christ, for if I had put my trust in the Lord Jesus, I should not be afraid to die, but I should be quite confident." I do not doubt that many a person is saying, "I cannot follow Christ, because I am afraid to die; I cannot believe that Jesus Christ will save me, because the thought of death makes me tremble." Ah, poor soul, there are many of God's blessed ones, who through fear of death have been much of their lifetime subject to bondage! I know precious children of God now: I believe that, when they die, they will die triumphantly; but I know this, that the thought of death is never pleasing to them. And this is accounted for, because God has stamped on nature that law, the love of life and self-preservation; and it is natural enough that the man who has kindred and friends should scarcely like to leave behind those who are so dear. I know that, when he gets more grace, he will rejoice in the thought of death; but I do know that there are many quite safe, who will die rejoicing in Christ, who now, in the prospect of death, feel afraid of it. My aged grand-father once preached a sermon which I have not yet forgotten. He was preaching from the text, "The God of all grace," and he some-what interested the assembly, after describing the different kinds of grace that God gave, by saying at the end of each period, "But there is one kind of grace that you do not want." After each part of his theme, there came the like sentence, "But there is one kind of grace you do not want." And then he wound up by saying, "You don't want dying grace in living moments, but you shall have dying grace when you need it. When you are in the condition to require it, you shall have grace enough if you put your trust in Christ." In a party of friends, we were discussing the question whether, if the days of martyrdom should come, we were prepared to be burned. I said, "I must frankly tell you that, speaking as I feel to-day, I am not prepared to be burned; but I do believe that, if there were a stake at Smithfield, and I knew that I was to be burned there at one o'clock, I should have grace enough to be burned there when one o'clock came."

*   *   *

I was much impressed, in my younger days, by hearing a minister, blind with age, speak at the communion table, and bear witness to us who had just joined the church, that it was well for us that we had come to put our trust in a faithful God; and as the good man, with great feebleness and yet with great earnestness, said to us that he had never regretted having given himself to Christ as a boy, I felt my heart leap within me with delight that I had such a God to be my God. His testimony was such as a younger man could not have borne: he might have spoken more fluently, but the weight of those eighty years at the back of it made the old man eloquent to my young heart. For twenty years he had not seen the light of the sun. His snow-white locks hung from his brow, and floated over his shoulders, and he stood up at the table of the Lord, and thus addressed us: "Brethren and sisters, I shall soon be taken from you; in a few more months, I shall gather up my feet in my bed, and sleep with my fathers. I have not the mind of the learned, nor the tongue of the eloquent; but I desire, before I go, to bear one public testimony to my God. Fifty and six years have I served Him, and I have never once found Him unfaithful. I can say, 'Surely goodness and mercy have followed me all the days of my life, and not one good thing hath failed of all the Lord God has promised.'" There stood the dear old man, tottering into his tomb, deprived of the light of heaven naturally, and yet having the Light of Heaven in a better sense shining into his soul; and though he could not look upon us, yet he turned towards us, and he seemed to say, "Young people, trust God in early life, for I have not to regret that I sought Him too soon. I have only to mourn that so many of my years ran to waste." There is nothing that more tends to strengthen the faith of the young believer than to hear the veteran Christian, covered with scars from the battle, testifying that the service of his Master is a happy service, and that, if he could have served any other master, he would not have done so, for His service is pleasant, and His reward everlasting joy.

In my early days, I knew a good man, who has now gone to his reward, who was the means of producing, under God, a library of useful lives. I do not mean books in paper, but books in boots! Many young men were decided for the Lord by his means, and became preachers, teachers, deacons, and other workers; and no one would wonder that it was so, if he knew the man who trained them. He was ready for every good word and work, but he gave special attention to his Bible-class, in which he set forth the gospel with clearness and zeal. Whenever any one of his young men left the country town in which he lived, he would be sure to arrange a parting interview. There was a wide-spreading oak down in the fields; and there he was wont to keep an early morning appointment with John, or Thomas, or William; and that appointment very much consisted of earnest pleading with the Lord that, in going up to the great city, the young man might be kept from sin, and made useful. Under that tree several decided for the Saviour. It was an impressive act, and left its influence upon them, for many men came, in after years, to see the spot, made sacred by their teacher's prayers.

Oh! how my young heart once ached in boyhood, when I first loved the Saviour. I was far away from father and mother, and all I loved, and I thought my heart would burst, for I was an usher in a school, in a place where I could meet with little sympathy or help. Well, I went to my chamber, and told my little griefs into the ears of Jesus. They were great griefs to me then, though they are nothing now. When on my knees I just whispered them into the ear of Him who had loved me with an everlasting love, oh, it was so sweet! If I had told them to others, they would have told them again; but He, my blessed Confidant, knows all my secrets, and He never tells again.

There is one verse of Scripture which, as a young believer, I used often to repeat, for it was very dear to me; it is this: "Bind the sacrifice with cords, even unto the horns of the altar." I did feel then that I was wholly Christ's. In the marriage covenant of which the Lord speaks, when the Husband put the ring upon His bride's finger, He said to her, "Thou hast become Mine;" and I remember when I felt upon my finger the ring of infinite, everlasting, covenant love that Christ put there. Oh, it was a joyful day, a blessed day! Happy day, happy day, when His choice was known to me, and He fixed my choice on Him! That blessed rest of soul, which comes of a sure possession of Christ, is not to be imitated, but it is greatly to be desired. I know that some good people, who I believe will be saved, nevertheless do not attain to this sweet rest. They keep on thinking that it is something that they may get when they are very

old, or when they are about to die, but they look upon the full assurance of faith, and the personal grasping of Christ, and saying, "My
Beloved is mine," as something very dangerous. I began my Christian
life in this happy fashion as a boy fifteen years of age; I believed fully
and without hesitation in the Lord Jesus Christ, and when I went to
see a good Christian woman, I was simple enough to tell her that I
believed in Christ, that He was mine, and that He had saved me. I
expressed myself very confidently concerning the great truth that
God would ne'er forsake His people, nor leave His work undone. I
was at once chid, and told that I had no right to speak so confidently,
for it was presumptuous. The good woman said to me, "Ah! I don't
like such assurance as that," and then she added, "I trust you are
believing in Christ—I hope so; but I have never got beyond a hope
or a trust, and I am an old woman." Bless the old woman, she was
no example for us who know whom we have believed; we ought to
rise far above that grovelling kind of life. The man who begins right,
and the boy who begins right, and the girl who begins right, will
begin by saying, "God hath said it: 'He that believeth on Him is not
condemned.' I believe on Him, therefore I am not condemned;
Christ is mine."

Before my conversion, I was accustomed to read the Scriptures to
admire their grandeur, to feel the charm of their history, and wonder
at the majesty of their language; but I altogether missed the Lord's
intent therein. But when the Spirit came with His Divine life, and
quickened all the Book to my newly-enlightened soul, the inner
meaning shone forth with wondrous glory. I was not in a frame of
mind to judge God's Word, but I accepted it all without demur; I
did not venture to sit in judgment upon my Judge, and become the
reviser of the unerring God. Whatever I found to be in His Word,
I received with intense joy. From that hour, I bless God that, being
not exempt from trouble, and especially not free from a tendency to
despondency which is always with me, I yet rejoice and will rejoice,
and am happy, unspeakably happy in resting upon Jesus Christ.
Moreover, I have found that those points of my character which were
most weak have been strengthened, while strong passions have been
subdued, evil propensities have been kept under, and new principles
have been implanted. I am changed; I am as different from what I
was as a man could be who had been annihilated, and had then been
made over again. Nor do I claim any of the credit for this change—
far from it. God has done great things for me, but He has done the
same for others, and is willing to do it for any soul that seeks His face
through Jesus Christ and His great atoning sacrifice.

I have known some men who were almost idiots before conversion, but they afterwards had their faculties wonderfully developed. Some time ago, there was a man who was so ignorant that he could not read, and he never spoke anything like grammar in his life, unless by mistake; and, moreover, he was considered to be what the people in his neighbourhood called "daft". But when he was converted, the first thing he did was to pray. He stammered out a few words, and in a little time his powers of speaking began to develop themselves. Then he thought he would like to read the Scriptures, and after long, long months of labour, he learned to read. And what was the next thing? He thought he could preach; and he did preach a little, in his own homely way, in his house. Then he thought, "I must read a few more books." And so his mind expanded, until, I believe he is at the present day a useful minister, settled in a country village, labouring for God.

An idea has long possessed the public mind, that a religious man can scarcely be a wise man. It has been the custom to talk of infidels, atheists, and deists, as men of deep thought and comprehensive intellect; and to tremble for the Christian controversialist as if he must surely fall by the hand of his enemy. But this is purely a mistake, for the gospel is the sum of wisdom, an epitome of knowledge, a treasure-house of truth, and a revelation of mysterious secrets. In it we see how justice and mercy may be married; here we behold inexorable law entirely satisfied, and sovereign love bearing away the sinner in triumph. Our meditation upon it enlarges the mind; and as it opens to our soul in successive flashes of glory, we stand astonished at the profound wisdom manifest in it. I have often said that, before I knew the gospel, I had gathered up a heterogeneous mass of all kinds of knowledge from here, there, and everywhere—a bit of chemistry, a bit of botany, a bit of astronomy, and a bit of this, that, and the other. I put them all together, in one great confused chaos, but when I learned the gospel, I got a shelf in my head to put everything upon just where it should be. It seemed to me as if, when I had discovered Christ and Him crucified, I had found the centre of the system, so that I could see every other science revolving in due order. From the earth, the planets appear to move in a very irregular manner—they are progressive, retrograde, or stationary; but if you could get upon the sun, you would see them marching round in their constant, uniform, circular motion. So is it with knowledge. Begin with any other science you like, and truth will seem to be all awry. Begin with the science of Christ crucified, and you will begin with the sun, you will see every other science moving round it in complete harmony.

The greatest mind in the world will be evolved by beginning at the right end. The old saying is, "Go from nature up to nature's God," but it is hard work going up-hill. The best thing is to go from nature's God down to nature; and if you once get to nature's God, and believe Him, and love Him, it is surprising how easy it is to hear music in the waves, and songs in the wild whisperings of the winds, to see God everywhere, in the stones, in the rocks, in the rippling brooks, and to hear Him everywhere, in the lowing of cattle, in the rolling of thunders, and in the fury of tempests. Christ is to me the wisdom of God. I can learn everything now that I know the science of Christ crucified.

Late into the night of January 6, 1850, the snow on Hythe Hill was still reflecting a light burning from the home of the Spurgeons which overlooked the street. The evening had been spent around the fireside reading the Bible, but when John Spurgeon at last said, "Come boys, it's time to go to bed," his eldest son replied, "Father, I don't want to go to bed yet." "We sat up long into the night," Spurgeon's father recalled many years later, "and he talked to me of his being saved which had taken place that day, and right glad I was to hear him talk. 'In the text, *Look, look, look,*' Charles said to me, holding up his hands, 'I found salvation this morning. In the text, *Accepted in the Beloved,* preached at the Baptist Church in the evening, I found peace and pardon.' "

From the commencement of his spiritual life Spurgeon thus shared his experiences with his parents. The following letters, written to them after his return to Newmarket, reveal him in the joy of his first love at the age of fifteen.

Chapter 9

Letters to Father and Mother, January to June, 1850

"Newmarket,
January 30th, 1850.

My Dear Father,

I am most happy and comfortable, I could not be more so whilst sojourning on earth, 'like a pilgrim or a stranger, as all my fathers were.' There are but four boarders, and about twelve day-boys. I have a nice little mathematical class, and have quite as much time for study as I had before. I can get good religious conversations with Mr. Swindell, which is what I most need. Oh, how unprofitable has my past life been! Oh, that I should have been so long time blind to those celestial wonders, which now I can in a measure behold! Who can refrain from speaking of the marvellous love of Jesus which, I hope, has opened mine eyes! Now I see Him, I can firmly trust to Him for my eternal salvation. Yet soon I doubt again; then I am sorrowful; again faith appears, and I become confident of my interest in Him. I feel now as if I could do everything, and give up everything for Christ, and then I know it would be nothing in comparison with His love. I am hopeless of ever making anything like a return. How sweet is prayer! I would be always engaged in it. How beautiful is the Bible! I never loved it so before; it seems to me as necessary food. I feel that I have not one particle of spiritual life in me but what the Spirit placed there. I feel that I cannot live if He depart; I tremble and fear lest I should grieve Him. I dread lest sloth or pride should overcome me, and I should dishonour the gospel by neglect of prayer, or the Scriptures, or by sinning against God. Truly, that will be a happy place where we shall get rid of sin and this depraved, corrupt nature. When I look at the horrible pit and the hole from which I have been digged, I tremble lest I should fall into it, and yet rejoice that I am on the King's highway. I hope you will forgive me for taking up so much space about myself, but at present my thoughts are most about it.

From the Scriptures, is it not apparent that, immediately upon receiving the Lord Jesus, it is a part of duty openly to profess Him? I firmly believe and consider that baptism is the command of Christ, and shall not feel quite comfortable if I do not receive it. I am unworthy of such things, but so am I unworthy of Jesu's love. I hope I have received the blessing of the one, and think I ought to take the other also.

My very best love to you and my dear Mother; I seem to love you more than ever, because you love my Lord Jesus. I hope yourself, dear Mother, Archer, Eliza, Emily, Louisa, and Lottie, are well; love to all. . . .

May we all, after this fighting life is over, meet in—

'That Kingdom of immense delight,
Where health, and peace, and joy unite,
Where undeclining pleasures rise,
And every wish hath full supplies;'

and while you are here, may the blessings of the gospel abound toward you, and may we as a family be all devoted to the Lord! May all blessings be upon us, and may—

I ever remain,
Your dutiful and affectionate son,
CHAS. H. SPURGEON."

*   *   *

"Newmarket,
Feb. 19th, 1850.

My Dear Mother,

I hope the long space between my letters will be excused, as I assure you I am fully occupied. I read French exercises every night with Mr. Swindell—Monsr. Perret comes once every week for an hour. I have 33 houses at present where I leave tracts—I happened to take a district formerly supplied by Mrs. Andrews, who last lived in this house, and Miss Anna Swindell. Next Wednesday—I mean to-morrow—I am to go to a meeting of the tract-distributors. They have been at a standstill, and hope now to start afresh. On Thursday, Mr. Simpson intends coming to talk with me upon the most important of all subjects. Oh, how I wish that I could do something for Christ! Tract-distribution is so pleasant and easy that it is a nothing—nothing in itself, much less when it is compared with the amazing debt of gratitude I owe.

I have written to grandfather, and have received a very nice letter. I have been in the miry Slough of Despond; he sends me strong consolation, but is that what I want? Ought I not rather to be reproved for my deadness and coldness? I pray as if I did not pray, hear as if I did not hear, and read as if I did not read—such is my deadness and coldness. I had a glorious revival on Saturday and Sunday. When I can do anything, I am not quite so dead. Oh, what a horrid state! It seems as if no real child of God could ever look so coldly on, and think so little of, the love of Jesus, and His glorious atonement. Why is not my heart always warm? Is it not because of my own sins? I fear lest this deadness be but the prelude to death—spiritual death. I have still a sense of my own weakness, nothingness, and utter inability to do anything in and of myself—I pray God that I may never lose it— I am sure I must if left to myself, and then, when I am cut off from Him, in whom my great strength lieth, I shall be taken by the Philistines in my own wicked heart, and have mine eyes for ever closed to all spiritual good. Pray for me, O my dear Father and Mother! Oh, that Jesus would pray for me! Then I shall be delivered, and everlastingly saved. I should like to be always reading my Bible, and be daily gaining greater insight into it *by the help of the Spirit*. I can get but very little time, as Mr. S. pushes me on in Greek and French.

I have come to a resolution that, by God's help, I will profess the name of Jesus as soon as possible if I may be admitted into His Church on earth. It is an honour—on difficulty—grandfather encourages me to do so, and I hope to do so both as a duty and privilege. I trust that I shall then feel that the bonds of the Lord are upon me, and have a more powerful sense of my duty to walk circumspectly. Conscience has convinced me that it is a duty to be buried with Christ in baptism, although I am sure it constitutes no part of salvation. I am very glad that you have no objection to my doing so. Mr. Swindell is a Baptist.

You must have been terribly frightened when the chimney fell down, what a mercy that none were hurt! There was a great deal of damage here from the wind. My cold is about the same as it was at home, it has been worse. I take all the care I can, I suppose it will go away soon. How are all the little ones? Give my love to them, and to Archer and Eliza. How does Archer get on? Accept my best love for yourself and Father. I hope you are well,

And remain,

Your affectionate son,

CHARLES HADDON SPURGEON."

*   *   *

"Newmarket,
March 12th, 1850.

My Dear Father,

Many thanks to you for your kind, instructive, and unexpected letter. . . . My very best love to dear Mother; I hope she will soon be better.

At our last church-meeting, I was proposed. No one has been to see me yet. I hope that now I may be doubly circumspect, and doubly prayerful. How could a Christian live happily, or live at all, if he had not the assurance that his life is in Christ, and his support, the Lord's undertaking? I am sure I would not have dared to take this great decisive step were it not that I am assured that Omnipotence will be my support, and the Shepherd of Israel my constant Protector. Prayer is to me now what the sucking of the milk was to me in my infancy. Although I do not always feel the same relish for it, yet I am sure I cannot live without it.

> 'When by sin overwhelm'd, shame covers my face,
> I look unto Jesus, who saves by His grace;
> I call on His name from the gulf of despair,
> And He plucks me from hell in answer to prayer.
>   Prayer, sweet prayer!
> Be it ever so feeble, there's nothing like prayer.'

Even the Slough of Despond can be passed by the supports of prayer and faith. Blessed be the name of the Lord, despondency has vanished, like a mist, before the Sun of righteousness, who has shone into my heart! 'Truly, God is good to Israel.' In the blackest darkness, I resolved that, if I never had another ray of comfort, and even if I was everlastingly lost, yet I would love Jesus, and endeavour to run in the way of His commandments: from the time that I was enabled thus to resolve, all these clouds have fled. If they return, I fear not to meet them in the strength of the Beloved. One trial to me is that I have nothing to give up for Christ, nothing wherein to show my love to Him. What I *can* do, is *little*; and what I DO do, is less. The tempter says, 'You don't leave anything for Christ; you only follow Him to be saved by it. Where are your evidences?' Then I tell him that I have given up my self-righteousness, and he says, 'Yes, but not till you saw it was filthy rags!' All I have to answer is, that my sufficiency is not of myself.

(Thursday afternoon.)

I have just now received a very nice note from my dear Mother.

Many thanks to you for the P.O. order. I do not know what money obligations are imposed upon members; I must do as you tell me.

(Here a piece of the letter has been cut out.)

I am glad brother and sister are better. Again my best love to you all.

I am,

Dear Father,

Your affectionate son,

CHARLES."

*   *   *

"Newmarket,

April 6th, 1850.

My Dear Father,

You will be pleased to hear that, last Thursday night, I was admitted as a member. Oh, that I may henceforth live more for the glory of Him, by whom I feel assured that I shall be everlastingly saved! Owing to my scruples on account of baptism, I did not sit down at the Lord's table, and cannot in conscience do so until I am baptized. To one who does not see the necessity of baptism, it is perfectly right and proper to partake of this blessed privilege; but were *I* to do so, I conceive would be to tumble over the wall, since I feel persuaded it is Christ's appointed way of professing Him. I am sure this is the only view which I have of baptism. I detest the idea that I can do a single thing towards my own salvation. I trust that I feel sufficiently the corruption of my own heart to know that, instead of doing one iota to forward my own salvation, my old corrupt heart would impede it, were it not that my Redeemer is mighty, and works as He pleases.

Since last Thursday, I have been unwell in body, but I may say that my soul has been almost in Heaven. I have been able to see my title clear, and to know and believe that, sooner than one of God's little ones shall perish, God Himself will *cease to be*, Satan will conquer the King of kings, and Jesus will no longer be the Saviour of the elect. Doubts and fears may soon assail me, but I will not dread to meet them if my Father has so ordained it; He knows best. Were I never to have another visit of grace, and be always doubting from now until the day of my death, yet 'the foundation of the Lord standeth sure, having this seal, the Lord knoweth them that are His.' I see now the secret, how it was that you were enabled to bear up under all your late trials. This faith is far more than any of us deserve; all beyond hell is mercy, but this is a mighty one. Were it not all of sovereign, electing, almighty grace, I, for one, could never hope to be saved. God says, '*You shall*,' and not all the devils in hell, let loose upon a real Christian, can stop the workings of God's sovereign grace, for in due time the Christian cries, '*I will*.' Oh, how little love have I for One who has thus promised to save me by so great a salvation, and who will certainly perform His promise!

I trust that the Lord is working among my tract people, and blessing my little effort. I have had most interesting and encouraging conversation with many of them. Oh, that I could see but one sinner constrained to come to Jesus! How I long for the time when it may please God to make me, like you, my Father, a successful preacher of the gospel! I almost envy you your exalted privilege. May the dew of Hermon and the increase of the Spirit rest upon your labours! Your unworthy son tries to pray for you and his Mother, that grace and peace may be with you. Oh, that the God of mercy would incline Archer's heart to Him, and make him a partaker of His grace! Ask him if he will believe me when I say that one drop of the pleasure of religion is worth ten thousand oceans of the pleasures of the unconverted, and then ask him if he is not willing to prove the fact by experience. Give my love to my dear Mother. . . .

As Mr. Cantlow's baptizing season will come round this month, I have humbly to beg your consent, as I will not act against your will, and should very much like to commune next month. I have no doubt of your permission. We are all one in Christ Jesus; forms and ceremonies, I trust, will not make us divided. . . .

With my best love and hopes that you are all well,

> I remain,
>> Your affectionate *son*,
>>> Not only as to the flesh, but in the faith,
>>> CHARLES HADDON SPURGEON."

*   *   *

> "Newmarket,
> April 20th.

My Dear Mother,

I have every morning looked for a letter from Father, I long for an answer; it is now a month since I have had one from him. Do, if you please, send me either permission or refusal to be baptized; I have been kept in painful suspense. This is the 20th, and Mr. Cantlow's baptizing day is to be the latter end of the month; I think, next week. I should be so sorry to lose another Ordinance Sunday; and with my present convictions, I hope I shall never so violate my conscience as to sit down unbaptized. When requested, I assured the members at the church-meeting that I would never do so.

I often think of you poor starving creatures, following Mr.—— for the bony rhetoric and oratory which he gives you. What a mercy that you are not dependent upon him for spiritual comfort! I hope you will soon give up following that empty cloud without rain, that type-and-shadow preacher, for I don't think there is much substance. But, my dear Mother, why do you not go and hear my friend, Mr. Langford? He is an open-communion Baptist, and I have no doubt will receive you without baptism. Perhaps his preaching may be blest to Archer, Eliza, and my sisters, as well as to myself; would it not be worth giving up a little difference of persuasion for? God can save whom He will, when He will, and where He will, but I think Mr.——'s Mount Sinai roarings are the last things to do it, to all human appearance.

I think I might date this letter from a place in the Enchanted Ground, with the warm air of Beulah blowing upon me. One drop of the pleasures I have felt is worth a life of agony. I am afraid of becoming satisfied with this world.

My very best love to yourself, dear Father, Eliza, Archer, Emily, Louisa, and Lottie. I hope you are well. I am very much better; thanks for the prescription; and with my love to you again,

I remain,

Dear Mother,

Your affectionate son,

CHARLES.

P.S.—If baptized, it will be in an open river; go in just as I am, with some others. . . . I trust the good confession before many witnesses will be a bond betwixt me and my Master, my Saviour, and my King."

*   *   *

"Newmarket,

May 1st, 1850.

My Dear Mother,

Many very happy returns of your Birthday! In this instance, my wish will certainly be realized, for in Heaven you are sure to have an eternity of happy days. May you, in your coming years, live beneath the sweet smiles of the God of peace; may joy and singing attend your footsteps to a blissful haven of rest and tranquillity! Your birthday will now be doubly memorable, for on the third of May, the boy for whom you have so often prayed, the boy of hopes and fears, your first-born, will join the visible Church of the redeemed on earth, and will bind himself doubly to the Lord his God, by open profession. You, my Mother, have been the great means in God's hand of rendering me what I hope I am. Your kind, warning Sabbath-evening addresses were too deeply settled on my heart to be forgotten. You, by God's blessing, prepared the way for the preached Word, and for that holy book, *The Rise and Progress*. If I have any courage, if I feel prepared to follow my Saviour, not only into the water, but should He call me, even into the fire, I love you as the preacher to my heart of such courage, as my praying, watching Mother. Impossible, I think it is, that I should ever cease to love you, or you to love me, yet not nearly so impossible as that the Lord our Father should cease to love either of us, be we ever so doubtful of it, or ever so disobedient. I hope you may one day have cause to rejoice, should you see me, the unworthy instrument of God, preaching to others—yet have I vowed in the strength of my only Strength, in the name of my Beloved, to devote myself for ever to His cause. Do you not think it would be a bad beginning were I, knowing it to be my duty to be baptized, to shrink from it? If you are now as happy as I am, I can wish no more than that you may continue so. I am the happiest creature, I think, upon this globe.

I hope you have enjoyed your visit, and that it will help much to establish your health. I dare not ask you to write, for I know you are always so busy that it is quite a task to you. I hope my letter did not pain you, dear Mother; my best love to you, be assured that I would not do anything to grieve you, and I am sure that I remain,

Your affectionate son,

CHARLES HADDON.

Mr. and Mrs. Swindell's respects to you and dear Father."

*   *   *

"Newmarket Academy,
June 11th, 1850.

My Dear Mother,

Many thanks to you for your valuable letter. Your notes are so few and far between, and are such a trouble to you, that one now and then is quite a treasure.

Truly, indeed, I have much for which to bless the Lord, when I contemplate His Divine Sovereignty, and see that my salvation is entirely of His free electing love. He has chosen me to be one of His vessels of mercy, and, despite all opposition from without and from within, He will surely accomplish His own work. I have more than sufficient to induce me to give up myself entirely to Him who has bought me and purchased me with an everlasting redemption. I am now enabled to rely upon His precious promises, and to feel that I am as safe, though not so holy, as the greatest saint in Heaven.

I have had two opportunities of addressing the Sunday-school children, and have endeavoured to do so as a dying being to dying beings. I am bound to Newmarket by holy bonds. I have 70 people whom I regularly visit on Saturday. I do not give a tract, and go away, but I sit down, and endeavour to draw their attention to spiritual realities. I have great reason to believe the Lord is working—the people are so kind, and so pleased to see me. I cannot bear to leave them. We are so feeble here that the weakest cannot be spared. We have a pretty good attendance at prayer-meetings, but so few praying men, that I am constantly called upon. . . .

One of our Deacons, Mr. ———, is constantly inviting me to his house. He is rather an Arminian, but so are the majority of Newmarket Christians. Grandfather has written to me; he does not blame me for being a Baptist, but hopes I shall not be one of the tight-laced, strict-communion sort. In that, we are agreed. I certainly think we ought to forget such things in others when we come to the Lord's table. I can, and hope I shall be, charitable to unbaptized Christians, though I think they are mistaken. It is not a great matter; men will differ; we ought both to follow our own consciences, and let others do the same. I think the time would be better spent in talking upon vital godliness than in disputing about forms. I trust the Lord is weaning me daily from all self-dependence, and teaching me to look at myself as less than nothing. I know that I am perfectly dead without Him; it is His work; I am confident that He will accomplish it, and that I shall see the face of my Beloved in His own house in glory.

My enemies are many, and they hate me with cruel hatred, yet with Jehovah Jesus on my side, why should I fear? I will march on in His Almighty strength to certain conquest and victory. I am so glad that Sarah, too, is called, that two of us in one household at one time should thus openly profess the Saviour's name. We are brother and sister in the Lord; may our Father often give each of us the refreshing visits of His grace! I feel as if I could say with Paul, 'Would that I were even accursed, so that my brethren according to the flesh might be saved!' What a joy if God should prove that they are redeemed ones included in the covenant of grace! I long to see your face, and let my heart beat with yours, whilst we talk of the glorious things pertaining to eternal life. My best love to you and Father; may the Angel of the covenant dwell with you, and enchant you by the visions of His grace! Love to Eliza, Archer (many happy returns to him), Emily, Lottie, and Louisa; may they become members of the church in our house! I am very glad you are so well. I am so, but hard at work for the Examination, so allow me to remain,

Your most affectionate son,
CHARLES.

Master H—— shall be attended to; be ye always ready for every good work. I have no time, but it shall be done."

"Saved men and women date from the dawn of their true life; not from their first birthday, but from the day wherein they were born again. Their calendar has been altered and amended by a deed of Divine grace."—C. H. S.

"I have sometimes said, when I have become the prey of doubting thoughts, 'Well, now, I dare not doubt whether there be a God, for I can look back in my Diary, and say, On such a day, in the depths of trouble, I bent my knee to God, and or ever I had risen from my knees, the answer was given me.' "—C. H. S.

Chapter 10

Diary, April to June, 1850

INTRODUCTION, BY MRS. C. H. SPURGEON

Not very long after our marriage, my husband brought to me, one day, a small clasped book, and putting it into my hand with a grave and serious air, he said, "That book contains a record of some of my past spiritual experiences, wifey; take care of it, but I never want to see it again." He never did, and to me also it was a sealed book, for I did not dare to open it; and it has lain, unrevealed, for certainly forty years since the day I first saw it. But now, with reverent hands, I take it from its hiding-place, and, as I look upon the boyish hand-writing, and begin to read the thoughts of my dear one's heart in the bygone years, I wonder whether I *can* undertake the duty of tran-scription, whether my eyes will see through the tears which must come, and my fingers will hold the pen without much trembling, and my heart, which loved him so well, will be able to thank God that the past *is past*, and the struggles and sorrows of earth are for ever for-gotten in the ecstasies of eternal glory. Lord, strengthen and help me!

The contents of the little book prove to be a continuous Diary of nearly three months' duration, commencing April 6th, 1850, and ending on June 20th in the same year. As its pages cover the season of baptism, and the young convert's first efforts in service for the Lord, it is full of deep interest and pathos to all who afterward knew and loved the great preacher. I feel that I am justified in at last reveal-ing the long-kept secret of the book, for a perusal of its soul-confessions and holy resolutions can only redound to the glory of God, and show how He was leading His young servant by a way which he knew not. And I believe God would have me do this.

The words of the boy of sixteen are very touching when read in the light of his subsequent marvellous career. As the trunk and branches of the future tree may, in some cases, be seen faintly outlined in the fruit it bears, so we can here discern something of the form and beauty of the fair character which the Lord was preparing for a glorious service.

How marked is his *humility*, even though he must have felt within him the stirrings and throes of the wonderful powers which were afterwards developed. "Forgive me, Lord," he says, in one place, "if

I have ever had high thoughts of myself"—so early did the Master implant the precious seeds of that rare grace of meekness, which adorned his after life. After each youthful effort at public exhortation, whether it be engaging in prayer, or addressing Sunday-school children, he seems to be surprised at his own success, and intensely anxious to be kept from pride and self-glory, again and again confessing his own utter weakness, and pleading for God-given strength. What deep foundations were laid in this chosen soul, upon what massive pillars of truth and doctrine did God construct the spiritual consciousness of the man who was to do so great a work in the world for his Master! He was truly a "building fitly framed together", and he grew into "a holy temple in the Lord", "a habitation of God through the Spirit". So young in years, when he wrote these thoughts, yet so old in grace, and possessing an experience in spiritual matters richer and broader than most Christians attain to at an advanced age! How plainly revealed in these pages are the workings and teachings of the Divine Spirit, and how equally clear are the docility, and earnestness, and humility of the pupil! Many of the sentences in the Diary are strangely prophetic of his future position and work— notably these two: "Make me Thy faithful servant, O my God; may I honour Thee in my day and generation, and be consecrated for ever to Thy service!" And again, "Make me to be an eminent servant of Thine, and to be blessed with the power to serve Thee, like Thy great servant Paul!"

In these breathings, too, we see where the secret of his great strength lay. He believed and trusted God absolutely, and his faith was honoured in a God-like fashion. Deeply realizing his own weakness, he rested with child-like and complete dependence on his Lord. And God carried him, as a father bears his little one in his arms; and God's Spirit dwelt in him, to teach him all things. His *whole heart* was given to God and His service, God's promises were verities to him; and as "He abideth faithful, He cannot deny Himself", it was with both hands that He heaped gifts and grace upon His dear servant until the time came to receive him into glory.

Perhaps of greatest price among the precious things which this little book reveals, is the beloved author's personal and intense love to the Lord Jesus. He lived in His embrace; like the apostle John, his head leaned on Jesu's bosom. The endearing terms used in the Diary, *and never discontinued*, were not empty words; they were the overflowings of the love of God shed abroad in his heart by the Holy Ghost. One of the last things he said to me at Mentone, before unconsciousness had sealed his dear lips, was this, "O Wifey, I have had such a blessed time with my Lord!" And it was always so, the Saviour was as real to him as if his eyes could look upon Him, and it was his delight to dwell in the very presence of God, in his daily, hourly life.

Full of a sweet pain has been the task I set myself to write out these details of my dear one's life for three short months, but if anyone shall be the gainer by it, through being drawn nearer to God, and having clearer views of Divine truth, I shall deem the pain a pleasure, and the sorrow will bring me joy.

*   *   *

THE DIARY

1850

Born,	January 6, 1850.
Admitted to Fellowship,	April 4
Baptized,	May 3
Communed first,	May 5
Commenced as S.S. Teacher,	,,
Joined Church at Cambridge,	Oct. 2

CONSECRATION

O great and unsearchable God, who knowest my heart, and triest all my ways; with a humble dependence upon the support of Thy Holy Spirit, I yield up myself to Thee; as Thy own reasonable sacrifice, I return to Thee Thine own. I would be for ever, unreservedly, perpetually Thine; whilst I am on earth, I would serve Thee; and may I enjoy Thee and praise Thee for ever! Amen.

Feb. 1, 1850.   CHARLES HADDON SPURGEON.

1850—A BLESSED YEAR OF JUBILEE

April 6.—I have had a blessed day of refreshing from the Lord, and from the glory of His face. Went round my Station District, and had a talk with several people. I trust the Lord is working here. Had some serious thoughts about baptism. "The Lord is my strength and my song; He also is become my salvation."

April 7.—Not well; the body bears the soul down. Heard Mr. S. from Gen. xxii. 8; could not take it in to heart, headache would not let me. Arminianism does not suit me now. If I were long to be so heavy as I now am, I could scarcely live. Evening, could not attend to the sermon; was happier without it. I feasted all the time on—

"When I soar to worlds unknown,
See Thee on Thy judgment throne,
Rock of Ages! cleft for me,
I *shall* hide myself in Thee."

Cannot think how Mr. S. could say that Esau, he trusted, was converted, when the Lord says, "Esau have I *hated*."

April 8.—Walked out after breakfast, never saw more plainly the
sovereignty of God's will. He has called me; I feel sure that He will
carry me to glory. Not well. O God of grace, take me home when
Thou pleasest! It is, "Mercy, mercy, mercy," from first to last.

April 9.—Happy again to-day; if such days continue, earth and
Heaven will be but one;—but what have I written? I know I have
sinned this day; in Heaven, I cannot. Oh, to be holy, to be like God!
I trust I shall be one day. O glorious hour, O blest abode, when I am
near, and like my God. Jesus, how can I e'er forget Thee, Thou
life of my delights? Hold Thou me by Thy free Spirit, and pour down
upon me more love to Thee! Can hardly pray, yet, O my God,
remember A———! Oh, that I could do more for God! "By grace
ye are saved."

April 10.—Much better in health. All more than hell, is mercy. How
small is my sphere, yet what a great Being condescended to fix my
state before I had a being! All things are ordered by God. Blessed be
His name, though He slay me, yet will I trust in Him. Sin is all
cleansed by Jesu's blood. Doubts and fears will soon come. "Desire
of my soul," prepare me to meet them. The Lord's presence has not
departed yet; had I the tongue of an archangel, I could not praise
Him enough for this. I hope all is well at home with my dear mother;
I must expect the cross soon. "He that taketh not his cross, and
followeth after Me, is not worthy of Me."

April 11.—Have had sweet thoughts upon, "I am the good
Shepherd, and know My sheep, and am known of Mine." How can
one of His sheep be lost if He knows all His own?

I have read to-day of the iniquities of some in high places. Father,
forgive them, and grant that Thy name may not be blasphemed
through them! O my Beloved, sooner may I perish everlastingly than
thus dishonour Thee, Thou sole desire of my heart! Heard Mr. S.
from Psalm lxviii. 18-20. I love to hear him give all the honour of
our salvation to God. Shepherd of Israel, guide Thy flock into all
truth! Quicken me, and make me love Thee more and more!

April 12.—Earthly things have engaged too much of my thoughts
this day. I have not been able to fix my attention entirely upon my

Saviour. Yet, even yet, the Lord has not hidden His face from me. Though tempted, I am not cast down; tried, but not overcome; truly it is of the Lord's sovereign mercy. I would desire again this day to make a fresh application to the sin-atoning blood of Jesus to cleanse away my sins. O God, do Thou keep me down, and then I need fear no fall! O visit Zion, and preserve Thy Church; let her yet shine forth in glory! April showers have been coming down to-day; the Lord does not forget His promises. Jesus took my heart: "or ever I was aware, my soul made me like the chariots of Amminadib." "Tell me, O Thou whom my soul loveth, where Thou feedest, where Thou makest Thy flock to rest at noon;" I would be ever with Thee, O my spotless, fairest Beloved! Daily meet me, for Thy embrace is Heaven; sanctify me, prepare me, help me to bring forth fruit, and to be Thine for ever!

April 13.—Did not feel so tired at the end of this week; one reason is that every day has been Sunday with me. Blessed be the Shepherd, I walk now beside the still waters. What events are transpiring in the world! Things are quite at a crisis in the Church of England. I love my little work; Lord, be with me! "O the depth of the riches both of the wisdom and knowledge of God!" Trust in Him, my soul; follow hard after Him.

April 14.—Heard Mr. S., this morning, from 3 John 4—the great subject of justification by faith. Who could dare to hope of going to Heaven, if works are the price? I could not; it would be like offering me a possession in the sun, if I could jump up to it, and take it in my hand! Afternoon—some of last Sunday over again. Esau does not give us a very interesting sermon. Evening subject was, Decision. I am quite encouraged. Hope I shall soon have an answer from home upon baptism.

> "Through floods and flames, if Jesus lead,
> I'll follow where He goes."

I would not desert Him in any one point, but keep close to Him.

April 15.—Quite well to-day, and tolerably happy. First day of the races. O God, Thou makest me to differ! Had a nice prayer-meeting. "Also unto Thee, O Lord, belongeth mercy." What else have I to trust to? Mr. P. came in this evening, and talked till past eleven, so that I lost some of the time I should have spent in devotion.

> "What various hindrances we meet
> In coming to a mercy-seat!
> Yet who that knows the worth of prayer,
> But wishes to be often there?"

K

April 16.—This evening, the friends at the Hythe will be assembled. Grant Thy gracious blessing! Read of the land Beulah. I have been there, and that, too, before coming to Giant Despair. Comfort we must not always have, or I am afraid I should go to sleep. I am now getting drowsy in spirit. Strong Deliverer, keep my eyes open! My soul seems to long after the flesh-pots of Egypt, and that after eating Heavenly manna; help and forgive me, O my Saviour!

April 17.—Read some of "Fuller upon Antinomianism". My God, what a gulf is near me! I think I can say that I hate this religion; I would desire to love God, and to be as holy as my Father-God Himself. There is a little cloud betwixt me and my Sun of righteousness but I doubt not that He still shines upon me. He has not left me. I am a living miracle, a walking wonder of grace that I am alive at all; much more, following on. May I from this time live nearer to Him, and honour His name more!

April 18.—I trust the cloud has burst. I have seen some few gleams of sunshine to-day. I will walk on in His strength, whether it be through clouds or not. Went to chapel, very few there. I have been enabled to renew my strength; may I now run in the ways of the Lord! I begin to wonder why father has not written; he has good reason, no doubt. Lord, strengthen Thy people, and revive Thy Church by Thine enlivening grace!

April 19.—I do not live near enough to God. I have to lament my coldness and indifference in the ways of the Lord. O God of restoring grace, visit Thy servant in the midst of the days! I will trust Him, I cannot doubt His power or His love. Yes.

> "I love Thee, and adore,
>   O for grace to love Thee more!"

I shall yet have another visit, and see again His smiling face. "Whatsoever ye shall ask the Father in My name, He will give it you."

April 20.—Went round with my tracts; could not feel the Spirit of the Lord upon me. I seemed to have a clog upon my feet and my tongue. I have richly deserved this, for I have not prayed, or studied my Bible as I ought. I confess mine iniquity, and my sin is ever before me. Mercy! it is all mercy! Wash me anew, O Saviour, in Thy sin-atoning blood!

> "Firm as the earth Thy gospel stands,
>   My Lord, my hope, my trust."

I cannot perish if God protects me. I can do nothing. Weak and sinful worm am I.

April 21 —This morning, Mr. S. preached from 2 Thess. iii. 3. This is the great hope of a Christian, the main comfort of my life—the Lord will do it. Afternoon, Matt. ix. 22. Here again it is the Saviour's working; earthly physicians could not do it. Blessed art Thou, O God, for this great salvation! Evening, 3 John 4. I am not very much interested with these twice-preached sermons. On the whole, I have enjoyed much this day; little have I deserved it, nay, not at all. No merit in me, I am sure; vilest of the vile, for so long shutting mine eyes to this great salvation and glorious state of God's people.

April 22.—The Lord has not forsaken me. Went this evening to the prayer-meeting; engaged in prayer. Why should I fear to speak of my only Friend? I shall not be timid another time, I hope the Lord has helped me in this; He will in other things. The spirit is more brisk to-day, more soaring, and more enchanted with that Saviour who is the life of all my joy. Faith is the precious gift of God, and love is His gift; it is all of God from first to last.

April 23.—My prayer is in some measure answered; I trust the work has again revived. No desert is there in me; 'tis all of mercy, I must acknowledge. I feel that I am dependent on the Lord for all, for growing grace, and for living grace. I have my daily supply, and sure enough, I do not have two days' portion at a time. 'Tis a mercy to feel one's own dependence, and to be able to trust the Lord for all. Sing, O my soul, sing, for the Lord has redeemed thee, thou art safe!

April 24.—Letter from Mr. Cantlow. Baptism on Thursday week. God help me to live worthy of Him, and that my open confession of Him may make me more diligent! Letter from Mr. Leeding better than I had thought. Truly, O Lord, my lot is in pleasant places, and I have a goodly heritage. I am to do as I please about baptism. Never do I lose anything by zeal for the truth, and close walk with my Saviour; rather, I gain everything. Lord, Thou art my life; guide me, and allot my portion on this earth according to Thine own wisdom and love!

April 25.—Went to Burwell. Heard the examination of the children. Education is indeed a talent from the Lord. What a weight of responsibility rests upon me! I trust I shall one day employ this more to His honour. A letter from father; in truth, he is rather hard upon me. When I followed my conscience, and did not presumptuously break through the fences of the Lord about His Church, I might have expected this. My business is to follow my Saviour and not to pick out smooth paths for myself. If in any measure I have walked worthily, I would desire to give all the glory to the great Author of my salvation. I now feel so bold that, if the devil were to reproach me, I could answer him. Lord, I would ascribe it all to Thee, that I have not yet turned back, and that no enemies have yet made me to quail with terror! Onward may I press, with Heaven itself in view, trusting my salvation entirely in the hands of my Jesus, my life, my all in all!

April 26.—How my father's fears lest I should *trust* to baptism stir up my soul! My God, Thou knowest that I hate such a thought! No, I know that, could I from this day be as holy as God Himself, yet I could not atone for past sin. I have had a pretty good day. Fear, Mistrust, and Timorous are yet at sword's length. May I be Valiant-for-Truth, and live and die in my Master's glorious war!

April 27.—Fear, begone! Doubts, fall back! In the name of the Lord of hosts I would set up my banner. Come on, ye demons of the pit, my Captain is more than a match for you; in His name, armed with His weapons, and in His strength, I dare defy you all. How glorious 'twould be to die by the side of such a Leader! I am a worm, and no man, a vanity, a nothing; yet hath He set His love upon me, and why should I tremble or fear? I have been round with my tracts; may the good seed prosper, and take root! I have again to lament that I do not live so near to God as I ought. Blessed be the name of the Lord for that measure of grace which He has given me; I can trust Him for the rest.

April 28.—Mr. S. addressed us both morning and evening from John i. 5. I could not fix upon the subject, so as to see the train of his thought. Afternoon, how I did rejoice when I brought a man to chapel, and a boy to the Sunday-school! It is the Lord! By this encouragement, in Thy strength, I pledge myself to live yet more for Thee, to fight more constantly, and to work harder. Hold Thou me up! Support me, for I can do nothing. The Lord has been with me to-day, though my heart has not been in such transports as heretofore. I will follow through shade as well as sunshine. Saviour, dwell with me; Thine I am, help me to serve Thee, and adore Thee, world without end!

April 29.—Went to prayer-meeting. Thought upon Matt. viii. 20. When I have the presence of the Lord, nothing is a hardship to me. I would love to lodge with my Master, and to endure all things for Him. Let not my first love chill. I have no fire within to keep it alight, Thou alone canst do this, my Lord and my God. I would anew devote myself to Thee, and glory only in Thy cross, and in Thy shame.

April 30.—Another month has passed, time rolls away, I am nearer home. This month has brought me much holy enjoyment, much privilege; how little I have done when compared with what Jesus has done for me! What a slothful servant am I of so good a Master! Roll on, ye months; bring joy or sorrow as ye will, if God be with me, all is mine! How much like Vanity Fair is this place (Newmarket)! It is crowded with visitors; I saw two engines required to take them to London. Lord, give me strength, like the engine, to go straight on, guided by Thee, my great Conductor!

May 1.—Another month now dawns upon me. I have lived through one, I will bless the Lord for it, and trust Him for this also. Help me to live more to Thy glory, and to honour Thee in my daily walk and conversation. The time of my baptism approaches. May I die to the world, and live alone for Thee! I would serve Thee, O Lord, but I feel a weight, a law working against this law, and holding me in partial bondage; let Thy grace break every fetter that withholds my heart from Thee!

May 2.—Went to the lecture, very few there, not enough for a church-meeting. Lord, revive Thy Church in Newmarket! A far happier day than I deserve, I have been able to soar a little, and see the Canaan which I desire—though with a feeble eye. To-morrow will be a solemn day. I have been enabled more than usual to pour out my heart in prayer. I need support now, and I feel that I shall have it. How safe are all God's people! Not one of the least of them can be lost, the oath and promise of the Lord cannot be broken. 'Tis a sin to think that God, a God of truth, will ever desert His people; it is a shame, a blasphemy. "Fear thou not, for I am with thee; be not dismayed, for I am thy God." "I will never leave thee, nor forsake thee."

May 3.—My mother's birthday. May the sun of heaven shine upon her, and revive her, even as it has done upon the natural world this day! Started with Mr. Cantlow at eleven, reached Isleham at one o'clock. In the afternoon, I was privileged to follow my Lord, and to be buried with Him in baptism. Blest pool! Sweet emblem of my death to all the world! May I, henceforward, live alone for Jesus! Accept my body and soul as a poor sacrifice, tie me unto Thee; in Thy strength I now devote myself to Thy service for ever; never may I shrink from owning Thy name!

> "Witness, ye men and angels now,
> If I forsake the Lord!"

I vow to glory alone in Jesus and His cross, and to spend my life in the extension of His cause, in whatsoever way He pleases. I desire to be sincere in this solemn profession, having but one object in view, and that to glorify God. Blessing upon Thy name that Thou hast supported me through the day; it is Thy strength alone that could do this. Thou hast—Thou wilt. Thou hast enabled me to profess Thee, help me now to honour Thee, and carry out my profession, and live the life of Christ on earth!

May 4.—Reached Newmarket at 9; feel high in spirit, have been round with my tracts; help me to serve Thee, O my Lord! There is a report in the church that Mr. S. and I have been on the heath. Mr. A. told me of it very gruffly. Mr. H. will not commune because so many have been to the races. My master knows, I have no need to tell Him I am innocent. Though I be cast out and rejected of the disciples, the Lord will not cast off one of His chosen. I can, in this respect, wash my hands in innocency.

May 5.—A third, but very strong sermon, from John i. 5. How ought the people of God to be a peculiar people, zealous for good works! Lord, help me to honour Thee! This afternoon, partook of the Lord's supper; a royal feast for me, worthy of a King's son. Mr. S. addressed me before all the people. Sunday-school for the first time, and went visiting the people with friend M. I quite like my new work. Teachers' prayer-meeting after evening service, from 8 to 9; five of us engaged in prayer. Went to Mr. B.'s to supper, talked with young C., stopped to family prayer, past 10 o'clock! I have been too excited to-day, amidst the busy whirl of constant action, to feel myself so solid as I could wish. Rock of Ages, bind me to Thyself! I can feel the bad law working yet. All is of God, He will perform His promise.

> "His honour is engaged to save
> The meanest of His sheep."

May 6.—Went to prayer-meeting. Missionary meeting in the afternoon, upon the glory of Christ's kingdom. "He must reign." Saviour, come and extend Thy kingdom over all the world, sway Thy sceptre over all hearts! Make me Thy temple, and honour me by making me an instrument of good in Thy hands! Lord, save me from pride and from sloth, my two great enemies; keep me, oh, keep and preserve me! I am an erring sheep. It is in Thy power that I trust, upon Thy strength I rely; I am less than nothing, hold me by Thine own right hand.

May 7.—I have again to confess my lukewarmness; I fear I am losing my first love. Coldness and deadness seem to be natural to me; I have no inward warmth, it all comes from the Sun of righteousness, by rich, free, and sovereign grace. What a mercy that I have not been altogether frozen to death, and left to perish in my sinful distance from God! Lord, help me to follow Thee, and may Thy right hand uphold me! Strength, O Lord, I need! I would not fear, but trust in Thine omnipotence.

May 8.—Teachers' business meeting. Too much joking and levity to agree with my notions of what a Sunday-school teacher should be. Lord, keep me from the evil of the world, let me not be led away; but if these are Thy people, help me to serve Thee better than they, and to be more like my Master! O my God, keep me ever near to Thee, help me to live more to Thy glory, and to honour Thee more than I have hitherto done, to live alone for Thee, and to spend and be spent in Thy service! Preserve, perfect, keep, and bless me!

> "Keep me, oh, keep me, King of kings,
> Beneath Thine own almighty wings!"

May 9.—Prayer-meeting. Mr. S. has resigned. Well, we have a better Pastor, who cannot, who will not leave us. Truly, I have sunk very low; my lamp seems going out in obscurity. Lord, fan it, keep it burning yet! I know that I can never perish; yet be pleased, my God, to visit me again, to revive and uphold me, so that I may honour Thee more; make me to be an eminent servant of Thine, and to be blessed with the power to serve Thee, like Thy great servant Paul.

May 10.—Blessed be the name of the Lord, He has not left His servant, or turned away from His chosen! Though I have often sinned, and neglected the sweet privilege of prayer, yet He hath not deserted me. Had a letter from Mr. L. I hope that the Lord will bless him, and give him many souls as seals for his hire. I wonder how they are at home. Time flies away. Seasons come and go. Lord, grant me Thy Holy Spirit to enable me to improve each moment! I am "bought with a price".

May 11.—Went round my district. I trust the Lord is moving upon the face of this people. It is Thy work, O Lord; accomplish it! I feel encouraged to go on in the ways of the Lord, and still to spend my spare time in His service. Prosper Thou the work of my hands! My own soul is encouraged, my life is revived, and I hope soon to enjoy the presence of the Lord.

May 12.—One of the days of the Son of man—happy day when Sabbath shall never end! Went to Sunday-school at 9, stayed till service at 10.30, out at 12.15; Sunday-school at 1.45, service 3 till 4, visiting till 5. The day has thus been closely occupied. The morning's discourse was upon 1 Corinthians iv. 7. Truly, I have nothing which I have not received; I can boast of no inherent righteousness. Had the Lord not chosen me, I should not have chosen Him. Grace! Grace! Grace! 'Tis all of grace. I can do nothing, I am less than nothing, yet what a difference—once a slave of hell, now the son of the God of Heaven! Help me to walk worthy of my lofty and exalted vocation! Afternoon, Psalm xlviii. 14, "This God is *my* God for ever and ever; HE WILL be *my* Guide even unto death." I can wish for no better Guide, or more lasting Friend; He shall lead me in His own way.

Lord, permit me not to choose the road, allow me not to wander into By-path meadow; rather carry me straight to glory! Evening, Acts xvii. 11. The Word of God is my chart. Lord, give me more of Berean nobility; grant me Thy grace to search the Scriptures, and to become wise unto life eternal! Thine is the gift, I cannot do it without Thee. Again would I give myself anew to Thee; bind Thou the sacrifice with cords, even to the horns of Thine altar! Let me not go away from Thee; hold me firmly in Thy gracious arms! Let Thine omnipotence be my protection, Thy wisdom my direction, Thy grace my salvation. "Lord, I believe; help Thou mine unbelief!"

May 13.—A day of great, unmerited mercy. Happiness cannot exist here without some cloy. How sweet the joys of religion, of communion with God! Letter from home. All well. I thank Thee, Father, for such good tidings; bless me, even me also, O my Father! I would devote myself to Thee; it is my highest privilege to be able to give myself to Thee. Thy service is the greatest pleasure, the most untiring delight; I would, more than ever, wear Thy livery, be known as Thy servant, and become one of Thy peculiar people.

May 14.—In the evening, enjoyed an ecstasy of delight. I seemed transported, and able to fly beyond the bounds of this poor atom of an earth. Spiritual realities were present to view, while the flesh, like Abraham's servant, tarried at the foot of the mountain. How much do I owe; how little good do I deserve, yea, none at all!

> "Let Thy grace, Lord, like a fetter,
> Bind my wandering heart to Thee!"

Blessed be Thy name for evermore! Bless the Lord, O my soul; follow hard after Him, love and serve Him!

May 15.—How feeble I am! I am not able to keep myself near to God. I am compelled to acknowledge my own deadness. I confess how greatly I have strayed from Thee, Thou great Fountain of living waters; but—

"Since I've not forgot Thy law,
Restore Thy wandering sheep."

Revive me in the midst of the years, and make Thy face to shine upon me! How much do I deserve eternal damnation! But salvation is not of desert, but of free grace. This is the plank whereon I hope to float to glory, when this world shall be a wreck, and perish in the vast abyss.

May 16.—Went to chapel. Sermon on Psalm xxiii. 3. How much do I need this restoration! If the Lord does not do it, I cannot. "Turn out Thine enemy and mine." I would be passive, submitting to Thy sovereign will; Thou wilt do what is right. Lord, keep me; I will wait Thy time of revival; teach me both to work and wait, expecting and hoping that Thou wilt soon come, and restore unto me the joy of Thy salvation! I am in a low condition, yet I am eternally safe. He will lead me.

May 17.—It is now a fortnight since my baptism. How solemnly have I devoted myself to Thee! I would now repeat my vows, and again solemnly devote myself to Thee.

"Witness, ye men and angels now,
If I forsake the Lord."

In His strength I can do all things. Thou hast sworn to save, and death and hell cannot thwart Thine everlasting purpose. Hold me! Thou hast blessed me, Thou alone canst do it. If Thou dost not save, I must perish. Thou wilt not leave me, Thou hast showed me a portion of the glory of Thy face.

May 18.—Station District. When I first set out, I was all but dumb concerning spiritual things. Soon I felt the working of the Lord in some degree. Blessed be His holy name for ever and ever, and let all the redeemed say, Amen! His is the power. Beloved, Thine is enduring beauty! Thou art glorious to behold. Give me more of the entrancing visions of Thy face, the looks of Thy love, and more constant communion with Thee! Lord, move Thou upon the earth, and bring in Thine elect from among the condemned sinners of the world!

May 19.—Went to the Sunday-school. Mr. S. preached, this morning, from 2 Cor. iii. 6–8. How glorious is the ministration of life, how beautiful the tables of stone, when enclosed in the blessed ark of the covenant! Afternoon, Ezek. xxxvi. 27. Evening, "What is truth?" As to interest, the sermons to-day have been a failure. Addressed the children upon Prayer. Went visiting with Mr. M., six fresh children.

Evening at Mr. B.'s. Engaged in prayer at his family altar. To-day has been a sunny day with me. The Lord has visited me from on high. Rejoice, O my soul, leap for joy, renew thy strength; run, run, in the name of the Lord! He is with me, He has been with me. Weakness He has made strength! Mighty to save, Thou shalt have all my noblest songs! Let Thy grace constrain me to love Thee, and live for Thee! I am buried with my Lord and Saviour; may I be crucified to the world, and die daily! How sure is it that Thy yoke is easy, and Thy burden is light! I can do all things through Christ Jesus.

May 20.—Went to the prayer-meeting, and engaged in prayer. How inexhaustible is the source from whence my life proceeds! How boundless the store from whence my provision comes! I must be saved, for Omnipotence has undertaken it. Another glorious day, another visit of His reviving grace, blessed be the name of the Lord! The service of the Lord were a happy service, even if such enjoyment as this was the only reward. How sweet are the visits of His grace, sweeter than honey and the honey-comb!

May 21.—Glorious day, happy were all like this! Oh, the safety of a Christian, as sure, but not so blest, as any saint in Heaven! Lord, how can I leave Thee? To whom, or whither should I go? Thou centre of my love, all glorious names in one, Thou brightest, sweetest, fairest One, that eyes have seen or angels known, I trust to Thee for salvation; without Thee, I can do nothing. I am utter weakness, Thou must do it all, or I shall perish! Love of loves, all love excelling, fix my wandering heart on Thee!

May 22.—My weakness is my greatest strength, for then I trust alone on Jesus, when I feel my own dependence. I am an earthen vessel, I have been among the pots of the unregenerate; make me now a vessel for Thy use! Thy blood is my trust, I am washed; who shall now blacken me so as not to leave me spotless at the last? Joy, joy unspeakable, rapture divine, I fly beyond the bounds of earth, my Husband folds me in His arms, I am His, and He is mine, my glorious Prince, Redeemer, Love!

May 23.—Went to chapel, very few there. "He restoreth my soul." The same subject again! How true is this, how has He revived me! Short, but glorious, are the days of my refreshing—worthy of years of sorrow and distress. O my Beloved, did my way lie over the embers of hell all my life, didst Thou but show Thyself, I would rush through the fire to meet Thee! I have not been quite so ecstatic as for some days past. I am the Lord's for ever, how much do I owe to Him! My Advocate, Brother, Husband, let not my first love chill and grow cold! Keep me and preserve in Thy hands!

May 24.—A day of undeserved joy. I am not altogether banished from the presence of the Lord. Though He slay me, I cannot but trust Him, since I have had such tokens of His love. Lord, when in darkness and distress, when my head is bowed down, then return unto Thy servant to encourage and support him! For ever, oh, for ever, lashed to the Ark, and safe from the floods, I shall get at last upon the *terra firma* of glory! Oh, let me not dishonour Thee! Never may I bring a disgrace upon the cause of Christ! Keep me, and I shall be infinitely safe, and rest securely.

May 25.—Free grace, sovereign love, eternal security are my safeguards; what shall keep me from consecrating all to Thee, even to the last drop of my blood? Went to my district with tracts, a woman gave me 24 new ones. I fear Mr. T. is doing much harm by telling the people that the Lord's supper will save them. Work, Lord, work! Thou hast encouraged me; may I not be disappointed! "Bless the Lord, O my soul." The Covenant is my trust, the agreement signed between my Elder Brother and the Almighty standeth sure. "None shall pluck them out of My hand."

May 26.—Went round for the children. Sunday-school in the morning. Mr. S. preached from, "All these things are against me." Stayed in the chapel the dinner-time, had a sweet season of prayer and communion with God. Afternoon, Jacob's consecration of himself at Bethel. I would give myself in the same manner to Thee, my best-loved King. Evening subject, Paul's great labours. Oh, could I emulate such a man, I should be the greatest on this earth!

May 27.—Life of my soul, forgive me when I am so blind as to look upon an earthly object, and forget Thine own Divine beauties! Oh, for a love as strong as death, fierce as hell, and lasting as eternity!

May 28.—Thou hast hedged me about with thorns so that I cannot get out; this is my comfort. What name can I devise for Thee, O Beloved, equal to Thy desert? All beauties joined in one perfection, "Thou art all fair, my Love, there is no spot in Thee." Thou didst die for me, and shall not I live for Thee? What a love is that of Jesus to me, surpassing knowledge! I can do nothing in return, but give Thee my worthless self. What! shall I dare to doubt Thy love? Can I conceive that Thou wilt leave me? Yes, I may sin so as to distrust Thee; but Thou wilt never let me go. No thief can steal away Thy precious purchase; never, never, can I be lost. Redeemed and purchased; then, how can I be snatched away? How is my soul a battlefield between the corruptions of nature and the principle of grace! They tear up the earth of my soul with the trampling of their armies; but I cannot be destroyed.

May 29.—To the Lord belongeth strength, He has given me my portion. He putteth His treasure in earthen vessels. How happy am I to be one of His chosen, His elect, in whom His soul delighteth! But I do not live up to my Heavenly calling; I could not at all without the Lord, He has helped—He will help—this is my comfort. His everlasting promises are my rest, my bread, my support. Make me Thy faithful servant, O my God; may I honour Thee in my day and generation, and be consecrated for ever to Thy service!

May 30.—The stormy commotion has somewhat passed away; the sun is still shining, though a cloud may pass between. I desire more constant communion with God. Went to church-meeting, had some nice cheering conversation with old Mrs. A. Two candidates proposed; we shall have no Ordinance next Sunday. The Lord can and will feed us without it. He has kept me, and He will. The strife in my soul is now hushed, peace returns as a river upon the dry places.

May 31.—Weakness am I in every point, I cannot keep myself in the least. Forgive me that I have tried it! I would now come, naked, stript, exhausted, dead. I would cry, "Lash me tighter, firmer, to Thy free-grace raft of life!" Mercy is all I ask for—continued mercy. Those whom He once loves, He loves to the end; He has once loved me, I am now secure. May the live coal within be shown to the world by the burning flames of love to Thee! May that love burn up the stubble and sin!

June 1.—A new month; time soon glides away. How much more ought I to do this month than last! Desire of my heart, keep me nearer to Thy bosom this month! Went to South District. Talked with a woman who says there are contradictions in the Bible. Some good may be doing. He that can work, will work; and who shall hinder Him? In the Lord's time it shall be accomplished; His time is best. Arise, O Sun of righteousness, why should this people lie in darkness?

June 2.—Heard Mr. J. the first part of the day, Num. xxi. 4. Interesting, but rather too weak. Afternoon, Rev. xix. 12. Many crowns indeed does my Lord deserve; crowns of glory shall be around His sacred, blessed head. Evening, 1 John v. 4. Strong meat; the Lord has sent the manna down this evening. "Overcometh the world!" Glorious victory, amazing conquest, triumph Divine; and shall I, with such a promise, dare to doubt the power of God to keep, and guide, and preserve me?

Had a large class at Sunday-school, gave an address upon Death—the dreadful sword hanging by a single hair above the head of the ungodly. Had tea at Mr. B.'s, and combated with him for what I consider "the form of sound words". Prayer-meeting after evening service. Seven present, six of us engaged in prayer. Bless the Sunday-school, great King! Honour thy Master, O my soul; live *for* Him, live *in* Him! I am a prince; ought I not to be a good soldier, and fight for my Lord? Give me, lend me a sword, O God, and strength to wield it; let my foes and Thine be as furious as lions, Thy sword shall destroy them!

June 3.—Prayer-meeting, engaged in prayer. Lord, when shall Thy set time to favour Zion come? When shall Thine elect be gathered in? "Who shall separate us from the love of Christ?" For ever, yes, for ever, safe. Rejoice, rejoice, O my soul, and let thy joy constrain thee to work more earnestly and more zealously for Him! Redeemed and purchased, I am not my own. Letter from grandfather. How glad I am he does not differ!

June 4.—I have had evidence this day of the changeableness of all mortal things. How little does it matter to me, so that my eternal inheritance is secure! Lord, help me now to mount my watch-tower against pride and sloth! Keep me always upon the look-out, lest an enemy should come unawares; forgive me, if I have ever had high thoughts of myself! Thou makest me to feel my weakness in every part; may I now trust and rely upon the arm of Omnipotence, the mercies of the Lord! Give strength, Lord, strength!

June 5.—Awake, my soul, record the mercies of the Lord!

> "He justly claims a song from me,
> His loving kindness, O how free!"

Mercy, I breathe Another's air, I am a tenant of this earth at my Master's will; sovereign grace has kept me hitherto, upon sovereign grace I now rely. What sweet moments have I had in answer to prayer; blessed be the Lord for His rich mercy thus bestowed upon me! I would now live in close communion with my King, and feast upon the riches of His love.

June 6.—Prayer-meeting. Mr. S. spoke to us upon the Babylonian Captivity. Teachers' meeting after the service. What a want of spirituality and vital godliness! O Lord, give me *life*; increase the vital spark, fan it to a flame! I can never perish, yet would I keep upon my watch-tower, for my enemies are many, and they hate me with cruel hatred. Help me to hate sin, and pride, and sloth! I live only as Thou givest me life. I have not one atom of life of my own, I must perish if Thou desert me for one moment.

June 7.—How manifold are Thy mercies toward me, O Lord! When

I think of the great salvation which has been worked out for me, and remember that Heaven is secure, it seems too good to be true. Yet do I now believe Thy promise; may I now be entirely Thine, Thy glory my only aim! Could I but be like Paul, how honoured should I be! Happy is the man whom Thou teachest, O Lord! I am happy; how can I be otherwise, since my Beloved has looked upon me, and I have seen His glorious face?

June 8.—Could not burn with zeal as oft I have done. When, Lord, wilt Thou arise, and let Thy power be known and felt? How sweet to flap my wings to Heaven, with others following me; then lay my crown beneath His feet, and call Him Lord of all! He is deserving of all honour and praise; dominion and power are His due, and He shall have them. Many honours on His ever-blessed head! Worthy is the Lamb who has died for me. All glorious is my Beloved.

June 9.—Mr. S. preached. Acts xvi. 19. Did not hear to profit. Afternoon, "Who is this that cometh up from the wilderness, leaning upon her Beloved?" Did not hear enough about *the Beloved*. Evening, "Prepare to meet thy God." Oh, what a mercy to be prepared!

> "So whene'er the signal's given,
>   Us from earth to call away,
> Borne on angels' wings to Heaven,
>   Glad the summons to obey,
>   We shall surely
>   Reign with Christ in endless day!"

Felt rather hurt by Mr. C., he does not act quite rightly; but I hereby forgive him. I desire to look alone to Jesus, and regard His glory only. I am too proud, I am weak in every point; keep me, for I have no strength! I would look up to Thee—the Strong—for strength. I am Thine, keep me!

June 10.—Letter from dear mother. Mr. S. made her his text at the prayer-meeting. Engaged in prayer. Have not been able to be much in private prayer to-day. The joy of my Lord, however, is not gone. I can yet trust in the God of my salvation. If I ever forget Thee, let my right hand forget her fellow. What! has He done so much for me, and shall I ever leave Him? No—

> "While a breath, a pulse remains,
>   *I will remember Thee!*"

June 11.—Prayer seems like labour to me, the chariot wheels drag heavily; yet they are not taken off. I will still rely upon almighty strength; and, helpless, throw myself into the arms of my Redeemer. "Leave, ah, leave me not alone!" "I will never leave Thee." I shall yet walk the golden street of the New Jerusalem, I shall yet see His beauteous face. He loved me before the foundations of the earth, before I was created or called by grace.

June 12.—The Lord is my Helper, He shall plead my cause. I would desire to record the gratitude I feel for the sparing mercies of the Lord, but especially for His great grace in electing me, by the sovereign counsels of His love, to be one of His redeemed ones. What! shall I not live for Him, shall I keep back a single particle of my heart, and of myself, from my charming Redeemer, my King, Husband, Brother, Friend? No; oh, give me strength to say, "I will never dishonour Thee"!

June 13.—Dangers are around me, Satan stands in the way; I have no hope but in the Lord, no safety but in keeping straight on in the Heavenly road. In the Lord Jehovah is everlasting strength, and inexhaustible mines of eternal love are mine; the Lord reserves them for His chosen people. Went to prayer-meeting. Tried to address my Lord in prayer. Come, my Beloved, Thou art ever mine; leave me not, O do not forsake me, my King, my Saviour! Saved everlastingly!

June 14.—Examination. Mr. M. gave me 10s. for the Missionary Society. I would thank the Lord for thus opening his hand to do good. Gave a Missionary speech. Lord, keep Thy servant low and humble at Thy feet! How prone am I to pride and vain-glory! Keep me always mindful that I have nothing which I have not received; 'tis grace, free, sovereign grace that has made me to differ. Why should I be chosen an elect vessel? Not that I deserve it, I am sure; but it is rich love.

June 15.—Went round my S. District and divided my stock amongst the people, and now, Lord, I desire to commend them to Thy keeping; look upon them with pity, let them not be as sheep without a shepherd! Let Thy work go on and prosper among this people! I can do nothing; how is it that I have lived so long in my spiritual life? It is by sovereign power I stand, by Omnipotence I shall be supported. "My grace is sufficient for thee." I trust in Him; He will perfect His own work.

June 16.—Old Mr. W. preached; could not hear him, he spoke so low. Was set upon by him and Mr. S. Lord, help me to take firm hold of the truth, and never yield an inch! Addressed the Sunday-school children. Oh, may I be kept humble! Pride dwells in my heart. I am now to leave Newmarket; perhaps, for ever. What a scene of changes is this world! How blest to have a house above the skies, eternal in the Heavens!

June 17.—Left Newmarket at 6. Reached Stambourne about 12. Grandfather quite well. I have had journeying mercies to-day. This life is a journey; I know that I shall one day reach the blessed end, in bliss, unfading bliss. What can I write equal to the theme of sovereign grace? It is a miracle, a perfect miracle, that God should so love man as to die for him, and to choose him before the foundation of the world.

June 19.—My birthday. Sixteen years have I lived upon this earth, and yet I am only—scarcely six months old! I am very young in grace. Yet how much time have I wasted, dead in trespasses and sins, without life, without God, in the world! What a mercy that I did not perish in my sin! How glorious is my calling, how exalted my election, born of the Lord—regenerate! Help me more than ever to walk worthily, as becomes a saint!

June 20.—Truly my lot is cast in pleasant places, and I have a goodly heritage. I can love religion now in the sunshine; may I love it and prize it under all circumstances![1]

Storms have raged around me; yet, blessed be my Father's name, I have now some peace! "But more the treacherous calm I dread, than tempests breaking overhead." Let me not be left even here; let Thy grace still flow into my heart! O Lord, my King, reign in me, and be glorified by me! May it please Thee to dwell in such a bramble-bush as I am, so that, though burning, I may not be consumed! Ordered in all things and sure is the everlasting covenant of redeeming love. For ever settled and eternally complete in Him is my salvation. May it be completed in myself, and may I grow up to be a man in Christ Jesus, a perfect man, prepared for the inheritance of the saints in light! Oh, that my spirituality may be revived! My matchless Immanuel, let me see once more Thy face in the temple of my heart! May I know the joy, and have the faith of God's elect; may I rejoice in free and sovereign grace, saving me from the guilt and power of sin! Grace is a glorious theme, above the loftiest flights of the most soaring angel, or the most exalted conceptions of one of the joint-heirs with Jesus. All power is God's, and all is engaged to protect and preserve me. Let me have my daily grace, peace and comfort, zeal and love, give me some work, and give me strength to do it to Thy glory!

Heard Mr. C., of Bumpstead. Morning, "What doest thou here,

---

[1] The continuous Diary abruptly closes at this date. The fragmentary entries which follow are undated.

Elijah?" Afternoon, "I am the door." Went to the prayer-meeting before and after chapel, engaged in prayer, read the hymns, and addressed the children. What an honour it is to be but a door-keeper in the house of the Lord! Oh, to be humble, and to be always at the feet of Jesus! Then should I grow more in grace, and increase in the knowledge of the Lord. The Lord is able to keep me from falling, and He will, for He has promised never to leave one of His called children.

Fair Day.—Spoke to Mr. R. How can a child of God go there? "Vanity of vanities, all is vanity." Forgive him, Lord, for so forgetting his high calling! I, too, should be there, but for the grace of God. I have the seeds of all evil in my own heart; pride is yet my darling sin, I cannot shake it off. Awake, O my Lord, against the mighty, for I shall die by his hand if Thou do not help me, and lead me on to triumph! Leave me, ye vain thoughts! I have nothing but what I have received; it is the Lord's goodness that I even have my reason.

How could I live without prayer when troubles come? How blessed to carry them to the throne! I will now say that the Lord heareth prayer, for He hath removed from me that which I feared. But, oh! could I feel the presence of the Lord as in days gone by, how joyful! Could I enjoy His face, and feast upon His love, then would it be a sort of Heaven below the skies. Yes, Thou art mine, my Saviour and my King; I am bound to Thee by love, by Thine own dying love, not mine! Fairest of beings, best-beloved, come, let me yet see Thy smiling face!

Chapter 11

A Good Confession

I REMEMBER the difficulty that I had, when I was converted, and wished to join the Christian Church in Newmarket. I called upon the minister four successive days before I could see him; each time there was some obstacle in the way of an interview; and as I could not see him, I wrote and told him that I would go down to the church-meeting, and propose myself as a member. He looked upon me as a strange character, but I meant what I said, for I felt that I could not be happy without fellowship with the people of God. I wanted to be wherever they were, and if anybody ridiculed them, I wished to be ridiculed with them, and if people had an ugly name for them, I wanted to be called by that ugly name, for I felt that, unless I suffered with Christ in His humiliation, I could not expect to reign with Him in His glory.

When I had been accepted as a member of the Congregational Church at Newmarket, I was invited to the communion table, although I had not been baptized. I refused, because it did not appear to me to be according to the New Testament order: "Then they that gladly received his word were baptized: and the same day there were added unto them about three thousand souls. And they continued stedfastly in the apostles' doctrine and fellowship, and in breaking of bread, and in prayers." I waited until I could go to the Lord's table as one who had believed, and who had been baptized. I had attended the house of God with my father, and my grandfather, but I thought, when I read the Scriptures, that it was my business to judge for myself. I knew that my father and my grandfather took little children in their arms, put a few drops of water on their faces, and said they were baptized; but I could not see anything in my Bible about babes being baptized. I learned a little Greek, but I could not discover that the word "baptize" meant to sprinkle, so I said to myself, "They are good men, yet they may be wrong; and though I love and revere them, that is no reason why I should imitate them." And they acknowledged, when they knew of my honest conviction, that it was quite right for me to act according to my conscience. I consider the "baptism" of an unconscious infant is just as foolish as the "baptism" of a ship or a bell, for there is as much Scripture for the one as for the other. Therefore I left my relations, and became what I am to-day, a

Baptist, so-called, but I hope a great deal more a Christian than a Baptist. Many a man will go to chapel, because his grandmother did. Well, she was a good old soul, but I do not see that she ought to influence your judgment. "That does not signify," says one, "I do not like to leave the church of my fathers." No more do I, for I would rather belong to the same denomination as my father, I would not wilfully differ from any of my friends, or leave their sect and denomination, but I must let God be above my parents. Though our parents are at the very top of our hearts, and we love them, and reverence them, and in all other matters render them strict obedience, yet, with regard to religion, to our own Master we stand or fall, and we claim to have the right of judging for ourselves as men, and then we think it our duty, having judged, to carry out our conscientious convictions.

I once met a man who had been forty years a Christian, and believed it to be his duty to be baptized, but when I spoke to him about it, he said, "He that believeth shall not make haste." After forty years' delay, he talked about not making haste. I quoted to him another passage, "I made haste, and delayed not to keep Thy commandments," and showed him what the meaning of his misapplied passage was. A person who was present when John Gill preached his very *first* sermon at Kettering, also heard him deliver his *last* in London, more than fifty years after. *After his death*, she joined the church over which he had presided, relating, at some length, a truly interesting experience, which gave universal pleasure to all who heard it. Her name was Mary Bailey, and it is to be hoped that none will imitate her by postponing the confession of their faith in Jesus for so long a time. She lived half a century in disobedience to her Lord, and even when she avowed His name it must have caused her deep regret that she had lingered so long in neglect of the Redeemer's ordinance.

When I was a boy of fifteen, I believed in the Lord Jesus, was baptized, and joined the Church of Christ, and nothing upon earth would please me more than to hear of other boys having been led to do the same. I have never been sorry for what I did then; no, not even once. I have had plenty of time to think it over, and many temptations to try some other course, and if I had found out that I had been deceived, or that I had blundered, I would have made a change before now, and would do my best to prevent others from falling into the same delusion. The day I gave myself up to the Lord Jesus, to be His servant, was the very best day of my life; then I began to be safe and to be happy; then I found out the secret of living, and had a worthy object for my life's exertions, and an unfailing comfort for life's

troubles. Because I would wish every boy, who reads these lines, to
have a bright eye, a light tread, a joyful heart, and overflowing spirits,
I therefore plead with him to consider whether he will not follow my
example, for I speak from experience, and know what I say.

Baptism is the mark of distinction between the Church and the
world. It very beautifully sets forth the death of the baptized person
to the world. Professedly, he is no longer of the world; he is buried
to it, and he rises again to a new life. No symbol could be more
significant. In the immersion of a believer, there seems to me to be a
wondrous setting forth of the burial of the Christian to all the world
in the burial of Christ Jesus. It is the crossing of the Rubicon. If
Cæsar crosses the Rubicon, there will never be peace between him
and the Senate again. He draws his sword, and he throws away his
scabbard. Such is the act of baptism to the believer. It is the burning
of the boats: it is as much as to say, "I cannot come back again to
you, I am dead to you; and to prove that I am, I am absolutely buried
to you, I have nothing more to do with the world; I am Christ's, and
Christ's for ever." Then, the Lord's supper: how beautifully that
ordinance sets forth the distinction of the believer from the world
in his life and that by which his life is nourished. He eats the flesh of
Christ, and drinks His blood. Both these ordinances bring a cross
with them to some degree, especially the first. I was noting, when
reading the life of good Andrew Fuller, that, after he had been
baptized, some of the young men in the village were wont to mock
him, asking him how he liked being dipped, and such like questions
which are common enough nowadays. I could but notice that the
scoff of a hundred years ago is just the scoff of to-day.

This is the way of salvation—worship, prayer, faith, profession—
and the profession, if men would be obedient, if they would follow
the Bible, must be done in Christ's way, by a baptism in water, in the
name of the Father, and of the Son, and of the Holy Ghost. God
requireth this, and though men are saved without any baptism, and
multitudes fly to Heaven who are never plunged in the stream;
though baptism is not saving, yet, if men would be saved, they must
not be disobedient. And inasmuch as God gives the command, it is
mine to enforce it. Jesus said to His disciples, "Go ye therefore, and
preach the gospel to every creature: he that believeth, and is immersed,
shall be saved; he that believeth not shall be damned." The Church
of England Prayer-book approves dipping. It only says, if children
be weak, they are to be sprinkled, and it is marvellous how many
weakly children there have been born lately. The dear little ones are
so tender, that a few drops suffice instead of the dipping which their

own Church endorses. I would that all churchmen were better church-men; if they would be more consistent with their own articles of faith, they would be more consistent with Scripture; and if they were a little more consistent with some of the rubrics of their own Church, they would be a little more consistent with themselves. I became a Baptist through reading the New Testament—especially in the Greek —and was strengthened in my resolve by a perusal of the Church of England Catechism, which declared as necessary to baptism, repent-ance and the forsaking of sin.

Doddridge has recommended a solemn covenant between the soul and God, to be signed and sealed with due deliberation and most fervent prayer. Many of the most eminent of the saints have adopted this excellent method of devoting themselves in very deed unto the Lord, and have reaped no little benefit from the re-perusal of that solemn document when they have afresh renewed the act of dedication. I conceive that burial with Christ in baptism is a far more Scriptural and expressive sign of dedication, but I am not inclined to deny my brethren the liberty of confirming that act by the other, if it seem good unto them, as I myself did soon after my conversion. According to my reading of Holy Scripture, the believer in Christ should be buried with Him in baptism, and so enter upon his open Christian life. I therefore cast about to find a Baptist minister, and I failed to discover one nearer than Isleham, in the Fen country, where resided a certain Mr. W. W. Cantlow. My parents wished me to follow my own con-victions, Mr. Cantlow arranged to baptize me, and my employer gave me a day's holiday for the purpose.

I can never forget May 3, 1850; it was my mother's birthday, and I myself was within a few weeks of being sixteen years of age. I was up early, to have a couple of hours for quiet prayer and dedication to God. Then I had some eight miles to walk, to reach the spot where I was to be immersed into the Triune Name according to the sacred command. What a walk it was! What thoughts and prayers thronged my soul during that morning's journey! It was by no means a warm day, and therefore all the better for the two or three hours of quiet foot-travel which I enjoyed. The sight of Mr. Cantlow's smiling face was a full reward for that country tramp. I think I see the good man now, and the white ashes of the peat-fire, by which we stood and talked together about the solemn exercise which lay before us. We went together to the Ferry, for the Isleham friends had not degenerated to indoor immersion in a bath made by the art of man, but used the ampler baptistery of the flowing river. Isleham Ferry, on the River Lark, is a very quiet spot, half-a-mile from the village, and rarely

disturbed by traffic at any time of the year. The river itself is a beautiful
stream, dividing Cambridgeshire from Suffolk, and is dear to local
anglers. The navigation of this little River Lark is possible between
Bury St. Edmunds and the sea at Lynn, but at Isleham it is more in
its infancy.

The ferry-house, hidden in the picture (Plate 8) by the trees, is
freely opened for the convenience of minister and candidates at a
baptizing. Where the barge is hauled up for repairs, the preacher
takes his stand, when the baptizing is on a week-day, and there are
few spectators present. But on Lord's-day, when great numbers are
attracted, the preacher, standing in a barge moored mid-stream,
speaks the Word to the crowds on both sides of the river. This can be
done the more easily, as the river is not very wide. The bank
at the prow of the barge is the usual place for entering the water.
The right depth, with sure footing, may soon be found, and so the
delightful service proceeds in the gently-flowing stream. No accident
or disorder has ever marred the proceedings. In the course of seven
or eight miles, the Lark serves no fewer than five Baptist churches,
and they would on no account give up baptizing out of doors.

The first baptizing at Isleham is recorded thus: "Sept. 13, 1798.
John Webber, sen., John Webber, jun., William Brown, John
Wibrow, and Mary Gunstone were baptized by Mr. Fuller, of
Kettering, at Isleham Ferry."

To me, there seemed to be a great concourse on that week-day.
Dressed, I believe, in a jacket, with a boy's turn-down collar, I
attended the service previous to the ordinance, but all remembrance
of it has gone from me: my thoughts were in the water, sometimes
with my Lord in joy, and sometimes with myself in trembling awe at
making so public a confession. There were first to be baptized two
women—Diana Wilkinson and Eunice Fuller—and I was asked to
conduct them through the water to the minister, but this I most
timidly declined. It was a new experience to me, never having seen a
baptism before, and I was afraid of making some mistake. The wind
blew down the river with a cutting blast, as my turn came to wade
into the flood, but after I had walked a few steps, and noted the people
on the ferry-boat, and in boats, and on either shore, I felt as if Heaven,
and earth, and hell, might all gaze upon me, for I was not ashamed,
there and then, to own myself a follower of the Lamb. My timidity
was washed away; it floated down the river into the sea, and must
have been devoured by the fishes, for I have never felt anything of the
kind since. Baptism also loosed my tongue, and from that day it has
never been quiet. I lost a thousand fears in that River Lark, and found

that "in keeping His commandments there is great reward". It was a thrice-happy day to me. God be praised for the preserving goodness which allows me to write of it with delight so long afterwards!

> "Many days have passed since then,
> Many changes I have seen;
> Yet have been upheld till now;
> Who could hold me up but Thou?"

In the Isleham Vestry, in the extremely gentle and cordial companionship of the pastor, I spent a very happy evening,[1] which I recollect was very cold, so that a peat-fire, whose white appearance I still remember, was needed to warm the room. Cantlow was for some time a missionary in Jamaica, and is mentioned three times in Hinton's *Life of Knibb*. For thirty-two years this excellent man resided at Isleham, and was pastor of the church till age enfeebled him, and he welcomed our worthy student, Mr. Wilson, as his successor. He was great at giving the "soft answer which turneth away wrath"; he was beloved by his people, and universally respected in the village. His death serves as a landmark in my life, reminding me that the days are long past since I was generally spoken of as "the boy-preacher".

Stevenson, in *The Rev. C. H. Spurgeon, his Life and Work*, makes it out that I joined the Baptist Church a year before I was baptized, but it was not so. I never dreamed of entering the Church except by Christ's own way, and I wish that all other believers were led to make a serious point of commencing their visible connection with the Church by the ordinance which symbolizes death to the world, burial with Christ, and resurrection to newness of life. That open stream, the crowded banks, and the solemn plunge, have never faded from my mind, but have often operated as a spur to duty, and a seal of consecration. From henceforth let no man trouble me, for He who first saved me, afterwards accepted me—spirit, soul, and body—as His servant, in token whereof this mortal frame was immersed beneath the wave. The outward sign has often served to bring vividly before mind and heart the spiritual meaning, and therefore is it dearly loved, for His sake who both ordained the ordinance and Himself submitted to it.

*   *   *

---

[1] A Christian who recollected the day of Spurgeon's baptism wrote many years later, "The most precious memory of that day is the prayer-meeting in the vestry in the evening, where Mr. Spurgeon prayed, and people wondered, and wept for joy, as they listened to the lad."—P.

Mr. Wilson also explains the picture, and adds an amusing story: "In the view of the Ferry, the chaise and cart are waiting to cross the river by the ferry-boat. One old lighter is rotting away in the water, and another lies high and dry under repair. The box is for keeping eels until they can be sent to market, and there is also a small boat to be seen if you look closely. The late vicar of Isleham, a very solemn man, meeting a deacon of ready wit at the Ferry, began to find fault with a recent baptizing there. Said the vicar, 'I suppose this is the place where the people came crowding, the other Sunday, showing the little respect they had for the Sabbath-day.' 'There was, indeed, a great crowd,' replied the deacon, 'but they were all as still and attentive as in the house of God.' 'Is it true that the man, J. S——, was baptized?' enquired the vicar. 'Yes, quite true,' said the deacon, 'and he seemed to be full of joy at the time.' 'What!' exclaimed the vicar, 'a man who never went to school, and cannot read a word! How much can he know about the religion he came here to profess?' 'Well,' answered the deacon, with a smile, 'very likely the poor man knows little as yet; still, he told us how he found the Saviour, and became happy in His love. But,' added the deacon, 'do not you, sir, christen little children, declaring that you make them children of God, while you are perfectly aware that the children know nothing at all?' "

If any ask, Why was I thus baptized?—I answer, because I believed it to be an ordinance of Christ, very specially joined by Him with faith in His name. "He that believeth and is baptized shall be saved." I had no superstitious idea that baptism would save me, for I was saved. I did not seek to have sin washed away by water, for I believed that my sins were forgiven me through faith in Christ Jesus. Yet I regarded baptism as the token to the believer of cleansing, the emblem of his burial with his Lord, and the outward avowal of his new birth. I did not trust in *it*; but, because I trusted in Jesus as my Saviour, I felt bound to obey Him as my Lord, and follow the example which He set us in Jordan, in His own baptism. I did not fulfil the outward ordinance to join a party, and to become a Baptist, but to be a Christian after the apostolic fashion, for they, when they believed, were baptized. It is now questioned whether John Bunyan was baptized; but the same question can never be raised concerning *me*. I, who scarcely belong to any sect, am, nevertheless, by no means willing to have it doubted in time to come whether or no I followed the conviction of my heart. I read the New Testament for myself, and found believers' baptism there, and I had no mind to neglect what I saw to be the

Lord's order. If others see not as I do, to their own Master they stand or fall, but for me, the perceptions of my understanding in spiritual things were the law of my life, and I hope they will always be so.

If I thought it wrong to be a Baptist, I should give it up, and become what I believed to be right. The particular doctrine adhered to by Baptists is that they acknowledge no authority unless it comes from the Word of God. They attach no importance to the authority of the Fathers—they care not for the authority of the mothers—if what they say does not agree with the teaching of the Evangelists, Apostles, and Prophets, and, most of all, with the teaching of the Lord Himself. If we could find infant baptism in the Word of God, we should adopt it. It would help us out of a great difficulty, for it would take away from us that reproach which is attached to us—that we are odd, and do not as other people do. But we have looked well through the Bible, and cannot find it, and do not believe that it is there; nor do we believe that others can find infant baptism in the Scriptures, unless they themselves first put it there.

Our forefathers were called *Ana*-baptists, because it was said by their opponents that they re-baptized those who had been already baptized. Of course, they did nothing of the kind; they immersed, on profession of their faith, those who had previously been sprinkled as unconscious infants. There was no ana-baptism or re-baptism there, the two things were altogether distinct. I could tell a good many stories of that kind of ana-baptism. There was one of the elders of the Tabernacle Church who was—as the word is usually understood—"baptized" four times. The first time the babe was sprinkled, he was so ill that he was only half-done, according to the ritual provided for that purpose in the Prayer-book. When he got better, he was taken to the church to be properly finished off, but the parson gave the child a girl's name instead of the one which had been selected for him. His father and mother did not like their boy running the risk of being called by the name that had been given to him, so they took him for the third time, and the clergyman then gave him his right name. When he grew up, he was converted, and I baptized him after the Scriptural order; but the Church of England had made three attempts to baptize him, and had failed every time!

"When you bewail the world's iniquity, let not your emotions end in tears; mere weeping will do nothing without action. Get on your feet; ye that have voices and knowledge, go forth and preach the gospel, preach it in every street and lane of this huge city; ye that have wealth, go forth and spend it for the poor, and sick, and needy, and dying, the uneducated, the unenlightened; ye that have time, go forth and occupy it in deeds of goodness; ye that have power in prayer, go forth and pray; ye that can handle the pen, go forth and write down iniquity—every man to his post, every one of you to your gun in this day of battle; now for God and for His truth; for God and for the right; let every one of us who knows the Lord seek to fight under His banner!"—C. H. S.

Chapter 12

Beginning to Serve the Lord

I DO not see how our sense of oneness to Christ could ever have been perfected if we had not been permitted to work for Him. If He had been pleased to save us by His precious blood, and then leave us with nothing to do, we should have had fellowship with Christ up to a certain point, but (I speak from experience) there is no fellowship with Christ that seems to me to be so vivid, so real to the soul, as when I try to win a soul for Him. Oh, when I come to battle with that soul's difficulties, to weep over that soul's hardness; when I begin to set the arguments of Divine mercy before it, and find myself foiled; when I am in a very agony of spirit, and feel that I could die sooner than that soul should perish, then I get to read the heart of Him whose flowing tears, and bloody sweat, and dying wounds showed how much He loved poor fallen mankind.

I think that, when I was first converted to God, if the Lord had said "I have taken you into My house, and I am going to make use of you, and you shall be a door-mat for the saints to wipe their feet on," I should have said, "Ah, happy shall I be if I may but take the filth off their blessed feet, for I love God's people, and if I may minister to them in the slightest degree, it shall be my delight!" I know it did not come into my head, at that time, that I should be a leader in God's Israel. Ah, no; if I might but sit in the corner of His house, or be a door-keeper, it had been enough for me! If, like the dog under the table, I might get a crumb of His mercy, were it but flavoured by His hand, because He had broken it off, that was all I wanted. In that day when I surrendered myself to my Saviour, I gave Him my body, my soul, my spirit; I gave Him all I had, and all I shall have for time and for eternity. I gave Him all my talents, my powers, my faculties, my eyes, my ears, my limbs, my emotions, my judgment, my whole manhood, and all that could come of it, whatever fresh capacity or new capability I might be endowed with. Were I, at this good hour, to change the note of gladness for one of sadness, it would be to wail out my penitent confession of the times and circumstances in which I have failed to observe the strict and unwavering allegiance I promised to my Lord. So far from regretting what I then did, I would fain renew my vows, and make them over again. I pray God, if I have a drop of blood in my body which is not His, to let it bleed away; and if there be one hair in my head which is not consecrated to Him, I would have it plucked out.

The very first service which my youthful heart rendered to Christ was the placing of tracts in envelopes, and then sealing them up, that I might send them, with the hope that, by choosing pertinent tracts, applicable to persons I knew, God would bless them. And I well remember taking other tracts, and distributing them in certain districts in the town of Newmarket, going from house to house, and telling, in humble language, the things of the Kingdom of God. I might have done nothing for Christ if I had not been encouraged by finding myself able to do a little. Then I sought to do something more, and from that something more, and I do not doubt that many of the servants of God have been led on to higher and nobler labours for their Lord, because they began to serve Him in the right spirit and manner. I look upon the giving away of a religious tract as only the first step, not to be compared with many another deed done for Christ; but were it not for the first step, we might never reach to the second; but that being attained, we are encouraged to take the next, and so, at the last, God helping us, we may be made extensively useful.

I think I never felt so much earnestness after the souls of my fellow-creatures as when I first loved the Saviour's name, and though I could not preach, and never thought I should be able to testify to the multitude, I used to write texts on little scraps of paper, and drop them anywhere, that some poor creatures might pick them up, and receive them as messages of mercy to their souls. I could scarcely content myself even for five minutes without trying to do something for Christ. If I walked along the street, I must have a few tracts with me; if I went into a railway carriage, I must drop a tract out of the window; if I had a moment's leisure, I must be upon my knees or at my Bible; if I were in company, I must turn the subject of conversation to Christ, that I might serve my Master. It may be that, in the young dawn of my Christian life, I did imprudent things in order to serve the cause of Christ, but I still say, give me back that time again, with all its imprudence and with all its hastiness, if I may but have the same love to my Master, the same overwhelming influence in my spirit, making me obey my Lord's commands because it was a pleasure to me to do anything to serve my God.

How I did then delight to sit in that upper room where stars looked between the tiles, and hear the heavenly conversation which, from a miserable pallet surrounded by ragged hangings, an enfeebled saint of the Lord did hold with me! Like divers, I valued the pearl, even though the shell might be a broken one; nor did I care where I went to win it. When those creaking stairs trembled beneath my weight, when that bottomless chair afforded me uneasy rest, and when the heat and effluvia of that sick room drove my companion away, did I not feel more than doubly repaid while that friend of Jesus told me of all His love, His faithfulness, and His grace? It is frequently the case that the most despised servants of the Lord are made the chosen instruments of comforting distressed souls, and building them up in the faith.

* * *

I love to see persons of some standing in society take an interest in Sabbath-schools. One great fault in many of our churches is that the children are left for the young people to take care of; the older members, who have more wisdom, taking but very little notice of them; and very often, the wealthier members of the church stand aside as if the teaching of the poor were not (as indeed it is) the special business of the rich. I hope for the day when the mighty men of Israel shall be found helping in this great warfare against the enemy. In the United States, we have heard of presidents, judges, members of Congress, and persons in the highest positions, not condescending—for I scorn to use such a term—but honouring themselves by teaching little children in Sabbath-schools. He who teaches a class in a Sabbath-school has earned a good degree. I had rather receive the title of S.S.T. than M.A., B.A., or any other honour that ever was conferred by men.

There is no time for work like the first hours of the day; and there is no time for serving the Lord like the very earliest days of youth. I recollect the joy I had in the little service I was able to render to God when first I knew Him. I was engaged in a school all the week, but I had the Saturday afternoon at liberty, and though I was but a boy myself, and might rightly have used that time for rest, it was given to a tract-district, and to visiting the very poor within my reach; and the Sabbath-day was devoted to teaching a class, and later on, also to addressing the Sunday-school. When I began to teach—I was very young in grace then—I said to the class of boys whom I was teaching, that Jesus Christ saved all those who believed in Him. One of them at once asked me the question, "Teacher, do *you* believe in Him?" I replied, "Yes, I hope I do." Then he enquired again, "But are you not sure?" I had to think carefully what answer I should give. The lad was not content with my repeating, "I hope so." He would have it, "If you have believed in Christ, you *are* saved." And I felt at that time that I could not teach effectually until I could say positively, "I know that it is so. I must be able to speak of what I have heard, and seen, and tasted, and handled of the good Word of life." The boy was right; there can be no true testimony except that which springs from assured conviction of our own safety and joy in the Lord. If I was ever a little dull, my scholars began to make wheels of themselves, twisting round on the forms on which they sat. That was a very plain intimation to me that I must give them an illustration or an anecdote, and I learned to tell stories partly by being obliged to tell them. One boy, whom I had in the class used to say to me, "This is very dull, teacher; can't you pitch us a yarn?" Of course he was a naughty boy, and it might be supposed that he went to the bad when he grew up, though I am not at all sure that he did, but I used to try and pitch him the yarn that he wanted, in order to get his attention again.

At one of the teachers' meetings, the suggestion was adopted that the male teachers should, in turn, give a few words of address on the lesson at the close of the teaching, alternating in so doing with the superintendent. My turn came in due course. After I had spoken, the superintendent requested me to take his place in addressing the school on the following Sabbath, and when I had done this, he asked me, as I did so well, to speak to the children each Lord's day. But to this I demurred, not deeming it fair to the other teachers. "Well," he said, "on Sunday week, I shall expect you to give the address in my stead." The precedent thus instituted soon became a kind of usage, so that, for a time, it was usual for one of the teachers and myself to speak on alternate Sabbaths. Speedily something else followed. The older people also took to coming when I spoke; and that, ere long, in such numbers that the auditory looked more like that of a chapel than a school—a circumstance which the old pastor, jealous of the seeming invasion of his province, did not quite like. I always spoke as best I could, after carefully preparing my subject. Though only a youth, I said, "I think I am bound to give myself unto reading and study and prayer, and not to grieve the Spirit by unthought-of effusions;" and I soon found that my hearers appreciated what I said. Oh, but, how earnestly I did it all! I often think that I spoke better then than I did in later years, for I spoke so tremblingly, but my heart went with it all. And when I began to talk a little in the villages on the Sunday, and afterwards every night in the week, I know that I used to speak then what came fresh from my heart. There was little time for gathering much from books; my chief library was the Word of God and my own experience, but I spoke out from my very soul—no doubt with much blundering, and much weakness, and much youthful folly, but oh, with such an intense desire to bring men to Christ! I often felt that I could cheerfully lay down my life if I might but be the means of saving a poor old man, or bring a boy of my own age to the Saviour's feet. I feel it a great joy to have been called to work for my Lord in the early hours of my life's day; and I hope by-and-by to be able to say, "O God, Thou hast taught me from my youth: and hitherto have I declared Thy wondrous works. Now also when I am old and grey-headed, O God, forsake me not; until I have shewed Thy strength unto this generation, and Thy power to every one that is to come." I do not think my Lord will turn His old servant off; when I get old, men may become tired of me, but He will not; He will hear my prayer—

"Dismiss me not Thy service, Lord."

I can truly say, that I never did anything which was a blessing to my fellow-creatures without feeling compelled to do it. For instance, before I thought of going to a Sabbath-school to teach, someone called—asked me—begged me—prayed me to take his class. I could not refuse to go; and there I was, held hand and foot by the super-intendent, and was compelled to go on. Then I was asked to address the children; I thought I could not, but I stood up, and stammered out a few words. It was the same on the first occasion when I attempted to preach to the people—I am sure I had no wish to do it—but there was no one else in the place who could, and the little congregation must have gone away without a single word of warning or invitation. How could I suffer it? I felt forced to address them, and so it has been with whatever I have laid my hand to. I have always felt a kind of impulse which I could not resist; but, moreover, I have felt placed by Providence in such a position that I had no wish to avoid the duty, and if I had desired it, I could not have helped myself.

I shall never forget standing by the bed-side of a youth who had been in my Sunday-school class; he had received very little good training at home, and though he was but a lad of seventeen, he became a drunkard, and drank himself to death at one debauch. I saw him, and talked to him, and tried to point him to the Saviour, and heard at last the death-rattle in his throat, and as I went downstairs, I thought everybody a fool for doing anything except preparing to die. I began to look upon the men who drove the carts in the street, those who were busy at their shops, and those who were selling their wares, as being all foolish for attending to anything except their eternal busi-ness, and myself most of all foolish for not pointing dying sinners to a living Christ, and inviting them to trust in His precious blood. And

M

yet, in an hour or so, all things took their usual shape, and I began to think that I was not dying after all, and I could go away and be as unconcerned as before—I could begin to think that men were, after all, wise in thinking of this world, and not the next; I mean not that I really thought so, but I fear I acted as if I thought so; the impression of the death-bed was so soon obliterated. It is sadly true, that even a Christian will grow by degrees so callous, that the sin which once startled him, and made his blood run cold, does not alarm him in the least. I can speak from my own experience. When first I heard an oath, I stood aghast, and knew not where to hide myself; yet now, if I hear an imprecation or blasphemy against God, though a shudder still runs through my veins, there is not that solemn feeling, that intense anguish, which I felt when first I heard such evil utterances. By degrees we get familiar with sin. I am fearful that even preaching against sin may have an injurious effect upon the preacher. I frankly confess that there is a tendency, with those of us who have to speak upon these themes, to treat them professionally, rather than to make application of them to ourselves; and thus we lose our dread of evil in some degree, just as young doctors soon lose their tender nervousness in the dissecting-room. We are compelled in our office to see ten thousand things which at first are heart-breakers to us. In our young ministry, when we meet with hypocrisy and inconsistency, we are ready to lie down and die, but the tendency in after years is to take these terrible evils as matters of course. Worldliness, covetousness, and carnality, shock us most at the outset of our work: is not this a sad sign, that even God's ministers may feel the hardening effect of sin? I daily feel that the atmosphere of earth has as much a tendency to harden my heart as to harden plaster which is newly spread upon the wall; and unless I am baptized anew with the Spirit of God, and constantly stand at the foot of the cross, reading the curse of sin in the crimson hieroglyphics of my Saviour's dying agonies, I shall become as steeled and insensible as many professors already are.

"We only use the term 'Calvinism' for shortness. That doctrine which is called 'Calvinism' did not spring from Calvin; we believe that it sprang from the great founder of all truth. Perhaps Calvin himself derived it mainly from the writings of Augustine. Augustine obtained his views, without doubt, through the Spirit of God, from the diligent study of the writings of Paul, and Paul received them of the Holy Ghost, from Jesus Christ the great founder of the Christian dispensation. We use the term then, not because we impute any extraordinary importance to Calvin's having taught these doctrines. We would be just as willing to call them by any other name, if we could find one which would be better understood, and which on the whole would be as consistent with fact."—C. H. S.

"The old truth that Calvin preached, that Augustine preached, is the truth that I must preach to-day, or else be false to my conscience and my God. I cannot shape the truth; I know of no such thing as paring off the rough edges of a doctrine. John Knox's gospel is my gospel. That which thundered through Scotland must thunder through England again."—C. H. S.

Chapter 13

A Defence of Calvinism

It is a great thing to begin the Christian life by believing good solid doctrine. Some people have received twenty different "gospels" in as many years; how many more they will accept before they get to their journey's end, it would be difficult to predict. I thank God that He early taught me *the* gospel, and I have been so perfectly satisfied with it, that I do not want to know any other. Constant change of creed is sure loss. If a tree has to be taken up two or three times a year, you will not need to build a very large loft in which to store the apples. When people are always shifting their doctrinal principles, they are not likely to bring forth much fruit to the glory of God. It is good for young believers to begin with a firm hold upon those great fundamental doctrines which the Lord has taught in His Word. Why, if I believed what some preach about the temporary, trumpery salvation which only lasts for a time, I would scarcely be at all grateful for it; but when I know that those whom God saves He saves with an everlasting salvation, when I know that He gives to them an everlasting righteousness, when I know that He settles them on an everlasting foundation of everlasting love, and that He will bring them to His everlasting kingdom, oh, then I do wonder, and I am astonished that such a blessing as this should ever have been given to me!

> "Pause, my soul! adore, and wonder!
> Ask, 'Oh, why such love to me?'
> Grace hath put me in the number
> Of the Saviour's family:
> Hallelujah!
> Thanks, eternal thanks, to Thee!"

I suppose there are some persons whose minds naturally incline towards the doctrine of free-will. I can only say that mine inclines as naturally towards the doctrines of sovereign grace. Sometimes, when I see some of the worst characters in the street, I feel as if my heart must burst forth in tears of gratitude that God has never let me act as they have done! I have thought, if God had left me alone, and had not touched me by His grace, what a great sinner I should have been! I should have run to the utmost lengths of sin, dived into the very depths of evil, nor should I have stopped at any vice or folly, if God had not restrained me. I feel that I should have been a very king of sinners, if God had let me alone. I cannot understand the reason why I am saved, except upon the ground that God would have it so. I cannot, if I look ever so earnestly, discover any kind of reason in myself why I should be a partaker of Divine grace. If I am not at this moment without Christ, it is only because Christ Jesus would have His will with me, and that will was that I should be with Him where He is, and should share His glory. I can put the crown nowhere but upon the head of Him whose mighty grace has saved me from going down into the pit. Looking back on my past life, I can see that the dawning of it all was of God; of God effectively. I took no torch with which to light the sun, but the sun enlightened me. I did not commence my spiritual life—no, I rather kicked, and struggled against the things of the Spirit: when He drew me, for a time I did not run after Him: there was a natural hatred in my soul of everything holy and good. Wooings were lost upon me—warnings were cast to the wind—thunders were despised; and as for the whispers of His love, they were rejected as being less than nothing and vanity. But, sure I am, I can say now, speaking on behalf of myself, "He only is my salvation." It was He who turned my heart, and brought me down on my knees before Him. I can in very deed, say with Doddridge and Toplady—

> "Grace taught my soul to pray,
> And made my eyes o'erflow;"

and coming to this moment, I can add—

> " 'Tis grace *has* kept me to this day,
> And will not let me go."

Well can I remember the manner in which I learned the doctrines of grace in a single instant. Born, as all of us are by nature, an Arminian, I still believed the old things I had heard continually from the pulpit, and did not see the grace of God. When I was coming to Christ, I thought I was doing it all myself, and though I sought the Lord earnestly, I had no idea the Lord was seeking me. I do not think the young convert is at first aware of this. I can recall the very day and hour when first I received those truths in my own soul[1]—when they were, as John Bunyan says, burnt into my heart as with a hot iron, and I can recollect how I felt that I had grown on a sudden from a babe into a man—that I had made progress in Scriptural knowledge,

---

[1] See the letter, dated April 6, 1850, on page 115, and the entry in Diary on page 125— April 7:—"Arminianism does not suit me now."

through having found, once for all, the clue to the truth of God. One week night, when I was sitting in the house of God, I was not thinking much about the preacher's sermon, for I did not believe it. The thought struck me, "*How did you come to be a Christian?*" I sought the Lord. "*But how did you come to seek the Lord?*" The truth flashed across my mind in a moment—I should not have sought Him unless there had been some previous influence in my mind to *make me* seek Him. I prayed, thought I, but then I asked myself, *How came I to pray?* I was induced to pray by reading the Scriptures. *How came I to read the Scriptures?* I did read them, but what led me to do so? Then, in a moment, I saw that God was at the bottom of it all, and that He was the Author of my faith, and so the whole doctrine of grace opened up to me, and from that doctrine I have not departed to this day, and I desire to make this my constant confession, "I ascribe my change wholly to God."

I once attended a service where the text happened to be, "*He* shall choose our inheritance for us;" and the good man who occupied the pulpit was more than a little of an Arminian. Therefore, when he commenced, he said, "This passage refers entirely to our temporal inheritance, it has nothing whatever to do with our everlasting destiny, for," said he, "we do not want Christ to choose for us in the matter of Heaven or hell. It is so plain and easy, that every man who has a grain of common sense will choose Heaven, and any person would know better than to choose hell. We have no need of any superior intelligence, or any greater Being, to choose Heaven or hell for us. It is left to our own free-will, and we have enough wisdom given us, sufficiently correct means to judge for ourselves," and therefore, as he very logically inferred, there was no necessity for Jesus Christ, or anyone, to make a choice for us. We could choose the inheritance for ourselves without any assistance. "Ah!" I thought, "but, my good brother, it may be very true that we *could*, but I think we should want something more than common sense before we *should* choose aright."

*   *   *

First, let me ask, must we not all of us admit an over-ruling Providence, and the appointment of Jehovah's hand, as to the means whereby we came into this world? Those men who think that, afterwards, we are left to our own free-will to choose this one or the other to direct our steps, must admit that our entrance into the world was not of our own will, but that God had then to choose for us. What circumstances were those in our power which led us to elect certain persons to be our parents? Had we anything to do with it? Did not

God Himself appoint our parents, native place, and friends? Could He not have caused me to be born with the skin of the Hottentot, brought forth by a filthy mother who would nurse me in her "kraal", and teach me to bow down to Pagan gods, quite as easily as to have given me a pious mother, who would each morning and night bend her knee in prayer on my behalf? Or, might He not, if He had pleased, have given me some profligate to have been my parent, from whose lips I might have early heard fearful, filthy, and obscene language? Might He not have placed me where I should have had a drunken father, who would have immured me in a very dungeon of ignorance, and brought me up in the chains of crime? Was it not God's Providence that I had so happy a lot, that both my parents were His children, and endeavoured to train me up in the fear of the Lord?

John Newton used to tell a whimsical story, and laugh at it, too, of a good woman who said, in order to prove the doctrine of election, "Ah! sir, the Lord must have loved me before I was born, or else He would not have seen anything in me to love afterwards." I am sure it is true in my case; I believe the doctrine of election, because I am quite certain that, if God had not chosen me, I should never have chosen Him; and I am sure He chose me before I was born, or else He never would have chosen me afterwards; and He must have elected me for reasons unknown to me, for I never could find any reason in myself why He should have looked upon me with special love. So I am forced to accept that great Biblical doctrine. I recollect an Arminian brother telling me that he had read the Scriptures through a score or more times, and could never find the doctrine of election in them. He added that he was sure he would have done so if it had been there, for he read the Word on his knees. I said to him, "I think you read the Bible in a very uncomfortable posture, and if you had read it in your easy chair, you would have been more likely to understand it. Pray, by all means, and the more, the better, but it is a piece of superstition to think there is anything in the posture in which a man puts himself for reading: and as to reading through the Bible twenty times without having found anything about the doctrine of election, the wonder is that you found anything at all: you must have galloped through it at such a rate that you were not likely to have any intelligible idea of the meaning of the Scriptures."

If it would be marvellous to see one river leap up from the earth full-grown, what would it be to gaze upon a vast spring from which all the rivers of the earth should at once come bubbling up, a million of them born at a birth? What a vision would it be! Who can conceive it. And yet the love of God is that fountain, from which all the rivers of mercy, which have ever gladdened our race—all the rivers of grace in time, and of glory hereafter—take their rise. My soul, stand thou at that sacred fountain-head, and adore and magnify for ever and ever God, even our Father, who hath loved us! In the very beginning, when this great universe lay in the mind of God, like unborn forests in the acorn cup; long ere the echoes awoke the solitudes; before the mountains were brought forth; and long ere the light flashed through the sky, God loved His chosen creatures. Before there was any created being—when the ether was not fanned by an angel's wing, when space itself had not an existence, when there was nothing save God alone—even then, in that loneliness of Deity, and in that deep quiet and profundity, His bowels moved with love for His chosen. Their names were written on His heart, and then were they dear to His soul. Jesus loved His people before the foundation of the world— even from eternity! and when He called me by His grace, He said to me, "I have loved *thee* with an everlasting love: therefore with loving-kindness have I drawn thee."

Then, in the fulness of time, He purchased me with His blood; He let His heart run out in one deep gaping wound for me long ere I loved Him. Yea, when He first came to me, did I not spurn Him? When He knocked at the door, and asked for entrance, did I not drive Him away, and do despite to His grace? Ah! I can remember that I full often did so until, at last, by the power of His effectual grace, He said, "I must, I will come in;" and then He turned my heart, and made me love Him. But even till now I should have resisted Him, had it not been for His grace. Well, then, since He purchased me when I was dead in sins, does it not follow, as a consequence necessary and logical, that He must have loved me first? Did my Saviour die for me because I believed on Him? No; I was not then in existence; I had then no being. Could the Saviour, therefore, have died because I had faith, when I myself was not yet born? Could that have been possible? Could that have been the origin of the Saviour's love towards me? Oh! no; my Saviour died for me long before I believed. "But," says someone, "He foresaw that you would have faith; and, therefore, He loved you." What did He foresee about my faith? Did He foresee that I should get that faith myself, and that I should believe on Him of myself? No; Christ could not foresee that, because no Christian man will ever say that faith came of itself without the gift and without the working of the Holy Spirit. I have met with a great many believers, and talked with them about this matter; but I never knew one who could put his hand on his heart, and say, "I believed in Jesus without the assistance of the Holy Spirit."

I am bound to the doctrine of the depravity of the human heart, because I find myself depraved in heart, and have daily proofs that in my flesh there dwelleth no good thing. If God enters into covenant with unfallen man, man is so insignificant a creature that it must be an act of gracious condescension on the Lord's part; but if God enters into covenant with *sinful* man, he is then so offensive a creature that it must be, on God's part, an act of pure, free, rich, sovereign grace. When the Lord entered into covenant with me, I am sure that it was all of grace, nothing else but grace. When I remember what a den of unclean beasts and birds my heart was, and how strong was my unrenewed will, how obstinate and rebellious against the sovereignty of the Divine rule, I always feel inclined to take the very lowest room in my Father's house, and when I enter Heaven, it will be to go among the less than the least of all saints, and with the chief of sinners.

The late lamented Mr. Denham has put, at the foot of his portrait, a most admirable text, "Salvation is of the Lord." That is just an epitome of Calvinism; it is the sum and substance of it. If anyone should ask me what I mean by a Calvinist, I should reply, "He is one who says, *Salvation is of the Lord.*" I cannot find in Scripture any other doctrine than this. It is the essence of the Bible. "He *only* is my rock and my salvation." Tell me anything contrary to this truth, and it will be a heresy; tell me a heresy, and I shall find its essence here, that it has departed from this great, this fundamental, this rock-truth, "God is my rock and my salvation." What is the heresy of Rome, but the addition of something to the perfect merits of Jesus Christ—the bringing in of the works of the flesh, to assist in our justification? And what is the heresy of Arminianism but the addition of something to the work of the Redeemer? Every heresy, if brought to the touchstone, will discover itself here. I have my own private opinion that there is no such thing as preaching Christ and Him crucified, unless we preach what nowadays is called Calvinism. It is a nickname to call it Calvinism; Calvinism is the gospel, and nothing else. I do not believe we can preach the gospel, if we do not preach justification by faith, without works; nor unless we preach the sovereignty of God in His dispensation of grace; nor unless we exalt the electing, unchangeable, eternal, immutable, conquering love of Jehovah; nor do I think we can preach the gospel, unless we base it upon the special and particular redemption of His elect and chosen people which Christ wrought out upon the cross; nor can I comprehend a gospel which lets saints fall away after they are called, and suffers the children of God to be burned in the fires of damnation after having once believed in Jesus. Such a gospel I abhor.

"If ever it should come to pass,
  That sheep of Christ might fall away,
My fickle, feeble soul, alas!
  Would fall a thousand times a day."

If one dear saint of God had perished, so might all; if one of the covenant ones be lost, so may all be; and then there is no gospel promise true, but the Bible is a lie, and there is nothing in it worth my acceptance. I will be an infidel at once when I can believe that a saint of God can ever fall finally. If God hath loved me once, then He will love me for ever. God has a master-mind; He arranged everything in His gigantic intellect long before He did it; and once having settled it, He never alters it, "This shall be done," saith He, and the iron hand of destiny marks it down, and it is brought to pass. "This is My purpose," and it stands, nor can earth or hell alter it. "This is My decree," saith He, "promulgate it, ye holy angels; rend it down from the gate of Heaven, ye devils, if ye can; but ye cannot alter the decree, it shall stand for ever." God altereth not His plans; why should He? He is Almighty, and therefore can perform His pleasure. Why should He? He is the All-wise, and therefore cannot have planned wrongly. Why should He? He is the everlasting God, and therefore cannot die before His plan is accomplished. Why should He change? Ye worthless atoms of earth, ephemera of a day, ye creeping insects upon this bay-leaf of existence, ye may change *your* plans, but He shall never, never change *His*. Has He told me that His plan is to save me? If so, I am for ever safe.

"My name from the palms of His hands
  Eternity will not erase;
Impress'd on His heart it remains,
  In marks of indelible grace."

I do not know how some people, who believe that a Christian can fall from grace, manage to be happy. It must be a very commendable thing in them to be able to get through a day without despair. If I did not believe the doctrine of the final perseverance of the saints, I think I should be of all men the most miserable, because I should lack any ground of comfort. I could not say, whatever state of heart I came into, that I should be like a well-spring of water, whose stream fails not; I should rather have to take the comparison of an intermittent spring, that might stop on a sudden, or a reservoir, which I had no reason to expect would always be full. I believe that the happiest of Christians and the truest of Christians are those who never dare to doubt God, but who take His Word simply as it stands, and believe it, and ask no questions, just feeling assured that if God has said it, it will be so. I bear my willing testimony that I have no reason, nor even the shadow of a reason, to doubt my Lord, and I challenge Heaven, and earth, and hell to bring any proof that God is untrue. From the depths of hell I call the fiends, and from this earth I call the tried and afflicted believers, and to Heaven I appeal, and challenge the long experience of the blood-washed host, and there is not to be found in the three realms a single person who can bear witness to one fact which can disprove the faithfulness of God, or weaken His claim to be trusted by His servants. There are many things that may or may not happen, but this I know *shall* happen—

> "He *shall* present my soul,
>   Unblemish'd and complete,
> Before the glory of His face,
>   With joys divinely great."

All the purposes of man have been defeated, but not the purposes of God. The promises of man may be broken—many of them are made to be broken—but the promises of God shall all be fulfilled. He is a promise-maker, but He never was a promise-breaker; He is a promise-keeping God, and every one of His people shall prove it to be so. This is my grateful, personal confidence, "The Lord *will* perfect that which concerneth *me*"—unworthy *me*, lost and ruined *me*. He will yet save *me*; and—

> "I, among the blood-wash'd throng,
>   Shall wave the palm, and wear the crown,
>   And shout loud victory."

I go to a land which the plough of earth hath never upturned, where it is greener than earth's best pastures, and richer than her most abundant harvests ever saw. I go to a building of more gorgeous architecture than man hath ever builded; it is not of mortal design; it is "a building of God, a house not made with hands, eternal in the Heavens." All I shall know and enjoy in Heaven, will be given to me by the Lord, and I shall say, when at last I appear before Him—

> "Grace all the work shall crown
>   Through everlasting days;
> It lays in Heaven the topmost stone,
>   And well deserves the praise."

I know there are some who think it necessary to their system of theology to limit the merit of the blood of Jesus: if my theological system needed such a limitation, I would cast it to the winds. I cannot, I dare not allow the thought to find a lodging in my mind, it seems so near akin to blasphemy. In Christ's finished work I see an ocean of merit; my plummet finds no bottom, my eye discovers no shore. There must be sufficient efficacy in the blood of Christ, if God had so willed it, to have saved not only all in this world, but all in ten thousand worlds, had they transgressed their Maker's law. Once admit infinity into the matter, and limit is out of the question. Having a Divine Person for an offering, it is not consistent to conceive of limited value; bound and measure are terms inapplicable to the Divine sacrifice. The intent of the Divine purpose fixes the *application* of the infinite offering, but does not change it into a finite work. Think of the numbers upon whom God has bestowed His grace already. Think of the countless hosts in Heaven: if thou wert introduced there to-day, thou wouldst find it as easy to tell the stars, or the sands of the sea, as to count the multitudes that are before the throne even now. They have come from the East, and from the West, from the North, and from the South, and they are sitting down with Abraham, and with Isaac, and with Jacob in the Kingdom of God; and beside those in Heaven, think of the saved ones on earth. Blessed be God, His elect on earth are to be counted by millions, I believe, and the days are coming, brighter days than these, when there shall be multitudes upon multitudes brought to know the Saviour, and to rejoice in Him. The Father's love is not for a few only, but for an exceeding great company. "A great multitude, which no man could number," will be found in Heaven. A man can reckon up to very high figures; set to work your Newtons, your mightiest calculators, and they can count great numbers, but God and God alone can tell the multitude of His redeemed. I believe there will be more in Heaven than in hell. If anyone asks me why I think so, I answer, because Christ, in every-thing, is to "have the pre-eminence", and I cannot conceive how He could have the pre-eminence if there are to be more in the dominions of Satan than in Paradise. Moreover, I have never read that there is to be in hell a great multitude, which no man could number. I rejoice to know that the souls of all infants, as soon as they die, speed their way to Paradise. Think what a multitude there is of them! Then there are already in Heaven unnumbered myriads of the spirits of just men made perfect—the redeemed of all nations, and kindreds, and people, and tongues up till now; and there are better times coming, when the religion of Christ shall be universal; when—

"He shall reign from pole to pole,
With illimitable sway;"

when whole kingdoms shall bow down before Him, and nations shall
be born in a day, and in the thousand years of the great millennial
state there will be enough saved to make up all the deficiencies of the
thousands of years that have gone before. Christ shall be Master
everywhere, and His praise shall be sounded in every land. Christ
shall have the pre-eminence at last; His train shall be far larger than
that which shall attend the chariot of the grim monarch of hell.

Some persons love the doctrine of universal atonement because
they say, "It is so beautiful. It is a lovely idea that Christ should have
died for all men; it commends itself," they say, "to the instincts of
humanity; there is something in it full of joy and beauty." I admit there
is, but beauty may be often associated with falsehood. There is much
which I might admire in the theory of universal redemption, but I
will just show what the supposition necessarily involves. If Christ on
His cross intended to save every man, then He intended to save those
who were lost before He died. If the doctrine be true, that He died
for all men, then He died for some who were in hell before He came
into this world, for doubtless there were even then myriads there who
had been cast away because of their sins. Once again, if it was Christ's
intention to save all men, how deplorably has He been disappointed,
for we have His own testimony that there is a lake which burneth
with fire and brimstone, and into that pit of woe have been cast some
of the very persons who, according to the theory of universal redemption, were bought with His blood. That seems to me a conception a thousand times more repulsive than any of those consequences which are said to be associated with the Calvinistic and
Christian doctrine of special and particular redemption. To think that
my Saviour died for men who were or are in hell, seems a supposition
too horrible for me to entertain. To imagine for a moment that He
was the Substitute for all the sons of men, and that God, having first
punished the Substitute, afterwards punished the sinners themselves,
seems to conflict with all my ideas of Divine justice. That Christ
should offer an atonement and satisfaction for the sins of all men, and
that afterwards some of those very men should be punished for the
sins for which Christ had already atoned, appears to me to be the
most monstrous iniquity that could ever have been imputed to
Saturn, to Janus, to the goddess of the Thugs, or to the most
diabolical heathen deities. God forbid that we should ever think thus
of Jehovah, the just and wise and good!

There is no soul living who holds more firmly to the doctrines of grace than I do, and if any man asks me whether I am ashamed to be called a Calvinist, I answer—I wish to be called nothing but a Christian; but if you ask me, do I hold the doctrinal views which were held by John Calvin, I reply, I do in the main hold them, and rejoice to avow it. But far be it from me even to imagine that Zion contains none but Calvinistic Christians within her walls, or that there are none saved who do not hold our views. Most atrocious things have been spoken about the character and spiritual condition of John Wesley, the modern prince of Arminians. I can only say concerning him that, while I detest many of the doctrines which he preached, yet for the man himself I have a reverence second to no Wesleyan; and if there were wanted two apostles to be added to the number of the twelve, I do not believe that there could be found two men more fit to be so added than George Whitefield and John Wesley. The character of John Wesley stands beyond all imputation for self-sacrifice, zeal, holiness, and communion with God; he lived far above the ordinary level of common Christians, and was one "of whom the world was not worthy." I believe there are multitudes of men who cannot see these truths, or, at least, cannot see them in the way in which we put them, who nevertheless have received Christ as their Saviour, and are as dear to the heart of the God of grace as the soundest Calvinist in or out of Heaven.

I do not think I differ from any of my Hyper-Calvinistic brethren in what I do believe, but I differ from them in what they do not believe. I do not hold any less than they do, but I hold a little more, and, I think, a little more of the truth revealed in the Scriptures. Not only are there a few cardinal doctrines, by which we can steer our ship North, South, East, or West, but as we study the Word, we shall begin to learn something about the North-west and North-east, and all else that lies between the four cardinal points. The system of truth revealed in the Scriptures is not simply one straight line, but two; and no man will ever get a right view of the gospel until he knows how to look at the two lines at once. For instance, I read in one Book of the Bible, "The Spirit and the bride say, Come. And let him that heareth say, Come. And let him that is athirst come. And whosoever will, let him take the water of life freely." Yet I am taught, in another part of the same inspired Word, that "it is not of him that willeth, nor of him that runneth, but of God that sheweth mercy". I see, in one place, God in providence presiding over all, and yet I see, and I cannot help seeing, that man acts as he pleases, and that God has left his actions, in a great measure, to his own free-will. Now, if I were to declare that man was so free to act that there was no control of God over his actions, I should be driven very near to atheism; and if, on the other hand, I should declare that God so over-rules all things that man is not free enough to be responsible, I should be driven at once into Antinomianism or fatalism. That God predestines, and yet that man is responsible, are two facts that few can see clearly. They are believed to be inconsistent and contradictory, but they are not. The fault is in our weak judgment. Two truths cannot be contradictory to each other. If, then, I find taught in one part of the Bible that everything is fore-ordained, *that is true*; and if I find, in another Scripture, that man is responsible for all his actions, *that is true*; and it is only my folly that leads me to imagine that these two truths can ever contradict each other. I do not believe they can ever be welded into one upon any earthly anvil, but they certainly shall be one in eternity. They are two lines that are so nearly parallel, that the human mind which pursues them farthest will never discover that they converge, but they do converge, and they will meet somewhere in eternity, close to the throne of God, whence all truth doth spring.

It is often said that the doctrines we believe have a tendency to lead us to sin. I have heard it asserted most positively, that those high doctrines which we love, and which we find in the Scriptures, are licentious ones. I do not know who will have the hardihood to make that assertion, when they consider that the holiest of men have been believers in them. I ask the man who dares to say that Calvinism is a licentious religion, what he thinks of the character of Augustine, or Calvin, or Whitefield, who in successive ages were the great exponents of the system of grace; or what will he say of the Puritans, whose works are full of them? Had a man been an Arminian in those days, he would have been accounted the vilest heretic breathing, but now *we* are looked upon as the heretics, and they as the orthodox. *We* have gone back to the old school; *we* can trace our descent from the apostles. It is that vein of free-grace, running through the sermonizing of Baptists, which has saved us as a denomination. Were it not for that, we should not stand where we are to-day. We can run a golden line up to Jesus Christ Himself, through a holy succession of mighty fathers, who all held these glorious truths; and we can ask concerning them, "Where will you find holier and better men in the world?" No doctrine is so calculated to preserve a man from sin as the doctrine of the grace of God. Those who have called it "a licentious doctrine" did not know anything at all about it. Poor ignorant things, they little knew that their own vile stuff was the most licentious doctrine under Heaven. If they knew the grace of God in truth, they would soon see that there was no preservative from lying like a knowledge that we are elect of God from the foundation of the world. There is nothing like a belief in my eternal perseverance, and the immutability of my Father's affection, which can keep me near to Him from a motive of simple gratitude. Nothing makes a man so virtuous as belief of the truth. A lying doctrine will soon beget a lying practice. A man cannot have an erroneous belief without by-and-by having an erroneous life. I believe the one thing naturally begets the other. Of all men, those have the most disinterested piety, the sublimest reverence, the most ardent devotion, who believe that they are saved by grace, without works, through faith, and that not of themselves, it is the gift of God. Christians should take heed, and see that it always is so, lest by any means Christ should be crucified afresh, and put to an open shame.

At the same time as Spurgeon left his Colchester school for Maidstone, Mr. Leeding, who had taught him for three years, removed to Cambridge to conduct a small school of his own. On August 6, 1850, Mr. Leeding received a letter from John Spurgeon which proposed the free services of his eldest son in return for the opportunity of his continuing under his former master's instruction. The letter was replied to the same day: "I have more than once wished it possible," wrote the Cambridge schoolmaster, "that an arrangement could be made for securing your son's services in the event of an increase in my school; but my partial success has appeared to me a bar to such an engagement, for I have such an estimate of him, that I could never have started the proposal on such terms as have proceeded from you. I will readily engage to give him all the assistance in my power for the prosecution of his own studies, and his board and washing in return for his assistance. . . . Your offer, coming to me at this particular juncture, is a striking interposition of the Providence of God on my behalf."

The sixteen-year-old "tutor" who thus came to Cambridge, shared in the same consciousness of Divine Providence. "I can see", he later wrote, "a thousand chances, as men would call them, all working together, like wheels in a great piece of machinery, to fix me just where I am." In the next three years he was prepared more deeply by the hand of God for the life-long duty of preaching the Gospel to every creature which his voice or pen could reach, but meanwhile the boys of the Academy in Union Road and the rustic Chapel-goers of the Fens were to benefit from the presence of one of whom it was soon to be said, "That young man will yet shake England like a second Luther."

Chapter 14

The Boy Preacher of the Fens

IT was **my** privilege, at Cambridge, to live in a house where, at eight o'clock, every person, from the servant to the master, would have been found for half-an-hour in prayer and meditation in his or her chamber. As regularly as the time came round, that was done, just as we partook of our meals at appointed hours. If that were the rule in all households, it would be a grand thing for us. In the old Puritanic times, a servant would as often answer one who enquired for him, "Sir, my master is at prayers," as he would nowadays reply, "My master is engaged." It was then looked upon as a recognized fact that Christian men did meditate, and study the Word, and pray; and society respected the interval set apart for devotion. It is said that, in the days of Cromwell, if you had walked down Cheapside at a certain hour in the morning, you would have seen the blinds down at every house. Alas! where will you find such streets nowadays? I fear that what was once the rule, is now the exception.

When I joined the Baptist Church at Cambridge—one of the most respectable churches that can be found in the world, one of the most generous, one of the most intelligent—this was a good many years ago, when I was young—nobody spoke to me. On the Lord's-day, I sat at the communion table in a certain pew; there was one gentleman in it, and when the service was over, I said to him, "I hope you are quite well, sir?" He said, "You have the advantage of me." I answered, "I don't think I have, for you and I are brothers." "I don't quite know what you mean," said he. "Well," I replied, "when I took the bread and wine, just now, in token of our being one in Christ, I meant it, did not you?" We were by that time in the street; he put both his hands on my shoulders—I was about sixteen years old then—and he said, "Oh, sweet simplicity!" Then he added, "You are quite right, my dear brother, you are quite right; come in to tea with me. I am afraid I should not have spoken to you if you had not first addressed me." I went to tea with him that evening, and when I left, he asked me to go again the next Lord's-day, so I went, and that Sabbath day he said to me, "You will come here every Sunday evening, won't you?" That dear friend used to walk with me into the villages when I afterwards went out to preach, and he remains to this day one of the truest Christian friends I have, and often have we looked back, and laughed at the fact that I should have dared to assume that Christian fellowship was really a truth. I remember that he said to me at the time, "I am rather glad you spoke to me, for if you had gone to some of our deacons, I am afraid you would not have received quite as friendly a reply as I have given you."

*   *   *

[The following letters written during his first year in Cambridge reveal the speedy growth in grace of the young convert:

"No. 9, Union Road,
Cambridge,
19th Sept., '50.

My Dear Father,

I received your kind letter in due time. I joined the Church here at the Lord's table last Ordinance day. I shall write for my dismission; I intended to have done so before. The Baptists are by far the most respectable denomination in Cambridge; there are three Baptist Chapels—St. Andrew's Street, where we attend, Zion Chapel, and Eden Chapel. There is a very fine Wesleyan Chapel and some others. I teach in the Sunday-school all the afternoon. Mr. Leeding takes the morning work. Last Sabbath-day we had a funeral sermon from Hebrews vi. 11, 12. We have a prayer-meeting at 7 in the morning, and one after the evening service; they are precious means of grace, I trust, to my soul. How soon would the lamps go out did not our mighty Lord supply fresh oil; and if it were not for His unshaken promise to supply our need out of the fulness of His grace, poor indeed should we be.

Yes, where Jesus comes, He comes to reign: how I wish He would reign more in my heart; then I might hope that every atom of self, self-confidence, and self-righteousness, would be quite swept out of my soul. I am sure I long for the time when all evil affections, corrupt desires, and rebellious, doubting thoughts shall be overcome, and completely crushed beneath the Prince's feet, and my whole soul be made pure and holy. But so long as I am encaged within this house of clay, I know they will lurk about, and I must have hard fighting though the victory by grace is sure. Praying is the best fighting; nothing else will keep them down.

I have written a letter to grandfather; I am sorry he is so poorly. He wants the promises now, and why may not young and old live upon them? They are the bread-corn of Heaven, the meat of the Kingdom, and who that has once tasted them will turn to eat husks without any sweetness and comfort in them? God's power will keep all His children, while He says to them, 'How shall ye who are dead to sin live any longer therein?' I feel persuaded that I shall never fathom the depths of my own natural depravity, nor climb to the tops of the mountains of God's eternal love. I feel constrained day by day to fall flat down upon the promises, and leave my soul in Jesu's keeping. It is He that makes my feet move even in the slow obedience which marks them at present, and every attainment of grace must come from Him. I would go forth by prayer, like the Israelites, to gather up this Heavenly manna, and live upon free-grace.

Add to all your great kindness and love to me, through my life, a constant remembrance of me in your prayers. I thank you for those petitions which you and dear Mother have so often sent up to the mercy-seat for me. Give my love to my sisters and brother, and accept the same for yourself and dear Mother. Hoping you are all quite well,

I remain,

Your obedient, affectionate son,

CHAS. H. SPURGEON."

*   *   *

"My Dear Uncle,

Dumb men make no mischief. Your silence, and my neglect, make one think of the days when letters were costly, and not of penny postage. You have doubtless heard of me as a top-tree Antinomian. I trust you know enough of me to disbelieve it. It is one object of my life to disprove the slander. I groan daily under a body of sin and corruption. Oh, for the time when I shall drop this flesh, and be free from sin! I become more and more convinced that, to attempt to be saved by a mixed covenant of works and faith is, in the words of Berridge, 'To yoke a snail with an elephant.' I desire to press forward for direction to my Master in all things; but as to trusting to my own obedience and righteousness, I should be worse than a fool, and ten times worse than a madman. Poor dependent creatures, prayer had need be our constant employment, the foot of the throne our continued dwelling-place; for the Rock of ages is our only safe Hiding-place. I rejoice in an assured knowledge by faith of my interest in Christ, and of the certainty of my eternal salvation. Yet what strivings, what conflicts, what dangers, what enemies stand in my way! The foes in my heart are so strong, that they would have killed me, and sent me to hell long ere this, had the Lord left me; but, blessed be His name, His electing, redeeming, and saving love has got fast hold of me; and who is able to pluck me out of my Father's hand? On my bended knees, I have often to cry for succour; and, bless His name, He has hitherto heard my cry. Oh, if I did not know that all the Lord's people had soul-contention, I should give up all for lost! I rejoice that the promises left on record are meant for me, as well as for every saint of His, and as such I desire to grasp them. Let the whole earth, and even God's professing people, cast out my name as evil; my Lord and Master, He will not. I glory in the distinguishing grace of God, and will not, by the grace of God, step one inch from my principles, or think of adhering to the present fashionable sort of religion.

Oh, could I become like holy men of past ages—fearless of men—holding sweet communion with God—weaned more from the world, and enabled to fix my thoughts on spiritual things entirely! But when I would serve God, I find my old deceitful heart full of the very essence of hell, rising up into my mouth, polluting all I say and all I do. What should I do if, like you, I were called to be engaged about things of time and sense? I fear I should be neither diligent in business, nor fervent in spirit. 'But,' (say you) 'he keeps talking all about himself.' True, he does; he cannot help it. Self is too much his master. I am proud of my own ignorance: and, like a toad, bloated with my own venomous pride—proud of what I have not got, and boasting when I should be bemoaning. I trust you have greater freedom from your own corruptions than I have; and in secret, social, and family prayer enjoy more blessed, sanctified liberty at the footstool of mercy.

Rejoice! for Heaven awaits us, and all the Lord's family! The mansion is ready; the crown is made; the harp is strung; there are no willows there. May we be enabled to go on, brave as lions, and valiant for the truth and cause of King Jesus, and by the help of the Spirit, vow eternal warfare with every sin, and rest not until the sword of the Spirit has destroyed all the enemies in our hearts! May we be enabled to trust the Lord, for He will help us; we must conquer; we cannot be lost. Lost? Impossible! For who is able to snatch us out of our Father's hand?

May the Lord bless you exceedingly!

Your affectionate nephew,
C. H. SPURGEON."

*   *   *

"Cambridge,
May 1, 1851.[1]

My Dear Mother,

Many happy returns of this day, I pray for you. Another year's journey of the vast howling wilderness have you gone; you have leaned on the arm of your Beloved, and are now nearer the gates of bliss. Happy as the year has been, I trust, to you, yet I do not think you would wish to traverse it over again, or to go back one step of the way. Glorious, wondrous, has been the grace shown to all of us, as members of the mystical body of Christ, in preservation, restraint from sin, constraint to holiness, and perseverance in the Christian state. What shall a babe say to a mother in Israel? And yet, if I might speak, I would say, 'Take this year's mercies as earnests of next year's blessings.' The God who has kept you so long, you may rest assured will never leave you. If He had not meant to do good continually to you, He would not have done it at all. His love in time past, in the past year, forbids you—

'FORBIDS YOU to think,
He'll leave you at last in trouble to sink.'

The rapturous moments of enjoyment, the hallowed hours of communion, the blest days of sunshine in His presence, are pledges of sure, certain, infallible glory. Mark the providences of this year; how clearly have you seen His hand in things which others esteem chance! God, who has moved the world, has exercised His own vast heart and thought for you. All your life, your spiritual life, all things have worked together for good; nothing has gone wrong, for God has directed, controlled all. 'Why, sayest thou O Jacob, and speakest, O Israel, My way is hid from the Lord, and my judgment is passed over from my God?' He who counts the hairs of our heads, and keeps us as the apple of His eye, has not forgotten you, but still loves you with an everlasting love. The mountains have not departed yet, nor the hills been removed, and till then we may have confidence that we, His own people, are secure.

But I am writing what to you are everyday meditations. Well, dear Mother, you know where this comes from, only from your boy. Let us rejoice together; your prayers for us I know will be answered, they are sure to be, for God has said so. May God give you a feast—honey, wine, milk—may you be satisfied with marrow and fatness, satiated

---

[1] The date in the *Autobiography* was given as May 3, 1851, but a comparison with the original letter revealed that it should be as above. Spurgeon intended it to arrive on May 3, which was his mother's birthday.—P.

with the dainties and luxuries of religion, and rejoice exceedingly in the Lord! I remember that, a year ago, I publicly professed the name of Jesus by baptism. Pray for me, that I may not dishonour my profession, and break my solemn vow. While I look back through the year, I can see a Great Exhibition of love and grace to me, more marvellous than even that now opened in Hyde Park. Give my love to dear Father, Archer, and sisters, and accept the same doubly. I trust all are well. I have nothing the matter with me. Mr. and Mrs. L. desire respects. Many thanks for the postal order.

I am,

Your affectionate son,

CHARLES."]

MY FIRST SERMON

There is a Preachers' Association in Cambridge, connected with St. Andrew's Street Chapel, once the scene of the ministry of Robert Robinson and Robert Hall. A number of worthy brethren preach the gospel in the various villages surrounding Cambridge, taking each one his turn according to plan. In my day, the presiding genius was the venerable Mr. James Vinter, whom we were wont to address as Bishop Vinter. His genial soul, warm heart, and kindly manner were enough to keep a whole fraternity stocked with love; and, accordingly, a goodly company of zealous workers belonged to the Association, and laboured as true yoke-fellows. My suspicion is, that he not only preached himself, and helped his brethren, but that he was a sort of recruiting sergeant, and drew in young men to keep up the number of the host; at least, I can speak from personal experience as to one case.[1]

I had, one Saturday, finished morning school, and the boys were all going home for the half-holiday, when in came the aforesaid "Bishop" to ask me to go over to Teversham, the next evening, for a young man was to preach there who was not much used to services, and very likely would be glad of company. That was a cunningly-devised sentence, if I remember it rightly, and I think I do, for, at the time, in the light of that Sunday evening's revelation, I turned it over, and vastly admired its ingenuity. A request to go and preach, would have met with a decided negative, but merely to act as company to a good brother who did not like to be lonely, and perhaps might ask me to

[1] Mr. Vinter was a deacon at St. Andrew's Street Chapel and seems to have been one of a select number of friends who saw in young Spurgeon a genius that would one day be manifested. A fellow deacon declared of Spurgeon, "Whoever lives to see it, he will become one of the greatest men in England."—P.

give out a hymn or to pray, was not at all a difficult matter, and the request, understood in that fashion, was cheerfully complied with. LIttle did the lad know what Jonathan and David were doing when he was made to run for the arrow, and as little did I know when I was cajoled into accompanying a young man to Teversham.

My Sunday-school work was over, tea had been taken, and I set off through Barnwell, and away along the Newmarket Road, with a gentleman some few years my senior. We talked of good things, and at last I expressed my hope that he would feel the presence of God while preaching. He seemed to start, and assured me that he had never preached in his life, and could nŏt attempt such a thing; he was looking to his young friend, Mr. Spurgeon, for that. This was a new view of the situation, and I could only reply that I was no minister, and that, even if I had been, I was quite unprepared. My companion only repeated that *he*, in a still more emphatic sense, was not a preacher, that he would help *me* in any other part of the service, but that there would be no sermon unless I delivered one. He told me that, if I repeated one of my Sunday-school addresses, it would just suit the poor people, and would probably give them more satisfaction than the studied sermon of a learned divine. I felt that I was fairly committed to do my best. I walked along quietly, lifting up my soul to God, and it seemed to me that I could surely tell a few poor cottagers of the sweetness and love of Jesus, for I felt them in my own soul. Praying for Divine help, I resolved to make the attempt. My text should be, "Unto you therefore which believe He is precious," and I would trust the Lord to open my mouth in honour of His dear Son. It seemed a great risk and a serious trial, but depending upon the power of the Holy Ghost, I would at least tell out the story of the cross, and not allow the people to go home without a word.

We entered the low-pitched room of the thatched cottage, where a few simple-minded farm-labourers and their wives were gathered together; we sang, and prayed, and read the Scriptures, and then came my first sermon. How long, or how short it was, I cannot now remember. It was not half such a task as I had feared it would be, but I was glad to see my way to a fair conclusion, and to the giving out of the last hymn. To my own delight, I had not broken down, nor stopped short in the middle, nor been destitute of ideas, and the desired haven was in view. I made a finish, and took up the hymn-book, but, to my astonishment, an aged voice cried out, "Bless your dear heart, how old are you?" My very solemn reply was, "You must wait till the service is over before making any such enquiries. Let us

now sing." We did sing, the young preacher pronounced the benediction, and then there began a dialogue which enlarged into a warm,
friendly talk, in which everybody appeared to take part. "How old
are you?" was the leading question. "I am under sixty," was the reply.
"Yes, and under sixteen," was the old lady's rejoinder. "Never mind
my age, think of the Lord Jesus and His preciousness," was all that
I could say, after promising to come again, if the gentlemen at Cambridge thought me fit to do so. Very great and profound was my awe
of "the gentlemen at Cambridge" in those days.

Are there not other young men who might begin to speak for Jesus
in some such lowly fashion—young men who hitherto have been as
mute as fishes? Our villages and hamlets offer fine opportunities for
youthful speakers. Let them not wait till they are invited to a chapel,
or have prepared a fine essay, or have secured an intelligent audience.
If they will go and tell out from their hearts what the Lord Jesus has
done for them, they will find ready listeners. Many of our young folks
want to commence their service for Christ by doing great things, and
therefore do nothing at all; let none of my readers become the victims
of such an unreasonable ambition. He who is willing to teach infants,
or to give away tracts, and so to begin at the beginning, is far more
likely to be useful than the youth who is full of affectations, and sleeps
in a white necktie, who is aspiring to the ministry, and is touching up
certain superior manuscripts which he hopes ere long to read from
the pastor's pulpit. He who talks upon plain gospel themes in a
farmer's kitchen, and is able to interest the carter's boy and the dairy-
maid, has more of the minister in him than the prim little man who
keeps prating about being cultured, and means by that—being taught
to use words which nobody can understand. To make the very poorest
listen with pleasure and profit, is in itself an achievement; and beyond
this, it is the best possible promise and preparation for an influential
ministry. Let our younger brethren go in for cottage preaching, and
plenty of it. If there is no Lay Preachers' Association, let them work
by themselves. The expense is not very great for rent, candles, and a
few forms: many a young man's own pocket-money would cover it
all. No isolated group of houses should be left without its preaching-
room, no hamlet without its evening service. This is the lesson of the
thatched cottage at Teversham.

*   *   *

Considerable weight is to be given to the judgment of men and
women who live near to God, and in most instances their verdict will
not be a mistaken one. Yet this appeal is not final nor infallible, and is

only to be estimated in proportion to the intelligence and piety of those consulted. I remember well how earnestly I was dissuaded from preaching by as godly a Christian matron as ever breathed; I endeavoured to estimate, with candour and patience, the value of her opinion, but it was outweighed by the judgment of persons of wider experience. If a man be truly called of God to the ministry, I will defy him to withhold himself from it. A man who has really within him the inspiration of the Holy Ghost calling him to preach, cannot help it—he must preach. As fire within the bones, so will that influence be until it blazes forth. Friends may check him, foes criticize him, despisers sneer at him, the man is indomitable; he must preach if he has the call of Heaven. All earth might forsake him, but he would preach to the barren mountain-tops. If he has the call of Heaven, if he had no congregation, he would preach to the rippling waterfalls, and let the brooks hear his voice. He could not be silent. He would become a voice crying in the wilderness, "Prepare ye the way of the Lord." I no more believe it possible to stop ministers than to stop the stars of heaven. I think it no more possible to make a man cease from preaching, if he is really called, than to stay some mighty cataract, by seeking, in an infant's cup, to catch the rushing torrent. The man has been moved of Heaven, who shall stop him? He has been touched of God, who shall impede him? With an eagle's wing, he must fly; who shall chain him to the earth? With a seraph's voice, he must speak; who shall seal his lips? And when a man does speak as the Spirit gives him utterance, he will feel a holy joy akin to that of Heaven; and when it is over, he wishes to be at his work again, he longs to be once more preaching. Is not the Lord's Word like a fire within *me*? Must I not speak if God has placed it there?

I was for three years a Cambridge man, though I never entered the University. I could not have obtained a degree, because I was a Nonconformist;[1] and, moreover, it was a better thing for me to pursue my studies under an admirable scholar and tender friend, and to preach at the same time. I was, by my tutor's own expressed verdict, considered to be sufficiently proficient in my studies to have taken a good place on the list had the way been open. "You could win in a canter," said he to me. I had, however, a better College course, for, when I first began to preach, this was my usual way of working. I was up in the morning early, praying and reading the Word; all the day, I was either teaching my scholars or studying theology as much as I could; then, at five in the evening, I became a travelling preacher, and went

[1] The Act of Uniformity of 1662 had excluded Nonconformists from the Universities; it was not until 1871 that this part of the Act was repealed.—P.

into the villages around Cambridge,[1] to tell out what I had learned. My quiet meditation during the walk helped me to digest what I had read, and the rehearsal of my lesson in public, by preaching it to the people, fixed it on my memory. I do not mean that I ever repeated a single sentence from memory, but I thought my reading over again while on my legs, and thus worked it into my very soul, and I can bear my testimony that I never learned so much, or learned it so thoroughly, as when I used to tell out, simply and earnestly, what I had first received into my own mind and heart. I found that I derived greater benefit by proclaiming to others what I had learned than if I had kept it all to myself.

I must have been a singular-looking youth on wet evenings, for I walked three, five, or even eight miles out and back again on my preaching work, and when it rained, I dressed myself in waterproof leggings and a mackintosh coat, and a hat with a waterproof covering, and I carried a dark lantern to show me the way across the fields. I am sure that I was greatly profited by those early services for my Lord. How many times I enjoyed preaching the gospel in a farmer's kitchen, or in a cottage, or in a barn! Perhaps many people came to hear me because I was then only a boy. In my young days, I fear that I said many odd things, and made many blunders, but my audience was not hypercritical, and no newspaper writers dogged my heels; so I had a happy training-school, in which, by continual practice, I attained such a degree of ready speech as I now possess.

I had many adventures, and a great variety of experiences in this itinerating work. I recollect one summer's evening, when I had engaged to preach at a village not far from Waterbeach, before I could reach my destination, the sky darkened, and a severe thunderstorm burst over the district. Some people are terrified at lightning, but ever since I believed in the Lord Jesus Christ, I have had no fear in a storm, however severe it might be. I distinctly remember, while quite a lad, being in my uncle's house one night during a tremendous tempest. The older folks were all afraid, but I had really trusted myself with the Lord Jesus, and I did not dare to fear. The baby was upstairs, and nobody was brave enough to fetch it down because of a big window on the stairs. I went up to the bedroom, and brought the child to its mother, and then read a Psalm, and prayed with my relatives, who were trembling in terror. There was real danger, for a stack was set on fire a short distance away, but I was as calm as in the sunshine of a summer's day, not because I was naturally courageous,

---

[1] There were thirteen villages comprised in the district which came within the operation of the Lay Preachers' Association.—P.

but because I had unshaken confidence in my Lord. I love the lightnings, God's thunder is my delight; I never feel so well as when there
is a great thunder and lightning storm. Then I feel as if I could mount
up as with the wings of eagles, and my whole heart loves then to
sing—

> "The God that rules on high,
>   And thunders when He please,
> That rides upon the stormy sky,
>   And manages the seas,
>
> This awful God is ours,
>   Our Father and our love;
> He shall send down His Heavenly powers
>   To carry us above."

Men are by nature afraid of the heavens; the superstitious dread the
signs in the sky, and even the bravest spirit is sometimes made to
tremble when the firmament is ablaze with lightning, and the pealing
thunder seems to make the vast concave of heaven to tremble and to
reverberate, but I always feel ashamed to keep indoors when the
thunder shakes the solid earth, and the lightnings flash like arrows
from the sky. Then God is abroad, and I love to walk out in some
wide space, and to look up and mark the opening gates of heaven, as
the lightning reveals far beyond, and enables me to gaze into the
unseen. I like to hear my Heavenly Father's voice in the thunder.

On this particular occasion, while walking to the place where I
was to preach, I was enjoying the storm, but as I was passing a cottage
on the road, I noticed a woman who seemed to be greatly alarmed
and in sore distress because of the tempest. I did not like to pass by,
and leave a fellow-creature in trouble, so I entered the house, read a
few verses of Scripture, and prayed, and so comforted the woman. I
then proceeded to my destination, to fulfil my engagement. On entering the village, I took off my waterproof coat, because the smooth
surface appeared to reflect the vivid flashes of lightning in a way that
might alarm the timid. I found that, because of the severity of the
tempest, the people were not expecting that there would be a service,
so I went round from house to house, and invited them to come to the
regular meeting-place. This unusual method of gathering a congregation brought me many hearers; the service was held, and, at its
close, I walked back to my Cambridge home.

One night, having been preaching the Word in a country village, I
was walking home, all by myself, along a lonely footpath. I do not

know what it was that ailed me, but I was prepared to be alarmed; when, of a surety, I saw something standing in the hedge—ghastly, giant-like, and with outstretched arms. Surely, I thought, for once I have come across the supernatural; here is some restless spirit performing its midnight march beneath the moon, or some demon of the pit wandering abroad. I deliberated with myself a moment, and having no faith in ghosts, I plucked up courage, and determined to solve the mystery. The monster stood on the other side of a ditch, right in the hedge. I jumped the ditch, and found myself grasping an old tree, which some waggish body had taken pains to cover with whitewash, with a view to frighten simpletons. That old tree has served me a good turn full often, for I have learned from it to leap at difficulties, and find them vanish or turn to triumphs.

Frequently, in those country places, when preaching in a low-pitched building crowded with people, I have seen the candles burn dimly for want of air—a clear indication that we were killing ourselves by inhaling an atmosphere from which the vitalizing principle had almost all gone. I have been afraid of the lights going out, and have thought it better to let the congregation depart rather sooner than usual. On one occasion, having a candle on each side of me in a small pulpit, I was somewhat vigorous, and dashed one of my luminaries from its place. It fell upon the bald head of a friend below, who looked up with an expression which I can see at this moment, and it makes me smile still. I took no more notice of the accident than to weave it into what I was saying, and I believe most of my hearers considered it to have been a striking practical illustration of the remark which accompanied it, "How soon is the glory of life dashed down!"

In my earlier days, I read, somewhere or other, in a volume of lectures upon homiletics, a statement which considerably alarmed me at the time; it was something to this effect: "If any man shall find a difficulty in selecting a text, he had better at once go back to the grocer's shop, or to the plough, for he evidently has not the capacity required for a minister." Now, as such had been very frequently my cross and burden, I enquired within myself whether I should resort to some form of secular labour, and leave the ministry, but I have not done so, for I still have the conviction that, although condemned by the sweeping judgment of the lecturer, I follow a call to which God has manifestly set His seal. I was so much in trouble of conscience through the aforesaid severe remark, that I asked my grandfather, who had been in the ministry some fifty years, whether he was ever perplexed in choosing his theme. He told me frankly that this had always been his greatest trouble, compared with which, preaching in itself was no anxiety at all. I remember the venerable man's remark, "The difficulty is not because there are not enough texts, but because there are so many, that I am in a strait betwixt them." We are something like the lover of choice flowers, who finds himself surrounded by all the beauties of the garden, with permission to select but one. How long he lingers between the rose and the lily, and how great the difficulty to prefer one among ten thousand lovely blooms! To me, still, I must admit, my text-selection is a very great embarrassment— *embarras de richesse*, as the French say—an embarrassment of riches, very different from the bewilderment of poverty—the anxiety of attending to the most pressing of so many truths, all clamouring for a hearing, so many duties all needing enforcing, and so many spiritual needs of the people all demanding supply. I confess that I frequently sit hour after hour praying and waiting for a subject, and that this is the main part of my study; much hard labour have I spent in manipulating topics, ruminating upon points of doctrine, making skeletons out of verses, and then burying every bone of them in the catacombs of oblivion, drifting on and on over leagues of broken water, till I see the red lights, and make sail direct to the desired haven. I believe that, almost any Saturday in my life, I prepare enough outlines of Sermons, if I felt at liberty to preach them, to last me for a month, but I no more dare to use them than an honest mariner would run to shore a cargo of contraband goods.

I am always sure to have the most happy day when I get a good text in the morning from my Master. When I have had to preach two or three sermons in a day, I have asked Him for the morning subject, and preached from it; and I have asked Him for the afternoon's topic or the evening's portion, and preached from it, after meditating on it for my own soul's comfort—not in the professional style of a regular sermon-maker, but feasting upon it for myself. Such simple food has done the people far more good than if I had been a week in manufacturing a sermon, for it has come warm from the heart just after it has been received in my own soul; and therefore it has been well spoken, because well known, well tasted, and well felt. Sometimes, my texts have come to me in a very remarkable way. While I was living at Cambridge, I had, as usual, to preach in the evening at a neighbouring village, to which I had to walk. After reading and meditating all day, I could not meet with the right text. Do what I would, no response came from the sacred oracle, no light flashed from the Urim and Thummim; I prayed, I searched the Scriptures, I turned from one verse to another, but my mind would not take hold of a text; I was, as Bunyan would say, "much tumbled up and down in my thoughts". Just then, I walked to the window, and looked out. On the other side of the narrow street in which I lived, I saw a poor solitary canary bird upon the slates, surrounded by a crowd of sparrows, who were all pecking at it as if they would tear it to pieces. At that moment the verse came to my mind, "Mine heritage is unto me as a speckled bird, the birds round about are against her." I walked off with the greatest possible composure, considered the passage during my long and lonely walk, and preached upon the peculiar people, and the persecutions of their enemies, with freedom and ease to myself, and I believe with comfort to my rustic audience. The text was sent to me, and if the ravens did not bring it, certainly the sparrows did.

While I was living at Cambridge, I once heard William Jay, of Bath, preach. His text was, "Let your conversation be as it becometh the gospel of Christ." I remember with what dignity he preached, and yet how simply. He made one remark which deeply impressed my youthful mind, and which I have never forgotten; it was this, "You do need a Mediator between yourselves and God, but you do not need a Mediator between yourselves and Christ; you may come to Him just as you are." Another of his striking sayings was this, "Popery is a lie, Puseyism is a lie, baptismal regeneration is a lie." I recollect also that, in the course of his sermon, Jay said that ladies were sometimes charged with dressing in too costly a fashion. He told us that he did not himself know much about that matter, but, if they would let him hear what their income was, he would tell them how many yards of silk, satin, lace, or ribbon, they could afford. My recollections of Jay were such as I would not like to lose. It usually happens that, when we listen to a venerable patriarch, such as he then was, there is all the greater weight in his words because of his age. I fancy that, if I had heard the same sermon preached by a young man, I should not have thought much of it, but there appeared all the greater depth in it because it came from an old man standing almost on the borders of the grave.

In an early part of my ministry, while but a lad, I was seized with an intense desire to hear John Angell James, and, though my finances were somewhat meagre, I performed a pilgrimage to Birmingham, solely with that object in view. I heard him deliver a week-evening lecture, in his large vestry, on that precious text, "Ye are complete in Him." The savour of that very sweet discourse abides with me to this day, and I shall never read the passage without associating therewith the quiet but earnest utterances of that eminent man of God.

Years afterwards, on being in James's company, I told him that I went all the way from Cambridge to Birmingham to hear him preach. On my mentioning the text, he replied, "Ah! that was a Calvinistic sermon. You would enjoy that, but you would not get on with me always." I was glad also to have the opportunity of thanking him for that precious book of his, *The Anxious Enquirer*, which has been the means of bringing so many sinners to the Saviour, and which I had found exceedingly helpful when I was seeking the Lord.

"C. H. Spurgeon's secret then, as ever afterwards, was his absolute dependence upon God and his whole-hearted earnestness and zeal. A typical instance of the latter occurred on his first visit to Waterbeach. He was put up for the night at the house of Mr. Smith, and shared a bed with Mr. Smith's son, then a young boy. Before retiring, C. H. Spurgeon went upon his knees, but his companion tumbled into bed without prayer and lay down. No sooner had young Spurgeon finished his devotions than he inquired of his bedfellow if he were not afraid to go to bed without asking God for protection during the night. "What a fearful thing would it be," he said, "if you went to your last sleep without a prayer and a Saviour." For an hour or more the young preacher talked to the boy, and his earnestness was so evident that the boy was moved. The youthful preacher had him out of bed and prayed with him, and that night the lad was converted. He is now an honoured deacon at Waterbeach. The same boy was sleeping with C. H. Spurgeon on another occasion, when in the early hours the young preacher, in great distress, awoke his companion and told him that his mind was filled with thoughts of the Judgment. He described, as in a vision, the fiery torments of the lost and the ascending smoke of the wrath of God, and never will his listener forget that Saturday night, or, rather ,Sunday morning. The matter was so laid upon the preacher's heart, that on the Sunday evening he embodied the thoughts in his sermon and preached the most terrible address ever delivered by him. . . . Strong men grew afraid and cried for mercy, and women sobbed and fainted. The memory of that dreadful picture, painted before their eyes, startles those who were present in the chapel, even to this day."—Charles Ray, *Life of C. H. Spurgeon* (1903).

Chapter 15

The Young Soul-winner at Waterbeach

DID you ever walk through a village notorious for its drunkenness and profanity? Did you ever see poor wretched beings, that once were men, standing, or rather leaning, against the posts of the ale-house, or staggering along the street? Have you ever looked into the houses of the people, and beheld them as dens of iniquity, at which your soul stood aghast? Have you ever seen the poverty, and degradation, and misery of the inhabitants, and sighed over it? "Yes," you say, "we have." But was it ever your privilege to walk through that village again, in after years, when the gospel had been preached there? It has been mine. I once knew just such a village as I have pictured—perhaps, in some respects, one of the worst in England—where many an illicit still was yielding its noxious liquor to a manufacturer without payment of the duty to the government, and where, in connection with that evil, all manner of riot and iniquity was rife.

There went into that village a lad, who had no great scholarship, but who was earnest in seeking the souls of men. He began to preach there, and it pleased God to turn the whole place upside down. In a short time, the little thatched chapel[1] was crammed, the biggest vagabonds of the village were weeping floods of tears, and those who had been the curse of the parish became its blessing. Where there had been robberies and villainies of every kind, all round the neighbourhood, there were none, because the men who used to do the mischief were themselves in the house of God, rejoicing to hear of Jesus crucified. I am not telling an exaggerated story, nor a thing that I do not know, for it was my delight to labour for the Lord in that village. It was a pleasant thing to walk through that place, when drunkenness had almost ceased, when debauchery in the case of many was dead, when men and women went forth to labour with joyful hearts, singing the praises of the ever-living God; and when, at sunset, the humble cottager called his children together, read them some portion from the Book of Truth, and then together they bent their knees in prayer

---

[1] "A curious little structure with a thatched roof, that had once been a dovecote, and was purchased by the local Baptists for a hundred pounds. It had a bricked floor, below the level of the road, and the pews were of the old-fashioned high-backed kind, whilst on the fronts of the galleries and on the square posts supporting them were placed hooks for the garments of the worshippers." (Charles Ray.) The Church had forty members when Spurgeon became their minister at the age of seventeen.—P.

to God. I can say, with joy and happiness, that almost from one end of the village to the other, at the hour of eventide, one might have heard the voice of song coming from nearly every roof-tree, and echoing from almost every heart. I do testify, to the praise of God's grace, that it pleased the Lord to work wonders in our midst. He showed the power of Jesu's name, and made me a witness of that gospel which can win souls, draw reluctant hearts, and mould afresh the life and conduct of sinful men and women.

[The village here referred to is, of course, WATERBEACH, where Spurgeon first preached in October, 1851, as the following letter proves:

> "No. 9, Union Road,
> Cambridge,
> October 15th (1851).

My Dear Father,

I received your most welcome note, and beg pardon if you think me negligent in returning thanks. I have been busily employed every Lord's-day; not at home once yet, nor do I expect to be this year. Last Sunday, I went to a place called Waterbeach, where there is an old-established church, but not able to support a minister. I have engaged to supply to the end of the month. They had, for twenty years, a minister who went over from Cambridge in the same way as you go to Tollesbury. After that, they tried to have a minister, but as they could not keep him, he has left, and they will have to do as they used to do. There is rail there and back, and it is only six miles.

I am glad you have such good congregations. I feel no doubt there is a great work doing there—the fields are ripe unto the harvest, the seed you have sown has yielded plenty of green, let us hope there will be abundance of wheat. Give my love to dear Mother; you have indeed had trials. I always like to see how you bear them. I think I shall never forget that time when Mother and all were so ill. How you were supported! How cheerful you were! You said, in a letter to me—

> 'When troubles, like a gloomy cloud,
>   Have gathered thick, and thundered loud,
>   He near my side has always stood;
>   His loving-kindness, O how good!'

I trust that you are all well, and that the clouds are blown away. I am quite well, I am happy to say. Where is Aunt? It is four months since I have heard anything from her, or about her. We have no settled minister yet, nor do we expect any. I thank you much for your sermon; it will just do for me.

How greatly must I admire the love that could choose me to speak the gospel, and to be the happy recipient of it! I trust my greatest concern is to grow in grace, and to go onward in the blessed course. I feel jealous lest my motive should change, fearing lest I should be my own servant instead of the Lord's. How soon may we turn aside without knowing it, and begin to seek objects below the sacred office!

Mr. and Mrs. L. are well, and send their respects. Grandfather has asked me to go to Stambourne, but I cannot afford to go his way. With love to you, dear Mother, and all at home,

I am,
Your affectionate son,
CHAS. H. SPURGEON."

The text of Spurgeon's *first* Sermon at Waterbeach was Matthew i. 21. One of the deacons, Robert Coe, later described his impression of the youth from Cambridge at the beginning of the service: "He sat on one side of the table-pew and I on the other side. I shall never forget it. He looked so white, and I thought to myself, *he'll* never be able to preach—what a boy he is. I despised his youth, you know, and thought all this while the congregation was singing. Then when the hymn was over, he jumped up and began to read and expound the chapter about the Scribes and Pharisees and lawyers, and as he went on about their garments, their phylacteries, and long prayers, I knew that *he* could preach." The following is the outline of the first Sermon at Waterbeach:

OUTLINE XXXIII.—SALVATION FROM SIN

"*Thou shalt call His name JESUS: for He shall save His people from their sins.*"—Matthew i. 21.

The two parts of this Salvation are Justification and Sanctification.

I. JUSTIFICATION, INCLUDING PARDON AND IMPUTATION OF RIGHTEOUSNESS

1. Pardon—free, perfect, instantaneous, irreversible, bringing with it deliverance from the consequences of sin, which are—

God's just displeasure.
The curse of the law.
Incapacity for Heaven.
Liability, yea, certain destination to eternal punishment.

2. Imputation of righteousness, causing a man to be regarded as holy, sinless, worthy of commendation and reward.

Its accompaniments are—God's love.

Blessing of the law.

Capacity for Heaven.

A right and title, yea, certain possession of Heaven.

This Jesus effected. As to the first, by His sufferings and death; as to the second, by His holy obedience to the law.

II. SANCTIFICATION, INCLUDING DELIVERANCE FROM SIN, AND POSITIVE HOLINESS.

1. Victory over—(1) our natural depravity, (2) the habits of sin, (3) temptations, (4) backslidings.

2. Working in us all holy affections. (1) Holy nature. (2) Holy habits. (3) Desires for holiness. (4) Progress in Divine grace.

Sanctification is unlike Justification, in that it is gradual, imperfect, progressional, never consummated but in Heaven.

This is the work of Jesus—(1) by showing us His example and commands, (2) by the Holy Spirit.

This is the beauteous salvation Jesus gives, complete deliverance from the guilt, consequences, and effects of sin.]

*　　　　*　　　　*

When I began to preach in the little thatched chapel at Waterbeach, my first concern was, Would God save any souls through me? They called me a ragged-headed boy, and I think I was just that; I know I wore a jacket. After I had preached for some little time, I thought, "This gospel has saved me, but then somebody else preached it; will it save anybody else now that I preach it?" Some Sundays went over, and I used to say to the deacons, "Have you heard of anybody finding the Lord under my ministry? Do you know of anyone brought to Christ through my preaching?" My good old friend and deacon said, "I am sure somebody must have received the Saviour; I am quite certain it is so." "Oh!" I answered, "but I want to know it, I want to prove that it is so."

How my heart leaped for joy when I heard tidings of my first convert! I could never be satisfied with a full congregation, and the kind expressions of friends; I longed to hear that hearts had been broken, that tears had been seen streaming from the eyes of penitents. How I did rejoice, as one that findeth great spoil, one Sunday afternoon, when my good deacon said to me, "God has set His seal on your ministry in this place, sir." Oh, if anybody had said to me, "Someone has left you twenty thousand pounds," I should not have given a snap of my fingers for it, compared with the joy which I felt when I was told that God had saved a soul through my ministry! "Who is it?" I asked. "Oh, it is a poor labouring man's wife over at such-and-such a place! She went home broken-hearted by your sermon two or three Sundays ago, and she has been in great trouble of soul, but she has found peace, and she says she would like to speak to you." I said, "Will you drive me over there? I must go to see her;" and early on the Monday morning I was driving down to the village my deacon had mentioned, to see my first spiritual child. I have in my eye now the cottage in which she lived; believe me, it always appears picturesque. I felt like the boy who has earned his first guinea, or like a diver who has been down to the depths of the sea, and brought up a rare pearl. I prize each one whom God has given me, but I prize that woman most. Since then, my Lord has blessed me to many thousands of souls, who have found the Saviour by hearing or reading words which have come from my lips. I have had a great many spiritual children born of the preaching of the Word, but I still think that woman was the best of the lot. At least, she did not live long enough for me to find many faults in her. After a year or two of faithful witness-bearing, she went home, to lead the way for a goodly number who have followed her. I remember well her being received into the church, and dying, and going to heaven. She was the first seal to my ministry, and a very precious one. No mother was ever more full of happiness at the sight of her first-born son. Then could I have sung the song of the Virgin Mary, for my soul did magnify the Lord for remembering my low estate, and giving me the great honour to do a work for which all generations should call me blessed, for so I counted and still count the conversion of one soul. I would rather be the means of saving a soul from death than be the greatest orator on earth. I would rather bring the poorest woman in the world to the feet of Jesus than I would be made Archbishop of Canterbury. I would sooner pluck one single brand from the burning than explain all mysteries. To win a soul from going down into the pit, is a more glorious achievement than to be crowned in the arena of theological controversy as *Dr. Sufficientissimus*; to have faithfully unveiled the glory of God in the face of Jesus Christ will be, in the final judgment, accounted worthier service than to have solved the problems of the religious Sphinx, or to have cut the Gordian knot of Apocalyptic difficulty. One of my happiest thoughts is that, when I die, it shall be my privilege to enter into rest in the bosom of Christ, and I know that

I shall not enjoy my heaven alone. Thousands have already entered there, who have been drawn to Christ under my ministry. Oh! what bliss it will be to fly to heaven, and to have a multitude of converts before and behind, and, on entering the glory, to be able to say, "Here am I, Father, and the children Thou hast given me."

*   *   *

A minister will never, I should think, forget his earliest converts. He lives to see hundreds begotten unto God by his means, but of these who were the children of his youth he still treasures delightful memories, for are they not his first-born, his might, and the beginning of his strength? I can recall an elderly woman who had found peace with God through my youthful ministry, and especially do I recollect her wail of woe as she told of the days of her ignorance, and the consequent godless bringing up of her children. Her words were somewhat as follows, and I write them down for the good of mothers who labour hard out of love to their dear ones, and provide them with all necessaries for this life, but never think of the life to come:

"Oh, sir!" said she, "I should be quite happy now, only I have one sore trouble which keeps me very low. I am so sad about my dear children. I was left with eight of them, and I worked hard at the wash-tub, and in other ways, morning, noon, and night, to find bread for them. I did feed and clothe them all, but I am sure I don't know how I did it. I had often to deny myself, both in food and clothing, and times were very hard with me. Nobody could have slaved worse than I did, to mend, and clean, and keep a roof over our heads. I cannot blame myself for any neglect about their bodies, but as to their souls, I never cared about my own, and of course I never thought of theirs. Two of them died. I dare not think about them. God has forgiven me, but I can't forget my sin against my poor children; I never taught them a word which could be of any use to them. The others are all alive, but there is not one of them in the least religious. How could they be when they saw how their mother lived? It troubles me more a good deal than all the working for them ever did, for I'm afraid they are going down to destruction, and *all through their cruel mother*."

Here she burst into tears, and I pitied her so much that I said I hardly thought she was *cruel*, for she was in ignorance, and would never intentionally have neglected anything that was for her children's good. "Don't excuse me," said she, "for if I had used my common sense, I might have known that my children were not like the sheep and the horses which die, and there's an end of them. I never thought about it at all, or I might have known better, and I feel that I was a cruel mother never to have considered their souls at all. They are all worldly, and none of them go to a place of worship, year in and year out. I never took them there, and how can I blame them? As soon as I was converted, I went down to my eldest son, who has a large family, and I told him what the Lord had done for me, and entreated him to come here with me to the services, but he said he wondered what next, and he had no time. When I pleaded hard with him, he said he was sure I meant well, but 'it was no go,'—he liked his Sunday at home too well to go to hear parsons. You know, sir, you can't bend a tree; I ought to have bent the twig when I could have done it. Oh, if I had but led him to the house of God when he was little! He would have gone then, for he loved his mother, and so he does now, but not enough to go where I want him. So, you see, I can do nothing with my son now. I was a cruel mother, and let the boy go into the fields, or the streets, when he should have been in the Sunday-school. Oh, that I could have my time back again, and have all my children around me as little ones, that I might teach them about my blessed Saviour! They are all beyond me now. What can I do?"

She sat down and wept bitterly, and I heartily wish all unconverted mothers could have seen her, and heard her lamentations. It was very pleasant to know that she was herself saved, and to see in her very sorrow the evidence of her genuine repentance; but, still, the evil which she lamented was a very terrible one, and might well demand a lifetime of mourning. Young mother, do not, as you love your babe, suffer it to grow up without Divine instruction. But you cannot teach your child if you do not know the Lord Jesus yourself. May the good Lord lead you to give your heart to Christ at once, and then help you to train your dear little ones for Heaven!

There was one woman in Waterbeach who bore among her neighbours the reputation of being a regular virago, and I was told that, sooner or later, she would give me a specimen of her tongue-music. I said, "All right; but that's a game at which two can play." I am not sure whether anybody reported to her my answer, but, not long afterwards, I was passing her gate, one morning, and there stood the lady herself; and I must say that her vigorous mode of speech fully justified all that I had heard concerning her. The typical Billingsgate fish-woman would have been nowhere in comparison with her. I made up my mind how to act, so I smiled, and said, "Yes, thank you; I am quite well, I hope you are the same." Then came another outburst of vituperation, pitched in a still higher key, to which I replied, still smiling, "Yes, it does look rather as if it is going to rain; I think I had better be getting on." "Bless the man!" she exclaimed, "he's as deaf as a post; what's the use of storming at him?" So I bade her, "Good morning," and I am not sure whether she ever came to the chapel to hear the "deaf" preacher who knew it was no use to give any heed to her mad ravings.

If I could have had a hope of doing her any good, I would have gone into her house, and talked with her, for I certainly went into some queer places while I was in that region. I used to think that, where my Master went, I need never be ashamed to go, and I have gone into some persons' houses, before I came to London, that I should have felt ashamed to enter if they had not invited me on a Sabbath-day. As I have stepped in there for the purpose of giving them religious advice, some have said to me, "What! going into that house?" "Yes, and quite right, too. 'The whole have no need of a physician, but they that are sick.' " I have gone after "the lost sheep of the house of Israel", and I have won their hearts because I went there, and talked to them of their sins. But had I stayed away, there would have been something of this spirit, "Stand by, for I am holier than you are; I cannot enter your house, because you are such an outrageous sinner." But when I go and talk to a man, and lay my hand on his shoulder, and ask him questions, he does not mind telling out his state of mind when I am under his own roof; and when I am gone, he says, "That man is not ashamed to speak to his fellows, I like that kind of preacher."

*   *   *

While I was at Waterbeach, I had one man who caused me many bitter tears. When I first knew him, he was the ringleader in all that was bad; a tall, fine, big fellow, and one who could, perhaps, drink more than any man for miles around him—a man who would curse and swear, and never knew a thought of fear. He was the terror of the neighbourhood; there were many incendiary fires in the region, and most people attributed them to him. Sometimes, he would be drunk for two or three weeks at a spell, and then he raved and raged like a madman. That man came to hear me; I recollect the sensation that went through the little chapel when he entered. He sat there, and fell in love with me; I think that was the only conversion that he experienced, but he professed to be converted. He had, apparently, been the subject of genuine repentance, and he became outwardly quite a changed character; he gave up his drinking and his swearing, and was in many respects an exemplary individual. All the parish was astonished. There was old Tom So-and-so weeping, and it was rumoured about that he felt impressed; he began regularly to attend the chapel, and was manifestly an altered man. The public-house lost an excellent customer; he was not seen in the skittle-alley, nor was he detected in the drunken rows that were so common in the neighbourhood. After a while, he ventured to come forward at the prayer-meeting; he talked about what he had experienced, what he had felt and known. I heard him pray; it was rough, rugged language, but there was such impassioned earnestness, I set him down as being a bright jewel in the Redeemer's crown. He held out six, nay, nine months he persevered in our midst. If there was rough work to be done, he would do it; if there was a Sunday-school to be maintained, six or seven miles away, he would walk there. At any risk, he would be out to help in the Lord's work; if he could but be of service to the meanest member of the Church of Christ, he rejoiced greatly. I remember seeing him tugging a barge, with perhaps a hundred people on board, whom he was drawing up to a place where I was going to preach; and he was glorying in the work, and singing as gladly and happily as any one of them. If anybody spoke a word against the Lord or His servant, he did not hesitate a moment, but knocked him over.

So he went on for a time, but, at last, the laughter to which he was exposed, the jeers and scoffs of his old companions—though at first he bore them like a man—became too much for him. He began to think he had been a little too fanatical, a little too earnest. He slunk up to the place of worship instead of coming boldly in; he gradually forsook the week-night service, and then neglected the Sabbath-day; and, though often warned, and often rebuked, he returned to his old habits, and any thoughts of God or godliness that he had ever known, seemed to die away. He could again utter the blasphemer's oath; once more he could act wickedly with the profane; and he—of whom we had often boasted, and said, in our prayer-meetings, "Oh! how much is God glorified by this man's conversion! What cannot Divine grace do?"—to the confusion of us all, was to be seen sometimes drunk in our streets, and then it was thrown in our teeth, "This is one of your Christians, is it?—one of your converts gone back again, and become as bad as he was before?" Before I left the district, I was afraid that there was no real work of grace in him. He was a wild Red Indian sort of a man; and I have heard of him taking a bird, plucking it, and eating it raw in the field. That was not the act of a Christian man, it was not one of the things that are comely, and of good repute. After I left the neighbourhood, I asked after him, and I could hear nothing good of him; he became worse than he was before, if that was possible; certainly, he was no better, and seemed to be unreachable by any agency.

Among my early hearers at Waterbeach was one good old woman whom I called "Mrs. Much-afraid". I feel quite sure she has been many years in Heaven, but she was always fearing that she should néver enter the gates of glory. She was very regular in her attendance at the house of God, and was a wonderfully good listener. She used to drink in the gospel; but, nevertheless, she was always doubting, and fearing, and trembling about her own spiritual condition. She had been a believer in Christ, I should think, for fifty years, yet she had always remained in that timid, fearful, anxious state. She was a kind old soul, ever ready to help her neighbours, or to speak a word to the unconverted; she seemed to me to have enough grace for two people, yet, in her own opinion, she had not half enough grace for one.

One day, when I was talking with her, she told me that she had not any hope at all; she had no faith; she believed that she was a hypocrite. I said, "Then don't come to the chapel any more; we don't want hypocrites there. Why do you come?" She answered, "I come because I can't stop away. I love the people of God; I love the house of God; and I love to worship God." "Well," I said, "you are an odd sort of hypocrite; you are a queer kind of unconverted woman." "Ah!" she sighed, "you may say what you please, but I have not any hope of being saved." So I said to her, "Well, next Sunday, I will let you go into the pulpit, that you may tell the people that Jesus Christ is a liar, and that you cannot trust Him." "Oh!" she cried, "I would be torn in pieces before I would say such a thing as that. Why, He cannot lie! Every word He says is true." "Then," I asked, "why do you not believe it?" She replied, "I do believe it; but, somehow, I do not believe it for myself; I am afraid whether it is for me." "Have you not any hope at all?" I asked. "No," she answered; so I pulled out my purse, and I said to her, "Now, I have got £5 here, it is all the money I have, but I will give you that £5 for your hope if you will sell it." She looked at me, wondering what I meant. "Why!" she exclaimed, "I would not sell it for a thousand worlds." She had just told me that she had not any hope of salvation, yet she would not sell it for a thousand worlds!

I fully expect to see that good old soul when I get to Heaven, and I am certain she will say to me, "Oh, dear sir, how foolish I was when I lived down there at Waterbeach! I went groaning all the way to glory when I might just as well have gone there singing. I was always troubled and afraid, but my dear Lord kept me by His grace, and brought me safely here." She died very sweetly; it was with her as John Bunyan said it was with Miss Much-afraid, Mr. Despondency's daughter. Mr. Great-heart had much trouble with those poor pilgrims on the road to the Celestial City, for, if there was only a straw in the way, they were fearful that they would stumble over it. Yet Bunyan says, "When the time was come for them to depart, they went to the brink of the river. The last words of Mr. Despondency were, 'Farewell night, welcome day.' His daughter went through the river singing." Our Lord often makes it calm and peaceful, or even joyous and triumphant, for His departing timid ones. He puts some of His greatest saints to bed in the dark, and they wake up in the eternal light, but He frequently keeps the candle burning for Mr. Little-faith, Mr. Feeble-mind, Mr. Ready-to-halt, Mr. Despondency, and Miss Much-afraid. They go to sleep in the light, and they also wake up in the land where the Lamb is all the glory for ever and ever.

Overleaf is a Facsimile *of one of the Sermons preached at Waterbeach in the early part of the year* 1852.

Luke XIX. 41 — The Redeemer's tears over sinners.

Jesus had a triumphant entrance into Jerusalem; he rode not on the forbidden horse of Egypt, but on the noble ass of Palestine; all around were shouting, palm branches were waving, clothes spread on the ass and on the ground, while the whole city was stirred. 'Tis a man riding on the ass, and in triumph, too, and yet this triumphant man weeps;— he is looking on a fair & beautiful city, and yet he weeps —.   There were pleasing associations connected with it; there, Abraham offered Isaac; there, David danced before the ark, & dwelt in solemn state. Through its streets Solomon once rode in regal splendour;— there Josiah held his great passover.— Once, happy feet ransomed from Babylon had trod its stones;— thither the tribes went up every year in joyful procession; but these are not in his mind, for see he weeps.......— He wept at the grave of Lazarus, but then he lost a friend; but now 'tis for a city flourishing, blooming, gorgeous with a temple surpassing all edifices on earth. —— ——

I. He wept at the remembrance of what she had been.

1 A city abounding with privileges, but having not at all improved them.

2. A city to whom prophets had been sent, but she had spilt their blood, and disregarded all.

3. A city of the highest order & degree about to be brought down to the lowest depths.

II. What she then was —

1. A city filled with those whom he had benefited,

and those same persons remaining most ungrateful.

2. He knew her state of sinfulness, & wept at the remembrance that she was a sink of sin, — cruel, bloody, vile hypocrites there.

3. A city he had lived and preached in.

4. a city given over - condemned —

III. What she would be —

1. She was to be stript of all her privileges.

2. Utterly ruined and destroyed —

now let Jesus stand up, and weep over Waterbeach, & over this congregation —

You have been distinguished for sin; yes, many here, and your sin is aggravated by your many privileges.

You are now many, yea, most of you, dead in trespasses and sins, and some especially vile —

You have long resisted divine calls, — you will yet go on in sin, and many of you will be damned.

Weep, oh preacher! Weep. Weep. Weep, — men, women,

Now let Jesus stand up, & weep over you one by one.

1. Over the open reprobate, — despisers, drunkards.

2. Over the unconverted many-year hearer.

3. Over the hopeful young, who yet will go aside.

4. Over convinced sinners wiping their tears away.

5. Over many feast-goers, who go despite warnings.

6. Over old men, on the brink of hell.

7. Over hypocrites, deceiving their own souls.

8. Over those who are given up & let alone.

9. Over careless, laughing, critical, &c, hearers —

Weep one by one. Oh, that mine eyes were fountains of tears.

168.

Bless. Bless —

"The life of Jonah cannot be written without God; take God out of the prophet's history, and there is no history to write. This is equally true of each one of us. Apart from God, there is no life, nor thought, nor act, nor career of any man, however lowly or however high. Leave out God, and you cannot write the story of anyone's career. If you attempt it, it will be so ill-written that it shall be clearly perceived that you have tried to make bricks without straw, and that you have sought to fashion a potter's vessel without clay. I believe that, in a man's life, the great secret of strength, and holiness, and righteousness, is the acknowledgment of God. When a man has no fear of God before his eyes, there is no wonder that he should run to an excess of meanness, and even to an excess of riot. In proportion as the thought of God dominates the mind, we may expect to find a life that shall be true, and really worth living; but in proportion as we forget God, we shall play the fool. It is the fool who says in his heart, 'No God,' and it is the fool who lives and acts as if there were no God. In every godly life there is a set time for each event; and there is no need for us to ask, 'Why is the white here and the black there; why this gleam of sunlight and that roar of tempest; why here a marriage and there a funeral; why sometimes a harp and at other times a sackbut?' God knows, and it is a great blessing for us when we can leave it all in His hands."—C. H. S.

Chapter 16

The Lord's Hand behind the Maid's Mistake

SOON after I had begun to preach the Word in the village of Water-beach, I was strongly advised to enter Stepney, now Regent's Park College, to prepare more fully for the ministry.[1] Knowing that solid learning is never an encumbrance, and is often a great means of useful-ness, I felt inclined to avail myself of the opportunity of attaining it: although I hoped that I might be useful without a College training, I consented to the opinion of friends that I should be more useful with it. Dr. Angus, the tutor of the College, visited Cambridge, and it was arranged that we should meet at the house of Mr. Macmillan, the publisher. Thinking and praying over the matter, I entered the house exactly at the time appointed, and was shown into a room where I waited patiently a couple of hours, feeling too much impressed with my own insignificance, and the greatness of the tutor from London, to venture to ring the bell, and make enquiries as to the unreasonably long delay. At last, patience having had her perfect work, and my school-engagements requiring me to attend to my duties as an usher, the bell was set in motion, and on the arrival of the servant, the waiting young man was informed that the Doctor had tarried in another room until he could stay no longer, and had gone off to London by train. The stupid girl had given no information to the family that any-one had called, and had been shown into the drawing-room; and, consequently, the meeting never came about, although designed by both parties. I was not a little disappointed at the moment, but have a thousand times since thanked the Lord very heartily for the strange Providence which forced my steps into another path.

Still holding to the idea of entering the Collegiate Institution, I thought of writing and making an immediate application, but this was not to be. That afternoon, having to preach at one of the village-stations of the Cambridge Lay Preachers' Association, I walked slowly, in a meditative frame of mind, over Midsummer Common to the little wooden bridge which leads to Chesterton, and in the midst of the Common I was startled by what seemed a loud voice, but which

---

[1] At that time the Baptist College at Stepney had existed for just over forty years. Though the surroundings at the time of its establishment in 1810 may have been of a semi-rural kind, they had now all the characteristics of a murky, East-end London parish. In 1856 the College was moved from Stepney and became known as Regent's Park College.—P.

may have been a singular illusion. Whichever it was, the impression was vivid to an intense degree; I seemed very distinctly to hear the words, "Seekest thou great things for thyself? Seek them not!" This led me to look at my position from another point of view, and to challenge my motives and intentions. I remembered the poor but loving people to whom I ministered, and the souls which had been given me in my humble charge; and, although at that time I anticipated obscurity and poverty as the result of the resolve, yet I did there and then solemnly renounce the offer of Collegiate instruction, determining to abide for a season at least with my people, and to remain preaching the Word so long as I had strength to do it. Had it not been for those words, in all probability I had never been where and what I now am. I was conscientious in my obedience to the monition, and I have never seen cause to regret it.

Waiting upon the Lord for direction will never fail to afford us timely intimation of His will, for though the ephod is no more worn by a ministering priest, the Lord still guides His people by His wisdom, and orders all their paths in love; and in times of perplexity, by ways mysterious and remarkable, He makes them to "hear a voice behind them, saying, 'This is the way, walk ye in it.' " Probably, if our hearts were more tender, we might be favoured with more of these sacred monitions; but, alas! instead thereof, we are like the horse and the mule, which have no understanding, and therefore the bit and bridle of affliction take the place of gentler means, else might that happier method be more often used, to which the psalmist alludes when he says, "Thou shalt guide me with Thine eye."

[The following letters give further particulars concerning the proposed College course:

"Cambridge,
Feb. 24, 1852.

My Dear Father,

Mr. Angus, the tutor of Stepney College, preached for us on Sunday, Feb. 1. Being at my own place, I had no opportunity of seeing him, and was very surprised when, on Monday, I was told that he wanted to see me. I assure you, I never mentioned myself to him, nor to anyone—this came quite unexpectedly. I suppose the deacons of our church, hearing of my doings at Waterbeach, had thought right to mention me to him.

Well, I went to the place of meeting, but, by a very singular occurrence, we missed each other; he waited in the parlour, while I was shown into the drawing-room, and the servant forgot to tell him I had come. As he was going to London, and could not wait, he wrote the enclosed."

(On the envelope containing the following letter, there is this note in Spurgeon's handwriting:

"Sent to Mr. Watts because he is my dear friend, and Mr. A. knew he would give it to me. Mr. Watts treats me like a son; he is well qualified to be a father: he will do anything for me, I know."

"College,
Tuesday, Feb. 3, 1852.

Dear Sir,

I am sorry that I missed seeing Mr. Spurgeon yesterday, and now write, through you, in the hope that you will lay this note before him. I cannot, of course, in any way pledge our Committee in the matter, but if, on prayerfully considering the whole case, he apply for admission here, I can assure him of a candid, friendly consideration of his application. There is a great need of hearty, devoted ministers; and to form such, so that they may occupy important posts, and wear well, we need to have them thoroughly furnished, especially with Bible knowledge. I should regret for your friend to settle without thorough preparation. He may be useful in either case, but his usefulness will be very much greater, it will at all events fill a wider sphere, with preparation than without it.

Applications must be sent to us before May, our Session beginning in September; and if Mr. S. think further of it, I shall be glad in due time to hear from him.

Yours truly,
JOSEPH ANGUS."

Mr. Watts,
    Wood Merchant, &c.,
        Cambridge.")

Spurgeon's letter to his father continues:

"I have waited thus long because (1) I wanted to get a little more to tell you; (2) I do not want to appear to desire to go to College at your expense. I do not wish to go until I can pay for it with my own money, or until friends offer to help, because I do not want to burden you. It is said by almost all friends that I ought to go to College. I have no very great desire for it; in fact, none at all. Yet I have made it a matter of prayer, and I trust, yea, I am confident, God will guide me.

Of course, you are my only earthly director and guide in these matters; your judgment always has been best; you must know best. But perhaps you will allow me just to state my own opinion, not because I shall trust in it, but only that you may see my inclination. I think, then (with all deference to you) that I had better not go to College *yet*, at least not just now, for—

1. Whatever advantages are to be derived from such a course of study, I shall be more able to improve when my powers are more developed than they are at present. When I know more, I shall be more able to learn.

2. Providence has thrown me into a great sphere of usefulness— a congregation of often 450, a loving and praying church, and an awakened audience. Many already own that the preaching has been with power from Heaven. Now, ought I to leave them?

3. In a few years' time, I hope to improve my financial position, so as to be at no expense to you, or at least not for all. I should not like to know that you were burdening yourself for me. I should love to work my own way as much as possible. I know you like this feeling.

4. I am not uneducated. I have many opportunities of improvement now; all I want is more time; but even that, Mr. Leeding would give me, if it were so arranged.[1] I have plenty of practice, and do we not learn to preach by preaching? You know what my style is. I fancy it is not very College-like. Let it be never so bad, God has blessed it, and I believe He will yet more. All I do right, He does in me, and the might is of Him. I am now well off; I think as well off as anyone of my age, and I am sure quite as happy. If I were in need, I think the people might be able to raise more for me. Now, shall I throw myself out, and trust to Providence as to whether I shall ever get another place as soon as I leave College?

5. But, no; I have said enough—you are to judge, not I. I leave it to God and yourself, but, still, I should like you to decide in this way. Of course, I have a will, and you now know it, but I say, 'Not mine, but your will, and God's will.'

---

[1] Spurgeon's devotion to study is an important factor in estimating his future influence. His brother's testimony was that "he never did anything else but study. I kept rabbits, chickens, and pigs, and a horse; he kept to books. While I was busy here and there, meddling with anything and everything that a boy could touch, he kept to books, and could not be kept away from study. But, though he had nothing to do with other things, he could have told you all about them because he used to read about everything with a memory as tenacious as a vice and as copious as a barn. . . . He made such progress in his studies that I am sure there were few young men that were his equals and I do not know any that were his superiors."—P.

I have just acknowledged the letter, and said that I could make no reply until I had consulted my friends. I think it might be as well, if you think so, too, to let Mr. Angus know as much as is right of my present position, that he may be favourable toward me at any future time. . . .

I hope you will excuse my scrawl, for, believe me, I am fully employed. Last night, I thought of writing, but was called out to see a dying man, and I thought I dare not refuse. The people at W—— would not like to get even a hint of my leaving them. I do not know why they love me, but they do; it is the Lord's doing.

Give my love and many thanks to dear Mother, Archer, and sisters. If at any time you think a letter from me would be useful, just hint as much, and I will write one. May God keep me, in every place, from every evil, and dwell with you, and abide with you for ever; and with my best love,

I am,

Dear Father,

Your affectionate son,

CHARLES."

*   *   *

Extract from C. H. Spurgeon's letter to his father, March 9th, 1852:

"I have all along had an aversion to College, and nothing but a feeling that I must not consult myself, but Jesus, could have made me think of it. It appears to my friends at Cambridge that it is my duty to remain with my dear people at Waterbeach; so says the church there, unanimously, and so say three of our deacons at Cambridge."

*   *   *

Letter from Deacon King to C. H. Spurgeon's father:

"Waterbeach,

March 20, '52.

Dear Sir,

Having heard, with deep regret, of your intention of placing your son at Stepney College, I write to say that, if you were aware of all the circumstances connected with his ministry at Waterbeach, I think you would defer doing so, at least for a time.

Allow me to say that, since his coming, the congregation is very much increased, the aisles and vestry being often full, and many go away for want of room; there are several cases of his being made useful in awakening the careless; and although we have only known him about five months, the attachment is as strong as if we had been acquainted with him as many years, and if he were to leave us just now, it would be the occasion of general '*Lamentation, Mourning, and Woe.*' Added to which, he has no wish to go, but rather the reverse; and his friends in Cambridge, who previously recommended his going, now hesitate, and feel disposed to alter their opinion. If you, sir, could come over, and see for yourself, you would find that this account is not exaggerated, but perhaps would be ready to exclaim, 'The half was not told me.' That we may be Divinely directed to act as shall be most conducive to the promotion of the Redeemer's glory, in connection with the best interests of those around us, is the sincere and earnest prayer of—

Yours respectfully,

C. KING, on behalf of the Church and Congregation.

P.S.—Our friends are very anxious that Mr. S. should continue with us at least a year. Your acceding to this would cause many devout thanksgivings to God, and we hope would be attended with lasting benefit to many amongst us. A line to this effect would much oblige."

*   *   *

"April 6th, 1852.

My Dear Father,

I am sorry that anything I said in my letter should have grieved you. It was nothing you *said* that made your letter a sad one; it was only my thoughts of leaving the people at 'Beach. I thank you most sincerely for your very kind offer, and also for your assurance that I am at perfect liberty to act as I think it is the will of God I should act. I am sure I never imagined that you would force me—it was only my poor way of expressing myself that caused the blunder—and I do now most affectionately entreat forgiveness of you if I said anything that had a shadow of wrong in it, or if I have thought in any wrong manner. I have desired, all along, to act the part of a dutiful son to an affectionate parent, and if I fail, I feel sure that you and dear Mother will impute it rather to my weakness in act, than to a want of love.

With regard to my decision—I have said so much in my last that more would be unnecessary. I do really think it to be my duty to continue in the place which I now occupy—for a short time at least. I have been assured that never were more tears shed in Waterbeach, at any time, than when I only hinted at leaving. They could not give me stronger tokens of their affection than they *did* give. One prayer went up from all, 'Lord, keep him here!' I am assured by Mr. King that the people have had ministers whom one lot were very pleased with, but there always was a party opposed, but now, though he has a good scope for observation, he has not heard one opinion contrary to me. The Lord gave me favour with the people, and I am so young that they look over many faults; I believe this is one of the facts of the case. The worst is, I am in a dangerous place; the pinnacle is not so safe as the quiet vale. I know you pray that I may be kept humble, and I know I do. Oh, if the clouds pass without rain, how sorrowful I shall feel! When I have been thinking on the many difficulties in preaching the Word, the doctrine of election has been a great comfort to me. I *do* want men to be saved, and it is my consolation that a multitude no man can number are by God's immutable decree ordained to eternal life. So we cannot labour in vain, we must have *some*; the covenant renders that secure.

I shall always be glad of some of your skeletons, for though I do not want them to make me lazy, yet they give some hints when a passage does not open at once. It will be too much trouble for you to write them, but I have no doubt Archer will copy them for me. . . . As to my cash, I have bought a great many books lately, for my constant work requires them, and you know Mr. L. would not have many of the class of books I want. Yet I calculate on having £15 in hand at Midsummer, or by God's blessing, more. I think that (of course, I mean, if God prosper me) I shall be able to save enough to put myself to College, and if not, if I should go, which, as you say, is not very certain, why then friends at Cambridge would help me if I could not manage it. Has —— taken the positive steps yet with regard to joining the church? If not, tell her, *I blush that she should blush to own her Lord*. Do not forget me in earnest prayer. . . . My very best love to my dear Mother. I am sure she can tell all the mothers in the world that parents' prayers are not forgotten. I daresay you think God saved the worst first; if you do not, I do. I believe I have given you more trouble than any of the others, but I did not mean it, and I still believe that I have given you joy, too, and I hope the trouble, though not repaid, will yet be recompensed by a comfort arising from seeing me walk in the truth. Remember me to Emily. . . . The little ones are getting big, I suppose; my love to them, I hope they will be God's daughters.

I remain,
Your affectionate son,
CHARLES."

*   *   *

Part of undated letter from C. H. Spurgeon to his mother; the first portion is missing:

"I need your prayers doubly at this time. I know I shall have them, and I believe I have felt the blessing of them more than once. The Lord visit you both, and bear you up in His everlasting arms! Troubles you have had, but I believe the comforts have always kept you joyful in tribulation; cast down, but not in despair.

Bless the Lord, I must say, for making me His son; 'tis of His own sovereign mercy. Not one good thing has failed. I have felt corruptions rise, and the old man is strong—but grace always comes in just at the critical time, and saves me from myself. The Lord keep me! I have no hope of going on well but by His power. I know that His almighty arm is all-sufficient. Get everyone you can to pray for me; a prayer is more precious than gold, it makes me rich. Lift up your arms, like Moses; there is a great battle both in me and out of me. Jesus intercedes; sweet thought, to one who needs just such a Pleader. Jehovah-Jesus, His people's buckler, is near; an ever-present help in time of trouble, not afar off. We live in Him, He is all around us; who shall destroy His favourites, His darlings? I have had for one of my sermons, John xv. 9: 'As the Father hath loved Me, so have I loved you: continue ye in My love.' Here is (1.) *Love without beginning.* God never began to love Jesus. (2.) *Love without limit.* God loves Jesus with an unbounded love. (3.) *Love without change.* God always loved Jesus alike, equally. (4.) *Love without end.* When will God leave off loving Jesus? Even so does Jesus love you and me.

> 'The weakest saint shall win the day,
> Though death and hell obstruct the way.'

How are all Christian friends? Love to Mr. Langford, and my best respects; tell him I desire a special interest in his prayers. I want to feel 'less than nothing', but this is a very great attainment. Thank Father for his letter; the Lord of hosts prosper his labours abundantly! My very best love to yourself. I hope, if it is right, that your hands are well. Kiss the little ones, and give them my love. May they learn of Jesus! I am glad Archer gets on so well; may your ten thousand prayers for us be answered by Him that heareth prayer! Emily is stronger, I hope; ask her to think whether she loves Jesus with all her heart.

I should very much like to know where Aunt lives. I have asked several times, but I have not learned yet. I do not expect many letters from home. Father is so much engaged, that I wonder I get so many. If you want to know any points in which I am not quite explicit enough, write and ask at any time. My affairs are your affairs. I hope always to do that which you would approve of.

Love to all once more—

From your affectionate son,

CHARLES."

*   *   *

Extract from letter from C. H. Spurgeon to his mother, November, 1852:

"I am more and more glad that I never went to College. God sends such sunshine on my path, such smiles of grace, that I cannot regret if I have forfeited all my prospects for it. I am conscious that I held back from love to God and His cause, and I had *rather be poor in His service than rich in my own*. I have all that heart can wish for; yea, God giveth more than my desire. My congregation is as great and loving as ever. During all the time that I have been at Waterbeach, I have had a different house for my home every Sabbath day. Fifty-two families have thus taken me in, and I have still six other invitations not yet accepted. Talk about the people not caring for me, because they give me so little! I dare tell anybody under heaven 'tis false! They do all they can. Our anniversary passed off grandly: six were baptized; crowds on crowds stood by the river; the chapel was afterwards crammed, both to the tea and the sermon."]

*   *   *

At this anniversary (in 1852) my venerable friend, Cornelius Elven, of Bury St. Edmunds, as a man of mark in that region, was requested to preach, and right well do I remember his hearty compliance with my request. I met him at the station as he alighted from a third-class carriage, which he had selected in order to put the friends to the least possible expense for his travelling. His bulk was stupendous, and one soon saw that his heart was as large as his body. There was a baptismal service in the river in connection with the anniversary, but Mr. Elven said that he could not go into the water with us, for if he got wet through, there were no garments nearer than Bury St. Edmunds that would fit him. He gave me much sage and holy advice during his visit, advice which came to me with much the same weight as Paul's words came to Timothy.[1] He bade me study hard, and mind and keep abreast

[1] Elven delighted to tell the story of this visit. In his Diary, that evening, he wrote: "Have preached to-day at Waterbeach for C. H. Spurgeon. He is a rising star. He will one day make his mark upon the denomination." Mr. Elven used to say:—"That day, I preached for Mr. Spurgeon, and he gave out the hymns for me; I should be very glad to give out the hymns for him if he would preach for me." This service Spurgeon very cheerfully rendered to Mr. Elven at Bury St. Edmunds on more than one occasion.

of the foremost Christians in our little church; "for," said he, "if these men, either in their knowledge of Scripture, or their power to edify the people, once outstrip you, the temptation will arise among them to be dissatisfied with your ministry; and, however good they are, they will feel their superiority, and others will perceive it, too, and then your place in the church will become very difficult to hold." I felt the common sense of the observation, and the spur was useful. The sermons of the day were very homely in style, and pre-eminently practical. I remember his reading the narrative of Naaman the Syrian, and his pithy comments thereon. He seemed to have taken Matthew Henry for his model, and in the course of one of the services he gave us Henry's inimitable description of the Father receiving the prodigal, which occurs in the commentator's exposition of Luke xv. With a voice deep-toned and graciously tender, he said: " 'When he was yet a great way off, his father saw him'—here were *eyes of mercy*; 'and had compassion'—here were *bowels of mercy*; 'and ran'—here were *feet of mercy*; 'and fell on his neck'—here were *arms of mercy*; 'and kissed him'—here were *lips of mercy*;—it was all mercy!" But one thing above all others fixed itself upon my memory, and when I heard of the good man's departure, it came before me with great vividness; he told me anecdotes of the usefulness of addressing individuals one by one about their souls, and urged the duty upon me with great earnestness, quoting again and again from the life of a certain Harlan Page. Being busy with a thousand matters, I had never looked up the biography which he so strongly recommended, but my first thought, when I learned of his death, was, Harlan Page. Cornelius Elven completed an honourable ministry of fifty years in his native town, and passed away amid the respectful regrets of all the inhabitants, and the deep affection of his church. He was a man of large and loving heart, with a vivacious mind, and interesting manner of utterance. He was not only the friend of my youth, but he also preached for me in London in after days. He used, with a merry laugh, to tell the story of a lady who came to hear me at New Park Street, but putting her head inside the door, and seeing the vast form of Cornelius Elven, she retreated, exclaiming, "No, no; the man has too much of the flesh about him, I cannot hear him." It was a very unjust judgment, for the dear man's great bulk was a sore affliction to him. Peace to his memory! I weave no fading wreath for his tomb, but I catch the gleaming of that immortal crown which the Master has placed upon his brow. He was a good man, full of faith and of the Holy Ghost.

*   *   *

[Professor Everett—see page 39—has preserved the following reminiscence of this period:

"In or about 1852, I was occupying a post in a high-class school—Mr. Thorowgood's, at Totteridge, near London—and there being a vacancy for another assistant, I wrote, with Mr. Thorowgood's approval, to my old friend Spurgeon, proposing that he should come and fill it. He asked for a few days to decide definitely, and then wrote declining, chiefly on the ground that he was unwilling to renounce the evangelistic work which he combined with the position he then held. He stated, then, or in a subsequent letter, that he had preached more than three hundred times in the previous twelve months, and that the chapel at Waterbeach was not only full, but crowded with outside listeners at the open windows."]

"The village of Waterbeach should not be unknown to fame, for the records of the Baptist Church prove that Rowland Hill first exercised in Waterbeach his gifts as a minister of Jesus, after riding over from Cambridge by stealth between the hours of College duty. The house still stands in which he is said to have commenced his labours as a preacher. Long before that time, the sainted Francis Holcroft, the apostle of Cambridgeshire, ejected by the Act of Uniformity from his living at Bassingbourne, had founded a church in this village, as in many others around. When confined in Cambridge Castle for the truth's sake, he obtained favour in the eyes of his jailer, who allowed him by night to visit Waterbeach, where he preached and administered the ordinances of the Lord to his little band of followers, returning always before morning light awoke his slumbering foes."— C. H. S.

Chapter 17

Reminiscences as a Village Pastor

WHEN I became Pastor at Waterbeach, the people could do very little for my support, and therefore I was an usher in a school at Cambridge at the same time. After a while, I was obliged to give up the latter occupation, and was thrown on the generosity of the people. They gave me a salary of £45 a year, but as I had to pay 12s. a week for two rooms which I occupied, my income was not sufficient to support me, but the people, though they had not money, had produce, and I do not think there was a pig killed by any one of the congregation without my having some portion of it, and one or other of them, when coming to the market at Cambridge, would bring me bread, so that I had enough bread and meat to pay my rent with, and I often paid my landlady in that fashion.

There was one old man at Waterbeach who was a great miser. On one of my visits to the place, after I had removed to London, I heard that, in his last illness, he had a bed made up in the sitting-room downstairs, and ordered his grave to be dug just outside the window, so as to reduce the cost of his funeral as much as possible. One of the friends who was talking about him said, "He was never known to give anything to anybody." "Well," I replied, "I know better than that, for, one Sunday afternoon, he gave me three half-crowns; and as I was wanting a new hat at the time, I got it with the money." "Well," rejoined the friend, "I am quite sure he never forgave himself for such extravagance as that, and that he must have wanted his three half-crowns back again." "Ah, but!" I answered, "you have not heard the whole of the story yet, for, the following Sunday, the old man came to me again, and asked me to pray for him that he might be saved from the sin of covetousness, 'for,' said he, 'the Lord told me to give you half-a-sovereign, but I kept back half-a-crown, and I can't rest of a night for thinking of it.'"

[Dr. D. A. Doudney, describing an interview with Spurgeon at "Westwood", wrote in *The Gospel Magazine* for March, 1892: "Among other subjects brought up was that of Dr. Gill's *Commentary*. I was asked by Mr. Spurgeon how it was that I was led to reproduce it. Its truthful character was urged as a reason, as well as its great price putting it beyond the power of ministers in general to possess it. My own copy—simply bound in plain canvas boards—had cost me

£6 10s. Moreover, I was anxious to set up an Industrial School, and thus find occupation for the youths of the parish. 'In what volume,' asked Mr. Spurgeon, 'did the names of the subscribers appear?' I could not recollect, but, withdrawing for a moment to his study, he quickly reappeared with the fourth volume of the Old Testament—the last issued upon the completion of the work—and, pointing to his own name, said, 'You published it in half-crown parts, or else I could not have taken it in.' Here was a fair specimen of Mr. Spurgeon's character—his proverbial simplicity and honesty. How few, in like manner, amid such surroundings, and having attained, as he had, to such a name, and such a popularity, would have made that frank statement, 'You published it in half-crown parts, or I could not have taken it in.' "

The following inscriptions, in Spurgeon's handwriting, are in his set of volumes of Dr. Gill's *Commentary*:

In Vol. I.—"I subscribed for this, and took the monthly parts.
          C. H. SPURGEON, 1852.
   To this Author's Pulpit I was permitted to succeed in 1854.
           C. H. SPURGEON."

In Vol. V.—"I subscribed for these vols. of Gill in monthly parts, and had them bound. December, 1852.
         C. H. SPURGEON,
          living in Cambridge,
       Baptist Minister of Waterbeach.
  In April, 1854, unanimously elected Pastor of the same Church, which once met in Carter Lane, under Dr. Gill, and then Dr. Rippon—now New Park Street, Southwark.
  In the year 1861, this Church migrated to the Metropolitan Tabernacle, Newington Butts, having far outgrown the space of New Park Street Chapel."

In Vol. VI.—"Many sneer at Gill, but he is not to be dispensed with. In some respects, he has no superior. He is always well worth consulting.
         C. H. S. 1886."

In Vol. IV, as stated by Dr. Doudney, Spurgeon's name appears in the list of subscribers to the work:
   "Spurgeon, C., Union Road, Cambridge."]

     *   *   *

Of late years, I have heard a great deal against deacons, and have read discussions as to their office, evidently suggested by no idolatrous reverence for their persons. Many of my brethren in the ministry bitterly rate them, others tremble at the mention of their very name, and a few put on their armour, and prepare to do battle with them wherever they go, as if they were the dragons of ministerial life. I have been accused of saying that "a deacon is worse than a devil, for if you resist the devil, he will flee from you, but if you resist a deacon, he will fly at you." This is no saying of mine; I never had any cause to speak so severely, and although, in some cases, it may be true, I have never had any experimental proof that it is so. Not one in a hundred of the sayings that are fathered upon me are mine at all; and as to this one, it was in vogue before I was born. I pardon the man who preached from James i. 6 before that drunken Solomon, James I of England and VI of Scotland—the temptation was too great to be resisted; but let the wretch be for ever execrated, if such a man really lived, who celebrated the decease of a deacon by a tirade from the words, "It came to pass that the beggar died." I forgive the liar who attributed such an outrage to me, but I hope he will not try his infamous arts upon anyone else.

My observation of deacons leads me to say that, as a rule, they are quite as good men as the pastors, and the bad and good in the ministry and the diaconate are to be found in very much the same proportions. If there be lordly deacons, are there not lordly pastors? If there be ignorant, crotchety men among deacons, are there not their rivals in our pulpits? The Church owes an immeasurable debt of gratitude to those thousands of godly men who study her interests day and night, contribute largely of their substance, care for her poor, cheer her ministers, and in times of trouble as well as prosperity, remain faithfully at their posts. Whatever there may be here and there of mistake, infirmity, and even wrong, I am sure, from wide and close observation, that the most of our deacons are an honour to our faith, and we may style them, as the apostle did his brethren, "the glory of Christ". The deacons of my first village pastorate were in my esteem the excellent of the earth, in whom I took great delight. Hard-working men on the week-day, they spared no toil for their Lord on the Sabbath; I loved them sincerely, and do love them still. In my opinion, they were as nearly the perfection of deacons of a country church as the kingdom could afford.

Yet, good as my deacons were, they were not perfect in all respects. I proposed to them, on one occasion, that I should preach on the Sunday evening by the river side, and the remark was made by one of them, "Ah! I do not like it, it is imitating the Methodists." To him, as a sound Calvinist, it was a dreadful thing to do anything which Methodists were guilty of; to me, however, that was rather a recommendation than otherwise, and I was happy to run the risk of being Methodistical. All over England, in our cities, towns, villages, and hamlets, there are tens of thousands who never will hear the gospel while open-air preaching is neglected. I rejoice that God *allows* us to preach in churches and chapels, but I do not pretend that we have any apostolical precedent for it, certainly none for confining our ministry to such places. I believe that we are permitted, if it promotes order and edification, to set apart buildings for our worship, but there is no warrant for calling these places sanctuaries and houses of God, for all places are alike holy where holy men assemble. It is altogether a mischievous thing that we should confine our preaching within walls. Our Lord, it is true, preached in the synagogues, but He often spake on the mountain side, or from a boat, or in the court of a house, or in the public thoroughfares. To Him, an audience was the only necessity. He was a Fisher of souls of the true sort, and not like those who sit still in their houses, and expect the fish to come to them to be caught. Did our Lord intend a minister to go on preaching from his pulpit to empty pews, when, by standing on a chair or a table outside the meeting-house, he might be heard by hundreds? I believe not, and I held the same opinion at the very beginning of my ministry, so I preached by the river side, even though my good deacon thought that, by so doing, I was imitating the Methodists.

Another of those worthy brethren, a dear old Christian man, said to me, one day, when I was at his house to dinner, "My dear sir, I wish you would not preach those *invitation sermons*. You are too general in your appeals; you seem to press the people so much to come to Christ. I do not like it; for it is not at all consistent with my doctrinal views." "Well," I replied, "what would you have me preach?" "Well, sir," he said, "though I don't like such preaching, yet it is evident that the Lord does, for my son-in-law was converted to God under one of those sermons, and when I came home, the other Sunday, so angry with you for being such a Fullerite, there was my daughter crying fit to break her heart; so," he added, "don't you take any notice of an old man like me. As long as God blesses you, you go on in your own way." I said to him, "But, my dear brother, don't you think, if God approves of this kind of preaching, that you ought to like it, too?" "Well," he answered, "perhaps I ought; but I am an old man, and I have always been brought up in those views. I am afraid I shall not get out of them, but don't you take the slightest notice of what I say." That was exactly what I had determined in my own mind that I would do, so we agreed after all.

One of my Waterbeach deacons was named King. He was a very methodical man, and kept the accounts and the church-books in admirable order. He was a calm, thoughtful, judicious brother, but he had a full proportion of zeal and warmth. His wife was made to match, and the pair were second to none in the village for grace and wisdom. Mr. King was a miller, and in his cottage by the mill I have often spent a happy night, and have met his excellent son, who was then the Pastor of the Baptist Church in Aldreth, Cambridgeshire. I remember our hearty laugh at the junior King, for borrowing a horse to ride to a preaching engagement, and then appearing at the place *leading the horse*, having only ridden him a very little way, and walked with him all the rest of the road because he seemed skittish. The elder Mr. King once gave me a kindly hint in a very delicate manner. He did not tell me that I should speak more guardedly in the pulpit, but when I left his house, one Monday morning, I found a pin in my Bible, stuck through Titus ii. 8: "Sound speech, that cannot be condemned; that he that is of the contrary part may be ashamed, having no evil thing to say of you." Nothing could have been in better taste. The wise rebuke was well deserved and lovingly taken. It was so deftly given that its value was thereby increased indefinitely. Mr. King was a deacon of deacons to me, and to the Waterbeach Church, and his son was worthy of such a father.

On one occasion, there had been a meeting to raise money for home-mission work; the collection had just been made, and the deacons had brought all the plates to the table-pew, when an old gentleman entered. He could not help being late at the meeting, though his heart was there all the time. His feet would have carried him down to the chapel two hours before, only duty forbade. As soon, however, as he had concluded his business, off he walked, saying to himself, "I'm afraid I shall be too late, but I shall at least hear how they have got on. The Lord grant a blessing on the meeting, and on the good work in hand!" It was Father Sewell—an Israelite indeed—the very image of Old Mr. Honest in Bunyan's *Pilgrim's Progress*. As soon as I caught sight of my aged friend, I said, "Our brother who has just come in will, I am sure, close the meeting by offering prayer for God's blessing on the proceedings of this evening." He stood up, but he did not pray. He did not shut his eyes, but, on the contrary, he seemed to be looking for something. He did not clasp his hands, but put them into his pockets, and fumbled there with much perseverance. "I am afraid,"

I said, "that my brother did not understand me. Friend Sewell, I did not ask you to *give*, but to *pray*." "Ay, ay!" replied the straightforward, bluff old saint, "but I could not pray till I had given; it would be hypocrisy to ask a blessing on that which I did not think worth giving to." There was not the least ostentation in the good man; it was his honest heart pouring out its true feelings, and, odd as his behaviour seemed, his conduct preached the whole congregation such a sermon as they would not readily forget.

*   *   *

In my first pastorate, I had often to battle with Antinomians—that is, people who held that, because they believed themselves to be elect, they might live as they liked. I hope that heresy has to a great extent died out, but it was sadly prevalent in my early ministerial days. I knew one man, who stood on the table of a public-house, and held a glass of gin in his hand, declaring all the while that he was one of the chosen people of God. They kicked him out of the public-house, and when I heard of it, I felt that it served him right. Even those ungodly men said that they did not want any such "elect" people there. There is no one who can live in sin—drinking, swearing, lying, and so on— who can truly declare that he is one of the Lord's chosen people. I recollect one such man—and he was a very bad fellow—yet he had the hardihood to say, "I know that I am one of God's dear people." "So you are," said I; "dear at any price, either to be given or thrown away!" He did not like my plain speaking, but it was true, for that was the only sense in which he was one of God's dear people. From my very soul, I detest everything that in the least savours of the Antinomianism which leads people to prate about being secure in Christ while they are living in sin. We cannot be saved *by* or *for* our good works, neither can we be saved *without* good works. Christ never will save any of His people *in* their sins; He saves His people *from* their sins. If a man is not desiring to live a holy life in the sight of God, with the help of the Holy Spirit, he is still "in the gall of bitterness, and in the bond of iniquity". I used to know a man of this class, who talked a great deal about "*saving faith*". He was notorious for his evil life, so I could not make out what he meant by saving faith, until the collection was taken, and I noticed how carefully he put his finger-nail round a threepenny piece for fear lest it should be a fourpenny; then I understood his meaning. But the idea of "saving faith" apart from good works, is ridiculous. The saved man is not a perfect man, but his heart's desire is to become perfect, he is always panting after perfection, and the day will come when he will be perfected, after the image of his once crucified and now glorified Saviour, in knowledge and true holiness.

While I was minister at Waterbeach, I used to have a man sitting in front of the gallery, who would always nod his head when I was preaching what he considered sound doctrine, although he was about as bad an old hypocrite as ever lived. When I talked about justification, down went his head; when I preached about imputed righteousness, down it went again. I was a dear good man in his estimation, without doubt. So I thought I would cure him of nodding, or at least make his head keep still for once; so I remarked, "There is a great deal of difference between God electing you, and your electing yourself; a vast deal of difference between God justifying you by His Spirit, and your justifying yourself by a false belief, or presumption; this is the difference," said I—and the old man at once put me down as a rank Arminian—"you who have elected yourselves, and justified yourselves, have no marks of the Spirit of God; you have no evidence of genuine piety, you are not holy men and women, you can live in sin, you can walk as sinners walk, you have the image of the devil upon you, and yet you call yourselves the children of God. One of the first evidences that anyone is a child of God is that he hates sin with a perfect hatred, and seeks to live a holy, Christlike life." The old Antinomian did not approve of that doctrine, but I knew that I was preaching what was revealed in the Word of God.

There was another man of that sort who at one time frequently walked out with me into the villages where I was going to preach. I was glad of his company till I found out certain facts as to his manner of life, and then I shook him off, and I believe he hooked himself on to somebody else, for he must needs be gadding abroad every evening of the week. He had many children, and they grew up to be wicked men and women, and the reason was, that the father, while he was constantly busy at this meeting and that, never tried to bring his own boys and girls to the Saviour. He said to me, one day, "I never laid my hand upon my children;" so I answered, "Then I think it is very likely that God will lay His hand upon you." "Oh!" he said, "I have not even spoken sharply to them." "Then," I replied, "it is highly probable that God will speak very sharply to you, for it is not His will that parents should leave their children unrestrained in their sin."

I knew another man, in those early days, who used to travel a long distance every Sabbath to hear what he called "the truth". Neither his wife nor any of his children went to any place of worship, and when I talked to him very seriously about them, he told me that "the Lord would save His own"; to which I could not help replying that the Lord would not "own" him. He demanded my authority for that statement, so I gave him this proof-text, "If any provide not for his own, and specially for those of his own house, he hath denied the faith, and is worse than an infidel." One of his companions said to me, one day, that he knew how many children of God there were in the parish where he lived; there were exactly *five*. I was curious to learn their names, so I asked him who the five were, and much to my amusement he began by saying, "There is *myself*." I stopped him at this point, with the query whether he was quite sure about the *first* one. Since then, his character has gone I know not where, but certainly he will get on better without it than with it; yet he was the first on his own list, and a few others of the same black sort made up the five. There were, in the other places of worship to which he did not go, men, whose characters for integrity and uprightness, ay, and for spirituality and prayerfulness, would have been degraded by being put into comparison with his; yet *he* set himself up as judge in Israel, and pretended to know exactly how many people of God were in the village. "The Lord knoweth them that are His." I bless God that I have learned to have very little respect for the vision of *the man* with the measuring line. When I see an angel with it, I am glad enough, but when I see *a man* with it, I tell him that he must give me a warrant from God, and show me how he is to know the elect by any other method than that laid down by our Lord Jesus Christ: "By their fruits shall ye know them."

*　　　*　　　*

I have sometimes been greatly obliged to a wicked world for what it has done to inconsistent professors of religion. While I was Pastor at Waterbeach, a certain young man joined the church. We thought he was a changed character, but there used to be in the village, once a year, a great temptation in the form of a feast; and when the feast came round, this foolish fellow was there in very evil company. He was in the long room of a public-house, in the evening, and when I heard what happened, I really felt intense gratitude to the landlady of that place. When she came in, and saw him there, she said, "Halloa, Jack So-and-so, are *you* here? Why, you are one of Spurgeon's lot, yet you are here; you ought to be ashamed of yourself. This is not fit company for you. Put him out of the window, boys." And they did put him out of the window on the Friday night, and we put him out of the door on the Sunday, for we removed his name from our church-book. Where was he to go to? The world would not have him, and the church would not have him; if he had been all for the world, the world would have made something of him; and if he had been all for Christ, Christ would have made something of him. But as he tried to be a little for each, and so nothing to either, his life became a wretched one; as he walked the streets, people pointed at him with scorn. The Christians turned away, thinking him a hypocrite, as I fear he was; and the worldlings called him one, and made his name a by-word and a proverb.

In those early days, I had sometimes to contend with the Antinominian preachers as well as with their people. I once found myself in the midst of a company of ministers and friends, who were disputing whether it was a sin in men that they did not believe the gospel. Whilst they were discussing, I said, "Gentlemen, am I in the presence of Christians? Are you believers in the Bible, or are you not?" They said, "We are Christians, of course." "Then," said I, "does not the Scripture say, 'of sin, because they believe not on Me?' And is it not the damning sin of men, that they do not believe on Christ?" I should not have imagined, if I had not myself heard them, that any persons would be so wicked as to venture to assert that "it is no sin for a sinner not to believe on Christ". I should have thought that, however far they might wish to push their sentiments, they would not tell a lie to uphold the truth, and, in my opinion, this is what such men really do. Truth is a strong tower, and never requires to be buttressed with error. God's Word will stand against all man's devices. I would never invent a sophism to prove that it is no sin on the part of the ungodly not to believe, for I am sure it is. When I am taught in the Scriptures that "this is the condemnation, that light is come into the world, and men loved darkness rather than light", and when I read, "He that believeth not is condemned already, because he hath not believed in the name of the only begotten Son of God," I affirm, and the Word declares it, *unbelief is a sin.* Surely, with rational and unprejudiced persons, it cannot require any reasoning to prove it. Is it not a sin for a creature to doubt the Word of its Maker? Is it not a crime and an insult to the Deity, for me, an atom, a particle of dust, to dare to deny His Words? Is it not the very summit of arrogance and the height of pride for a son of Adam to say, even in his heart, "God, I doubt Thy grace; God, I doubt Thy love; God, I doubt Thy power"? I feel that, could we roll all sins into one mass—could we take murder, blasphemy, lust, adultery, fornication, and everything that is vile, and unite them all into one vast globe of black corruption—they would not even then equal the sin of unbelief. This is the monarch sin, the quintessence of guilt, the mixture of the venom of all crimes the dregs of the wine of Gomorrah; it is the A1 sin, the masterpiece of Satan, the chief work of the devil. Unbelief hardened the heart of Pharaoh—it gave licence to the tongue of blaspheming Rabshakeh—yea, it became a deicide, and murdered the Lord Jesus Christ. Unbelief! it has mixed many a cup of poison; it has brought thousands to the gallows, and many to a shameful grave, who have murdered themselves, and rushed with bloody hands before their Creator's tribunal, because of unbelief. Give me an unbeliever—let me know that he doubts God's Word—let me know that he distrusts His promise and His threatening; and with that for a premise, I will conclude that the man shall, by-and-by, unless there is amazing restraining power exerted upon him, be guilty of the foulest and blackest crimes. Unbelief is a Beelzebub sin; like Beelzebub, it is the leader of all evil spirits. It is said of Jeroboam that he sinned, and made Israel to sin; and it may be said of unbelief that it not only itself sins, but it makes others sin; it is the egg of all crime, the seed of every offence; in fact, everything that is evil and vile lies couched in that one word—unbelief.

*   *   *

In striking contrast to those apologists for sin, I met in my first pastorate, as I have often done since, a number of persons who professed to be perfect, and who said that they had lived so many months or years without sinning against God. One man, who told me that he was perfect, was hump-backed, and when I remarked that I thought, if he were a perfect man, he ought to have a perfect body, he became so angry that I said to him, "Well, my friend, if *you* are perfect, there are a great many more as near perfection as you are." "Oh!" he exclaimed, "I shall feel it for having been betrayed into anger." He said that he had not been angry for many years; I had brought him back to his old state of infirmity, and painful as it might be for him, I have no doubt that it did him good to see himself as he really was. When a man thinks that he is a full-grown Christian, he reminds me of a poor boy whom I used to see. He had such a splendid head for his body that he had often to lay it on a pillow, for it was too weighty for his shoulders to carry, and his mother told me that, when he tried to stand up, he often tumbled down, overbalanced by his heavy head. There are some people who appear to grow very fast, but they have water on the brain, and are out of due proportion, but he who truly grows in grace does not say, "Dear me! I can feel that I am growing; bless the Lord! Let's sing a hymn, 'I'm a growing! I'm a growing!' " I have often felt that I was growing smaller; I think that is very probable, and a good thing, too. If we are very great in our own estimation, it is because we have a number of cancers, or foul gatherings, that need to be lanced, so as to let out the bad matter that causes us to boast of our bigness.

Our Wesleyan brethren have a notion that they are going to be perfect here on earth. I should be very glad to see them when they are perfect, and if any of them happen to be in the position of servants, wanting situations, I would be happy to give them any amount of wages I could spare, for I should feel myself highly honoured and greatly blessed in having perfect servants; and what is more, if any of them are masters, and need servants, I would undertake to come and serve them without any wages at all if I could but find a perfect master. I have had one perfect Master ever since I first knew the Lord, and if I could be sure that there is another perfect master, I should be greatly pleased to have him as an under-master, while the great Supreme must ever be chief of all. One man, who said he was perfect, called upon me once, and asked me to go and see him, for I should receive valuable instruction from him if I did. I said, "I have no doubt it would be so, but I should not like to go to your house, I think I should hardly be able to get into one of your rooms." "How is that?" he enquired. "Well," I replied, "I suppose that your house would be so full of angels that there would be no room for me." He did not like that remark; and when I made one or two other playful observations, he went into a towering rage. "Well, friend," I said to him, "I think, after all, I am as perfect as you are; but do *perfect men* ever get angry?" He denied that he was angry, although there was a peculiar redness about his cheeks, and a fiery flash in his eyes, that is very common to persons when they are in a passion. At any rate, I think I rather spoiled his perfection, for he evidently went home much less satisfied with himself than when he came out.

My own experience is a daily struggle with the evil within. I wish I could find in myself something friendly to grace, but, hitherto, I have searched my nature through, and have found everything in rebellion against God. At one time, there comes the torpor of sloth, when one ought to be active every moment, having so much to do for God, and for the souls of men, and so little time in which to do it. At another time, there comes the quickness of passion; when one should be calm and cool, and play the Christian, bearing with patience whatever has to be endured, there come the unadvised word and the rash expression. Anon, I am troubled with conceit, the devilish whisper—I can call it no less—"How well thou hast done! How nobly thou hast played thy part!" Then crawls out distrust—foul and faithless—suggesting that God does not regard the affairs of men, and will not interpose on my

behalf. Yet, what would I not give if I might but be perfect! Sometimes, I think that, if God's people mentioned in the Old and New
Testaments had all been perfect, I should have despaired, but, because
they seem to have had just the kind of faults I grieve over in myself,
I do not feel any more lenient toward my faults, but I do rejoice that
I also may say with each of them, "The Lord will *perfect* that which
concerneth me." He will most assuredly, beyond a doubt, bring to
perfection my faith, my love, my hope, and every grace. He will
perfect His own purposes; He will perfect His promises, He will
perfect my body, and perfect my soul. While I am fully persuaded that
perfection is absolutely impossible to any man beneath the sky, I feel
equally sure that, to every believer, future perfection is certain
beyond a doubt. The day shall come when the Lord shall not only
make us better, but shall make us perfectly pure and holy; when He
shall not merely subdue our lusts, but when He shall cast the demons
out altogether; when He shall make us holy, and unblameable, and
unreproveable in His sight. That day, however, I believe, shall not
come until we enter into the joy of our Lord, and are glorified
together with Christ in Heaven. Then, but not till then, shall He
present us "*faultless* before the presence of His glory with exceeding
joy".

*   *   *

While I was going about the Cambridgeshire villages, preaching
and visiting, it often saddened me to see, especially in the houses of
the poor, Roman Catholic pictures hanging on the walls—I suppose,
because they happened to be rather pretty, and very cheap. Popish
publishers have very cleverly managed to get up pictures of the Virgin
Mary, and the lying fable of her assumption to Heaven, and all sorts
of legends of saints and saintesses; and being brightly coloured, and
sold at a low price, these vile productions have been introduced into
thousands of houses. I have seen, to my horror, a picture of God the
Father represented as an old man—a conception almost too hideous
to mention—yet the picture is hung up in the cottages of England;
whereas the Lord has expressly commanded us not to make any likeness or image of Him, or to try to represent His appearance in any
way, and any attempt to do so is disobedient and even blasphemous.

It was grievous also to find what gross ignorance prevailed among
many of the villagers concerning the way of salvation. They seemed,
somehow, to have got into their heads the notion that they could not
be saved because they could not read, and did not know much.
Frequently, when I asked anything about personal salvation, I

received the answer, "Oh, sir, I never had any learning!" and that was supposed to be a sufficient excuse for not having repented of sin, and trusted in the Saviour. Yet the unlearned need not stay away from Christ. It was said of an old Greek philosopher, that he wrote over his door, "None but the learned may enter here;" but Christ, on the contrary, writes over His door, "He that is simple, let him turn in hither." I can testify that great numbers of those humble country folk accepted the Saviour's invitation, and it was delightful to see what a firm grip they afterwards had of the verities of the faith; many of them became perfect masters in divinity. I used to think, sometimes, that if they had degrees who deserved them, diplomas would often be transferred, and given to those who hold the plough-handle or work at the carpenter's bench, for there is often more divinity in the little finger of a ploughman than there is in the whole body of some of our modern divines. "Don't they understand divinity?" someone asks. Yes, in the letter of it, but as to the spirit and life of it, D.D. often means DOUBLY DESTITUTE.

An incident that I once witnessed at Waterbeach furnished me with an illustration concerning death. A company of villagers, the younger branches of a family, were about to emigrate to another land. The aged mother, who had not for some years left her cottage fireside, came to the railway-station from which they must start. I stood among the sorrowful group as their friend and minister. I think I see the many embraces which the fond mother gave to her son and daughter, and her little grandchildren; I can picture them folding their arms about her aged neck, and then saying farewell to all the friends in the village who had come to bid them adieu. A shrill sound is heard; it sends a pang through all hearts, as if it were the messenger of death to her who is about to lose the props of her household. In great haste, at the small village station, the passengers are hurried to their seats; they thrust their heads out of the carriage window; the aged parent stands on the very edge of the platform that she may take her last look at them. There is a whistle from the engine, and away goes the train. In an instant, the poor woman, jumping from the platform, rushes along the railway, with all her might crying, "My children! My children! My children! They are gone, and I shall never see them again." The illustration may not be classical; but, nevertheless, I have been reminded of it by many a death, when I have seen the godly suddenly snatched away. They have gone from us, swiftly as the wind itself could bear them, or as the hasty waves of the sea could bury them out of our sight. It is our affliction and trouble that we must remain behind and weep, for they are gone beyond recall; yet there is something pleasant in the picture. It is but a departure—they are not destroyed; they are not blown to atoms; they are not taken away to prison—'tis but a departure from one place to another. They still live; they still are blessed. While we weep, they are rejoicing; while we mourn, they are singing psalms of praise; and, by-and-by, in God's good time, we shall meet them again, to be parted no more for ever.

        *   *   *

There was an amusing incident in my early Waterbeach ministry which I have never forgotten. One day, a gentleman, who was then mayor of Cambridge, and who had more than once tried to correct my youthful mistakes, asked me if I really had told my congregation that, if a thief got into Heaven, he would begin picking the angels' pockets. "Yes, sir," I replied, "I told them that, if it were possible for an ungodly man to go to Heaven without having his nature changed, he would be none the better for being there; and then, by way of illustration, I said that, were a thief to get in among the glorified, he would remain a thief still, and he would go round the place picking the angels' pockets!" "But, my dear young friend," asked Mr. Brimley, very seriously, "don't you know that the angels haven't any pockets?" "No, sir," I replied, with equal gravity, "I did not know that, but I am glad to be assured of the fact from a gentleman who does know. I will take care to put it all right the first opportunity I get." The following Monday morning, I walked into Mr. Brimley's shop, and said to him, "I set that matter right yesterday, sir," "What matter?" he enquired. "Why, about the angels' pockets!" "What *did* you say?" he asked, in a tone almost of despair at what he might hear next. "Oh, sir, I just told the people I was sorry to say that I had made a mistake the last time I preached to them; but that I had met a gentleman—the mayor of Cambridge—who had assured me that the angels had no pockets, so I must correct what I had said, as I did not want anybody to go away with a false notion about Heaven. I would therefore say that, if a thief got among the angels without having his nature changed, he would try to steal the feathers out of their wings!" "Surely, you did not say that?" said Mr. Brimley. "I did, though," I replied. "Then," he exclaimed, "I'll never try to set you right again," which was just exactly what I wanted him to say.

Once, while I was at Waterbeach, I had a sleepy congregation. It was on a Sabbath afternoon—those afternoon services in our English villages are usually a doleful waste of effort. Roast beef and pudding lie heavy on the hearers' souls, and the preacher himself is deadened in his mental processes while digestion claims the mastery of the hour. The people had been eating too much dinner, so they came to chapel heavy and dull and, before long many of them were nodding. So I tried an old expedient to rouse them. I shouted with all my might, "Fire! Fire! Fire!" When, starting from their seats, some of my hearers asked where it was, I answered, as other preachers had done in similar circumstances, "In hell, for sinners who will not accept the Saviour."

"Let every man, called of God to preach the Word, be as his Maker has fashioned him. Neither Paul, nor Apollos, nor Cephas is to be imitated by John; nor are John's ways, habits, and modes of utterance to be the basis for a condemnation of any one or all of the other three. As God gives to every seed its own body as it rises from the soil, so to each man will He grant his own appropriate development, if he will but be content to let his inner self reveal itself in its true form. The good and the evil in men of eminence are both of them mischievous when they become objects of servile imitation; the good when slavishly copied is exaggerated into formality, and the evil becomes wholly intolerable. If each teacher of others went himself to the school of our one only Master, a thousand errors might be avoided."—C. H. S.

Chapter 18

Memorable Services away from Waterbeach

AFTER I had been preaching at Waterbeach for about a year or so, I was invited to conduct anniversary and other special services in various places. On several occasions I had very curious experiences. One eccentric individual whose acquaintance I made in those early days, was Potto Brown, "the miller of Houghton". He asked me over to preach in his chapel, and from Saturday night to Monday morning I had the felicitous misery of being his guest—I can use no other term to describe the strange mixture of emotions that I felt while under his roof. Nothing of special interest occurred the first night, but when I came downstairs the following morning, Mr. Brown said to me, "We always provide two eggs for the minister's breakfast on Sunday morning; the phosphorus in them feeds the brain, and it looks as though you will need plenty of mental nourishment to-day." I made no reply to this remark, thinking it was better to bide my time, and when I did open fire, to give him such a broadside as he did not expect. There were three services during the day; Mr. Brown preached in the morning, a neighbouring minister in the afternoon, and myself at night. After we had returned to my host's house, and had taken supper, the good man leaned back in his easy chair, with his eyes closed and the fingertips of each hand touching, and began to soliloquize aloud: "O Lord, we thank Thee for a good day all through! In the morning, Lord, Thy unworthy servant was privileged to speak in Thy name—with some degree of liberty, and he hopes also with some measure of acceptance to the people. In the afternoon, a worthy brother preached a good, sound, solid, gospel sermon—nothing very brilliant; but, still, likely to be useful. In the evening, Lord, we had a regular steam-engine—ran over everything and everybody." Then, opening his eyes, and looking across at me, he began a dialogue which, as nearly as I can recollect it, ran as follows:

Brown.—Young man, whoever persuaded you that you could preach?

Spurgeon.—I believe, sir, that the Lord called me to this work, and I have found a good many people who are of the same opinion.

B.—How long have you been a minister?

S.—A little more than twelve months.

B.—How many souls did you save, last year?

S.—None, sir.

B.—None? You have been a minister twelve months, and yet there have been no souls saved. You ought to be ashamed to confess it; though, if you have preached the same doctrines as you gave us to-night, I am not surprised to hear that no souls have been saved.

S.—I did not say that souls had not been saved; I said that I did not save any. I am happy to know that the Lord *has* saved some through my instrumentality.

B.—Most of your brethren would have said, "*humble* instrumentality", when, all the while, they were as proud as Lucifer. But that is only the common ministerial cant; you knew well enough what I meant. Well, how many were converted?

S.—Twenty-one, I believe, sir.

B.—How often do you preach?

S.—Three times on the Sunday, and once in the week, at Waterbeach; and nearly every night in the week somewhere else.

B.—We will only reckon the Sunday morning and evening sermons; afternoon services never save anybody, the people are too sleepy to listen after dinner. So, let us say, a hundred and four sermons, and twenty-one souls saved; that is eighty-three sermons wasted! Indeed, we might say, a hundred and three, for the whole twenty-one souls might just as well have been saved under one sermon. Do you live at Waterbeach?

S.—No, sir; I live at Cambridge, where I teach in a school.

B.—Oh, then; you are only an apprentice boy at present, just trying your hand at preaching! Your ministry is a sort of off-hand farm, to be cultivated at odd times. What salary do your people give you?

S.—£45 a year.

B.—Oh, that accounts for everything! Souls can't be saved under £100 a year; that is, of course, where the people can afford to pay it, and that amount is little enough for any minister. Well, now, my young friend, let me give you a bit of good advice. You'll never make a preacher; so just give it up, and stick to your teaching.

When, in after years, I reminded him of his advice and prophecy, he used waggishly to say, "Ah! there's no knowing how much good a man may do by a little timely correction; no doubt my sharp speech put you on your mettle." That was really the case, though not in the sense he meant. I soon discovered that he was a rank Arminian, and when he attacked the Calvinism that was so dear to me, I denounced his system of doctrine as being worthless theology. I found that he used to give his money to different Missionary Societies according to the proportion of converts they reported as brought to the Lord at the lowest possible cost! He would take the various Annual Reports, divide the amount expended by the number of additions to the churches, and then subscribe the most where the amount per head was the least! There was a modicum of truth at the back of what he said; but I was really shocked by the way he talked about conversions being dependent upon the money contributed, so I spoke out my opinion as freely as he did his, and gave him a Roland for his Oliver without the slightest compunction. It was a battle royal, and both the old gentleman and the 'prentice boy grew sufficiently warm, but no scars remained on either combatant. On the Monday morning, Mr. Brown walked to Huntingdon with me in loving conversation, and afterwards sent me Haldane's "Life" as a present, with his sincere regards; and I, whom he had horrified with his doctrinal statements, felt an inward drawing towards the bluff heretic. No doubt he purposely put forward his most *outré* views of doctrine on that occasion to draw out the youthful preacher, probably intending to set him right on many points, but he had an unpromising pupil to deal with, one who had no fear of Potto Brown, or Professor Finney, or any other Arminian, before his eyes, but held his own opinion with a firmness which interested and did not displease the good but eccentric miller, who had usually dealt with softer material when criticizing the young gentlemen who preached in his chapel on Sundays.

*   *   *

Another singular character with whom I became acquainted early in my ministry, was old Mr. Sutton, of Cottenham. He had never seen me, but he heard that I was a popular young minister, so he invited me over to preach his anniversary sermons. I was in the vestry of the chapel before the morning service, and when the aged man came in, and saw me, he seemed greatly surprised to find that I was so young. After gruffly exchanging the usual greetings, he remarked, "I shouldn't have asked you here, had I known you were such a bit of a boy. Why, the people have been pouring into the place all the morning in waggons, and dickey-carts, and all kinds of vehicles! More fools they!" he added. I said, "Well, sir, I suppose it will be so much the better for your anniversary; still, I can go back as easily as I came, and my people at Waterbeach will be very glad to see me." "No, no," said the old pastor; "now you are here, you must do the best you can. There is a young fellow over from Cambridge, who will help you, and we shan't expect much from you;" and thereupon he paced the room, moaning out, "Oh, dear! what a pass the world is coming to when we get as preachers a parcel of boys who have not got their mother's milk out of their mouths!"

I was in due time conducted to the pulpit, and the old minister sat upon the stairs—I suppose, ready to go on with the service in case I should break down. After prayer and singing, I read, from the Book of Proverbs, the chapter containing the words, "The hoary head is a crown of glory." When I had gone so far, I stopped, and remarked, "I doubt it, for, this very morning, I met with a man who has a hoary head, yet he has not learnt common civility to his fellow-men." Proceeding with the reading, I finished the verse—"if it be found in the way of righteousness." "Ah!" I said, "that's another thing; a hoary head would then be a crown of glory, and, for the matter of that, so would a red head, or a head of any other colour." I went on with the service, and preached as best I could, and as I came down from the pulpit, Mr. Sutton slapped me on the back, and exclaimed, "Bless your heart! I have been a minister nearly forty years, and I was never better pleased with a sermon in all my life, but you are the sauciest dog that ever barked in a pulpit." All the way home from the chapel, he kept on going across the road to speak to little groups of people who were discussing the service. I heard him say, "I never knew anything like it in all my life; and to think that I should have talked to him as I did!" We had a good time for the rest of the day, the Lord blessed the Word, and Mr. Sutton and I were ever afterwards the best of friends.[1]

I shall never forget Mr. Sutton's description of a sermon he had preached; I had the notes of the discourse from his own lips, and I trust they will remain as notes, and never be preached from again in this world. The text was, "The night-hawk, the owl, and the cuckoo." That might not strike anyone as being exceedingly rich in matter; it did not so strike me, and therefore I innocently enquired, "And what were the heads?" He replied most archly, "Heads? why, wring the birds' necks, and there are three directly, 'the night-hawk, the owl, and the cuckoo'." He showed that these birds were all unclean under the law, and were plain types of unclean sinners. Night-hawks were persons who pilfered on the sly, also people who adulterated their goods, and cheated their neighbours in an underhand way without being suspected to be rogues. As for the owls, they typified drunkards, who are always liveliest at night, while by day they will

---

[1] In Mr. Spurgeon's second volume of Outlines, there is the following note evidently referring to this day's services:—"Three joined the church at Cottenham through the sermons on Sabbath 179."

almost knock their heads against a post because they are so sleepy. There were owls also among professors. The owl is a very small bird when he is plucked; he only looks big because he wears so many feathers; so, many professors are all feathers, and if you could take away their boastful professions, there would be very little left of them. Then the cuckoos were the church clergy, who always utter the same note whenever they open their mouths in the church, and live on other birds' eggs with their church-rates and tithes. The cuckoos were also, I think, the free-willers, who were always saying, "Do-do-do-do." Was not this rather too much of a good thing? Yet, from the man who delivered it, the discourse would not seem at all remarkable or odd.

The same venerable brother preached a sermon equally singular, but far more original and useful; those who heard it will remember it to their dying day. It was from this text: "The slothful man roasteth not that which he took in hunting." The good old man leaned upon the top of the pulpit, and said, "Then, my brethren, he *was* a lazy fellow!" That was the exordium; and then he went on to say, "He went out a-hunting, and after much trouble he caught his hare, and then was too idle to roast it. He was a lazy fellow indeed!" The preacher made us all feel how ridiculous such idleness was, and then he said, "But, then, you are very likely quite as much to blame as this man, for you do just the same. You hear of a popular minister coming down from London, and you put the horse in the cart, and drive ten or twenty miles to hear him, and, then, when you have heard the sermon, you forget to profit by it. You catch the hare, and do not roast it; you go hunting after the truth, and then you do not receive it." Then he went on to show that, just as meat needs cooking to prepare it for assimilation in the bodily system—I do not think he used that word, though—so the truth needs to go through a certain process before it can be received into the mind, that we may feed thereon and grow. He said he should show us how to cook a sermon, and he did so most instructively. He began as the cookery books do— "First, catch your hare." "So," he said, "first, get a gospel sermon." Then he declared that a great many sermons were not worth hunting for, and that good sermons were mournfully scarce, and it was worth while to go any distance to hear a solid, old-fashioned, Calvinistic discourse. Then, after the sermon had been caught, there was much about it which might be necessary because of the preacher's infirmity, but which was not profitable, and must be put away. Here he enlarged upon discerning and judging what we heard, and not believing every word of any man. Then followed directions as to roasting a sermon—

R

run the spit of memory through it from end to end, turn it round upon the roasting-jack of meditation, before the fire of a really warm and earnest heart, and in that way the sermon would be cooked, and ready to yield real spiritual nourishment. I am only giving just the outline of the discourse, and though it may look somewhat laughable, it was not so esteemed by the hearers. It was full of allegory, and kept up the attention of the people from the beginning to the end.

Such was Mr. Sutton's usual talk, and such was his ministry. Peace to his ashes. He was a quaint old man, who, after being a shepherd of sheep for between thirty and forty years, became a shepherd of men for a similar period; and he often told me that his second flock was "a deal more sheepish than the first." The converts, who found the road to heaven under his preaching, were so many that, when we remember them, we are like those who saw the lame man leaping after he heard the word of Peter and John; they were disposed to criticize, but "beholding the man that was healed standing with Peter and John, they could say nothing against it."

*　　　　　*　　　　　*

In the beginning of my preaching experience, there was a dear good man who, when I took the service for him, would persist in announcing the hymn commencing—

> "Mighty God! while angels bless Thee,
> May *an infant* lisp Thy name?"

That was to be sung with special reference to me, and at first it was all very proper, for the veteran saint might well regard me as "an infant" in spiritual things, but, ten years later, when I went down into the country to preach for him again, there was still the same hymn to be sung before my sermon—

> "Mighty God! while angels bless Thee,
> May *an infant* lisp Thy name?"

And when I was forty years of age, and the venerable man was near the close of his long life, and I went once more to help him by a sermon, I still had to join the congregation in singing—

> "Mighty God! while angels bless Thee,
> May *an infant* lisp Thy name?"

I thought that I was rather a largish infant, and felt that I would have preferred to choose my own hymns.

On another occasion, the minister of the place where I was preaching would give out the hymns, and the hymn-book in use was that one by Dr. Watts in which there are first the Psalms, and then Books I, II, and III of Hymns. I had selected a hymn out of one of the divisions, but by some mistake the minister had turned to the wrong part of the book, and before he had discovered his error, he was reading—

> "When the Eternal bows the skies
> To visit earthly things,
> With scorn Divine He turns His eyes
> From towers of haughty kings.
>
> He bids His awful chariot roll
> Far downward from the skies,
> To visit every humble soul
> With pleasure in His eyes."

Those who are familiar with the hymns of Dr. Watts, know that the last verse begins—

> "Just like His nature is His grace,
> All sov'reign and all free;"

and when the minister had read these two lines, he said, "We won't sing this hymn." I felt that, under the circumstances, the hymn ought to be sung, so I said, "If you please, we *will* sing that hymn; or we will not have any at all if we do not have that one." So the minister shut up the book, and I went on with the sermon. I had fixed upon quite a different subject for my discourse, but when such a challenge was given to me, I felt compelled to change my theme, so I announced as my text, "I will have mercy on whom I will have mercy, and I will have compassion on whom I will have compassion. So then it is not of him that willeth, nor of him that runneth, but of God that sheweth mercy," and I preached from those words a discourse full of good sound doctrine—sixteen ounces to the pound—which filled with delight the hearts of all the brethren and sisters who loved the marrow and fatness of the faith which some call Calvinism, but which we trace back to our Lord Himself and His apostles.

*   *   *

In my early ministerial days, I was invited to preach at Isleham, Cambridgeshire, where I was baptized. I was to conduct the morning service; my Brother Aldis, I think it was, preached in the afternoon; and then I was to take my turn again in the evening. The people at Isleham had such a belief that I should draw a congregation, that they went and borrowed the largest chapel in the place. I shall never forget it, because I preached that morning at eleven o'clock to seven persons! That was all the people I had; and I remember how I told them that they reminded me of the way ducks act when they go through a doorway, they always lower their heads; they will do it even when they are going in or out of a barn. The entrance may be twenty feet high, but a duck never goes through it without putting his head down, for fear he might possibly hit the top of the door! So I said to the people, "You were so afraid of your place being overcrowded that you borrowed that big chapel for seven people!" Well, being there, I resolved that I would preach that morning at my very best, although the congregation was so small. The brother, who took the afternoon service, said to me, "I can't think how you did it; you were as earnest, and you preached as well as if you had had the place crowded." "Yes," I replied, "I thought that was the only way to make sure of getting it full in the evening; so I determined that I would lay out all my guns, and make the greatest possible impression upon those few people." In the afternoon, we had a very decent audience of, perhaps, a hundred or a hundred and fifty; but when I preached at night, there was not standing room in the place. Though I did not compliment myself upon gathering the crowd, yet I could not help saying that, if I had not preached at my best to the seven people in the morning, I should not have had the large company at night, for those who were there at the first service went away, and talked about how well they had got on, and so induced many others to come out in the evening to hear for themselves.

"With regard to coming for a week to preach at Stambourne and neighbouring villages, I am yours to serve to the utmost. Not on the Sabbath, but all the week. I have a good sphere of labour here, but I want to do more, if possible. It is a great field, and the labourers must work with all their might. I often wish I were in China, Hindostan, or Africa, so that I might preach, preach, preach all day long. It would be sweet to die preaching. But I want more of the Holy Spirit; I do not feel enough—no, not half enough—of His divine energy."—C. H. S. in letter to his Uncle dated September 27, 1853.

"It was Richard Knill, that blessed missionary of the cross to whom I am personally so deeply indebted, who said that, if there were only one unconverted person in the whole world, and if that person lived in the wilds of Siberia, and if every Christian minister and every private believer in the world had to make a pilgrimage to that spot before that soul were brought to Christ, the labour would be well expended if that one soul were so saved. This is putting the truth in a striking way, but in a way in which everyone who realizes the value of immortal souls, will heartily concur."—C. H. S.

Chapter 19

The Call to London

IN the year 1853, I was asked to give an address at the annual meeting of the Cambridge Sunday School Union, in the Guildhall of that town. There were two other ministers to speak, both of them much older than myself, and, as a natural consequence, I was called upon first. I do not now recollect anything that I said on that occasion, but I have no doubt that I spoke in my usual straightforward fashion. I do not think there was anything in my remarks to cause the other speakers to turn upon me so savagely as they did when it came to their turn to address the large gathering. One of them, in particular, was very personal and also most insulting in his observations, specially referring to my youth, and then, in what he seemed to regard as a climax, saying that it was a pity that boys did not adopt the Scriptural practice of tarrying at Jericho till their beards were grown before they tried to instruct their seniors.

Having obtained the chairman's permission, I reminded the audience that those who were bidden to tarry at Jericho were not boys, but full-grown men, whose beards had been shaved off by their enemies as the greatest indignity they could be made to suffer, and who were, therefore, ashamed to return home until their beards had grown again. I added that the true parallel to their case could be found in a minister who, through falling into open sin, had disgraced his sacred calling, and so needed to go into seclusion for a while until his character had been to some extent restored. As it happened, I had given an exact description of the man who had attacked me so unjustly, and for that reason all who were present, and knew the circumstances, would be the more likely to remember the incident. There was in the hall that evening a gentleman from Essex—George Gould, of Loughton—who felt so deeply sympathetic with me in the trying position in which I had been placed through no fault of my own, and who also was so much impressed by what he had heard that, shortly afterwards, meeting in London old Thomas Olney, one of the deacons of the church worshipping in New Park Street Chapel, he pressed him to try to secure my services as a supply for the vacant pulpit, and thus became, in the hand of God, the means of my transference from Cambridgeshire to the metropolis.

On the last Sabbath morning in November, 1853, I walked, according to my wont, from Cambridge to the village of Waterbeach, in order to occupy the pulpit of the little Baptist Chapel. It was a country road, and there were five or six honest miles of it, which I usually measured, each Sunday, foot by foot, unless I happened to be met by a certain little pony and cart which came half-way, but could not by any possibility venture further because of the enormous expense which would have been incurred by driving through the toll-gate at Milton! That winter's morning, I was all aglow with my walk, and ready for my pulpit exercises. As I sat down in the table-pew, a letter, bearing the postmark of London, was passed to me. It was an unusual missive, and was opened with curiosity. It contained an invitation to preach at New Park Street Chapel, Southwark, the pulpit of which had formerly been occupied by Dr. Rippon—the very Dr. Rippon whose hymn-book was then before me upon the table—the great Dr. Rippon, out of whose Selection I was about to choose the hymns for our worship. The late Dr. Rippon seemed to hover over me as an immeasurably great man, the glory of whose name covered New Park Street Chapel and its pulpit with awe unspeakable. I quietly passed the letter across the table to the deacon who gave out the hymns, observing that there was some mistake, and that the letter must have been intended for a Mr. Spurgeon who preached somewhere down in Norfolk. He shook his head, and remarked that he was afraid there was no mistake, as he always knew that his minister would be run away with by some large church or other, but that he was a little surprised that the Londoners should have heard of me quite so soon. "Had it been Cottenham, or St. Ives, or Huntingdon," said he, "I should not have wondered at all, but going to London is rather a great step from this little place." He shook his head very gravely; but the time had come for me to look out the hymns, therefore the letter was put away, and, as far as I can remember, was for the day quite forgotten.

The next day, this answer was sent to the letter from the London deacon:

> "No. 60, Park Street,
> Cambridge,
> November 28th, 1853.

My Dear Sir,

I do not reside at Waterbeach, and therefore your letter did not reach me till yesterday, although the friends ought to have forwarded it at once. My people at Waterbeach are hardly to be persuaded to let me come, but I am prepared to serve you on the 11th [December]. On the 4th, I could not leave them; and the impossibility of finding a supply at all agreeable to them, prevents me from leaving home two following Sabbaths. I have been wondering very much how you could have heard of me, and I think I ought to give some account of myself, lest I should come and be out of my right place. Although I have been more than two years minister of a church, which has in that time doubled, yet my last birthday was only my nineteenth. I have hardly ever known what the fear of man means, and have all but uniformly had large congregations, and frequently crowded ones, but if you think my years would unqualify me for your pulpit, then, by all means, I entreat you, do not let me come. The Great God, my Helper, will not leave me to myself. Almost every night, for two years, I have been aided to proclaim His truth. I am therefore able to promise you for the 11th, and should you accept the offer, I will come on Saturday afternoon, and return on Monday. As I shall have to procure a supply, an early answer will oblige—

Yours most truly,

C. H. SPURGEON."

In due time came another epistle, setting forth that the former letter had been written in perfect knowledge of the young preacher's age, and had been intended for him and him alone. The request of the former letter was repeated and pressed, a date mentioned for the journey to London, and the place appointed at which the preacher would find lodging. That invitation was accepted, and as the result thereof the boy-preacher of the Fens travelled to London. Though it is so long ago, yet it seems but yesterday that I lodged for the night at a boarding-house in Queen Square, Bloomsbury, to which the worthy deacon had directed me. As I wore a huge black satin stock, and used a blue handkerchief with white spots, the young gentlemen of that boarding-house marvelled greatly at the youth from the country who had come up to preach in London, but who was evidently in the condition known as "verdant green". They were mainly of the Evangelical Church persuasion, and seemed greatly tickled that the country lad should be a preacher. They did not propose to go and hear the youth, but they seemed to tacitly agree to *encourage* me after their own fashion, and I was encouraged accordingly! What tales were narrated of the great divines of the metropolis, and their congregations! One, I remember, had a thousand *city* men to hear him; another had his church filled with *thoughtful* people, such as could hardly be matched all over England; while a third had an immense audience

almost entirely composed of the *young men* of London, who were spell-
bound by his eloquence. The study which these men underwent in
composing their sermons, their herculean toils in keeping up their
congregations, and the matchless oratory which they exhibited on all
occasions, were duly rehearsed in my hearing, and when I was shown
to bed in a cupboard over the front door, I was not in an advantageous condition for pleasant dreams. New Park Street hospitality
never sent the young minister to that far-away hired room again; but,
assuredly, that Saturday evening in a London boarding-house was
about the most depressing agency which could have been brought to
bear upon my spirit. On the narrow bed I tossed in solitary misery,
and found no pity. Pitiless was the grind of the cabs in the street,
pitiless the recollection of the young city clerks, whose grim propriety
had gazed upon my rusticity with such amusement, pitiless the spare
room which scarcely afforded me space to kneel, pitiless even the gas-
lamps which seemed to wink at me as they flickered amid the December
darkness. I had no friend in all that city full of human beings, but felt
myself to be among strangers and foreigners, and hoped to be helped
through the scrape into which I had been brought, and to escape
safely to the serene abodes of Cambridge and Waterbeach, which then
seemed to be Eden itself. The Sabbath morning was clear and cold,
and I wended my way along Holborn Hill towards Blackfriars and
certain tortuous lanes and alleys at the foot of Southwark Bridge.
Wondering, praying, fearing, hoping, believing—I felt all alone, and
yet not alone. Expectant of Divine help, and inwardly borne down
by my sense of the need of it, I traversed a dreary wilderness of brick
to find the spot where my message was to be delivered. One text rose
to my lips many times, I scarcely know why—"He must needs go
through Samaria." The necessity of our Lord's journeying in a certain
direction, is no doubt repeated in His servants; and as my journey
was not of my seeking, and had been by no means pleasing so far as
it had gone—the one thought of a "needs be" for it seemed to overtop
every other. At sight of New Park Street Chapel, I felt for a moment
amazed at my own temerity, for it seemed to my eyes to be a large,
ornate, and imposing structure, suggesting an audience wealthy and
critical, and far removed from the humble folk to whom my ministry
had been sweetness and light. It was early, so there were no persons
entering, and when the set time was fully come, there were no signs
to support the suggestion raised by the exterior of the building, and
I felt that, by God's help, I was not yet out of my depth, and was not
likely to be with so small an audience. The Lord helped me very
graciously, I had a happy Sabbath in the pulpit, and spent the interval

with warm-hearted friends; and when, at night, I trudged back to the Queen Square narrow lodging, I was not alone, and I no longer looked on Londoners as flinty-hearted barbarians. My tone was altered; I wanted no pity of anyone, I did not care a penny for the young gentlemen lodgers and their miraculous ministers, nor for the grind of the cabs, nor for anything else under the sun. The lion had been looked at all round, and his majesty did not appear to be a tenth as majestic as when I had only heard his roar miles away.

[Mr. Spurgeon wrote two letters to his father, recounting his first experiences in London. A considerable portion of the earlier one is missing, including the first sheet, and also the end of the epistle. Evidently, the young preacher had been relating what the deacons had told him concerning the falling-off in the congregations, for the part of his letter that has been preserved begins as follows:

". . . me that the people would be back at the first blast of the trumpet which gives a certain sound. . . . The people are Calvinistic, and they could not get on with anything else. They raised £100 last week for a city missionary, so that they have the sinews of war. The deacons told me that, if I were there three Sundays, there would be no room anywhere. They say that all the London popular ministers are gospel-men, and are plain, simple, and original. They have had most of the good preachers of our denomination out of the country, but they have never asked one of them twice, for they gave them such philosophical, or dry, learned sermons, that once was enough. I am the only one who has been asked twice, the only one who has been heard with pleasure by all. I told them they did not know what they were doing, nor whether they were in the body or out of the body; they were so starved, that a morsel of gospel was a treat to them. The portraits of Gill and Rippon—large as life—hang in the vestry. Lots of them said I was Rippon over again.

It is God's doing. I do not deserve it—they are mistaken. I only mention facts. I have not exaggerated; nor am I very exalted by it, for to leave my own dear people makes it a painful pleasure. God wills it.

The only thing which pleases me is, as you will guess, that I am right about College. I told the deacons that I was not a College man, and they said, 'That is to us a special recommendation, for you would not have much savour or unction if you came from College.'

As to a school, or writing to my deacons in case I do not go, I shall feel happiest if left to manage alone, for I am sure that any letter to my deacons would not do any good. A church is free to manage its own affairs. We are in loving unity now, and they will improve. But churches of the Baptist denomination would think it an infringement of their rules and liberties to be touched in the least by persons of other denominations in any matter which is their own concern. I should at once say, and you would not mind my saying so, '*I had nothing to do with the note; I never asked my father to write it; and the deacons must do as they please about laying it before the church.*'

I feel pleasure in the thought that it will not now be necessary, and I feel that, if it had been, I should have been equally contented. Many other ministers have schools;[1] it is a usual thing. It is not right to say, 'If you mean to be a minister;' for I *am* one, and have been for two years as much a minister as any man in England, and probably very much more so, since in that time I have preached more than 600 times.

More soon."

*   *   *

"No. 60, Park Street,
Cambridge,
December, —, 1853.

My Dear Father,

I concluded rather abruptly before—but you are often called out from your writing, and therefore can excuse it in me. I hardly know what I left unsaid. I hope to be at home three days. I think of running down from London on Tuesday (January) 3rd, and to go home by Bury on Friday, 6th. I hope it will be a sweet visit although a short one.

Should I be settled in London, I will come and see you often. I do not anticipate going there with much pleasure. I am contented where I am; but if God has more for me to do, then let me go and trust in Him. The London people are rather higher in Calvinism than I am; but I have succeeded in bringing one church to my own views, and will trust, with Divine assistance, to do the same with another. I am a

---

[1] The following advertisement which appeared in a Cambridge newspaper in December, 1853, makes it clear that Spurgeon had intended to open his own school in the New Year:

"No. 60, Park Street, Cambridge. Mr. C. H. Spurgeon begs to inform his numerous friends that, after Christmas, he intends taking six or seven young gentlemen as day pupils. He will endeavour to the utmost to impart a good commercial Education. The ordinary routine will include Arithmetic, Algebra, Geometry, and Mensuration; Grammar and Composition; Ancient and Modern History; Geography, Natural History, Astronomy, Scripture, and Drawing. Latin and the elements of Greek and French, if required. Terms, £5 per annum."

Calvinist; I love what someone called 'glorious Calvinism', but 'Hyperism' is too hot-spiced for my palate.

I found a relation in London; a daughter of Thomas Spurgeon, at Ballingdon. On the Monday, she came and brought the unmarried sister, who you will remember was at home when we called last Christmas. I shall have no objection to preach for Mr. Langford on Wednesday, January 4th, if he wishes it.

I spent the Monday in going about London, climbed to the top of St. Paul's, and left some money with the booksellers.[1]

My people are very sad; some wept bitterly at the sight of me, although I made no allusion to the subject in the pulpit, as it is too uncertain to speak of publicly. It is Calvinism they want in London, and any Arminian preaching will not be endured. Several in the church are far before me in theological acumen; they would not admit that it is so, but they all expressed their belief that my originality, or even eccentricity, was the very thing to draw a London audience. The chapel is one of the finest in the denomination; somewhat in the style of our Cambridge Museum. A Merry Christmas to you all; a Happy New Year; and the blessing of the God of Jacob!

Yours affectionately,
C. H. SPURGEON."

At the laying of the foundation stone of the Metropolitan Tabernacle, Mr. Spurgeon's father made the following interesting reference to the College incident and his son's coming to London:

"My Lord Mayor, I am very happy to meet you to-night. We are Essex men; we come from Colchester. Colchester has something to boast of great men. The chief physician of London comes from Colchester; the Lord Mayor comes from Colchester; and I need not tell you who else. I have never had the headache in my life, friends; but if I ever had it, it would have been to-day. I feel nervous and excited. But I do feel very happy to-day to acknowledge my faults, and when a man confesses his faults, he has done a great deal towards amending them. I always thought my son did wrong in coming to London; now you see that I was wrong. I always thought he was wrong in not going to College; I tried three or four hours with him,

---

[1] Spurgeon's volume, *Commenting and Commentaries*, explains this allusion:

Among entire commentators of modern date, a high place is usually awarded to THOMAS SCOTT, and I shall not dispute his right to it. He is the expositor of Evangelical Episcopalians, even as Adam Clarke is the prophet of the Wesleyans; but to me he has seldom given a thought, and I have almost discontinued consulting him. *The very first money I ever received for pulpit services in London was invested in Thomas Scott*, and I neither regretted the investment, nor became exhilarated thereby.

one night, with a dear friend who loved him, but it was no use. He said, 'No, I will never go to College, except in strict obedience to you as a father.' There I left the matter; and I see that God has been with him, though I thought it was a wrong step in him to go to London. And I thought it was a wrong step for me to come here to-night, but perhaps I may be mistaken again. I can tell you it is one of the happiest days of my life. I feel beyond myself when I think of the kindness that has been shown to my son when but a youth. I ascribe it all to God's goodness, and the earnest prayers of His people. He has been exposed to temptation from every source, and even now, my friends, he is not free from it. You have prayed for him, and God has sustained him. Let me entreat you to continue your prayers. Every one here to-night, go home, and pray for your Pastor. A meeting like this is enough to carry a man beyond himself, and fill his heart with pride, but the grace of God is all-sufficient. Several persons said to me—I do not know what their motive was—'Your son will never last in London six months; he has no education.' I said, 'You are terribly mistaken; he has the best education that can possibly be had; God has been his Teacher, and he has had earthly teachers, too.' I knew, as far as education went, he could manage London very well. Then they said his health would fail; but it has not failed him yet. He has had enough to shake his constitution, it is true; but God has been very merciful to him. I think, if there is one thing that would crown my happiness to-day, it would have been to see his grandfather here. I should have loved to see him with us. He said, 'Boy, don't ask me to go, I am too old; I am overcome with God's goodness and mercy to me.' He is always talking about your Pastor. Old people like to have something to talk about, so he always talks about his grandson. And next to that, I should like, my dear friends, to have seen his mother here. I believe, under God's grace, his mother was the means of leading him to Christ."

*   *   *

After his first visit to New Park Street Spurgeon had agreed to preach there again on the three Sabbaths, January 1st, 15th, and 29th, 1854, but before the last-named date, the church had already taken definite action with a view to securing his services permanently. He had preserved, amongst his most treasured papers, the following letter, which is now published for the first time, together with a correct copy of his reply to the invitation to supply the pulpit at New Park Street Chapel for six months:

"15, Creed Lane,
Ludgate Hill,
London,
Jan. 25, 1854.

My Dear Sir,

It is with pleasure that I write these few lines to you hoping, through Divine grace, you are well and happy.

You will remember that I gave you a hint of the intention of the members of the church to request the deacons to call a special church-meeting for the purpose of inviting you to preach for a certain period. That special meeting has taken place this evening, and I am most happy to tell you that, at the private request of Mr. W. Olney, I moved a resolution that you should be invited for six months. Old Mr. Olney was in the chair—Mr. Low being unwell, but strongly in favour of your coming. We had a full vestry, and there were only five against you; three out of the five rarely occupy their places with us. It was a happy meeting, and I hope that God, in His tender mercy, will send you to us, and that you will see your way clear to come; and should the Great Shepherd of the flock make you the instrument to revive this ancient church, we shall be glad indeed, and shall give God all the glory. For my own part, since I have been at Park Street, I never saw such a desire on the part of the brethren toward a minister as there is at the present time toward you. We are cast down, but not destroyed. It has been a trying time to us; our church is scattered, but there is a goodly remnant filling their places constantly, and a band of young members growing up, requiring the watchful care of a good Pastor. I know you are being persuaded not to come among us, but I will say, 'Come and try us.' I hope next week to spend half a day with you, if possible, and then I will tell you more than I can write. I should have written before, but I thought I would wait for the result of this evening's meeting. We don't want an idle preacher; I know we shall not have *that* in you. As I have said before, we are cast down, but there is room to rise; and I believe God is about to answer our poor prayers, though they have been offered weak in faith. The different societies in connection with the chapel will be revived with an active Pastor as our leader. There may be a few against you, but I assure you it is only on the part of those who are as unstable as water, and seldom are at chapel. You will find a great many faithful friends; and should the Holy Spirit lead you to decide for New Park Street after you have received the request from the deacons, I hope and pray that you will prove a blessing to *thousands*—that God will give you a great number of souls for your crown of rejoicing, that, like Rippon, and Cox, Collier, Bennet, and others, you will be a guide to thousands of ignorant travellers to conduct them to the cross of Jesus. I hope I shall soon see you, and if it shall please God that it shall add to His glory for you to come among us, I will thank Him, and do all I can so far as my influence is concerned, for your temporal and spiritual happiness.

I have enclosed a copy of the resolution which I moved at the meeting, and which Mr. Ward seconded. I conclude with my Christian love to you, hoping you will be wisely directed in all your ways, and believe me to be,

Your sincere friend and brother in Christ,
WILLIAM CUTLER, Superintendent of the Sunday School."

"To the Rev. C. H. Spurgeon.

Resolved, That the ministry of the Rev. Charles H. Spurgeon having been very generally appreciated, he be invited to supply the pulpit for six months; and that the deacons be requested to communicate this resolution to him, and to make the necessary arrangements with him."

Spurgeon's reply to the official letter from the deacons was as follows:

"No. 60, Park Street,
Cambridge,
January 27th, 1854.

To James Low, Esq.,

My Dear Sir,

I cannot help feeling intense gratification at the unanimity of the church at New Park Street in relation to their invitation to me. Had I been uncomfortable in my present situation, I should have felt unmixed pleasure at the prospect Providence seems to open up before me; but having a devoted and loving people, I feel I know not how.

One thing I know, namely, that I must soon be severed from them by necessity, for they do not raise sufficient to maintain me in comfort. Had they done so, I should have turned a deaf ear to any request to leave them, at least for the present. But now my Heavenly Father drives me forth from this little Garden of Eden; and whilst I see that I must go out, I leave it with reluctance, and tremble to tread the unknown land before me.

When I first ventured to preach at Waterbeach, I only accepted an invitation for three months, on the condition that if, in that time, I should see good reason for leaving, or they on their part should wish for it, I should be at liberty to cease supplying, or they should have the same power to request me to do so before the expiration of the time.

Now, with regard to a six months' invitation from you, I have no objection to the length of time, but rather approve of the prudence of the church in wishing to have one so young as myself on an extended period of probation. But I write, after well weighing the matter, to say positively that I cannot, I *dare* not, accept an unqualified invitation for so long a time. My objection is not to the length of the time of probation, but it ill becomes a youth to promise to preach to a London congregation so long, until he knows *them* and they know *him*. I would engage to supply for three months of that time, and then, should the congregation fail, or the church disagree, I would reserve to myself liberty, without breach of engagement, to retire; and you could, on your part, have the right to dismiss me without seeming to treat me ill. Should I see no reason for so doing, and the church still retain their wish for me, I can remain the other three months, either with or without the formality of a further invitation; but even during that time (the second three months), I should not like to regard myself as a fixture, in case of ill-success, but would only be a supply, liable to a fortnight's dismissal or resignation.

Perhaps this is not business-like—I do not know; but this is the course I should prefer, if it would be agreeable to the church. Enthusiasm and popularity are often the crackling of thorns, and soon expire. I do not wish to be a hindrance if I cannot be a help.

With regard to coming *at once*, I think I must not. My own deacons just hint that I ought to finish the quarter here; though, by *ought*, they mean simply, 'Pray do so, if you can.' This would be too long a delay. I wish to help them until they can get supplies, which is only to be done with great difficulty; and as I have given you four Sabbaths, I hope you will allow me to give them four in return. I would give them the first and second Sabbaths in February, and two more in a month or six weeks' time. I owe them much for their kindness, although they insist that the debt lies on their side. Some of them hope, and almost pray, that you may be tired in three months, so that I may be again sent back to them.

Thus, my dear sir, I have honestly poured out my heart to you. You are too kind. You will excuse me if I err, for I wish to do right to you, to my people, and to all, as being not mine own, but bought with a price.

S

I respect the honesty and boldness of the small minority, and only wonder that the number was not greater. I pray God that, if He does not see fit that I should remain with you, the majority may be quite as much the other way at the end of six months, so that I may never divide you into parties.

Pecuniary matters I am well satisfied with. And now one thing is due to every minister, and I pray you to remind the church of it, namely, that in private, as well as in public, they must all earnestly wrestle in prayer to the God of our Lord Jesus Christ, that I may be sustained in the great work.

I am, with the best wishes for your health, and the greatest respect,

Yours truly,

C. H. Spurgeon."

*   *   *

The following letter was written to an Uncle at Stambourne. The swift transition from innocent mirth to deep solemnity was characteristic of Mr. Spurgeon to the end of his days.

"75, Dover Road,
Borough,
March 2, 1854.

Dear Uncle,

I shall be extremely obliged if you will, at the earliest opportunity, forward to my address, as above, by rail or otherwise, the books I purchased of you. I have been expecting them for many months; but thought that, perhaps, you had no means of sending them. Send them to any station, carriage I will pay.

Of course, I shall not look for an answer to my note; I never shall again expect to see your handwriting to me. 'Hope deferred maketh'—never mind—let Solomon finish the sentence. I have a birch in pickle for you; and when I come to your house, I shall use it with but little mercy, so you had need have on your very thickest skin. I might say some sharp things about the matter, but I will save them until I sit in your easy chair, or you are seated in mine. When you are in London, you will be in for a sound scolding if you do not come to see me. I do not think you dare come, and I am sure you will not venture to stay away. I promise you a hearty welcome.

75, Dover Road,
          Borough of Southwark,
                    London.

Can you see my address? I send my very best respects to your good wife; she is certainly worth more than you, if I am to value her by the number of letters I have received.

But, to joke no more, you have heard that I am now a Londoner, and a little bit of a celebrity. No College could have put me in a higher situation. Our place is one of the pinnacles of the denomination. But I have a great work to do, and have need of all the prayers the sons of God can offer for me.

I shall be glad to hear of your temporal and spiritual prosperity. Do not, for a moment, imagine that I am cold towards you. My Master's one aim was to spread the spirit of love among His disciples; and I trust little things will never chill my love to the brethren. Permit me, most respectfully and lovingly, to enquire, 'How does the cause of God prosper?' 'How does your soul prosper?' 'How is your love to the precious name of Jesus?' I wish for myself and you much soul-prosperity. We cannot afford to live a useless life; the sands of time are too valuable to be allowed to run on unheeded. We have a work before us, and woe be unto us if we are idle or unfaithful servants! Blessed is the man who often talks with his God alone, and comes forth from his closet, like Moses from the mountain top, with a celestial glory on his brow! Let us seek that blessing, and may God be ever with us! Do not forget the books, and believe me to be—

                    Yours truly,
                    C. H. SPURGEON."

*   *   *

The following letter was written by Spurgeon to the ladies with whom he had lodged at Cambridge:

                    "75, Dover Road,
                         Borough,
                              March, 1854.
To the Misses Blunson,

My Dear Friends,

I have not forgotten you, although I have been silent so long. I have thought of your trials, and have requested of my Master that

He would comfort and sustain you. If you have a portion in Him, your troubles will be blessings, and every grief will be turned into a mercy.

I am very well, and everything goes on even better than I could have hoped. My chapel, though large, is crowded; the aisles are blocked up, and every niche is packed as full as possible. I expect to come and see you in about a month. I hope to be at Waterbeach the fourth Sabbath in April. I get on very well in my present lodgings— but not better than with you, for that would be impossible. I had nothing to wish for better than I had, for your attention to me was beyond all praise. I cannot but feel very much for you, and only wish that I knew how I could serve you.

I hope you will not give way to doubts and despondency; but do what you can, and leave the rest to God. Blessed is the man who has the God of Jacob for his Helper; he need not fear either want, or pain, or death. The more you can realize this, the happier will you become, and the only means for so doing is to hold frequent communion with God in prayer. Get alone with Jesus, and He will comfort your hearts, and restore your weary souls. I hope you have let your rooms. I think I shall stop at Mrs. Warricker's, but I will be sure to come and see you, and leave something to remember me by. Trust in God, and be glad, and—

Believe me to be,
Yours truly,
C. H. SPURGEON."

*   *   *

The six months' probation was never fulfilled, for there was no need. The place was filled, the prayer-meetings were full of power, and the work of conversion was going on. A requisition for a special church-meeting, signed by fifty of the male members, was sent in to the deacons on April 12, the meeting was held on April 19, with the result mentioned in the following letter:

"30, Gracechurch Street,
April 20th, 1854.

My Dear Young Brother,

I annex a copy of a resolution passed last evening at a numerously-attended special church-meeting held at New Park Street Chapel.

If you feel it your duty to accept the invitation of the Church to become its Pastor, it will be desirable that you should obtain your dismission from the Church at Waterbeach to our Church as early as

you can, in order that you may be in a position as a member to attend
our church-meetings.

I remain,

My dear young brother,

Yours affectionately,

JAMES LOW, Chairman.

Rev. C. H. Spurgeon."

Spurgeon's letter, accepting the invitation to the pastorate, was as
follows:

"75, Dover Road,

Borough,

April 28th, 1854.

To the Baptist Church of Christ worshipping in
New Park Street Chapel, Southwark,

Dearly Beloved in Christ Jesus,

I have received your unanimous invitation, as contained in a
resolution passed by you on the 19th instant, desiring me to accept
the pastorate among you. No lengthened reply is required; there is
but one answer to so loving and cordial an invitation. I ACCEPT IT.
I have not been perplexed as to what my reply should be, for many
things constrain me thus to answer.

I sought not to come to you, for I was the minister of an obscure
but affectionate people; I never solicited advancement. The first note
of invitation from your deacons came quite unlooked-for, and I
trembled at the idea of preaching in London. I could not understand
how it had come about, and even now I am filled with astonishment
at the wondrous Providence. I would wish to give myself into the
hands of our covenant God, whose wisdom directs all things. He shall
choose for me; and so far as I can judge, this *is* His choice.

I feel it to be a high honour to be the Pastor of a people who can
mention glorious names as my predecessors, and I entreat of you to
remember me in prayer, that I may realize the solemn responsibility
of my trust. Remember my youth and inexperience, and pray that
these may not hinder my usefulness. I trust also that the remembrance
of these will lead you to forgive mistakes I may make, or unguarded
words I may utter.

Blessed be the name of the Most High, if He has called me to this
office, He will support me in it—otherwise, how should a child, a
youth, have the presumption thus to attempt the work which filled
the heart and hands of Jesus?

Your kindness to me has been very great, and my heart is knit unto you. I fear not *your* steadfastness, I fear my own. The gospel, I believe, enables me to venture great things, and by faith I venture this.

I ask your co-operation in every good work; in visiting the sick, in bringing in enquirers, and in mutual edification.

Oh, that I may be no injury to you, but a lasting benefit! I have no more to say, saving this, that if I have expressed myself in these few words in a manner unbecoming my youth and inexperience, you will not impute it to arrogance, but forgive my mistake.

And now, commending you to our covenant God, the Triune Jehovah,

I am,

Yours to serve in the gospel,

C. H. Spurgeon."

Professor Everett says, concerning this period in Spurgeon's life: "He gave me prompt intimation of his call to New Park Street Chapel; and soon after his settlement there, I called upon him by appointment. I spent half a day with him, and he poured forth to me, without reserve, the full tale of his successes, telling me of the distinguished men who continually came to hear him, and of the encomiums pronounced on his delivery by elocutionists like Sheridan Knowles."

Pastor G. H. Davies, of Lisbon, North Dakota, thus records Sheridan Knowles' remarkable prophecy:

"I was a student at Stepney, now Regent's Park College. Sheridan Knowles, the celebrated actor and play-writer, had just been baptized by Dr. Brock, and appointed our tutor in elocution. We had collected funds to give the grand old man a handsome Bible. The presentation was made one Wednesday afternoon. It was an occasion never to be forgotten, not only for the sake of Sheridan Knowles himself, but because of his prophecy concerning one of whom till then we knew nothing. Immediately on entering, Mr. Knowles exclaimed, 'Boys, have you heard the Cambridgeshire lad?' None of us had heard him. 'Then, boys,' he continued, 'go and hear him at once.' This was after Spurgeon had been preaching at New Park Street Chapel two Sundays. 'Go and hear him at once if you want to know how to preach. His name is Charles Spurgeon. He is only a boy, but he is the most wonderful preacher in the world. He is absolutely perfect in his oratory; and, beside that, a master in the art of acting. He has nothing to learn from me, or anyone else. He is simply perfect. He knows

everything. He can do anything. I was once lessee of Drury Lane
Theatre; and were I still in that position, I would offer him a fortune
to play for one season on the boards of that house. Why, boys, he
can do anything he pleases with his audience! He can make them
laugh, and cry, and laugh again, in five minutes. His power was never
equalled. Now, mark my word, boys, *that young man will live to be the
greatest preacher of this or any other age. He will bring more souls to Christ
than any man who ever proclaimed the gospel, not excepting the apostle Paul.
His name will be known everywhere, and his Sermons will be translated into
many of the languages of the world.'* "]

The congregation into whose midst Spurgeon was now called could trace their history back to the seventeenth century when they met in a private house in Southwark. William Rider became the first pastor in 1652. The length of his ministry is not known for he had "been dead for some time" when Benjamin Keach succeeded him in 1668. The days of Charles II were a dark era for Nonconformity and Keach had himself suffered in the pillory for his faith, nevertheless upon the Indulgence of 1672 the congregation erected a large meeting house in Goat's Yard Passage, Fair Street, Southwark. After thirty-six years Keach was followed by Benjamin Stinton whose fourteen years' pastorate was terminated by his sudden death at the age of forty-two. From that point, the witness was continued, from 1720 to 1771, by the eminent scholar and author, Dr. John Gill.

In Gill's latter years the congregation declined but the call of John Rippon in 1773 led to a new period of blessing. That period passed, however, before Rippon's long ministry of sixty-three years was over and frequently before his death in 1836 he would pray for a successor who would be used to restore the church to brighter days. The succeeding years saw little alteration, and the position was worsened by the fact that the congregation which had moved its meeting house to Carter Lane in 1757, had again to move in 1830 owing to the making of roads to the new London Bridge. Some cheap, freehold ground in a low-lying lane called New Park Street, close to the river bank and overshadowed by breweries and factories, was purchased as though "with the design of burying the church alive." The nearest approach from the City was Southwark Bridge at which a toll was then charged. Nevertheless some remembered Rippon's prayer and in the first twenty years of New Park Street Chapel (built 1833), though three ministers came and went, "there were a few in its midst" says Spurgeon, "who never ceased to pray for a gracious revival. The congregation became smaller and smaller; yet they hoped on, and hoped ever. Let it never be forgotten," says Spurgeon, "that, when they were at their worst, the Lord remembered them and gave to them such a tide of prosperity that they have since had no mourning, or doubting, but many, many years of continued rejoicing."

Chapter 20

The Long Pastorate Commenced, 1854

WHEN I came to New Park Street Chapel, it was but a mere handful of people[1] to whom I first preached, yet I can never forget how earnestly they prayed. Sometimes they seemed to plead as though they could really see the Angel of the covenant present with them, and as if they must have a blessing from Him. More than once, we were all so awe-struck with the solemnity of the meeting, that we sat silent for some moments while the Lord's power appeared to over-shadow us; and all I could do on such occasions was to pronounce the Benediction, and say, "Dear friends, we have had the Spirit of God here very manifestly to-night; let us go home, and take care not to lose His gracious influences." Then down came the blessing; the house was filled with hearers, and many souls were saved. I always give all the glory to God, but I do not forget that He gave me the privilege of ministering from the first to a praying people. We had prayer-meetings in New Park Street that moved our very souls. Every man seemed like a crusader besieging the New Jerusalem, each one appeared determined to storm the Celestial City by the might of intercession, and soon the blessing came upon us in such abundance that we had not room to receive it.

There is a confidence in one's own powers which must ever be of service to those who are called to eminent positions, provided the confidence is well-grounded, seasoned with humility, and attended with that holy gratitude which refers all honour and glory to the Giver of every good and perfect gift. But, at the same time, there is nothing more true than the fact that the self-confident are near a fall, that those who lean on themselves must be overthrown, and that carnal security has but a baseless fabric in which to dwell. When I first became a Pastor in London, my success appalled me, and the thought of the career which it seemed to open up, so far from elating me, cast me into the lowest depth, out of which I uttered my *miserere*, and found no room for a *gloria in excelsis*. Who was I that I should continue to lead so great a multitude? I would betake me to my village obscurity, or emigrate to America, and find a solitary nest in the backwoods, where I might be sufficient for the things which would be demanded of me. It

[1] About 200. The chapel had accommodation for 1,200 persons.—P.

was just then that the curtain was rising upon my life-work, and I dreaded what it might reveal. I hope I was not faithless, but I was timorous, and filled with a sense of my own unfitness. I dreaded the work which a gracious Providence had prepared for me. I felt myself a mere child, and trembled as I heard the voice which said, "Arise, and thresh the mountains, and make them as chaff." This depression comes over me whenever the Lord is preparing a larger blessing for my ministry; the cloud is black before it breaks, and over-shadows before it yields its deluge of mercy. Depression has now become to me as a prophet in rough clothing, a John the Baptist, heralding the nearer coming of my Lord's richer benison. So have far better men found it. The scouring of the vessel has fitted it for the Master's use. Immersion in suffering has preceded the baptism of the Holy Ghost. Fasting gives an appetite for the banquet. The Lord is revealed in the backside of the desert, while His servant keepeth the sheep, and waits in solitary awe. The wilderness is the way to Canaan. The low valley leads to the towering mountain. Defeat prepares for victory. The raven is sent forth before the dove. The darkest hour of the night precedes the day-dawn. The mariners go down to the depths, but the next wave makes them mount towards the heavens; and their soul is melted because of trouble before the Lord bringeth them to their desired haven.

*   *   *

Not long after I was chosen Pastor at Park Street, I was interviewed by a good man who had left the church, having been, as he said, "treated shamefully." He mentioned the names of half-a-dozen persons, all prominent members of the church, who had behaved in a very unchristian manner to him—he, poor innocent sufferer, having been a model of patience and holiness! I learned his character at once from what he said about others (a mode of judging which has never misled me), and I made up my mind how to act. I told him that the church had been in a sadly unsettled state, and that the only way out of the snarl was for every one to forget the past, and begin again. He said that the lapse of years did not alter facts; and I replied that it would alter a man's view of them if in that time he had become a wiser and a better man. I added that all the past had gone away with my predecessors, that he must follow them to their new spheres, and settle matters with *them*, for I would not touch the affair with a pair of tongs. He waxed somewhat warm, but I allowed him to radiate until he was cool again, and we shook hands, and parted. He was a good man, but constructed upon an uncomfortable principle, so that, at times, he crossed the path of other people in a very awkward manner, and if I had gone into his case, and taken his side, there would have been no end to the strife. I am quite certain that, for my own success, and for the prosperity of the church, I took the wisest course by applying my blind eye to all disputes which dated previously to my advent. It is the extremity of unwisdom for a young man, fresh from College, or from another charge, to suffer himself to be earwigged by a clique, and to be bribed by kindness and flattery to become a partisan, and so to ruin himself with one-half of his people.

I do not find, at the present time, nearly so much advice being given to young men as when I first came to London. Dear me, what quantities I had! I believe I had as much as that American humourist, who said he found enough advice lying loose round about him to ruin three worlds at least; I am sure I had quite enough to have done that. But now, instead of advising our young brethren, and hinting at their indiscretions, we rather rejoice in their impetuosity and earnestness. We like to see much freshness and vigour about utthem: and if they do kick over the traces now and then, we feel that time will moderate their zeal, and probably a very few years will add to them the prudence which they now lack.

*   *   *

I could tell many stories of the remarkable conversions that were wrought in those early days. Once, when I was in the vestry, an Irishman came to see me. Pat began by making a low bow, and saying, "Now, your *Riverence*, I have come to ax you a question." "Oh!" said I, "Pat, I am not a *Riverence*; it is not a title I care for; but what is your question, and how is it you have not been to your priest about it?" He said, "I have been to him, but I don't like his answer." "Well, what is your question?" Said he, "God is just; and if God be just, He must punish my sins. I deserve to be punished. If He is a just God, He ought to punish me; yet you say God is merciful, and will forgive sins. I cannot see how that is right; He has no right to do that. He ought to be just, and punish those who deserve it. Tell me how God can be just, and yet be merciful." I replied, "That is through the blood of Christ." "Yes," said he, "that is what my priest said, you are very much alike there; but he said a good deal besides, that I did not understand; and that short answer does not satisfy me. I want to know how it is that the blood of Jesus Christ enables God to be just, and yet to be merciful." Then I saw what he wanted to know, and explained the plan of salvation thus: "Now, Pat, suppose you had been killing a man, and the judge had said, 'That Irishman must be hanged.' " He said quickly, "And I should have richly deserved to be hanged." "But, Pat, suppose I was very fond of you, can you see any way by which I could save you from being hanged?" "No, sir, I cannot." "Then, suppose I went to the Queen, and said, 'Please your Majesty, I am very fond of this Irishman; I think the judge was quite right in saying that he must be hanged, but let me be hanged instead, and you will then carry out the law.' Now, the Queen could not agree to my proposal; but suppose she could—and God can, for He has power greater than all kings and queens—and suppose the Queen should have me hanged instead of you, do you think the policemen would take you up afterwards?" He at once said, "No, I should think not; they would not meddle with me; but if they did, I should say, 'What are you doing? Did not that gintleman condescind to be hung for me? Let me alone; shure, you don't want to hang two people for the same thing, do ye?' " I replied to the Irishman, "Ah, my friend, you have hit it; that is the way whereby we are saved! God must punish sin. Christ said, 'My Father, punish Me instead of the sinner;' and His Father did. God laid on His beloved Son, Jesus Christ, the whole burden of our sins, and all their punishment and chastisement; and now that Christ is punished instead of us, God would not be just if He were to punish any sinner who believes on the Lord Jesus Christ. If thou believest in Jesus Christ, the well-beloved and only begotten Son of God, thou art saved, and thou mayest go on thy way rejoicing." "Faith," said the man, clapping his hands, "that's the gospel. Pat is safe now; with all his sins about him, he'll trust in the Man that died for him, and so he shall be saved."

Another singular conversion, wrought at New Park Street, was that of a man who had been accustomed to go to a gin-palace to fetch in gin for his Sunday evening's drinking. He saw a crowd round the door of the chapel, so he looked in, and forced his way to the top of the gallery stairs. Just then, I turned in the direction where he stood; I do not know why I did so, but I remarked that there might be a man in the gallery who had come in with no very good motive, for even then he had a gin-bottle in his pocket. The singularity of the expression struck the man, and being startled because the preacher so exactly described him, he listened attentively to the warnings which followed, the Word reached his heart, the grace of God met with him, he became converted, and soon was walking humbly in the fear of God. On another occasion, a poor harlot found the Saviour in the same building. She had determined to go and take her own life on Blackfriars Bridge, but, passing the chapel on a Sunday evening, she thought she would step in, and for the last time hear something that might prepare her to stand before her Maker. She forced her way into the aisle, and being once in, she could not get out even if she had wanted to do so. The text that night was, "Seest thou this woman?" I described the woman in the city who was a notorious public sinner, and pictured her washing her Saviour's feet with her tears, and wiping them with the hair of her head, loving much because she had been forgiven much. While I was preaching, the wretched woman was melted to tears by the thought that her own evil life was being depicted to the congregation. It was, first, my great joy to be the means of saving the poor creature from death by suicide, and, then, to be the instrument of saving her soul from destruction.

Deeds of grace have been wrought in the Tabernacle after the same fashion. Men and women have come in, simply out of curiosity—a curiosity often created by some unfounded story, or malicious slander of prejudiced minds; yet Jesus Christ has called them, and they have become both *His* disciples and *our* warm-hearted friends. Some of the most unlikely recruits have been, in after days, our most valuable soldiers. They began with aversion, and ended with enthusiasm. They came to scoff, but remained to pray. Such cases are not at all uncommon. They were not unusual in the days of Whitefield and Wesley. They tell us in their Journals of persons who came with stones in their pockets to throw at the Methodists, but whose enmity was slain by a stone from the sling of the Son of David. Others came to create disturbances, but a disturbance was created in their hearts which could never be quelled till they came to Jesus Christ, and found peace in Him. The history of the Church of God is studded with the remarkable conversions of persons who did not wish to be converted, who were not looking for grace, but were even opposed to it, and yet, by the interposing arm of eternal mercy, were struck down and transformed into earnest and devoted followers of the Lamb.

*   *   *

Ever since I have been in London, in order to get into the habit of speaking extemporaneously, I have never studied or prepared anything for the Monday evening prayer-meeting. I have all along selected that occasion as the opportunity for off-hand exhortation; but I do not on such occasions select difficult expository topics, or abstruse themes, but restrict myself to simple, homely talk about the elements of our faith. When standing up, on such occasions, my mind makes a review, and enquires, "What subject has already occupied my thought during the day? What have I met with in my reading during the past week? What is most laid upon my heart at this hour? What is suggested by the hymns or the prayers ?" It is of no use to rise before an assembly, and hope to be inspired upon subjects of which one knows nothing; if anyone is so unwise, the result will be that, as he knows nothing, he will probably say it, and the people will not be edified. But I do not see why a man cannot speak extemporaneously upon a subject which he fully understands. Any tradesman, well versed in his line of business, could explain it without needing to retire for meditation, and surely I ought to be equally familiar with the first principles of our holy faith; I ought not to feel at a loss when called upon to speak upon topics which constitute the daily bread of my soul. I do not see what benefit is gained, in such a case, by the mere manual labour of writing before speaking, because, in so doing, a man would write extemporaneously, and extemporaneous writing is likely to be even feebler than extemporaneous speech. The gain of the writing lies in the opportunity of careful revision, but, as thoroughly able writers can express their thoughts correctly at the first, so also may able speakers. The thought of a man who finds himself upon his legs, dilating upon a theme with which he is familiar, may be very far from being his first thought; it may be the cream of his meditations warmed by the glow of his heart. He having studied the subject well before, though not at that moment, may deliver himself most powerfully; whereas another man, sitting down to write, may only be penning his first ideas, which may be vague and vapid.

I once had a very singular experience while preaching at New Park Street Chapel. I had passed happily through all the early parts of Divine service on the Sabbath evening, and was giving out the hymn before the sermon. I opened the Bible to find the text, which I had carefully studied as the topic of discourse, when, on the opposite page, another passage of Scripture sprang upon me, like a lion from a thicket, with vastly more power than I had felt when considering the text which I had chosen. The people were singing, and I was sighing. I was in a strait betwixt two, and my mind hung as in the balances. I was naturally desirous to run in the track which I had carefully planned, but the other text would take no refusal, and seemed to tug at my skirts, crying, "No, no, you must preach from me! God would have you follow me." I deliberated within myself as to my duty, for I would neither be fanatical nor unbelieving, and at last I thought within myself, "Well, I should like to preach the sermon which I have prepared, and it is a great risk to run to strike out a new line of thought, but, still, as this text constrains me, it may be of the Lord, and therefore I will venture upon it, come what may." I almost always announce my divisions very soon after the exordium, but, on this occasion, contrary to my usual custom, I did not do so, for a very good reason. I passed through the first head with considerable liberty, speaking perfectly extemporaneously both as to thought and word. The second point was dwelt upon with a consciousness of unusual quiet efficient power, but I had no idea what the third would or could be, for the text yielded no more matter just then; nor can I tell even now what I could have done had not an event occurred upon which I had never calculated. I had brought myself into great difficulty by obeying what I thought to be a Divine impulse, and I felt comparatively easy about it, believing that God would help me, and knowing that I could at least close the service should there be nothing more to be said. I had no need to deliberate, for in one moment we were in total darkness—the gas had gone out; and, as the aisles were choked with people, and the place was crowded everywhere, it was a great peril, but a great blessing. What was I to do then? The people were a little frightened, but I quieted them instantly by telling them not to be at all alarmed, though the gas was out, for it would soon be re-lighted; and as for myself, having no manuscript, I could speak just as well in the dark as in the light, if they would be so good as to sit or stand still, and listen. Had my discourse been ever so elaborate, it would have been absurd to have continued it, and, as my plight was, I was all the less embarrassed. I turned at once mentally to the well-known text which speaks of the child of light walking in darkness, and of the child of darkness walking in the light, and found appropriate remarks and illustrations pouring in upon me; and when the lamps were again lit, I saw before me an audience as rapt and subdued as ever a man beheld in his life. The odd thing of all was that, some few church-meetings afterwards, two persons came forward to make confession of their faith, who professed to have been converted that evening; the first owed her conversion to the former part of the discourse, which was on the new text that came to me, and the other traced his awakening to the latter part, which was occasioned by the sudden darkness. Thus, Providence befriended me. I cast myself upon God, and His arrangements quenched the light at the proper time for me. Some may ridicule, but I adore; others may even censure, but I rejoice.

When New Park Street Chapel was sold, I had the pulpit stairs removed to my garden at Nightingale Lane, and fixed them to a huge willow tree. I remember reading, with some amusement, of Lorenzo Dow, who is reported, many years ago, to have slipped down a tree in the backwoods, in order to illustrate the easiness of backsliding. He had previously pulled himself up, with extreme difficulty, in order to show how hard a thing it is to regain lost ground. I was all the more diverted by the story because it has so happened that this pretty piece of nonsense has been imputed to myself. I was represented as sliding down the banisters of my pulpit, and that at a time when the pulpit was fixed in the wall, and was entered from behind! I never gave even the remotest occasion for that falsehood; and yet it is daily repeated, and I have even heard of persons who have declared that they were present when I did so, and, with their own eyes, saw me perform the silly trick.

It is possible for a person to repeat a falsehood so many times that he at length imposes upon himself, and believes that he is stating the truth. When men mean to say what is untrue and unkind, they are not very careful as to the back upon which they stick the slander. For my own part, I have so long lived under a glass case that, like the bees which I have seen at the Crystal Palace, I go on with my work, and try to be indifferent to spectators; and when my personal habits are truthfully reported, though they really are not the concern of any-body but myself, I feel utterly indifferent about it, except in times of depression, when I sigh "for a lodge in some vast wilderness", where rumours of newspaper men and interviewers might never reach me more. I am quite willing to take my fair share of the current criticism allotted to public men, but I cannot help saying that I very seldom read in print any story connected with myself which has a shade of truth in it. Old Joe Miller's anecdotes of Rowland Hill, Sydney Smith, and John Berridge, and tales of remotest and fustiest antiquity, are imputed to me as they have been to men who went before, and will be to men who follow after. Many of the tales told about me, even to this day, are not only without a shadow of truth, but some of them border on blas-phemy, or are positively profane. On the whole, I am inclined to believe that the trade in falsehood is rather brisk, or so many untruths would not be manufactured. Why, I actually heard, not long since, of a minister, who said that a certain thing occurred to him, the other day; yet I told the original story twenty years ago! When I related it, I said it had been my experience, the other day, and I believed it was so, but after hearing that this man says that it happened to him, it makes me question whether it really did occur to me at all. I think it is a great pity for a preacher, or any speaker, to try to make a story appear interesting by saying that the incident related happened to him, when it really did not. Scrupulous truthfulness should always characterize everyone who stands up to proclaim the truth of God.

I mentioned to my New Park Street deacons, several times, my opinion that the upper panes of the iron-framed windows had better

9. *A humble beginning. The thatched cottage at Teversham where, by a strange providence, Spurgeon preached his first sermon to a few farm-labourers and their wives*

10. *The curious old Baptist Chapel (formerly a dovecote) at Waterbeach where Spurgeon became pastor at the age of 17. Before long the place was filled with hearers and a moral reformation swept through the village*

11. *The young preacher in action at New Park Street*

Better is the end of life than the beginning.
Better the end of labour than the starting.
These sketches are so many proofs of the
power of faith ... By faith I got them. —
They are evidences of God's love ... for oft
have they come just at the moment when
had they tarried, I had been undone.
Blessed be God — for making men so much
his darlings as to let them speak his word.
May it be my topmost desire to live
as much to God's glory as possible — and,
When I shall die
Receive me I'll cry
For Jesus has lov'd me
I cannot tell why ...
In health, contentment and peace June 19/52
Only feeling the thorns of sin & sin's effects. —

12. *A comment on the inside back cover of the second slim volume of his
manuscript sermon-outlines. It reveals the spirit in which his sermons
were prepared*

THE FAMILY REGISTER

Charles Haddon Spurgeon and Susannah Thompson were by the gracious arrangement of Divine Providence, most happily married at New Park Street Chapel by Dr Alexander Fletcher on Tuesday, January 8th 1856.

"And as year rolls after year
"Each to other still more dear

EXCEPT THE LORD BUILD THE HOUSE.

THEY LABOR IN VAIN THAT BUILD IT

13. *Marriage entry in the Family Bible*

14. *One of the many contemporary cartoons that reveal the attention*

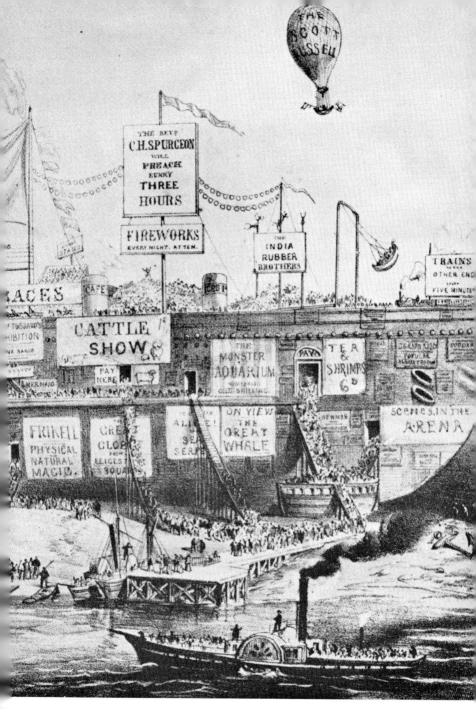

young preacher commanded even in the secular world of his time

15. *The Spurgeons' first home in New Kent Road still stands. It is the second from the right in this picture.* 16. [right] *A close-up of the entrance and commemoration plaque*

17. *The house as it was last century*

18. *An informal study of the pastor's wife*

19. [overleaf] *A rare snapshot!*

be taken out, as the windows were not made to open, yet nothing came of my remarks; but it providentially happened, one Monday, that somebody removed most of those panes in a masterly manner, almost as well as if they had been taken out by a glazier. There was considerable consternation, and much conjecture, as to who had committed the crime, and I proposed that a reward of five pounds should be offered for the discovery of the offender, who when found should receive the amount as a present. The reward was not forthcoming, and therefore I have not felt it to be my duty to inform against the individual. I trust none will suspect *me*, but if they do, I shall have to confess that I have walked with the stick which let the oxygen into that stifling structure. In a very short time after I began to preach in London, the congregation so multiplied as to make the chapel, in the evening, when the gas was burning, like the Black Hole of Calcutta. One night, in 1854, while preaching there, I exclaimed, "By faith, the walls of Jericho fell down, and by faith, this wall at the back shall come down, too." An aged and prudent deacon, in somewhat domineering terms, observed to me, at the close of the sermon, "Let us never hear of that again." "What do you mean?" I enquired; "you will hear no more about it *when it is done*, and therefore the sooner you set about doing it, the better." The following extract from the church-book shows that the members did set about doing it in real earnest:

"Church-meeting, 30th August, 1854.

Resolved—That we desire, as a church, to record our devout and grateful acknowledgments to our Heavenly Father for the success that has attended the ministry of our esteemed Pastor, and we consider it important, at as early a period as possible, that increased accommodation should be provided for the numbers that flock to the chapel on Lord's-days; and we would affectionately request our respected deacons to give the subject their full and careful consideration, and to favour us with their report at the church-meeting in October."

A considerable, but unavoidable delay, took place, in consequence of the vestry and school-rooms being held on a different Trust from that of the chapel, so that it became necessary to apply to the Charity Commissioners before including those rooms in the main building. After fully investigating the circumstances, they did not interpose any obstacle, so the alterations were commenced early in 1855, and in due course the chapel was enlarged as proposed, and a new school-room was erected along the side of the chapel, with windows which

T

could be let down, to allow those who were seated in the school to hear the preacher.

THE CHOLERA YEAR IN LONDON

In the year 1854, when I had scarcely been in London twelve months, the neighbourhood in which I laboured was visited by Asiatic cholera, and my congregation suffered from its inroads. Family after family summoned me to the bedside of the smitten, and almost every day I was called to visit the grave. At first, I gave myself up with youthful ardour to the visitation of the sick, and was sent for from all corners of the district by persons of all ranks and religions, but soon I became weary in body, and sick at heart. My friends seemed falling one by one, and I felt or fancied that I was sickening like those around me. A little more work and weeping would have laid me low among the rest; I felt that my burden was heavier than I could bear, and I was ready to sink under it.

I was returning mournfully home from a funeral, when, as God would have it, my curiosity led me to read a paper which was wafered up in a shoemaker's window in the Great Dover Road. It did not look like a trade announcement, nor was it, for it bore, in a good bold handwriting, these words:

"Because thou hast made the Lord, which is my refuge, even the Most High, thy habitation; there shall no evil befall thee, neither shall any plague come nigh thy dwelling."

The effect upon my heart was immediate. Faith appropriated the passage as her own. I felt secure, refreshed, girt with immortality. I went on with my visitation of the dying, in a calm and peaceful spirit; I felt no fear of evil, and I suffered no harm. The Providence which moved the tradesman to place those verses in his window, I gratefully acknowledge, and in the remembrance of its marvellous power, I adore the Lord my God.

[In a pamphlet entitled, "The Best Refuge in Times of Trouble", published about the time of Spurgeon's "home-going", Mr. W. Ford, of 19H, Peabody Buildings, Orchard Street, Westminster, wrote:

"In the year 1854, the first year of Mr. Spurgeon in London, the cholera raged in the locality of his church, and the neighbourhood where he resided. The parochial authorities were very thoughtful for the poor, and caused bills to be placed at the corners of the streets, headed CHOLERA—in large type—informing the public where advice and medicines would be supplied gratis. At that time, I lived in the Great Dover Road, and Mr. Spurgeon lived a little further towards Greenwich, in Virginia Terrace. Seeing the bills above-named at every turning, I was forcibly impressed that they were very much calculated to terrify the people. With the concurrence of a friend, I procured one, and wrote in the centre these words: 'Because thou hast made the Lord, which is my refuge, even the Most High, thy habitation; there shall no evil befall thee, neither shall any plague come nigh thy dwelling.' This bill I placed in my shop-window, hundreds read it, and I am not aware of one jeer or improper remark —so subdued and solemnized were the people by the awful visitation. Among the readers of the bill, was Mr. Spurgeon."]

During that epidemic of cholera, though I had many engagements in the country, I gave them up that I might remain in London to visit the sick and the dying. I felt that it was my duty to be on the spot in such a time of disease and death and sorrow. One Monday morning, I was awakened, about three o'clock, by a sharp ring of the door-bell. I was urged, without delay, to visit a house not very far from London Bridge. I went; and up two pairs of stairs I was shown into a room, the only occupants of which were a nurse and a dying man. "Oh, sir!" exclaimed the nurse, as I entered, "about half-an-hour ago, Mr. So-and-so begged me to send for you." "What does he want?" I asked. "He is dying, sir," she replied. I said, "Yes, I see that he is; what sort of a man was he?" The nurse answered, "He came home from Brighton, last night, sir; he had been out all day. I looked for a Bible, sir, but there is not one in the house; I hope you have brought one with you." "Oh!" I said, "a Bible would be of no use to him now. If he could understand me, I could tell him the way of salvation in the very words of Scripture." I stood by his side, and spoke to him, but he gave me no answer. I spoke again, but the only consciousness he had was a foreboding of terror, mingled with the stupor of approaching death. Soon, even that was gone, for sense had fled, and I stood there, a few minutes, sighing with the poor woman who had watched over him, and altogether hopeless about his soul. Gazing at his face, I perceived that he was dead, and that his soul had departed.

That man, in his lifetime, had been wont to jeer at me. In strong language, he had often denounced me as a hypocrite. Yet he was no sooner smitten by the darts of death than he sought my presence and counsel, no doubt feeling in his heart that I was a servant of God, though he did not care to own it with his lips. There I stood, unable to help him. Promptly as I had responded to his call, what could I do but look at his corpse, and mourn over a lost soul? He had, when in health, wickedly refused Christ, yet in his death-agony he had superstitiously sent for me. Too late, he sighed for the ministry of reconciliation, and sought to enter in at the closed door, but he was not able. There was no space left him then for repentance, for he had wasted the opportunities which God had long granted to him. I went home, and was soon called away again; that time, to see a young woman. She also was in the last extremity, but it was a fair, fair sight. She was singing—though she knew she was dying—and talking to those round about her, telling her brothers and sisters to follow her to Heaven, bidding good-bye to her father, and all the while smiling as if it had been her marriage day. She was happy and blessed. I never saw more conspicuously in my life, than I did that morning, the difference there is between one who feareth God and one who feareth Him not.

Chapter 21

Love, Courtship, and Marriage

By Mrs. C. H. Spurgeon

When I came to deal with the sacred and delicate task of writing this chapter, to record the events of the years 1854 and 1855, two courses only seemed to open before me—the one, to conceal, as gracefully as possible, under conventional phraseology and common-place details, the tender truth and sweetness of our mutual love-story —the other, to write out of the fulness of my very soul, and suffer my pen to describe the fair visions of the past as, one by one, they grew again before my eyes into living and loving realities. I chose the latter alternative, I felt *compelled* to do so. My hand has but obeyed the dictates of my heart, and, I trust also, the guidance of the unerring Spirit.

It may be an unusual thing thus to reveal the dearest secrets of one's past life, but I think, in this case, I am justified in the course I have taken. My husband once said, "You may write my life across the sky, I have nothing to conceal;" and I cannot withhold the precious testimony which these hitherto sealed pages of his history bear to his singularly holy and blameless character.

So, I have unlocked my heart, and poured out its choicest memories. Some people may blame my prodigality, but I am convinced that the majority of readers will gather up, with reverent hands, the treasures I have thus scattered, and find themselves greatly enriched by their possession.

It has cost me sighs, and multiplied sorrows, as I have mourned over my vanished joys; but, on the other hand, it has drawn me very near to "the God of all consolation", and taught me to bless Him again and again for having ever given me the priceless privilege of such a husband's love.

Many years ago, I read a most pathetic story, which is constantly recalled to mind as the duties of this compilation compel me to read the records of past years, and re-peruse the long-closed letters of my beloved, and live over again the happy days when we were all-in-all to each other. I do not remember all the details of the incident which so impressed me, but the chief facts were these. A married couple were crossing one of the great glaciers of Alpine regions, when a fatal accident occurred. The husband fell down one of the huge crevasses which abound on all glaciers—the rope broke, and the depth of the chasm was so great that no help could be rendered, nor could the body be recovered. Over the wife's anguish at her loss, we must draw the veil of silence.

Forty years afterwards saw her, with the guide who had accompanied them at the time of the accident, staying at the nearest hotel to the foot of the glacier, waiting for the sea of ice to give up its dead; for, by the well-known law of glacier-progression, the form of her long-lost husband might be expected to appear, expelled from the mouth of the torrent, about that date. Patiently, and with unfailing constancy, they watched and waited, and their hopes were at last rewarded. One day, the body was released from its prison in the ice, and the wife looked again on the features of him who had been so long parted from her!

But the pathos of the story lay in the fact that she was then an old woman, while the newly-rescued body was that of quite a young and robust man, so faithfully had the crystal casket preserved the jewel which it held so long. The forty years had left no wrinkles on that marble brow, Time's withering fingers could not touch him in *that* tomb, and so, for a few brief moments, the aged lady saw the husband of her youth, *as he was in the days which were gone for ever!*

Somewhat similar has been my experience while preparing these chapters. I have stood, as it were, at the foot of the great glacier of Time, and looked with unspeakable tenderness on my beloved as I knew him in the days of his strength, when the dew of his youth was upon him, and the Lord had made him a mighty man among men. True, the cases are not altogether parallel, for I had my beloved with me all the forty years, and we grew old together, but his seven years in glory seem like half a century to me; and now, with the burden of declining years upon me, I am watching and waiting to see my loved one again—not as he was forty years or even seven years ago, but as he will be when I am called to rejoin him through the avenue of the grave, or at the coming of our Lord Jesus Christ with all His saints. So I am waiting, and "looking for that blessed hope, and the glorious papearing of the great God and our Saviour Jesus Christ."

*　　　　　*　　　　　*

The first time I saw my future husband, he occupied the pulpit of New Park Street Chapel on the memorable Sunday when he preached his first sermons there. I was no stranger to the place. Many a discourse had I there listened to from Pastor James Smith (afterwards of

Cheltenham)—a quaint and rugged preacher, but one well versed in the blessed art of bringing souls to Christ. Often had I seen him administer the ordinance of baptism to the candidates, wondering with a tearful longing whether I should ever be able thus to confess my faith in the Lord Jesus.

I can recall the old-fashioned, dapper figure of the senior deacon, of whom I stood very much in awe. He was a lawyer, and wore the silk stockings and knee-breeches dear to a former generation. When the time came to give out the hymns, he mounted an open desk immediately beneath the pulpit, and from where I sat, I had a side view of him. To the best of my remembrance, he was a short, stout man, and his rotund body, perched on his undraped legs, and clothed in a long-tailed coat, gave him an unmistakable resemblance to a gigantic robin; and when he chirped out the verses of the hymn in a piping, twittering voice, I thought the likeness was complete!

Well also did I know the curious pulpit without any stairs; it looked like a magnified swallow's-nest, and was entered from behind through a door in the wall. My childish imagination was always excited by the silent and "creepy" manner in which the minister made his appearance therein. One moment the big box would be empty—the next, if I had but glanced down at Bible or hymn-book, and raised my eyes again—there was the preacher, comfortably seated, or standing ready to commence the service! I found it very interesting, and though I knew there was a matter-of-fact *door*, through which the good man stepped into his rostrum, this knowledge was not allowed to interfere with, or even explain, the fanciful notions I loved to indulge in concerning that mysterious entrance and exit. It was certainly somewhat singular that, in the very pulpit which had exercised such a charm over me, I should have my first glimpse of the one who was to be the love of my heart, and the light of my earthly life. After Mr. Smith left, there came, with the passing years, a sad time of barrenness and desolation upon the church at New Park Street; the cause languished, and almost died, and none even dreamed of the overwhelming blessing which the Lord had in store for the remnant of faithful people worshipping there.

*   *   *

From my childhood, I had been a greatly-privileged favourite with Mr. and Mrs. Olney, Senr. ("Father Olney" and his wife), and I was a constant visitor at their homes, both in the Borough and West Croydon, and it was by reason of this mutual love that I found myself in their pew at the dear old chapel on that Sabbath evening, December

18th, 1853. There had been much excitement and anxiety concerning the invitation to the country lad from Waterbeach to come and preach in the honoured, but almost empty sanctuary; it was a risky experiment, so some thought, but I believe that, from the very first sermon he heard him preach, dear old "Father Olney's" heart was fixed in its faith that God was going to do great things by this young David.

When the family returned from the morning service, varied emotions filled their souls. They had never before heard just such preaching; they were bewildered, and amazed, but they had been fed with royal dainties. They were, however, in much concern for the young preacher himself, who was greatly discouraged by the sight of so many empty pews, and manifestly wished himself back again with his loving people, in his crowded chapel in Cambridgeshire. "What can be done?" good Deacon Olney said; "we *must* get him a better congregation to-night, or we shall lose him!" So, all that Sabbath afternoon, there ensued a determined looking-up of friends and acquaintances, who, by some means or other, were coaxed into giving a promise that they would be at Park Street in the evening to hear the wonderful boy preacher. "And little Susie must come, too," dear old Mrs. Olney pleaded. I do not think that "little Susie" particularly cared about being present; her ideas of the dignity and propriety of the ministry were rather shocked and upset by the reports which the morning worshippers had brought back concerning the young man's unconventional outward appearance! However, to please my dear friends, I went with them, and thus was present at the second sermon which my precious husband preached in London.

Ah! how little I then thought that my eyes looked on him who was to be my life's beloved; how little I dreamed of the honour God was preparing for me in the near future! It is a mercy that our lives are not left for us to plan, but that our Father chooses for us; else might we sometimes turn away from our best blessings, and put from us the choicest and loveliest gifts of His providence. For, if the whole truth be told, I was not at all fascinated by the young orator's eloquence, while his countrified manner and speech excited more regret than reverence. Alas, for my vain and foolish heart! I was not spiritually-minded enough to understand his earnest presentation of the gospel, and his powerful pleading with sinners, but the huge black satin stock, the long, badly-trimmed hair, and the blue pocket-handkerchief with white spots, which he himself has so graphically described—these attracted most of my attention, and, I fear, awakened some feelings of amusement. There was only one sentence of the whole sermon which I carried away with me, and that solely on account of its quaintness, for it seemed to me an extraordinary thing for the preacher to speak of the "living stones in the Heavenly Temple perfectly joined together with the vermilion cement of Christ's blood."

*   *   *

I do not recollect my first introduction to him; it is probable that he spoke to me, as to many others, on that same Sabbath evening, but when the final arrangement was made for him to occupy New Park Street pulpit, with a view to the permanent pastorate, I used to meet him occasionally at the house of our mutual friends, Mr. and Mrs. Olney, and I sometimes went to hear him preach.

I had not at that time made any open profession of religion, though I was brought to see my need of a Saviour under the ministry of the Rev. S. B. Bergne, of the Poultry Chapel, about a year before Mr. Spurgeon came to London. He preached, one Sunday evening, from the text, "The word is nigh thee, even in thy mouth, and in thy heart" (Romans x. 8), and from that service I date the dawning of the true light in my soul. The Lord said to me, through His servant, "Give Me thine heart," and, constrained by His love, that night witnessed my solemn resolution of entire surrender to Himself. But I had since become cold and indifferent to the things of God; seasons of darkness, despondency, and doubt, had passed over me, but I had kept all my religious experiences carefully concealed in my own breast, and perhaps this guilty hesitancy and reserve had much to do with the sickly and sleepy condition of my soul when I was first brought under the ministry of my beloved. None could have more needed the quickening and awakening which I received from the earnest pleadings and warnings of that voice—soon to be the sweetest in all the world to me.

Gradually I became alarmed at my backsliding state, and then, by a great effort, I sought spiritual help and guidance from William Olney ("Father Olney's" second son, and my cousin by marriage), who was an active worker in the Sunday-school at New Park Street, and a true Mr. Greatheart, and comforter of young pilgrims. He may have told the new Pastor about me—I cannot say; but, one day, I was greatly surprised to receive from Mr. Spurgeon an illustrated copy of *The Pilgrim's Progress*, in which he had written the inscription which is reproduced in *facsimile* overpage.

Miss. Thompson
with desires for her progress
in the blessed pilgrimage.
from
C H Spurgeon
Ap. 20. 1854.

I do not think my beloved had, at that time, any other thought concerning me than to help a struggling soul Heavenward, but I was greatly impressed by his concern for me, and the book became very precious as well as helpful. By degrees, though with much trembling, I told him of my state before God; and he gently led me, by his preaching, and by his conversations, through the power of the Holy Spirit, to the cross of Christ for the peace and pardon my weary soul was longing for.

Thus things went quietly on for a little while; our friendship steadily grew, and I was happier than I had been since the days at the Poultry Chapel, but no bright dream of the future flashed distinctly before my eyes till the day of the opening of the Crystal Palace at Sydenham, on June 10, 1854. A large party of our friends, including Mr. Spurgeon, were present at the inauguration, and we occupied some raised seats at the end of the Palace where the great clock is now fixed. As we sat there talking, laughing, and amusing ourselves as best we could, while waiting for the procession to pass by, Mr. Spurgeon handed me a book, into which he had been occasionally dipping, and, pointing to some particular lines, said, "What do you think of the poet's suggestion in those verses?" The volume was Martin Tupper's *Proverbial Philosophy*, then recently published, and already beginning to feel the stir of the breezes of adverse criticism, which afterwards gathered into a howling tempest of disparagement and scathing sarcasm. No thought had I for authors and their woes at that moment. The pointing finger guided my eyes to the chapter on "Marriage", of which the opening sentences ran thus—

"Seek a good wife of thy God, for she is the best gift of His providence;
Yet ask not in bold confidence that which He hath not promised:
Thou knowest not His good will; be thy prayer then submissive there-
    unto,
And leave thy petition to His mercy, assured that He will deal well
    with thee.
If thou art to have a wife of thy youth, she is now living on the earth;
Therefore think of her, and pray for her weal."

"Do you pray for him who is to be your husband?" said a soft low
voice in my ear—so soft that no one else heard the whisper.

I do not remember that the question received any vocal answer, but
my fast-beating heart, which sent a tell-tale flush to my cheeks, and
my downcast eyes, which feared to reveal the light which at once
dawned in them, may have spoken a language which love understood.
From that moment, a very quiet and subdued little maiden sat by the
young Pastor's side, and while the brilliant procession passed round
the Palace, I do not think she took so much note of the glittering
pageant defiling before her, as of the crowd of newly-awakened
emotions which were palpitating within her heart. Neither the book
nor its theories were again alluded to, but when the formalities of the
opening were over, and the visitors were allowed to leave their seats,
the same low voice whispered again, "Will you come and walk round
the Palace with me?" How we obtained leave of absence from the
rest of the party, I know not, but we wandered together, for a long
time, not only in the wonderful building itself, but in the gardens, and
even down to the lake, beside which the colossal forms of extinct
monsters were being cunningly modelled. During that walk, on that
memorable day in June, I believe God Himself united our hearts in
indissoluble bonds of true affection, and, though we knew it not, gave
us to each other for ever. From that time our friendship grew apace,
and quickly ripened into deepest love—a love which lives in my heart
to-day as truly, aye, and more solemnly and strongly than it did in
those early days; for, though God has seen fit to call my beloved up
to higher service, He has left me the consolation of still loving him
with all my heart, and believing that our love shall be perfected when
we meet in that blessed land where Love reigns supreme and eternal.

*   *   *

It was not very long (August 2, 1854) before the sweet secret
between us was openly revealed. Loving looks, and tender tones, and
clasping hands had all told "the old, old story", and yet, when the
verbal confession of it came, how wonderful it was! Was there ever

quite such bliss on earth before? I can see the place where the marvel was wrought, as plainly, at this distance of over forty years, as I saw it then. It was in a little, old-fashioned garden (my grandfather's), which had high brick walls on three sides, and was laid out with straight, formal gravel paths, and a small lawn, in the midst of which flourished a large and very fruitful pear tree—the pride of old grandad's heart. Rather a dreary and unromantic place, one would imagine, for a declaration of love; but people are not particularly careful as to the selection of their surroundings at such a moment, and do not often take pains to secure a delightful background to the picture which will for ever be photographed on their hearts. To this day, I think of that old garden as a sacred place, a paradise of happiness, since there my beloved sought me for his very own, and told me how much he loved me. Though I thought I knew this already, it was a very different matter to hear him say it, and I trembled and was silent for very joy and gladness. The sweet ceremony of betrothal needs no description; every loving and true heart can fill up the details either from experience or anticipation. To me, it was a time as *solemn* as it was sweet, and, with a great awe in my heart, I left my beloved, and hastening to the house, and to an upper room, I knelt before God, and praised and thanked Him, with happy tears, for His great mercy in giving me the love of so good a man. If I had known, then, *how* good he was, and how great he would become, I should have been overwhelmed, not so much with the happiness of being his, as with the responsibility which such a position would entail. But, thank God, throughout all my blessed married life, the perfect love which drew us together never slackened or faltered, and, though I can now see how undeserving I was to be the life companion of so eminent a servant of God, I know *he* did not think this, but looked upon his wife as God's best earthly gift to him.

In the diary I then kept, I find this brief but joyful entry: "August 2, 1854.—It is impossible to write down all that occurred this morning. I can only adore in silence the mercy of my God, and praise Him for all His benefits."

*   *   *

My dear husband used often to write his name and a brief comment in any of his books which he specially valued. His first volume of Calvin's *Commentaries* contains an inscription which is a direct confirmation of what I have written above.

The volumes making up a complete set of Calvin were a gift to me from my own most dear, & tender wife. Blessed may she be among women. How much of comfort & strength she has ministered unto me it is not in my power to estimate, She has been to me God's best earthly gift, & not a little even of heavenly treasure has come to me by her means. She has often been as an angel of God unto me.

C. H. Spurgeon

*   *   *

After our engagement, we met pretty constantly; I attended the services at New Park Street Chapel as often as possible, and on February 1, 1855, I was baptized there by my beloved, upon my profession of repentance towards God, and faith in our Lord Jesus Christ. When I had to "come before the church", he endeavoured to keep the matter as quiet as possible, lest inconvenient curiosity should be aroused, but the fact must have found some small leakage, for we were amused to hear afterwards of the following little incident. An old man, named Johnny Dear, preceded me in the list of candidates, and when he had given in his experience, and been questioned and dismissed, two maiden ladies, sitting at the back of the room, were overheard to say, "What was that man's name?" "Johnny Dear." "Oh, well, I suppose it will be 'sister dear' next!" And I am thankful to say her surmise was correct, and that I happily passed through the somewhat severe ordeal.

Mr. Spurgeon had expressed a wish that I should write out my confession of repentance and faith, which I accordingly did. I do not know whether it was read to the officers of the church, or retained solely for his own perusal, but it is preserved among his papers, and in the following words he gave me assurance of his satisfaction with my testimony:

"75, Dover Road,
January 11, 1855.

My Dearest,

The letter is all I can desire. Oh! I could weep for joy (as I certainly am doing now) to think that my beloved can so well testify to a work of grace in her soul. I knew you were *really* a child of God, but I did not think you had been led in such a path. I see my Master has been ploughing deep, and it is the deep-sown seed, struggling with the clods, which now makes your bosom heave with distress. If I know anything of spiritual symptoms, I think I know a cure for you. Your position is not the sphere for earnest labour for Christ. You have done all you could in more ways than one, but you are not brought into actual contact either with the saints, or with the sinful, sick, or miserable, whom you could serve. Active service brings with it warmth, and this tends to remove doubting, for our works thus become evidences of our calling and election.

I flatter no one, but allow me to say, honestly, that few cases which have come under my notice are so satisfactory as yours. Mark, I write not now as your *admiring friend*, but impartially as your Pastor. If the Lord had intended your destruction, He would not have told you such things as these, nor would He enable you so unreservedly to cast yourself upon His faithful promise. As I hope to stand at the bar of God, clear of the blood of all men, it would ill become me to flatter; and as I love you with the deepest and purest affection, far be it from me to trifle with your immortal interests; but I will say again that my gratitude to God ought to be great, as well on my own behalf as yours, that you have been so deeply schooled in the lessons of the heart, and have so frequently looked into the charnel-house of your own corruption. There are other lessons to come, that you may be thoroughly furnished, but, oh! my dear one, how good to learn the first lesson well! I loved you once, but feared you might not be an heir of Heaven—God in His mercy showed me that you were indeed *elect*. I then thought I might without sin reveal my affection to you—but up to the time I saw your note, I could not imagine that you had seen such great sights, and were so thoroughly versed in soul-knowledge. God is good, very good, infinitely good. Oh, how I prize this last gift, because I now know, more than ever, that the Giver loves the gift, and so I may love it, too, but only in subservience to Him. Dear purchase of a Saviour's blood, you are to me a Saviour's gift, and my

heart is full to overflowing with the thought of such continued goodness. I do not wonder at His goodness, for it is just like Him; but I
cannot but lift up the voice of joy at His manifold mercies.

Whatever befall us, trouble and adversity, sickness or death, we
need not fear a final separation, either from each other, or our God. I
am glad you are not here just at this moment, for I feel so deeply that
I could only throw my arms around you and weep. May the choicest
favours be thine, may the Angel of the Covenant be thy companion,
may thy supplications be answered, and may thy conversation be
with Jesus in Heaven! Farewell; unto my God and my father's God
I commend you.

Yours, with pure and holy affection, as well as terrestrial love,

C. H. SPURGEON."

*   *   *

At this time, the Crystal Palace was a favourite resort with us. It
possessed great attractions of its own, and perhaps the associations
of the opening day gave it an added grace in our eyes. In common
with many of our friends, we had season tickets, and we used them
to good purpose, as my beloved found that an hour or two of rest and
relaxation in those lovely gardens, and that pure air, braced him for
the constant toil of preaching to crowded congregations, and relieved
him somewhat from the ill effects of London's smoky atmosphere. It
was so easy for him to run down to Sydenham from London Bridge
that, as often as once a week, if possible, we arranged to meet there for
a quiet walk and talk. After the close of the Thursday evening service,
there would be a whispered word to me in the aisle, "Three o'clock
to-morrow," which meant that, if I would be at the Palace by that
hour, "somebody" would meet me at the Crystal Fountain. I was then
living at 7, St. Ann's Terrace, Brixton Road, in the house which my
parents, Mr. and Mrs. R. B. Thompson, shared with my uncle,
H. Kilvington, Esq., and the long walk from there to Sydenham was
a pleasant task to me, with such a meeting in view, and such delightful
companionship as a reward. We wandered amid the many Courts,
which were then chiefly instructive and educational in character; we
gazed with almost solemn awe at the reproductions of Egypt, Assyria,
and Pompeii, and I think we learned many things beside the tenderness of our own hearts towards each other, as the bright blissful hours
sped by.

The young minister had not much time to spare from his duties,
but he usually came to see me on a Monday, bringing his sermon with

U

him to revise for the press; and I learned to be quiet, and mind my own business, while this important work was going on. It was good discipline for the Pastor's intended wife, who needed no inconsiderable amount of training to fit her in any measure for the post she was ordained to occupy. I remember, however, that there was one instance of preparation for future duty, which was by no means agreeable to my feelings, and which, I regret to say, I resented. As a chronicler must be truthful, I tell the story, and to show how, from the very beginning of his public life, my dear husband's devotion to his sacred work dominated and even absorbed every other passion and purpose of his heart. He was a "called, and chosen, and faithful" servant of Christ in the very highest degree, and during all his life he put God's service first, and all earthly things second. I have known him to be so abstracted, on a Sabbath morning at the Tabernacle, just before preaching, that if I left his vestry for a few moments, he would, on my return, rise and greet me with a handshake, and a grave "How are you?" as if I were a strange visitor; then, noting the amused look on my face, he would discover his mistake, and laughingly say, "Never mind, wifey dear, I was thinking about my hymns." This happened not once only, but several times, and when the service was over, and we were driving home, he would make very merry over it.

But I must tell the promised story of the earlier days, though it is not at all to my own credit; yet, even as I write it, I smile at the remembrance of his enjoyment of the tale in later years. If I wanted to amuse him much, or chase some gloom from his dear face, I would remind him of the time when he took his sweetheart to a certain service, and there was so preoccupied with the discourse he was about to deliver, that he forgot all about her, and left her to take care of herself as best she could. As I recalled the incident, which really was to me a very serious one at the time, and might have had an untoward ending, he would laugh at the ludicrous side of it till the tears ran down his cheeks, and then he would lovingly kiss me, and say how glad he was that I had borne with his ill manners, and how much I must have loved him.

This is the story. He was to preach at the large hall of "The Horns", Kennington, which was not very far from where we then resided. He asked me to accompany him, and dined with us at St. Ann's Terrace, the service being in the afternoon. We went together, happily enough, in a cab, and I well remember trying to keep close by his side as we mingled with the mass of people thronging up the staircase. But, by the time we had reached the landing, he had forgotten my existence; the burden of the message he had to proclaim to that crowd of immortal souls was upon him, and he turned into the small side door where the officials were awaiting him, without for a moment realizing that I was left to struggle as best I could with the rough and eager throng around me. At first, I was utterly bewildered, and then, I am sorry to have to confess, I was *angry*. I at once returned home, and told my grief to my gentle mother, who tried to soothe my ruffled spirit, and bring me to a better frame of mind. She wisely reasoned that my chosen husband was no ordinary man, that his whole life was absolutely dedicated to God and His service, and that I must never, *never* hinder him by trying to put myself first in his heart. Presently, after much good and loving counsel, my heart grew soft, and I saw I had been very foolish and wilful; and then a cab drew up at the door, and dear Mr. Spurgeon came running into the house, in great excitement, calling, "Where's Susie? I have been searching for her everywhere, and cannot find her; has she come back by herself?" My dear mother went to him, took him aside, and told him all the truth; and I think, when he realized the state of things, she had to soothe him also, for he was so innocent at heart of having offended me in any way, that he must have felt I had done him an injustice in thus doubting him. At last, mother came to fetch me to him, and I went downstairs. Quietly he let me tell him how indignant I had felt, and then he repeated mother's little lesson, assuring me of his deep affection for me, but pointing out that, before all things, he was *God's servant*, and I must be prepared to yield my claims to His.

I never forgot the teaching of that day; I had learned my hard lesson *by heart*, for I do not recollect ever again seeking to assert my right to his time and attention when any service for God demanded them. It was ever the settled purpose of my married life that I should never hinder him in his work for the Lord, never try to keep him from fulfilling his engagements, never plead my own ill-health as a reason why he should remain at home with me. I thank God, now, that He enabled me to carry out this determination, and rejoice that I have no cause to reproach myself with being a drag on the swift wheels of his consecrated life. I do not take any credit to myself for this; it was the Lord's will concerning me, and He saw to it that I received the necessary training whereby, in after years, I could cheerfully surrender His chosen servant to the incessant demands of his ministry, his literary work, and the multiplied labours of his exceptionally busy life. And now I can bless God for what happened on that memorable afternoon when my beloved preached at "The Horns", Kennington. What a delightfully cosy tea we three had together that evening, and how sweet was the calm in our hearts after the storm, and how much we both loved and honoured mother for her wise counsels and her tender diplomacy!

Some little time afterwards, when Mr. Spurgeon had an engagement at Windsor, I was asked to accompany him, and in forwarding the invitation, he referred to the above incident thus: "My Own Darling—What do you say to this? As you wish me to express my desire, I will say, 'Go'; but I should have left it to your own choice if I did not know that my wishes always please you. Possibly, I may be again inattentive to you if you do go, but this will be nice for us both —that 'Charles' may have space for mending, and that 'Susie' may exhibit her growth in knowledge of his character, by patiently enduring his failings." So the end of this little "rift in the lute" was no patched-up peace between us, but a deepening of our confidence in each other, and an increase of that fervent love which can look a misunderstanding in the face till it melts away and vanishes, as a morning cloud before the ardent glances of the sun.

Two tender little notes, written by my husband sixteen years later (1871), will show what an abundant reward of loving approval was bestowed on me for merely doing what it was my duty to do:

"My Own Dear One,—None know how grateful I am to God for you. In all I have ever done for Him, you have a large share, for in making me so happy you have fitted me for service. Not an ounce of power has ever been lost to the good cause through you. I have served the Lord far more, and never less, for your sweet companionship. The Lord God Almighty bless you now and for ever!

"I have been thinking over my strange history, and musing on eternal love's great river-head from which such streams of mercy have flowed to me. I dwell devoutly on many points—the building of the Tabernacle—what a business it was, and how little it seems now! Do you remember a Miss Thompson who collected for the enlargement of New Park Street Chapel as much as £100? Bless her dear heart! Think of the love which gave me that dear lady for a wife, and made her such a wife; to me, the ideal wife, and, as I believe, without exaggeration or love-flourishing, the precise form in which God would make a woman for such a man as I am, if He designed her to be the greatest of all earthly blessings to him; and in some sense a spiritual blessing, too, for in that also am I richly profited by you, though you would not believe it. I will leave this 'good matter' ere the paper is covered, but not till I have sent you as many kisses as there are waves on the sea."

*   *   *

It was our mutual desire to pay a visit to Colchester, that I might be introduced to Mr. Spurgeon's parents as their future daughter-in-law, and, after some trouble and disappointment, my father's consent was obtained, and we set off on our first important journey together, with very keen and vivid perceptions of the delightful novelty of our experience. It is not to be wondered at that my memories of the visit are somewhat hazy, although intensely happy. I was welcomed, petted, and entertained most affectionately by all the family, and I remember being taken to see every place and object of interest in and around Colchester, but *what* I saw, I know not; the joy of being all the day long with my beloved, and this for three or four days together, was enough to fill my heart with gladness, and render me oblivious of any other pleasure. I think we must have returned on the Friday of our week's holiday, for, according to our custom, we exchanged letters on the Saturday as usual, and this is what we said to each other:

"75, Dover Road,
April, '55.

My Own Doubly-dear Susie,

How much we have enjoyed in each other's society! It seems almost impossible that I could either have conferred or received so much happiness. I feel now, like you, very low in spirits, but a sweet promise in Ezekiel cheers me, 'I will give thee the opening of the mouth in the midst of them.' Surely my God has not forgotten me. Pray for me, my love; and may our united petitions win a blessing through the Saviour's merit! Let us take heed of putting ourselves too prominently in our own hearts, but let us commit our way unto the Lord. 'What I have in my own hand, I usually lose,' said Luther; 'but what I put into God's hand, is still, and ever will be, in my possession.' I need not send my love to you, for, though absent in body, my heart is with you still, and I am, your much-loved, and ardently-loving, C. H. S.

P.S.—The devil has barked again in *The Essex Standard*. It contains another letter. Never mind; when Satan opens his mouth, he gives me an opportunity of ramming my sword down his throat."

MY REPLY
"St. Ann's Terrace,
April, '55.

My Dearest,

I thank you with warm and hearty thanks for the note just received. It is useless for me to attempt to tell you how much happiness I have had during the past week. Words are but cold dishes on which to serve up thoughts and feelings which come warm and glowing from the heart. I should like to express my appreciation of all the tenderness and care you have shown towards me during this happy week, but I fear to pain you by thanks for what I know was a pleasure to you. I expect your thoughts have been busy to-day about 'the crown jewels.' The gems may differ in size, colour, richness, and beauty, but even the smallest are 'precious stones', are they not?

That *Standard* certainly does not bear 'Excelsior' as its motto; nor can 'Good will to men' be the device of its floating pennon, but it matters not; *we know* that all is under the control of One of whom Asaph said, 'Surely the wrath of man shall praise Thee; the remainder of wrath shalt Thou restrain.' May His blessing rest in an especial manner on you to-night, my dearly-beloved, and on the approaching Sabbath, when you stand before the great congregation, may you be 'filled with all the fulness of God'! Good-night. Fondly and faithfully yours,—SUSIE."

The mention of *The Essex Standard*, in the foregoing letters, points to the fact that, even thus early in his ministerial career, the strife of tongues had commenced against God's servant, and the cruel arrows of the wicked had sorely wounded him. He had also begun to learn that some of his severest critics were the very men who ought to have been his heartiest friends and warmest sympathizers. The first reference to this persecution is in a letter to me, written January 1, 1855, where he says: "I find much stir has been made by 'Job's letter', and hosts of unknown persons have risen up on my behalf. It seems very likely that King James (James Wells) will shake his own throne by lifting his hand against one of the Lord's little ones." Then, in May, in one of the Saturday letters, there occur these sentences: "I am down in the valley, partly because of two desperate attacks in *The Sheffield Independent*, and *The Empire*, and partly because I cannot find a subject. Yet faith fails not. I know and believe the promise, and am not afraid to rest upon it. All the scars I receive, are scars of honour; so, faint heart, on to the battle! My love, were you here, how you would comfort me, but since you are not, I shall do what is better still, go upstairs alone, and pour out my griefs into my Saviour's ear. 'Jesus, *Lover* of *my soul* I *can* to Thy bosom fly!' "

These were only the first few drops of the terrible storm of detraction, calumny, and malice, which afterward burst upon him with unexampled fury, but which, blessed be God, he lived through, and

lived down. I do not say more concerning these slanders, as they wil
be described in detail in the following chapters.

When my parents removed to a house in Falcon Square, City, we
met much more frequently, and grew to know each other better,
while our hearts were knit closer and closer in purest love. A little
more "training" also took place, for one day my beloved brought
with him an ancient, rusty-looking book, and, to my amazement, said,
"Now, darling, I want you to go carefully through this volume,
marking all those paragraphs and sentences that strike you as being
particularly sweet, or quaint, or instructive; will you do this for me?"
Of course, I at once complied, but he did not know with what a
trembling sense of my own inability the promise was given, nor how
disqualified I then was to appreciate the spiritual beauty of his favourite
Puritan writers. It was the simplest kind of literary work which he
asked me to do, but I was such an utter stranger to such service, that
it seemed a most important and difficult task to discover in that "dry"
old book the bright diamonds and red gold which he evidently
reckoned were therein enshrined. Love, however, is a matchless
teacher, and I was a willing pupil, and so, with help and suggestion
from so dear a tutor, the work went on from day to day till, in due
time, a small volume made its appearance, which he called, *Smooth
Stones taken from Ancient Brooks.* This title was a pleasant and Puritanic
play upon the author's name, and I think the compilers were well
pleased with the results of this happy work together. I believe the
little book is out of print now, and copies are very rarely to be met
with, but those who possess them may feel an added interest in their
perusal, now that they know the sweet love-story which hides
between their pages.

As the days went by, my beloved's preaching engagements multiplied exceedingly, yet he found time to make me very happy by his
loving visits and letters, and, on Sunday mornings, I was nearly
always allowed by my parents to enjoy his ministry. Yet this pleasure
was mingled with much of pain, for, during the early part of the year
1855, he was preaching in Exeter Hall to vast crowds of people, and
the strain on his physical power was terrible. Sometimes his voice
would almost break and fail as he pleaded with sinners to come to
Christ, or magnified the Lord in His sovereignty and righteousness.
A glass of Chili vinegar always stood on a shelf under the desk before
him, and I knew what to expect when he had recourse to that remedy.
Oh, how my heart ached for him! What self-control I had to exercise

to appear calm and collected, and keep quietly in my seat up in that little side gallery! How I longed to have the *right* to go and comfort and cheer him when the service was over! But I had to walk away, as other people did—I, who belonged to him, and was closer to his heart than anyone there! It was severe discipline for a young and loving spirit. I remember, with strange vividness at this long distance of time, the Sunday evening when he preached from the text, "His Name shall endure for ever." It was a subject in which he revelled, it was his chief delight to exalt his glorious Saviour, and he seemed in that discourse to be pouring out his very soul and life in homage and adoration before his gracious King. But I really thought he would have died there, in face of all those people! At the end of the sermon, he made a mighty effort to recover his voice, but utterance well-nigh failed, and only in broken accents could the pathetic peroration be heard—"Let my name perish, but let Christ's Name last for ever! Jesus! *Jesus!* JESUS! Crown Him Lord of all! You will not hear me say anything else. These are my last words in Exeter Hall for this time. Jesus! *Jesus!* JESUS! Crown *Him* Lord of all!" and then he fell back almost fainting in the chair behind him.

In after days, when the Lord had fully perfected for him that silver-toned voice which ravished men's ears, while it melted their hearts, there was seldom any recurrence of the painful scene I have attempted to describe. On the contrary, he spoke with the utmost ease, in the largest buildings, to assembled thousands, and, as a master musician playing on a priceless instrument, he could at will either charm his audience with notes of dulcet sweetness, or ring forth the clarion tones of warning and alarm.

He used to say, playfully, that his throat had been macadamized; but, as a matter of fact, I believe that the constant and natural use of his voice, in the delivery of so many sermons and addresses, was the secret of his entire freedom from the serious malady generally known as "clergyman's sore throat". During this first visit to Exeter Hall, New Park Street Chapel was enlarged, and when this improvement was completed, he returned to his own pulpit, the services at the hall ceased, and for a short time at least, my fears for him were silenced.

But his work went on increasing almost daily, and his popularity grew with rapid strides. Many notable services in the open-air were held about this time, and my letters give a glimpse of two of these occasions. On June 2, 1855, he writes: "Last evening, about 500 persons came to the field, and afterwards adjourned to the chapel kindly lent by Mr. Eldridge. My Master gave me power and liberty. I am persuaded souls were saved; and, as for myself, I preached like the chief of sinners, to those who, like me, were chief sinners too. Many were the tears, and not a few the smiles."

Then, on the 23rd of the same month, I had a jubilant letter, which commenced thus: "Yesterday, I climbed to the summit of a minister's glory. My congregation was enormous, I think 10,000 (this was in a field at Hackney); but certainly twice as many as at Exeter Hall. The Lord was with me, and the profoundest silence was observed, but, oh, the close—never did mortal man receive a more enthusiastic ovation! I wonder I am alive! After the service, five or six gentlemen endeavoured to clear a passage, but I was borne along, amid cheers, and prayers, and shouts, for about a quarter of an hour—it really seemed more like a week! I was hurried round and round the field without hope of escape until, suddenly seeing a nice open carriage, with two occupants, standing near, I sprang in, and begged them to drive away. This they most kindly did, and I stood up, waving my hat, and crying, 'The blessing of God be with you!' while, from thousands of heads the hats were lifted, and cheer after cheer was given. Surely, amid these plaudits I can hear the low rumblings of an advancing storm of reproaches, but even this I can bear for the Master's sake."

This was a true prophecy, for the time did come when the hatred of men to the truths he preached rose to such a height, that no scorn seemed too bitter, no sneer too contemptuous, to fling at the preacher who boldly declared the gospel of the grace of God, as he had himself learned it at the cross of Christ; but, thank God, he lived to be honoured above most men for his uprightness and fidelity, and never, to the last moment of his life, did he change one jot or tittle of his belief, or vary an iota of his whole-hearted testimony to the divinity of the doctrines of free grace.

*   *   *

In July of this year (1855), my dear one went to Scotland, intending to combine a holiday with the fulfilment of many preaching engagements—a very bad plan this, as he afterwards found, for an over-taxed mind needs absolute repose during resting times, and sermons and spirits both suffer if this reasonable rule be broken. His letters to me during this journey are not altogether joyful ones. I give a few extracts from them, which will serve to outline his first experiences in a form of service into which he so fully entered in after years. On this occasion, he was not happy, or "at home", and was constantly longing to return. This was, too, his *first* long journey by rail, and it is curious to note what physical pain the inexperienced traveller endured. In those days, there were no Pullman cars, or luxurious saloon carriages, fitted up with all the comforts and appliances of a first-class hotel, so our poor voyager fared badly. He writes a note from Carlisle, just to assure me of his safety, and then, on reaching Glasgow, he gives this account of his ride: "At Watford, I went with the guard, and enjoyed some conversation with him, which I hope God will bless to his good. At 10.45, I went inside—people asleep. I could not manage a wink, but felt very queer. At morning-light, went into a second-class carriage with another guard, and rejoiced in the splendid view as well as my uncomfortable sensations would allow. Arrived here tired, begrimed with dust, sleepy, not over high in spirits, and with a dreadful cold in my head. Last night, I slept twelve hours without waking, but I still feel as tired as before I slept. I will, I think, never travel so far at once again. I certainly shall not come home in one day, for if I do, my trip will have been an injury instead of a benefit. I am so glad you did not have my *horrid* ride, but if I could spirit you here, I would soon do it. Pray for me, my love."

The next epistle I will give at length. I have been trying in these pages to leave the "love" out of the letters as much as possible, lest my precious things should appear but platitudes to my readers, but it is a difficult task, for little rills of tenderness run between all the sentences, like the singing, dancing waters among the boulders of a brook, and I cannot still the music altogether. To the end of his beautiful life it was the same, his letters were always those of a devoted lover, as well as of a tender husband; not only did the brook never dry up, but the stream grew deeper and broader, and the rhythm of its song waxed sweeter and stronger.

> "Aberfeldy,
> July 17th, 1855.

My Precious Love,

Your dearly-prized note came safely to hand, and verily it did excel all I have ever read, even from your own loving pen. Well, I am all right now. Last Sabbath, I preached twice, and to sum up all in a word, the services were 'glorious'. In the morning, Dr. Patterson's placed was crammed, and in the evening, Dr. Wardlaw's Chapel was crowded to suffocation by more than 2,500 people, while persons outside declared that quite as many went away. My reception was enthusiastic; never was greater honour given to mortal man. They were just as delighted as are the people at Park Street. To-day, I have had a fine drive with my host and his daughter. To-morrow, I am to preach *here*. It is quite impossible for me to be left in quiet. Already, letters come in, begging me to go here, there, and everywhere. Unless I go to the North Pole, I never can get away from my holy labour.

Now to return to you again, I have had day-dreams of you while driving along, I thought you were very near me. It is not long, dearest, before I shall again enjoy your sweet society, if the providence of God permit. I knew I loved you very much before, but now I feel how necessary you are to me, and you will not lose much by my absence, if you find me, on my return, more attentive to your feelings, as well as equally affectionate. I can now thoroughly sympathize with your tears, because I feel in no little degree that pang of absence which my constant engagements prevented me from noticing when in London. How then must you, with so much leisure, have felt my absence from you, even though you well knew that it was unavoidable on my part! My darling, accept love of the deepest and purest kind from one who is not prone to exaggerate, but who feels that here there is no room for hyperbole. Think not that I weary myself by writing, for, dearest, it is my delight to please you, and solace an absence which must be even more dreary to you than to me, since travelling and preaching lead me to forget it. My eyes ache for sleep, but they shall keep open till I have invoked the blessings from above —mercies temporal and eternal—to rest on the head of one whose name is sweet to me, and who equally loves the name of her own, her much-loved, C. H. S."

The dear traveller seems to have had his Scottish visit interrupted by the necessity of a journey to fulfil preaching engagements at Bradford and Stockton. On his way to these towns, he stayed to see the beauties of Windermere, and sought to enjoy a little relaxation and rest, but he writes very sadly of these experiences. "This is a bad way of spending time," he says, "I had rather be preaching five times a day than be here. Idleness is my *labour*. I long for the traces again, and want to be in the shafts, pulling the old coach. Oh, for the quiet of my own closet! I think, if I have one reason for wishing to return, more cogent than even my vehement desire to see you, it is that I may see *my Lord*, so as I have seen Him in my retirement."

Of the services at Bradford, he gives this brief record: "Last Sabbath was a day of even greater triumph than at Glasgow. The hall, which holds more people than Exeter Hall, was crammed to excess at both services, and in the evening the crowds outside who went away were immense, and would have furnished another hall with an audience. At Stockton, I had a full house, and my Master's smile; I left there this morning at 8 o'clock."

Returning to Glasgow, *via* Edinburgh, he preached in that city, and I afterwards had a doleful little note, in which he wrote bitter things against himself—perhaps without reason. His words, however, show with what tenderness of conscience he served his God, how quick he was to discover in himself anything which might displease his Master, and how worthless was the applause of the people if the face of his Lord were hidden. He says: "I preached in Edinburgh, and returned here, full of anguish at my ill-success. Ah! my darling, your beloved behaved like Jonah, and half wished never more to testify against Nineveh. Though it rained, the hall was crowded, and there was I—*without my God!* It was a sad failure on my part; nevertheless, God can bless my words to poor souls."

A hurried excursion to the Highlands—a day's sight-seeing in Glasgow—another Sabbath of services, when enormous crowds were disappointed—20,000 people being turned away, because admittance was impossible—and then the Scottish journey (the forerunner of so many similar events) was a thing of the past, and work at home was recommenced with earnestness and vigour.

Even at this early period of my beloved's ministry, while he was still so youthful that none need have wondered had he been puffed up by his popularity and success, there was in his heart a deep and sweet humility, which kept him low at the Master's feet, and fitted him to bear the ever-increasing burden of celebrity and fame. This is manifest in so many of these letters of 1855, that I have felt constrained to refer to it, since even now some dare to speak of him as self-confident and arrogant, when, had they known him as his dearest friends knew him, they would have marvelled at his lowliness, and borne witness—as these have often done—that "the meekness and gentleness of Christ" was one of the many charms of his radiant character. His dear son in the faith, Pastor Hugh D. Brown, of Dublin, speaks truly when he says of him, in a lately-published eulogy, "So wonderful a man, and yet so simple—with a great child-heart; or rather, so simple because so great, needing no scaffoldings of pompous mannerism to buttress up an uncertain reputation, but universally esteemed, because he cared nought for human opinion, but only for what was upright, open-hearted, and transparent, both in ministry and life; we never knew a public man who had less of self about him, for over and above aught else, his sole ambition seemed to be, 'How can I most extol my Lord?'" These thoughtful, discriminating words would have been applicable to him if they had been written in the long-past days, when his marvellous career had but just commenced, and his glorious life-work lay all before him.

The following letter reveals his inmost heart, and it costs me a pang to give it publicity, but it should silence for ever the untrue charges of egotism and self-conceit which have been brought against him by those who ought to have known better: "I shall feel deeply indebted to you, if you will pray very earnestly for me. I fear I am not so full of love to God as I used to be. I lament my sad decline in spiritual things. You and others may not have observed it, but I am now conscious of it, and a sense thereof has put bitterness in my cup of joy. Oh! what is it to be popular, to be successful, to have abundance, even to have love so sweet as yours—if I should be left of God to fall, and to depart from His ways? I tremble at the giddy height on which I stand, and could wish myself unknown, for indeed I am unworthy of all my honours and my fame. I trust I shall now commence anew, and wear no longer the linsey-woolsey garment, but I beseech you, blend your hearty prayers with mine, that two of us may be agreed, and thus will you promote the usefulness, and holiness, and happiness of one whom you love."

Then, some months later, he wrote: "*The Patriot* has a glowing account of me, which will tend to make me more popular than ever. MAY GOD PRESERVE ME! I believe all my little troubles have just kept me right. I should have been upset by flattery, had it not been for this long balancing rod."

Let any impartial reader decide whether these are the words of a vain and self-complacent man!

*   *   *

The year 1855 was now drawing to a close, and we were looking forward, with unutterable joy, to having a home of our own, and being united by the holy ties of a marriage "made in Heaven". My beloved went to spend Christmas with his parents in Colchester, and after a personal "Good-bye," wrote again thus: "Sweet One,—How I love you! I long to see you; and yet it is but half-an-hour since I left you. Comfort yourself in my absence by the thought that my heart is with you. My own gracious God bless you in all things—in heart, in feeling, in life, in death, in Heaven! May your virtues be perfected, your prospects realized, your zeal continued, your love to Him increased, and your knowledge of Him rendered deeper, higher, broader—in fact, may more than even *my heart* can wish, or *my* hope anticipate, be yours for ever! May we be mutual blessings—wherein I shall err, you will pardon, and wherein you may mistake, I will more than overlook. Yours, till Heaven, *and then*—C. H. S."

Ah! my husband, the blessed earthly ties which we welcomed so rapturously are dissolved now, and death has hidden thee from my mortal eyes, but not even death can divide thee from me, or sever the love which united our hearts so closely. I feel it living and growing still, and I believe it will find its full and spiritual development only when we shall meet in the glory-land, and worship "together before the throne".

There is just one relic of this memorable time. On my desk, as I write this chapter, there is a book bearing the title of *The Pulpit Library*; it is the *first* published volume of my beloved's sermons, and its fly-leaf has the following inscription:

> In a few days it will be out of my power to present anything to Miss Thompson. Let this be a remembrance of our happy meetings & sweet conversations
>
> Dec 22 / 55
>
> *C. H. Spurgeon*

The wedding-day was fixed for January 8, 1856, and I think, till it came, and passed, I lived in a dreamland of excitement and emotion, the atmosphere of which was unfriendly to the remembrance of any definite incidents. Our feet were on the threshold of the gate which stands at the entry of the new and untrodden pathway of married life, but it was with a deep and tender gladness that the travellers clasped each other's hand, and then placed them both in that of the Master, and thus set out on their journey, assured that He would be their Guide, "*even unto death*".

I have been trying to recall in detail the events of the—to me—

notable day on which I became the loved, and loving wife of the best man on God's earth; but most of its hours are veiled in a golden mist, through which they look luminous, but indistinct only a few things stand out clearly in my memory.

I see a young girl kneeling by her bedside in the early morning; she is awed and deeply moved by a sense of the responsibilities to be taken up that day, yet happy beyond expression that the Lord has so favoured her; and there alone with Him she earnestly seeks strength, and blessing, and guidance through the new life opening before her. The tiny upper chamber in Falcon Square was a very sacred place that morning.

Anon, I see a very simply-dressed damsel, sitting by her father's side, and driving through the City streets to New Park Street Chapel —vaguely wondering, as the passers-by cast astonished glances at the wedding equipage, whether they all knew what a wonderful bridegroom she was going to meet!

As we neared our destination, it was evident that many hundreds of people *did* know and care about the man who had chosen her to be his bride, for the building was full to overflowing, and crowds of the young preacher's admirers thronged the streets around the chapel. I do not remember much more. Within the densely-packed place, I can dimly see a large wedding party in the table-pew, dear old Dr Alexander Fletcher beaming benignly on the bride and bridegroom before him, and the deacons endeavouring to calm and satisfy the excited and eager onlookers.

Then followed the service, which made "us twain most truly one", and with a solemn joy in our hearts we stood hand in hand, and spake the few brief words which legally bound us to each other in blessed bonds while life lasted. But the golden circlet then placed on my finger, though worn and thin now, speaks of love beyond the grave, and is the cherished pledge of a spiritual union which shall last throughout eternity.

"In these days, there is a growing hatred of the pulpit. The pulpit has maintained its ground full many a year, but partially by its becoming inefficient, it is losing its high position. Through a timid abuse of it, instead of a strong stiff use of the pulpit, the world has come to despise it; and now most certainly we are not a priest-ridden people one-half so much as we are a press-ridden people. By the press we are ridden indeed. *Mercuries, Despatches, Journals, Gazettes,* and *Magazines* are now the judges of pulpit eloquence and style. They thrust themselves into the censor's seat, and censure those whose office it should rather be to censure them. For my own part, I cheerfully accord to all men the liberty of abusing me; but I must protest against the conduct of at least one Editor, who has misquoted in order to pervert my meaning, and who has done even more than that; he has manufactured a "quotation" from his own head, which never did occur in my works or words."—C. H. S., *in sermon preached at the Music Hall, Royal Surrey Gardens, January* 25, 1857.

Chapter 22

Early Criticisms and Slanders

WHILE reading again the letters referred to in the preceding chapter, Mrs. Spurgeon has been reminded that before her marriage she made a collection of newspaper cuttings relating to her beloved. As the different articles appeared, Mr. Spurgeon sent them on to her, usually saying with regard to each one, "Here's another contribution for your museum." It would not be difficult to fill a volume with reprints of the notices—favourable and otherwise—of the young preacher's first years in London, but it is not likely that any useful purpose would be thereby served. It will probably suffice if a selection is given from the contents of this first scrap-book, especially as the papers it contains were published in various parts of the kingdom at considerable intervals during the years 1855 and 1856. They are therefore fairly representative of the press notices of the period, and they will be of greater interest to many readers because they were gathered by the dear preacher himself. The book in which the extracts are preserved bears upon its title-page, in his handwriting, the following inscription:

Facts, Fiction, and Facetiæ.

The last word might have been Falsehood, for there is much that is untrue, and very little that can be regarded as facetious in the whole series. Some of the paragraphs are too abusive or too blasphemous to be inserted in this work, and one cannot read them without wondering how any man could have written in such a cruel fashion concerning so young and so earnest a servant of the Lord Jesus Christ, who was labouring with all his might to bring sinners to the Saviour. At that early stage of his ministry, he had not become so accustomed as he was in later years to attacks from all quarters, and his letters show that he felt very keenly the aspersions and slanders to which he was subjected. Occasionally, also, he alluded from the pulpit to this form of fiery trial. In a sermon, preached March 15, 1857, he said: "I shall never forget the circumstance, when, after I thought I had made a full consecration to Christ, a slanderous report against my character came to my ears, and my heart was broken in agony because I should have to lose that, in preaching Christ's gospel. I fell on my

W

knees, and said, 'Master, I will not keep back even my character for Thee. If I must lose that, too, then let it go; it is the dearest thing I have, but it shall go, if, like my Master, they shall say I have a devil, and am mad, or, like Him, I am a drunken man and a wine-bibber." In after years, he was less affected by the notices which appeared. Perhaps this was all the easier as the tone adopted by most of the writers very greatly improved, while the friendly articles and paragraphs were so much more numerous than the unfavourable ones that they obliterated the memory of any that might have caused sorrow and pain. The habit of preserving newspaper and other records of his career was continued by Spurgeon to the last; and as each caricature, criticism, or commendation came to hand, he would say, "That is one more for my collection," while the praise or blame it contained would be of less importance in his esteem than his concern to have a conscience void of offence toward God and men. Preaching in the Tabernacle, in 1884, he thus referred to his early experience, and to the change the intervening period had witnessed:

" 'They compassed me about like bees,' says David; that is to say, they were very many, and very furious. When bees are excited, they are amongst the most terrible of assailants; sharp are their stings, and they inject a venom which sets the blood on fire. I read, the other day, of a traveller in Africa, who learned this by experience. Certain negroes were pulling his boat up the river, and as the rope trailed along it disturbed a bees' nest, and in a moment the bees were upon him in his cabin. He said that he was stung in the face, the hands, and the eyes. He was all over a mass of fire, and to escape from his assailants he plunged into the river, but they persecuted him still, attacking his head whenever it emerged from the water. After what he suffered from them, he said he would sooner meet two lions at once, or a whole herd of buffaloes, than ever be attacked by bees again; so that the simile which David gives is a very striking one. A company of mean-spirited, wicked men, who are no bigger than bees, mentally or spiritually, can get together, and sting a good man in a thousand places, till he is well-nigh maddened by their scorn, their ridicule, their slander, and their misrepresentation. Their very littleness gives them the power to wound with impunity. Such has been the experience of some of us, especially in days now happily past. For one, I can say, I grew inured to falsehood and spite. The stings at last caused me no more pain than if I had been made of iron, but at first they were galling enough. Do not be surprised, dear friends, if you have the same experience, and if it comes, count it no strange thing, for in this way the saints have been treated in all time. Thank

God, the wounds are not fatal, nor of long continuance! Time brings ease, and use creates hardihood. No real harm has come to any of us who have run the gauntlet of abuse; not even a bruise remains."

*   *   *

According to chronological order, the first serious attack resulted from the publication, by Rev. Charles Waters Banks, in *The Earthen Vessel*, December, 1854, of an article, from which we give the following paragraph.

"Mr. C. H. Spurgeon is the present Pastor of New Park Street Chapel, in the Borough of Southwark. He is a young man of very considerable ministerial talent, and his labours have been amazingly successful in raising up the before drooping cause at Park Street to a state of prosperity almost unequalled. We know of no Baptist minister in all the metropolis—with the exception of our highly-favoured and long-tried brother, James Wells, of the Surrey Tabernacle—who has such crowded auditories, and continued overflowing congregations, as Mr. Spurgeon has. But, then, very solemn questions arise. 'WHAT IS HE DOING?' WHOSE SERVANT IS HE?' '*What proof does he give that, instrumentally, his is a heart-searching, a Christ-exalting, a truth-unfolding, a sinner-converting, a church-feeding, a soul-saving ministry?*' This is the point at issue with many whom we know—a point which we should rejoice to see clearly settled—in the best sense—and demonstrated beyond a doubt in the confidence of all the true churches of Christ in Christendom. In introducing this subject to the notice of our readers, we have no object in view further than a desire to furnish all the material which has been thrown into our hands—a careful and discriminating examination of which may, to some extent, be edifying and profitable. We wish our present remarks to be considered merely *introductory*, not *conclusive*; but seeing that the minds of so many are aroused to *enquiry* as to what may be considered the *real position* of this young Samuel in the *professing* church, we are disposed to search the records now before us, and from thence fetch out all the evidence we can find expressive of a real work of grace in the soul, and a Divine call to publish the tidings of salvation, the mysteries of the cross, and the work of the Holy Spirit, in the hearts of the living in Jerusalem."

The article contained a kindly reference to Spurgeon's spiritual experience, and included the friendly testimony of a recent hearer, whose judgment carried weight with Mr. Banks, though his name was not given; but most of the space was devoted to extracts from the young preacher's published discourses. In *The Earthen Vessel* for the following month (January, 1855), a long communication was inserted, bearing the signature, "Job". Spurgeon believed that the writer was the redoubtable James Wells.[1]

The following extracts will show how the veteran wrote concerning the stripling who was destined far to surpass his critic in fame and usefulness:

"I have no personal antipathy to Mr. Spurgeon; nor should I have written concerning him, but for your review of his ministry. His ministry is a public matter, and therefore open to public opinion, and as you assure us that the sermon on 1 Cor. i. 6, 'The Testimony of Christ Confirmed in You,' by Mr. Spurgeon, is *by far* the best, I will, by your permission, lay before you my opinion of the same. But I will first make a few remarks concerning Mr. Spurgeon, to which remarks I think he is entitled.

It is, then, in the first place, clear that he has been, from his childhood, a very industrious and ardent reader of books, especially those of a theological kind, and that he has united with his theological researches books of classic and of scientific caste, and has thus possessed himself of every kind of information which, by the law of association, he can deal out at pleasure; and these acquirements, by reading, are united, in Mr. Spurgeon, with good speaking gifts. The laws of oratory have been well studied, and he suits the action to his words. This mode of public speaking was, in the theatres of ancient Greece, carried to such an extent that one person had to speak the words, and another had to perform the gestures, and suit, with every variety of face and form, the movement to the subject in hand. Mr. Spurgeon has caught the idea, only with this difference, that he performs both parts himself. Mr. Spurgeon is too well acquainted with Elisha Coles not to see in the Bible the sovereignty of God; and too well acquainted with the writings of Toplady and Tucker not to see in the Bible the doctrine of predestination, and an overruling providence; and too well versed in the subtleties of the late Dr. Chalmers not to philosophize upon rolling planets, and methodically-moving particles of earth and water, each particle having its ordained sphere.

But, in addition to this, he appears to be a well-disposed person—kind, benevolent, courteous, full of goodwill to his fellow-creatures—endearing in his manners, social—a kind of person whom it would seem almost a cruelty to dislike. The same may be, with equal truth, said both of Dr. Pusey and of Cardinal Wiseman. But, then, it becomes us to be aware, not only of the rough garment of a mock and 'arrogant humility', but also of Amalekite-measured and delicate steps; and

[1] "King James," see p. 292.

also of the soft raiment of refined and studied courtesy (Matt. xi. 8), and fascinating smile with, 'Surely the bitterness of death is past' (1 Sam. xv. 32). But Samuel had too much honesty about him to be thus deceived. We must, then, beware of words that are smoother than butter, and softer than oil (Psalm lv. 21). Not one of the Reformers appears to have been of this *amiable* caste, but these creature-refinements pass with thousands for religion, and tens of thousands are deluded thereby. It was by great, very great *politeness* that the serpent beguiled Eve; and, unhappily, her posterity love to have it so—so true is it that Satan is not only a prince of darkness, but transformed also as 'an angel of light', to deceive, if it were possible, even the very elect.

And yet further than all this, Mr. Spurgeon was, so says the *Vessel*, brought to know the Lord when he was only fifteen years old. Heaven grant it may prove to be so—for the young man's sake, and for that of others also! But I have—*most solemnly have*—*my doubts* as to the Divine reality of his conversion. I do not say—it is not for me to say—that he is not a regenerated man, but this I do know, that there are conversions which are not of God, and whatever convictions a man may have, whatever may be the agonies of his mind as to the possibility of his salvation, whatever terror anyone may experience, and however sincere they may be, and whatever deliverance they may have by dreams or visions, or by natural conscience, or the letter or even apparent power of the Word, yet, if they cannot stand, in their spirit and ministry, the test of the law of truth, and the testimony of God, there is no *true* light in them; for a person may be intellectually enlightened, he may taste of the Heavenly gift, and be made partaker of the Holy Ghost, *professionally*, and taste of the good Word of God (Hebrews vi.), and yet not be regenerated, and therefore not beyond the danger of falling away, even from that portion of truth which such do hold. Such are never thoroughly convinced of what they are by nature; Psalm xxxviii. and Romans vii. show a path to which they make some approaches, and of which they may eloquently talk, but at the same time give certain proofs that they are not truly walking therein. Mr. Spurgeon tells us, in his sermon on the Ministry of Angels, that he has more angelology about him than most people. Well, perhaps he has, but then, if a *real* angel from Heaven were to preach another gospel, he is not to be received. . . .

Concerning Mr. Spurgeon's ministry, I believe the following things:

1st. That it is most awfully deceptive; that it passes by the essentials of the work of the Holy Ghost, and sets people by shoals down for

Christians who are not Christians by the quickening and indwelling power of the Holy Ghost. Hence, freewillers, *intellectual* Calvinists, high and low, are delighted with him, together with the philosophic and classic-taste Christian! This is simply deceiving others with the deception wherewith he himself is deceived.

2nd. That, as he speaks some truth, convictions will in some cases take place under his ministry; such will go into real concern for their salvation, and will, after a time, leave his ministry, for a ministry that can accompany them in their rugged paths of wilderness experience.

3rd. Though I do not attach the moral worth to such a ministry as I should to the true ministry of the Spirit, yet it may be morally and socially beneficial to some people, who perhaps would care to hear only such an intellectually, or rather rhetorically-gifted man as is Mr. Spurgeon, but then they have this advantage at the cost of being *fatally deluded*.

4th. My opinion is, and my argument is, and my conclusion is, that no man who knows his own heart, who knows what the daily cross means, and who knows the difference between the form and the power, the name and the life itself, the semblance and the substance, the difference between the sounding brass or the tinkling cymbal and the voice of the turtle, pouring the plaintive, but healing notes of Calvary into the solitary and weary soul—he who walks in this path, could not hear with profit the ministry of Mr. Spurgeon.

5th. I believe that Mr. Spurgeon could not have fallen into a line of things more adapted to popularity: his ministry pays its address courteously to all; hence, in this sermon, he graciously receives us all —such a reception as it is—he who preaches all doctrine, and he who preaches no doctrine; he who preaches all experience, and he who preaches no experience; and, hence, *intellectually* High Calvinists of *easy virtue* receive such a ministry into their pulpits, at once showing that the man of sin, the spirit of apostacy, is lurking in their midst. Low Calvinists also receive him, showing that there is enough of their spirit about him to make him their *dear brother*; only his Hyperism does sometimes get a little in their way, but they hope *experience* will soon take away this Calvinistic taint, and so make things more agreeable. But in this I believe they will be disappointed; he has chosen his sphere, his orbit may seem to be eccentric, but he will go *intellectually* shining on, throwing out his cometary attractions, crossing the orbits of all the others, seeming friendly with all, yet belonging to none.

His originality lies not in the materials he uses, but in ranging them into an order that suits his own turn of mind; at this he industriously labours. (In this he is a reproof to some ministers of our own denomination who are not industrious, nor studious, nor diligent, but sluggish, slothful, negligent, empty-headed, and in the pulpit as well as in the parlour, empty-handed. Preaching then is like sowing the wind, and reaping the whirlwind, and many on this account leave our ministers, and prefer a half-way gospel, ingenuously and enthusiastic-ally preached, to a whole gospel, not half preached, or preached with-out variety, life, or power. May the Lord stir up His own servants, that they may work while it is day!)

. But, in conclusion, I say—I would make every allowance for his youth, but while I make this allowance, I am, nevertheless, thoroughly disposed to believe that we have a fair sample of what he will be even unto the end."

This letter was followed by editorial comments, and a long corres-pondence, *pro* and *con*. "JOB" wrote again, explaining one expression he had previously used, but making even more definite his assertion concerning what he supposed to be Spurgeon's lack of true spiritual life:

"Dear Mr. Editor,—In one part of my review of Mr. Spurgeon's sermon, I have said of him, as a *minister*, 'I am thoroughly (it should have been *strongly*) *disposed to believe that we have a fair sample of what he will be to the end.*' It is to be regretted that some persons have tried to make the above mean that, as Mr. Spurgeon is in a state of nature now, he will so continue even unto the end; whereas, I neither did, *nor do I mean*, any such thing: all I mean is, that his *ministry*, as it now is, is I am strongly disposed to believe a fair sample of what *it* will be even unto the end. I do not here refer to his personal destiny at all—though no doubt many would have been glad to have seen me commit myself, by rushing in 'where angels fear to tread'. . . .

I am, Mr. Editor, credibly informed that Mr. Spurgeon *himself* intends taking no notice of what I have written, and if I am to be counted an enemy because I have spoken what I believe to be the truth (Gal. iv. 16), I am perfectly willing to bear the reproach thereof, and most happy should I be to have just cause to think differently of his ministry; but I am at present (instead of being shaken) more than ever *confirmed* in what I have written. I beg therefore to say that any-thing said upon the subject by Mr. Spurgeon's friends will be to me as straws thrown against a stone wall (Jeremiah i. 18), and of which I shall take no notice. Only let them beware lest a voice from Him, by whom *actions* are weighed, say unto them, 'Ye have not spoken of Me the thing that is right, as My servant Job hath' (Job xlii. 7)."

Wells long continued his spirit of opposition to Spurgeon, even refusing to fulfil an engagement to preach because his brother-minister was to take one of the services on the same day; but many of his strict Baptist brethren did not sympathize with him in his action, and cordially welcomed the young preacher who held so many truths that were dear also to them.

The Editor of *The Earthen Vessel* (Mr. Banks) published, in later numbers of his Magazine for 1855, three articles from his own pen, in the course of which, reviewing Spurgeon's life and ministry up to that time, he wrote:

"It was a nice word of Richard Sibbes when he said, '*The office of a minister is to be a wooer, to make up the marriage between Christ and Christian souls:*' and we will plainly speak our minds—we have hoped that C. H. Spurgeon's work, in the hands of the Holy Ghost, is to woo and to win souls over unto Jesus Christ, and we have an impression, should his life be spared, that, through his instrumentality, all our churches will, by-and-by, be increased. God Almighty grant that we may be true prophets, and then, to all our cruel correspondents we will say, 'Fire away; cut up, cast out, and condemn *The Earthen Vessel* as much as ye may, ye will do us no harm.' . . . We have no ground for suspecting the genuineness of Mr. Spurgeon's motives, nor the honesty of his heart. We are bound to believe that his statements respecting his own experience are just and true. We are bound to believe that, in prosecuting his ministry, he is sincerely aiming at three things—THE GLORY OF CHRIST, *the good of immortal souls*, and *the well-being of Zion*—and that, in all this, the love of Christ constrains him. If, in thoroughly weighing the sermons before us, proof to the contrary appeared, we would not hide it up; but we sincerely trust no evidence of that kind can be produced. . . . In the course of Mr. Spurgeon's ministry, there are frequently to be found such gushings forth of love to God, of ravishing delights in Christ, of the powerful anointings of the Holy Ghost, as compel us to believe that God is in him of a truth. We must confess that is the deep-wrought conviction of our spirit; and we dare not conceal it. Why should we? We may be condemned by many; but, whatever it may cast upon us—whoever may discard us—we must acknowledge that, while in these sermons we have met with sentences that perplex us, and with what some might consider contradiction, still, we have found those things which have been powerful demonstrations of the indwelling of THE LIFE AND THE LOVE OF THE TRIUNE GOD in the preacher's heart.

In thus giving, without reserve, *an unbiased verdict* respecting the main drift of the sermons contained in *The New Park Street Pulpit*, we do not endorse every sentence, nor justify every mode of expression; our first work has been to search for that which, in *every new work* that comes to hand, we always search for—that which we search for in every candidate for church-membership—that is, LIFE, and if we have not found evidences of a Divine life in the ministry at New Park Street Chapel, we are deceived; yea, we are blind, and the powers of spiritual discernment are not with us. . . . We beseech all Christian people, who long for a revival in the midst of our churches, to pray for this young man, *whom we do earnestly hope* THE LORD HAS SENT AMONGST US. Let us not be found fighting against him, lest unhappily we be found fighting against God. Let us remember, he has not made himself, he has not qualified himself, he has not sent himself; all that he has, which is good, Godlike, and gracious, the Lord has given him—all that he is doing, that is of real benefit to immortal souls, the Lord is doing by him."

*　　　*　　　*

The next attack was of a very different character. It was contained in the following paragraph published by *The Ipswich Express*, February 27, 1855, in a letter from its London correspondent:

"*A Clerical Poltroon.*—There is some little excitement in the religious world, created by a young man, a Baptist minister, and whose father, I am told, is an Independent minister of the name of Spurgeon, in Colchester. This youth is fluent, and the consequences are most distressing. As his own chapel is under repair, he preaches in Exeter Hall every Sunday, and the place is crammed to suffocation. All his discourses are redolent of bad taste, are vulgar and theatrical, and yet he is so run after that, unless you go half-an-hour before the time, you will not be able to get in at all. I am told, one leading minister of the Independent denomination, after hearing this precocious youth, said that the exhibition was 'an insult to God and man.' Actually, I hear, the other Sunday, the gifted divine had the impudence, before preaching, to say, as there were many young ladies present, that he was engaged—that his heart it was another's, he wished them clearly to understand that—that he might have no presents sent him, no attentions paid him, no worsted slippers worked for him by the young ladies present. I suppose the dear divine has been rendered uncomfortable by the fondness of his female auditors; at any rate, such is the impression he wishes to leave. The only impression, however, he seems to have produced upon the judicious few is one of intense sorrow and regret that such things should be, and that such a man should draw."

Spurgeon's feeling about the matter can be judged by the following letter to his father:

"75, Dover Road,

4th March, 1855.

Dear Father,

Do not be grieved at the slanderous libel in this week's *Express*. . . .

Of course, it is *all a lie*, without an atom of foundation; and while the whole of London is talking of me, and thousands are unable to get near the door, the opinion of a penny-a-liner is of little consequence.

I beseech you not to write; but if you can see Mr. Harvey, or some official, it might do good. A full reply on all points will appear next week.

I only fear for you; I do not like you to be grieved. For myself, I WILL REJOICE; the devil is roused, the Church is awakening, and I am now counted worthy to suffer for Christ's sake. . . . Good ballast, father, good ballast; but, oh! remember what I have said before, and do not check me.

Last night, I could not sleep till morning light, but now my Master has cheered me, and I 'hail reproach, and welcome shame'.

Love to you all, especially to my dearest mother. I mean to come home April 16th. So, amen.

Your affectionate son,

C. H. SPURGEON."

On March 6, *The Ipswich Express* contained the following paragraphs:

"THE REV. C. H. SPURGEON

A gentleman of good position in London complains, as 'a friend of the Rev. C. H. Spurgeon', of the statements respecting that gentleman, last week, in the letter of our London correspondent, which are, he assures us, 'a tissue of falsehoods'. That being the case, we lose no time in contradicting them, and at the same time expressing our regret that they should have appeared in our columns. Of Mr. Spurgeon we know nothing personally, and, of course, can have no desire to say anything which should cause pain to him or his friends. It has been, and will still be, our constant desire in criticising public men to avoid anything like personalities. We much regret that our London correspondent should have reported mere hearsay (which we are now informed was incorrect) respecting Mr. Spurgeon, and also that we did not give his letter that revision before its appearance in print which all letters for the press should receive, but which Editors, in the hurry of the day of publication, are too apt to neglect.

A London publisher also sends us a sermon delivered by Mr. Spurgeon on the 11th ult., at Exeter Hall, stating that we ought to read and review it, in justice to the rev. gentleman. We have received, from an anonymous correspondent in London, another sermon delivered by Mr. Spurgeon last November, accompanied by a like request. It is not our habit to review sermons, but, under the circumstances, we admit the justice of these demands, and shall comply with them. Our correspondent having criticised Mr. Spurgeon's preaching (harshly, as the friends of the preacher think), we shall consider ourselves bound to take an opportunity of reviewing these discourses. In so doing, the friends of Mr. Spurgeon may be assured we shall bring to the task the best of our ability, and a perfectly unbiased judgment; we shall 'nothing extenuate, nor set down aught in malice'."

The Editor published several letters from those who wrote in Spurgeon's defence, as well as from others who attacked him, and on April 24 he commenced his promised review of the sermons, as follows:

"Some are born great, some achieve greatness, and some have greatness thrust upon them. We have had, in a measure, the reviewal of Mr. Spurgeon's sermons thrust upon us, and in the fulfilment of our task we may, perhaps, assist our readers to judge whether that gentleman has achieved any real, permanent greatness, or whether he has had a factitious, fleeting greatness thrust upon him by his ignorant admirers.

The *Express* of February 27th contained, as usual, a letter from our London correspondent, a gentleman favourably known as a writer on politics and general literature. This letter contained some rather severe criticism on Mr. Spurgeon's style of preaching, and a line or two respecting a rumour, heard by our correspondent, of some absurd remarks said to have been made on a certain occasion by Mr. Spurgeon previous to preaching. We did not read the letter until it appeared in print. . . . As soon as we saw the paragraph, we blamed ourselves for publishing, as well as our correspondent for forwarding, anything of *mere hearsay* which could possibly give annoyance to the preacher in question or his friends. And we have since learned, on the undoubted authority of his own published effusions, that Mr. Spurgeon really does run into so many extravagancies that to attribute to him any which he has never perpetrated would not only be a wrong, but a 'wasteful and ridiculous excess'.

However, in a day or two, we received from several of Mr. Spurgeon's acquaintances (some of them his intimate friends) a flat contradiction of the absurd story of 'the slippers'. For the credit of the ministry we were glad to have it thus authoritatively denied, and lost no time in stating our sincere regret that we had, through an inadvertence, given publicity to an incorrect report. More than this, we published several of the longest letters out of the many we received from Mr. Spurgeon's friends—stuffed full of the most glowing eulogiums of that gentleman as a minister and a man—and in compliance with the wishes of some very ardent in his cause, we promised to review Mr. Spurgeon's sermons. We printed about twenty times as much in his praise as had appeared in his dispraise—we courteously carried on for some time a considerable correspondence with the London Spurgeonites—and although we think theology is out of place in a newspaper, we agreed, for once, rather than the least injustice should be committed, to step out of our usual course, and criticise sermons. Could we do more? Indeed, the line we took showed so clearly the absence of any ill-feeling on our part to Mr. Spurgeon, that the gentleman who first (rather angrily) called our attention to the obnoxious paragraph, finished a lengthy correspondence with us by saying, 'I am perfectly satisfied with your explanation, and think it does you honour.' "

The "review" was continued on May 1, and concluded on May 29. The tone of it may be judged from the closing paragraphs: "There is enough foolishness in London to keep up, in flourishing style, Tom Thumb, Charles Kean, the Living Skeleton, C. H. Spurgeon, and many other delusions all at once, and yet to allow a vast mass of sober-minded citizens to go 'the even tenor of their way', quite unaffected by such transient turmoils. Our decided opinion is, that in no other place but London could Mr. Spurgeon have caused the *furor* that he has excited. It must not be forgotten that in London, or anywhere else, a religious delusion is, of all others, the most easy to inaugurate and carry on. When a man obtains possession of a pulpit, he has credit for meaning well, at any rate, and expressions are thenceforward often listened to from him, without hostile criticism, which would not be tolerated, if enunciated from any other position.

Mr. Spurgeon's career is suggestive of various interesting questions. If such a man can obtain, in a short time, the position he now certainly occupies, does that fact say much for the condition of a great portion of the religious world? If Mr. S. be, as is stated, the very best among a large section of preachers, what sort of a man is the very worst of that section? Does the pulpit, upon the whole, keep pace with the age, or does it lag behind? Will not the immense success of such as Spurgeon go far to account for that aversion of men of taste to the public profession of Evangelical Religion complained of long ago by John Foster?"

Although the falsehood published in *The Ipswich Express* was promptly contradicted, it was widely copied into other papers. *The Empire* (London) and *The Christian News* (Glasgow) published the paragraph in full, while portions of it were incorporated into articles that appeared in various parts of the kingdom, and the story of "the slippers" was repeated so often that probably many people were foolish enough to believe it, and others were wicked enough to say that they heard Spurgeon make the statement!

*   *   *

The Essex Standard, April 18, 1855,[1] contained a long letter, signed "Iconoclast", describing a Sunday evening service at Exeter Hall. The writer said: "The mighty gathering and the 'religious *furor*' made me think of Demosthenes haranguing the Athenians, Cicero before the Roman senate, Peter the Hermit preaching the Crusade, Wesley on his father's tomb at Epworth, and Whitefield stirring the breasts of the thousands in Hyde Park, and therefore I scanned somewhat curiously both 'orator' and auditors. A young man, in his 21st year, but looking much older, short in stature and thick set, with a broad massive face, a low forehead, an expressionless eye, a wide and sensual mouth, a voice strong but not musical—suggestive of *Stentor* rather than *Nestor*—the very reverse of a *beau ideal* of an orator: without the eye of fire, where was the heart of flame? Orpheus without his lyre (*flute*, Spurgeon says), what was the potent charm that was to change the 'swine of the metropolis' into men, and convert sinners into saints? We must wait for the thoughts that breathe, and the words that burn. The hymn was sung right lustily, and the preacher proceeded to read and expound the 3rd of Philippians. . . . It was evident that *exposition* was not his forte. Then followed what his audience called prayer. It was an apostrophe to the Invisible, containing certain

[1] See Spurgeon's comments on, p. 291.

petitions first for himself, then for the elect saints, and then for the outer-court worshippers. It was such an utterance as indicated low views of Deity, and exalted views of self. Indeed, self is never out of sight, and is presented to the listener as a 'little child', a 'babbler', a 'baby', a 'battering ram', '*little* David', 'this despised young man', 'this ranting fellow', and 'an empty ram's horn'. If reverence is the greatest mark of respect to an earthly parent, how much more is it due to the Supreme Father of all! . . . When the painful effect of this most arrogant dictation to Deity allowed me to think, I could not but rejoice in that 'form of sound words' by which the devotions of the Church are sustained from Sabbath to Sabbath, and by which, also, such outrageous violations of decorum are rendered impossible. The discourse was from Philippians iii. 10: '*That I may know Him.*' The various objects of human pursuit being designated and discussed, we had put before us the object, nature, and effects of Paul's knowledge. . . . Speaking of his study, Mr. Spurgeon said it was his '*dukedom*', where he could talk to Milton and Locke as *slaves*, and say, 'Come down here.' Mr. Spurgeon loves controversy, but with the modesty peculiar to himself told us that, nowadays, 'he found no foeman worthy of *his* steel.' His favourite action is that of washing his hands, and then rubbing them dry. He belongs to the peripatetic, or Walker school, perpetually walking up and down as an actor treading the boards of a theatre. His style is that of the vulgar colloquial varied by rant. . . . All the most solemn mysteries of our holy religion are by him rudely, roughly, and impiously handled. Mystery is vulgarised, sanctity profaned, common sense outraged, and decency disgusted. . . . His rantings are interspersed with coarse anecdotes that split the ears of the groundlings; and this is popularity! and this is the 'religious *furor*' of London! and this young divine it is that throws Wesley and Whitefield in the shade! and this is the preaching, and this the theology, that five thousand persons from Sabbath to Sabbath hear, receive, and approve, and––profit by it!"

The next issue of *The Essex Standard* contained another communication in a similar strain:

"Mr. Editor,—The letter of 'Iconoclast' in your Wednesday's impression is a faithful delineation of the young preacher who is making so great a stir just now. Had we seen it previously, we should have been kept from taking the trouble to go to Earl's Colne yesterday, to hear what extremely disgusted us—a young man of 21 years assuming airs, and adopting a language, which would be scarcely tolerated in the man of grey hairs. In common with many others, though obliged to smile during his performances, we felt more inclined to weep over such a prostitution of the pulpit and hours devoted to professedly religious worship. His prayer, to us, appeared most profanely familiar, and never were we impressed more with the contrast between this effusion and the beautifully-simple, reverential, and devout language of the Church of England Liturgy, and said, within our hearts, 'Would that Dissenters would bind down their ministers to use those forms of sound words, rather than allow of these rhapsodies, which, to all persons of taste and true devotion, must have been very offensive!' It is a matter of deep regret to many that one of the best Dissenting chapels in London should be occupied by a youth of Mr. Spurgeon's caste and doctrinal sentiments; and they very properly shrink from recognizing him among the regular ministers of the Baptist denomination; and we heard it regretted more than once yesterday that he should have been chosen to represent a Society so respectable as the Baptist Home Missionary Society. If gain were their object, they certainly obtained it, as we understand the collections were large, but we submit no such motive can be tolerated at the cost of so much propriety. I exceedingly regret to write thus of one who, until I heard him yesterday, I thought probably was raised up for usefulness; but a sense of duty to the public leads me to express my opinions and sentiments in this plain, unflinching manner.

I am, Mr. Editor,

Halstead,   Yours respectfully,
    April 18th, 1855.   A LOVER OF PROPRIETY."

The following week, a letter of quite another kind was published in the same paper:

"Sir,—Your readers have had the opinions of two supporters of the Established Church on the preaching of the Rev. C. H. Spurgeon, and I trust to your well-known fairness to allow a Dissenter an opportunity of expressing the sentiments held by many who have enjoyed the pleasure of listening to the fervid words of that distinguished minister of the gospel.

Mr. Spurgeon institutes a new era, or more correctly, revives the good old style of Bunyan, Wesley, and Whitefield—men whose burning eloquence carried conviction to the hearts of their hearers—men who cared nought for the applause of their fellow-mortals, but did all for God's glory. In the steps of these apostles does Mr. S. follow, and who could desire more noble leaders?

The pulpit is now too much abused by the mere display of intellect; instead of the indignant burst of a Luther against the iniquities of mankind, we have only the passive disapprobation of the silvery-tongued man of letters. The preachers address their cold, 'packed-in-ice' discourses to the educated portion of their audience; and the majority, the uneducated poor, are unable, in these 'scientific' sermons, to learn the way of holiness, from the simple fact that they are above their comprehension. How unlike these ministers—who appear to consider the gospel so frail that it would lose its power if delivered with unflinching candour—are to the holy Saviour! His words were always characterized by the greatest simplicity, and by a thorough detestation of those 'blind guides who strain at a gnat, and swallow a camel.'

Mr. Spurgeon goes to the root of the evil; his discourses are such as a child can understand, and yet filled with the most elevating philosophy and sound religious instruction. Taking the Word as his only guide, and casting aside the writings—however antiquated—of fallible men, he appeals to the *heart*, not to the *head*; puts the living truth forcibly before the mind, gains the attention, and then, as he himself says, fastens in the bow the messenger shaft, which, by the blessing and direction of the Almighty, strikes home to the heart of the sinner.

He holds that irreligion is to be fought against, not to be handled with 'fingers of down', and hence Exeter Hall is crammed. It is objected that these are the lowest of the London poor. What of that? They, above all, need religious training. I suppose there are few advocates in this country for the opinion that the aristocracy of the land *alone* have souls; Jehovah has breathed His spirit into the democracy, and Mr. S. is the man for them. In my humble opinion, if there were more C. H. Spurgeons, there would be fewer Sabbath desecrationists, fewer tendencies to the idol-worship of Rome, and fewer disciples of Holyoake and Paine.

In conclusion, let me suggest that, even if Mr. Spurgeon were guilty of all laid to his charge, would it not be better for Christians to gloss over the failings of a brother-worker (for no one doubts the sincerity of the young man's efforts), than to seek here and there for the dross amongst the pure metal—making mountains out of mole-hills, and wantonly refusing the golden ears because mixed with the necessary chaff?

I am, Sir,
Your obedient servant,
Vox Populi."

*   *   *

To the Editor of *The Chelmsford Chronicle*, who had published an article of a more friendly character than those in other East Anglian papers, Spurgeon wrote:

> "75, Dover Road,
>
>   April 24th, 1855.
>
> My Dear Sir,
>
> I am usually careless of the notices of papers concerning myself— referring all honour to my Master, and believing that dishonourable articles are but advertisements for me, and bring more under the sound of the gospel. But you, my dear sir (I know not why), have been pleased to speak so favourably of my labours that I think it only right that I should thank you. If I could have done so personally, I would have availed myself of the pleasure, but the best substitute is by letter. Amid a constant din of abuse, it is pleasant to poor flesh and blood to hear *one* favourable voice. I am far from deserving much that you have said in my praise, but as I am equally undeserving of the coarse censure poured on me by *The Essex Standard*, &c., &c., I will set the one against the other. I am neither eloquent nor learned, but the Head of the Church has given me sympathy with the masses, love to the poor, and the means of winning the attention of the ignorant and un- enlightened. I never sought popularity, and I cannot tell how it is so many come to hear me; but shall I now change? To please the polite critic, shall I leave '*the people*', who so much require a simple and stirring style? I am, perhaps, 'vulgar', and so on, but it is not inten- tional, save that I *must* and *will* make the people listen. My firm con- viction is, that we have quite enough *polite* preachers, and that 'the many' require a change. God has owned me to the most degraded and off-cast; let others serve their class: these are mine, and to them I must keep. My sole reason for thus troubling you is one of gratitude to a disinterested friend. You may another time have good cause to censure me—do so, as I am sure you will, with all heartiness, but my young heart shall not soon forget 'a friend'.
>
>   Believe me,
>
>   My dear sir,
>
>   Yours very sincerely,
>
>   C. H. SPURGEON."

The Bucks Chronicle, April 28, 1855, published an article signed, "A BRITON", of which the following portion sufficiently indicates the character of the whole:

x

"THE POPULAR MINISTER
(From our London correspondent)

Scarcity produces dearness; rarity, curiosity. Great preachers are as scarce as Queen Anne's farthings. The market is glutted with mediocrity—a star is looked upon, in the theological world, as a prize equally with green peas in Covent Garden Market at Christmas. We have been inundated with the slang phrases of the profession until they have acquired the sameness of our milkman's cry, when he places his pails upon the ground, and, as he gives the bell-handle a spasmodic twitch, utters his well-known 'M-i-l-k'.

We had thought the day for dogmatic, theologic dramatising, was past—that we should never more see the massive congregation listening to outrageous manifestations of insanity—no more hear the fanatical effervescence of ginger-pop sermonising, or be called upon to wipe away the froth, that the people might see the colour of the stuff. In this we were mistaken. A star has appeared in the misty plain of orthodoxy, and such a star that, were it not for the badge which encircles that part of it called neck, we should, for the more distinguishing characteristic, write comet. It has made its appearance in Exeter Hall, and is to be seen on the first day of the week, by putting a few 'browns' into a basket. The star is a Spurgeon—not a carp, but much resembling a pike. Thousands flock weekly to see it; and it shines grandiloquently. It is a parson—a young parson. Merciful goodness! such a parson seldom talks. It is a railway speed of joining sentences, conflabergasticated into a discourse. It is now near eleven o'clock a.m. He rises to read; and, as if the Book of Inspiration was not fine enough in its composition, enters into explanations of his own as apt as a coal-heaver would give of Thucidydes (*sic*). Never mind! the great gun of starology in theology has a mission. Not to convert the doggerelisms of Timbuctoo into rationalisms—not to demonstrate the loving-kindness of the great Fatherhood—not to teach the forgiveness of Jehovah Jirah (*sic*) in His great heart of mercy —not to proclaim the extension of the kingdom of the Master of assemblies. No! but to teach that, if Jack Scroggins was put down in the black book, before the great curtain of events was unfolded, that the said Jack Scroggins, in spite of all he may do or say, will and must tumble into the limbo of a brimstone hell, to be punished and roasted, without any prospect of cessation, or shrinking into a dried cinder; because Jack Scroggins had done what Jack Scroggins could not help doing. . . . It is not pleasant to be frightened into the portal of bliss by the hissing bubbles of the seething cauldron. It is not Christian-like to say, 'God must wash brains in the Hyper-Calvinism a Spurgeon teaches before man can enter Heaven.' It does not harmonize with the quiet majesty of the Nazarene. It does not fall like manna for hungry souls, but is like the gush of the pouring rain in a thunderstorm, which makes the flowers to hang their heads, looking up afterwards as if nothing had happened. When the Exeter Hall stripling talks of Deity, let him remember that He is superior to profanity, and that blasphemy from a parson is as great a crime as when the lowest grade of humanity utters the brutal oath at which the virtuous stand aghast."

*   *   *

The *Sheffield and Rotherham Independent*, April 28, 1855, to which Spurgeon alludes on page 292, had an article somewhat similar to the one in the Buckinghamshire paper of the same date:

"Just now, the great lion, star, meteor, or whatever else he may be called, of the Baptists, is the Rev. M. (*sic*) Spurgeon, minister of Park Street Chapel, Southwark. He has created a perfect *furor* in the religious world. Every Sunday, crowds throng to Exeter Hall—where for some weeks past he has been preaching during the enlargement of his own chapel—as to some great dramatic entertainment. The huge hall is crowded to overflowing, morning and evening, with an excited auditory, whose good fortune in obtaining admission is often envied by the hundreds outside who throng the closed doors. For a parallel to such popularity, we must go back to Dr. Chalmers, Edward Irving, or the earlier days of James Parsons. But I will not dishonour such men by comparison with the Exeter Hall religious demagogue.[1] They preached the gospel with all the fervour of earnest natures. Mr. Spurgeon preaches *himself*. He is nothing unless he is an actor—unless exhibiting that matchless impudence which is his great characteristic, indulging in coarse familiarity with holy things, declaiming in a ranting and colloquial style, strutting up and down the platform as though he were at the Surrey Theatre, and boasting of his own intimacy with Heaven with nauseating frequency. His fluency, self-possession, oratorical tricks, and daring utterances, seem to fascinate his less-thoughtful hearers, who love excitement more than devotion. . . . I have glanced at one or two of Mr. Spurgeon's published sermons, and turned away in disgust from the coarse sentiments, the scholastical expressions, and clap-trap style I have discovered. It would seem that

[1] It is worthy of note that the paper which, in 1855, thus described Spurgeon, in 1898, in reviewing his *Autobiography*, spoke of him as "this noble Puritan preacher and saintly Christian."

the poor young man's brain is turned by the notoriety he has acquired and the incense offered at his shrine. From the very pulpit he boasts of the crowds that flock to listen to his rodomontade. Only lately, he told his fair friends to send him no more slippers, as he was already engaged; and on another occasion gloried in the belief that, by the end of the year, not less than 200,000 of his published trashy sermons would be scattered over the length and breadth of the land. This is but a mild picture of the great religious lion of the metropolis. To their credit be it spoken, Mr. Spurgeon receives no countenance or encouragement from the ornaments of his denomination. I don't think he has been invited to take part in any of their meetings. Nor, indeed, does he seek such fellowship. He glories in his position of lofty isolation, and is intoxicated by the draughts of popularity that have fired his feverish brain. He is a nine days' wonder—a comet that has suddenly shot across the religious atmosphere. He has gone up like a rocket, and ere long will come down like a stick. The most melancholy consideration in the case is the diseased craving for excitement which this running after Mr. Spurgeon by the 'religious world' indicates. I would charitably conclude that the greater part of the multitude that weekly crowd to his theatrical exhibitions consists of people who are not in the habit of frequenting a place of worship."

What higher compliment than this could the slanderer have paid the dear young preacher! Spurgeon's own testimony, concerning many of his first London hearers, was that they had not been accustomed to attend any house of prayer until they came to New Park Street Chapel, Exeter Hall, or the Surrey Gardens Music Hall. Best of all, many of them became truly converted, and so helped to build up the great church which afterwards worshipped in the Metropolitan Tabernacle.

The Lambeth Gazette was a paper published so near to the scene of Spurgeon's ministry that it would have been easy for the Editor to ascertain *facts* concerning his life and work, yet its issue for September 1, 1855, contained an article from which the following is an extract:

"The fact cannot be concealed, mountebankism is, to a certain class of minds, quite as attractive in the pulpit as in the fields of a country town. The Rev. C. H. Spurgeon is now the star of Southwark. Mr. Wells (commonly known by the curious *sobriquet* of 'Wheelbarrow Wells'), of the Borough Road, has, for some years past, had the run in this line, but he has, at last, got a rival well up in his 'tip', and likely to prove the favourite for a long time. He is a very young man, too, and the young 'sisters' are dancing mad after him. He has received slippers enough from these lowly-minded damsels to open a shoe shop, and were it not that he recently advertised them that he was 'engaged', he would very soon have been able to open a fancy bazaar with the nicknacks that were pouring in upon him. No doubt he is a very good young man, with the best of intentions, but will not this man-worship spoil him? Between the parts of the service, his mannerism in the pulpit is suggestive of affectation and vanity; it might be only an overpowering sense of responsibility, yet it would do for either state of feeling. Who can wonder at it? . . . "

The Bristol Advertiser, April 12, 1856, speaks thus in its report of a sermon by Spurgeon in that city:

"Now, what is there in Mr. Spurgeon to account for the extra-ordinary sensation he makes everywhere? It is not the doctrine he preaches, for that is 'orthodox'; that is, it is preached by a thousand other clergymen. It is not his personal appearance, for that is but ordinary: his forehead is low, his eye is small, and though capable of vivid flashes of self-appreciation, not radiant with those 'heavenly' rays by which sentimental ladies are usually fascinated; his figure is broad and stumpy; his manners are rude and awkward. In short, we can find no genuine qualities in this gentleman sufficient to explain the unrivalled notoriety he has acquired. If he were simple in his pre-tensions, and had the serene and sacred dignity of religious earnest-ness to support him, his destitution of refinement, his evident ignor-ance, his positive vulgarities of expression and of manner might be forgiven. We should feel that he was doing good in an important direction, and that to follow him with criticism or contempt would be, in a sort, profane. Or if he possessed unusual powers of mind, imagination, or speech, we could understand how many would seek to hear him. But his intellect not only lacks culture, it is evidently of meagre grasp. He has fancy, but all his larger illustrations failed, either in fitness or in development. He is fluent; he talks on without stopping; he has certain theatrical attitudes of which he knows how to make the most; his voice is powerful, and his enunciation clear; and thus many of the *mechanical* effects of oratory are under his sway. But his thoughts are commonplace, and his figures false, though striking. He says good things smartly, but his best things are his tritest, and his most striking are his most audacious sentences. . . . Solemnly do we express our regret that insolence so unblushing, intellect so feeble, flippancy so ostentatious, and manners so rude should, in the name of religion, and in connection with the church, receive the acknowledgment of even a momentary popularity. To our minds, it speaks sad things as to the state of intelligence, and calm, respectful, and dignified piety among a mass of people who call themselves the disciples of Jesus. Where curiosity is stronger than faith, and astonishment easier to excite than reverence to edify, religious life must either be at a very low ebb, or associated with some other deleterious elements."

*   *   *

The Daily News, a paper from which something better might have been expected, had, in its issue of September 9, 1856, a long article on "Popular Preachers—The Rev. Mr. Spurgeon," in which it said: "In Protestant countries in general, and in England in particular, we shrink from undue familiarity with holy words and things. We have just as much aversion to see a church turned into a theatre as to see a theatre turned into a church. We hold an opinion, grounded as much on the principles of good taste as of religion, that it is almost as offensive to see a clergyman perform in his pulpit as to hear actors invoke Heaven in a theatre. This opinion, however, is not quite universally entertained. Let any person who wishes to convince himself of the truth of this, take his station opposite to Exeter Hall on Sunday evening at about a few minutes before six o'clock. We say opposite, because, unless he arrives some time before the hour mentioned, there will be no standing-room on the pavement from which the entrance to the hall ascends. At six, the doors open, and a dense mass of human beings pours in. There is no interruption now to the continuous stream until half-past six o'clock, when the whole of the vast hall, with its galleries and platform, will be filled with the closely-packed crowd.

If the spectator has not taken care to enter before this time, he will have but small chance of finding even standing-room. Suppose him to have entered early enough to have found a seat, he will naturally look around him to scan the features of the scene. They are remarkable enough to excite attention in the minds of the most listless. Stretching far away to the back are thousands of persons evidently eager for the appearance of someone. Towering up the platform, the seats are all crowded. Nearly all the eyes in this multitude are directed to the front of the platform. The breathless suspense is only broken occasionally by the struggle, in the body of the hall, of those who are endeavouring to gain or maintain a position. Suddenly, even this noise is stopped. A short, squarely-built man, with piercing eyes, with thick black hair parted down the middle, with a sallow countenance only redeemed from heaviness by the restlessness of the eyes, advances along the platform towards the seat of honour. A cataract of short coughs, indicative of the relief afforded to the ill-repressed impatience of the assembly, announces to the stranger that the business of the evening has commenced. He will be told with a certain degree of awe by those whom he asks for information, that the person just arrived is the Rev. C. H. Spurgeon. He will perhaps hear, in addition to this, that Mr. Spurgeon is beyond all question the most popular preacher in London; that he is obliged to leave off preaching in the evening at his chapel in New Park Street, Southwark, on account of the want of room to accommodate more than a mere fraction of the thousands who flock to hear him; that Exeter Hall has been taken for the purpose of diminishing in a slight degree the disappointment experienced, but that nothing will be done to afford effectual relief until the new chapel which is in contemplation is built, and which is intended to hold 15,000 persons."[1]

The article concluded thus: "We might fill columns with specimens of this pulpit buffoonery, but we have given enough to show the nature of Mr. Spurgeon's preaching. We might have brought forward instances of his utter ignorance of any theology except that current among the sect to which he belongs; and of his ludicrous misinterpretations of Scripture, occasioned by his want of even a moderate acquaintance with Oriental customs and forms of language. . . . A congregation that constantly listens to the spiritual dram-drinking that Mr. Spurgeon encourages, will become not only bigoted, but greedy after stronger doses of excitement. What excited them once, will fall flat upon their palate. The preacher will be obliged to become more and more extravagant as his audience becomes more and more exacting, and the end may be an extensive development of dangerous fanaticism."

The Illustrated Times, October 11, 1856, published a portrait—or rather, a caricature—of Spurgeon, with a lengthy article containing one of the many prophecies that subsequent events proved to be false. The writer said:

"Mr. Spurgeon's popularity is unprecedented; at all events, there has been nothing like it since the days of Wesley and Whitefield. Park Street Chapel cannot hold half the people who pant to hear him, and even Exeter Hall is too small. Indeed, it is reported on good authority

---

[1] This figure is, of course, only an example of the inaccuracies of many of the press attacks. The building of a chapel with such a capacity was never envisaged.

that his friends mean to hire the Concert Room at the Surrey Gardens, and firmly believe that he will fill that. Nor is his popularity confined to London; in Scotland, he was very much followed, and, lately, we ourselves saw, on a week-day, in a remote agricultural district, long lines of people all converging to one point, and on enquiring of one of the party where they were going, received for answer, 'We're a go'in' to hear *Maester Spudgin*, sir.'

WILL HIS POPULARITY LAST?

We more than doubt it. It stands on no firm basis. Thousands who go now to hear him only go through curiosity. Men are very much like sheep; one goes through a hedge, then another, and another; at last the stream gathers *crescit eundo*, and the whole flock rushes madly forward. This has been a good deal the case with Mr. Spurgeon's congregation, but the current will soon turn and leave him; and as to those who have gone from a slightly different, if not better, motive, it is hardly likely that he will retain them long. He must bid high if he does—offering them every Sunday a stronger dram than they had the last."

POSTSCRIPT BY MRS. C. H. SPURGEON

No defence of my beloved is needed now. God has taken him to Himself, and "there the wicked cease from troubling; and there the weary be at rest". The points of these arrows are all blunted—the stings of these scorpions are all plucked out—the edge of these sharp swords is rusted away. "And where is the fury of the oppressor?"

A strange serenity has brooded over my spirit as these chapters have recalled the heartless attacks made on God's servant; I have even smiled as I read once again the unjust and cruel words written by his enemies; for he is so safe now, "with God eternally shut in"; and I can bless the Lord for the suffering all ended, and the eternity of bliss begun. "For Thou hast made him most blessed for ever: Thou hast made him exceeding glad with Thy countenance."

But, at the time of their publication, what a grievous affliction these slanders were to me! My heart alternately sorrowed over him, and flamed with indignation against his detractors. For a long time, I wondered how I could set continual comfort before his eyes, till, at last, I hit upon the expedient of having the following verses printed in large Old English type, and enclosed in a pretty Oxford frame. (This was before the days of the illuminated mottoes which at present are so conspicuous in our homes, and so often silently speak a message from God to us.)

> "Blessed are ye, when men shall revile you, and persecute you, and shall say all manner of evil against you falsely, for My sake. Rejoice, and be exceeding glad: for great is your reward in Heaven: for so persecuted they the prophets which were before you."— *Matthew* v. 11, 12.

The text was hung up in our own room, and was read over by the dear preacher every morning—fulfilling its purpose most blessedly, for it strengthened his heart, and enabled him to buckle on the invisible armour, whereby he could calmly walk among men, unruffled by their calumnies, and concerned only for their best and highest interests.

"Observe how sovereign the operations of God are. When Elijah wanted rain, there was a cloud seen, and he heard a sound as of abundance of rain, and by-and-by the water descended in floods; but when God would send the water to Elisha, he heard no sound of rain, nor did a drop descend. God is not tied to this or that mode or form. He may in one district work a revival, and persons may be stricken down, and made to cry aloud; but in another place there may be great crowds, and yet all may be still and quiet, as though no deep excitement existed at all. God blesses often by the open ministry, and frequently by the personal and more secret action of His people. He *can* bless as He wills and He *will* bless as He wills. Let us not dictate to God. Many a blessing has been lost by Christians not believing it to be a blessing, because it did not come in the particular shape which they had conceived to be proper and right."— C. H. S.

"Shall we ever forget Park Street, these prayer meetings, when I felt compelled to let you go without a word from my lips, because the Spirit of God was so awfully present that we felt bowed to the dust. And what listening there was at Park Street, where we scarcely had air enough to breathe! The Holy Spirit came down like showers which saturate the soil till the clods are ready for the breaking; and then it was not long before we heard on the right and on the left the cry, 'What must we do to be saved?' "—C. H. S.

Chapter 23

Revival at New Park Street

GREAT numbers of the converts of those early days came as the direct result of the slanders with which I was so mercilessly assailed. My name was so often reviled in the public press that it became the common talk of the street, and many a man, going by the door of our house of prayer, has said, "I'll go in, and hear old Spurgeon." He came in to make merriment of the preacher (and very little that troubled *him*), but the man stood there until the Word went home to his heart, and he who was wont to beat his wife, and to make his home a hell, has before long been to see me, and has given me a grip of the hand, and said, "God Almighty bless you, sir; there is something in true religion!" "Well, let me hear your tale." I have heard it, and very delightful has it been in hundreds of instances. I have said to the man, "Send your wife to me, that I may hear what she says about you." The woman has come, and I have asked her, "What do you think of your husband now, ma'am?" "Oh, sir, such a change I never saw in my life! He is so kind to us; he is like an angel now, and he seemed like a fiend before. Oh, that cursed drink, sir! Everything went to the public-house; and then, if I came up to the house of God, he did nothing but abuse me. Oh! to think that now he comes with me on Sunday; and the shop is shut up, sir; and the children, who used to be running about without a bit of shoe or stocking, he takes them on his knee, and prays with them so sweetly. Oh, there is such a change!"

One Sabbath evening, two brothers were brought to the Lord at New Park Street Chapel the very first time they met with us. These were the circumstances of the case. A widowed mother had two sons, who had nearly come to man's estate. They had been excellent children in their boyhood, but they began to be headstrong, as too many young people are prone to be, and they would not brook maternal control; they would spend their Sunday as they pleased, and sometimes in places where they should not have been seen. Their mother determined that she would never give up praying for them, and one night she thought she would stop at home from the house of God, shut herself up in her room, and pray for her sons' conversion.

The very night she had thus set apart for prayer on their behalf, the elder son said to her, "I am going to hear the minister that preaches down Southwark way; I am told he is an odd man, and I want to hear him preach." The mother herself did not think much of that minister, but she was so glad that her boy was going anywhere within the sound of the Word, that she said, "Go, my son." He added, "My brother is going with me." Those two young men came to the house of God, and that odd minister was blessed to the conversion of both of them.

When the mother opened the door, on their return home, the elder son fell upon her neck, weeping as if his heart would break. "Mother," he said, "I have found the Saviour; I am a believer in the Lord Jesus Christ." She looked at him a moment, and then said, "I knew it, my son; to-night I have had power in prayer, and I felt that I had prevailed." "But," said the younger brother, "oh, mother! I, too, have been cut to the heart, and I also have given myself to the Lord Jesus Christ." Happy was that mother, and I was happy, too, when she came to me, and said, "You have been the means of the conversion of my two sons; I have never thought of baptism before, but I see it now to be the Lord's own ordinance, so I will be baptized with my children." It was my great joy to lead the whole three down into the water, and to baptize them "into the Name of the Father, and of the Son, and of the Holy Ghost".

Not only were many converted who had been indifferent or careless about their souls, but I had peculiar joy in receiving not a few, who had themselves been numbered amongst the slanderers and blasphemers who seemed as if they could not say anything cruel and wicked enough concerning me, even though they had never been to hear me. Many a man has come to me, when he was about to be added to the church, and his first speech has been, "Will you ever forgive me, sir?" I have said, "Forgive you for what?" "Why, because," he has answered, "there was no word in the English language that was bad enough for me to say of you; and yet I had never seen you in my life, and I had no reason for speaking like that. I have cursed God's people, and said all manner of evil of them; will you forgive me?" My reply has been, "I have nothing to forgive; if you have sinned against the Lord's people, I am heartily glad that you are ready to confess the sin to God, but as far as I was concerned, there was no offence given, and none taken." How glad I have been when the man has said that his heart was broken, that he had repented of his sins, that Christ had put away all his iniquities, and that he wished to follow the Lord, and make confession of his faith! I think there is only one joy I have had greater than this; that has been when those converted through my instrumentality have been the means of the conversion of others. Constantly has this happened during my ministry, until I have not only been surrounded by those who look upon me as their father in Christ, but I have had quite a numerous company of spiritual grandchildren, whom my sons and daughters in the faith have led to the Saviour.

The love that exists between a pastor and his converts is of a very special character, and I am sure that mine was so from the very beginning of my ministry. The bond that united me to the members at New Park Street was probably all the stronger because of the opposition and calumny that, for a time at least, they had to share with me. The attacks of our adversaries only united us more closely to one another, and, with whole-hearted devotion, the people willingly followed wherever I led them. I have never brought any project before them, or asked them to aid me in any holy enterprise, but they have been ready to respond to the call, no matter what amount of self-sacrifice might be required. Truly I may say, without the slightest flattery, that I never met with any people, on the face of the earth, who lived more truly up to this doctrine—that, chosen of God, and loved by Him with special love, they should do extraordinary things for Him—than those among whom it has been my privilege to minister. I have often gone on my knees before God to thank Him for the wondrous deeds I have seen done by some of the Christians with whom I have been so long and so happily associated. In service, they have gone beyond anything I could have asked. I should think they would have considered me unreasonable if I had requested it, but they have done it without request. At the risk of everything, they have served their Master, and not only spent all that they could spare, but have even spared what they could ill afford to devote to the service of Jesus. Often have I brushed the tears from my eyes when I have received from some of them offerings for the Lord's work which utterly surpassed all my ideas of giving. The consecration of their substance has been truly apostolic. I have known some who have, even in their poverty, given all that they had; and when I have even hinted at their exceeding the bounds of prudence, they have seemed hurt, and pressed the gift again for some other work of the Master whom they love. A man once said to me, "If you want a subscription from me, sir, you must get at my heart, and then you will get at my purse." "Yes," I answered, "I have no doubt I shall, for I believe that is where your purse lies." But that was not the case with the great bulk of my dear friends at New Park Street; their hearts were in the Lord's work, and therefore they generously gave of their substance for the advancement of their Saviour's Kingdom.

*   *   *

Our first sojourn at Exeter Hall, from February 11 to May 27, 1855, like the later assemblies in that historic building, was one long series of "special" services, which gave the church at New Park Street a position it had not previously attained. The simple record in our church-book scarcely conveys an adequate idea of the importance of the "forward movement" that was about to be inaugurated:

"Our Pastor announced from the pulpit that our place of worship would be closed for enlargement for the eight following Lord's-days, during which period the church and congregation would worship in the large room[1] at Exeter Hall, Strand, on Lord's-days, morning and evening, and that accommodation had also been provided for the usual week-evening services to be held at Maze Pond Chapel."

The following paragraph, published in *The Globe*, March 22, was extensively copied into other papers, and the comments upon it, both favourable and otherwise, helped still further to attract public attention to our services:

"The circumstances under which the Rev. C. H. Spurgeon has recently come before the public are curious, and demand a passing notice. Some months since, he became minister of New Park Street Chapel, and it was soon found that the building, capacious as it was, was far too small to accommodate the crowds of persons who flocked to hear the young and eloquent divine. In this state of affairs, there was no alternative but to enlarge the chapel, and while this process was going on, Exeter Hall was engaged for him. For some weeks past, he has been preaching there every Sunday morning and evening; but he has filled the great hall, just as easily as he filled New Park Street Chapel. A traveller along the Strand, about six o'clock on a Sunday evening, would wonder what could be the meaning of a crowd which literally stopped the progress of public vehicles, and sent unhappy pedestrians round the by-streets, in utter hopelessness of getting along the wider thoroughfare. Since the days of Wesley and White-field—whose honoured names seem to be in danger of being thrown into the shade by this new candidate for public honours—so thorough a religious *furor* has never existed. Mr. Spurgeon is likely to become a great preacher; at present, his fervid and impassioned eloquence sometimes leads him a little astray, and sometimes there is a

---

[1] It was capable of holding from 4,000 to 5,000 persons. Prior to this time it was used chiefly by the Sacred Harmonic Society and the conveners of May meetings.—P

want of solemnity, which mars the beauty of his singularly happy style."

Before we had completed the two months for which we had engaged Exeter Hall, we found that it was advisable to continue there for eight more Sabbaths (making sixteen in all). Our return to our own chapel is thus recorded in the church-book:

"The meeting-house in New Park Street was re-opened, after the enlargement, on Thursday, May 31st, 1855, when two sermons were preached, that in the forenoon by the Rev. James Sherman, of Blackheath, and that in the evening by our Pastor."

It was a very wet day, and, although I am not a believer in omens, I told the people that I regarded it as a prognostication of the "showers of blessing" we hoped to receive in the enlarged building; and that, as it had rained literally at the re-opening services, I prayed that we might have the rain spiritually as long as we worshipped there. To the glory of God, I am grateful to testify that it was so. I also quoted to the crowded congregation Malachi iii. 10—"Bring ye all the tithes into the storehouse, that there may be meat in Mine house, and prove Me now herewith, saith the Lord of hosts, if I will not open you the windows of heaven, and pour you out a blessing, that there shall not be room enough to receive it;"—and reminded the friends that, if they wished to have the promised blessing, they must comply with the condition attached to it. This they were quite ready to do, and from the time of our return to our much-loved sanctuary until the day when we finally left it, we never had "room enough to receive" the blessings which the Lord so copiously poured out for us.

There were two evenings—June 22, and September 4, 1855—when I preached in the open air in a field in King Edward's Road, Hackney. On the first occasion,[1] I had the largest congregation I had ever addressed up to that time, but at the next service the crowd was still greater.[2] By careful calculation, it was estimated that from twelve to

[1] This was the service which is referred to in his letter on page 295.

[2] The text on the second occasion was Matthew viii. 11, 12; and the sermon was printed in *The New Park Street Pulpit* (Nos. 39–40), under the title, "Heaven and Hell". Translations were published in various languages, including Russian and French. Copies of the Russian version reached Mr. Spurgeon from time to time, each one bearing on its front cover the "Alpha and Omega" in the centre of the official stamp certifying that it might be read and circulated by faithful members of the Greek Church; on the back, was a list of nine more of the sermons issued by the same publisher. As soon as the permission of the censor had been obtained, the gentleman who had sought it ordered a million copies of the sermons to be printed, and scattered over the Russian Empire. "That day" alone will reveal how many souls have been saved through this method of spreading the truth in that dark region.

fourteen thousand persons were present. I think I shall never forget the impression I received then when, before we separated, that vast multitude joined in singing—

"Praise God from whom all blessings flow."

That night, I could understand better than ever before why the apostle John, in the Revelation, compared the "new song" in Heaven to "the voice of many waters". In that glorious hallelujah, the mighty waves of praise seemed to roll up towards the sky, in majestic grandeur, even as the billows of old ocean break upon the beach.

*   *   *

[Preaching at New Park Street Chapel on the last Lord's-day morning in 1855 Spurgeon said: "Ought we to let this year pass without rehearsing the works of the Lord? Hath He not been with us, and prospered us exceeding abundantly? . . . We shall not soon forget our sojourn in Exeter Hall—shall we? During those months, the Lord brought in many of His own elect, and multitudes, who had been up to that time unsaved, were called by Divine mercy, and brought into the fold. How God protected us there! What peace and prosperity hath He given to us! How hath He enlarged our borders, and multiplied our numbers, so that we are not few; and increased us, so that we are not weak! I do think we were not thankful enough for the goodness of the Lord which carried us there, and gave us so many who have now become useful to us in our church. . . . Some old writer has said, 'Every hour that a Christian remains a Christian, is an hour of miracle.' It is true; and every year that the church is kept a united church, is a year of miracle. This has been a year of miracles.[1] Tell it to the wide, wide world; tell it everywhere: 'The eyes of the Lord' have been upon us, 'from the beginning of the year even unto the end of the year.' Two hundred and ten

[1] There are many references in Spurgeon's sermons at this period to his conviction that they were in the midst of an outpouring of the Holy Spirit. In a sermon preached on January 7, 1855, he said to his unconverted hearers, "Unbelief makes you sit here in times of revival and of the outpouring of God's grace, unmoved, uncalled, unsaved." In a sermon on June 28, 1857, he said, "A certain race of croaking souls are always crying out about the badness of the times. They cry, 'O! for the good old times!' Why, these are the good old times . . . I do think that many an old puritan would jump out of his grave if he knew what was doing now." In later years he would remind his congregation of the days they had once witnessed, "Oh, my hearers, some of you have been here in times of revival; you have seen drunkards saved, you have seen the most unlikely converted." *Metropolitan Tabernacle Pulpit*, 1881, p. 459.—P.

persons[1] have this year united with us in church-fellowship—about enough to have formed a church. One half the churches in London cannot number so many in their entire body; yet the Lord has brought so many into our midst. And still they come; whenever I have an opportunity of seeing those who are converted to God, they come in such numbers that many have to be sent away; and I am well assured that I have as many still in this congregation who will, during the next year, come forward to put on the Lord Jesus Christ."

*   *   *

One of the earliest descriptions of Spurgeon's preaching at New Park Street is given by John Anderson, a man thirty years older than Spurgeon who had been ministering in Helensburgh, Scotland, since 1827. Visiting London, he was at New Park Street on March 30, 1856, and on returning home he related the following experience:

"When Mr. Spurgeon was in Glasgow last summer, the fame of his eloquence had reached me in my seclusion here, by the shores of the sounding sea, the noise of whose waves delight me more than the 'din of cities' or the tumult of the people. I had heard him 'spoken against' by some, but spoken of by others as a preacher of remarkable and, since the days of Whitefield himself, of unprecedented popularity. But being one of those who judge for themselves in the matter of preaching, and whose opinions as to what constitutes good preaching are somewhat peculiar, I did not attach much—I may almost say any —importance whatever to what I heard of Mr. Spurgeon and his popularity in Glasgow. One of his printed sermons, however, having fallen in my way, I had no sooner read a few paragraphs of it than I said, 'Here, at last, is a preacher to my mind; one whom not only I, but whom Paul himself, I am persuaded, were he on earth, would hear, approve, and own.' I forget what was the subject of the discourse; but I remember well saying to myself, 'I would rather have been the author of that sermon than of all the sermons, or volumes of sermons, published in my day.' I had lately before this been reading Guthrie and Caird, but here was something entirely different, and to my mind, in all that constitutes a genuine and good Gospel sermon, infinitely superior.

For some time after this I heard little, and thought little, about Mr. Spurgeon. Having been, however, in London on the last Sabbath of March, and having been unexpectedly released from an engagement to

---

[1] It appears from the New Park Street church-book that the number was even larger than this. At the end of 1854, there were 313 names on the roll; during 1855, there was a net increase of 282; and the following year the net increase was 265, making the total membership 860.

preach, I thought I could not do better than go and hear for myself the preacher of whom I had heard so much in my own country. Along with two young friends, see me, then, early on the beautiful morning of that beautiful Sabbath day, when as yet there were few people on the streets, and all the 'mighty heart' of that great city was 'lying still', on my way from Islington to New Park Street Chapel, Southwark, a distance of nearly four miles. We arrived at the chapel about eleven, but found that the service had commenced a quarter before eleven. The church was filled, and there were crowds of people at the gate uncertain what to do. Seeing one of the doorkeepers near the great entrance, I went up to him and said 'that I was from Scotland, and that having come so far I really *must* get in.' He asked me from what 'part of Scotland I came.' I said, 'Glasgow.' He asked no more, but said, 'Come, follow me; I really must get you in', or words to that effect. He led the way into a wing of the building, fitted up and evidently used as a school; and here, where there were many assembled, we found seats; and though, from the crowd which choked the doors and passages, we did not see the preacher very well, we—and this was what we wanted—heard him distinctly. When we entered he was expounding, as is his custom, a portion of the Scriptures. The passage expounded was Exodus, fourteenth chapter, which contains an account of the Israelites at the Red Sea—a passage of Scripture peculiarly interesting to me, having stood on its shore and sailed on the very spot where the waters were so wondrously divided. The remarks of the preacher on each of the verses were very much in the style of Henry, and were rich and racy. His text was from the 106th Psalm, and the subject of the discourse was the same with that of the chapter he had just expounded—'The Israelites at the Red Sea'.

Regarding them as typical of the people of God under the Gospel, he said there were two things which he intended to consider. First, their difficulties; secondly, their resources. Their difficulties, he said were occasioned by three things—first, the Red Sea before them; second, the Egyptians behind them; and third, the weakness of their faith. These difficulties were in the way, he said, of believers: first, the Red Sea of trials—trials peculiar to them as Christians, and caused by their coming out of Egypt, or their renouncing the world; second, the Egyptians are behind them—sin, Satan, and the world, seeking to recover them to their yoke, and, failing this, to harass and distress them. But the greatest difficulty in the way of both was unbelief. Had they trusted in Him that was *for* them, they would have made little of all them that were *against* them.

Second, their resources. These were three—first, the providence of God. He had brought them to the Red Sea; and He who had brought them *to* it, was able and wise enough to bring them *through* it. Second, His covenant, in virtue of which He was under engagement to do so, and was bound in honour to do so. Third, the intercession of Moses. He prayed for them when they knew it not. So Christ prays for His people, and Him the Father heareth always; and in answer to His prayers, delivers, and will continue to deliver, them out of all their troubles, etc.

Such was the method of one of the richest and ripest sermons, as regards Christian experience, all the more wonderful as being the sermon of so young a man, I ever heard. It was a sermon far in advance of the experience of many of his hearers; and the preacher evidently felt this. But, notwithstanding this, such was the simplicity of his style, the richness and quaintness of his illustrations, his intense earnestness, and the absolute and admirable naturalness of his delivery, it told upon his audience generally, and told powerfully. Many, most of them, were of the 'common people', and when I looked upon their plebeian faces, their hands brown with labour, and, in many cases, their faded attire, I could not help remembering Him of whom it is said, 'And the common people heard Him gladly.' Yes, Mr. Spurgeon is the minister of the 'common people'; he considers himself, I am told, to be such, and well he may. Happy London people, if they but knew their happiness, to have such a minister! But to return to the sermon, and its effects on the faces! How intensely fixed were they on the preacher—how eager to hear every word he uttered—how fearful lest they should fail to catch the least! Tears were now to be seen trickling down them; and then, again, pale and careworn though many of them were, they might be seen beaming with light and joy, and brightening into smiles. One man I noticed in particular. He was evidently of humble rank, but had a noble and intelligent countenance; his face was a perfect study; every time the preacher said a striking thing, he looked expressively to me and I to him. At the close of the service I could have given him a hearty, brotherly shake of the hand, but I lost him in the crowd, and did not see him again.

Thus much for the morning. A word or two now about the evening sermon. We were told that, if we wanted to get in, to come early, as the crowd would be greater than in the morning. With two friends, I returned about six; the service was to commence at half-past six. To our dismay, when we arrived, we found crowds already at the door waiting for admission. Those only who had tickets were now permitted to enter; as we had none, we almost despaired of getting in.

One of my friends, however, knowing how I had got in in the morning, went up to a police officer, and told him I was a clergyman from Scotland, and was anxious to be admitted. The police officer, hearing this, said, very politely, he would allow us to enter the church, but would not promise us seats. This was all we wanted. One of us (a lady) was kindly favoured with a seat; my other friend and myself thought ourselves happy, like Eutychus of old, in being permitted to sit 'in a window', with a dense crowd in the passage at our feet. I asked a man near me if he came regularly; he said he did. 'Why, then,' I asked, 'do you not take a seat?' 'Seat!' he replied; 'such a thing is not to be had for love or money. I got a ticket for leave to stand.' The church, I was told, is seated for 1,500; but what with the school-room and the passages, which were choke-full, there could not have been fewer in it than 3,000. The service commenced with a hymn, which was sung by the congregation standing. Never did I hear such singing; it was like the 'voice of many waters', or the roll of thunder. No need was there of an organ in that congregation; the most powerful organ would not have been heard in the loud swell of so many living human voices. Then came the prayer. Phrenologically speaking, I should say veneration is not largely developed in Mr. Spurgeon; yet that prayer was one of the most remarkable and impressive I ever heard. He prayed first for confirmed believers, then for declining ones, then for sundry other conditions. Then there was a pause, after which he prayed for the unconverted. 'Some,' he said, 'were present who were in this state, who, in all likelihood, would never be in that or any other church again—who were that night to hear their last sermon—who, ere next Lord's day, would not be in this world; and where would they be? There was but one place where they would be—in hell!' He then said, or rather cried out, 'O God, God! must they perish? wilt Thou not save them, and make that sermon the means of their conversion?' The effect was overwhelming; many wept, and I am not ashamed to say I was one of them. The text was in Psalm cxxvi. 1, 2—'When the Lord turned again the captivity of Zion, we were like them that dream. Then was our mouth filled with laughter, and our tongue with singing.' The subject raised from the text was the 'joy of the young convert'. This sermon, in some respects, was not equal to the one in the morning, but in other respects, and in particular in its suitableness to a large and promiscuous audience, was superior.

Some of the sketches, and that in particular of a slave newly emancipated, drunk with joy that he was free, were equal to anything ever drawn by a Dickens, or any of our great masters of fiction. Equally fine was that of the sick man restored to health, and going forth for the first time after his recovery to take his walk in the streets of London. But it would be impossible to mention all the fine touches of nature in that sermon, which made the whole of that vast congregation for the moment 'kin'. His denunciations of the Sabbath-breaker and others were as terrible as his delineations of the penitent were tender and melting. Mr. Spurgeon is equally great in the tender and the terrible. Nor is he without humour. Here many will refuse him their sympathy, and think him censurable. I scarcely think he is. Others will think, and do think, differently. His taste, according to others, is bad. It is, I admit, often so. But, then, think of the immaturity of his years. I was told he was conceited. I saw no proofs of it; and if I had, was I on that account to think less of his sermons? I do not say I will not eat good bread, because the maker of it is conceited. His conceit may be a bad thing for himself—his bread is very good for me. I am far from thinking Mr. Spurgeon perfect. In this respect he is not like Whitefield, who from the first was as perfect an orator as he was at the last. In respect of his power over an audience, and a London one in particular, I should say he is not inferior to Whitefield himself. Mr. Spurgeon is a Calvinist, which few of the dissenting ministers in London now are. He preaches salvation, not of man's *free will*, but of the Lord's *good will*, which few in London, it is to be feared, now do. On all these accounts, we hail the appearance of Mr. Spurgeon with no ordinary delight, and anticipate for him a career of no ordinary usefulness. 'Happy are they which stand continually before him, and hear his words of wisdom.' As for myself, I shall long remember with delight the day on which I stood among them, and recommend such of my countrymen as may have a Lord's day to spend in London, to spend it as I did at New Park Street Chapel in hearing Mr. Spurgeon."

*   *   *

The following letters, written by Spurgeon to his very intimate friend, Mr. J. S. Watts, Regent Street, Cambridge, record the young Pastor's experiences during the period 1854–1856, and throw a vivid light on many of the notable incidents which occurred then:

"75, Dover Road,
August 25, 1854.

My Very Dear Friend,

I am astonished to find that fame has become so inveterate a fabricator of untruths, for I assure you that I had no more idea of coming to Cambridge on Wednesday than of being dead last week.

I have been, this week, to Tring, in Hertfordshire, on the border of Bucks. I have climbed the goodly hills, and seen the fair vale of Aylesbury below. In the morning, I startled the hare from her form, and at eve talked with the countless stars. I love the glades and dells, the hills and vales, and I have had my fill of them. The week before, I was preaching at Ramsgate, and then tarried awhile at Margate, and came home by boat. Kent is indeed made to rejoice in her God, for in the parts I traversed the harvest was luxuriant, and all seemed thankful.

The Crystal Palace is likewise a favourite haunt of mine; I shall rejoice to take your arm one day, and survey its beauties with you.

Now for the cause at New Park Street. We are getting on too fast. Our harvest is too rich for the barn. We have had one meeting to consider an enlargement—quite unanimous—meet again on Wednesday, and then a committee will be chosen immediately to provide larger accommodation. On Thursday evenings, people can scarcely find a vacant seat—I should think not a dozen in the whole chapel. On Sabbath days, the crowd is immense, and seat-holders cannot get into their seats; half-an-hour before time, the aisles are a solid block, and many stand through the whole service, wedged in by their fellows, and prevented from escaping by the crowd outside, who seal up the doors, and fill the yard in front, and stand in throngs as far as the sound can reach. I refer mainly to the evening, although the morning is nearly the same.

Souls are being saved. I have more enquirers than I can attend to. From six to seven o'clock on Monday and Thursday evenings, I spend in my vestry; I give but brief interviews then, and have to send many away without being able to see them. The Lord is wondrous in praises. A friend has, in a letter, expressed his hope that my initials may be prophetic—

C.	H.	S.
COMFORT	HAPPINESS	SATISFACTION

I can truly say they are, for I have *comfort* in my soul, *happiness* in my work, and *satisfaction* with my glorious Lord. I am deeply in debt for your offer of hospitality; many thanks to you. My kindest regards to all my friends, and yours, especially your sons and daughters. I am sure it gives me delight to be remembered by them, and I hope it will not be long before I run down to see them. Hoping you will be *blessed* in going out, and coming in,

I am,

Yours truly,

C. H. SPURGEON."

"75, Dover Road,
Saturday [Oct. or Nov., 1854].

My Dear Friend,

I do not think I can by any means manage to see you. There is just a bare possibility that I may be down by the half-past-one train on Monday morning, but do not prepare for me, or expect me. I can only write very briefly to-day, as it is Saturday. Congregations as crowded as ever. Twenty-five added to the church last month; twelve proposed this month. Enlargement of chapel to be commenced speedily. £1,000 required. Only one meeting held, last Friday evening, £700 or £800 already raised; we shall have more than enough. I gave £100 myself to start the people off. Friends firm. Enemies alarmed. Devil angry. Sinners saved. Christ exalted. Self not well. Enlargement to comprise 300 seats to let, and 300 free sittings; 200 more to be decided on. I have received anonymously in one month for distribution, £18 5s., and have given it to poor Christians and sick persons.

Love to you all. Excuse haste. Forgot to say—Prayer-meeting, 500 in regular attendance. Glory to the Master!

Yours in Jesus,
C. H. SPURGEON."

"75, Dover Road,
March 23, 1855.

My Dear Friend and Brother,

Often have I looked for a note from you, but I have not reproached you, for I, too, have been negligent. Really, I never seem to have an hour to call my own. I am always at it, and the people are teasing me almost to death to get me to let them hear my voice. It is strange that such a power should be in one small body to crowd Exeter Hall to suffocation, and block up the Strand, so that pedestrians have to turn down by-ways, and all other traffic is at a standstill.

The Globe, of last evening, says that, never since the days of White-field was there such a religious furor, and that the glories of Wesley and Whitefield seem in danger of being thrown into the shade. Well, the press has kicked me quite long enough, now they are beginning to lick me; but one is as good as the other so long as it helps to fill our place of worship. I believe I could secure a crowded audience at dead of night in a deep snow.

On Fast-day, all Falcon Square was full—police active, women shrieking—and at the sight of me the rush was fearful. . . . Strange to say, nine-tenths of my hearers are men; but one reason is, that women cannot endure the awful pressure, the rending of clothes, &c., &c.

I have heard of parties coming to the hall, from ten or twelve miles distance, being there half-an-hour before time, and then never getting so much as near the door.

Dear me, how little satisfies the crowd! What on earth are other preachers up to, when, with ten times the talent, they are snoring along with prosy sermons, and sending the world away? The reason is, I believe, they do not know what *the gospel* is; they are afraid of *real gospel Calvinism*, and therefore the Lord does not own them.

And now for spiritual matters. I have had knocking about enough to kill a dozen, but the Lord has kept me. Somewhere in *nubibus* there lies a vast mass of *nebulæ* made of advice given to me by friends—most of it about humility. Now, my Master is the only one who can humble me. My pride is so infernal that there is not a man on earth who can hold it in, and all their silly attempts are futile; but then my Master can do it, and He will. Sometimes, I get such a view of my own insignificance that I call myself all the fools in the world for even letting pride pass my door without frowning at him. I am now, as ever, able to join with Paul in saying, 'Having nothing, and yet possessing all things.'

Souls are being converted, and flying like doves to their windows. The saints are more zealous, and more earnest in prayer.

Many of the man-made parsons are mad, and revile me, but many others are putting the steam on, for this is not the time to sleep in.

The Lord is abroad. The enemy trembles. Mark how the devil roars —see *Era*, last week, a theatrical paper, where you can read about 'EXETER HALL THEATRE' linked with Drury Lane, Princess's, &c. Read the slander in *Ipswich Express* and the London *Empire*. The two latter have made an apology.

What a fool the devil is! If he had not vilified me, I should not have had so many precious souls as my hearers.

I long to come and throw one of my *bombs* into Cambridge; you are a sleepy set, and want an explosion to wake you. (Here omit a gentleman whose initials are J. S. W.) I am coming on Good Friday; is your house still the Bishop's Hostel? Of course it is. Now, DO write me; I love you as much as ever, and owe you a vast debt. Why not come and see me? I know you pray for me.

With Christian love to you, and kind remembrances to all your family,

I am,

Yours ever truly,

C. H. SPURGEON."

"75, Dover Road,
Tuesday [April, 1855].

Dear Friend and Brother,

(D.V.) Thursday, I shall be with you at 1.30 by the mail train. I shall be glad to preach in St. Andrew's Street Chapel, but shall disappoint you all. The people are silly to follow me so much. It now gets worse. *Crowds awful* on Sunday last. Collected £90 morning and evening at the hall. At Shoreditch, on Tuesday, there were eight or nine hundred where only six hundred should have been admitted; upon *personally* appealing to the throng outside, disappointed at not getting in, most of them dispersed, and allowed the rest of us to worship as well as we could with windows open to let those hear who remained outside.

Joseph is still shot at by the archers, and sorely grieved (see *Baptist Reporter, United Presbyterian Magazine, Critic, Christian News*, &c., with a lot of small fry), but his bow abides in strength, neither does he tremble. Oh, my dear brother, envy has vexed me sorely—scarcely a Baptist minister of standing will own me! I am sick of *man*; but when I find a good one, I love him all the better because of the contrast to others.

I have just received a handsome silver inkstand, bearing this inscription: 'Presented to Mr. C. H. Spurgeon by J. and S. Alldis, as a token of sincere gratitude to him as the instrument, under Almighty God, of turning them from darkness to light, March 30, 1855.' The devil may look at *that* as often as he pleases; it will afford him sorry comfort.

And now, farewell. Christian love to you and yours, from—

Yours deeply in debt,
C. H. SPURGEON."

"New Kent Road,
Southwark,
Feb. 23, 1856.

My Dear Brother,

A wearied soldier finds one moment of leisure to write a despatch to his brother in arms. Eleven times this week have I gone forth to battle, and at least thirteen services are announced for next week. Additions to the church, last year, 282; received this year, in three months, more than 80—30 more proposed for next month—hundreds, who are equally sincere, are asking for admission; but time will not allow us to take in more. Congregation more than immense—even *The Times* has noticed it. Everywhere, at all hours, places are crammed to the doors. The devil is wide awake, but so, too, is the Master.

The Lord Mayor, though a Jew, has been to our chapel; he came up to my vestry to thank me. I am to go and see him at the Mansion House. The Chief Commissioner of Police also came, and paid me a visit in the vestry; but, better still, some thieves, thimbleriggers, harlots, &c., have come, and some are now in the church, as also a right honourable hot-potato man, who is prominently known as 'a hot Spurgeonite'.

The sale of sermons is going up—some have sold 15,000. *Wife*, first-rate; beloved by all my people, we have good reason mutually to rejoice.

I write mere heads, for you can fill up details.

I have been this week to Leighton Buzzard, Foots Cray, and Chatham; everywhere, no room for the crowd. Next week, I am to be thus occupied:

Sabbath	Morning and evening, New Park Street.
	Afternoon, to address the schools.
Monday	Morning, at Howard Hinton's Chapel.
	Afternoon, New Park Street.
	Evening, „ „
Tuesday	Afternoon, } Leighton
	Evening, }
Wednesday	Morning, } Zion Chapel, Whitechapel.
	Evening, }
Thursday	Morning, Dalston.
	Evening, New Park Street.
Friday	Morning, Dr. Fletcher's Chapel.
	Evening, Mr. Rogers' Chapel, Brixton.

With best love,
Yours in haste,
C. H. Spurgeon."]

"I have striven, with all my might, to attain the position of complete independence of all men. I have found, at times, if I have been much praised, and if my heart has given way a little, and I have taken notice of it, and felt pleased, that the next time I was censured and abused I felt the censure and abuse very keenly, for the very fact that I accepted the commendation, rendered me more sensitive to the censure. So that I have tried, especially of late, to take no more notice of man's praise than of his blame, but to rest simply upon this truth—I know that I have a pure motive in what I attempt to do, I am conscious that I endeavour to serve God with a single eye to His glory, and therefore it is not for me to take either praise or censure from man, but to stand independently upon the solid rock of right doing."—C. H. S.

Chapter 24

First Literary Friends

ALTHOUGH many assailed Spurgeon through the press in the first years of his ministry in London, there were always loyal and true hearts ready to come to his help, and write in his defence. The following pages contain some of the principal favourable articles published during 1855 and 1856; they furnish a marked contrast to the slanders and calumnies which the young preacher had to endure at that time.

One of the first and one of the ablest of Spurgeon's champions among literary men was James Grant, the Editor of *The Morning Advertiser*, which, under his management, a contemporary writer testifies, was raised "to the position of a first-class morning paper, second only to *The Times*, either in circulation or influence." In its columns, on February 19, 1855, he published an article, the tenor of which may be judged by the following extracts:

"THE REV. MR. SPURGEON

A young man, in the twenty-first year of his age, has just appeared, under this name, among our metropolitan preachers, and is creating a great sensation in the religious world. He had only been a few weeks settled as minister of Park Street Chapel, Southwark, before that commodious place was filled to overflowing, while hundreds at each service went away who were unable to effect an entrance. The result was, that it was agreed to enlarge the chapel, and that the youthful minister should preach in the large room of Exeter Hall for eight Sundays, until the re-opening of his own place of worship. It will easily be believed how great must be the popularity of this almost boyish preacher, when we mention that, yesterday, both morning and evening, the large hall, capable of containing from 4,000 to 5,000 persons, was filled in every part. Mr. Spurgeon belongs to the Baptist denomination. . . . He is short in stature, and somewhat thickly built, which, with an exceedingly broad, massive face, gives him the appearance of a man twenty-six or twenty-seven years of age instead of twenty-one. His doctrines are of the Hyper-Calvinist school. He is a young man, we are told, of extensive information, especially on theological subjects, and of a highly cultivated mind. There can be no doubt that he possesses superior talents, while, in some of his happier flights, he rises to a high order of pulpit oratory. It is in pathos that he excels, though he does not himself seem to be aware of the fact. But for some sad drawbacks in the young divine, we should anticipate great usefulness from him, because he not only possesses qualities peculiarly adapted to attract and rivet the attention of the masses, but he makes faithful and powerful appeals to the consciences of the unconverted. In the spirit of sincere friendship, we would advise him to study to exhibit an aspect of greater gravity and seriousness. Let us also impress upon him the indispensable necessity of relinquishing those theatrical—we had almost said melo-dramatic—attitudes into which he is in the habit of throwing himself. In Exeter Hall, yesterday, instead of confining himself to the little spot converted into a sort of pulpit for him, he walked about on the platform just as if he had been treading the boards of Drury Lane Theatre, while performing some exciting tragedy. Altogether, he seems to want the reverence of manner which is essential to the success of a minister of the gospel. We hope, however, that in these respects he will improve. It is with that view we give him our friendly counsels. He is quite an original preacher, and therefore will always draw large congregations, and, consequently, may be eminently made the means of doing great good to classes of persons who might never otherwise be brought within the sound of a faithfully-preached gospel. He has evidently made George Whitefield his model; and, like that unparalleled preacher, that prince of pulpit orators, is very fond of striking apostrophes. Like him, too, he has a powerful voice, which would, at times, be more pleasing, and not less impressive, were it not raised to so high a pitch."

Spurgeon's own testimony confirms James Grant's assertion that he had "evidently made George Whitefield his model". He wrote, in 1879: "There is no end to the interest which attaches to such a man as George Whitefield. Often as I have read his life, I am conscious of distinct quickening whenever I turn to it. *He lived.* Other men seem to be only half-alive, but Whitefield was all life, fire, wing, force. My own model, if I may have such a thing in due subordination to my Lord, is George Whitefield; but with unequal footsteps must I follow in his glorious track."

*   *   *

An account of Spurgeon's life and work was published in *The Patriot*, on September 21, 1855. The following are some of the writer's kind expressions concerning the young preacher:

"Although the name of the Rev. C. H. Spurgeon has been frequently mentioned in the columns of this Journal, we have not introduced him to our readers by any formal description of his preaching. Such, however, is its effect, that curiosity cannot but have been awakened by intelligence of the immense crowds collected to hear him while occupying Exeter Hall from Sunday to Sunday, and also when he returned to his own enlarged chapel in New Park Street, over Southwark Bridge. There must surely be something extraordinary in a mere youth who could command an attendance of from ten to twelve thousand persons in the open field, and who, on visiting the North, though received with cold suspicion at first, soon compelled the fixed and admiring attention of the reluctant Scotch; though, he says, 'they seemed to be all made of lumps of ice fetched from Wenham Lake.' Those who go to hear Mr. Spurgeon, enquiring, 'What will this babbler say?' are not long left in doubt as to either the manner or the matter of his discourses. . . . We have ourselves heard Mr. Spurgeon but once, and, on that occasion, not having succeeded in gaining an entrance to the chapel, we squeezed ourselves into a side vestry, from which the speaker could be heard, but not seen. We found him neither extravagant nor extraordinary. His voice is clear and musical; his language is plain; his style flowing, yet terse; his method lucid and orderly; his matter sound and suitable; his tone and spirit cordial; his remarks always pithy and pungent, sometimes familiar and colloquial, yet never light or coarse, much less profane. Judging from this single sermon, we supposed that he would become a plain, faithful, forcible, and affectionate preacher of the gospel in the form called Calvinistic; and our judgment was the more favourable because, while there was a solidity beyond his years, we detected little of the wild luxuriance naturally characteristic of very young preachers.

Our opinion of Mr. Spurgeon as a preacher has been somewhat modified by a perusal of his published discourses, which, issued in a cheap form, appear to be bought up with great eagerness. These show him to be a more extraordinary person than we supposed, and not to be quite so far from extravagance as at first we thought him. But it is more for the sake of information than with a view to criticism that we refer to the subject. From whatsoever cause it springs, whether from force of native character, or from a vigour superinduced upon that basis by the grace of God, there is that in Mr. Spurgeon's reported sermons which marks him a superior man.

Models of different styles of preaching are so numerous, that originality must be of rare occurrence; but he appears to be an original genius. To the pith of Jay, and the plainness of Rowland Hill, he adds much of the familiarity, not to say the coarseness, of the Huntingtonian order of ultra-Calvinistic preachers. 'It has been my privilege,' he says, 'to give more prominence in the religious world to those old doctrines of the gospel.' But the traits referred to present themselves in shapes and with accompaniments which forbid the notion of imitation, and favour the opinion of a peculiar bent. Neither in the style and structure, nor in handling, is there appearance of art, study, or elaboration. Yet, each discourse has a beginning, a middle, and an end, and the subject is duly introduced and stated, divided and discussed, enforced and applied. But all is done without effort, with the ease and freedom of common conversation, and with the artlessness, but also with the force, of spontaneous expression.

Mr. Spurgeon waits for nothing which requires what we understand by composition, and he rejects nothing by which attention may be arrested, interest sustained, and impression made permanent. The vehicle of his thoughts is constructed of well-seasoned Saxon speech, and they are conveyed to the hearer's mind in terms highly pictorial and often vividly dramatic. Great governing principles are freely personified, and religious experience, past, present, and future, appears in life-like action upon the scene. Tried by such tests as the unities, Mr. Spurgeon might sometimes be found wanting, but it is enough for him that, as face answers to face in the glass, so do his words elicit a response in the hearts of those who hear him. This end secured, what cares he for a mixed metaphor or a rhetorical anachronism? Were it his aim to rival the Melvilles and Harrises of the day, he lacks neither the talent nor the taste; and, with these, he has the faculty of gathering what is to be learned from men or from books, and of turning all to account. But his single aim is to preach the gospel, and he depends for success, not upon the enticing words of man's wisdom, but upon the influence of the Spirit of God, and, with a view to that, the prayers of his people.

Mr. Spurgeon evinces much aptitude in borrowing illustrations, not only from the pages of antiquity, and from modern life and literature, but also from the most familiar incidents, as well as from public events. Thus, the war suggests to him the idea that even the believer 'carries within him a bomb-shell, ready to burst at the slightest spark of temptation.' In like manner, the fatal exposure of the officers to the sharp-shooting of the enemy, furnishes him with a comparison by which to illustrate the peculiar liability of Christian ministers to hostile attack, though with a great difference in the result.

'Some of us,' he says, 'are the officers of God's regiments, and we are the mark of all the riflemen of the enemy. Standing forward, we have to bear all the shots. What a mercy it is, that not one of God's officers ever falls in battle! God always keeps them.'

His sermons abound with aphoristic and pointed sayings, which often afford a striking proof of his genius. . . . Many instances might easily be given of a force and beauty of language indicative of a high degree of eloquence. 'Bright-eyed cheerfulness and airy-footed love,' are fine phrases. Winter is described as not killing the flowers, but as 'coating them with the ermine of its snows'. Again, the sun is not quenched, but is behind the clouds, 'brewing up summer; and, when he cometh forth again, he will have made those clouds fit to drop in April showers, all of them mothers of the sweet May flowers.' God 'puts our prayers, like rose-leaves, between the pages of His book of remembrance, and when the volume is opened at last, there shall be a precious fragrance springing up therefrom'. 'There is one thing,' the sinner is told, 'that doth outstrip the telegraph: "Before they call, I will answer, and while they are yet speaking, I will hear." ' The memory, infected by the Fall, is described as 'suffering the glorious timbers from the forest of Lebanon to swim down the stream of oblivion; but she stoppeth all the draff that floateth from the foul city of Sodom'. With quaintness, yet with force and truth, the caste feeling of society is hit off: 'In England, a sovereign will not speak to a shilling, a shilling will not notice a sixpence, and a sixpence will sneer at a penny.' A singular quaintness and vigour may be remarked in Mr. Spurgeon's diction; as when he speaks of the lightning 'splitting the clouds, and rending the heavens'; of 'the mighty hand wherein the callow comets are brooded by the sun'; and of 'the very spheres stopping their music while God speaks with His wondrous bass voice.'

The manly tone of Mr. Spurgeon's mind might be illustrated from the admirable thoughts which he expresses on the connection between the diffusion of the gospel and the increase of civil liberty. His graphic skill in delineating character might be demonstrated from his life-like pictures of the prejudiced Jew and the scoffing Greek of modern times; his unsparing fidelity, from the sarcastic severity with which he rebukes the neglect of the Bible by modern professors; his powers of personification and dramatic presentation, from the scene which he paints between the dying Christian and Death, or between Jesus and Justice and the justified sinner; his refined skill in the treatment of a delicate subject, in the veiled yet impressive description of the trial of Joseph; the use that he can make of a single metaphor by his powerful comparison of the sinner to 'Mazeppa bound on the wild horse of his lust, galloping on with hell's wolves behind him,' till stopped and liberated by a mighty hand. The sermon entitled, 'The People's Christ', contains a very striking description of the resurrection of our Lord. In that on 'The Eternal Home', the contrast between the dying thief before and after his conversion, is powerfully drawn. The rage of Satan, on the rescue of a sinner from his grasp, forms a picture of terrific grandeur. In the sermon on 'The Bible', the respective characteristics of the holy penmen are sketched with a masterly comprehension of their peculiarities and command of words. . . . The beautiful sermon on the words, 'So He giveth His beloved sleep,' exhibits a variety and force which stamp the master."

*   *   *

On February 18, 1856, just a year after his first article, Mr. James Grant wrote as follows in *The Morning Advertiser*:

"Never, since the days of George Whitefield, has any minister of religion acquired so great a reputation as this Baptist preacher, in so short a time. Here is a mere youth—a perfect stripling, only twenty-one years of age—incomparably the most popular preacher of the day. There is no man within her Majesty's dominions who could draw such immense audiences; and none who, in his happier efforts, can so completely enthral the attention, and delight the minds of his hearers. Some of his appeals to the conscience, some of his remonstrances with the careless, constitute specimens of a very high order of oratorical power. . . . When this able and eloquent preacher first made his appearance in the horizon of the religious world, and dazzled the masses in the metropolis by his brilliancy, we were afraid that he might either get intoxicated by the large draughts of popularity which he had daily to drink, or that he would not be able, owing to a want of variety, to sustain the reputation he had so suddenly acquired. Neither result has happened. Whatever may be his defects, either as a man or as a preacher of the gospel, it is due to him to state that he has not been spoiled by popular applause. Constitutionally he has in him no small amount of self-esteem, but so far from its growing with his daily-extending fame, he appears to be more humble and more subdued than when he first burst on our astonished gaze. With regard again to our other fear, that his excellence as a preacher would not be sustained, the event has, we rejoice to say, no less agreeably proved the groundlessness of our apprehensions. There is no falling off whatever. On the contrary, he is, in some respects, improving with the

lapse of time. We fancy we can see his striking originality to greater
advantage than at first."

As a specimen of the early friendly notices in the provincial press,
the following may be given from *The Western Times*, February 23, 1856:

"ANOTHER EXTRAORDINARY PREACHER

It is a remarkable fact that, in the Baptist denomination of Christians
in this country, there have sprung up, from time to time, ministers of
extraordinary Biblical and other learning, and of great talent and
pulpit eloquence. We may refer to Dr. Carey, Dr. Gill, Dr. Rippon,
the distinguished Robert Hall of Bristol (whose discourses
Brougham and Canning were glad to listen to), and many others,
in proof of this peculiarity. It seems that another light has now sprung
up among the Baptists, which bids fair to rival, if not to eclipse, the
departed luminaries: we mean, the Rev. C. H. Spurgeon, who,
although but just arrived at twenty-one years of age, seems in the
pulpit and the press to have astonished the religious world. This
young Baptist minister's preaching created a great sensation in
Bristol a short time since, and his visits to other places have excited
intense interest. In Glasgow and other parts of Scotland, this gifted
young minister has also, with marvellous effect, carried home to the
hearts of crowded audiences the saving truths of 'the everlasting
gospel'. There is a singularity also about Mr. Spurgeon, for he is
emphatically 'one of the people'; and, by the gifts and graces with
which he is endowed, he shows to the world that the great Head of
the Church of Christ, as He called His apostles from the class of
humble fishermen, when He 'tabernacled on earth in the flesh', so
now that He is in Heaven, He continues to call labourers into His
vineyard from the working-men of polished society."

Another favourable notice appeared in *The Christian Weekly News*,
March 4, 1856: "Great orators, whether pulpit, platform, or senatorial, make many friends and many foes. This is inevitable, but it is
not our purpose, just now, to investigate or set forth the reasons for
this result. The fact being granted, we are at no loss to account for
the applause and contumely which have been heaped upon the young
minister whose sermons are before us. His appearance and labours in
this metropolis have excited in all religious circles, and even beyond
them, attention and surprise, if not admiration. Scarcely more than a
youth in years, comparatively untutored, and without a name, he
enters the greatest city in the world, and almost simultaneously

commands audiences larger than have usually listened to her most favoured preachers. Almost daily has he occupied pulpits in various parts of town and country, and everywhere been greeted by overflowing congregations. As might be expected, many who have listened to him have gone away to speak ill of his name; while others, and by far the larger number, have been stimulated by his earnestness, instructed by his arguments, and melted by his appeals. We have seen, among his hearers, ministers of mark of nearly every section of the Christian Church, laymen well known in all circles as the supporters of the benevolent and Evangelical institutions of the day, and citizens of renown from the chief magistrate down to the parish beadle. That the man who causes such a *furor* must possess some power not commonly found in men of his profession, will only be doubted by his detractors. Whether that power be physical, intellectual, or moral, or a happy blending of them all, is, perhaps, a question not yet fully decided even in the minds of many of his warmest admirers. The sermons before us would, we think, if carefully examined, help them to a decision. . . . Among the reasons to which, in our opinion, may be attributed the unbounded popularity of our author, we would name his youth, his devotedness, his earnestness, but especially that thrilling eloquence which can at once open the floodgates of the hearts of the thousands forming a Sabbath morning audience within the walls of Exeter Hall. May the Lord continue to hold him as a star in His right hand, and through his instrumentality bring many souls to bow to the sceptre of His love and mercy!"

*   *   *

The list of "first literary friends" would not be complete unless it included Rev. Edwin Paxton Hood. His volume, *The Lamps of the Temple*, published in 1856, contained a long and appreciative article on Spurgeon, in the course of which the writer said:

"It is not too much to say that this mere lad—this boy preacher—is the most remarkable pulpit celebrity of his day; it must be admitted that, amidst all the popularities, there is no popularity like his. . . . Among things—remarkable or not remarkable according to the reader's ideas—is the treatment of the young preacher by his brethren—shall we say, brethren?—in the ministry. We understand they have pretty generally agreed to regard him as a black sheep. His character is good—unexceptionable; his doctrines have no dangerous heresy in them; still, he is tabooed. The other day, a very eminent minister, whose portrait we have attempted to sketch in this volume, and whom

we certainly regarded as incapable of so much meanness when we
were sketching it—perhaps the most eminent of the London Dissenting ministers—was invited to open a chapel in the country—at
any rate, to take the evening service, but he found that Spurgeon was
to take the morning, and he smartly refused to mix in the affair: it
was pitiable, and we discharged ourselves, as in duty bound, of an
immense quantity of pity upon the head of the poor jealous man, who
dreaded lest the shadow of a rival should fall prematurely over his
pulpit. No; usually the ministers have not admired this advent; the
tens of thousands of persons, who flock to hear the youth preach his
strong nervous gospel, do not at all conciliate them—perhaps rather
exasperate them. It would be easy to pick up a thousand criticisms on
the preacher; many, not to say most of them, very severe. He is
flattered by a hurricane of acrimonious remark and abuse, and perhaps
owes his popularity in no small degree to this sweeping condemnation. One thing is certain—Spurgeon's back is broad, and his skin is
thick; he can, we fancy, bear a good deal, and bear a good deal without wincing. Little more than twenty-one years of age, he is the topic
and theme of remark now in every part of England; and severe as
some of his castigators are, he returns their castigation frequently
with a careless, downright, hearty goodwill. Beyond a doubt, the lad
is impudent, very impudent—were he not, he could not, at such an
age, be where he is, or what he is. . . .

We hear that Mr. Spurgeon has models upon which he forms his
mind and style. We think it very doubtful, but, at any rate, he does
not follow them slavishly; he has in his speech true mental and moral
independence. Robert Hall was charged with imitating Robert
Robinson, of Cambridge—in fact, there was not the slightest resemblance between those two minds. Spurgeon is said to imitate Robert
Hall and William Jay. No doubt he has read them both, but his style
is wholly unlike theirs; he, perhaps, has something of William Jay's
plan and method, and that is all; but to Robert Hall there is not the
most remote resemblance. He has not the purity, power, nor speed
of that inimitable master; he is not at all qualified to shine in the
brilliant intellectual firmament in which he held his place. We should
give to him a very different location. He has the unbridled and un-
disciplined fancy of Hervey, without his elegance; but, instead of that,
the drollery of Berridge and the ubiquitous earnestness of Rowland
Hill, in his best days. But it is probable that many of us walk far too
gingerly in our estimate of public speech. He who determines never
to use a word that shall grate harshly on the ears of a refined taste,
may be certain that he will never be very extensively useful; the people

love the man who will condescend to their idiom, and the greatest preachers—those who have been the great apostles of a nation—have always condescended to this. Bossuet, Massillon, Hall, Chalmers, McAll, were the doctors of the pulpit; at their feet sat the refinement, the scholarship, the politeness of their times; but such men as Luther and Latimer, St. Clara and Knox, Whitefield and Christmas Evans—such men have always seized on the prevailing dialect, and made it tell with immense power on their auditors.

A question repeatedly asked by many persons, when they have either heard, or heard of, this young man is, 'Will he last, will he wear?' To which we have always replied, 'Why not?' There is, apparently, no strain in the production of these discourses; they bear every appearance of being, on the whole, spontaneous talkings. The preacher speaks from the full and overflowing spring within him, and speaks, as we have said, many times during the week. Some of his sermons are characterized by great mental poverty; some, and most, by a great mental wealth; so is it with all preachers, even those who consume the midnight oil, and make it their boast that they can only produce one sermon a week. . . . Our preacher's fulness and readiness is, to our mind, a guarantee that he will wear, and not wear out. His present amazing popularity will of course subside, but he still will be amazingly followed, and what he is now, we prophesy, he will on the whole remain: for polished diction, we shall not look to him; for the long and stately argument, we shall not look to him; for the original and profound thought, we shall not look to him; for the clear and lucid criticism, we shall not look to him—but for bold and convincing statements of Evangelical truth, for a faithful grappling with convictions, for happy and pertinent illustrations, for graphic description, and for searching common sense, we shall look, and we believe we shall seldom look in vain. In a word, he preaches—not to metaphysicians or logicians—neither to poets nor to *savants*, to masters of erudition or masters of rhetoric; he preaches to men."

This chapter may be fitly closed with an extract from a pamphlet entitled, *Why so Popular? An Hour with Rev. C. H. Spurgeon*, by a Doctor of Divinity. It caused a great stir in the religious world when it appeared, and there is a special appropriateness in the poetical conclusion now that the beloved preacher, as a star, has melted into the light of Heaven. The writer, addressing his remarks personally to Spurgeon, says:

"I am fully aware that, if I asked yourself the question, 'Why so popular, and why so useful?' you would reply, in a self-humbling, God-exalting spirit, 'I am nothing: God is all; and to His sovereignty I ascribe all my popularity and all my success.' While admiring the spirit of this declaration, I decline to accept it as an answer to my question. God *is* a Sovereign, and in His sovereignty—essential to his Godhead—He has a right to give His Spirit when, where, to whom, and in what proportion He pleases, but He has no caprice, no senseless, reasonless arbitrariness in His administration. He never acts without reason, though, in His sovereign right, He often withholds from His creature, man, the reasons which influence the Divine mind. This, and not caprice, is God's sovereignty.

If I cannot discover the secret of your popularity in *what* you preach, can I find it in any peculiarity in your mode of preaching? Here is, in my judgment, the explanation of the secret. *You have strong faith, and, as the result,* INTENSE EARNESTNESS. *In this lies,* as in the hair of Samson, *the secret of your power.* Go on, my brother, and may God give you a still larger amount of ministerial success! 'Preach the Word,' the old theology, that 'glorious gospel of the blessed God' for which apostles laboured and martyrs died. In all your teachings, continue to exhibit the cross of Christ as occupying, in the Christian revelation, like the sun in our planetary system, the very centre, and imparting to all their light and heat. Tell the people that every doctrine, duty, or promise of the Scriptures stands intimately connected with the cross, and from that connection derives its meaning and value to us. Thus exhibiting the whole system of Divine Truth in its harmony and symmetry, what a glorious prospect of honour, happiness, and usefulness presents itself to your view! A star in the churches—a star of no mean magnitude, of no ordinary brilliancy—you may be honoured to diffuse, very luminously, the derived glories you possess, and, having run your appointed course, ultimately set—but far distant be the day!—as sets the morning star—

'Which falls not down behind the darkened West,
Nor hides obscured amid the tempests of the sky,
But melts away into the light of Heaven!' "

"If Christ should leave the upper world, and come into the midst of this hall, this morning, what answer could you give, if, after showing you His wounded hands and feet, and His rent side, He should put this question, 'I have suffered thus for thee, what hast thou done for Me?' Let me put that question for Him, and in His behalf. You have known His love, some of you fifty years, some of you thirty, twenty, ten, three, one. For you He gave His precious life, and died upon the cross, in agonies most exquisite. What have you done for Him? Turn over your diary. Can you remember the contributions you have given out of your wealth? What do they amount to? Add them up. Think of what you have done for Jesus, how much of your time you have spent in His service. Add that up, turn over another leaf, and then observe how much time you have spent in praying for the progress of His Kingdom. What have you done there? Add that up. I will do so for myself; and I can say, without a boast, that I have zealously served my God, and have been 'in labours more abundant;' but when I come to add all up, and set what I have done side by side with what I owe to Christ, it is less than nothing and vanity; I pour contempt upon it all, it is but dust of vanity. And though, from this day forward, I should preach every hour in the day; though I should spend myself and be spent for Christ; though by night I should know no rest, and by day I should never cease from toil, and year should succeed to year till this hair was hoary and this frame exhausted; when I come to render up my account, He might say, 'Well done;' but I should not feel it was so, but should rather say, 'I am still an unprofitable servant; I have not done that which it was even my bare duty to do, much less have I done all I would to show the love I owe.' Now, as you think what you have done, dear brother and sister, surely your account must fall short equally with mine."— C. H. S., *in sermon preached at the Music Hall, Royal Surrey Gardens, June 26, 1859.*

Chapter 25

"In Labours More Abundant"

BEFORE I came to London I usually preached three times on the Lord's-day, and five nights every week; and after I became Pastor at New Park Street Chapel that average was fully maintained. Within two or three years, it was considerably exceeded, for it was no uncommon experience for me to preach twelve or thirteen times a week, and to travel hundreds of miles by road or rail. Requests to take services in all parts of the metropolis and the provinces poured in upon me, and being in the full vigour of early manhood, I gladly availed myself of every opportunity of preaching the gospel which had been so greatly blessed to my own soul. In after years, when weakness and pain prevented me from doing all that I would willingly have done for my dear Lord, I often comforted myself with the thought that I did serve Him with all my might while I could, though even then I always felt that I could never do enough for Him who had loved me, and given Himself for me. Some of my ministerial brethren used to mourn over the heavy burden that rested upon them because they had to deliver their Master's message twice on the Sabbath, and once on a week-night, but I could not sympathize with them in their complaints, for the more often I preached, the more joy I found in the happy service. I was also specially sustained under the strain of such constant labour by continual tokens of the Lord's approval. I find that, preaching to my own people at New Park Street, on the last Sabbath of 1855, from Deuteronomy xi. 10–12—"For the land, whither thou goest in to possess it, is not as the land of Egypt, from whence ye came out, where thou sowedst thy seed, and wateredst it with thy foot, as a garden of herbs: but the land, whither ye go to possess it, is a land of hills and valleys, and drinketh water of the rain of heaven: a land which the Lord thy God careth for: the eyes of the Lord thy God are always upon it, from the beginning of the year even unto the end of the year;"—I was able to bear this testimony to the Divine power that had accompanied the Word:

"Beloved friends, I can say that, as a minister of the gospel, the eyes of the Lord have been specially upon me all this year. It has been my privilege very frequently to preach His Word; I think, during the past twelve months, I have stood in the pulpit to testify His truth more than four hundred times, and blessed be His Name, whether it has been in the North, in the South, in the East, or in the West, I have never lacked a congregation; nor have I ever gone again to any of the places where I have preached, without hearing of souls converted. I cannot remember a single village, or town, that I have visited a second time, without meeting with some who praised the Lord that they heard the Word of truth there from my lips. When I went to Bradford last time, I stated in the pulpit that I had never heard of a soul being converted through my preaching there, and the good pew-opener came to Brother Dowson, and said, 'Why didn't you tell Mr. Spurgeon that So-and-so joined the church through hearing him?' and instantly that dear man of God told me the cheering news."

It would not be possible for me to make more than a very incomplete list of my multitudinous engagements during those early years; and, indeed, there is no occasion for me to attempt to do so, for the record of them is on high; yet certain circumstances impressed a few of the services so powerfully upon my mind that I can distinctly recall them even after this long interval.

*   *   *

I had promised to give some of my "Personal Reminiscences" at the annual meeting of the Pastors' College held in the Tabernacle on December 1, 1880; and while I sat in my study that morning, with my two secretaries, Mr. Keys and Mr. Harrald, I said to the former: "I recollect an incident, which occurred during my first year in London, in which you were concerned." This is the story. Old Thomas Olney—"Father Olney", as he was affectionately called by our Park Street friends—was very anxious that I should go and preach at Tring, the little Hertfordshire town where he was born, and where his father, Daniel Olney, was for many years a deacon in one of the three Baptist churches. He found it was not a very easy matter to arrange, for the people had heard either so much or so little about me that I could not be allowed to appear in one of the chapels because I was too high in doctrine for the good folk who worshipped there, and permission could not be obtained for the use of another chapel because I was too low in doctrine for the dear Hyper-Calvinist friends who met there, and sang, with a meaning good Dr. Watts never intended—

> "We are a garden wall'd around,
>   Chosen and made peculiar ground;
>   A little spot, enclosed by grace
>   Out of the world's wide wilderness."

But there was a third place—the West End Chapel—the minister of which was a William Skelton, who thought that I was all right in doctrine, so Mr. Olney obtained consent for me to preach there. If I remember rightly, the worthy man's stipend only amounted to about fifteen shillings a week. He had invited us to tea at his house; but while we sat in his humble home, my conscience rather smote me because my good deacon and I were consuming some of his scanty store of provisions, and I began to think of some plan by which we could repay him for his kindness. I noticed that our friend was wearing an alpaca coat, which was very shiny, and in places was so worn that I could see through it. We went to the chapel, and the service proceeded, and all the while I was pondering in my mind what could be done for the worthy man who had lent us his chapel, and entertained us so generously. During the singing of one of the hymns, Mr. Keys came up to the pulpit, and said to me, "The pastor of this church is a very poor man, the people are able to give him very little; it would be a great kindness, sir, if you could have a collection for him, and get him a new coat." That was just what I had been thinking, so at the close of the service I said to the congregation: "Now, dear friends, I have preached to you as well as I could, and you know that our Saviour said to His disciples, 'Freely ye have received, freely give.' I don't want anything from you for myself, but the minister of this chapel looks to me as though he would not object to a new suit of clothes." I pointed down to my worthy deacon, and said, "Father Olney, down there, I am sure will start the collection with half a sovereign (he at once nodded his head to confirm my statement); I will gladly give the same amount, and if you will all help as much as you can, our brother will soon have a new suit, and a good one, too."

The collection was made, it realized a very fair sum, and the minister was in due time provided with suitable garments. I apologised to him, after the service, for my rudeness in calling public attention to his worn coat, but he heartily thanked me for what I had done, and then added, "Ever since I have been in the service of the Lord Jesus Christ, my Master has always found me my livery. I have often wondered where the next suit would come from, and I really was wanting a new one very badly, but now you have provided it for me, and I am very grateful both to the Lord and also to you." I don't remember doing quite the same thing on any other occasion, though I may have helped some of the Lord's poor servants in a different way.

I believe the friends at Tring were pleased with the service, for, not long afterwards, I was invited to go there again, to preach the Sunday-school anniversary sermons. This was, I think, at one of the other

Baptist chapels in the town. I addressed the children in the afternoon, and preached to the adults in the evening. At the close of the afternoon service, some of the Hyper-Calvinist friends, who had been present, found fault with what they called my unsound teaching. The Holy Spirit had very graciously helped me in speaking to the many young people who were gathered together, and I believe that some of them were brought to the Saviour; but, among other things, I had said to them that God had answered my prayers while I was a child, and before I was converted. That was certainly true, for, on many occasions, long before I knew the Lord, I had gone to Him with my childish petitions, and He had given me what I had asked of Him. I told the children that this fact had greatly impressed me while I was a boy, and it led me to believe more firmly in God's overruling power, and in the efficacy of prayer, and I urged them also to pray to Him. This gave great offence to my critics, so five or six of those grave old men gathered round me, and tried to set me right in their peculiar fashion. Did I not know that the Scripture declared that "the prayer of a sinner is abomination unto the Lord"? That is a sentence which I have never been able to find in my Bible, and I told them so. Then they asked, "How can a dead man pray?" I could not tell, but I knew that *I* prayed even while I was "dead in trespasses and sins". They said that it was impossible; but I was equally positive that it could be done, for I had done it. They still maintained that it was not sound doctrine, and that God did not hear the prayers of sinners. There was quite a little ring formed around me, and I did my best to answer the objections, but, after all, the victory was won, not by Barak, but by Deborah. A very old woman, in a red cloak, managed to squeeze herself into the circle, and turning to my accusers, she said, "What are you battling about with this young man? You say that God does not hear the prayers of unconverted people, that He hears no cry but that of His own children. What do you know about the Scriptures? Your precious passage is not in the Bible at all, but the psalmist did say, 'He giveth to the beast his food, and to the young ravens which cry' (Psalm cxlvii. 9). Is there any grace in *them*? If God hears the cry of the ravens, don't you think He will hear the prayers of those who are made in His own image? You don't know anything at all about the matter, so leave the young man alone, and let him go on with his Master's work." After that vigorous speech, my opponents quickly vanished, and I walked away in happy conversation with the dear old soul who had so wisely delivered me from the cavillers.

*   *   *

I had quite a different experience on the occasion when I went to preach at Haverhill, in Suffolk. The congregation that day had the somewhat unusual privilege, or affliction, of listening to two preachers discoursing by turns upon the same text! The passage was that grand declaration of the apostle Paul, "For by grace are ye saved through faith; and that not of yourselves: it is the gift of God" (Ephesians ii. 8). It does not often happen to me to be late for service, for I feel that punctuality is one of those little virtues which may prevent great sins. But we have no control over railways and breakdowns, and so it happened that I reached the appointed place considerably behind time. Like sensible people, they had begun their worship, and had proceeded as far as the sermon. As I neared the chapel, I perceived that someone was in the pulpit preaching, and who should the preacher be but my dear and venerable grandfather! He saw me as I came in at the front door, and made my way up the aisle, and at once he said, "Here comes my grandson! He may preach the gospel better than I can, but he cannot preach a better gospel; can you, Charles?" As I pressed through the throng, I answered, "You can preach better than I can. Pray go on." But he would not agree to *that*. I must take the sermon, and so I did, going on with the subject there and then, just where he left off. "There," said he, "I was preaching on 'For by grace are ye saved'. I have been setting forth the source and fountain-head of salvation, and I am now showing them the channel of it, 'through faith.' Now, you take it up, and go on."

I am so much at home with these glorious truths, that I could not feel any difficulty in taking from my grandfather the thread of his discourse, and joining my thread to it, so as to continue without a break. Our agreement in the things of God made it easy for us to be joint-preachers of the same discourse. I went on with "through faith", and then I proceeded to the next point, "and that not of your-selves". Upon this, I was explaining the weakness and inability of human nature, and the certainty that salvation could not be of our-selves, when I had my coat-tail pulled, and my well-beloved grandsire took his turn again. When I spoke of our depraved human nature, the good old man said, "I know most about that, dear friends;" so he took up the parable, and for the next five minutes set forth a solemn and humbling description of our lost estate, the depravity of our nature, and the spiritual death under which we were found. When he had said his say in a very gracious manner, his grandson was allowed to go on again, to the dear old man's great delight, for now and then he would say, in a gentle tone, "Good! Good!" Once he said, "Tell them that again, Charles," and of course I did tell them *that* again. It was a happy exercise to me to take my share in bearing witness to truths of such vital importance, which are so deeply impressed upon my heart. Whenever I read this text, I seem to hear that dear voice, which has been so long lost to earth, saying to me, "TELL THEM THAT AGAIN." I am not contradicting the testimony of forefathers who are now with God. If my grandfather could return to earth, he would find me where he left me, steadfast in the faith, and true to that form of doctrine which was once for all delivered to the saints. I preach the doctrines of grace because I believe them to be true; because I see them in the Scriptures; because my experience endears them to me; and because I see the holy result of them in the lives of believers. I confess they are none the less dear to me because the advanced school despises them: their censures are to me a commendation. I confess also that I should never think the better of a doctrine because it was said to be "new". Those truths which have enlightened so many ages appear to me to be ordained to remain throughout eternity. The doctrine which I preach is that of the Puritans: it is the doctrine of Calvin, the doctrine of Augustine, the doctrine of Paul, the doctrine of the Holy Ghost. The Author and Finisher of our faith Himself taught most blessed truth which well agreed with Paul's declaration, "By grace are ye saved." The doctrine of grace is the substance of the testimony of Jesus.

*   *   *

Some of the special services it was my privilege to conduct in London, in those long-past days, remain in my memory with great vividness. The first time I was asked to preach at one of the representative gatherings of the denomination was on January 10, 1855, when the annual meetings of the London Association of Baptist Churches were held at New Park Street Chapel, which was crowded both afternoon and evening, to the manifest astonishment of the grave and venerable ministers and delegates who had usually met on such occasions in much smaller numbers. My subject was, "The Holy War", the text being 2 Cor. x. 4: "For the weapons of our warfare are not carnal, but mighty through God to the pulling down of strong holds." Rev. Thomas Binney, of the Weigh House Chapel, near the Monument, was in the congregation that afternoon, and as he walked away, one of our friends heard him say, concerning the service, "It is an insult to God and man; I never heard such things in my life before." Our brother was so indignant that he turned to him, and said, "The man who can speak like that of a young minister of Jesus Christ is one of whom I shall be ashamed as long as I live, unless he repents having uttered such unkind remarks." I know this story is true, for I had it from the lips of the good man himself. Many years afterwards, he was again in Mr. Binney's company, so he reminded him of the incident, and our friend told me that no one could have spoken of me with more intense and hearty esteem than did the venerable man at that time. "But," he added, "you know, my dear sir, that your minister has greatly improved since those early days. I very soon found out my mistake, and you may depend upon it that my sentiments with regard to Mr. Spurgeon are completely changed. I did not at all blame you for rebuking me as you did; I only wish I had as many friends to stick to me, and speak up for me, as your minister has always had. If I ever said anything against him, I might just as well have pulled down a skep of bees about my head, but now I have no feeling towards him but that of the utmost regard and affection." I also know that, long before this confession, Mr. Binney, while addressing the students of one of the Congregational Colleges, had said, in reply to some disparaging remarks concerning me which he had overheard: "I have enjoyed some amount of popularity, I have always been able to draw together a congregation; but, in the person of Mr. Spurgeon, we see a young man, be he who he may, and come whence he will, who at twenty-four hours' notice can command a congregation of twenty thousand people. Now, I have never been able to do that, and I never knew of anyone else who could do it."

The Freeman thus reported the meetings of the day:

"LONDON BAPTIST ASSOCIATION.—Whatever reason may be assigned for the fact, it is certain that an Association meeting in London is very different from one in the country. Perhaps the ministers and members of the several churches meet so often that an annual gathering is no novelty; perhaps the walk through London streets, or the jolt in an omnibus or cab, has fewer attractions than the Whitsuntide jaunt by railroad or pleasant country lane—or perhaps the thing has escaped due attention amid the throng of metropolitan claims—but certain it is, that the London Particular Baptist Association, holding, as it does from a sense of duty, a meeting every year, has only given generally the impression of being a somewhat dull affair. Indeed, it is not enlivening either to preacher or hearer to find one's self in New Park Street Chapel with a congregation of seventy people, on a January week-day afternoon!

This year, we are bound to say, all was different. The popularity of the Rev. C. H. Spurgeon, the recently-settled Pastor at New Park Street, attracted a crowded audience on the afternoon of the 10th instant. The metropolitan churches of the denomination appeared for the most part well represented, the only noticeable exception being the absence of several leading ministers, owing, as was explained, to the Quarterly Mission Committee being holden by some mischance which will probably not occur again, upon the same day. The preacher treated with much earnestness on the 'strongholds' of the evil one that we are called to subdue, and on 'the weapons of our warfare', which are 'mighty through God' to the task. The vigour and originality of the sermon, we cannot forbear remarking, sufficiently accounted to us for the popularity of the youthful preacher, and indicated powers which, with due culture, may by the Divine blessing greatly and usefully serve the Church in days to come. A very large company remained in the chapel to tea, and in the evening the place was thronged to overflowing for the public meeting —which, however, was not distinguished by any feature worthy of remark, save the delivery of two or three brief, simple, evangelical addresses. It appears that many churches in London are not connected with the Association, and of those which are, several sent no reports. No complete statistics, therefore, could be presented. Of those churches from which letters were read, most seemed stationary— some were prosperous. The accounts, perhaps, on the whole, were quite equal to the average."

*　　　　*　　　　*

Among the notable gatherings in various provincial towns, my visit to Trowbridge has a special interest because of the singularity of an extra service that was crowded into my programme. I had promised to preach in one place of worship in the afternoon and evening of Monday, April 7, 1856, and in another chapel the following morning. At both the services on the Monday, the building was densely packed, and hundreds had to go away, unable to gain admission, so I offered to preach again at ten o'clock at night if the friends could make it known, and bring in a fresh congregation. Many remained after the first evening service, and before the appointed hour others came in such numbers that the place was again crowded.

That was a memorable night, but it was quite eclipsed by another, which I spent in a meeting-house not far from the place which was the scene of the terrible explosion in the Risca colliery in December, 1860. That charming spot in South Wales has frequently yielded me a quiet and delightful retreat. Beautiful for situation, surrounded by lofty mountains, pierced by romantic valleys, the breathing of its air refreshes the body, and the sight of the eyes makes glad the heart. I have climbed its hills, I have seen the ever-widening landscape, the mountains of Wales, the plains of England, and the sea sparkling afar. I have mingled with its godly men and women, and worshipped God in their assemblies. I have been fired with the glorious enthusiasm of the people when they have listened to the Word; but that night I shall never forget in time or in eternity, when, crowded together in the place of worship, hearty Welsh miners responded to every word I uttered, with their "Gogoniants" encouraging me to preach the gospel, and crying "Glory to God!" while the message was proclaimed. They kept me well-nigh to midnight, preaching three sermons, one after another, almost without a break, for they loved to listen to the gospel. God was present with us, and many a time has the baptismal pool been stirred since then by the fruit of that night's labour.

Nor shall I ever forget when, standing in the open air beneath God's blue sky, I addressed a mighty gathering within a short distance of that same place, when the Spirit of God was poured upon us, and men and women were swayed to and fro under the Heavenly message, as the corn is moved in waves by the summer winds. Great was our joy that day when the people met together in thousands, and with songs and praises separated to their homes, talking of what they had heard.

*   *   *

I must mention the visit I paid to Stambourne, on May 27, 1856, when I preached, at my dear grandfather's request, in commemoration of his ministerial jubilee. He had then been Pastor of the Congregational Church at Stambourne for forty-six years, and he had previously been minister at Clare, in Suffolk, for four years. I suppose such a service is almost unique; certainly, I have no recollection of any other instance in which a grandson has had the privilege of preaching for his grandfather under similar circumstances, and I bless God that this was my happy lot. On the previous Sabbath morning, at New Park Street Chapel, I delivered substantially the same discourse from Isaiah xlvi. 4, and it was published under the title, "The God of the Aged". Some fifteen hundred or two thousand persons assembled at Stambourne for the celebration; and to accommodate them, a large covered space was extemporized by the use of a barn, and tents, and tarpaulins. The proceedings were, naturally, full of interest. My venerable friend, Rev. Benjamin Beddow, who assisted me in the compilation of *Memories of Stambourne*, has recorded the following incident which, otherwise, I might have forgotten:

"In the afternoon, Mr. C. H. Spurgeon made some allusions to Thomas Binney's volume, *How to Make the Best of Both Worlds*, and expressed his opinion that no man could serve two masters, or live for more than one world. The ardent spirit of a Congregationalist minister was aroused, and he interrupted the speaker. This was a mistake; but though it raised discussion, it produced no result upon the evening congregation, which was as thronged and as enthusiastic as that which preceded it. We only refer to it for the sake of the sequel to the anecdote. Years after, the gentleman who interrupted had such an opinion of C. H. Spurgeon that, in a very kind and genial letter, he reminded him of the incident, and asking for a sermon from him, pressed the request by quoting the old saying about Cranmer, 'If you do my Lord of Canterbury an ill turn, he will be your friend all the days of your life.' At that time it was not in the power of C. H. Spurgeon to grant the request, for the season had long been promised to others, but he felt that he would right gladly have done so had it been within the region of the possible.

Great were the crowds of that day: very busy were all the ladies of the region in making tea, and very liberal were the gifts. The venerable old man, whose ministerial jubilee was thus celebrated, seemed to feel rather the weight of the years than any special exhilaration because of their having reached to fifty. Within himself he held a quiet jubilee of rest, which the world could neither give nor take away."

My experiences in those early years were very varied, and some of them were so singular that I cannot easily forget them. At one place, I was preaching to a great crowd of people, and during the sermon many in the congregation were visibly affected. I felt that the power of the Lord was working there very manifestly; one poor creature absolutely shrieked out because of the wrath of God against sin.

On another occasion, I had scarcely finished my discourse, when a Christian woman, who had been listening to it, dropped dead in her pew. That was at a village in Kent. Not very long afterwards, I went to Tollesbury, in Essex, to preach on a week-day afternoon on behalf of the Sunday-school at my father's chapel. There was a large assembly of friends from the surrounding district; and at the close of the service, tea was provided for them in a tent. Before they had finished, the wife of one of the deacons was seized with a fit, and died in a few minutes. I had not arranged to preach in the evening, but, under the circumstances, I did so, taking for my text Paul's words, "For to me to live is Christ, and to die is gain."

In another part of the country, I was preaching once to people who kept continually looking round, and I adopted the expedient of saying, "Now, friends, as it is so very interesting to you to know who comes in, and it disturbs me so very much for you to look round, I will, if you like, describe each one as he comes in, so that you may sit and look at me, and keep up at least a show of decency." I described one gentleman who came in, who happened to be a friend whom I could depict without offence, as "a very respectable gentleman who had just taken his hat off," and so on; and after that one attempt I found it was not necessary to describe any more, because they felt shocked at what I was doing, and I assured them that I was much more shocked that they should render it necessary for me to reduce their conduct to such an absurdity. It cured them for the time being, and I hope for ever, much to their pastor's joy.

On one of my many early journeys by the Eastern Counties Railway —as the G.E.R. was then called—I had a singular adventure, upon which I have often looked back with pleasurable recollections. I had been into the country to preach, and was returning to London. All at once, I discovered that my ticket was gone, and a gentleman—the only other occupant of the compartment—noticing that I was fumbling about in my pockets as though in search of something I could not find, said to me, "I hope you have not lost anything, sir?" I thanked him, and told him that it was my ticket that was missing, and that, by a remarkable coincidence, I had neither watch nor money with me. I seldom wear a watch, and probably the brother whom I had gone to help had seemed to me in need of any coin that I might have had in my possession before I started on my homeward journey. "But," I added, "I am not at all troubled, for I have been on my Master's business, and I am quite sure all will be well. I have had so many interpositions of Divine providence, in small matters as well as great ones, that I feel as if, whatever happens to me, I am bound to fall on my feet, like the man on the Manx penny." The gentleman seemed interested, and said that no doubt it would be all right, and we had a very pleasant, and, I hope, profitable conversation until the train had nearly reached Bishopsgate Station, and the collectors came for the tickets. As the official opened the door of our compartment, he touched his hat to my travelling companion, who simply said, "All right, William!" whereupon the man again saluted, and retired. After he had gone, I said to the gentleman, "It is very strange that the collector did not ask for my ticket." "No, Mr. Spurgeon," he replied —calling me by my name for the first time—"it is only another illustration of what you told me about the providence of God watching over you even in little things; I am the General Manager of this line, and it was no doubt Divinely arranged that I should happen to be your companion just when I could be of service to you. I knew you were all right, and it has been a great pleasure to meet you under such happy circumstances."

A somewhat similar instance of the presence of "a friend in need" occurred at a later period of my life, but it follows so appropriately upon the previous one that it may as well be related here. I was going to preach somewhere in the North of London, and to reach my destination, I had to pass through the City. When I was in Princes Street, near the Bank, my horse fell, some of the harness gave way, and one of the shafts of the carriage was broken. Almost at the instant that the accident happened, a hand was thrust in at the window, and the owner of it gave me his card, and said, "I know where you are going, Mr. Spurgeon; you have no time to lose in getting to the chapel. Take a cab, and go on about your Master's business; I'll stay with the coachman, and see what can be done with the horse and carriage." I did as the gentleman suggested, and after I had preached, and was ready to return, there was the carriage at the chapel door, ready for me, and the coachman gave me the message that there was "nothing to pay". I wrote to thank the generous friend for his timely and welcome help and gift, and in his reply he said, "I only hope that, next time your horse goes down, I may be close at hand, or that somebody else may be there who will feel it as great a pleasure to be of service to you as I have done. You do not know me, but I am well acquainted with one of your deacons, and through him I have heard a good deal about you." So he took care of me for my deacon's sake, and still more for my Lord's sake; and many and many a time have I had kindnesses shown to me by those who, until then, had been complete strangers to me. Other people may not think much of such incidents, but to me they are intensely interesting, and they fill me with adoring gratitude to God.

"Coming, one Thursday in the late autumn, from an engagement beyond Dulwich, my way lay up to the top of the Herne Hill ridge. I came along the level out of which rises the steep hill I had to ascend. While I was on the lower ground, riding in a hansom cab, I saw a light before me, and when I came near the hill, I marked that light gradually go up the hill, leaving a train of stars behind it. This line of new-born stars remained in the form of one lamp, and then another, and another. It reached from the foot of the hill to its summit. I did not see the lamplighter. I do not know his name, nor his age, nor his residence; but I saw the lights which he had kindled, and these remained when he himself had gone his way. As I rode along, I thought to myself, 'How earnestly do I wish that my life may be spent in lighting one soul after another with the sacred flame of eternal life! I would myself be as much as possible unseen while at my work, and would vanish into the eternal brilliance above when my work is done.'" —C. H. S.

Chapter 26

Seeking the Souls of Men

I OFTEN envy those of my brethren who can go up to individuals, and talk to them with freedom about their souls. I do not always find myself able to do so, though, when I have been Divinely aided in such service, I have had a large reward. When a Christian can get hold of a man, and talk thus personally to him, it is like one of the old British men-of-war lying alongside a French ship, and giving her a broadside, making every timber shiver, and at last sending her to the bottom.

How many precious souls have been brought to Christ by the loving personal exhortations of Christian people who have learned this holy art! It is wonderful how God blesses very little efforts to serve Him. One night, many years ago, after preaching, I had been driven home by a cabman, and after I had alighted, and given him the fare, he took a little Testament out of his pocket, and showing it to me, said, "It is about fifteen years since you gave me that, and spoke a word to me about my soul. I have never forgotten your words, and I have not let a day pass since without reading the Book you gave me." I felt glad that, in that instance, the seed had, apparently, fallen into good ground.

Having promised to preach one evening at a certain river-side town, I went to the place early in the day, as I thought I should like to have a little time in a boat on the river. So, hailing a waterman, I made arrangements with him to take me, and, whilst sitting in the boat, wishing to talk with him about religious matters, I began the conversation by asking him about his family. He told me that the cholera had visited his home, and that he had lost no less than thirteen of his relatives, one after another, by death. My question, and the man's answer, prepared the way for a dialogue somewhat in this fashion:

Spurgeon.—Have you, my friend, a good hope of Heaven if you should die?

Waterman.—Well, sir, I think as how I have.

S.—Pray tell me, then, what your hope is, for no man need ever be ashamed of a good hope.

W.—Well, sir, I have been on this here river for five-and-twenty or thirty years, and I don't know that anybody ever saw me drunk.

S.—Oh, dear! Oh, dear! Is that all you have to trust to?

W.—Well, sir, when the cholera was about, and my poor neighbours were bad, I went for the doctor for 'em, and was up a good many nights, and I do think as how I am as good as most folk that I know.

Of course, I told him that I was very glad to hear that he had sympathy for the suffering, and that I considered it far better to be charitable than to be churlish; but I did not see how his good conduct could carry him to Heaven. Then he said:

"Well, sir, perhaps it can't; but I think, when I get a little older, I shall give up the boat, and take to going to church, and then I hope that all will be right—won't it, sir?"

"No," I answered, "certainly not; your going to church won't change your heart, or take away your sins. Begin to go to church as soon as possible, but you will not be an inch nearer Heaven if you think that, by attending the sanctuary, you will be saved."

The poor man seemed perfectly astounded, while I went on knocking down his hopes one after another. So I resumed the dialogue by putting another question to him:

S.—You have sometimes sinned in your life, have you not?

W.—Yes, sir, that I have, many a time.

S.—On what ground, then, do you think that your sins will be forgiven?

W.—Well, sir, I have been sorry about them, and I think they are all gone—they don't trouble me now.

S.—Now, my friend, suppose you were to go and get into debt with the grocer where you deal, and you should say to her, "Look here, missus, you have a long score against me, I am sorry to say that I cannot pay you for all those goods that I have had; but I'll tell you what I will do, I'll never get into your debt any more." She would very soon tell you that was not her style of doing business; and do you suppose that is the way in which you can treat the great God? Do you imagine that He is going to strike out your past sins because you say you will not go on sinning against Him?

W.—Well, sir, I should like to know how my sins are to be forgiven. Are you a parson?

S.—I preach the gospel, I hope, but I do not go by the name of a parson; I am only a Dissenting minister.

Then I told him, as plainly as I could, how the Lord Jesus Christ had taken the place of sinners, and how those who trusted in Him, and rested in His blood and righteousness, would find pardon and peace. The man was delighted with the simple story of the cross; he said that he wished he had heard it years before, and then he added, "To tell the truth, master, I did not feel quite easy, after all, when I saw those poor creatures taken away to the graveyard; I did think there was something I wanted, but I did not know what it was."

I cannot say what was the final result of our conversation, but I had the satisfaction of knowing that I had at least set before him God's way of salvation in language that he could easily understand.

Sometimes, I have found it less easy, than it might otherwise have been, to influence certain persons for good, because of the neglect of those who ought to have done the work before me. I was trying to say a word for my Master to a coachman, one day, when he said to me, "Do you know the Rev. Mr. So-and-so?" "Yes," I replied, "I know him very well; what have you to say about him?" "Well," said the man, "he's the sort of minister I like, and I like his religion very much." "What sort of a religion is it?" I asked. "Why!" he answered, "he has ridden on this box-seat every day for six months, and he has never said anything about religion all the while; that is the kind of minister I like." It seemed to me a very doubtful compliment for a man who professed to be a servant of the Lord Jesus Christ.

At other times, the difficulty in dealing with individuals has arisen from their ignorance of the plan of salvation. When I have spoken of my own hope in Christ to two or three people in a railway carriage, I have often found myself telling my listeners perfect novelties. I have seen the look of astonishment upon the face of many an intelligent Englishman when I have explained the doctrine of the substitutionary sacrifice of Christ; I have even met with persons who had attended their parish church from their youth up, yet who were totally ignorant of the simple truth of justification by faith; ay, and some who have been to Dissenting places of worship do not seem to have laid hold of the fundamental truth that no man is saved by his own doings, but that salvation is procured by faith in the blood and righteousness of Jesus Christ. This nation is steeped up to the throat in self-righteousness, and the Protestantism of Martin Luther is very generally unknown. The truth is held by as many as God's grace has called, but the great outlying masses still talk of doing their best, and then hoping in God's mercy, and I know not what besides of legal self-confidence; while the master-doctrine, that he who believes in Jesus is saved by His finished work, is sneered at as the utterance of misguided enthusiasm, or attacked as leading to licentiousness. Luther talked of beating the heads of the Wittenbergers with the Bible, so as to get the great doctrine of justification by faith into their brains. But beating is of no use; we must have much patience with those we are trying to teach, and we must be willing to repeat over, and over, and over again the elements of truth. Someone asked a mother once, "Why do you teach your child the same thing twenty times?" She answered, very wisely, "Because I find that nineteen times are not sufficient;" and it will often be the same with those who need to be taught the A B C of the gospel.

*   *   *

Though this is a Protestant land, it is beyond all question that there are in it people who are Popish enough to perform great religious acts by way of merit. What a goodly row of almshouses was erected by that miserly old grinder of the poor as an atonement for his hoarding propensities! What a splendid legacy somebody else left to that hospital! That was a very proper thing, but the man who left it never gave a farthing to a beggar in his life, and he would not have given anything when he died only he could not take his money with him, so he left it to a charity as an atonement for his sin.

Sometimes, persons are so foolish as to think that the doing of some professedly religious act will take them to Heaven; attending church prayers twice a day, fasting in Lent, decorating the altar with needlework, putting stained glass in the window, or giving a new organ; at the suggestion of their priest, they do many such things; and thus they go on working like blind asses in a mill, from morning to night, and making no more real progress than the poor donkeys do. Many who are nominally Christians appear to me to believe in a sort of sincere-obedience covenant, in which, if a man does as much as he can, Christ will do the rest, and so the sinner will be saved; but it is not so. God will never accept any composition from the man who is in debt to Divine justice; there is no Heavenly Court of Bankruptcy where so much in the pound may be accepted, and the debtor then be discharged. It must be all or nothing; he who would pay his debt must bring all, even to the uttermost farthing, and that can never be, for God's Word declares that "by the deeds of the law there shall no flesh be justified in His sight". Some people have a notion that going to church and chapel, taking the sacrament, and doing certain good deeds that appertain to a respectable profession of religion, are the way to Heaven. If they are put in the place of Christ, they are rather the way to hell; although it is strewn with clean gravel, and there be grassy paths on either side, it is not the road to Heaven, but the way to everlasting death.

Strange as it may seem at the first glance, yet the very fact that a person has been brought up in a system of error will, sometimes, by force of contrast, make it all the easier to bring home the truth to the heart and conscience. I can bear personal witness that the simple statement of the gospel has often proved, in God's hand, enough to lead a soul into immediate peace. I once met with a lady who held sentiments of almost undiluted Popery, and in conversing with her, I was delighted to see how interesting and attractive a thing the gospel was to her. She complained that she enjoyed no peace of mind as the result of her religion, and never seemed to have done enough to bring her any rest of soul. She had a high idea of priestly absolution, but it had evidently been quite unable to yield repose to her spirit. Death was feared, God was terrible, even Christ was an object of awe rather than of love. When I told her that whosoever believeth on Jesus is perfectly forgiven, and that I knew I was forgiven—that I was as sure of it as of my own existence, that I feared neither to live nor to die, for all would be well with me in either case, because God had given to me eternal life in His Son—I saw that a new set of thoughts had begun to astonish her mind. She said, "If I could believe as you do, I should be the happiest person in the world." I did not deny the inference, but claimed to have proved its truth, and I have reason to think that the little simple talk we had has not been forgotten, or unprofitable.

One advantage of dealing personally with souls is, that it is not so easy for them to turn aside the message as when they are spoken to in the mass. I have often marvelled when I have been preaching. I have thought that I have exactly described certain people; I have marked in them special sins, and as Christ's faithful servant, I have not shunned to picture their case in the pulpit, that they might receive a well-deserved rebuke; but I have wondered when I have spoken to them afterwards, that they have thanked me for what I have said, because they thought it so applicable to another person in the assembly. I had intended it wholly for them, and had, as I thought, made the description so accurate, and brought out all their peculiar points, that it must have been received by them. But, on at least one occasion, a direct word to one of my hearers was not only taken by him in a sense I did not mean, but it was resented in a fashion which I did not anticipate. I felt constrained to say that I hoped the gentleman who was reporting my discourse would not do it as a mere matter of business routine, but that he would take the Word as addressed to himself as well as to the rest of the audience. I certainly did not think there was anything offensive in the remark, and I was astonished to see the reporter fling down his pen in anger, as though resolved not to take down anything more that I might say. Before long, however, his better judgment prevailed, he went on with his work, and the sermon duly appeared in *The New Park Street Pulpit* —under the circumstances, of course, with the omission of the personal reference which had unintentionally caused offence.[1]

Whatever may have been the feelings of my hearers, I can honestly say that scores, and, indeed, hundreds of times I have gone from my pulpit groaning because I could not preach as I wished; but this has been my comfort, "Well, I did desire to glorify Christ, I did try to clear my conscience of the blood of all men, I did seek to tell them the whole truth, whether they liked it or not." It will be an awful thing for any man, who has been professedly a minister of Christ, and yet has not preached the gospel, to go before the bar of God, and to answer for the souls committed to him. That ancient message still needs to be heard: "If the watchman see the sword come, and blow not the trumpet, and the people be not warned; if the sword come, and take any person from among them, he is taken away in his iniquity, but his blood will I require at the watchman's hand." This it is that makes our work so weighty that our knees sometimes knock together when we are thinking of going up to our pulpit again. It is no child's play, if there is to be a judgment, and we are to answer for our faithfulness or unfaithfulness. What must be our account if we are not true to God and to man? I have prayed, many a time, that I might be able, at the end of my ministry, to say what George Fox, the Quaker, said when he was dying, "I am clear, I am clear."

It has often been a marvel to me how some old ministers have continued to labour for twenty, or thirty, or even forty years in one place without gathering any fruit from all their toil. I will not judge them—to their own Master they stand or fall; but if I had been in such a position, although I should not have dared to leave the vine-yard in which my Lord bade me work while I was yet a youth, I should have concluded that He had need of me in some other part of

---

[1] Mr. Passmore, Spurgeon's publisher, preserved a letter written to himself by Spurgeon in which there was the following allusion to the incident here described:— "You may tell Mr. —— that I was so far from intending to insult him by what I said that I uttered the sentence in the purest love for his soul; and that I dare not be unfaithful to him any more than to anyone else in my congregation. God is my witness, how earnestly I long for the salvation of all my hearers, and I would far rather err by too great personality than by unfaithfulness. At the last great day, none of us will be offended with Christ's ministers for speaking plainly to us. I am sorry that Mr. —— was vexed, and have prayed that the sermon may be blessed to him."

His field where my efforts might be more productive of blessing. I thank God that I have not had to labour in vain, or to spend my strength for nought. He has given me a long period of happy and successful service, for which, with all my heart, I praise and magnify His holy Name. There has been a greater increase sometimes, or a little diminution now and then; but, for the most part, the unbroken stream of blessing has run on at much the same rate all the while. It has ever been my desire, not to "compass sea and land to make proselytes" from other denominations, but to gather into our ranks those who have not been previously connected with any body of believers, or, indeed, who have attended any house of prayer. Of course, many persons have joined us from other communities, when it has seemed to them a wise and right step, but I should reckon it to be a burning disgrace if it could be truthfully said, "The large church under that man's pastoral care is composed of members whom he has stolen away from other Christian churches," but I value beyond all price the godless and the careless, who have been brought out from the world into communion with Christ. These are true prizes—not stealthily removed from friendly shores, but captured at the edge of the sword from the enemy's dominions. We welcome brethren from other churches, if in the providence of God, they are drifted into our midst, but we would never hang out the wrecker's beacon, to dash other churches in pieces in order to enrich ourselves with the wreckage. Far rather would we be busy, looking after perishing souls, than cajoling unstable ones from their present place of worship. To recruit one regiment from another, is no real strengthening of the army; to bring in fresh men, should be the aim of all.

*   *   *

From the very early days of my ministry in London, the Lord gave such an abundant blessing upon the proclamation of His truth that, whenever I was able to appoint a time for seeing converts and enquirers, it was seldom, if ever, that I waited in vain; and, usually, so many came, that I was quite overwhelmed with gratitude and thanksgiving to God. On one occasion, I had a very singular experience, which enabled me to realize the meaning of our Lord's answer to His disciples' question at the well of Sychar, "Hath any man brought Him aught to eat? Jesus saith unto them, My meat is to do the will of Him that sent Me, and to finish His work." Leaving home early in the morning, I went to the chapel, and sat there all day long seeing those who had been brought to Christ through the preaching of the Word. Their stories were so interesting to me that the hours flew by without my noticing how fast they were going. I may have seen some thirty or more persons during the day, one after the other, and I was so delighted with the tales of mercy they had to tell me, and the wonders of grace God had wrought in them, that I did not know anything about how the time passed. At seven o'clock, we had our prayer-meeting; I went in, and prayed with the brethren. After that, came the church-meeting. A little before ten o'clock, I felt faint, and I began to think at what hour I had my dinner, and I then for the first time remembered that I had not had any! I never thought of it, I never even felt hungry, because God had made me so glad, and so satisfied with the Divine manna, the Heavenly food of success in winning souls.

I am not sure that I ever had another day quite like that, but I had much to interest me, and sometimes a good deal to humble me, in the different cases with which I had to deal. I have seen very much of my own stupidity while in conversation with seeking souls. I have been baffled by a poor lad while trying to bring him to the Saviour; I thought I had him fast, but he has eluded me again and again with perverse ingenuity of unbelief. Sometimes, enquirers, who are really anxious, surprise me with their singular skill in battling against hope; their arguments are endless, and their difficulties countless. They have put me to a nonplus again and again. The grace of God has at last enabled me to bring them to the light, but not until I have seen my own inefficiency, and realized that, without the Holy Spirit's aid, I should be utterly powerless to lead them into the liberty of the gospel. Occasionally, I have met with a poor troubled soul who has refused to be comforted. There was one good Christian man who, through feebleness of mind, had fallen into the deepest despair; I have hardly ever met with a person in such an awful condition as he was, and it puzzled me to give him any sort of comfort; indeed, I fear that I failed to do so after all. He said, "I'm too big a sinner to be saved." So I told him that God's Word says, "the blood of Jesus Christ His Son cleanseth us from *all* sin". "Ay!" he replied, "but you must remember the context, which is, 'If we walk in the light, as He is in the light, we have fellowship one with another, and the blood of Jesus Christ His Son cleanseth us from all sin.' Now, I do not walk in the light; I walk in the dark, and I have no fellowship with the people of God now, and therefore that passage does not apply to me." "Well," I rejoined, "but Christ is able to save to the uttermost all them that come unto God by Him." "That is the only text," he admitted, "I never can get over, for it says 'to the uttermost', and I know I cannot have gone beyond that; yet it does not yield me any comfort." I said, "But God asks nothing of you but that you will believe Him; and you know, if you have ever so feeble a faith, you are like a child—the feeble hand of a child can receive, and that is the mark of a Christian: 'of His fulness have all we received', and if you only receive with your hand, that is enough." "Ay!" said he, "but I have not the hand of faith." "Very well," I answered, "but you have the mouth of desire; you can ask with your lips if you cannot receive with your hand." "No," said he, "I do not pray, and I cannot pray; I have not the mouth of desire." "Then," I pleaded, "all that is wanted is an empty place, a vacuum, so that God can put the grace in." "Ah, sir!" said he, "you have me there; I have a vacuum; I have an aching void; if there was ever an empty sinner in this world, I am one." "Well," I exclaimed, "Christ will fill that vacuum; there is a full Christ for empty sinners," and there I had to leave the matter.

Very often, when enquirers have come to me to relate the story of their spiritual history, they have told their little tale with an air of the greatest possible wonder, and asked me, as soon as they have finished it, whether it is not extremely unusual. One has said, "Do you know, sir, I used to be so happy in the things of the world, but conviction entered into my heart, and I began to seek the Saviour; and for a long time, when I was under concern of soul, I was so miserable that I could not bear myself. Surely, sir, this is a strange thing?" And when I have looked the friend in the face, and said, "No, it is not at all strange; I have had a dozen people here to-night, and they have all told me the same tale; that is the way almost all God's people go to Heaven"—he has stared at me, as if he did not think I would tell an untruth, but as if he thought it the queerest thing in the world that anybody else should have felt as he had done.

"Now, sit down," I say sometimes, when I am seeing an enquirer or a candidate for church-membership, "and I will tell you what were my feelings when I first sought and found the Saviour." "Why, sir!" he exclaims, "that is just how I have felt, but I did not think anyone else had ever gone over the same path that I have trodden." It is no wonder that, when we have little acquaintance with each other's spiritual experience, our way should seem to be a solitary one, but he who knows much of the dealings of God with poor seeking sinners, is well aware that their experiences are, in the main, very much alike.

Sometimes, a desperate case requires a desperate remedy. I had once to deal with a man who assented to everything I said. When I talked about the evil of sin, he agreed with me, and said that I was very faithful. When I set before him the way of salvation, he assented to it, but it was evident that his heart was not affected by the truth. I could almost have wished that he had flatly denied what I said, for that would have given me the opportunity of arguing the matter with him, and pressing him to come to a decision. At last, I felt that it was quite hopeless to talk to him any longer, so I said, "The fact is, one of these days you will die, and be damned"—and I walked away without saying another word. As I expected, it was not very long before he sent for me, and when I went to him, he begged me to tell him why I had said such a dreadful thing to him. I answered, "It seems quite useless for me to talk to you about the salvation of your soul, for you never appear to feel the force of anything that I say. I might almost as well pour oil down a slab of marble as expect you to be impressed by the truth that I set before you, and my solid conviction is that you will be damned." He was quite angry with me for speaking so plainly; and I went away again, leaving him very cross. Before many hours were over, he was in an awful state of mind; the Holy Spirit had convinced him of his state as a sinner, and he was in an agony of soul. That sharp sentence of mine was like the hook in a fish's gills, but that fish was landed all right. The man was brought to repentance and faith; he was baptized, joined the church, and a few years ago went home to Heaven.

" 'I have made thee a watchman.' Ezek. iii. 17. Here we read a true account of the making of a minister. God alone can do it. Two things are absolutely requisite to make a man a preacher, viz.—(1) Special gifts—such as perception of truth, simplicity, aptness to impart instruction, some degree of eloquence, and intense earnestness. (2) Special call. Every man who is rightly in the ministry must have been moved thereto of the Holy Ghost. He must feel an irresistible desire to spend his whole life in his Master's cause. No college, no bishop, no human ordination, can make a man a minister; but he who can feel, as did Bunyan, Whitefield, Berridge, or Rowland Hill, the strugglings of an impassioned longing to win the souls of men, may hear in the air the voice of God saying, 'Son of man, I have made thee a watchman.' "—C. H. S.

"No College at that time appeared to me to be suitable for the class of men that the providence and grace of God drew around me. . . . It must be frankly admitted that my views of the gospel and of the mode of training preachers were, and are, somewhat peculiar. I may have been uncharitable in my judgment, but I thought the Calvinism of the theology usually taught to be very doubtful, and the fervour of the generality of the students to be far behind their literary attainments. It seemed to me that preachers of the grand old truths of the gospel, ministers suitable for the masses, were more likely to be found in an institution where preaching and divinity would be the main objects, and not degrees and other insignia of human learning."—C. H. S.

Chapter 27

A New School of the Prophets

WHEN, in early days, God's Holy Spirit had gone forth with my ministry at New Park Street, several zealous young men were brought to a knowledge of the truth; and among them some whose preaching in the street was blessed of God to the conversion of souls. Knowing that these men had capacities for usefulness, but laboured under the serious disadvantage of having no education, and were, moreover, in such circumstances that they would not be likely to obtain admission into any of our Colleges, it entered into my heart to provide them with a course of elementary instruction, which might, at least, correct their inaccuracies of speech, and put them in the way of obtaining information by reading. One young man of especial promise seemed to be thrust in my way by Providence, so that I must commence with him at once, and, not long after, the very man of all others the most suitable to assist in carrying out my design was brought before me. The Rev. George Rogers, of Camberwell, had been waiting and ripening for the office and work of a tutor, and while the idea of educating young men was simmering in my brain, he was on the lookout for some such service. We met, and entered into a fellowship which every succeeding year has strengthened.

With a solitary student, our labour of love commenced. Funds were forthcoming for the support of this one brother, but, at the time, it seemed to me to be a very weighty enterprise and a great responsibility. With a limited income, it was no easy thing for a young minister to guarantee £50 a year. This, however, was a small matter ere long, for other brethren, who required the same aid, and were equally worthy, came forward to ask for similar instruction, and we could not deny them. The single student, in 1856, grew into eight ere long; and then into twenty; and, anon, the number rose to nearly one hundred men. Faith trembled when tried with the weight of the support of one man, but the Lord has strengthened her by exercise, so that she has rejoiced under the load when multiplied a hundred-fold.

The work did not begin with any scheme—it grew out of necessity. It was no choice with him who first moved in it, he simply acted because he was acted upon by a higher power. He had no idea whereunto the matter would grow, nor did he contemplate the institution of any far-reaching and wide-spread agency. To meet the present need, and follow the immediate movement of Providence, was all that was intended, and no idea of the future presented itself at the commencement. It seems to be God's plan that works of usefulness should develop themselves in obedience to a living force within, rather than by scheme and plan from without.

When the Pastors' College was fairly moulded into shape, we had before us but one object, and that was, the glory of God by the preaching of the gospel. To preach with acceptance, men, lacking in education, need to be instructed; and therefore our Institution set itself further to instruct *those whom God had evidently called to preach the gospel*, but who laboured under early disadvantages. We never dreamed of making men preachers, but we desired to help those whom God had already called to be such. Hence, we laid down, as a basis, the condition that a man must, during about two years, have been engaged in preaching, and must have had some seals to his ministry, before we could entertain his application. No matter how talented or promising he might appear to be, the College could not act upon mere hopes, but must have evident marks of a Divine call, so far as human judgment can discover them. This became a main point with us, for we wanted, not men whom our tutors could make into scholars, but men whom the Lord had ordained to be preachers.

Firmly fixing this landmark, we proceeded to sweep away every hindrance to the admission of fit men. We determined never to refuse a man on account of absolute poverty, but rather to provide him with needful lodging, board, and raiment, that he might not be hindered on that account. We also placed the literary qualifications of admission so low that even brethren who could not read have been able to enter, and have been among the most useful of our students in after days. A man of real ability as a speaker, of deep piety, and genuine faith, may be, by force of birth and circumstances, deprived of educational advantages, and yet, when helped a little, he may develop into a mighty worker for Christ; it would be a serious loss to the Church to deny such a man instruction because it was his misfortune to miss it in his youth. Our College began by inviting men of God to her bosom, whether they were poor and illiterate, or wealthy and educated. We sought for earnest preachers, not for readers of sermons, or makers of philosophical essays. "Have you won souls for Jesus?" was and is our leading enquiry of all applicants. "If so, come thou with us, and we will do thee good." If the brother has any pecuniary means, we feel that he should bear his own charges, and many have done so; but if he cannot contribute a sixpence, he is equally welcome, and is received upon the same footing in all respects. If we can but find men who love

Jesus, and love the people, and will seek to bring Jesus and the people together, the College will receive two hundred of such as readily as one, and trust in God for their food; but if men of learning and wealth should come, the College will not accept them unless they prove their calling by power to deliver the truth, and by the blessing of God upon their labours. Our men seek no Collegiate degrees, or classical honours—though many of them could readily attain them; but to preach efficiently, to get at the hearts of the masses, to evangelize the poor—this is the College ambition, this and nothing else.

We endeavour to teach the Scriptures, but, as everybody else claims to do the same, and we wish to be known and read of all men, we say distinctly that the theology of the Pastors' College is Puritanic. We know nothing of the new *ologies*; we stand by the old ways. The improvements brought forth by what is called "modern thought" we regard with suspicion, and believe them to be, at best, dilutions of the truth, and most of them old, rusted heresies, tinkered up again and sent abroad with a new face put upon them, to repeat the mischief which they wrought in ages past. We are old-fashioned enough to prefer Manton to Maurice, Charnock to Robertson, and Owen to Voysey. Both our experience and our reading of the Scriptures confirm us in the belief of the unfashionable doctrines of grace; and among us, upon those grand fundamentals, there is no uncertain sound. Young minds are not to be cast into one rigid mould, neither can maturity of doctrine be expected of beginners in the ministry; as a rule, our men have not only gone out from us clear and sound in the faith, but, with very few exceptions, they have continued so. Some few have ascended into Hyper-Calvinism, and, on the other hand, one or two have wandered into Arminian sentiments, but even these have remained earnestly Evangelical, while the bulk of the brethren abide in the faith in which their Alma Mater nourished them. The general acceptance of our students in Scotland is one remarkable proof that they stand by the old Calvinistic evangelical doctrines. The Presbyterian Churches of Rotterdam and Amsterdam, which are frequently supplied by our students, and are resolutely orthodox, have again and again sent us pleasing testimony that our men carry to them the old theology of the Westminster Assembly's Confession. Let wiseacres say what they will, there is more truth in that venerable Confession than could be found in ten thousand volumes of the school of affected culture and pretentious thoughtfulness. Want of knowing what the old theology is, is in most cases the reason for ridiculing it. Believing that the Puritanic school embodied more of gospel truth in it than any other since the days of the apostles, we continue in the same line of things, and, by God's help, hope to have a share in that revival of Evangelical doctrine which is as sure to come as the Lord Himself. Those who think otherwise can go elsewhere; but, for our own part, we shall never consent to leave the doctrinal teaching of the Institution vague and undefined, after the manner of the bigoted liberalism of the present day. The College motto is *Et Teneo Et Teneor*, "I hold and am held". We labour to hold forth the cross of Christ with a bold hand among the sons of men, because that cross holds us fast by its attractive power. Our desire is, that every man may hold the truth, and be held by it; especially the truth of Christ crucified.

There were many interesting incidents associated with the earliest days of the Pastors' College, or which occurred even before it was actually in existence. When Medhurst[1] began to preach in the street, some of the very precise friends, who were at that time members at New Park Street, were greatly shocked at his want of education, so they complained to me about it, and said that I ought to stop him, for, if I did not, disgrace would be brought upon the cause. Accordingly, I had a talk with the earnest young brother, and, while he did not deny that his English was imperfect, and that he might have made mistakes in other respects, yet he said, "I must preach, sir; and I shall preach unless you cut off my head." I went to our friends, and told them what he had said, and they took it in all seriousness. "Oh!" they exclaimed, "you can't cut off Mr. Medhurst's head, so you must let him go on preaching." I quite agreed with them, and I added, "As our young brother is evidently bent on serving the Lord with all his might, I must do what I can to get him an education that will fit him for the ministry."

The next one to come to me in trouble was Medhurst himself. One day, with a very sad countenance, he said to me, "I have been preaching for three months, and I don't know of a single soul having been converted." Meaning to catch him by guile, and at the same time to teach him a lesson he would never forget, I asked, "Do you expect the Lord to save souls every time you open your mouth?" "Oh, no, sir!" he replied. "Then," I said, "that is just the reason why you have not had conversions: 'According to your faith be it unto you.' "

During the time Medhurst was studying at Bexley Heath,[2] he used to conduct services in the open air. On one occasion, when I went

[1] T. W. Medhurst first heard Spurgeon at Maze Pond Chapel early in 1854. After a period of soul-distress he was converted through a Thursday night sermon at New Park Street, and soon after began to act as described above.—P.

[2] Medhurst was receiving tuition from Rev. C. H. Hosken, who lived at Bexley Heath and was pastor of the Baptist Church at Crayford. Once a week he spent several hours with Spurgeon at his lodgings studying theology. This continued after Spurgeon's

there to preach, I was much amused, after the service, by overhearing the remarks of two good souls who were manifestly very much attached to the young student. "Well," enquired the first, "how did you like Mr. Spurgeon?" "Oh!" answered her companion, "very well; but *I should have enjoyed the service more if he hadn't imitated our dear Mr. Medhurst so much.*"

There was another explanation, which did not seem to have occurred to the old lady, and, in after days, when relating the story to other students, I pointed out how serious the consequences might be if any of them imitated me!

At a later date, when I visited Kingston-on-Thames, after Medhurst had become pastor of the church there, I wanted to find out what the people thought of him, so I spoke of him with apparent coolness to an estimable lady of his congregation. In a very few moments, she began to speak quite warmly in his favour. She said, "You must not say anything against him, sir; if you do, it is because you do not know him." "Oh!" I replied, "I knew him long before you did; he is not much, is he?" "Well," she answered, "I must speak well of him, for he has been a blessing to my family and servants." I went out into the street, and saw some men and women standing about, so I said to them, "I must take your minister away." "If you do," they exclaimed, "we will follow you all over the world to get him back; you surely will not be so unkind as to take away a man who has done so much good to our souls?" After collecting the testimony of fifteen or sixteen persons, I said, "If the man gets such witnesses as these to the power of his ministry, I will gladly let him go on where he is; for it is clear that the Lord has called him into His service."

Medhurst himself told me of an incident that occurred to him in connection with one young man whom I had accepted for training, because I could see that he might do good service after proper tuition. So extraordinarily ignorant was he of his Bible that, upon hearing Medhurst mention the story of Nebuchadnezzar's being driven out from men, until his nails grew like birds' claws, and his hair like eagles' feathers, he said to the preacher, at the close of the sermon, "That was a queer story you told the people, certainly; where did you fish that up?" "Why!" replied our friend, "have you never read your Bible? Can you not find it in the Book of Daniel?" The young man had read a great many other books, but he had never read his Bible through, yet he was going to be a teacher of it! I fear that such ignorance is very

---

marriage. On March 21, 1857, Medhurst went to reside with Rev. George Rogers, at Albany Road, Camberwell; a second student joined him and thus began the Pastors' College.—P.

current in many persons; they do not know what is in the Bible: they could tell you what is in *The Churchman's Magazine,* or *The Wesleyan Magazine,* or *The Baptist Magazine,* or *The Evangelical Magazine,* but there is one old magazine, a magazine of arms, a magazine of wealth, that they have forgotten to read—that old-fashioned Book called the Bible. I remember saying, of a later student, that if he had been as well acquainted with his Bible as he was with *The Baptist Handbook,* he would have made a good minister; and he was not the only one to whom such a remark might have been applied.

There was one of the early students, who gave me great cause to fear concerning his future, when he began his petition at the Monday night prayer-meeting thus: "O Thou that art encinctured with an auriferous zodiac!" This was, of course, a grandiloquent paraphrase of Revelation i. 13. Alas! my fears proved to be only too well founded; after he left the College, he went from the Baptists to the Congregationalists, then became a play-writer and play-actor; and where he is now, I do not know. For many years I had the sad privilege of helping to support his godly wife, whom he had deserted. I thank God that, among so many hundreds of men, so few have caused me such sorrow of heart as he did.

"How many souls may be converted by what some men are privileged to *write and print*! There is, for instance, Dr. Doddridge's *Rise and Progress of Religion in the Soul*. Though I decidedly object to some things in it, I could wish that everybody had read that book, so many have been the conversions it has produced. I think it more honour to have composed Watts's *Psalms and Hymns* than Milton's *Paradise Lost*; and more glory to have written old Thomas Wilcocks' book, *A Choice Drop of Honey from the Rock Christ*, or the booklet that God has used so much, *The Sinner's Friend*, than all the works of Homer. I value books for the good they may do to men's souls. Much as I respect the genius of Pope, or Dryden, or Burns, give me the simple lines of Cowper, that God has owned in bringing souls to Him. Oh, to think that I may write and print books which shall reach poor sinners' hearts! The other day, my soul was gladdened exceedingly by an invitation from a pious woman to go and see her. She told me she had been ten years on her bed, and had not been able to stir from it. 'Nine years,' she said, 'I was dark, and blind, and unthinking; but my husband brought me one of your sermons. I read it, and God blessed it to the opening of my eyes. He converted my soul by it; and now, all glory to Him, I love His Name! Each Sabbath morning,' she added, 'I wait for your sermon. I live on it all the week, it is marrow and fatness to my spirit.' Ah! thought I, there is something to cheer the printers, and all of us who labour in that good work. A country friend wrote to me, this week, 'Brother Spurgeon, keep your courage up; you are known in multitudes of the households of England, and you are loved, too; though we cannot hear you, or see your living form, yet throughout our villages your sermons are scattered; and I know of cases of conversion from them, more than I can tell you.' Another friend mentioned to me an instance of a clergyman of the Church of England, a canon of a cathedral, who frequently preaches the sermons on the Sabbath—whether in the cathedral or not, I cannot say, but I hope he does. Oh! who can tell, when these words are printed, what hearts they may reach, or what good they may effect?"—C. H. S., *in sermon preached at New Park Street Chapel, October 7, 1855.*

Chapter 10

First Printed Works

THE first product of my pen which found its way into print was No. 1
of a short series of *Waterbeach Tracts*, which bore upon its front page
the announcement, "PUBLISHED BY REQUEST OF NUMEROUS FRIENDS".
This was issued in 1853, and in the same year I sent to *The Baptist
Reporter* an account of the conversation I had with the clergyman at
Maidstone which was the means of leading me to search the Scriptures,
and to find out the teaching of the New Testament concerning
believers' baptism. My letter was printed, although I only gave, for
publication, initials for my name and sphere of labour. Soon after I
was settled in London, the Editor of *The Baptist Messenger*, then
recently started, asked me to write some articles for his Magazine, so I
wrote a brief Exposition of Psalm lxxxiv. 6, which was published in
September, 1854, under the title, "The Valley of Weeping". The
following month, the next verse furnished me with a sequel, which
appeared in the October number under the heading, "Onward and
Heavenward". Month by month, I continued to contribute short
meditations to the pages of the *Messenger* until my other work absorbed
all my time and strength, and from then up to the present, one of my
sermons has regularly occupied the first page of each issue of the little
Magazine.

On August 20, 1854, I preached at New Park Street Chapel from the
words in 1 Samuel xii. 17: "Is it not wheat harvest to-day?" The
sermon was published by James Paul, as No. 2,234 in his *Penny Pulpit*,
under the title, "Harvest Time," and was, I believe, the first of my
discourses to appear in print. Before I ever entered a pulpit, the
thought had occurred to me that I should one day preach sermons
which would be printed. While reading the penny sermons of Joseph
Irons,[1] which were great favourites with me, I conceived in my heart
the idea that, some time or other, I should have a "Penny Pulpit" of
my own. In due course, the dream became an accomplished fact.
There was so good a demand for the discourses as they appeared in the
Penny Pulpit and *Baptist Messenger*, that the notion of occasional
publication was indulged, but with no idea of continuance week by
week for a lengthened period; *that* came to pass as a development and a

[1] Minister of Grove Chapel, Camberwell, 1819–1852. His weekly sermons, characterized by a strong Evangelical Calvinism, were widely circulated.—P.

growth. With much fear and trembling, my consent was given to the proposal of my present worthy publishers to commence the regular weekly publication of a sermon. We began with the one preached at New Park Street Chapel, on Lord's-day morning, January 7, 1855, upon the text, "I am the Lord, I change not; therefore ye sons of Jacob are not consumed" (Malachi iii. 6); and now, after all these years,[1] it is a glad thing to be able to say, "Having therefore obtained help of God, I continue unto this day, witnessing both to small and great." How many "Penny Pulpits" have been set up and pulled down in the course of these years, it would be hard to tell; certainly, very many attempts have been made to publish weekly the sermons of most eminent men, and they have all run to their end with more or less rapidity, in some cases through the preacher's ill-health or death, but in several others, to my knowledge, from an insufficient sale. Perhaps the discourses were too good: the public evidently did not think them too interesting. Those who know what dull reading sermons are usually supposed to be, will count that man happy who has for over thirty years been favoured with a circle of willing supporters, who not only purchase but actually *read* his discourses. I am more astonished at the fact than any other man can possibly be, and I see no other reason for it but this—the sermons contain the gospel, preached in plain language, and this is precisely what multitudes need beyond anything else. The gospel, ever fresh and ever new, has held my vast congregation together these many long years, and the same power has kept around me a host of readers. A French farmer, when accused of witchcraft by his neighbours, because his crops were so large, exhibited his industrious sons, his laborious ox, his spade, and his plough, as the only witchcraft which he had used; and, under the Divine blessing, I can only ascribe the continued acceptableness of the sermons to the gospel which they contain, and the plainness of the speech in which that gospel is uttered.

When the time arrived for issuing Vol. I of *The New Park Street Pulpit*, I wrote in the Preface: "Little can be said in praise of these sermons, and nothing can be said against them more bitter than has been already spoken. Happily, the author has heard abuse exhaust itself; he has seen its vocabulary used up, and its utmost venom entirely spent; and yet, the printed discourses have for that very reason

---

[1] Thirty-seven annual volumes, each containing fifty-two or more sermons, had been published by the time of Spurgeon's death in 1892; but such was the material available that a weekly sermon continued to be published until May 10, 1917; the last to appear was No. 3,563! Surveying some of these volumes, Mrs. Spurgeon once wrote, "My heart blessed God, not only for what He has done by them, but for all they shall yet accomplish by His grace till HE COME of whom they speak." *Ten Years of My Life*, p. 206.—P.

found a readier sale, and more have been led to peruse them with deep attention.

One thing alone places this book above contempt—and that accomplishes the deed so triumphantly, that the preacher defies the opinion of man—it is the fact that, to his certain knowledge, there is scarcely a sermon here which has not been stamped by the hand of the Almighty, by the conversion of a soul. Some single sermons, here brought into the society of their brethren, have been, under God, the means of the salvation of not less than twenty souls; at least, that number has come under the preacher's notice from one sermon only; and, doubtless, more shall be discovered at the last day. This, together with the fact that hundreds of the children of God have been made to leap for joy by their message, makes their author invulnerable either to criticism or abuse.

The reader will, perhaps, remark considerable progress in some of the sentiments here made public, particularly in the case of the doctrine of the Second Coming of our Lord; but he will remember that he who is learning truth will learn it by degrees, and if he teaches as he learns, it is to be expected that his lessons will become fuller every day.

There are also many expressions which may provoke a smile; but let it be remembered that every man has his moments when his lighter feelings indulge themselves, and the preacher must be allowed to have the same passions as his fellow-men; and since he lives in the pulpit more than anywhere else, it is but natural that his whole man should be there developed; besides, he is not quite sure about a smile being a sin, and, at any rate, he thinks it less a crime to cause a momentary laughter than a half-hour's profound slumber.

With all faults, the purchaser has bought this book; and, as it was not warranted to be perfect, if he thinks ill of it, he must make the best of his bargain—which can be done, either by asking a blessing on its reading to himself, or entreating greater light for his friend the preacher."

The first seven volumes were printed in small type, and each discourse formed only eight pages; but the abolition of the paper duty enabled the publishers to give a more readable type and twelve pages of matter. This has been better in every way, and marks an epoch in the history of the sermons, for their name was at about the same period changed from *The New Park Street Pulpit* to *The Metropolitan Tabernacle Pulpit*, and their sale was largely increased. Constant habit enables me generally to give the same amount of matter on each occasion, the very slight variation almost surprises myself; from forty to forty-five minutes' speaking exactly fills the available space, and saves the labour of additions, and the still more difficult task of cutting down. The earlier sermons, owing to my constant wanderings abroad, received scarcely any revision, and consequently they abound in colloquialisms, and other offences, very venial in extempore discourse, but scarcely tolerable in print; the later specimens are more carefully corrected, and the work of revision has been a very useful exercise to me, supplying in great measure that training in correct language which is obtained by those who write their productions before they deliver them. The labour has been far greater than some suppose, and has usually occupied the best hours of Monday, and involved the burning of no inconsiderable portion of midnight oil. Feeling that I had a constituency well deserving my best efforts, I have never grudged the hours, though often the brain has been wearied, and the pleasure has hardened into a task.

I have commenced revising the small-type sermons in preparation for their re-issue in type similar to that used for the rest of the series. There were mistakes in orthography and typography, which needed to be corrected, but I was happy to find that I had no occasion to alter any of the doctrines which I preached in those early days of my ministry. I might, here and there, slightly modify the expressions used thirty or five-and-thirty years ago, but, as to the truths themselves, I stand just where I did when the Lord first revealed them to me by His unerring Spirit.

Before the first volume of my sermons was completed, W. H. Collingridge had published for me, under the title of *Smooth Stones taken from Ancient Brooks*, a small volume containing "a collection of sentences, illustrations, and quaint sayings, from the works of that renowned Puritan, Thomas Brooks." (See page 293.) In the same year (1855), James Paul issued Vol. I of *The Pulpit Library*, which contained ten of my sermons. Being printed in clear, leaded type, and bound in cloth, the volume was much appreciated, and had a large sale, although half-a-crown was charged for it.

It contained, amongst other discourses, the one preached the night before I came of age,[1] "Pictures of Life, and Birthday Reflections";

---

[1] On March 30, 1884, just after the sudden death of the Duke of Albany, I preached again from the same text: "What is your life?" The sermon was published as No. 1,773 in the *Metropolitan Tabernacle Pulpit*, and during the following week a gentleman, who came to see me at the Tabernacle upon some matter of business, said to me, "I felt quite overwhelmed with emotion a minute ago." I asked him the reason; and he answered, "As I entered this building, I saw an announcement that you had lately preached from the words, 'What is your life?'" "Well," I enquired, "what is there special about that?" "Why!" he replied, "the night before you came of age, you preached from the same text." I told the friend that I had no doubt it was a very different discourse from the one I had

another delivered on the Sabbath following the marriage of Mr. and Mrs. Henry Olney, and in the midst of the terrible visitation of cholera, "The House of Mourning and the House of Feasting"; and a third, preached from Isaiah liv. 17, on November 5, 1854 (at the very moment when the battle of Inkermann was being fought), in which I urged the importance of Christians and Protestants remembering the day which had been made memorable in English history by the discovery of the Guy Fawkes' plot on November 5, 1605, and by the landing at Torbay of William III, on November 5, 1688. The title of the discourse was, "The Saints' Heritage and Watchword". The volume also included my first printed sermon—"Harvest Time"; and another entitled, "A Promise for the Blind", preached at the Baptist Chapel, Church Street, Blackfriars Road, on behalf of the Christian Blind Relief Society, in the course of which I referred to three institutions in the neighbourhood which represented the three classes of blind people: "The physically blind, the mentally blind, and the spiritually blind. . . . In the London Road, you will find the School for the blind—the physically blind. Just before you is the Roman Catholic Cathedral—there you have the spiritually blind. And further on is the Bethlehem Hospital (Bedlam), where you have the mentally blind."

*   *   *

In 1855—partly as an answer to the slanders and calumnies by which I was assailed, and partly that my own people might be furnished with a plain statement of "the faith once for all delivered to the saints"— Messrs. Alabaster and Passmore brought out, under my direction, a new edition of "*The Baptist Confession of Faith,* with Scripture proofs, adopted by the ministers and messengers of the General Assembly which met in London in July, 1689"; amongst whom were such notable men as Hanserd Knollys, William Kiffin, Andrew Gifford, and my own illustrious predecessor, Benjamin Keach.

In two Prefatory Notes, one to Christians in general, and the other to my own people, I wrote as follows:

---

just delivered, and then he said, "I have never been able to shake hands with you before to-day; but I have great pleasure in doing so now. When you were twenty-one years old, I was dreadfully depressed in spirit; I was so melancholy that I believe I should have destroyed myself if I had not heard you preach that sermon in celebration of your twenty-first birthday. It encouraged me to keep on in the battle of life; and, what is better, it made such an impression on me that I have never gone back to what I was before. Though I live a long way from here, no one loves you more than I do, for you were the means of bringing me up out of the horrible pit, and out of the miry clay." I was very glad to have that testimony to the usefulness of one of my early sermons.

"To all the Household of Faith, who Rejoice in the
Glorious Doctrines of Free Grace—
Dearly-beloved,
                 I have thought it meet to reprint in a cheap form this
most excellent list of doctrines, which was subscribed unto by the
Baptist ministers in the year 1689.

We need a banner, because of the truth; it may be that this small
volume may aid the cause of the glorious gospel, by testifying plainly
what are its leading doctrines. Known unto many of you by face in the
flesh, I trust we are also kindred in spirit, and are striving together for
the glory of our Three-one God. May the Lord soon restore unto His
Zion a pure language, and may the watchmen see eye to eye!

He who has preserved this faith among us, will doubtless bless our
gospel evermore.

So prays your brother in the gospel of Jesus,

C. H. Spurgeon."

"To the Church in New Park Street, among whom it is
my Delight to Minister—
Dearly-beloved,
                 This ancient document is a most excellent epitome of
the things most surely believed among us. By the preserving hand of
the Triune Jehovah, we have been kept faithful to the great points of
our glorious gospel, and we feel more resolved perpetually to abide by
them.

This little volume is not issued as an authoritative rule, or code of
faith, whereby you are to be fettered, but as an assistance to you in
controversy, a confirmation in faith, and a means of edification in
righteousness. Here, the younger members of our church will have a
Body of Divinity in small compass, and by means of the Scriptural
proofs, will be ready to give a reason for the hope that is in them.

Be not ashamed of your faith; remember it is the ancient gospel of
martyrs, confessors, Reformers, and saints. Above all, it is *the truth of
God*, against which the gates of hell cannot prevail.

Let your lives adorn your faith, let your example recommend your
creed. Above all, live in Christ Jesus, and walk in Him, giving credence
to no teaching but that which is manifestly approved of Him, and
owned by the Holy Spirit. Cleave fast to the Word of God, which is
here mapped out to you. May our Father, who is in Heaven, smile on
us as ever! Brethren, pray for—

Your affectionate Minister,

C. H. Spurgeon."

I have never seen any reason to alter what I then wrote, and I would, at the present time, just as earnestly commend to my fellow-Christians the prayerful study of *The Baptist Confession of Faith* as I did in the early years of my ministry in London, for I believe it would greatly tend to the strengthening of their faith.

I have already stated that, as soon as the publication of the sermons was commenced, the Lord set His seal upon them in the conversion of sinners, the restoration of backsliders, and the edification of believers, and, to His praise, I rejoice to write that, ever since, it has been the same. For many years, seldom has a day passed, and certainly never a week, without letters reaching me from all sorts of places, even at the utmost ends of the earth, telling me of the salvation of souls by means of one or other of the sermons. There are, in the long series, discourses of which I may say, without exaggeration, that the Holy Spirit has blessed them to hundreds of precious souls; and long after their delivery, fresh instances of their usefulness have come to light. For this, to God be all the glory!

There were certain remarkable cases of blessing through the reading of some of the very earliest of the sermons; I mention these, not merely because of the interest naturally attaching to them, but because they are representative of many similar miracles of mercy that have been wrought by the Holy Ghost all through the years which have followed. On June 8, 1856, I preached in Exeter Hall from Hebrews vii. 25: "Wherefore He is able also to save them to the uttermost that come unto God by Him, seeing He ever liveth to make intercession for them." The sermon was published under the title, "Salvation to the Uttermost"; and, more than thirty years afterwards, I received the joyful tidings that a murderer in South America had been brought to the Saviour through reading it. A friend, living not far from the Tabernacle, had been in the city of Pará, in Brazil. There he heard of an Englishman in prison, who had, in a state of drunkenness, committed a murder, for which he was confined for life. Our friend went to see him, and found him deeply penitent, but quietly restful, and happy in the Lord. He had felt the terrible wound of blood-guiltiness in his soul, but it had been healed, and he was enjoying the bliss of pardon.

Here is the story of the poor fellow's conversion as told in his own words: "A young man, who had just completed his contract at the gas-works, was returning to England; but, before doing so, he called to see me, and brought with him a parcel of books. When I opened it, I found that they were novels; but, being able to read, I was thankful for anything. After I had read several of the books, I found one of Mr. Spurgeon's sermons (No. 84), in which he referred to Palmer, who

cc

was then lying under sentence of death in Stafford Gaol, and in order to bring home the truth of his text to his hearers, he said that, if Palmer had committed many other murders, if he repented, and sought God's pardoning love in Christ, even he would be forgiven! I then felt that, if Palmer could be forgiven, so might I. I sought the Saviour, and, blessed be God, I found Him, and now I am pardoned, I am free; I am a sinner saved by grace. Though a murderer, I have not yet sinned beyond 'the uttermost', blessed be His holy Name!"

It made me very happy when I heard the glad news that a poor condemned murderer had thus been converted, and I am thankful to know that he is not the only one who, although he had committed the awful crime of murder, had, through the Spirit's blessing upon the printed sermons, been brought to repentance, and to faith in our Lord Jesus Christ. There was another man, who had lived a life of drunkenness and unchastity, and who had even shed human blood with his bowie knife and his revolver, yet he, too, found the Saviour, and became a new man; and when he was dying, he charged someone who was with him to tell me that one of my discourses had brought him to Christ. "I shall never see Mr. Spurgeon on earth," he said, "but I shall tell the Lord Jesus Christ about him when I get to Heaven." It was a sermon, read far away in the backwoods, that, through sovereign grace, was the means of the salvation of this great sinner.

One Saturday morning in November, 1856, when my mind and heart were occupied with preparation for the great congregation I expected to address the next day at the Surrey Gardens Music Hall, I received a long letter from Norwich, from a man who had been one of the leaders of an infidel society in that city. It was most cheering to me, amid the opposition and slander I was then enduring, to read what he wrote:

"I purchased one of the pamphlets entitled, 'Who is this Spurgeon?' and also your portrait (or a portrait sold as yours) for 3d. I brought these home, and exhibited them in my shop-window. I was induced to do so from a feeling of derisive pleasure. The title of the pamphlet is, naturally, suggestive of caricature, and it was especially to convey that impression that I attached it to your portrait, and placed it in my window. But I also had another object in view, I thought by its attraction to improve my trade. I am not at all in the book or paper business, which rendered its exposure and my motive the more conspicuous. I have taken it down now: *I am taken down, too. . . .* I had bought one of your sermons of an infidel a day or two previously. In that sermon I read these words, 'They go on; that step is safe—they take it; the next is apparently safe—they take that; their foot hangs over a gulf of darkness.' I read on, but the word darkness staggered me; it was all dark with me. I said to myself, 'True, the way has been safe so far, but I am lost in bewilderment; I cannot go on as I have been going. No, no, no; I will not risk it.' I left the apartment in which I had been musing, and as I did so, the three words, 'Who can tell?' seemed to be whispered to my heart. I determined not to let another Sunday pass without visiting a place of worship. How soon my soul might be required of me, I knew not, but I felt that it would be mean, base, cowardly, not to give it a chance of salvation. 'Ay!' I thought, 'my associates may laugh, scoff, deride, and call me coward and turncoat, I will do an act of justice to my soul.' I went to chapel; I was just stupefied with awe. What could I want there? The doorkeeper opened his eyes wide, and involuntarily asked, 'It's Mr. ——, isn't it?' 'Yes,' I said, 'it is.' He conducted me to a seat, and afterwards brought me a hymn-book. I was fit to burst with anguish. 'Now,' I thought, 'I am here, if it be the house of God, Heaven grant me an audience, and I will make a full surrender. O God, show me some token by which I may know that Thou art, and that Thou wilt in no wise cast out the vile deserter who has ventured to seek Thy face and Thy pardoning mercy!' I opened the hymn-book to divert my mind from the feelings that were rending me, and the first words that caught my eyes were—

> 'Dark, dark indeed the grave would be
> Had we no light, O God, from Thee!' "

After mentioning some things which he looked upon as evidences that he was a true convert, the man closed up by saying, "O sir, tell this to the poor wretch whose pride, like mine, has made him league himself with hell; tell it to the hesitating and the timid; tell it to the desponding Christian, that God is a very present help to all that are in need! ... Think of the poor sinner who may never look upon you in this world, but who will live to bless and pray for you here, and long to meet you in the world exempt from sinful doubts, from human pride, and backsliding hearts."

After that letter, I heard again and again from the good brother, and I rejoiced to learn that, the following Christmas-day, he went into the market-place at Norwich, and there made a public recantation of his errors, and a profession of his faith in Christ. Then, taking up all the infidel books he had written, or that he had in his possession, he burned them in the sight of all the people. I blessed God with my whole heart for such a wonder of grace as that man was, and I afterwards had the joy of learning from his own lips what the Lord had done for his soul, and together we praised and magnified Him for His marvellous mercy.

Many singular things have happened in connection with the publication of the sermons. One brother, whose name I must not mention, purchased and gave away no less than 250,000 copies. He had volumes bound in the best style, and presented to every crowned head in Europe. He gave copies, each containing twelve or more sermons, to all the students of the Universities,[1] and to all the members of the two Houses of Parliament, and he even commenced the work of distributing volumes to the principal householders in the towns of Ireland. May the good results of his laborious seed-sowing be seen many days hence! The self-denial with which this brother saved the expense from a very limited income, and worked personally in the distribution, was beyond all commendation, but praise was evaded and observation dreaded by him; the work was done without his left hand knowing what his right hand did.

In the first days of our publishing, a city merchant advertised the sermons in all sorts of papers, offering to supply them from his own office. He thus sold large quantities to persons who might otherwise never have heard of them. He was not a Baptist, but held the views of the Society of Friends. It was very long before I knew who he was, and I trust he will pardon me for thus calling attention to a deed for which I shall ever feel grateful to him. By my permission, the sermons were printed *as advertisements* in several of the Australian papers, one gentleman spending week by week a sum which I scarcely dare to mention, lest it should not be believed. By this means, they were read far away in the Bush, and never were results more manifest, for numbers of letters were received—in answer to the enquiry as to whether the advertisements should be continued—all bearing testimony to the good accomplished by their being inserted in the newspapers. A selection of these letters was sent to me, and made my heart leap for joy, for they detailed conversions marvellous indeed. Beside these, many epistles of like character came direct to me, show-ing that the rough dwellers in the wilds were glad to find in their

[1] During the compilation of the *Autobiography*, Mrs. Spurgeon received from a Church of England clergyman a letter containing the following reference to this distribution of sermons to the students in the Universities:—

"Over thirty years ago, when an undergraduate at Oxford, one of our men came into College with a volume of your husband's sermons, saying that someone was distributing them to the 'men' who would accept them. I was one of those who had the privileged gift, and have since read it through and through with advantage. I have never preached knowingly other than the doctrines of grace; and though the clergy round about are mostly Ritualists and Sacerdotalists, thank God the error taught by them has never tempted me!"

secular paper the best of all news, the story of pardon bought with blood.

In America, the sale of the first volume reached 20,000 in a very short time; and, many years ago, it was calculated that half a million volumes had been sold there. Beside this, dozens of religious papers in the United States, and Canada, and elsewhere, appropriate the sermons bodily, and therefore it is quite impossible to tell where they go, or rather, where they do not go. For all these opportunities of speaking to so large a portion of the human race, I cannot but be thankful to God, neither can I refrain from asking the prayers of God's people that the gospel thus widely scattered may not be in vain.

Brethren in the ministry will be best able to judge the mental wear and tear involved in printing one sermon a week, and they will most sympathize in the overflowing gratitude which reviews between thirty and forty years of sermons, and magnifies the God of grace for help so long continued. The quarry of Holy Scripture is inexhaustible, I seem hardly to have begun to labour in it, but the selection of the next block, and the consideration as to how to work it into form, are matters not so easy as some think. Those who count preaching and its needful preparations to be slight matters, have never occupied a pulpit continuously month after month, or they would know better. Chief of all is the responsibility which the preaching of the Word involves: I do not wish to feel this less heavily, rather would I feel it more, but it enters largely into the account of a minister's life-work, and tells upon him more than any other part of his mission. Let those preach lightly who dare do so; to me, it is "the burden of the Lord"— joyfully carried as grace is given; but, still, a burden which at times crushes my whole manhood into the dust of humiliation, and occasionally, when ill-health unites with the mental strain, into depression and anguish of heart.

However, let no man mistake me. I would sooner have my work to do than any other under the sun. Preaching Jesus Christ is sweet work, joyful work, Heavenly work. Whitefield used to call his pulpit his throne, and those who know the bliss of forgetting everything beside the glorious, all-absorbing topic of Christ crucified, will bear witness that the term was aptly used. It is a bath in the waters of Paradise to preach with the Holy Ghost sent down from Heaven. Scarcely is it possible for a man, this side the grave, to be nearer Heaven than is a preacher when his Master's presence bears him right away from every care and thought, save the one business in hand, and that the greatest that ever occupied a creature's mind and heart. No tongue can tell the amount of happiness which I have enjoyed in delivering these sermons, and so, gentle reader, forgive me if I have wearied you with this grateful record, for I could not refrain from inviting others to aid me in praising my gracious Master. "Bless the Lord, O my soul, and all that is within me, bless His holy Name."

*   *   *

In my early experience as an author, I made one mistake which I have never repeated. For my volume, *The Saint and his Saviour*, which contained 480 small octavo pages, I accepted from James S. Virtue the sum of £50. At the time I entered into the agreement—within about a year of my coming to London—the amount seemed to me large; but in comparison with what the book must have brought to the publisher, it was ridiculously small, and as he never deemed it wise to add anything to it, I took good care not to put any other of my works into his hands, but entrusted them to publishers who knew how to treat me more generously. After the volume had been on sale for more than thirty years, the copyright was offered to me for considerably more than I had originally received for it! Neither my publishers nor I myself thought it was worth while to buy it back under the circumstances, so it passed into the possession of my good friends, Messrs. Hodder and Stoughton.

[The book was issued in the United States soon after it was published in England, and it had a large sale there. In a letter to Spurgeon, dated "New York, Sept. 17, 1857," Messrs. Sheldon, Blakeman, & Co., who for many years republished his works on mutually advantageous terms, wrote: "Messrs. Virtue and Son sold to D. Appleton & Co. the advance sheets of *The Saint and his Saviour*, and they have sold them to us. We have the book stereotyped as far as we have received the sheets; we expect the rest from London by next steamer, and shall then immediately issue the book. We are delighted with it, and think it will take well with our people."]

My own experiences in the production of the work are faithfully described in the Preface:

"Never was a book written amid more incessant toil. Only the fragments of time could be allotted to it, and intense mental and bodily exertions have often rendered me incapable of turning even those fragments to advantage. Writing is, to me, the work of a slave. It is a delight, a joy, a rapture, to talk out my thoughts in words that flash upon the mind at the instant when they are required, but it is poor drudgery to sit still, and groan for thoughts and words without succeeding in obtaining them. Well may a man's books be called his 'works', for, if every mind were constituted as mine is, it would be work indeed to produce a quarto volume. Nothing but a sense of duty has impelled me to finish this little book, which has been more than two years on hand. Yet have I, at times, so enjoyed the meditation which my writing has induced, that I would not discontinue the labour were it ten times more irksome; and, moreover, I have some hopes that it may yet be a pleasure to me to serve God with the pen as well as the lip."

Those who are familiar with my literary career know how abundantly those "hopes" have been realized; yet, at the time, my faithful friend, Dr. John Campbell, doubtless expressed what many beside himself felt when he wrote: "Such hopes are innocent, and, should they never be realized, the disappointment will not be viewed as a calamity. We think it will be wise in Mr. Spurgeon, however, to moderate his expectations in this quarter. The number of those who, either in past or present times, have attained to eminence both with tongue and pen, is small. The Greeks produced none, and the Romans only one; and Great Britain has hardly been more successful. Charles Fox, not satisfied with peerless eminence in the House of Commons, aspired to honour in the field of history. Thomas Erskine, without an equal at the Bar, also thirsted for literary renown. Each made the attempt, and gave to the world a fragment, presenting not the slightest impress of their towering genius as orators, and otherwise adding nothing to their fame. These illustrious men, however, were perfectly capable, had they foresworn eloquence, and given themselves to letters, in early life, to have taken a foremost place in the ranks of literature, and so is Mr. Spurgeon; but they were early ensnared by their rhetorical successes, and so is he. By incessant speaking, they developed to the full, and cultivated to the highest extent, oral eloquence, and so has he. After this, they could not endure the drudgery necessary to cultivate the habit of composition till it became a pleasure and a luxury, and neither can he. Their indisposition to use the pen increased with time, and so will his; and to such a length did their self-created incapacity grow on them, that they became almost incapable of correspondence; and so will he. We believe he is well-nigh so now!

If we might use the liberty, we would say, it is Mr. Spurgeon's wisdom to know his place, and be satisfied to occupy it. Let him rejoice in his glorious mission, and continue to fulfil, as he now does, its exalted obligations. It is surely enough to satisfy all the ambition for which there is room in the bosom of a Christian man, to remain supreme in the realm of sacred eloquence—an instrument, beyond all others, intended to promote the salvation of sinners. . . . The volume throughout bears the stamp of a rhetorical genius, and indicates a practised speaker rather than writer, and breathes a most intense concern for the souls of men. This is everywhere the prominent idea, to the utter exclusion of everything that savours of display. We dismiss the work with the most cordial wish for its success in further-ance of the great object with which it was prepared, and doubt not that, however tame and gentle as compared with the powerful stream of life and fire which pervades the sermons, it will, in its own way, amply contribute to the same grand result—the turning of men from darkness to light, and from the power of Satan unto God."

In the long interval which necessarily elapsed between my undertak-ing to write *The Saint and his Saviour* and the date of the publication of the volume, I had become so attached to my friends, Joseph Passmore and James Alabaster, that I had no wish to have any other publishers as long as I lived. Our relationship has been one of the closest in-timacy, and I think they would join with me in saying that it has been of mutual benefit; and our business arrangements have been such as Christian men would desire to make so that in all things God might be glorified. The young partners began in a very humble fashion in Wilson Street, Finsbury, and they were afterwards able to tell a wonderful story of how the Lord prospered and blessed them there. The very speedy and unprecedented success of the publications made it difficult at times to cope with the extraordinary rush of orders; but, by setting themselves manfully to the task, and using all the help available, they were able to lay a solid foundation for the future well-being of the firm, which afterwards migrated to Little Britain, and then to Fann Street, Aldersgate Street. I have often asked Mr. Pass-more the question whether I wrote for him, or he prints for me—whether he is my employer, or I am his. He says that I am "the Governor", so perhaps that settles the point.

*   *   *

[The following selection from the hundreds of letters written by Spurgeon to Mr. or Mrs. Passmore, during their long and intimate association, will afford just a glimpse of the happy friendship which existed between them, and also of the business relationship which remained throughout one of unbroken harmony. This communication was so characteristic that it was deemed worthy of reproduction in *facsimile*:

A respectful epistle from a poor author
to an eminent publisher

Respected Sir,

I humbly suggest the enclosed as an advertisement in the Advertising sheet of Sword & Trowel for this month. If your majestic highness sees fit, please see it inserted & oblige

Your humble
& obed^t servant

C. H. Spurgeon

To my friend
Joe.
What an impertinent rascal that author is!

This letter was written by Spurgeon at the close of one of the many Continental tours on which Mr. Passmore had been his companion:

"Boulogne,
Dec. 23.

My Dear Mrs. Passmore,

Your noble husband is sitting before the fire on one chair, with his legs up on another, and as it seemed to be a pity to disturb His Royal Highness, I offered to write to you for him, and he accepted the offer. I am happy to say that our mutually respected and beloved Joseph is much better, and will, I hope, arrive at Park Lodge in first-rate condition about 7 or 8 o'clock on Friday. The sea is in an excited condition, and I fear none of us will need an emetic when crossing to-morrow: but it will be better arranged than if we had the management of it, no doubt.

I am very much obliged to you for lending me your worser half so kindly. He is a dear, kind, generous soul, and worth his weight in angels any day. I hope all the young folk are quite well. My dear wife says you are bonnie, which is vastly better than being bony.

My kindest regards are always with you and yours. Pray accept my love, and I daresay His Royal Highness, the King of Little Britain,[1] would send his also; but he is so much engrossed in reading *The Standard*, that I have not asked about it.

Yours ever truly,
C. H. SPURGEON."

The next letter needs scarcely any explanation; yet it would be interesting to know whether *all* authors write in as genial a spirit when promised "proofs" do not arrive at the appointed time.

"Dear Mr. Passmore,

Have you retired from business? For, if not, I should be glad of proofs for the month of November of a book entitled *Morning by Morning* which, unless my memory fails me, you began to print. I was to have had some matter on Monday; and it is now Wednesday. Please jog the friend who has taken your business, and tell him that YOU always were the very soul of punctuality, and that he must imitate you.

[1] Where the printing-offices were situated at that time.

I send a piece for October 31, for I can't find any proof for that date. Please let the gentleman who has taken your business have it soon.

Yours ever truly,

C. H. SPURGEON.

P.S.—Has Mr. Alabaster retired, too? I congratulate you both, and hope the new firm will do as well. What is the name? I'll make a guess —MESSRS. QUICK AND SPEEDY."

Although the following letter is of much later date than the preceding ones, it is inserted here to show that Spurgeon had as much consideration for the welfare of a little messenger-boy as he had for the principals of the firm—

"Westwood,
Beulah Hill,
Upper Norwood,
March 11th, 1891.

Dear Mr. Passmore,

When that good little lad came here on Monday with the sermon, late at night, it was needful. But please blow somebody up for sending the poor little creature here, late to-night, in all this snow, with a parcel much heavier than he ought to carry. He could not get home till eleven, I fear; and I feel like a cruel brute in being the innocent cause of having a poor lad out at such an hour on such a night. There was no need at all for it. Do kick somebody for me, so that it may not happen again.

Yours ever heartily,
C. H. SPURGEON."]

"Sometimes we have seen a model marriage, founded on pure love, and cemented in mutual esteem. Therein, the husband acts as a tender head; and the wife, as a true spouse, realizes the model marriage-relation, and sets forth what our oneness with the Lord ought to be. She delights in her husband, in his person, his character, his affection; to her, he is not only the chief and foremost of mankind, but in her eyes he is all-in-all; her heart's love belongs to him, and to him only. She finds sweetest content and solace in his company, his fellowship, his fondness; he is her little world, her Paradise, her choice treasure. At any time, she would gladly lay aside her own pleasure to find it doubled in gratifying him. She is glad to sink her individuality in his. She seeks no renown for herself; his honour is reflected upon her, and she rejoices in it. She would defend his name with her dying breath; safe enough is he where she can speak for him. The domestic circle is her kingdom; that she may there create happiness and comfort, is her life-work; and his smiling gratitude is all the reward she seeks. Even in her dress, she thinks of him; without constraint she consults his taste, and considers nothing beautiful which is distasteful to him. A tear from his eye, because of any unkindness on her part, would grievously torment her. She asks not how her behaviour may please a stranger, or how another's judgment may approve her conduct; let her beloved be content, and she is glad. He has many objects in life, some of which she does not quite understand; but she believes in them all, and anything that she can do to promote them, she delights to perform. He lavishes love on her, and, in return, she lavishes love on him. Their object in life is common. There are points where their affections so intimately unite that none could tell which is first and which is second. To watch their children growing up in health and strength, to see them holding posts of usefulness and honour, is their mutual concern; in this and other matters, they are fully one. Their wishes blend, their hearts are indivisible. By degrees, they come to think very much the same thoughts. Intimate association creates conformity; I have known this to become so complete that, at the same moment, the same utterance has leaped to both their lips.

Happy woman and happy man! If Heaven be found on earth, they have it! At last, the two are so blended, so engrafted on one stem, that their old age presents a lovely attachment, a common sympathy, by which its infirmities are greatly alleviated, and its burdens are transformed into fresh bonds of love. So happy a union of will, sentiment, thought, and heart exists between them, that the two streams of their life have washed away the dividing bank, and run on as one broad current of united existence till their common joy falls into the ocean of eternal felicity."—C. H. S.

Chapter 29

Early Wedded Life

BY MRS. C. H. SPURGEON

Again the responsible task lies before me of interweaving my own dearest personal memories with my beloved's *Autobiography*, that the picture of his life's history may glow with the fair colours and present some of the finishing touches which are needed to render it as complete as possible. Alas, that his dear hand is powerless to furnish them! Every line I write fills me with regret that I cannot better set forth the remembrance of his worth and goodness.

Someone wrote to me, lately, saying that it was impossible for a man's nearest friends to give a true and impartial idea of him; they lived in too close proximity to him, their vision was interrupted by their admiration, they could not see many things that others, looking on from a remoter and broader coign of vantage, could distinctly discern. This seems to me a great mistake, except indeed in cases where "distance lends enchantment to the view"; for who could so reasonably be supposed to understand and recognize the inner qualities and disposition of an individual's character as the one who lived in constant and familiar intercourse with him, and to whom his heart was as a clear, calm lake, reflecting Heaven's own light and beauty? Those who knew my husband best, can testify that intimate knowledge of his character, and close companionship with him, did but more clearly reveal how very near, by God's grace, he had "come in the unity of the faith, and of the knowledge of the Son of God, unto a perfect man, unto the measure of the stature of the fulness of Christ." *Not in his own estimation*, be it well understood—he never spoke of himself as "having apprehended"—he was always "a poor sinner, and nothing at all". So pre-eminently and gloriously was "Jesus Christ his All-in-all" that his gracious, gentle, lovely life testified daily to the indwelling of the Holy Spirit in his heart, and the exceeding power of God which kept him through faith, and enabled him to "walk worthy of the vocation wherewith he was called". Robert Murray M'Cheyne used to pray: "O God, make me as holy as a pardoned sinner can be made!" and, to judge by my husband's *life*, a similar petition must have been constantly in his heart if not on his lips.

Our brief wedding trip was spent in Paris, and, as I had made many previous visits to the fair city, beside spending some months in the Christian household of Pastor Audebez, in order to acquire the language, I felt quite at home there, and had the intense gratification of introducing my husband to all the places and sights which were worthy of arousing his interest and admiration. We had a cosy suite of rooms (by special favour) in the *entresol* of the Hôtel Meurice, and every day we explored some fresh *musée,* or church, or picture-gallery, or drove to some place of historic fame, all the charms of Paris seeming ten times more charming in my eyes than they had ever been before, because of those other loving eyes which now looked upon them with me.

The city was then in the days of her luxury and prosperity; no Communistic fires had scorched and blackened her streets, no turbulent mobs had despoiled her temples and palaces, and laid her glories in the dust; she was triumphant and radiant, and in the pride of her heart was saying, "I sit a queen, ... and shall see no sorrow." Alas! there were days of calamity and tribulation in store for her, when war, and bloodshed, and fire, and famine ravaged her beauty, and laid waste her choice habitations. But no forecast of such terrible visitations troubled our hearts; the halo of the present illumined all the future. We went to Versailles, to Sèvres, to the Louvre, the Madeleine, the Jardin des Plantes, the Luxembourg, the Hôtel de Cluny; in fact, to every place we could find time for, where Christian people might go, and yet bring away with them a clear conscience. A peep at the Bourse interested us very much. What a scene of strife it was! What a deafening noise the men made! My husband quaintly depicted the excitement in a few words: "The pot boiled more and more furiously as the hour of three approached, and then the brokers, like the foam on the top, ran over, and all the black contents followed by degrees!" Anyone acquainted with the place and its customs will recognize the accuracy and humour of this graphic description.

Naturally, the interiors of the churches attracted much of our attention; we always found something to admire, though, alas! there was also much to deplore. When we visited the Cathedral of Notre Dame, I was able to interest my companion by telling him that I had seen it in full gala dress on the occasion of the marriage of the Emperor Napoleon III to his charming Empress Eugenie, and how glittering and gorgeous it then looked, with its abundant draperies of imperial purple velvet, embroidered all over with golden bees! All the wealth and riches of the great sanctuary were then pressed into service, and the result was magnificent. Without such adornments, the church has a simple and solemn grandeur of its own, very soothing to the mind, and, at the time of which I am writing, its sanctity was enhanced—in the opinion of its Roman Catholic worshippers—by its possession of such sacred relics as part of the true cross, and the crown of thorns! These were shown to visitors on payment of an extra fee, as was also an amazing number of splendid vestments encrusted with gold and jewels, and worth a prince's ransom. I believe that, at the time of the Commune, much of this treasure was carried away, or ruthlessly destroyed.

The beauty of the Sainte Chapelle specially delighted us, and we went there more than once. "It is a little heaven of stained glass," was my beloved's verdict; and, truly, its loveliness looked almost celestial, as we stood enwrapped in its radiance, the light of the sinking sun glorifying its matchless windows into a very dream of dazzling grace and harmony of colour.

Then there were St. Roch, St. Sulpice, Ste. Clotilde, and hosts of other churches, not forgetting St. Etienne du Mont, a grand edifice, containing the sumptuous shrine of Ste. Geneviève—in its way, a perfect gem—nor St. Germain l'Auxerrois, with its ancient rose windows, and its pathetic memories of the betrayed Huguenots.

The Panthéon, too, once a temple, now a church, received a share of our interested attention. So far as I can remember, the building itself was almost empty, except for some statues ranged around it; but we descended to the crypt, which contains the tombs of Rousseau, Voltaire, and other notable or notorious men, and we listened, with something like fear, to the thunderous echo which lurks there, and attracts visitors to these subterranean vaults. It is very loud and terrible, like a cannon fired off, and it gives one quite an uncanny feeling to hear such a deafening roar down in the bowels of the earth. After this experience, we were very glad to get into the fresh air again.

Of course, we went to St. Cloud (now, alas! in ruins). There is—or was—a lonely, lovely walk through the Park to the summit of an eminence crowned by the lantern of Diogenes. From there, the view was glorious. The Seine flowed far below, the suburbs of the city lay beyond; Mont Valérien on the right, Paris straight before one's eyes, with the gilded dome of the Invalides shining in the clear air; St. Sulpice, and the Panthéon, and countless spires and towers forming landmarks in the great sea of houses and streets, the twin heights of Montmartre and Père la Chaise in the background; all these grouped together, and viewed from the hill, formed an indescribably charming picture.

I tried to be a good cicerone, and I think I fairly succeeded, for my companion was greatly delighted, and in after years, in his frequent visits to the French capital with friends and fellow-voyagers, he took upon himself the *rôle* of conductor, with the happiest and most satisfactory results. He was never at a loss where to go, or how to spend the time in the most pleasant and profitable manner. A little note, written from Paris, twenty years after our wedding trip, contains the following sentences: "My heart flies to you, as I remember my first visit to this city under your dear guidance. I love you now as then, only multiplied many times."

Ah! "tender grace of a day that is dead", thy joy is not lessened by distance, nor lost by separation; rather is it stored both in Heaven and in my heart's deepest chambers, and some day, when that casket is broken, it will "come back to me", not here, but in that happy land where the days die not, where "the touch of a vanished hand" shall be felt again, and "the sound of a voice that is still" shall again make music in my ravished ears!

'Twas a brief, bright season, this wedding trip of ours, lasting about ten days, for my husband could not leave his sacred work for a longer time, and we were both eager to return that we might discover the delights of having a home of our own, and enjoy the new sensation of feeling ourselves master and mistress of all we surveyed! What a pure unsullied joy was that home-coming! How we thanked and praised the Lord for His exceeding goodness to us in bringing us there, and how earnestly and tenderly my husband prayed that God's blessing might rest upon us then and evermore! How we admired everything in the house, and thought there never was quite such a delightful home before, will be best understood by those who have lived in Love-land, and are well acquainted with the felicity of setting up house-keeping there. On the table, in the little sitting-room, lay a small parcel, which, when opened, proved to be a wedding present from Mr. W. Poole Balfern.

I think the circumstances under which my beloved and Mr. Balfern met, are worthy of a passing notice. One Saturday, the time for sermon-preparation had arrived, and the dear preacher had shut himself up in his study, when a ministerial visitor was announced. He would not give his name, but said, "Tell Mr. Spurgeon that a servant of the Lord wishes to see him." To this my husband replied, "Tell the gentleman that I am so busy with his Master, that I cannot attend to the servant." Then word was sent that W. Poole Balfern was the visitor, and no sooner did Mr. Spurgeon hear the name, than he ran out to him, clasped his hand in both his own, and exclaimed, "W. Poole Balfern! The man who wrote *Glimpses of Jesus!* Come in, thou blessed of the Lord!" Describing that interview, long afterwards, Mr. Balfern said, "I learned then that the secret of Mr. Spurgeon's success was, that he was *cradled in the Holy Ghost.*" It was a very remarkable expression, which I do not remember to have met with anywhere else; but it was as true as it was striking.

So many memories cling about our first home, and so many notable events of early married life transpired within its walls, that I must ask my readers kindly to refer to the view given on Plate 17, that they may the more readily understand the description which follows. On the ground floor, the single window—now almost hidden by a tree, planted since the days of which I write—marks the little front parlour or "living-room", in old-fashioned parlance, where the greater part of the home-life was spent; above this, and boasting two windows, was a very fair-sized room, the best in the house, and, therefore, devoted to the best of uses—the master's study; and the two windows immediately over this belonged to a bed-chamber of the same size, where afterwards our twin-boys first saw the light of day. It may not be out of place to say here that in all the houses we have lived in— four in all—we never encumbered ourselves with what a modern writer calls, "the drawback of a drawing-room"; perhaps for the good reason that we were such homely, busy people that we had no need of so useless a place—but more especially, I think, because the "best room" was always felt to belong by right to the one who "laboured much in the Lord".

We began housekeeping on a very modest scale, and even then had to practise rigid economy in all things, for my dear husband earnestly longed to help young men to preach the gospel, and from our slender resources we had to contribute somewhat largely to the support and education of T. W. Medhurst, who was the first to receive training for the work. From so small a beginning sprang the present Pastors' College, with its splendid record of service both done and doing. I rejoice to remember how I shared my beloved's joy when he founded the Institution, and that, together we planned and pinched in order to carry out the purpose of his loving heart; it gave me quite a motherly interest in the College, and "our own men". The chief difficulty, with regard to money matters in those days, was to "make both ends meet"; we never had enough left over to "tie a bow and ends", but I can see now that this was God's way of preparing us to sympathize with and help poor pastors in the years which were to come.

One of these good men, when recounting to me the griefs of his poverty, once said, "You can scarcely understand, for you have never been in the same position;" but my thoughts flew back to this early time, and I could truly say, "I may not have been in such depths of need as seem now likely to swallow you up, but I well remember when we lived on the 'do without' system, and only 'God's providence was our inheritance', and when He often stretched forth His hand, and wrought signal deliverances for us, when our means were sorely straitened, and the coffers of both College and household were well-nigh empty." I recall a special time of need, supplied by great and unexpected mercy. Some demand came in for payment—I think it must have been a tax or rate, for I never had bills owing to tradesmen —and we had nothing wherewith to meet it. What a distressing condition of excitement seized us! "Wifey," said my beloved, "what can we do? I must give up hiring the horse, and walk to New Park Street every time I preach!" "Impossible," I replied, "with so many services, you simply could not do it." Long and anxiously we pondered over ways and means, and laid our burden before the Lord, entreating Him to come to our aid. And, of course, He heard and answered, for He is a faithful God. That night, or the next day, I am not sure which, a letter was received, containing £20 for our own use, and we never knew who sent it, save that it came in answer to prayer! This was our first united and personal home experience of special necessity provided for by our Heavenly Father, and our hearts felt a very solemn awe and gladness as we realized that He knew what things we had need of before we asked Him. As the years rolled by, such eventful passages in our history were graciously multiplied, and even excelled, but perhaps this first blessed deliverance was the foundation stone of my husband's strong and mighty faith, for I do not remember ever afterwards seeing him painfully anxious concerning supplies for any of his great works; he depended wholly on the Lord, his trust was perfect, and he lacked nothing.

*   *   *

There are one or two little pictures which memory has retained of events in that little front parlour whose window looks into the road. I will try to reproduce them, though the colours are somewhat faded, and the backgrounds blurred with age.

It is the Sabbath, and the day's work is done. The dear preacher has had a light repast, and now rests in his easy chair by a bright fire, while, on a low cushion at his feet, sits his wife, eager to minister in some way to her beloved's comfort. "Shall I read to you to-night, dear?" she says; for the excitement and labour of the Sabbath services sorely try him, and his mind needs some calm and soothing influence to set it at rest. "Will you have a page or two of good George Herbert?" "Yes, that will be very refreshing, wifey; I shall like that." So the book is procured, and he chooses a portion which I read slowly and with many pauses, that he may interpret to me the sweet mysteries hidden within the gracious words. Perhaps his enjoyment of the book is all the greater that he has thus to explain and open out to me the precious truths enwrapped in Herbert's quaint verse—anyhow, the time is delightfully spent. I read on and on for an hour or more, till the peace of Heaven flows into our souls, and the tired servant of the King of kings loses his sense of fatigue, and rejoices after his toil.

Another Sabbath night, and the scene is somewhat changed in character. The dear Pastor is not only weary, but sorely depressed in spirit. "Oh, darling!" he says, "I fear I have not been as faithful in my preaching to-day as I should have been; I have not been as much in earnest after poor souls as God would have me be. O Lord, pardon Thy servant!" "Go, dear," he continues, "to the study, and fetch down Baxter's *Reformed Pastor*, and read some of it to me; perhaps that will quicken my sluggish heart." So I bring the book, and with deep sighs he turns the pages till he finds some such passage as the following: "Oh, what a charge have we undertaken! And shall we be unfaithful? Have we the stewardship of God's own family, and shall we neglect it? Have we the conduct of those saints who must live for ever with God in glory, and shall we be unconcerned for them? God forbid! I beseech you, brethren, let this thought awaken the negligent! You that draw back from painful, displeasing, suffering duties, and will put off men's souls with ineffectual formalities; do you think this is an honourable usage of Christ's Spouse? Are the souls of men thought meet by God to see His face, and live for ever in His glory, and are they not worthy of your utmost cost and labour? Do you think so basely of the Church of God, as if it deserved not the best of your care and help? Were you the keepers of sheep or swine, you might better let them go, and say, 'They be not worth the looking after;' and yet you would scarcely do so, if they were your own. But dare you say so by the souls of men?"

I read page after page of such solemn pleadings, interrupted now and again by his stifled heart-sobs, till my voice fails from emotion and sympathy, my eyes grow dim, and my tears mingle with his as we weep together—he, from the smitings of a very tender conscience towards God, and I, simply and only because I love him, and want to share his grief. Not for a moment do I believe there is any real cause for his self-upbraidings, but as that is a matter between himself and his God, I can only comfort him by my quiet sympathy. "The burden of the Lord" is upon his heart, and He lets him feel the awful weight of it for a time, that "the excellency of the power may be of God," and not of man. "Who teacheth like Him?"

In the same small room occurred also a touching little scene which I have described in *Ten Years After!* but which cannot be left out of this history, for it has a right to a place here, revealing, as it does, the tenderness of my beloved's heart, while he still consistently put "first things first". He was constantly away from home fulfilling preaching engagements of long or short duration, and these frequent absences were a trial to me, though I kept faithfully to my purpose of never hindering him in his work. But I remember how, while waiting for his return, late at night, from some distant place, I would tire of the cramped space of the tiny parlour, and pace up and down the narrow passage—dignified by the name of a "hall"—watching and listening for the dear footstep I knew so well, and praying—oh, how fervently! —that the Lord would care for his precious life, and avert all danger from him as he travelled back by road or rail. I can even now recall the thrill of joy and thankfulness with which I opened the door, and welcomed him home.

One morning, after breakfast, when he was preparing to go out on one of his long journeys, the room looked so bright and cosy that a sudden depression seized me at the thought of its emptiness when he was gone, and the many anxious hours that must pass before I should see him again. Some tears would trickle down my cheeks, in spite of my efforts to restrain them. Seeing me look so sad, he said, very gently, "Wifey, do you think that, when any of the children of Israel brought a lamb to the Lord's altar as an offering to Him, they stood and wept over it when they had seen it laid there?" "Why, no!" I replied, startled by his strange question, "certainly not; the Lord would not have been pleased with an offering reluctantly given." "Well," said he, tenderly, "don't you see, you are giving me to God, in letting me go to preach the gospel to poor sinners, and do you think He likes to see you cry over your sacrifice?" Could ever a rebuke have been more sweetly and graciously given? It sank deep into my heart, carrying comfort with it, and, thenceforward, when I parted with him, the tears were scarcely ever allowed to show themselves, or if a stray one or two dared to run over the boundaries, he would say, "What! crying over your lamb, wifey!" and this reminder would quickly dry them up, and bring a smile in their place.

Ah, sweetheart! was there ever one like thee? These were the days of early married life, it is true, when love was young, and temper tranquil, and forbearance an easy task, but "the wife of thy youth" can testify that, with thee, these lovely things of good report strengthened rather than diminished as time went on, and that, during all the forty years she knew and loved thee, thou wert the most tender, gracious, and indulgent of husbands, ruling with perfect love and gentleness, maintaining the Divinely-ordained position of "the head of the wife, even as Christ is the Head of the Church", yet permitting her heart and hand to influence and share in every good word and work.

And now that I am parted from thee, not for a few days only, as in that long-ago time, but "until the day break, and the shadows flee away", I think I hear again thy loving voice saying, "Don't cry over your lamb, wifey," as I try to give thee up ungrudgingly to God— not without tears—ah, no! that is not possible, but with that full surrender of the heart which makes the sacrifice acceptable in His sight.

*   *   *

An extraordinary incident occurred in this early period of our history. One Saturday evening, my dear husband was deeply perplexed by the difficulties presented by a text on which he desired to preach the next morning. It was in Psalm cx. 3: "Thy people shall be willing in the day of Thy power, in the beauties of holiness from the womb of the morning: Thou hast the dew of Thy youth;" and, with his usual painstaking preparation, he consulted all the Commentaries he then possessed, seeking light from the Holy Spirit upon their words and his own thoughts, but, as it seemed, in vain. I was as much distressed as he was, but I could not help him in such an emergency. At least, I thought I could not; but the Lord had a great favour in store for me, and used me to deliver His servant out of his serious embarrassment. He sat up very late, and was utterly worn out and dispirited, for all his efforts to get at the heart of the text were unavailing. I advised him to retire to rest, and soothed him by suggesting that, if he would try to sleep then, he would probably in the morning feel quite refreshed, and able to study to better purpose. "If I go to sleep now, wifey, will you wake me very early, so that I may have plenty of time to prepare?" With my loving assurance that I would watch the time for him, and call him soon enough, he was satisfied, and, like a trusting, tired child, he laid his head upon the pillow, and slept soundly and sweetly at once.

By-and-by, a wonderful thing happened. During the first dawning hours of the Sabbath, I heard him talking in his sleep, and roused myself to listen attentively. Soon, I realized that he was going over the subject of the verse which had been so obscure to him, and was giving a clear and distinct exposition of its meaning, with much force and freshness. I set myself, with almost trembling joy, to understand and follow all that he was saying, for I knew that, if I could but seize and remember the salient points of the discourse, he would have no difficulty in developing and enlarging upon them. Never preacher had a more eager and anxious hearer! What if I should let the precious words slip? I had no means at hand of "taking notes", so, like Nehemiah, "I prayed to the God of Heaven," and asked that I might receive and retain the thoughts which He had given to His servant in his sleep, and which were so singularly entrusted to my keeping. As I lay, repeating over and over again the chief points I wished to remember, my happiness was very great in anticipation of his surprise and delight on awaking, but I had kept vigil so long, cherishing my joy, that I must have been overcome with slumber just when the usual time for rising came, for he awoke with a frightened start, and seeing the tell-tale clock, said, "Oh, wifey, you said you would wake me very early, and now see the time! Oh, why did you let me sleep? What shall I do? What shall I do?" "Listen, beloved," I answered; and I told him all I had heard. "Why! that's just what I wanted," he exclaimed; "that is the true explanation of the whole verse! And you say I preached it in my sleep?" "It is wonderful," he repeated again and again, and we both praised the Lord for so remarkable a manifestation of His power and love. Joyfully my dear one went down to his study, and prepared this God-given sermon, and it was delivered that same morning, April 13, 1856, at New Park Street Chapel. It can be found and read in Vol. II of the sermons (No. 74), and its opening paragraph gives the dear preacher's own account of the difficulty he experienced in dealing with the text. Naturally, he refrained from telling the congregation the special details which I have here recorded, but, many years after, he told the tale to his students at one of their ever-to-be-remembered Friday afternoon gatherings, and some of them still keep it fresh in their memories.

About this time, I recall a visit to Stambourne which I paid with my dear husband. I saw, and loved at first sight, the dear old grandfather, so proud of "the child" who had grown into a great and gracious preacher. How kindly he received his grandson's wife! With what tender, old-fashioned courtesy he cared for her! Everything about the place was then exactly as my beloved has described it earlier in this work; nothing had been altered. The old Manse was still standing, though not as upright as in its youth; the ivy grew inside the parlour, the old flowered chintz curtains still hung in their places, and the floor of the best bed-chamber where we slept was as "anxious to go out of the window" as ever; indeed, a watchful balancing of one's self was required to avoid a stumble or a fall. It was all very quaint, but very delightful, because of so many precious memories to him who had lived there. The occasion of our visit was the anniversary, either of the meeting-house, or the revered Pastor's ministry, and the house was crowded with visitors, and unremitting hospitality seemed the order of the day. How delighted and interested the home folks and neighbours all were, and how much loving fuss was made over the young Pastor and his wife! It was charming to see him in the midst of his own people. He was just "the child" again, the joy of the old man's heart; but when he preached, and the power of God's Spirit burned in his words, and he fed the people to the full, the grandfather's bliss must have been a foretaste of the joys of Heaven.

For my part, I had a considerable share of petting and kind attention, and but one black drop in my cup of pleasure. This I mean literally; I was enjoying a large cup of tea, and thinking how good and refreshing it was on a hot day, when, as the bottom of the cup was becoming visible, I saw, to my horror, a great spider—my special detestation—dead, of course, his black body swollen to a huge size, and his long legs describing a wheel-like circle in the remaining fluid. And I had been drinking the boiled juice of this monster! Oh, the disgust of it! Alas! that we can remember the evil, and let go the good! My beloved's *sermon* is forgotten; but the spider has the power to make me feel "creepy" even at this moment!

*　　　*　　　*

I make a passing reference to the birth of our twin-boys, in order to contradict emphatically a story, supposed to be very witty, which was circulated extensively, and believed in universally, not only at the time it was told, but through all the following years. It was said that my dear husband received the news of the addition to his household while he was preaching, and that he immediately communicated the fact to his congregation, adding in a serio-comic way—

> "Not more than others I deserve,
> But God has given me more."

I am sorry to say there are persons, still living, who declare that they were present at the service, and heard him say it!

Now the truth is, that the boys were born on *Saturday* morning, September 20, 1856, and my dear husband never left the house that day; nor, so far as I know, did he ever preach on the seventh day at any time, so the statement at once falls to the ground disproved. But I think I have discovered how the legend was manufactured. Looking through the sermons preached near to this date, I find that, on Thursday evening, September 25—five days after the event referred to— Mr. Spurgeon delivered a discourse on behalf of the Aged Pilgrims' Friend Society, and in the course of it made the following remarks: "When we take our walks abroad, and see the poor, he must be a very thankless Christian who does not lift up his eyes to Heaven, and praise his God thus—

> 'Not more than others I deserve,
> But God has given me more.'

If we were all made rich alike, if God had given us all abundance, we should never know the value of His mercies; but He puts the poor side by side with us, to make their trials, like a dark shadow, set forth the brightness which He is pleased to give to others in temporal matters."

I have no doubt that some facetious individual, present at this Thursday evening service, and being aware of the babies' advent, on hearing these lines repeated, pounced upon them as the nucleus of an attractive story, linked the two facts in his own mind, and then proclaimed them to the world as an undivided verity! Most of the stories told of my dear husband's jocoseness *in the pulpit* were "stories" in the severe sense of the word; or possessed just so small a modicum of truth internally that the narrators were able, by weaving a network of exaggeration and romance around them, to make a very presentable and alluring fiction. It was one of the penalties of his unique position and gifts that, all through his life, he had to bear the cross of cruel misrepresentation and injustice. Thank God, that is all left behind for ever!

Though I am quite certain that the lines in question were not quoted by my beloved in public in reference to the double blessing God gave to us, I should scarcely be surprised if he made use of them when speaking to friends in private. If his heart were full of joy and gratitude, it would be sure to bubble over in some child-like and natural fashion. I have quite recently received a letter from a lady in the country, telling me of her visit to an old man—an ex-policeman, named Coleman—who, though bedridden, never tires of relating his memories of Mr. Spurgeon in those early days. He was stationed at New Park Street Chapel, on special duty, when the crowds came to hear "the boy-preacher", and he delights to tell how, after a short while, the street became so blocked that the chapel-gates had to be closed, and the people admitted a hundred at a time. "Ah!" said he, "he was a dear, good young man, he did not make *himself* anything; he would shake hands with anyone, he would give me such a grip, and leave half-a-crown in my hand; he knew that we policemen had a rub to get along on our pay. I know there were many he helped with their rent. *He did look pleased, that Sunday morning, when he said, 'Coleman, what do you think? God has blessed me with two sons!'* I used to go in and sit just inside the door, and get a feast for my soul from his discourses. I shall see him again soon, I hope."

Of course, this little story lacks the piquancy and sparkle of the former one; but it has the advantage of being *true*.

There was one other notable time in the front parlour. It recurs to me, at this moment, as the first falling of that black shadow of sorrow which the Lord saw fit to cast over our young and happy lives. It was again a Sabbath evening. I lay on a couch under the window, thinking of my dear one who had gone to preach his first sermon at the Surrey Music Hall, and praying that the Lord would bless his message to the assembled thousands. It was just a month since our children were born, and I was dreaming of all sorts of lovely possibilities and pleasures, when I heard a carriage stop at the gate. It was far too early for my husband to come home, and I wondered who my unexpected visitor could be. Presently, one of the deacons was ushered into the room, and I saw at once, from his manner, that something unusual had happened. I besought him to tell me all quickly, and he did so, kindly, and with much sympathy; and he kneeled by the couch, and prayed that we might have grace and strength to bear the terrible trial which had so suddenly come upon us. But how thankful I was when he went away! I wanted to be alone, that I might cry to God in this hour of darkness and death! When my beloved was brought home, he looked a wreck of his former self—an hour's agony of mind had changed his whole appearance and bearing. The night that ensued was one of weeping, and wailing, and indescribable sorrow. He refused to be comforted. I thought the morning would never break; and when it did come, it brought no relief.

The Lord has mercifully blotted out from my mind most of the details of the time of grief which followed, when my beloved's anguish was so deep and violent that reason seemed to totter on her throne, and we sometimes feared he would never preach again. It was truly "the valley of the shadow of death" through which we then walked, and, like poor Christian, we here "sighed bitterly", for the pathway was so dark "that, ofttimes, when we lifted up our foot to set forward, we knew not where or upon what we should set it next!"

It was in the garden of a house belonging to one of the deacons, in the suburbs of Croydon, whither my beloved had been taken in hope that the change and quiet would be beneficial, that the Lord was pleased to restore his mental equilibrium, and unloose the bars which had kept his spirit in darkness. We had been walking together, as usual—he, restless and anguished; I, sorrowful and amazed, wondering what the end of these things would be—when, at the foot of the steps which gave access to the house, he stopped suddenly, and turned to me, and with the old sweet light in his eyes (ah! how grievous had been its absence!), he said, "Dearest, how foolish I have been! Why! what does it matter what becomes of me, if the Lord shall but be glorified?"—and he repeated, with eagerness and intense emphasis, Philippians ii. 9–11: "Wherefore God also hath highly exalted Him, and given Him a Name which is above every name; that at the Name of Jesus every knee should bow, of things in Heaven, and things in earth, and things under the earth; and that every tongue should confess that Jesus Christ is Lord, to the glory of God the Father." "If Christ be exalted," he said—and his face glowed with holy fervour —"let Him do as He pleases with me; my one prayer shall be, that I may die to self, and live wholly for Him and for His honour. Oh, wifey, I see it all now! Praise the Lord with me!"

In that moment his fetters were broken, the captive came forth from his dungeon, and rejoiced in the light of the Lord. The Sun of righteousness arose once more upon him, with healing in His wings. But he carried the scars of that conflict to his dying day, and never afterwards had he the physical vigour and strength which he possessed before passing through that fierce trial. Verily, it was a thorny path by which the Lord led him. Human love would have protected him at any cost from an ordeal so terrible, and suffering so acute, but God's love saw the end from the beginning, and "He never makes a mistake." Though we may not, at the time, see His purpose in the afflictions which He sends us, it will be plainly revealed when the light of eternity falls upon the road along which we have journeyed.

*   *   *

While staying at Mr. Winsor's hospitable home, where he so kindly received and sheltered us in the time of our trouble, it was decided that the babies should be there dedicated to the Lord, and His service. So, when our dear patient seemed sufficiently recovered to take part in the observance, a goodly number of friends gathered together, and we had a happy meeting for prayer and praise. Full details I am unable to give; the only photograph which my memory retains is that of the two little creatures being carried round the large room— after the dedicatory prayers were offered—to be admired, and kissed, and blessed. What choice mercies, what special favours, their dear father asked for them then, I do not remember; but the Lord has never forgotten that prayer, and the many petitions which followed it. He not only heard, but has been answering all through the years of their lives, and with the most abounding blessing since He saw fit to make them fatherless! No ceremonial was observed, no drops of "holy water" fell on the children's brows; but in that room, that evening, as truly as in the house, "by the farther side of Jordan", in the days gone by, our infants were brought to Christ the Lord "that He would touch them"; and it is not now a matter of faith, so much as of sight, that "He took them up in His arms, put His hands upon them, and blessed them".

Ah, me! it is not so many years ago since the elder of those twin-boys brought his firstborn son to "Westwood", and my beloved, in one of those tender outpourings of the heart which were so natural to him, gave the child to God; and, not many months afterwards —*God answered the prayer, and took him to Himself!* One of the brightest, bonniest babies ever seen, he was the delight and expectation of our hearts; but the gift was claimed suddenly, and the child, who was to have done, according to our ideas, so much service on earth, went to sing God's praises with the angels! I wonder, sometimes, whether the little ransomed spirit met and welcomed his warrior grandfather on the shores of the Glory-land!

"On a night which time will never erase from my memory, large numbers of my congregation were scattered, many of them wounded and some killed, by the malicious act of wicked men. Strong amid danger, I battled against the storm; nor did my spirit yield to the overwhelming pressure while my courage could reassure the wavering, or confirm the bold; but when, like a whirlwind, the destruction was overpast, when the whole of its devastation was visible to my eye, who can conceive the anguish of my sad spirit? I refused to be comforted; tears were my meat by day, and dreams my terror by night. I felt as I had never felt before. . . . My mind lay, like a wreck upon the sand, incapable of its usual motion. I was in a strange land, and a stranger in it. My Bible, once my daily food, was but a hand to lift the sluices of my woe. . . . Then came 'the slander of many'—barefaced fabrications, libellous insinuations, and barbarous accusations. These alone might have scooped out the last drop of consolation from my cup of happiness; but the worst had come to the worst, and the utmost malice of the enemy could do no more. Lower they cannot sink who are already in the nethermost depths.

On a sudden, like a flash of lightning from the sky, my soul returned to me. The burning lava of my brain cooled in an instant. The throbbings of my brow were still; the cool wind of comfort fanned my cheek, which had been scorched in the furnace. . . . On wings of a dove, my spirit mounted to the stars—yea, beyond them. Whither did it wing its flight, and where did it sing its song of gratitude? It was at the feet of Jesus, whose Name had charmed its fears, and placed an end to its mourning. The Name—the precious Name of Jesus—was like Ithuriel's spear, bringing back my soul to its own right and happy state. I was a man again, and what is more, a believer. The garden in which I stood became an Eden to me, and the spot was then most solemnly consecrated in my restored consciousness. . . . Never since the day of my conversion had I known so much of His infinite excellence, never had my spirit leaped with such unutterable delight. Scorn, tumult, and woe seemed less than nothing for His sake. I girded up my loins to run before His chariot, I began to shout forth His glory, for my soul was absorbed in the one idea of His glorious exaltation and Divine compassion.

Thus is the thought of the love of Jesus, in His delivering grace, most indelibly impressed upon my memory; and the fact that this experience is to me the most memorable crisis of my life, must be my apology for narrating it."—C. H. S., in *The Saint and his Saviour*, 1857.

Chapter 30

The Great Catastrophe at the
Surrey Gardens Music Hall

MANY of my friends are unacquainted with the transactions of the early years of my ministry in London, for a whole generation has passed away since then, and the mass of those who are with me now know little of "the brave days of old". Hence the necessity of telling the story, that later sympathizers and fellow-labourers may learn by what a wonderful way the Lord has led us. To return to New Park Street Chapel, greatly enlarged as it was during the time of our first sojourn at Exeter Hall, resembled the attempt to put the sea into a tea-pot. We were more inconvenienced than ever. To turn many hundreds away from the doors, was the general if not the universal necessity, and those who gained admission were but little better off, for the packing was dense in the extreme, and the heat something terrible even to remember. My enemies continued to make my name more and more widely known, by means of pamphlets, caricatures, and letters in the papers, which all tended to swell the crowd. Matters reached a crisis in the Spring of 1856, and at a church-meeting, held on May 26 in that year, two resolutions were passed, the first intended to meet the immediately pressing need of a larger meeting-place for our great congregation, and the second looking further ahead, and providing for the requirements of the future. The official record is as follows:

"Resolved—That arrangements be made as early as possible for this church to worship at Exeter Hall on the Sabbath evenings during the Summer months.

Resolved—That the male members of this church be called together, as speedily as possible, to consult as to the best means of providing better accommodation for the vast crowds who are anxious to hear the gospel in connection with the ministry of our Pastor."

Accordingly, services were held at New Park Street Chapel on the Sabbath mornings from June 8 to August 24, and in the evenings at Exeter Hall, but this plan was very inconvenient; and, therefore, in August, a fund was commenced to provide for the erection of a larger house of prayer, the first meeting in aid of that object being held at the house of "Father Olney". Meanwhile, the proprietors of Exeter Hall intimated that they were unable to let that building continuously to one congregation. Although we paid for the use of it, it was but natural that others should think that the Baptists were monopolizing a hall which pertained to all denominations. I felt this to be just, and began to look about for another shelter. It was an anxious time, for friends feared that it would be long before we could build a house of our own; but the Lord had prepared for us a place where we sojourned for three years—the Music Hall of the Royal Surrey Gardens.

Very curious is the story of the Surrey Gardens. Everybody has heard of the elephant and other animals which were to be seen at Exeter Change, near Waterloo Bridge. Mr. Cross, the proprietor of that exhibition, removed his menagerie, in 1831, to the Surrey Gardens. There were fountains, and caves, and summer-houses, a lake of three and a half acres, pleasant walks and lawns, and all the usual paraphernalia of public gardens. In Dr. Montgomery's *History of Kennington*, we read: "Perhaps the most remarkable fact, for temperance folk, is that the proprietors of the Gardens never made application for a licence to sell drink. It was started and made a success without the sale of intoxicants. This is a noteworthy fact. I do not know what happened in later years, but during the time of Mr. Cross, up to 1844, no licence was ever applied for. The hours kept were early. At the latest, in the middle of Summer, the Gardens closed at 10 p.m., and in the Autumn at 7 p.m. Our Queen, when she was quite a little girl, came here with the Duchess of Kent, and was shown over the Gardens by Mr. Warwick."

When I first came to London, the Zoological Gardens were a very respectable and quiet resort, but few persons availed themselves of them. The age which could be content with quiet amusements, free from loose associations, was passing away, and giving place to a generation which looked for more flavour in its recreation. The Gardens were kept up in part by subscription from families in the neighbourhood, and partly by displays of fireworks. The affair did not pay in that form, so a company was formed to continue the zoological collection, and add thereto the far greater attraction of the popular concerts of M. Jullien. A very fine hall was erected, which had three galleries, and would accommodate from six to ten thousand people. I cannot speak exactly as to numbers, nor correct my estimate by personal inspection, for no vestige of the hall is now remaining. I recollect going with William Olney to see the place, and though we felt it to be a venturesome experiment to attempt to preach in so large a building, we had faith in God, and dared to hope that He would bless an earnest attempt to proclaim the gospel to the multitude. One or two of our good members thought it wrong to go to what they persisted in calling "the devil's house". I did not agree with their hard names, but encouraged them to stop away, and not to violate their consciences. At the same time, I bade them not to discourage either their brethren or me, for we were willing to go even into "the devil's house" to win souls for Christ. We did not go to the Music Hall because we thought that it was a good thing to worship in a building usually devoted to amusement, but because we had no other place to go to.

On October 6, a special church-meeting was held, for the purpose which is thus recorded in our Minutes: "This meeting was convened to consider the propriety of engaging the use of the large hall in the Royal Surrey Gardens for our Sabbath evening worship, the directors of Exeter Hall having refused the church the further use of that place. After several of the brethren had expressed their concurrence, it was resolved that the Music Hall of the Royal Surrey Gardens be engaged for one month, commencing the third Sabbath in October."

When the appointed day arrived our anticipations ran high, but none of us dreamed of that which lay before us. Much prayer was offered, and I looked forward hopefully, but yet felt overweighted with a sense of responsibility, and filled with a mysterious premonition of some great trial shortly to befall me. In the Preface to Vol. II of *The Pulpit Library*, I wrote: "The first sermon in this volume—'Prove Me now', Malachi iii. 10—was preached at New Park Street Chapel in the morning of that Lord's-day on which the fatal accident occurred at the Surrey Gardens Music Hall. By many readers it will now be perused with curiosity, but the preacher himself reviews each sentence with thrilling emotion. Its subject was entirely suggested by the enlarged sphere of labour he was about to occupy, and the *then* unprecedented number of souls he was expecting ere nightfall to address. If any passage seems to forestall the calamity, he can only say it is genuine—a transcript from the reporter's notes. The Christian reader can understand many sore conflicts between the heart's feelings and its faith; yet no one *can* know, as the author's own soul, how, amidst fightings without and fears within, he was enabled to proclaim the strongest confidence in God. He has made that proof, which he counselled others to make, of the Divine faithfulness; and as to the result (notwithstanding a parenthesis of grievous tribulation), he dares to speak with abundant gratitude."

The sermon itself contained the following almost prophetic

passage: "Perhaps I may be called to stand where the thunder-clouds brew, where the lightnings play, and tempestuous winds are howling on the mountain-top. Well, then, I am born to prove the power and majesty of our God; amidst dangers, He will inspire me with courage; amidst toils, He will make me strong. . . . This old Bible speaks to me to-day. This sword of the Spirit hath been thrust into many of your hearts; and though they were hard as adamant, it has split them in sunder. I have wielded it in your midst as God's soldier, and some of you have had sturdy spirits broken in pieces by this good old Jerusalem blade. But we shall be gathered together, to-night, where an unprecedented mass of people will assemble, perhaps from idle curiosity, to hear the Word of God; and His voice cries in my ears, 'Prove Me now.' Many a man has come, during my ministrations, armed to his very teeth, and having on a coat of mail, yet hath this tried weapon cleft him in twain, and pierced to the dividing asunder of the joints and marrow. 'Prove Me now,' says God, 'go and prove Me before blasphemers; go and prove Me before reprobates, before the vilest of the vile, and the filthiest of the filthy; go and "prove Me now." Lift up that life-giving cross, and let it again be exhibited; into the regions of *death*, go and proclaim the Word of *life*; into the most plague-smitten parts of the city, go and carry the waving censer of the incense of a Saviour's merits, and prove now whether He is not able to stay the plague, and remove the disease.'

But what does God say to the church? 'You have proved Me afore-time, you have attempted great things; though some of you were faint-hearted, and said, "We should not have ventured," others of you had faith, and proved Me. I say again, "Prove Me now."' See what God can do, *just when a cloud is falling on the head of him whom God has raised up to preach to you*, go and prove Him now; and see if He will not pour you out such a blessing as ye had not even dreamed of, see if He will not give you a Pentecostal blessing. 'Prove Me now.' Why should we be unbelieving? Have we one thing to make us so? We are weak; what of that? Are we not strongest in our God when we are weakest in ourselves? We are fools, it is said, and so we are, we know it; but He maketh fools to confound the wise. We are base, but God hath chosen the base things of the world. We are unlearned—

'We know no schoolman's subtle arts,'

yet we glory in infirmity when Christ's power doth rest upon us. *Let them represent us as worse than we are;* let them give us the most odious character that hath ever been given to man, we will bless them, and

20. Exeter Hall in the Strand accommodated Spurgeon's hearers on Sunday evenings for two periods during 1855 and 1856

21. *The Music Hall in the Royal Surrey Gardens was erected for popular concerts, but for 3 years (1856–1859) provided a home for the New Park Street congregation and the ever-increasing crowds who wished to hear the young preacher*

22. [opposite] *Penned five days after the great disaster at the Music Hall this remarkable letter has the stamp of the ordeal through which Spurgeon had passed. (This reproduction is considerably smaller than the original.)*

Mr Winton's
Beulah House
Croydon
Friday

Dear Mother,

I could not write till now for my poor brain was lot with grief — but it is all right now — all right —

I shall rest for some days & then at it again.

God is on my side why should I fear

I am not dismayed for God shall help me

Dear Susie don't write she is so ill — The Doctor has been to day & says she is very, very ill — Then says but not seriously —

Do not mention the accident in the Gardens to me at present, but pray for me —

I am now almost restored to spirits, but I shall never forget

His burning furnace.

I will thrash the devil yet — I will seek to be yet more valiant for God.

The Lord nerved me that evening & no unaided man in the universe could have been as brave, as calm, as fearless as I by God's grace —

Ah Mother, this

is no small honour to be maligned for Jesus —

Tremble not I do not — In God's name I say to timid friends & boisterous foes my word is On still On — for Christ & for his truth —

My most fervent love to you & my dear father — all

your much tried son
Charles

23. *Surrey Gardens Music Hall with its three galt*

as probably capable of holding up to 10,000 people

24. *The Spurgeons' second home, "Helensburgh House", Nightingale Lane, Clapham—"a pretty and rural, but comparatively unknown region, and our delight in the change and interest it afforded was unbounded"*

25. *Charles and Thomas with their mot*

26. *Husband and wife in the garden at "Helensburgh House"*

27. *Father and the twins*

28. *Spurgeon with his friend and publisher, Joseph Passmore*

wish them well. What though the weapon be a stone, or even the jawbone of an ass, if the Lord direct it? 'Do you not know,' say some, 'what wise men say?' Yes, we do; but we can read their oracles backwards. Their words are the offspring of their wishes. We know *who* has instructed them, and we know he was a liar from the beginning. O fools, and slow of heart! do ye shrink from the truth, or do ye shrink from obloquy and disgrace? In either case, ye have not the love to your Master that ye should have. If ye be brave men and true, go on and conquer. *Fear not, ye shall yet win the day;* God's holy gospel shall yet shake the earth once more. The banner is lifted up, and multitudes are flocking to it; the Pharisees have taken counsel together, the learned stand confounded, the sages are baffled, they know not what to do. The little one, God has made great; and He that was despised, is exalted. Let us trust Him, then. He will be with us even to the end, for He has said, 'Lo, I am with you always, even unto the end of the world.' "

*　　　*　　　*

I can never forget that terrible night. Having preserved all the pamphlets and papers connected with "the great catastrophe", I have just now perused them in order to write this memorial. I have thereby revived within myself much that is painful; but much more that causes me to praise the name of the Lord. When I was nearing the house in Manor Street, which was the office of the company, and was to serve me as a private entrance, I was exceedingly surprised to find the streets thronged for a long distance. With difficulty I reached the door. There was a long private road from the entrance of the Gardens to the Music Hall itself, and this appeared to be filled up with a solid block of people, who were unable to get into the building. I felt overawed, and was taken with that faintness which was, in my youth, the usual fore-runner of every sermon. Still, I rallied, and was duly escorted to my pulpit in the midst of a dense throng. Here I was to pass through the greatest ordeal of my life.

But I will now give way to Dr. Campbell, then the Editor of *The British Banner*, for his is the description of an eye-witness, and of an impartial, self-possessed critic. He wrote: "Ecclesiastically viewed, Sunday last (October 19th) was one of the most eventful nights that have descended upon our metropolis for generations. On that occasion, the largest, most commodious, and most beautiful building erected for public amusement in this mighty city was taken possession of for the purpose of proclaiming the gospel of salvation. There, where, for a long period, wild beasts had been exhibited, and wilder men had been accustomed to congregate, in countless multitudes, for idle pastime, was gathered together the largest audience that ever met in any edifice in these isles, to listen to the voice of a Nonconformist minister. The spectacle, of its kind, was one of the most imposing, magnificent, and awful ever presented to the human eye. No adequate idea of it can be conveyed by description; to be understood, it must have been seen; and they who beheld it received an impression which no time will ever obliterate. The sight of 10,000 or 12,000 people, more or fewer, assembled to listen to the Word of the living God, in such a place, at such a time, and addressed by a man with a voice of such power and compass that the remotest might hear with ease and pleasure, was sufficient to excite intense joy in the hearts of all good men who witnessed it; nor is it extravagant to say that it was enough to wake the attention of the angelic world!

But, in proportion to the joy and the hope thus inspired, were the sorrow and disappointment arising from the terrible catastrophe by which the very first service was attended and cut short! At the most solemn moment of the occasion, the wicked rose in their strength, like a whirlwind, sin entered, followed by terror, flight, disorder, and death! The entire city has been filled with astonishment! From the cellar to the palace, the events of that dreadful night have been the theme of eager discourse. In the squares, the streets, the lanes, and alleys, as well as in the workshops and counting-houses, and all the chief places of concourse, it has been, through each successive day, the one great object of thought and converse.

Imagination, as usual, has been active in the work of exaggeration, and malice in that of mendacity. At one time, the beautiful building has been wrapped in flames, and reduced to ashes! At another, the roof has fallen in, and entombed 10,000 people! The human mind, voracious of the tragical and the marvellous, has greedily devoured even the most preposterous accounts. The more horrible, the more credible and the more welcome; and the public press, as is its wont, has not been backward to pander to the morbid appetite of the excited millions. It has lied as well as exaggerated, most fearfully! Fancy pictures have been drawn, suited to 'the chamber of horrors'. Having ourselves not only witnessed the spectacle, but been in the very vortex, we are able to speak from observation touching the various points which the public are mainly concerned to know, and every way able to distinguish between truth and error. We, therefore, feel in duty bound to clear away the bewildering mist and darkness which have gathered around the character and conduct of honourable men. We were among the very first to enter the building, where we took up a position before the pulpit, which had been erected in front of the orchestra, so that we had a perfect command of the entire house, hearing and seeing everything of importance to be either heard or seen. The simplest statement of facts as they occurred will form the best antidote to the flood of misrepresentation and falsehood which has welled forth from a portion of the metropolitan press.

The house, considering its magnitude, might be said to be very speedily filled, leaving, it is supposed, an equal number outside unable to gain admission. The process of packing the hall, as may be presumed, was gone about in a somewhat tumultuous manner. The people were deeply excited by the violent struggle which had to be encountered and overcome at the doors to obtain an entrance, which naturally led, after admission, to rapid movements in every direction where there seemed a probability of gaining a seat, or, at least, standing-room. The aspect of the hall during this period was, of course, anything but like that which obtains in places of regular worship, and somewhat fitted to do violence to the sober spirit of orderly people; but, certainly, it would have borne a very favourable comparison with the gatherings of the huge religious anniversary meetings at Exeter Hall, or any other vast place of general concourse. It was, 'Every man for himself;' and, as compared with the monster meetings of Whitefield on Kennington Common or Moorfields, in the High Churchyard, Glasgow, and the Orphan House Park, Edinburgh, so far as history has testified, there was nothing to complain of on the score of tumultuous levity.

The hall having been filled in every part, things began to assume a perfectly settled aspect. The commotion ceased, and the air of the assembly was every whit as tranquil as that of our great philanthropic or even worshipping assemblies. The hall being thus gorged, Mr. Spurgeon considerately and wisely commenced the service about ten minutes before the appointed time, surrounded by a large number of most respectable people, composed of his officers and flock, who led the psalmody. After a few words of a highly pertinent character, he briefly offered prayer, and then gave out a thoroughly Evangelical hymn, with a force, a feeling, and an unction seldom witnessed in a worshipping assembly, and which threw an air of deep solemnity over the immense multitude by whom it was sung as with the voice of many waters. That hymn itself was an important proclamation of the gospel. The reading of the sacred Scriptures immediately followed, with a running comment, as is the preacher's custom. The Scripture was well chosen, and the exposition admirably appropriate, and such as was well fitted to impress even the most frivolous. There was no dry disquisition, no curious criticism, but an address directed to the hearts of the hearers, showing, from the first, that the speaker came strongly intent upon most important business, and that nothing was to be regarded short of its accomplishment.

The general prayer next followed, and here, too, the same pertinent and peculiar air was manifested. The one great motive which animated the preacher was, most obviously, the salvation of men. . . . This was the moment chosen by the emissaries of darkness to spring the mine of mischief, which, in effect, resulted in manifold murder! To have made the attempt while the high praises of God were being sung, would have been certain failure. To have done so while a stream of eloquence was rolling on in the sermon, and all eyes open, would have been attended with no better success. Yes; and the inhuman miscreants—cunning as they were impious and cruel—knew it. They were obviously adepts in iniquity. They understood their business thoroughly. Their plans were skilfully formed, and executed with the precision of military science opening a masked battery. Just as the minds of the devout portion of the assembly were collected around the throne of the Great Eternal, far away from earth and its grovellings, abstracted, absorbed, prostrate, suppliant, and adoring, the fiendish conspiracy broke forth with the rapidity of lightning and the fury of a tempest! The effect was such as was anticipated and desired. To say it began with one or two cries of 'Fire!' as we view the matter, is wholly to misrepresent it. For our own part, we heard no such cries. Such, however, there doubtless were, but they were only signals. The thing bore the impress of a plan to which some hundreds of persons at least appeared to be parties. The mere cry of 'Fire!' would have produced more or less of a general commotion extending to all parts of the house, which was but slightly moved; whereas, the indescribable and terrible outbreak was limited to a large portion of people in a given locality surrounding the great entrance. The outbreak could be likened to nothing but the sudden bursting forth of an immense body of trained singers, or a vast reservoir of water, whose sluices were opened, or whose banks had given way. It is impossible that any cries of two or three individuals could ever have produced so sudden, so simultaneous, and so sustained a display of fear, horror, and consternation. We are strongly impressed with the conviction that the thing, from the adroitness of the performance, must have been well practised beforehand. So far as we could judge from appearances, the parties, or a portion of them, who led in the terrific uproar, also led in the rush, which appeared as an especial part of their infernal arrangement. Mr. Spurgeon, who instantly recovered from the horrible surprise with which he was overwhelmed, in the very act of prayer, of course saw in a moment that the alarm was false. There was no appearance whatever of fire, and the noble structure in no place gave any symptoms of fracture or rupture. His quick eye perceived in an instant the true origin of the movement, and he acted accordingly, adopting every method that seemed calculated to calm the tumult, and to reassure the assembly."

*   *   *

It may put the matter still more vividly before the reader, if I quote from a statement appended to a sermon, preached soon after the catastrophe, by the venerable Dr. Alexander Fletcher: "As early as five o'clock, thousands of persons were filling up the approaches to the Surrey Gardens. By five minutes after six, the hall was filled to overflow; it is supposed that not fewer than 12,000 persons were present, and many thousands were on the outside, and still as many more were unable to gain admittance even to the Gardens. While the service was being conducted in Mr. Spurgeon's usual way, during the second prayer, all of a sudden there were cries simultaneously, doubtless preconcerted, from all parts of the building, of 'Fire!' 'The galleries are giving way!' 'The place is falling!' the effect of which on the audience it is impossible to describe. Many hundreds of persons rushed towards the place of exit, at the risk of their own lives, and sacrificing those of their fellow-creatures. In vain did Mr. Spurgeon, with his stentorian voice and self-possession, assure the alarmed multitude that it was a *ruse* on the part of thieves and pickpockets; the people in the galleries rushed down, precipitating themselves almost headlong over, or breaking down the balustrade of the stairs, killing some and fearfully wounding others. Those who fell through force, or fainting, were trampled under foot, and several lives were lost in the *mêlée*. To make 'confusion worse confounded', it is also said that, as fast as one portion of the multitude made their exit, others from without entered. Mr. Spurgeon, who was ignorant of any of these fatal consequences, after a temporary lull, was persuaded to make an effort to preach; but, after one or two attempts, he found it impossible to proceed, owing to the noises which the swell-mobsmen continued to make. Wishing to get the people gradually out of the hall, he gave out a hymn, requesting the congregation to withdraw while it was being sung. He then pronounced the Benediction, and, at length, overcome by emotion, which he had long striven to repress, he was led from the platform in a state of apparent insensibility. The results of this dreadful panic are most calamitous and distressing. Seven lives have been sacrificed, and serious bodily injury inflicted upon a great number of persons."

[Spurgeon felt that it was impossible, under the circumstances, to say what he had prepared, but, notwithstanding the tumult, the people clamoured for him to go on preaching, so he spoke as follows—

"My friends, you bid me preach, but what shall I preach about? I am ready to do all I can, but, in the midst of all this confusion, what shall be my subject? May God's Holy Spirit give me a theme suited to this solemn occasion! My friends, there is a terrible day coming, when the terror and alarm of this evening shall be as nothing. That will be a time when the thunder and lightning and blackest darkness shall have their fullest power, when the earth shall reel to and fro beneath us, and when the arches of the solid heavens shall totter to their centre. The day is coming when the clouds shall reveal their wonders and portents, and Christ shall sit upon those clouds in glory, and shall call you to judgment. Many have gone away to-night, in the midst of this terrible confusion, and so shall it be on that great day. I can, however, believe that the results of that time of testing will show that there will be many—not a less proportion than those who now remain to those who have left—who will stand the ordeal even of that day. The alarm which has just arisen has been produced, in some measure, by that instinct which teaches us to seek self-preservation, but in the more numerous of the cases, it is not so much the dread of death which has influenced them, as 'the dread of something after death—the undiscovered country, from whose bourn no traveller returns'. 'Tis conscience that has made cowards of them. Many were afraid to stop here, because they thought, if they stayed, they might die, and then they would be damned. They were aware— and many of you are aware—that, if you were hurried before your Maker to-night, you would be brought there unshriven, unpardoned, and condemned. But what are your fears now to what they will be on that terrible day of reckoning of the Almighty, when the heavens shall shrink above you, and hell shall open her mouth beneath you? But know you not, my friends, that grace, sovereign grace, can yet save you? Have you never heard the welcome news that Jesus came into the world to save sinners? Even if you are the chief of sinners, believe that Christ died for you, and you shall be saved. Do you not know that you are lost and ruined, and that none but Jesus can do helpless sinners good? You are sick and diseased, but Jesus can heal you; and He will if you only trust Him. I thought of preaching to-night from the third chapter of Proverbs, at the 33rd verse: 'The curse of the Lord is in the house of the wicked: but He blesseth the habitation of the just.' I feel that, after what has happened, I cannot preach as I could have wished to do; I fear that you will have another alarm, and I would rather that some of you would seek to retire gradually, in order that no harm may be done to anyone."

Here there was a fresh disturbance; but after singing part of a hymn, comparative silence was obtained, and the preacher again attempted to begin his discourse: "Although, my hearers, you may suppose that there are fifty different classes of persons in the world, there are, in the eyes of God, but two. God knows nothing of any save the righteous and the unrighteous, the wicked and the just."

In the confusion that again ensued it was useless to try to preach, so Spurgeon said: "My brain is in a whirl, and I scarcely know where I am, so great are my apprehensions that many persons must have been injured by rushing out. I would rather that you retired gradually, and may God Almighty dismiss you with His blessing, and carry you in safety to your homes! If our friends will go out by the central doors, we will sing while they go, and pray that some good may, after all, come out of this great evil. Do not, however, be in a hurry. Let those nearest the door go first."]

*   *   *

All that I can remember of that awful night is the sight of a tumult, which I was then quite unable to understand. Even now it remains a mystery to me. I hope there was no concerted wickedness at the bottom of the sad event, though there may have been a love of mischief aiding at the first. We were all fresh to the place, and all more or less excited. I did my utmost to be calm, and to quiet the people, and I succeeded with the great mass of them, but away at the end of the building there was a something going on which I did not understand, while around the seated part of the hall there were rushes made by excited people again and again, for reasons quite incomprehensible to me. One can understand now, that those who had seen the accident on the staircase may have been trying to call attention to it, thinking it a strange thing that the service should have been continued after persons had been killed. Of this dread calamity I was unaware till, as I was led down faint from the pulpit, I heard a whisper of it. I know no more, for I lost almost all consciousness, and, amid the weeping and cries of many, I was carried by a private garden into the street, and taken home more dead than alive. There were seven corpses lying on the grass, and many have since told me how grievous was the sight. This I never saw, but what I had seen might have been sufficient to shatter my reason. It might well seem that the ministry which promised to be so largely influential was silenced for ever. There were persons who said so exultingly, but they knew not what they said. I was taken away to the house of a friend, early the following morning, and as I was assisted out of the carriage at Croydon, a working-man caught sight of me, and, in a frightened fashion, stammered out, "Why, sir!—it's Mr. Spurgeon, isn't it?" I answered, "Yes." "Then," he rejoined, "it must be his ghost, for, last night, I saw him carried out dead from the Surrey Gardens Music Hall!" I was not dead, thank God; but the bystanders might well have imagined that the terrible shock had killed me.

Of course there was an inquest; verdict, accidental death—on the whole, the only safe conclusion to arrive at. A fund was raised for the sufferers, and all was done that lay in the power of our people to help the injured. Our friends were crushed in spirit, but not driven from their faith or love, nor divided from their youthful minister. I was, for a short time, incapable of any mental effort. Who would not be? How great a trial to have a number of one's hearers killed or maimed! A word about the calamity, and even the sight of the Bible, brought from me a flood of tears, and utter distraction of mind.

During that time, I was not aware of the ferocious assaults which were made upon me by the public press; indeed, I heard no word of them until I was sufficiently recovered to bear them without injury. As we read of David, that they spake of stoning him, so was it with me. Here is a specimen of what was said by a popular daily paper, which I will not name, for it has long been of quite another mind, and most friendly to me:

"Mr. Spurgeon is a preacher who hurls damnation at the heads of his sinful hearers. Some men there are who, taking their precepts from Holy Writ, would beckon erring souls to a rightful path with fair words and gentle admonition; Mr. Spurgeon would take them by the nose, and bully them into religion. Let us set up a barrier to the encroachments and blasphemies of men like Spurgeon, saying to them, 'Thus far shalt thou come, but no further'; let us devise some powerful means which shall tell to the thousands who now stand in need of enlightenment—this man, in his own opinion, is a righteous Christian; but in ours, nothing more than a ranting charlatan. We are neither strait-laced nor Sabbatarian in our sentiments; but we would keep apart, widely apart, the theatre and the church; above all, would we place in the hand of every right-thinking man, a whip to scourge from society the authors of such vile blasphemies, as, on Sunday night, above the cries of the dead and the dying, and louder than the wails of misery from the maimed and suffering, resounded from the mouth of Spurgeon in the Music Hall of the Surrey Gardens."

Many other utterances were equally cruel and libellous. A gentleman applied to the magistrate at Lambeth, seeking an investigation by his Worship into the circumstances connected with the catastrophe, and into the necessity for a licence to use the Music Hall as a place of worship. He was not aware that, on the previous Saturday, the building had been licensed as a place for Dissenting worship. He stated that persons collecting money in an unlicensed place were liable to be treated as rogues and vagabonds, and went on to add that a further question might arise, as to whether the parties causing large congregations to assemble were not liable to a still graver charge. This liberal-minded person represented the mind of a considerable section whose thoughts of the preacher were bitterness itself. The magistrate, however, assured the applicant that the law permitted public buildings to be used as places of worship for temporary purposes.

The following article appeared in *The Saturday Review*,[1] October 25, 1856:

"MR. SPURGEON AT THE SURREY GARDENS.

If it be true, as has been said, that notables represent rather than create, public opinion, Mr. Spurgeon and his doings are worth a more serious consideration than their intrinsic value would justify. The manners of an age or people do not follow its literature—they produce it. Crebillon or Shaftesbury did not form the taste or principles of their contemporaries; Voltaire did not so much educate as embody his times; and, in like manner, Mr. Spurgeon does not create the state of feeling to which he owes his popularity. It is a melancholy reflection that such a personage is a notable at all. It is no new thing that there should be popular delusions; but we had flattered ourselves that we had outlived the days of religious, or so-called religious, epidemics. Yet the age of spirit-rapping and of Mr. Spurgeon—the times in which Dr. Cumming is an authority, and Joe Smith and Mr. Prince are prophets—cannot cast stones at any 'dark ages'. Whatever legitimate weapons, be they of argument or ridicule, can be employed to arrest

---

[1] Recalling this attack in *The Saturday Review*, W. P. Lockhart, an early friend of Spurgeon's, later wrote concerning the feeling that was stirred against the pastor of New Park Street: "One remembers that long years ago, on the occasion of some popular demonstration in London, his carriage was driven through the crowd, and when its occupant was recognized he was heartily hooted by the mob, and one remembers also the scornful notices of a portion of the Press, which drew from him one of the most striking things he ever uttered—"A true Christian is one who fears God and is hated by *The Saturday Review*."—P.

the progress of mere imposture, we hold to be justifiable. We should not deem Mr. Spurgeon entitled to the place which he at this moment occupies in public attention—and certainly we should not trouble ourselves with any reference to his proceedings—did we not consider him rather as a sign and a result than an original. His success is simply of the vulgarest and most commonplace type. Given a person of some natural talents, with matchless powers of acquired impudence, and a daring defiance of good taste, and often of common decency—and he will always produce an effect. Anybody who will give himself out as some great one, will find followers enough to accept his leadership. A charlatan will never be without dupes. The crowds who flock to the various Spurgeon conventicles are only of the class who would follow the bottle conjuror, or anyone who chose to advertise that he would fly from the Monument to the dome of St. Paul's. Mr. Spurgeon is perfectly aware that human nature is much the same now as it was five hundred years ago, and it is with humiliation that we concur in his estimate. His crowded congregations are part of his stock-in-trade. He hires Exeter Hall or the Surrey Gardens merely in the way of an advertisement. If he could have the Coliseum at Rome, it would be a safe investment. His scheme for building a conventicle to hold fifteen thousand persons is all in the way of business, just like the big shop, *toute la Rue du Coq,* in Paris.

All we can do is to warn the public; but we are afraid it will be to little purpose. *Populus vult decipi.* It is, we fear, scarcely more useless to caution people against joint-stock banks and public companies when there is a plethora of money, than seriously to hold up Mr. Spurgeon to the world as a very ordinary impostor. The only effectual remedy is, in the one case, to provide safe and honest investments for capital—in the other, to offer more healthful and rational counter-attractions. We have been accused, in some quarters, of recommending Sunday amusements in the place of religion. As a fact, we have done no such thing, for our arguments were all based on the compatibility of religious exercises with healthful and innocent recreation, and the policy of combining them. But if the question is between Sunday bands and Sunday doings of the Spurgeon character at the Surrey Gardens, by all means, we say, let the bands at least be admitted to un-restricted competition. We do not wish to silence Mr. Spurgeon; but, for the sake of the public safety, let there be a chance of thinning the crowds. Very judiciously, on a late occasion, we had fireworks simultaneously in the West End Parks, on Primrose Hill, and in the East of London; and we do not see why Mr. Spurgeon should have a monopoly of brazen instruments South of the Thames. Whitefield used to preach at fairs. In these days of open competition, we perceive no reason why this practice should not be inverted. The innovation would only be the substitution of one set of amusements for another—or, rather, an addition to our list of Sunday sports. Let religious people ask themselves whether this is not in fact the true way of putting the case. It is a profanation to religion to imagine that, as regards the crowds who flock to the Spurgeon show, there is any higher influence at work than the common love of excitement. Mr. Spurgeon's doings are, we believe, entirely discountenanced by his co-religionists. There is scarcely a Dissenting minister of any note who associates with him. We do not observe, in any of his schemes or building operations, the names, as trustees or the like, of any leaders in what is called the religious world. Nor can we attribute to mere envy the feelings with which Mr. Spurgeon is apparently regarded by those respectable persons who are his brethren in the Dissenting ministry. Somehow, it is generally felt that religion is not benefited by his abnormal proceedings. There is, at any rate, this most remarkable *differentia* between him and other revivalists—that he stands alone, or nearly so. The fact is an antecedent ground for grave suspicion and natural distrust.

This hiring of places of public amusement for Sunday preaching is a novelty, and a painful one. It looks as if religion were at its last shift. It is a confession of weakness rather than a sign of strength. It is not wrestling with Satan in his strongholds—to use the old earnest Puritan language—but entering into a very cowardly truce and alliance with the world. After all, Mr. Spurgeon only affects to be the Sunday Jullien. We are told of the profanity which must have been at the bottom of the clerical mind when the Church acted miracle-plays, and tolerated the Feast of the Ass; but the old thing reappears when popular preachers hire concert-rooms, and preach Particular Redemption in saloons reeking with the perfume of tobacco, and yet echoing with the chaste melodies of *Bobbing Around* and the valse from the *Traviata*. And where is this to end? If, as Mr. Spurgeon doubtless argued, Exeter Hall can be hired by a clergyman of the Establishment to read Mr. Caird's sermon, and if the enterprising divine who performed this notable feat was rewarded for it by the judicious Archbishop of Canterbury with a living of £500 per annum, why should not he hire the Surrey Gardens? Mr. Spurgeon has outbid Mr. Mansfield; but why should not somebody outbid Mr. Spurgeon? Or why should he be content with his present achievements? The Surrey Gardens affair was a great *coup*. The deplorable accident, in which seven people lost their lives, and scores were maimed, mutilated, or otherwise cruelly injured, Mr. Spurgeon only considers as an additional intervention of Providence in his favour. 'This event will, I trust, teach us the necessity of'—being sober, rational, and decent?—No—'having a building of our own.' Preach another crowd into a frenzy of terror; kill and smash a dozen or two more—and then the speculation will have succeeded.

Mr. Spurgeon, improving the occasion, is said to have remarked that 'this gathering had aroused Satan, and he would not allow the service to go on without endeavouring to interrupt it.' We do not profess that familiarity with Satan and his doings which is enjoyed by Mr. Spurgeon. Doubtless, he possesses more of Satan's confidence, and more knowledge of his character, than ordinary men; at least, with our estimate of the power of evil, we should judge so from this mode of dealing with the deplorable result of his vanity and cupidity. We certainly believe that Satan was busy enough on Sunday evening last. The reporters tell us that the publicans and pickpockets 'reaped a rich harvest' from the occasion. These are, at any rate, new fruits of a gospel ministry, and strange triumphs of the cross. Expostulation and advice are thrown away upon one who can act as Mr. Spurgeon is reported to have acted in the very presence of these unusual seals to his ministry. Yet it is always a public duty to show up selfishness and vanity; and we can only hope that it will prove in this instance to be a public benefit also."

*   *   *

Our church-book contains the following entry concerning the catastrophe; it shows the way in which this great affliction was viewed by our own friends: "Lord's-day, October 19, 1856. On the evening of this day, in accordance with the resolution passed at the church-meeting, October 6, the church and congregation assembled to hear our Pastor in the Music Hall of the Royal Surrey Gardens. A very large number of persons (about 7,000) were assembled on that occasion, and the service was commenced in the usual way, by singing, reading the Scriptures, and prayer. Just, however, after our Pastor had commenced his prayer, a disturbance was caused (as it is supposed, by some evil-disposed persons acting in concert), and the whole congregation was seized with a sudden panic. This caused a fearful rush to the doors, particularly from the galleries. Several persons, either in consequence of their heedless haste, or from the extreme pressure of the crowd behind, were thrown down on the stone steps of the north-west staircase, and were trampled on by the crowd pressing upon them. The lamentable result was that seven persons lost their lives, and twenty-eight were removed to the hospitals seriously bruised and injured. Our Pastor, not being aware that any loss of life had occurred, continued in the pulpit, endeavouring by every means in his power to alleviate the fear of the people, and was successful to a very consider-able extent. In attempting to renew the service, it was found that the people were too excited to listen to him, so the service was closed, and those who had remained dispersed quietly. This lamentable circum-stance produced very serious effects on the nervous system of our Pastor. He was entirely prostrated for some days, and compelled to relinquish his preaching engagements. Through the great mercy of our Heavenly Father, he was, however, restored so as to be able to occupy the pulpit in our own chapel on Sunday, November 2nd, and gradually recovered his wonted health and vigour. 'The Lord's name be praised!'

The church desires to note this event in their Minutes, and to record their devout thankfulness to God that, in this sad calamity, the lives of their beloved Pastor, and deacons, and members were all preserved and also with the hope that our Heavenly Father may, from this seeming evil, produce the greatest amount of real lasting good."

[Spurgeon did not approve of the printing of his prayers, as a rule, but the circumstances under which the church and congregation met on that Lord's-day morning (November 2, 1856) were so unusual, that an exception may be made in order to insert the record of the Pastor's first public utterance after the accident:

"We are assembled here, O Lord, this day, with mingled feelings of joy and sorrow—joy that we meet each other again, and sorrow for those who have suffered bereavements. Thanks to Thy Name! Thanks to Thy Name! Thy servant feared that he should never be able to meet this congregation again; but Thou hast brought him up out of the burning fiery furnace, and not even the smell of fire has passed upon him. Thou hast, moreover, given Thy servant special renewal of strength, and he desires now to confirm those great promises of free grace which the gospel affords. Thou knowest, O Lord, our feelings of sorrow! We must not open the sluices of our woe, but, O God, comfort those who are lingering in pain and suffering, and cheer those who have been bereaved! Let great blessings rest upon them—the blessings of the covenant of grace, and of this world, too. And now, O Lord, bless Thy people! We have loved one another with a pure heart fervently; we have rejoiced in each other's joy; we have wept together in our sorrow. Thou hast welded us together, and made us one in doctrine, one in practice, and one in holy love. Oh, that it may be said of each individual now present with us that he is bound up in the bundle of life! O Lord, we thank Thee even for all the slander, and calumny, and malice, with which Thou hast allowed the enemy to honour us; and we pray Thee to grant that we may never give them any real cause to blaspheme Thy holy Name! We ask this for our Lord Jesus Christ's sake. Amen."

The opening sentences of the discourse delivered on that occasion have a special and permanent interest from the fact that the Lord so abundantly fulfilled Spurgeon's prophecy concerning future services and blessing in the Music Hall:

"I almost regret, this morning, that I have ventured to occupy this pulpit, because I feel utterly unable to preach to you for your profit. I had thought that the quiet and repose of the last fortnight had removed the effects of that terrible catastrophe; but on coming back to this chapel again, and more especially, standing here to address you, I feel somewhat of those same painful emotions which well-nigh prostrated me before. You will therefore excuse me, this morning, if I make no allusion to that solemn event, or scarcely any. I could not preach to you upon a subject that should be in the least allied to it; I should be obliged to be silent if I should bring to my remembrance that terrific scene in the midst of which it was my solemn lot to stand. God will overrule it, doubtless.[1] It may not have been so much by *the malice* of men, as some have asserted; it was perhaps simple wickedness—an intention to disturb a congregation; but certainly with no thought of committing so terrible a crime as that of the murder of those unhappy creatures. God forgive those who were the instigators of that horrid act! They have my forgiveness from the depths of my soul. *It shall not stop us, however;* we are not in the least degree daunted by it. I shall preach there again yet; aye, and God will give us souls there, and Satan's empire shall tremble more than ever. God is with us; who is he that shall be against us? The text I have selected is

---

[1] Thirty years later a leading London newspaper wrote: "It was an accident of a serious nature that first drew the attention of the world in general to the rising influence of Mr. Spurgeon. The young preacher—he was then very young—had already secured an immense following on the south side of London. But the world on the other side, the world north of the Thames, the world of society and of the clubs and the West End, the world of Bloomsbury and Fitzroy Square, the world of Maida Vale and Highgate, all these various microcosms knew little or nothing of the powerful young preacher whose congregations had already far outgrown the capacity of New Park Street Chapel in Southwark. . . .

Mr Spurgeon, of course, would have been known to the whole public of these countries in time, even if there had never been a panic and a rush and a catastrophe in the Surrey Music Hall. But he found himself famous the morning after the accident, and he kept his fame."—P.

one that has comforted me, and, in a great measure, enabled me to come here to-day—the reflection upon it had such a power of comfort on my depressed spirit. It is this: 'Wherefore God also hath highly exalted Him, and given Him a Name which is above every name: that at the name of Jesus every knee should bow, of things in Heaven, and things in earth, and things under the earth; and that every tongue should confess that Jesus Christ is Lord, to the glory of God the Father.' I shall not attempt to preach upon this text; I shall only make a few remarks that have occurred to my own mind; for I could not preach to-day. I have been utterly unable to study, but I thought that even a few words might be acceptable to you this morning, and I trust to your loving hearts to excuse them. O Spirit of God, magnify Thy strength in Thy servant's weakness, and enable him to honour his Lord, even when his soul is cast down within him!"]

*   *   *

I have many times used the great calamity as an illustration of the truth that accidents are not to be regarded as Divine judgments; perhaps the most notable instance is the sermon I preached soon after the collision in the Clayton tunnel on the Brighton railway.[1] That discourse is to me the more memorable as I possess a copy of it which Dr. Livingstone had carried with him in his African journeys, and on the top of which he had written, "*Very good.*—D. L." It was found, after his death, in the volume of his Diary from November, 1861, to July, 1863, and was sent to me by his daughter, Mrs. Livingstone-Bruce. In the course of the sermon I said: "It has been most absurdly stated that those who travel on the first day of the week, and meet with an accident, ought to regard that accident as being a judgment from God upon them on account of their violating the Christian's day of worship. It has been stated, even by godly ministers, that the late deplorable collision should be looked upon as an exceedingly wonderful and remarkable visitation of the wrath of God against those unhappy persons who happened to be in the Clayton tunnel. Now I enter my solemn protest against such an inference as that, not in my own name, but in the Name of Him who is the Christian's Master and the Christian's Teacher. I say of those who were crushed in that tunnel, Suppose ye that they were sinners above all the other sinners? 'I tell you, Nay: but, except ye repent, ye shall all likewise perish.' Or those who were killed last Monday, think ye that they were sinners above all the sinners that were in London? 'I tell you, Nay: but, except ye repent, ye shall all likewise perish.' Now, mark, I would not

[1] See *Metropolitan Tabernacle Pulpit*, Vol. VII, p. 481.

deny that there have been judgments of God upon particular persons for sin; sometimes, and I think but exceedingly rarely, such things have occurred. Some of us have heard, in our experience, instances of men who have blasphemed God, and defied Him to destroy them, who have suddenly fallen dead; and in such cases, the punishment has so quickly followed the blasphemy that one could not help perceiving the hand of God in it. The man had wantonly asked for the judgment of God, his prayer was heard, and the judgment came. . . . But in cases of accident, such as that to which I refer, and in cases of sudden and instant death, again I say, I enter my earnest protest against the foolish and ridiculous idea that those who thus perish are sinners above all the sinners who survive unharmed. Let me just try to reason this matter out with Christian people, for there are some unenlightened Christians who will feel horrified by what I have said. Those who are ready at perversions may even dream that I would apologize for the desecration of the day of worship. Now, I do no such thing. I do not extenuate the sin, I only testify and declare that accidents are not to be viewed as punishments for sin, for punishment belongs not to this world, but the world to come. To all those who hastily look on every calamity as a judgment, I would speak in the earnest hope of setting them right.

Let me begin, then, by saying, my dear brethren, do you not see that *what you say is not true*, and that is the best of reasons why you should not say it? Do not your own experience and observation teach you that one event happeneth both to the righteous and to the wicked? It is true, the wicked man sometimes falls dead in the street, but has not the minister fallen dead in the pulpit? It is true that a boat, in which men were seeking their own pleasure on the Sunday, has suddenly gone down, but is it not equally true that a ship, which contained none but godly men, who were bound upon an excursion to preach the gospel, has gone down, too? The visible providence of God has no respect of persons, and a storm may gather around the *John Williams* missionary ship, quite as well as around a vessel filled with riotous sinners. Why, do you not perceive that the providence of God has been, in fact, in its outward dealings, rather harder upon the good than upon the bad? For, did not Paul say, as he looked upon the miseries of the righteous in his day, 'If in this life only we have hope in Christ, we are of all men most miserable'? The path of righteousness has often conducted men to the rack, to the prison, to the gibbet, to the stake; while the road of sin has often led a man to empire, to dominion, and to high esteem among his fellows. It is not true that, in this world, God does, as a rule, and of necessity, punish men for sin, and reward them for their good deeds; for, did not David say, 'I have seen the wicked in great power, and spreading himself like a green bay tree'; and did not this perplex the psalmist for a little season, until he went into the sanctuary of God, and then he understood their end?

Will you allow me also to remark that the supposition, against which I am earnestly contending, is *a very cruel and unkind one*? For, if it were the case that all persons who thus meet with their death in an extraordinary and terrible manner were greater sinners than the rest, would it not be a crushing blow to bereaved survivors, and is it not ungenerous on our part to indulge the idea unless we are compelled by unanswerable reasons to accept it as an awful truth? Now, I defy you to whisper it in the widow's ear. Go home to her, and say, 'Your husband was a worse sinner than the rest of men, therefore he died.' You have not brutality enough for that. A little unconscious infant, which had never sinned, though, doubtless, an inheritor of Adam's fall, is found crushed amidst the *débris* of the accident. Now, think for a moment, what would be the infamous consequence of the supposition that those who perished were worse than others; you would have to make it out that this unconscious infant was a worse sinner than many in the dens of infamy whose lives are yet spared. Do you not perceive that the thing is radically false? And I might perhaps show you the injustice of it best by reminding you that it may, one day, turn upon your own head. Let it be your own case that you should meet with sudden death in such a way, are you willing to be adjudged to damnation on that account? Such an event may happen in the house of God. Let me recall to my own, and to your sorrowful recollection, what occurred when once we met together. I can say, with a pure heart, we met for no object but to serve our God, and the minister had no aim in going to that place but that of gathering many to hear who otherwise would not have listened to his voice; and yet there were funerals as a result of that holy effort (for holy effort still we avow it to have been, and the aftersmile of God hath proved it so). There were deaths, and deaths among God's people—I was about to say, I am glad it was with God's people rather than with others. A fearful fright took hold upon the congregation, and they fled; and do you not see that, if accidents are to be viewed as judgments, then it is a fair inference that we were sinning in being there—an insinuation which our consciences repudiate with scorn? However, if that logic were true, it is as true against us as it is against others; and inasmuch as you would repel with indignation the accusation that any were wounded or hurt on account of sin in being there to worship God, what you repel for yourself repel for others, and be no party to the accusation which is brought against those who have been destroyed, during the last fortnight, that they perished on account of any great sin.

Here I anticipate the outcries of prudent and zealous persons who tremble for the ark of God, and would touch it with Uzzah's hand. 'Well,' says one, 'but we ought not to talk like this, for it is very serviceable superstition, because there are many people who will be kept from travelling on the Sunday by the accident, and we ought to tell them, therefore, that those who perished, perished because they travelled on Sunday.' Brethren, I would not tell a lie to save a soul; and this would be telling lies, for it is not the fact. I would do anything that is right to stop Sunday labour and sin, but I would not forge a falsehood even to do that. They might have perished on a Monday as well as on a Sunday. God gives no special immunity any day of the week, and accidents may occur as well at one time as at another; and it is only a pious fraud when we seek thus to play upon the superstition of men to make capital for Christ. The Roman Catholic priest might consistently use such an argument, but an honest Christian man, who believes that the religion of Christ can take care of itself without his telling falsehoods, scorns to do it. These men did not perish because they travelled on a Sunday. Witness the fact that others perished on the Monday when they were on an errand of mercy. I know not why or wherefore God sent the accident. God forbid that we should offer our own reason when God has not given us His reason, but we are not allowed to make the superstition of men an instrument for advancing the glory of God. You know, among Protestants, there is a great deal of Popery. I meet with people who uphold infant baptism on the plea, 'Well, it is not doing any hurt, and there is a great deal of good meaning in it, and it may do good; and even confirmation may be blessed to some people, therefore do not let us speak against it.' I have nothing to do with whether the thing does hurt or not; all I have to do with is whether it is right, whether it is Scriptural, whether it is true, and if truth does mischief—which is a supposition we can by no means allow—that mischief will not lie at our door. We have nothing to do but to speak the truth, even though the heavens should fall."

I thank God that, terrible as the great catastrophe was, there was never in my experience another like it, for I do not think I could have survived a second one. I have, on several occasions, seen some cause for alarm when I have been conducting services in places that have not seemed to me to be able to stand the strain of the multitudes gathered to hear the Word; and the sensation I felt at the Surrey Gardens has, in a moment, come over me again. Many years ago, I was preaching in a building which was exceedingly crowded, and, to my apprehension, there was a continuous tremor. I grew so anxious that I said to a friend, who understood such matters, "Go downstairs, and see whether this structure is really safe, for it seems hardly able to bear the weight of this crowd." When he returned, he looked anxious, but gave me no answer. The service ended quietly, and then he said, "I am so glad that everything has gone off safely. I do not think you should ever preach here again, for it is a very frail affair; but I thought that, if I frightened you, there would be more risk of a panic than there was in letting the service go on." The narrowest escape I ever had of a repetition of the Music Hall fatality was about eighteen months after the accident there; on the following Lord's-day morning (April 11, 1858), I thus described to my congregation the Lord's merciful interposition:

"During this week, my mind has been much directed to the subject of providence, and you will not wonder when I relate a portion of one day's story. I was engaged to preach, last Wednesday, at Halifax, where there was a heavy snowstorm. Preparations had been made for a congregation of 8,000 persons, and a huge wooden structure had been erected. I considered that, owing to the severe weather, few persons could possibly assemble, and I looked forward to the dreary task of addressing an insignificant handful of people in a vast place. However, when I arrived, I found from 5,000 to 6,000 people gathered together to hear the Word; and a more substantial-looking place it has not been my lot to see. It certainly was a great uncomely building; but, nevertheless, it seemed well adapted to answer the purpose. We met together in the afternoon, and again in the evening, and worshipped God; and we separated to our homes, or rather, we were about to separate, and all this while the kind providence of God was watching over us. Immediately in front of me there was a huge gallery, which looked an exceedingly massive structure, capable of holding 2,000 persons. This, in the afternoon, was crowded, and it seemed to stand as firm as a rock. Again, in the evening, there it stood, and neither moved nor shook. But mark the provident hand of God; in the evening, when the people were retiring, and when there were scarcely more than a hundred persons there, a great beam gave way, and down came a portion of the flooring of the gallery with a fearful crash. Several people were precipitated with the planks, but still the good hand of God watched over us, and only two persons were severely injured with broken legs, which it is trusted will be set so as to avoid the necessity of amputation. Now, had this happened any earlier, not only must many more have been injured, but there are a thousand chances to one, as we say, that a panic must necessarily have ensued similar to that which we still remember, and deplore as having occurred in this place. Had such a thing happened, and had I been the unhappy preacher on the occasion, I feel certain that I should never have been able to occupy the pulpit again. Such was the effect of the first calamity, that I marvel that I ever survived. No human tongue can possibly tell what I experienced. The Lord, however, graciously preserved us; the fewness of the people in the gallery prevented any such catastrophe, and thus a most fearful accident was averted. But there is a more marvellous providence still to record. Overloaded by the immense weight of snow which fell upon it, and beaten by a heavy wind, the entire structure fell with an enormous crash three hours after we had left it, splitting the huge timbers into shivers, and rendering very much of the material utterly useless for any future building. Now mark this—had the snow begun three hours earlier, the hall must have fallen upon us, and how few of us would have escaped, we cannot guess. But mark another thing. All day long it thawed so fast, that the snow as it fell seemed to leave a mass, not of white snow, but of snow and water together. This ran through the roof upon us, to our considerable annoyance, and I was almost ready to complain that we had hard dealings from God's providence. But if it had been a frost instead of a thaw, you can easily perceive that the place must have fallen several hours before it did; and then your minister, and the greater part of his congregation, would probably have been in the other world. Some there may be who deny providence altogether. I cannot conceive that there were any witnesses of that scene who could have done so. This I know, if I had been an unbeliever to this day in the doctrine of the supervision and wise care of God, I must have been a believer in it at this hour. Oh, magnify the Lord with me, and let us exalt His Name together! He hath been very gracious unto us, and remembered us for good."

*   *   *

[In his record of "The Life and Labours of Pastor C. H. Spurgeon", entitled, *From the Usher's Desk to the Tabernacle Pulpit*, Shindler says, concerning the catastrophe at the Surrey Gardens: "Twenty-five years afterwards, the writer witnessed the terribly depressing effect the memory of this sad event had on Mr. Spurgeon. During the session of the Baptist Union at Portsmouth and Southampton, in 1881, Mr. Spurgeon was announced to preach in the largest available room in the former town. Long before the service began, every available seat and all standing-room were occupied, and still there were hundreds pressing forward, and endeavouring to crowd in. There was some confusion just as the preacher was passing on to the platform to take his seat. He seemed entirely unmanned, and stood in the passage leaning his head on his hand. He told the writer that the circumstance so vividly recalled the terrible scene at the Surrey Music Hall, that he felt quite unable to preach. But he did preach, and preach well, though he could not entirely recover from the agitation of his nervous system. Prince Edward of Saxe-Weimar, a cousin of Queen Victoria, who was then the military commander of the district, was present with his suite, and cordially greeted 'the prince of preachers' after his sermon."

Pastor W. Williams, in his *Personal Reminiscences of Charles Haddon Spurgeon*, writes: " 'What are you going to preach from to-morrow?' he once asked me. ' "The curse of the Lord is in the house of the wicked: but He blesseth the habitation of the just;" ' I answered. He gave a deep sigh; his countenance changed even before I had finished the verse, brief as it was; and he said, in tones of deep solemnity, 'Ah, me!' 'What is the matter, sir?' I asked. 'Don't you know,' he replied, 'that is the text I had on that terrible night of the accident at the Surrey Music Hall?' I did not know it, but I learned, from the mere mention of it, how permanent was the effect upon his mind of that awful night's disaster. I never alluded either to this text or to the Surrey Gardens calamity after that. I cannot but think, from what I then saw, that his comparatively early death might be in some measure due to the furnace of mental suffering he endured on and after that fearful night."]

"I do not expect to see so many conversions in this place as I had a year ago, when I had far fewer hearers. Do you ask why? Why, a year ago, I was abused by everybody; to mention my name, was to mention the name of the most abominable buffoon that ever lived. The mere utterance of it brought forth oaths and curses; with many men it was the name of contempt, kicked about the street as a football; but then God gave me souls by hundreds, who were added to my church, and in one year it was my happiness personally to see not less than a thousand who had then been converted. I do not expect that now. My name is somewhat esteemed, and the great ones of the earth think it no dishonour to sit at my feet; but this makes me fear lest my God should forsake me while the world esteems me. I would rather be despised and slandered than aught else. This assembly, that you think so grand and fine, I would readily part with, if by such a loss I could gain a greater blessing. . . . It is for us to recollect, in all times of popularity, that 'Crucify Him! Crucify Him!' follows fast upon the heels of 'Hosanna!' and that the crowd of to-day, if dealt with faithfully, may turn into the handful of to-morrow; for men love not plain speaking. We should learn to be despised, learn to be condemned, learn to be slandered, and then we shall learn to be made useful by God. Down on my knees have I often fallen, with the hot sweat rising from my brow, under some fresh slander poured upon me; in an agony of grief, my heart has been well-nigh broken; till at last I learned the act of bearing all, and caring for none. And now my grief runneth in another line, it is just the opposite; I fear lest God should forsake me, to prove that He is the Author of salvation, that it is not in the preacher, that it is not in the crowd, that it is not in the attention I can attract, but in God, and in God alone. This I hope I can say from my heart—if to be made as the mire of the streets again, if to be the laughing-stock of fools and the song of the drunkard once more will make me more serviceable to my Master, and more useful to His cause, I will prefer it to all this multitude, or to all the applause that man could give."
—C. H. S.

Chapter 31

Varying Voices—*Pro* and *Con*

IN Chapter 30, mention was made of the cruel and libellous articles which appeared in various newspapers after the great catastrophe at the Music Hall, and extracts from two of them were given as specimens of the rest. There were other secular papers which published more favourable comments, one of the first being *The Evening Star*, November 5, 1856, which said:

"Other questions than that of the structure of the building, or the self-protection of the startled assemblage, are raised by the Surrey Gardens calamity. The vocation of the preacher, and the secret of his power are brought by it within the range of every man's thoughts, and, therefore, of newspaper discussion. The worldly-minded are forced to reflect on the nature of an institution which survives the most sweeping changes, defies alike persecution and rivalry, and is no less conspicuous in this nineteenth century, to which the press and platform are almost peculiar, than in the twelfth or sixteenth, when the altar and the pulpit had no competitors but in the throne. The devout, moreover, who prefer to think of all religious exercises as more or less supernatural, and the result of direct or indirect inspiration from on high, are compelled to observe the very different operations of the same Divine Spirit working through different human instrumentalities; so that, while a host of good, and perhaps able men, are discoursing from Scripture texts to their few hundreds of hearers each, one—and he a comparatively untrained youth—draws the multitude by ten and fifteen thousand at a time, and is even besought to continue his preaching while the dead and wounded are being carried from the doors of the meeting-house.

No one can go into a well-filled church, or into the majority of chapels, without being tempted to ask—'Where are the poor?' Preacher and hearers are alike emphatically of the middle class. The grey-headed, white-neckclothed, and otherwise respectable-looking men, in conspicuous seats, are prosperous traders, lawyers or doctors. The younger fathers of families are clerks or shopkeepers. A few Sunday-school teachers, unmarried shopmen and clerks, make up the males of the congregation. The female portion greatly preponderate in number, are almost exclusively connections of the before-mentioned; though, here and there, is some solitary wife or widowed mother, who has slipped away from a penurious home to snatch consolation from the lips that speak of Heaven. But where are the artisan classes—that keen-eyed, strong-minded race, who crowd the floor at political meetings or cheap concerts, fill the minor theatres, and struggle into the shilling gallery of the Lyceum or Princess's? So very scanty is their attendance upon the most noted preachers, that it is their adhesion to Mr. Spurgeon which has made that gentleman a prodigy and a phenomenon. The first that we heard of him, two or three years since, was that the Bankside labourers went to hear him on Sundays and week-nights. The summer before last, we found the artisans of Bethnal Green—a much more fastidious race—flocking round him in a field at Hackney. And in the list of the killed and wounded at the Music Hall, are journeymen painters, tanners, and milliners' girls. It is worth while to ask the reason why.

A single hearing is sufficient to answer the question—supposing the hearer can also see. There never yet was a popular orator who did not talk more and better with his arms than with his tongue. Mr. Spurgeon knows this instinctively. When he has read his text, he does not fasten his eyes on a manuscript, and his hands to a cushion. As soon as he begins to speak, he begins to act—and that not as if declaiming on the stage, but as if conversing with you in the street. He seems to shake hands with all around, and put everyone at his ease. There is no laboured exordium, making you wonder by what ingenious winding he will get back to his subject, but a trite saying, an apt quotation, a simple allegory, one or two familiar sentences, making all who hear feel interested and at home. Then there is no philosophical pomp of exposition, but just two or three catch-words, rather to guide than to confine attention. Presently comes, by way of illustration, a gleam of humour—perhaps a stroke of downright vulgarity—it may be, a wretched pun. The people are amused, but they are not left at liberty to laugh. The preacher's comedy does but light up his solemn earnestness. He is painting some scene of death-bed remorse, or of timely repentance; some Magdalene's forgiveness, or some prodigal's return. His colours are taken from the earth and sky of common human experience and aspiration. He dips his pencil, so to speak, in the veins of the nearest spectator, and makes his work a part of every man's nature. His images are drawn from the homes of the common people, the daily toil for daily bread, the nightly rest of tired labour, the mother's love for a wayward boy, the father's tenderness to a sick daughter. His anecdotes are not far-fetched, they have a natural pathos. He tells how some despairing unfortunate, hastening with her last penny to the suicide's bridge, was stopped by the sound of psalmody, and turned into his chapel; or how some widow's son, running away from his mother's home, was brought back by the recollection of a prayer, and sits now in that pew. He does not narrate occurrences, but describes them, with a rough, graphic force and faithfulness. He does not reason out his doctrines, but announces, explains, and applies them. He ventures a political allusion, and it goes right to the democratic heart. In the open air, someone may interrupt or interrogate, and the response is a new effect. In short, this man preaches Christianity—his Christianity, at any rate—as Ernest Jones preaches Chartism, and as Gough preaches temperance. Is it any wonder that he meets with like success? Or is he either to be blamed or scorned? Let it first be remembered that Latimer was not less homely when he preached before the king—nor South less humorous when he cowed Rochester—nor Whitefield less declamatory when he moved Hume and Franklin—nor Rowland Hill less vulgar, though brother to a baronet. To us, it appears that dullness is the worst fault possible to a man whose first business it is to interest—that the dignity of the pulpit is best consulted by making it attractive—and that the clergy of all denominations might get some frequent hints for the composition of their sermons from the young Baptist preacher who never went to College."

*   *   *

Soon after the services were resumed at the Music Hall, a correspondent of *The Sun* newspaper wrote: "If what we heard, last Sunday, be a specimen of Mr. Spurgeon's usual preaching, there was certainly nothing at all more extravagant than would be heard from most of the Evangelical clergymen and Dissenting preachers in the country. There were no outrageous descriptions of Divine anger and future punishment, nor any wiredrawn refinements on the theology of repentance. His statements on the latter point were characterized by remarkable common sense; they were forcibly expressed and illustrated, as were his arguments for the necessity of repentance. Indeed, there was little in which preachers of all creeds would not have concurred. His voice is a noble one, filling the whole place with the greatest ease; at the further end of the building, we did not miss a syllable. His manner was perfectly unrestrained, but not irreverent. His command of language is very considerable, but does not lead him, for an extempore speaker, into verbosity. His style is unfettered, homely, forcible, and abounds in pointed remarks. There was a total absence of anything humorous or ludicrous. The secret of his popularity, taking last Sunday as a specimen, appeared to us to be something very different.

It was impossible not to feel that the preacher was absorbed, not in himself, but in his audience. The formal separation of the pulpit did not separate him from his hearers. He conversed with them, he was one of them. He did not lecture them *ex cathedrâ*, or indulge in disquisitions or topics out of their line of thought, but spoke with them as he would have done on a solemn subject in their own houses. Most of our pulpits 'die of dignity'; but, while there was nothing unbecoming on Sunday, the preacher placed himself on a level with all. Of course, a vivid fancy, and considerable powers of expression, aided by a first-rate voice, will account for much, but we think what we have pointed out was the chief reason why, among so many thousands of hearers, we could not—and we looked carefully—detect a single sleeper.

Our more dignified preachers might study with advantage the phenomenon of this youth's popularity. We can only say that, for our part, his manner disarmed criticism, and we could think only of his probable usefulness to the thousands present who, we are confident, by their appearance, are not listeners to our customary pulpit prosaics. Lord Chief Justice Campbell, with his son, was present on the platform, and seemed to take the same view with ourselves; he remarked several times to one of the managers, after the service, in our hearing, and also to Sir Richard Mayne (Commissioner of Police), who was likewise present, 'He is doing great good, sir—great good.' London could find room for twenty such preachers; they are just what the populace needs."

Dr. John Campbell reprinted the foregoing letter in *The British Banner,* and added the following remarks:

"Such a testimony, from such a quarter, possesses a special value, and the deliberate language of the Lord Chief Justice of England will be duly estimated wherever it shall be read. There is no living man from whom a ranting, raving enthusiast would have so much to fear. A better judge of teaching or preaching, or eloquence, than Lord Campbell, is nowhere to be found. The friends of Mr. Spurgeon, therefore, may congratulate themselves on having anticipated the decision of this great legal luminary."[1]

---

[1] Other well-known figures attended the Music Hall services. Another eye-witness in 1857 wrote, "Dr. Livingstone sat on the platform; and the Princess Royal, as well as the Duchess of Sutherland, were said to be present." On one occasion, it was rumoured that Queen Victoria herself had attended *incognito.*—P.

The famous *Greville Memoirs* contain the following record relating to the period now under consideration: "8th February, 1857.—I have just come from hearing the celebrated Mr, Spurgeon preach in the Music Hall of the Surrey Gardens. It was quite full. He told us from the pulpit that there were 9,000 persons present. The service was like the Presbyterian—psalms, prayer, expounding a Psalm, and a sermon. He is certainly very remarkable, and, undeniably, a fine character; not remarkable in person; in face, rather resembling a smaller Macaulay; a very clear and powerful voice, which was heard through the hall; a manner natural, impassioned, and without affectation or extravagance, wonderful fluency and command of language, abounding in illustration, and very often of a very familiar kind, but without anything either ridiculous or irreverent. He gave me an impression of his earnestness and sincerity; speaking without book or notes, yet his discourse was evidently very carefully prepared. The text was, 'Cleanse Thou me from secret faults,' and he divided it into heads— the misery, the folly, the danger (and a fourth, which I have forgotten,) of secret sins, in all of which he was very eloquent and impressive. He preached for about three-quarters of an hour, and, to judge by the use of the handkerchiefs and the audible sobs, with great effect."

In the *Life of Principal Tulloch*, by Mrs. Oliphant, there is a description by the Scottish preacher, of a visit he made with his friend, Professor Ferrier, to the Music Hall in May, 1858:

"We have just been to hear Spurgeon," Tulloch wrote, "and have both been so much impressed that I wish to give you my impressions while they are fresh. As we came out we both confessed, 'There is no doubt about *that*, and I was struck with Ferrier's remarkable expression, 'I feel it would do me good to hear the like of that, it sat so close to reality.'

The sermon is about the most real thing I have come in contact with for a long while. Guthrie is as sounding brass and a tinkling cymbal to it; and although there is not the elevated thought and descriptive felicity of Caird (the latter especially, however, not wanting), there is more power. Power, in fact, and life are its characteristics.

The place is fully adapted for preaching, being the largest, lightest, and airiest building I ever saw. It was crammed, of course, but not in the least uncomfortable, as round all the thickly-studded benches there was a wide and open corridor, with window-doors open, out and in of which you could walk into the gardens (Surrey Gardens) as you liked; and Ferrier kept taking a turn now and then during the sermon. He began the service with a short prayer, then sang the twenty-third Psalm, but instead of our fine old version, some vile version, in which the simple beauty of the hymn is entirely lost. Then he read and expounded the thirty-second chapter (I think) of Numbers. His remarks were very good and to the point, with no display or misplaced emotion. He then prayed more at length, and this was the part of the service I least liked.

He preached from the same chapter he read, about the spies from the land of Canaan—the good and bad spies. It was a parable, he said, of religion. Canaan is not rightly taken as a type of heaven, but of the religious life. Then, after speaking of men of the world judging religion (which, however, they had no right to do) from those who professed it rather than from the Bible—which in thought and grasp was the fullest part of the sermon—he said he would speak of two classes of people, the bad spies first, those who made a great ado about religion and did not show its power, and then the good spies. His description here was graphic beyond what I can give you an idea of, the most telling satire, cutting home, yet not overdone, as he spoke of the gloomy religionist who brought up a bad report of the land of religion, making himself and his wife and children miserable, drawing down the blinds on a Sunday, 'almost most religious when most miserable, and most miserable when most religious'; then the meek-faced fellow, who can pray all Sunday and preach by the hour, and cheat all Monday, always ready with his prayer-book, but keeping a singular cash-book, wouldn't swear, but would cheat and lie. Then, again, he showed still higher powers of pathos in describing the good spies—the old blind saint who had served God for fifty years and never found Him fail; the consumptive girl testifying of the goodness of her Saviour as the dews of death gathered on her brow. And then of all who only lived as Christians—the good wife who converted her husband by her untiring gentleness, and having supper ready even at twelve o'clock at night; the servant who, because she was religious, cleaned knives better without losing their edge; the Christian merchant; the wife who, unknown to fame, and having no time for teaching or district visiting, achieved her household work day by day.

In fact, the whole was a wonderful display of mental vigour and Christian sense, and gave me a great idea of what good such a man may do. The impression made upon Ferrier, which he has just read over to me as he has written it to his wife, 'is driving downright.' He improves in look, too, a little, as he warms in preaching. At first he certainly is not interesting in face or figure—very fat and podgy; but there is no doubt of the fellow, look as he may. His voice is of rare felicity, as clear as a bell—not a syllable lost."

*   ♠   *

The letter which follows was published in *The Times*, April 13, 1857. Spurgeon thought it was worthy of preservation, for it came from the pen of a learned professor, and did much to turn the tide of public opinion in his favour.

"PREACHING *and* PREACHING.

To the Editor of *The Times*,

Sir,—One Sunday morning, about a month ago, my wife said, 'Let us send the children to St. Margaret's, to hear the Archbishop of —— preach on behalf of the Society of Aged Ecclesiastical Cripples, which is to celebrate to-day its three hundredth anniversary.' So the children went, though the parents, for reasons immaterial to mention, could not go with them. 'Well, children, how did you like the Archbishop of ——, and what did he say about "the Aged Ecclesiastical Cripples"?' Here the children—for it was during their dinner—attacked their food with great voracity; but never a word could we get out of their mouths about the spiritual feast of which they had just partaken. No! not even the text could they bring out. The more they were pressed, the more they blushed, and hung their heads over their plates, until, at last, in a rage, I accused them of having fallen asleep during the service. This charge threw my first-born on his defence, and he sobbed out the truth, for, by this time, their eyes were full of tears. 'Why, papa! we can't say what the Archbishop of —— said, because we could not hear a word. He is very old, and has got no teeth; and do you know, I don't think he has got any tongue either, for, though we saw his lips moving, we could not hear a single word.' On this I said no more, but I thought a good deal of 'the Aged Ecclesiastical Cripples,' and their venerable advocate, and, being something of a philologist, I indulged in dreamy speculations on the possibility of an alphabet composed entirely of labials; and if my wife had not roused me from my dream by some mere matter-of-fact question, I almost think I should have given my reflections to the world in the shape of a small pamphlet entitled, 'The Language of Labials; or, how to preach sermons without the aid of either tongue or teeth; published for the benefit of the Society of Aged Ecclesiastical Cripples, and dedicated, of course by permission, to the Archbishop of ——.'

Now listen to another story. A friend of mine, a Scotch Presbyterian, comes up to town, and says, 'I want to hear Spurgeon; let us go.' Now, I am supposed to be a High Churchman, so I answered, 'What! go and hear a Calvinist—a Baptist—a man who ought to be ashamed of himself for being so near the Church, and yet not within its pale?' 'Never mind, come and hear him.' Well, we went yesterday morning to the Music Hall in the Surrey Gardens. At first, I felt a strange sensation of wrong-doing. It was something like going to a morning theatrical performance on Sunday; nor did a terrific gust of wind (which sent the Arctic Regions, erected out of laths and pasteboard in a style regardless of expense, flying across the water of the lake) tend to cheer a mind depressed by the novelty of the scene. Fancy a congregation, consisting of ten thousand souls, streaming into the hall, mounting the galleries, humming, buzzing, and swarming—a mighty hive of bees—eager to secure at first the best places, and at last, any place at all. After waiting more than half-an-hour—for if you wish to have a seat, you must be there at least that space of time in advance—Mr Spurgeon ascended the tribune. To the hum, and rush, and trampling of men, succeeded a low, concentrated thrill and murmur of devotion, which seemed to run at once, like an electric current, through the breast of everyone present; and by this magnetic chain, the preacher held us fast bound for about two hours. It is not my purpose to give a summary of his discourse. It is enough to say of his voice, that its power and volume are sufficient to reach everyone in that vast assembly; of his language, that it is neither high-flown nor homely; of his style, that it is at times familiar, at times declamatory, but always happy, and often eloquent; of his doctrine, that neither the Calvinist nor the Baptist appears in the forefront of the battle which is waged by Mr. Spurgeon with relentless animosity, and with gospel weapons, against irreligion, cant, hypocrisy, pride, and those secret bosom sins which so easily beset a man in daily life; and to sum up all in a word, it is enough to say of the man himself that he impresses you with a perfect conviction of his sincerity.

But I have not written so much about my children's want of spiritual food when they listened to the mumbling of the Archbishop of ——, and my own banquet at the Surrey Gardens, without a desire to draw a practical conclusion from these two stories, and to point them by a moral. Here is a man not more Calvinistic than many an incumbent of the Established Church, who 'humbles and mumbles', as old Latimer says, over his liturgy and text. Here is a man who says the complete immersion, or something of the kind, of adults is necessary to baptism. These are his faults of doctrine; but, if I were the examining chaplain of the Archbishop of ——, I would say, 'May it please your Grace, here is a man able to preach eloquently, able to fill the largest church in England with his voice, and, what is more to the purpose, with people. And may it please your Grace, here are two churches in the metropolis, St. Paul's and Westminster Abbey. What does your Grace think of inviting Mr. Spurgeon, this heretical Calvinist and Baptist, who is able to draw ten thousand souls after him, just to try his voice, some Sunday morning, in the nave of either of those churches? At any rate, I will answer for one thing that, if he preaches in Westminster Abbey, we shall not have a repetition of the disgraceful practice, now common in that church, of having the sermon *before* the anthem, in order that those who would quit the church when the arid sermon begins, may be forced to stay it out for the sake of the music which follows it.' But I am not, I am sorry to say, examining chaplain to the Archbishop of ——, so I can only send you this letter from the devotional desert in which I reside, and sign myself—

Habitans in Sicco.

Broad Phylactery, Westminster."

The Times, of the same date, had the following leading article upon the letter: "Society, like the private individual, has its grievances—certain old-established sores, any allusion to which is sure to excite general sympathy in all companies. The extortions of cabmen, inn charges, rates and taxes—any reference to these veteran impositions kindles a spark of genial hostility in every circle. Everyone has had his particular collision with these offensive claims, and has his story to tell. Those compositions called sermons belong to this class of veteran grievances. An allusion to them will revive a drooping conversation, and awaken a spirit of rebellion in every breast. . . . Certainly, to hear the remarks that are generally made, a good preacher does seem to be a very rare production, and to require the lantern of Diogenes to discover him. The fact of the excessive dulness of sermons being indeed taken for granted, people are lost in perplexity how to account for it. Do the Canons require it? Do the Bishops enjoin it? The evil is altogether mysterious, and broods over the public like a nightmare. Its origin, like that of the source of the Nile, is unknown. Is it the result of volcanic influences? Will the same discovery explain it that will, some day, explain the phenomenon of the tides? Or does the enigma await a meteorological solution? There appears also to be something mysterious in the sensations of the sufferers. Language can give the superficial characteristics of what is experienced, but there seems to be something at the bottom which is indescribable. In fact, the whole thing is very mysterious, and we feel out of our depth when we attempt to penetrate it analytically. But, as metaphysicians say, the facts of consciousness in this department are plain; and, so long as we keep quite close to them, we feel ourselves tolerably safe.

Now, undoubtedly, preachers have something to say on their side of the question. As a class of public exhibitors, they labour under peculiar difficulties. For example, a good lecture and a good theatrical piece can be repeated, and we have Mr. Albert Smith and *The Corsican Brothers* night after night. But a good sermon has only one existence. It goes off like a rocket, and disappears for ever. The preacher cannot advertise a second delivery. If it takes place, it is by stealth. But success is not so frequent that it can afford this waste and extravagance without serious results. In other departments, the failures escape notice, because they are merely tentative, and are withdrawn as soon as they are discovered not to take, while one good hit is hammered for months running into the public mind. In the case of sermons, good and bad are on the same exhibitory level, and human nature is pinned forcibly to its average mark.

The reputation, however, of this class of compositions being thus low, it is not surprising if the sudden phenomenon of a monster preacher excites some astonishment; and if our correspondent, 'HABITANS IN SICCO', regrets that the Church has not the benefit of similar services, it is quite natural to ask why should such demonstrations be confined to Dissent? Why cannot the Church have a monster preacher drawing his crowds?

Physically speaking, there can be no reason why the Church should not have, at any rate once or twice in a generation, a natural orator in its clerical ranks endowed with a voice as loud as Mr. Spurgeon's; and, if she has, there can be no cogent reason why she should not use him. A loud voice is a decided gift, an endowment; it may be thrown away in the prodigality of nature upon a man who has no purpose to turn it to, no thought to utter from that splendid organ, upon a man, in fact, who is a mere pompous Stentor in a pulpit; but give it to one who has thought and a purpose, and see the effect. It collects a crowd to listen, but that is only the first step. Another crowd comes because there is a crowd to begin with, and a third follows the second. But this is not all. A multitude listens with a different feeling to a speaker from that with which a roomful of people or a churchful of people listen, for the multitude *feels* itself a multitude; it is conscious of its numbers, and every individual partakes in some degree the gigantic vibrations of the mass. The addition of power which is thus gained is immense; and, therefore, how is it that the Church never has a monster preacher?

The reason is, that a loud voice requires its proper material to exert itself upon. The voice is notoriously the most sympathetic thing in nature. It cannot be loud and soft indiscriminately. Some things are made to be shouted, and others to be whispered. Nobody shouts out an axiom in mathematics; nobody balances probabilities in thunder— *Nemo consilium cum clamore dat.* There must be a strong sentiment, some bold truth, to make a man shout. In religion, there must be something rather extravagant in the shape of doctrine. The doctrine of sudden conversion or of irresistible grace can be shouted, but if a man tried ever so hard to shout in delivering a moderate and sensible discourse on free-will, he would find himself talking quietly in spite of himself. A loud voice, then, must have 'loud' doctrine to develop it. But the Church of England has rather a distaste for 'loud' doctrine; her general standard is opposed to it, her basis is a balanced one, mixing opposite truths, and qualifying what she teaches with judicious pro- tests and disclaimers. She preaches Catholicity with a protest against Rome, and Protestantism with a protest against Geneva. This is very sensible, and very true, but it is not favourable to popular preaching. Of the two parties into which she is divided, one thinks it wrong to shout, as being against the principle of reverence. This school specially contrasts itself in this respect with 'the rude world', which is supposed to be always shouting, and doing everything that is noisy and vulgar, and with heretics who are audacious and immodest; and it plumes itself on its refinement and good taste in the delivery of religious truth, which it thinks ought to be done in a sort of veiled and fragmentary way, so as to reach the sensitive ears of the good, and pass over those of the profane. All this is very excellent and refined, but it is against popular preaching. So much for one party. The other party might speak loud if it liked; it has no theory against it, and its doctrines admit of it, but it does not like the trouble. And, besides, this party, though it professedly holds strong doctrine, practically tempers it considerably, and bends to the moderate standard of the Church. Thus, what with the fear of criticism, the deference to a recognized standard, idleness, reverence, and a great many other things—what with some thinking it heretical to shout, and others thinking it un- polite to be popular—there is no monster preaching in the English Church. It does certainly admit of a question whether, in our general policy, we are not over-cautious, and gain greater theoretical correct- ness at the cost of much practical efficiency. It admits of a question whether a little extravagance and a little onesidedness might not be tolerated for the sake of a good, substantial, natural, telling appeal to the human heart. We should have no objection, for our part, to an

Evangelical clergyman, with a strong voice, doing what Mr. Spurgeon does. The doctrines of the two are in reality much the same; and, that being the case, why should fear of criticism prevent the Evangelical school from making themselves as effective as they can? But such is the influence of a conventional standard, which, like conscience, 'makes cowards of us all.' "

The British Quarterly Review, June, 1857, contained a long article, of which the following were the opening and closing paragraphs:

"CHARLES SPURGEON AND THE PULPIT

Mr. Spurgeon is a notability. He filled Exeter Hall with eager listeners for months together. He has since done the same in the great Music Hall of the Surrey Gardens, though spacious enough to receive 9,000 persons. Hitherto, the prophets have been in the wrong. The feeling does not subside. The crowds gather even more than before. The 'common people' are there, as at the first; but with them there are now many who are of a much higher grade. Professional men, senatorial men, ministers of state, and peers of the realm, are among Mr. Spurgeon's auditory. These are facts that cannot be questioned. That there is something very extraordinary in them, everyone must feel. How is the matter to be explained? . . .

We believe that, to explain the fact presented in the Sunday meetings at the Surrey Gardens, we must go beyond the personal as found in the preacher, beyond the scheme of truth which he propounds—and we must rest in nothing short of the Divine hand itself. The All-wise has often worked by instruments, and in ways which would seem to have been chosen for the purpose of making a mock of the world's wisdom. He did so when he founded Christianity—He may do much like it again.

Certainly, a choice rebuke has been administered to a course of speculation which has become somewhat rife among us of late, especially among parties who account themselves as belonging to the far-seeing of their generation. It has come to be very much in fashion, with some persons, to speak of all things connected with religion as beset with great difficulty and mystery. On all such questions, we are told, there must be two sides; and the negative side, it is said, is generally much more formidable than is commonly imagined. It is assumed, accordingly, that, to be in a state of some hesitancy and doubt, is the sign of intelligence, while to be positive, very sure about anything, is the sign of a vulgar and shallow mind. Our people are said to be familiar with phrases about the doctrines of the gospel, but with little more. They may become bigots in their conceit on such subjects, and know nothing. Educated men now must not be expected to be content with phrases, or with assertions. The preacher, in consequence, owes it to himself to deal with matters much otherwise than formerly. To insist on the authority of Scripture now, as in past times, it is said, would be in vain. To set forth the doctrines of the gospel now as formerly, would be wasted labour. The preacher must be more considerate, more candid, more forbearing. He must acquit himself with more intelligence, more independence, and in a more philosophical spirit, presenting his topics on broader and more general grounds. In other words, the old mode of presenting what is called 'the old truth' has had its day. Whitefield himself, were he to come back, would produce little impression on our generation.

But here comes a man—no Whitefield in voice, in presence, in dignity, or genius, who, nevertheless, as with one stroke of his hand, sweeps away all this sickly sentimentalism, this craven misbelief. It is all to him as so much of the merest gossamer web that might have crossed his path. He not only gives forth the old doctrine of Paul in all the strength of Paul's language, but with exaggerations of his own, such as Paul would have been forward to disavow. This man knows nothing of doubt as to whence the gospel is, what it is, or wherefore it has its place amongst us. On all such subjects his mind is that of a made-up man. In place of suspecting that the old accredited doctrines of the gospel have pretty well done their work, he expects good from nothing else, and all that he clusters about them is for the sake of them.

The philosophical precision, the literary refinements, the nice discriminations between what we may know of a doctrine and what we may not, leaving us in the end, perhaps, scarcely anything to know about it—all this which, according to some, is so much needed by the age, is Mr. Spurgeon's utter scorn. He is the direct, dogmatic enunciator of the old Pauline truth, without the slightest attempt to soften its outline, its substance, or its results; and what has followed? Truly, Providence would seem once more to have made foolish the wisdom of this world. While the gentlemen, who know so well how people ought to preach, are left to exemplify their profound lessons before empty benches and in obscure corners, the young man at the Surrey Gardens can point to his 9,000 auditors, and ask, 'Who, with such a sight before him, dares despair of making the gospel, the good old gospel, a power in the great heart of humanity?'"

* * *

The following extracts from an article written by J. Ewing Ritchie

("Christopher Crayon"), and published in his volume entitled, *The London Pulpit*, will show that, even in 1857, "all men" did not "speak well" of the young preacher:

"THE REV. C. H. SPURGEON

I fear there is very little difference between the Church and the world. In both, the tide seems strongly set in favour of ignorance, presumption, and charlatanism. In the case of Mr. Spurgeon, they have both agreed to worship the same idol. Nowhere more abound the vulgar, be they great or little, than at the Surrey Music Hall on a Sunday morning. Mr. Spurgeon's service commences at a quarter to eleven, but the doors are opened an hour and a half previously, and all the while there will be a continuous stream of men and women— some on foot, some in cabs, many in carriages—all drawn together by this world's wonder. The motley crowd is worth a study. . . . A very mixed congregation is this one at the Surrey Gardens. The real flock—the aborigines from Park Street Chapel—are a peculiar people —very plain, much given to the wearing of clothes of an ancient cut —and easy of recognition. The men are narrow, hard, griping, to look at, the women stern and unlovely; yet they, and such as they alone, if we are to believe them, are to walk the pearly streets of the New Jerusalem, and to sit down with martyrs and prophets and saints— with Abraham, and Isaac, and Jacob—at the marriage supper of the Lamb. . . .

Here is a peer, and there his tailor. Here Lady Clara Vere de Vere kills a weary hour, and there is the poor girl who sat up all night to stitch her ladyship's costly robe. Here is a blasphemer come to laugh; there, a saint to pray. Can these dry bones live? Can the preacher touch the heart of this listening mass? Breathed on by a spell more potent than his own, will it in its anguish and agony exclaim, 'What must we do to be saved?' You think how this multitude would have melted beneath the consecrated genius of a Chalmers, or a Parsons, or a Melville, or an Irving—and look to see the same torrent of human emotions here. Ah, you are mistaken!—Mr. Spurgeon has not the power to wield 'all thoughts, all passions, all delights'. It is not in him to 'shake the arsenal, and fulmine over Greece'. In the very midst of his fiercest declamation, you will find his audience untouched; so coarse is the colouring, and clumsy the description, you can sit calm and unmoved through it all; and all the while the haughty beauty by your side will fan herself with a languor Charles Matthews in 'Used Up' might envy. Look at the preacher; the riddle is solved. You see at once that he is not the man to soar; and, soaring, bear his audience, trembling and enraptured, with him in his Heavenward flight. . . .

Of course, at times, there is a rude eloquence on his lips, or, rather, a fluent declamation, which the mob around takes for such. The orator always soars with his audience. With excited thousands waiting his lightest word, he cannot remain passionless and unmoved. Words and thoughts are borne to him from them. There is excitement in the hour; there is excitement in the theme; there is excitement in the living mass; and, it may be, as the preacher speaks of a physical hell and displays a physical heaven, some sensual nature is aroused, and a change may be effected in a man's career.

Little causes may produce great events; one chance word may be the beginning of a new and a better life; but the thoughtful hearer will learn nothing, will be induced to feel nothing, will find that, as regards Christian edification, he had much better have stayed at home. At the best, Mr. Spurgeon will seem to him a preacher of extra-ordinary volubility. Most probably he will return from one of Mr. Spurgeon's services disgusted with the noisy crowding, reminding him of the Adelphi rather than the house of God; disgusted with the commonplace prayer; disgusted with the questionable style of oratory; disgusted with the narrowness of the preacher's creed, and its pitiful misrepresentations of 'the glorious gospel of the blessed God'; disgusted with the stupidity that can take, for a Divine afflatus, brazen impudence and leathern lungs. Most probably, he will come back confessing that Mr. Spurgeon is the youngest, and the loudest, and the most notorious preacher in London—little more; the idol of people who dare not go to theatres, and yet pant for theatrical excitement. . . .

Will not Mr. Spurgeon's very converts, as they become older—as they understand Christianity better—as the excitement produced by dramatic dialogues in the midst of feverish audiences dies away—feel this themselves? And yet this man actually got nearly 24,000 to hear him on the Day of Humiliation. Such a thing seems marvellous. If popularity means anything, which, however, it does not, Mr. Spurgeon is one of our greatest orators. It is true, it is not difficult to collect a crowd in London. If I simply stand stock still in Cheapside, in the middle of the day, a crowd is immediately collected. The upper class of society requires finer weapons than any Mr. Spurgeon wields; but he preaches to the people in a homely style, and they like it, for he is always plain, and never dull. Then, his voice is wonderful; of itself, a thing worth going to hear; and he has a readiness rare in the pulpit, and which is invaluable to an orator. Then, again, the matter of his discourses commends itself to uneducated hearers. We have done with the old miracle-plays, wherein God the Father appeared upon the stage in a blue coat, and wherein the devil had very visible hoofs and tail; but the principle to which they appealed—the love of man for dramatic representations rather than abstract truths—remains, and Mr. Spurgeon avails himself of it successfully. Another singular fact—Mr. Spurgeon would quote it as a proof of its truth—is that what is called high doctrine—the doctrine Mr. Spurgeon preaches—the doctrine which lays down all human pride—which teaches us we are villains by necessity, and fools by a Divine thrusting on—is always popular, and, singular as it may seem, especially on the Surrey side of the water.

In conclusion, let me not be understood as blaming Mr. Spurgeon. We do not blame Stephano when Caliban falls at his feet, and swears that 'he's a brave god, and bears celestial liquor'. Few ministers get people to hear them. Mr. Spurgeon has succeeded in doing so. It may be a pity that the people will not go and hear better preachers; but, in the meanwhile, no one can blame Mr. Spurgeon that he fearlessly and honestly preaches what he deems the truth."

"As good stewards, we must maintain the cause of truth against all comers. 'Never get into religious controversies,' says one; that is to say, being interpreted, 'Be a Christian soldier, but let your sword rust in its scabbard, and sneak into Heaven like a coward.' Such advice I cannot endorse. If God has called you by the truth, maintain the truth which has been the means of your salvation. We are not to be pugnacious, always contending for every crotchet of our own; but wherein we have learned the truth of the Holy Spirit, we are not tamely to see that standard torn down which our fathers upheld at the peril of their lives. This is an age in which truth must be maintained zealously, vehemently, continually. Playing fast and loose, as many do, believing this to-day and that to-morrow, is the sure mark of children of wrath; but having received the truth, to hold fast the very form of it, as Paul bids Timothy to do, is one of the duties of heirs of Heaven. Stand fast for truth, and may God give the victory to the faithful!"
—C. H. S., 1867.

Chapter 32

The "Down-grade" Controversy Foreshadowed

WHEN, in 1887, there arose the great "Down-grade" controversy,[1] in which Spurgeon was to prove himself Christ's faithful witness and *martyr*, many people were foolish enough to suppose that he had adopted a new *rôle*, and some said that he would have done more good by simply preaching the gospel, and leaving the so-called "heretics" to go their own way! Such critics must have been strangely unfamiliar with his whole history, for, from the very beginning of his ministry, he had earnestly contended for the faith once for all delivered to the saints. Long before *The Sword and the Trowel* appeared, with its monthly "record of combat with sin and of labour for the Lord", its Editor had been busily occupied both in battling and building—vigorously combating error in all its forms, and, at the same time, edifying and establishing in the faith those who had been brought to a knowledge of the truth as it is in Jesus.

While the church under Spurgeon's pastoral charge was worshipping in New Park Street Chapel, there were two notable controversies —the first was caused by the issue of a book of hymns, written by the Rev. Thomas Toke Lynch, and entitled, *The Rivulet; or, Hymns for the Heart and Voice*. The other arose from the publication of a volume of sermons by Rev. James Baldwin Brown, B.A., entitled *The Divine Life in Man*. Mr. J. Ewing Ritchie, whose adverse opinion concerning Spurgeon, at that period, is given on page 466, wrote at about the same time in this friendly fashion with regard to Mr. Lynch:

"Some few years back, when Professor Scott, then of University College, London, now of Owens College, Manchester, was in town, it seemed as if an honest attempt was made to meet and win to Christianity the philosophy that was genuine and earnest and religious, though it squared with the creed of no church, and took for its text-

---

[1] The Downgrade Controversy is the name which Spurgeon gave to a battle-royal commencing in his own denomination in 1887. In August of that year he published an article in his monthly magazine, *The Sword and Trowel*, which drew attention to Baptist ministers who "scouted the atonement, derided the inspiration of Scripture, degraded the Holy Spirit into an influence, and turned the punishment of sin into a fiction and the resurrection into a myth". Parallel with these serious heresies ran endeavours to "unite church and stage, cards and prayer, dancing and sacraments". In other words, Spurgeon attacked modernism and worldliness simultaneously. Ultimately he resigned from the Baptist Union. Undoubtedly, the Downgrade Controversy helped to bring about his death at the comparatively early age of 57.—P.

book the living heart of man rather than the written Word. In our time, the same thing is attempted. The man who has had the courage to make the attempt—and to whom honour should be given for it— is the Rev. Thomas Lynch."

The Baptist Messenger, May, 1856, in reviewing James Grant's pamphlet upon "The Rivulet Controversy", gave the following *résumé* of the dispute, which will enable present-day readers to understand the merits of the subject then under discussion:

"A volume of poetry by Rev. T. T. Lynch, has lately been published. These 'hymns' were very highly commended in *The Eclectic Review*, and subsequently in *The Patriot*, and *The Nonconformist*. The Editor of *The Morning Advertiser* (Mr. James Grant), who has in his day done much service to the cause of Evangelical truth, also reviewed the volume; and while referring most respectfully to Mr. Lynch and his poetry, pronounced these 'hymns' to be seriously defective with regard to the essentials of vital Christianity; that, while in them there was no distinct recognition of the Divinity of Christ, or of the mediatorial work and vicarious sacrifice of the Saviour, or of the personality, office, and work of the Holy Ghost, at the same time there was an implied denial of the doctrine of innate and total depravity. In proof of this latter charge, the following stanzas, from one of the hymns in question, were quoted by Mr. Grant:

> 'Our heart is like a little pool,
>   Left by the ebbing sea;
> Of crystal waters still and cool,
>   When we rest musingly.
>
> *'And see what verdure exquisite,*
>   *Within it hidden grows;*
> We never should have had the sight,
>   But for this brief repose.'

'Only imagine,' says the Editor of *The Morning Advertiser*, 'this and other such kind of hymns being sung in a place of public worship, or being quoted to or by a person in the near prospect of the world to come. There is poetry,' says Mr. Grant, 'in the 63rd hymn, but we look in vain for the least atom of practical religion in it;' and he adds, 'if the materials of the reverend gentleman's sermons be substantially similar to those of his hymns, we should be much surprised were not the instances very rare indeed of persons crying out in intense agony of soul, under his ministrations, "What must we do to be saved?"

In a subsequent notice of the work, the same writer expressed his regret that *The Eclectic Review* should have endorsed this 'modified Deism' of Mr. Lynch, hoping that the objectionable article had crept into the pages of that Magazine unawares. To these animadversions, the Editor of *The Eclectic* replied, not ingenuously enough to escape further remonstrances from his sturdy opponent, at which *The Eclectic* took great umbrage, and accused Mr. Grant of being guilty of 'sordidness and calumny', and of being influenced by 'extreme personal prejudice'. For ourselves, we have no hesitation in saying that, from all we know of the Editor of *The Morning Advertiser*, we can testify that he is too much of a Christian and a gentleman to be influenced by mean and unworthy motives. So far from this, Mr. Grant has not been in the least degree backward to acknowledge the literary taste which the volume displayed, and spoke of Mr. Lynch as being both amiable and highly intellectual. It was his *theology* only that was condemned.

In the March number of *The Eclectic*, the strife was renewed with more than tenfold vigour. On this occasion, some fifteen of the leading metropolitan ministers, headed by the Revs. Allon, Binney, and Newman Hall, came to the help of the Editor of *The Eclectic*, and their *protégé*, the Rev. T. T. Lynch. The literary and devotional merits of these hymns, as well as the orthodoxy of their author, they endorsed and commended in the form of a protest signed by all the fifteen.

The Editor of *The Morning Advertiser*, nothing daunted by the *status* or talents of his reverend assailants, met the combined forces—an imposing phalanx—with a simple interrogatory: 'Can Mr. Newman Hall, Mr. Binney, Mr. Martin, or either of the remainder of the fifteen reverend protesters reconcile it with his views of right, to give out the "hymn" we have just quoted in his chapel? No one of the number will venture to return an affirmative answer to the question.' If this be so, then we ask, wherefore do these reverend gentlemen appear in the field at all? It had been far better for themselves, and for *The Eclectic Review*, had they heeded the counsel of the wise man, 'Leave off contention, before it be meddled with,' and had left the criticism and remonstrances of Mr. Grant to their own merits, than for them to have interfered at all in the affair. We do most deeply deplore the position these fifteen reverend gentlemen have voluntarily and needlessly taken in this business, inasmuch as we greatly fear it betokens, on their part, an evident leaning towards a transcendental theology, the blighting influences of which have proved most fatal to many once-flourishing churches.

In a series of powerfully-written articles, which have appeared in *The Banner*, headed 'The Theology of Nonconformity', Dr. Campbell has given the results of his searching analysis of Mr. Lynch's volume, which he pronou nces to be as destitute of poetic excellence as it is of the elementary principles of Christian doctrine, containing hymns which any infidel might compose or use. We thank Mr. Grant for the outspoken truths contained in his pamphlet. Although but a layman, he has, in its pages, contended nobly and earnestly for the faith once delivered to the saints—'an effort,' to adopt his own words, 'which may the Almig hty be pleased to crown with eminent success!' "

In *The Christian Cabinet*, May 23, Mr. Banks published the following article written by Spurgeon:

"MINE OPINION

The appearance of a volume entitled *The Rivulet* has excited a controversy of the most memorable character. I shall not enter into the details of that fierce affray; the champions on either side have been of noble rank, have done their best, and must await the verdict of the Master for whom they profess to strive. Some of the fighting has not appeared quite in keeping with fairness, and there are a few persons who have gained little but disgrace in the battle, while there are others who deserve the eternal thanks of the faithful for their valiant defence of the truth. It is my business, not to review the controversy, but the book of poems. Another time I may possibly give 'mine opinion' upon that subject. Suffice it here to say that my mind on doctrinal points is wholly with the men who have censured the theology of the writer of the hymns.

With the leave of Mr. Editor, I will forget the past for a moment, and give 'mine opinion'. It may be of little worth, but there are not a few who will give it a patient hearing. Concerning this book—*The Rivulet*—let me say, in the first place, I believe that, except in Kentish Town (Mr. Lynch's residence), there is scarcely to be found an individual who would ever think of using these *Hymns for the Heart and Voice* in the public assembly. A book may be very excellent, and yet unfit for certain purposes. Who would dream of giving out a verse from quaint old Quarles? Imagine the precentor saying, 'Let us sing to the praise and glory of God the ode on the 150th page of Quarles' *School of the Heart—*

'What!
Shall I
Always lie
Grov'ling on earth,
Where there is no mirth?
Why should I not ascend,
And climb up where I may mend
My mean estate of misery?
Happiness, I know, is exceeding high;
Yet sure there is some remedy for that.'

We should not find fault with Milton's *Paradise Lost*, Herbert's *Temple*, or Young's *Night Thoughts*, because we cannot sing them in our houses of prayer, for such was not their design. But *The Rivulet* professes to be a book of hymns 'suitable for the chamber or the church'; they may be 'said or sung'; and to facilitate their use in song, the author has appended tunes from *The Psalmist*. We are, therefore, called upon to judge it as a hymn-book, and it is our firm opinion that, until Butler's *Hudibras* is sung in Heaven, Mr. Lynch's *Rivulet* will not be adopted in the assemblies of the saints below.

There is scarcely an old woman in our churches who would not imitate that ancient dame in Scotland who hurled her stool at the minister's head, should any of us venture to mount our pulpits, and exclaim, 'Let us commence the present service by singing the 34th hymn in *The Rivulet*—

'When the wind is blowing
    Do not shrink and cower:
Firmly onward going,
    Feel the joy of power;
Heaviest the heart is
    In a heavy air,
Every wind that rises,
    Blows away despair.'

I ask, without fear of any but a negative reply—Could any man in Christendom sing the concluding 'l'Envoi'? I believe I shall never find an advocate for the singing of these hymns in churches, and will therefore have done with that point, only remarking that, if a book be not what it professes to be, it is a failure, however excellent it may be in other respects. One would fain hope that the intelligent author, should another edition be demanded, will preface it with other words, purporting another object for his book, and then one great objection would be quietly removed, while he could still use his work himself as a hymn-book, if any could be found to sing with him.

It is said that the new hymn-book matter omens badly; well, it is very likely, but that is not my business just now.

In the second place, when reading these hymns, simply as literary compositions, I found them far from despicable. There is true poetry in some of them, of a very delicate and refined order. Every now and then, the voices of the flowers or of the rain-drops are clear and soft, and perpetually the thinkings of the poet wake an echo in the soul. There is much mist, and a large proportion of fog, but, nevertheless, there is enough of poetic light to cheer the darkness. I believe there is a moderate quantity of unintelligible writing in the book. At any rate, there are many sentences of which I cannot see the connection, but, no doubt, these are grand thoughts which broke the backs of the words, or frightened them out of their propriety. There is nothing very wonderful in the book. We hope to see many productions far superior to it before we are very much older, and we hope at least to see many volumes which can endure the criticism of a daily journal, and yet keep up their spirits without the potent cordial of fifteen ministerial recommendations.

I should set this *Rivulet* on my shelf somewhere near Tennyson for its song, and sundry nondescript labyrinthine divines for its doctrine, but should I place it in the same bookcase with Watts, Cowper, Hart, and Toplady, I should be on the lookout for a tremendous hubbub if the worthy authors should arouse themselves from the covers of their volumes; and should it show itself in the region sacred to Owen, Baxter, Howe, Charnock, Bunyan, Crisp, Gill, &c., I am sure their ancient effigies would scarcely be able to display their indignation in the absence of those fists whereof the antique oval frame has bereaved them. Apart from all theological consideration, a man of reading would not regret the purchase of this volume; but the mass of book-skimmers would, with some qualification, apply to the present book the words of the wit concerning Tennyson's *Maud*—

> 'Dreadfully dry and dreadfully dawdling,
> Tennyson's *Maud* should be Tennyson's maudlin.'

This, I am aware, is no argument against the book; in fact, many writers think themselves complimented when they are told that only the few can appreciate them. I am midway between the many and the few; I shall not exclaim against a man's poem because I have not culture of mind enough to sympathize with his mode of expression, nor can I hope to claim the privilege which allows to the discerning few the right of decisive criticism. I can only say, I had rather have written *Divine and Moral Songs for Children* than these fine but comparatively useless verses. No man of even moderate education can despise the talent, the mind, and the research, which have together produced this 'rivulet singing as it flows along'; but he who desires to see talent well applied, and mind put out to the largest interest, will never consider the writing of these verses a profitable employment. A minister of Christ's holy gospel should ever be seeking after the conversion of his fellow-men; and I would be sorry to write so much, and expend so much labour, on a work so little calculated to arouse the careless, guide the wanderer, comfort the desponding, or edify the believer.

In the next place, what have I to say of the hymns theologically? I answer, there is so little of the doctrinal element in them that I am at a loss to judge; and that little is so indefinite that, apart from the author's antecedents, one could scarcely guess his doctrinal views at all. Certainly, some verses are bad—bad in the most unmitigated sense of that word, but others of them, like noses of wax, will fit more than one face.

There are sweet sentences which would become the lips of those rich poets of early times in whom quaintness of style and weight of matter were united, but an unkind observer will notice that even these are not angular enough to provoke the hostility of the Unitarian, and might be uttered alike by the lover and the hater of what we are well known to regard as the gospel.

Frequently, an honest tongue must pronounce unhesitating condemnation; but in many other places, one must pause lest, while cutting up the tares, we destroy the wheat also. The scale one moment descends with good truth, and for many a long hour it hangs aloft with emptiness for its only glory. There is nothing distinct in the book but its indistinctness; and one becomes painfully nervous while wandering through this pretty valley, lest it should turn out to be what some of its waymarks betoken—an enchanted ground full of 'deceivableness of unrighteousness.' There are in it doctrines which no man who knows the plague of his own heart can tolerate for a moment, and which the believer in free-grace will put aside as being nothing but husks, upon which he cannot feed. 'It is not my book,' the convinced sinner will exclaim; and the matured believer will say, 'Nor is it mine,' and yet it is more covertly unsound than openly so.

These hymns rise up in the *Rivulet* like mermaids—there is much form and comeliness upon the surface, but their nether parts, I ween, it were hard to describe. Perhaps they are not the fair things they seem: when I look below their glistening eyes and flowing hair, I think I discern some meaner nature joined with the form divine, but the surface of this *Rivulet* is green with beautifully-flowering weeds, and I can scarcely see into the depths where lurks the essence of the matter.

This much I think I can discover in this volume—viz., that it is not the song of an Isaiah speaking more of Jesus than all the rest, nor a canticle of Solomon concerning 'my Well-beloved'. It is doubtful who is the mother of this babe; and so little claim will orthodoxy ever lay to it, that its true parent may receive it into her loving arms, and there will be no demand for the half thereof. But, then, the writer never asked us to grant him the reputation of our orthodoxy; we need not, therefore, dispute with him concerning that to which he makes no claim.

If I should ever be on amicable terms with the chief of the Ojibewas, I might suggest several verses from Mr. Lynch as a portion of a liturgy to be used on the next occasion when he bows before the Great Spirit of the West wind, for there are some most appropriate sonnets for the worship of the God of nature which the unenlightened savage would understand quite as well as the believer in Revelation, and might perhaps receive rather more readily. Hark! O ye Delawares, Mohawks, Choctaws, Chickasaws, Blackfeet, Pawnees, Shawnees, and Cherokees, here is your primitive faith most sweetly rehearsed—not in your own wild notes, but in the white man's language:

> 'My God, in nature I confess
> A beauty fraught with holiness;
> Love written plainly I descry
> My life's commandment in the sky;
> Oh, still to me the days endear,
> When lengthening light leads on the year!'

It is, I conceive, but a fair judgment to which even the writer would give his assent that these are more the hymns of nature than the songs of Zion, though I am far from believing that even the voice of nature is here at all times faithfully interpreted. This rivulet runs through fair meadows, and between glorious hills, but it flows rather too far away from 'the oracle of God' to please me. It has some pure drops of God's own rain within its bosom, but its flood is not drawn from the river, 'the streams whereof shall make glad the city of God.' It has good thoughts, holy thoughts, from God's glorious temple of nature, commingled with a few of the words of the inspired prophets of the Lord; but, in the main, its characteristic is not Revelation, but nature. As such, it can never suit the taste of the spiritually-minded who delight in fellowship with the Divine Jesus. Those who would crown the Head of their Maker with wreaths of thought, may here find some little assistance, but she who would wash the feet of the God-man, Christ Jesus, with her tears, will never find a companion in this book. I can talk with it for an hour, and learn much from it, but I cannot love it as I do my favourite Herbert, and it does not open the door of Heaven to me as does the music of Zion which it is my wont to hear. But why am I to condemn a book because it does not touch a chord in my own soul? Why should I blame a man because he has not written for the old-fashioned piety which some of us inherit from our fathers? Why murmur if he speaks his own much-puzzled mind in language which the repose of an anchored faith cannot interpret? It were unfair to burn this book because it came forth, like some other queer things, on the fifth of November; and it is not very brave to be so desperately afraid of a plot because, on that day, a man was discovered, with a dark lantern, singing in the vaults beneath the house which ancient people call *the truth, against which the gates of hell shall not prevail.*

Liberty of conscience is every man's right; our writer has spoken his mind, why should he alone provoke attack when many others, who agree quite as little with our views, are allowed to escape? The battle is either a tribute to superior ability, or else a sign of the times; I believe it to be both. The work has its errors, in the estimation of one who does not fear to subscribe himself a Calvinistic Christian, but it has no more evil leaven than other books of far less merit. No one would have read it with a jealous eye unless it had been made the centre of a controversy, for we should either have let it quietly alone, or should have forgotten the deleterious mixture, and retained the little good which it certainly contains. The author did not write for us; he wrote for men of his own faith, he tells his little book—

> 'Thy haven shall the approval be
> Of hearts with faith like thine.'

The only wonder is that men, whom we thought to be of other mind, should endorse all therein; but private friendship operates largely, and perhaps some of them may have sympathized more with the *man censured* than with the *man singing*. This deed of men, who in standing are eminent, is not a theme for our present discussion. We must, however, observe that we cannot wonder that they themselves are attacked, and we cannot think that any other course was open to the original censor than to reply *with spirit*.

We are sure this book could not cheer us on a dying bed, or even nerve us with faith for a living conflict. Its sentiments are not ours; its aims, its teachings, are not enough akin to any which we hold dear to give us any aid in our labours; but if there be any goodness, doth not the bee suck honey from the nettle? We would do the same, believing it to be a nettle still; but one which does not grow in our garden, and is not of very gigantic stature, and therefore no great object of abhorrence. Had the author claimed to be one of the old school, we might be up in arms; but we know the men and their communications, therefore we need not read what we do not approve.

The book is out of our line as a theological work, it does not advocate what *we* believe; having said that, we have been but honest; and those who think with us need not malign the author; but, seeing that the fight is now in another quarter, let them respect the man, however much they may oppose the sentiments which have been for a while brought into fellowship with his volume. This controversy is but one volcano indicative of seas of latent fire in the bosom of our churches. It will, in a few more years, be hard to prove the orthodoxy of our churches if matters be not changed. It has manifested what existed already; it has dragged to light evils which were before unseen.

Would to God that the day were over when our churches tamely endure false doctrine; and would, moreover, that all champions of truth would keep the one point in view, and cease from all personalities! May God, of His infinite mercy, preserve the right, and may those who err from the faith be brought to the fold of Jesus, and be saved! The old doctrines of free-grace are gracious doctrines still; there are none of these in this book, what then? They are in our hearts, I trust, and the outspoken enunciation of them will do ten times more for these truths than the high-flying language of the pseudo-intellectual few can ever do against them. This book is important only as the hinge of a controversy, as such alone ought it to excite our minds, but the less we observe the hinge, and the more we look to the matter itself, the more easy will be our victory.

As long as the fight is thought to be concerning a man, or a book, the issue is doubtful, but let it be for God and for His truth, and the battle is the Lord's. The time is come for sterner men than the willows of the stream can afford; we shall soon have to handle truth, not with kid gloves, but with gauntlets—the gauntlets of holy courage and integrity. Go on, ye warriors of the cross, for the King is at the head of you. *The Evening Star* exhorts the ministers to stand fast in the liberty wherewith Cromwell and Milton made them free; but the apostle of the Son of God bids you stand fast in the liberty wherewith *Christ* has made you free. THE OLD FAITH MUST BE TRIUMPHANT.

C. H. SPURGEON."

Lynch thus commented on this article: "This review of Mr. Spurgeon's enjoys the credit with me of being the only thing on his side—that is, *against* me—that was impertinent, without being malevolent. It evinced far more ability and appreciation than Grant or Campbell had done, and indicated a man whose eyes, if they do not get blinded with the fumes of that strong, but unwholesome, incense, popularity, may glow with a heavenlier brightness than it seems to me they have yet done. Mr. Spurgeon concluded by remarking that 'the old faith must be triumphant', in which I entirely agree with him, doubting only whether he is yet old enough in experience of the world's sorrows and strifes to know what the old faith really is. He says, 'We shall soon have to handle truth, not with kid gloves, but with gauntlets—the gauntlets of holy courage and integrity.' Aye, that we shall, and some of us now do! And, perhaps, the man who has a soul that 'fights to music'—

> 'Calm 'mid the bewildering cry,
> Confident of victory,'—

is the likeliest to have a hand with a grip for battle, and a grasp for friendship alike strong and warm."

The controversy continued for a long time; *The Freeman* and *The Wesleyan Times* joined the other papers that had supported Mr. Lynch, but so powerful was the protest of Grant and Campbell, that the Congregational Union actually had to postpone its autumnal session. The ultimate result of this long-past "fight for the faith" appears to have been very much the same as followed the "Down-grade" controversy more than thirty years later: many ministers, and their people, too, were led back to the fundamental doctrines from which they had begun to wander; Evangelical truth was, at least for a time, more widely proclaimed; and, although some strayed yet further away from the great central verities of the inspired Word, yet, on the whole, the discussion was declared by contemporary and reliable witnesses to have been productive of "an untold amount of good to the Church of God."

*   *   *

Nearly four years elapsed before the next historic controversy, which was produced by Baldwin Brown's volume of sermons. The veteran Baptist minister, Rev. J. Howard Hinton, M.A., wrote two articles, which were published in *The Baptist Magazine*, March and April, 1860, under the title, "Strictures on some passages in the Rev. J. B. Brown's *Divine Life in Man*". The conclusion of his protest is such a pattern and justification of Spurgeon's similar action, twenty-seven years afterwards, that it must be inserted here. Mr. Hinton wrote:

"I offer no apology for these 'Strictures', since the matter on which they are made is before the public. I have written them with a feeling of perfect respect towards Mr. Brown, and I trust nothing inconsistent with that feeling has escaped from me. I submit them respectfully to my brethren in the ministry, and in 'the kingdom and patience of Jesus Christ', deeply feeling the importance of the subjects to which they relate, and not without hope that they may be deemed worthy of serious consideration.

To my own conviction, I am pleading for vital Evangelical truth— for the truth of God, and for the souls of men. I speak because I would fain contribute somewhat, however little, to withstand what I take to be the first open inroad, into English Evangelical Nonconformist churches, of a theology fatally deficient in the truth and power of the gospel. Whether this, or any similar system may have privately diffused itself to any considerable extent, I neither know, insinuate, nor conjecture; but, assuredly, I should regard the prevalence of it as a mischief of the gravest character, and whether I am heard or not, I cannot but lift up my voice against it.

It is true, I am now an old minister, and perhaps I ought, as is said to have been pleasantly suggested by some fast spirit of the rising generation of divines concerning old ministers in general, to be 'hung up in God's armoury', as the armour of ancient heroes is in the Tower, but words of truth and soberness may find a response, if breathed low from the verge of the grave. The aspect of the times emboldens me. It is not now, dear brethren—above all times, it is not now—when 'the end' must be so near, and when so many cheering tokens of revival enkindle our hopes, that a perversion, or even a dilution, of the truth as it is in Jesus should find welcome or entrance among us; and I trust in God it will be given to us to 'contend earnestly for the faith which was once delivered unto the saints.' "

The articles were afterwards reprinted, and issued as a pamphlet. The review of the "Strictures", published in *The Freeman*, was considered by several prominent Baptist ministers to be of so un-satisfactory a character that seven of them signed the following joint-protest, which duly appeared in the denominational paper on April 11—

"THE REV. J. B. BROWN, AND THE REV. J. H. HINTON.

To the Editors of *The Freeman*,

Dear Sirs,
                We are constrained to address you by considerations which, if we may not say they are imperative, appear to us too urgent and weighty to be resisted. We entertain, however, so high a sense of the value of free and unbiassed criticism, and are so jealous of in-fringing on the proper liberty of a public journal, that we address you with great reluctance, and only under the influence of what we deem our duty, at once to ourselves and to what we regard as important theological truth.

Our duty to ourselves seems to us to require that we should, with your permission, explicitly state in your columns that the review, in your last number, of Mr. Hinton's 'Strictures' on the recent work of the Rev. J. B. Brown, is so far from expressing *our* sentiments that we altogether disagree with the writer's estimate, both of the theological principles Mr. Brown avows, and of the services which Mr. Hinton has rendered to Evangelical truth by his strictures upon them. *The Freeman* is so generally assumed to be connected with the Baptist denomination that, but for such a disclaimer as we now send you, that review might be supposed to speak the sense of the body. A more erroneous opinion could not, so far as we know, be entertained. At all events, *our* position as Baptist ministers is well known, and we speak for ourselves.

We shall not indulge in any indefinite censures on the character and tendency of Mr. Brown's volume, but we feel constrained to say that the passages on which Mr. Hinton founds his 'Strictures' contain, in our judgment, pernicious error. We would not hold an author responsible for the inferences which may seem to another fairly deducible from his statements, and we entertain the hope that Mr. Brown does not see the consequences which we think inevitably follow from some of his principles. But we do not hesitate to avow our conviction, that both the principles and their consequences, whether categorically stated, or involved in a metaphor, go to subvert the whole scheme of God's moral government as revealed in the sacred Scriptures, and with it those precious truths which cluster round the cross, and centre in it, and which, for that reason, are most distinctive of the gospel, and most fundamental to it.

In our judgment, therefore, Mr. Hinton has rendered a timely and valuable service to Evangelical Christianity by his animadversions on those portions of Mr. Brown's book, and, for our part, we thank God that our brother's pen has been so well and so ably employed. We are no more lovers of controversy in the Church than is your reviewer, but if errors subversive of the gospel are advocated by some of her ministers, it is the duty of others to withstand them; and we honour Mr. Hinton that, at a period of life when he might be naturally desirous of repose, he has stepped forward in the vindication and defence of some of the vital doctrines of the faith.

Nor, in conclusion, can we refrain from expressing our earnest hope that our pulpits may be preserved from the sentiments which Mr. Brown has published, and which *we cannot but fear your reviewer approves.* Without conjuring up any 'phantasmal hydra' of heterodoxy, as your reviewer speaks, and imagining that it is beginning to be rampant in our churches, which we do not for a moment suppose or believe, we take the liberty of saying that we trust our ministers will continue to be students of Howe, and Charnock, and Hall, and Fuller, rather than draw their theology from Maurice, Professor Scott, and others of the same school, whom Mr. Brown so strongly recommends.

Above all, we desire affectionately to caution those in the ministry, who are younger than ourselves, against that style of preaching which, under the pretentious affectation of being intellectual, grows ashamed of the old and vulgar doctrines of man's guilt, as well as of his total depravity, of Christ's atonement and satisfaction for sin, of justification by the imputation of His righteousness through faith, of the new birth by the agency of the Holy Spirit, and, in a word, of that scheme of dogmatic Christian truth which is popularly known under the designation of 'the doctrines of grace'. Those doctrines are dear to us as epitomising and concentrating the theology of the Bible, and as constituting, through the presence and power of the Christian Comforter, the spiritual life of our churches.

Pardon us in one final word to yourselves. By whomsoever the evil work of lowering the estimate entertained of the value of these doctrines, and so diminishing their influence, may be perpetrated, let

it be far from you as the conductors of one of our public denominational journals, to further it with your countenance, or to lend even
the semblance of your aid.

We are,

Dear Sirs,

Yours very faithfully,

EDWARD STEANE.
DANIEL KATTERNS.
C. H. SPURGEON.
CHARLES STANFORD.
W. G. LEWIS, JUNR.
WILLIAM BROCK.
JOSEPH ANGUS."

London,
    April 9, 1860."

To this communication the Editors of *The Freeman* added the
following note:

"We have no hesitation in giving insertion to the above letter.
Notwithstanding that it is somewhat unusual, and generally inconvenient, to admit of discussion respecting reviews, the spirit of our
brethren who have favoured us with the above letter is at the same
time so excellent, and so kindly respectful to ourselves, that we should
be doing both ourselves and them an injustice if we hesitated about
admitting this expression of their views. At the same time, we cannot
but be somewhat surprised that they should have considered such an
expression necessary. In whatever sense *The Freeman* may be regarded
as 'the organ of the Baptist denomination', *we* had never been so vain
as to suppose that the editorial 'we' in our columns meant Messrs.
Steane, Katterns, Spurgeon, Stanford, Lewis, Junr., Brock, and
Angus; still less had we imagined that any judgment respecting a
work, which was formed and expressed by our reviewer, would be
regarded by anybody as the judgment of the Baptist denomination.
The modesty of our reviewer, at least, is so shocked at the very idea of
being supposed to review in this representative character, that he begs
us to state, once for all, that his judgment of the works which come
before him is simply *his own*, and that, neither the brethren who have
favoured us with the above letter, nor any other brethren, are at all
responsible for opinions of books which probably they have not seen,
and about which, assuredly, he has not consulted them.

As to our friend's review of Mr. Brown's book, we do not think it is needful to say anything. Our reviewer has already given *his* opinion of that work at considerable length, and his objections to the volume were by no means 'indefinite'. Indeed, he pointed out its deficiencies, in relation to the person and work of the Redeemer, with a precision that ought, we venture to say, to have secured him from the censures of our brethren. If he felt it his duty, as an impartial critic, to object to some things, also, in Mr. Hinton's 'Strictures', everyone who read the review would see at once that it was not the *doctrine* of the 'Strictures' that he had any doubt about—for the 'doctrine' he declared emphatically to be 'important to be upheld'—but the *style and character* of the 'Strictures', upon which he still retains his own opinion.

We hope it is not necessary for *us* to say that we also 'trust'—without thinking we are 'taking a liberty' in saying so—that 'our ministers will continue to be students of Howe, and Charnock, and Hall, and Fuller? We trust—and, what is more, *we thoroughly believe*—that our ministers will not grow ashamed of 'the old' (*we* will not venture to say, 'vulgar') doctrine of man's guilt as well as of his total depravity, of Christ's atonement and satisfaction for sin, of justification by the imputation of His righteousness through faith, of the new birth by the agency of the Holy Spirit, and, in a word, of that scheme of dogmatic Christian truth which is popularly known under the designation of 'the doctrines of grace'. At the same time, we must be permitted still to doubt whether 'our younger ministers' have given any cause to their 'elder' brethren—amongst whom, it seems, are Mr. Spurgeon, Mr. Stanford, and Mr. Lewis, Junr.—to 'caution' them publicly against becoming 'ashamed' of these doctrines. To our 'younger' ministers as well as to their 'elders', these doctrines are 'dear'. In the pulpits of our 'younger' ministers, as much, if not as ably, as in those of their elders, these doctrines are preached. We so far sympathize with our reviewer as to hope that 'the last days of our elder brethren may not be embittered by suspicions of their younger brethren's orthodoxy, from which souls such as theirs must naturally recoil.'—*Eds.*"

Preaching at New Park Street Chapel, on Lord's-day evening, April 15, 1860, from the text, "For He hath made Him to be sin for us, who knew no sin; that we might be made the righteousness of God in Him," the Pastor, in commencing his discourse, thus referred to the burning question of the hour—

"Some time ago, an excellent lady sought an interview with me, with the object, as she said, of enlisting my sympathy upon the question of 'Anti-Capital Punishment'. I heard the reasons she urged against hanging men who had committed murder, and, though they did not convince me, I did not seek to answer them. She proposed that, when a man committed murder, he should be confined for life. My remark was, that a great many men, who had been confined half their lives, were not a bit the better for it, and as for her belief that they would necessarily be brought to repentance, I was afraid it was but a dream. 'Ah!' she said, good soul as she was, 'that is because we have been all wrong about punishments. We punish people because we think they deserve to be punished. Now, we ought to show them that we love them; that we only punish them to make them better.' 'Indeed, madam,' I replied, 'I have heard that theory a great many times, and I have seen much fine writing upon the matter, but I am no believer in it. The design of punishment should be amendment, but the ground of punishment lies in the positive guilt of the offender. I believe that, when a man does wrong, he ought to be punished for it, and that there is a guilt in sin which justly merits punishment.' She could not see that. Sin was a very wrong thing, but punishment was not a proper idea. She thought that people were treated too cruelly in prison, and that they ought to be taught that we love them. If they were treated kindly in prison, and tenderly dealt with, they would grow up much better, she was sure. With a view of interpreting her own theory, I said, 'I suppose, then, you would give criminals all sorts of indulgences in prison. Some great vagabond, who has committed burglary dozens of times—I suppose you would let him sit in an easy chair in the evening, before a nice fire, and mix him a glass of spirits and water, and give him his pipe, and make him happy, to show how much we love him.' Well, no, she would not give him the spirits; but, still, all the rest would do him good. I thought that was a delightful picture, certainly. It seemed to me to be the most prolific method of cultivating rogues which ingenuity could invent. I imagine that you could grow any number of thieves in that way, for it would be a special means of propagating all manner of wickedness. These very beautiful theories, to such a simple mind as mine, were the source of much amusement; the idea of fondling villains, and treating their crimes as if they were the tumbles and falls of children, made me laugh heartily. I fancied I saw the Government resigning its functions to these excellent persons, and the grand results of their marvellously kind experiments—the sword of the magistrate being transformed into a gruel-spoon, and the jail becoming a sweet retreat for people with bad reputations.

Little, however, did I think I should live to see this kind of stuff taught in the pulpit; I had no idea that there would arise teaching which would bring down God's moral government from the solemn aspect in which Scripture reveals it, to a namby-pamby sentimentalism, which adores a deity destitute of every masculine virtue. But we never know to-day what may occur to-morrow. We have lived to see a certain sort of men—thank God, they are not Baptists!—though I am sorry to say there are a great many Baptists who are beginning to follow in their trail—who seek to teach, nowadays, that God is a universal Father, and that our ideas of His dealing with the impenitent as a Judge, and not as a Father, are remnants of antiquated error. Sin, according to these men, is a disorder rather than an offence, an error rather than a crime. Love is the only attribute they can discern, and the full-orbed Deity they have not known. Some of these men push their way very far into the bogs and mire of falsehood, until they inform us that eternal punishment is ridiculed as a dream. In fact, books now appear which teach us that there is no such thing as the vicarious sacrifice of our Lord Jesus Christ. They use the word atonement, it is true; but, in regard to its meaning they have removed the ancient landmark. They acknowledge that the Father has shown His great love to poor sinful man by sending His Son, but not that God was inflexibly just in the exhibition of His mercy, nor that He punished Christ on the behalf of His people, nor that, indeed, God ever will punish anybody in His wrath, or that there is such a thing as justice apart from discipline. Even *sin* and *hell* are but old words employed henceforth in a new and altered sense. Those are old-fashioned notions, and we poor souls, who go on talking about election and imputed righteousness, are behind our time. Aye, and the gentlemen who bring out books on this subject applaud Mr. Maurice, and Professor Scott, and the like, but are too cowardly to follow them, and boldly propound these sentiments. These are the new men whom God has sent down from Heaven, to tell us that the apostle Paul was all wrong, that our faith is vain, that we have been quite mistaken, that there was no need for propitiating blood to wash away our sins; that the fact was, our sins needed discipline, but penal vengeance and righteous wrath are quite out of the question! When I thus speak, I am free to confess that such ideas are not boldly taught by a certain individual whose volume excites these remarks, but as he puffs the books of gross perverters of the truth, I am compelled to believe that he endorses such theology.

Well, brethren, I am happy to say that sort of stuff has not gained entrance into this pulpit. I dare say the worms will eat the wood before there will be anything of that sort sounded in this place; and may these bones be picked by vultures, and this flesh be rent in sunder by lions, and may every nerve in this body suffer pangs and tortures, ere these lips shall give utterance to any such doctrines or sentiments! We are content to remain among the vulgar souls who believe the old doctrines of grace. We are willing still to be behind in the great march of intellect, and stand by that unmoving cross, which, like the pole star, never advances, because it never stirs, but always abides in its place, the guide of the soul to Heaven, the one foundation other than which no man can lay, and without building upon which no man shall ever see the face of God and live.

Thus much have I said upon a matter which just now is exciting controversy. It has been my high privilege to be associated with six of our ablest brethren in the ministry, in a letter of protest against the countenance which a certain newspaper seemed willing to lend to this modern heresy. We trust it may be the means, in the hands of God, of helping to check that downward march—that wandering from truth which seems, by a singular infatuation, to have unsettled the minds of some brethren in our denomination."

So far as that particular publication (*The Freeman*) was concerned, the protest was unavailing; and a few weeks later, Spurgeon forwarded to at least two other papers the following letter, which appears to have been his final contribution to the controversy:

"Clapham,
May 21, 1860.

Sir,

The fulfilment of irksome duties is the test of sincere obedience. When pleasure and service are identical, it is easy to be diligent in Heavenly business; but when flesh and blood rebel against a known duty, it is time to invoke the aid of Divine grace. Every personal feeling and private affection must give way before the imperative demands of our Lord and Master. Contention for the faith is far less pleasant than communion with Christ; but the neglect of the precept may involve the withdrawal of the privilege.

In the matter of *The Freeman* newspaper, I most sorrowfully enter upon a work as distasteful to my feelings as it is inconvenient to my circumstances. Excuses for silence have utterly failed me. Although my respect for the gentlemen who conduct that journal has given me great readiness in suggesting arguments for peace, my conscience permits me no longer to purchase peace at the expense of the truths in which my soul finds its solace and delight. Private resentment I have none; but, on the contrary, I cherish feelings of personal regard, which restrain me in this controversy from the use of a more vigorous style, and seriously encumber me in the conflict which lies before us. Can we not honour the gentlemen in their private capacity, and yet regret the fact that they have officially occupied a position which exposes them to severe criticism? I can honestly say that I can meet, with cordial charity, many men from whom I differ widely; and I never consider a blow dealt against my opinions in the light of a personal attack—nay, I respect an honest antagonist, and only despise the man who mingles resentment with public debate. We have solemn matters to discuss—in some degree, connected with one of the most serious heresies which ever afflicted the Christian Church—and it behoves us to use language which shall become the lips of men who know the value of the doctrines upon which they debate; and it will be our wisdom to cherish the spirit which shall be in consonance with the sentiments which we maintain. Solemnly, as in the sight of God, I believe *The Freeman* to have been very guilty; but to our own Master we must stand or fall. It is ours to reprove, but not to condemn; it will be the duty of the offender to defend, and not to recriminate.

The fact that seven brethren among the London Baptist ministers, led by one of the most venerable fathers of the denomination, had unitedly dissented from their opinion upon an important question, should have had some weight with the Editors. They are not so conspicuous for learning, ability, or success, as to be beyond the reach of friendly admonition; and surely they are not so immodest as to hold in contempt a solemn protest signed by brethren whom they are compelled to regard as honoured servants of Christ. Was the document in which that protest was contained insulting, contemptuous, or unfriendly? Far from it. Was it not written by one whose amiable spirit might rather tempt him to laxity than lead him to severity? What but the most weighty reasons and powerful motives could compel the most loving spirit in the universe, at a time of life when age and painful infirmity have brought him very low, to spend a great part of a weary night in penning a deliberate protest against a dangerous evil? This may be a joke to some men; to us, it was as devout an act as our baptism into the name of our Lord Jesus. Freely would I have signed that letter with my blood had it been needed; and I think I speak the sentiments of all. We saw in the matter before us one of the ramifications of a deadly evil, which has commenced by polluting our literature, and may conclude by debauching our pulpits. We wrote under a strong sense of duty as in the sight of God, and there has not been a moment since in which I would not have signed it again with all my heart. We did not attack *The Freeman;* we only deprecated its patronizing the new school of theology. It is true, we expressed our fear that the reviewer was a personal believer in the sentiments we denounced; that fear has since ripened into conviction, but it did not involve a suspicion of the Editors, as we had reason to believe the reviewer to be a person totally distinct from the managers of the journal. At the risk of being considered egotistical, I do not hesitate to say that a more judicious, generous, gentlemanly, and Christian letter was never written. It was worthy of its author, and honourable to the cause it vindicated.

But now the evil begins. How, think you, was the admirable document received? Why, Sir, it was supplemented by an editorial postscript, the marrow of which consisted in a joke upon the juvenility of three of the brethren, who are yet old enough to know some who are their juniors in years, and a few who are far more their juniors in decency. A ghastly smile, like that which flickers upon the face of a man who is confused and confounded, but who longs to conceal his fears with the mask of levity, was the only answer we received. We were dealing with Divine realities, and with verities which concern the very basis of our holy religion; the reply was a play upon a harmless sentence, highly appropriate in the mouth of most of the seven, and not indecorous upon the lip of any one of them. This absurd trifling was esteemed to be so terrible a piece of artillery that it must needs be fired off again at Exeter Hall on the missionary occasion, to the disgust of many of the audience, by a gentleman who was so alarmed at the stupendous engine with which he was entrusted, that the echo of his own voice seemed to startle him, and one word from an indignant hearer extorted a trembling apology.

A silence ensued. Discretion mounted guard, and hushed alike review and article, save one faint growl, which showed the animus within more surely than the most laboured writing. We will not hint that conscience was at work, and yet this is a better supposition than some have hinted at. However, the quietude was at last broken, and *The Freeman* came forth in a new and unexpected character. It refused to be styled an organ, or even to be suspected of such a relation to the body. Who in his senses could have thought it possible that a paper could represent even seven men, much less a denomination? The question was a singularly refreshing one. We had certainly been unreasonable enough to assist in the first circulation of the paper, and some of us in its continued maintenance, under the hallucination that it was, in some sense, the representative of the denomination.

In this belief, we wrote our letter. We now find that we were all the victims of a mistaken, if not ridiculous, idea. It is true that the irrational conception of a representative newspaper is embodied in scores of journals which are the advocates and organs of bodies political and religious; but facts, however stubborn, must give way before the powerful satire of *The Freeman*. It is equally true that the circulation of that paper is mainly owing to the absurd notion which our Editors so merrily repudiate; but, when a protest presents no other assailable point, common sense and interest are alike invaluable, and must be slaughtered if they stand in the way of revenge. Oh, sad result of this most rebellious protest! It has achieved its purpose in a manner the most unexpected. We thought to screen ourselves from complicity with error, and it is done more effectually than we could desire when *The Freeman* rejects the representative standing which was its greatest honour and the very breath of its nostrils. This is committing suicide in order to be avenged. The worst enemies of the paper could not have uttered a sentiment more damaging to it than that which it reiterates *ad nauseam*. The Member has taken his seat in the Parliament of the Press, but he is not now the representative of the men whose suffrages he sought. He laughs in your face if you have the impertinence to show him kindness in that capacity. Be it so, Mr. *Freeman;* follow your own sweet will, and utter your own opinions without restraint. From this day forth, we will never slander you by the supposition that there is any connection between you and our churches; you are your own spokesman, and not ours. We would not have touched the subject if we had not believed ourselves compromised; and, as we find we were labouring under a delusion, now happily dispelled, there is no need for protesting in a friendly manner. The field of battle now divides us; and, if the old Lutheran spirit be not buried for ever, we will be clear of the blood of all men by clearing ourselves each day from the errors of the times.

But, Sir, it seems that, in the performance of *The Freeman*, tragedy must always be followed by a farce. This marvellously-free actor has mounted the judgment-seat, put on the wig and gown, and tried the brethren who gently rebuked him, as if they had been guilty of misdemeanour. In mimic justice, he condemns; but, in comic mercy, he offers pardon. Forgive me, Sir, if I leave my place as a minister for a moment, and answer these brethren according to their folly. What brilliant wits these men are! They seem to expect the whole seven of us to perform a penitential pilgrimage to *The Freeman* office, and, with ropes about our necks, plead for pardon at the hands of the offended Editors. In truth, the offence is very grievous, and demands punishment the most exemplary. It is all in vain to plead that witnessing was of old an honoured service, and that protesting is sanctioned by the very name of our Protestant theology. It is equally in vain to hint that the opinions of seven ministers may be, in some cases, equal in value to the *dicta* of two or even three Editors. This is not to the point; the criminals are guilty, and let them plead so, that mercy may step in. It is a memorable proof of the longsuffering of a paper which, not long ago, pretended to exercise a sort of archiepiscopal oversight and authority, that the seven culprits were not executed upon the spot, and that space for repentance is still allowed. We are assured (and I do not doubt it) that our retractation, when tendered, will be received with all the lovingkindness with which the yearning bowels of our tender parent are so abundantly surcharged. Oh, hasten to be wise, my erring brethren, sorrowful comrades in crime! We have but to confess our great iniquity, and the forgiveness, which we so ill deserve, shall be poured in unctuous abundance upon our heads, low as they must be in the very dust. *The Freeman*, glorious in magnanimity, stretches out to you the hand of mercy; run into its gracious arms, and be smothered by its suffocating compliments. By dint of steady obedience, you may recover your lost position, and once more receive the paternal approbation. Yes, gentle *Freeman;* when we retract, when we ask your pardon, when we confess that our protest was anything but a needed tribute to the soundness of the Baptist denomination, and a most proper warning to yourself, then, and not till then, put us all in your portrait gallery, from which some of our ablest ministers have prayed to be excluded, and dandle us upon your knee in blissful companionship with Kingsley and J. B. Brown.

However agreeable this comedy may be to *The Freeman*, I am completely weary with it, and once more return to the sobriety which our subject demands. I must now refer to the injurious insinuations with which we have been personally assailed. *The Freeman* affirms that some of us had never read the book to which we referred. I am sure I had both read and marked it; but, as to inwardly digesting it, I am not nearly enough allied to an ostrich to be able to accomplish that feat. Next, it unfairly takes it for granted that the letter of Dr. Angus was a joint affair, although it is his writing, and his alone. Admirable as it is, that letter is no more the composition of the whole seven than is this epistle, which the Editor will take care to observe is mine, and mine alone.

A worse act than this imperiously demands enquiry. *The Freeman* must make good a statement to which I am now about to refer, or tacitly admit that its courage and truthfulness have vanished. *It dares to say that one of us had previously approved of Mr. Brown's book.* Name the man. Why stab the whole seven in the dark? In the name of common honesty, not to say religion, point out the individual. None of us would take the pains to deny an accusation so indefinitely worded. The charge is so serious that, to whomsoever it may be falsely applied, it will be his duty, for the protection of society, to visit the author of the libel with the fullest punishment the laws of his country can enforce, unless an ample apology be forthcoming. The imputation is tantamount to calling a man dishonest, if not a liar, and what remains to any of us when such charges are allowed to pass unchallenged?

This last item is weighty enough to allow me to pause for a reply. I have written to you rather than to *The Freeman*, because this last matter is a barrier to communication too serious to be overleaped.

I am, Sir,

Yours very truly,

C. H. SPURGEON."

Mr. Brown wrote the following letter to the Editors of *The Freeman;*

"Sirs,

I hold no controversy with the six Baptist ministers who have joined Mr. Spurgeon in a deliberate effort to prejudice my ministry, and the book which I have recently published on *The Divine Life of Man.*

So many Christian brethren have testified to me that they find the book full of the light of those truths which I am said to weaken or deny, that I am able to bear with great composure the judgment of my critics.

I content myself with declaring, in the belief that there are men in the Baptist ministry candid enough to find my words credible, that the doctrines of grace, in the broad, full, Evangelic sense of the term, have for nearly twenty years been the great theme of my ministry, and, if I know my own heart, will be till I die.

I pray these seven to bear more faithful witness to their Master's words in their ministry, than they have borne to mine, and am,

Yours faithfully,

J. BALDWIN BROWN.

P.S.—Is it too much to expect that those papers which have copied the protest, will do me the justice to insert this brief reply?"

One of the papers which published Brown's letter added this significant comment:

"While we feel it to be a matter of simple justice to give insertion to Mr. Baldwin Brown's letter, it is, to say the least of the matter, not a little remarkable that Mr Brown should hold to 'the doctrines of grace, in the broad, full, Evangelic sense of the term,' as he here professes to do; and that he should, at the same time, declare his full appreciation of Professors Maurice and Scott, as model teachers of truth, whose published works are most decidedly antagonistic to, and subversive of, the fundamental truths of the gospel."

The Inquirer, a Unitarian paper, in an article on the controversy, fully justified the protests of Mr. Hinton, and his seven brother ministers, when it said: "It is not a little encouraging to us, who have maintained a faithful confession through long years of ill-report, to find the most thoughtful and earnest of the younger school of orthodox ministers gradually and painfully struggling, amid much opposition, towards the recognition of the same conclusions which we have long advocated as the highest truth of the Scriptures. With deep sympathy do we watch their struggles, praying that they may have strength from above to quit themselves like true men in the contest, and to follow *the whole truth* faithfully wheresoever it may lead them."

The Dial, in quoting this extract, very pertinently adds: 'Mr. Brown will probably say, 'Save me from my friends!' " The writers in the Unitarian paper could see clearly enough whither his teaching was tending, just as, a whole generation afterwards, their successors plainly perceived the drift of the "Down-gradeism" which broke the heart of the brave champion of the faith—C. H. Spurgeon—who counted not even his life dear unto him if he might, in any degree, stem the torrent that was bearing away so much that he regarded as the priceless truth of the living God.

Chapter 33

"Helensburgh House" and Garden

BY MRS. C. H. SPURGEON

A WELL-KNOWN writer of to-day, in one of his pleasant little sketches, says: "There are certain scenes in one's early life which come before us in a somewhat confused fashion. One is quite sure of the facts, but where to place them as to time, and how to connect them with relation to other facts, is not easy. It is a curious medley that memory gives back to one, passing quickly 'from grave to gay, from lively to severe'."

This exactly describes my experience while trying to chronicle the further events of our early married life. I am embarrassed with the multitude and variety of the recollections which crowd upon me, but many of them are not important enough to be written down, and some are so disjointed that I fail to reproduce them connectedly. I seem to have before me a mass of bright, shining webs of precious memories, hopelessly disarranged and entwisted; and the question is —How can I bring these rebellious threads into something like order and beauty? I remember a story of my childhood's days, in which a little maiden—for a punishment of untidy habits, I think—was given a basket full of tangled skeins of silk, and told that she must, by a certain time, have them all sorted out, and laid in regular rows. The fairy "Order", pitying her distress, came to her relief, and, with a touch of her wand, did the work deftly, and thus disposed of all her difficulties. I want better help than a fairy could give. "Order" and dates are some little aid to me; but, beside this, I have earnestly asked to have brought to my full remembrance only those incidents, the relation of which shall not tend so much to gratify natural curiosity, as to render some immediate and lasting benefit to those who read them. My husband's whole life was "an example of the believers, in word, in conversation, in charity, in spirit, in faith, in purity"; and if, in any of the pages I have written, I have failed to set this bright example forth with due prominence, the fault is mine, and will be deeply grieved over; but if I have at all succeeded in magnifying the grace of God in him, it is simply because the Lord, for His own glory, has given skill for the service. I can say with Ezra, "I was strengthened as the hand of the Lord my God was upon me."

*　　　　*　　　　*

We left the New Kent Road, in 1857, to reside in Nightingale Lane, Clapham. This was then a pretty and rural, but comparatively unknown, region, and our delight in the change and interest it afforded, was unbounded. On the right hand of the road, if the visitor came from Clapham, stretched a glorious park, which, with its residential mansion, was then the property of J. Dent., Esq. Our house stood on the left side, facing the park and its palings. I do not think there were more than five or six houses, beside our own, the whole length of the "Lane" from one end to the other! This secludedness was a great attraction to my beloved, for he felt the need of absolute quiet and rest after the labours and toils of the day; and he found them here. We could walk abroad, too, in those days, in the leafy lanes, without fear of being accosted by too many people, and this privilege brought us very great pleasure. In one of these wanderings, an incident occurred which my dear husband has so tenderly described, and so aptly turned into an encouragement for a seeking sinner, that I introduce it here, as a diamond among my rock-crystals, praying that some longing soul may find it, appropriate it, and be rich for ever:

"We were walking up the lane near where I live, and there was a poor woman, who stopped us. She spoke in French. This poor soul had some children at Guildford, and she was wanting to find her way to them, but did not know a single sentence of English. She had knocked at the doors of all the gentlemen's houses down the lane, and of course the servants could do nothing for her, for they did not understand a word she said. So she went from one place to another, and at last she did not know what would become of her. She had some thirty miles to walk; she did not mind that, but then, she could not tell which way to go, so I suppose she had made up her mind she would ask everybody. All she knew was, she had written on a piece of paper the word 'Guildford', and she held it up, and began to ask in French which was the right road.

When, at last, she had met with someone who could tell her the path she must take, beautifully did she express both her distress and her gratitude; she said she felt like a poor bird who was hunted about, and did not know how to find her way to the nest. She poured a thousand blessings on us when we told her the way, and, I thought—how much this is like the sinner when he wants to find the way to Heaven! All he knows is, he wants Christ, but where to find Him, and how to get to Him, he cannot tell; and he knocks, first at one door, and then at another, and perhaps the minister at the place of worship does no know the language of human sympathy. He cannot comprehend thet sinner's need, for there are many servants in my Master's house, I am sorry to say, who do not understand the language of a sinner's cry. O sinner, thou shalt surely find Christ though thou knowest not how to find Him! He will ask thee, 'Whom seekest thou?' and thou wilt answer, 'I seek Jesus,' and He will say, 'I that speak unto thee am He.' I am much mistaken if He who speaks in thy heart is not the very Jesus whom thou art seeking. His speaking in thy heart is a token of His love. Trust Him, believe in Him, and Thou shalt be saved."

The house was a very old one, and, in its first estate, I should judge it had been an eight-roomed cottage, with underground cellars afterwards turned into kitchens. Some bygone owner had built another storey, and thrown the eight small rooms into four better-sized ones, but, even with this improvement, they were narrow and incommodious. To us, however, they were then all that we could desire, and the large garden made up for all the inconveniences indoors. Oh, what a delightsome place we thought it, though it was a very wilderness through long neglect—the blackberry bushes impertinently asserting themselves to be trees, and the fruit trees running wild for want of the pruning-knife! It was all the more interesting to us in this sweet confusion and artlessness because we had the happy task of bringing it gradually into accord with our ideas of what a garden should be. I must admit that we made many absurd mistakes both in house and garden management, in those young days of ours, but what did that matter? No two birds ever felt more exquisite joy in building their nest in the fork of a tree-branch, than did we in planning and placing, altering and rearranging our pretty country home.

What a boon such a retreat was to my beloved, can be well understood by all zealous workers who know the penalties exacted by weary brains and jaded powers. At this time, Mr. Spurgeon's sermons were having a phenomenal sale both at home and abroad, and the generous arrangements of the publishers, together with the increased income from the church, made possible the purchase of the freehold of this house and grounds; and the fact of the place being old and long untenanted, enabled him to obtain it on very easy terms. It had some queer corners in it, which we peopled with mysterious shadows for the mere gratification of afterwards dispersing them. A large brewhouse sort of erection at the side was a great puzzle to us, with its flagged floor, its great boiler in one corner, and its curious little rooms, like cells, which we converted into apple-chambers.

But *the* sensation of the place was *the well*, which altogether fascinated us, and did not withdraw its spell till the demolition of the house broke the charm by covering it up entirely, and leaving only a common pump-handle "en évidence". It was a wonderful well; the water came up pure, sparkling, and cold as ice. The story of it was, as far as I can recollect, as follows: A former occupant of the house had resolved, at any cost, to have water at that particular spot. So he hired well-diggers, and they began to dig. At one hundred feet depth, they stopped. There was no sign of water. "Go on," said the master; "you must go deeper." They dug another two hundred feet, and came to the solid rock! "Now," said he, "you must *bore*, for I am going to have water here if I bore to the centre of the earth for it." So they bored, and bored, and got quite disheartened, for they had now gone 460 feet into the bowels of the earth! But the master insisted that they should continue their efforts, and, one day, they came up as usual to have their dinner, but they never went down to the rock again, for the water had burst through, and covered up their tools, and risen high in the well! Was not the man right glad that he had not relinquished his object, and was he not well rewarded for his perseverance? He was a bene-factor to succeeding generations, too, for the delicious water had quite a fame round about the place, and residents in our time used to send and beg the favour of a large jugful of "water from the well".

Many years afterwards, when the main drainage works were in progress, its generous abundance diminished, and when the new house was built, though its services were still secured, it lost, as I have said, all its ancient attractiveness—*and danger*. Yes, there was danger in the old well, as we painfully realized, one day, when a man, while making some repairs, a short way down, lost his footing, and fell through many of the wooden stages (erected inside the well, and reached by ladders), and would have been precipitated into the deep water, with a very faint chance of life, but that, by God's great mercy, he was caught by the arms on one of the stagings, and there hung suspended, in horror and darkness, till his mates could reach and rescue him! I can never forget my dear husband's anguish of mind on that occasion. He paced to and fro, before the well-house door, in an agony of suspense. We were all white and trembling, and sick with frightful fears. But it pleased the Lord to avert the threatened tragedy; and, after a time, the man was brought up from the depths, to see again the blessed light of the sun. He looked more like a dead than a living creature when he was safely on *terra firma;* but, beyond being much bruised, he was uninjured. After that, my dear husband allowed no one to go down the well without having a stout rope round his body, securely fastened, or held by other men. We never again had an accident there.

In the little parlour of this old house—see the window of the room to the left of the porch in the picture—there occurred, one day, an incident of much interest, which, though it concerns a notable and still living author (John Ruskin), I think I may be permitted to reveal. It will but disclose the existence, at that time, in a very noble and gifted heart, of a sweet spring of brotherly love, which has long remained sealed-up and hidden. Towards the end of the year 1858, my beloved had a serious illness, which kept him out of his pulpit for three Sabbaths. In those early days, Mr. Ruskin was not only a frequent attendant at the Surrey Music Hall services, and a loving friend to my dear husband, but I believe he was also an ardent admirer of him as a preacher of the gospel. When Mr. Spurgeon was partly convalescent, but still painfully weak, Mr. Ruskin, knowing of his condition, called to see him. My beloved was downstairs for the first time that day, and was lying on the couch in the room I have indicated. How well I remember the intense love and devotion displayed by Mr. Ruskin, as he threw himself on his knees by the dear patient's side, and embraced him with tender affection and tears. "My brother, my dear brother," he said, "how grieved I am to see you thus!" His sorrow and sympathy were most touching and comforting. He had brought with him two charming engravings—gems of artistic taste, which still adorn the walls of one of the rooms at "Westwood"—and some bottles of wine of a rare vintage, which he hoped would prove a cordial to the sufferer's much-weakened frame. My husband was greatly moved by the love and consideration so graciously expressed, and he very often referred to it afterwards in grateful appreciation; especially when, in later years, there came a change of feeling on Mr. Ruskin's part, and he strongly repudiated some of the theological opinions to which Mr. Spurgeon closely clung to the end of his life.

I am not sure that it was on the occasion of the visit I have now described, or at some other time, that Mr. Ruskin told my husband a very remarkable story, for the truth of which he himself could answer. I think they had been talking together of the interpositions of God's providence, of His care over His people, and of the singular deliverances which He had vouchsafed to them when in danger or distress; and Mr. Ruskin then related, with an impassioned tenderness and power which my pen cannot possibly imitate, the following instance of direct and Divine preservation from a dreadful death.

A Christian gentleman, a widower, with several little ones, was in treaty for the occupancy of an old farm-house in the country, for the sake of his children's health. One day, he took them to see their new residence, before finally removing into it. While he talked with the landlord or agent, the young people set off on a tour of inspection, and scampered here, there, and everywhere over the garden and grounds. Then they proceeded to examine the house, and rushed up and down stairs, looking into every room, dancing with delight, full of fun and frolic, and shouting out their joy over every new discovery. Presently, when they seemed to have exhausted the wonders of the old house, one of them suggested that the underground premises had not yet been explored, and must therefore be visited at once. So the merry band went helter-skelter in search of a way below, found a door at the head of some dark stairs, and were rushing down them at great speed, when, midway, they suddenly stopped in startled amazement, for, standing at the bottom of the steps, they saw *their mother*, with outstretched arms and loving gesture, waving them back, and silently forbidding their further passage. With a cry of mingled fear and joy, they turned, and fled in haste to their father, telling him that they had seen "Mother", that she had smiled lovingly at them, but had eagerly motioned them to go back. In utter astonishment, the father listened to the children's tale, and at once perceived that something unusual had happened. Search was made, and close at the foot of those narrow, gloomy stairs, they found a deep and open well, entirely unguarded, into which, in their mad rush, every child must inevitably have fallen and perished, had not the Lord in His mercy interposed.

Stories of the supernatural are seldom worthy of credence, but, in this case, both my dear husband and Mr. Ruskin were convinced that God permitted the appearance of their mother to those dear children, in order to save them from a terrible death; and that nothing else, and nothing less than such a vision could have attained this object, and prevented the calamity.

I find, from data kindly supplied to me by Pastor J. W. Davies, of Lee, that on one occasion, "under the Oak" at "Westwood", the question was asked of Mr. Spurgeon, "Do you believe in supernatural visitations?" and for answer he repeated this story of Mr. Ruskin's. The students listened with eager interest, and then promptly requested their President to give his theory of the nature of the appearance. He replied that he could not explain it, but he thought that God had impressed on the retina of the children's eyes an object which would naturally cause them to return at once to their father, thus ensuring their safety.

There have been many other well-authenticated instances of similar appearances permitted by the Lord in seasons of special danger to His

children; and the calm and reverent consideration of such a subject, by
devout minds, might have the happy effect of bringing the soul very
close to the veil which separates the things that are seen, and are
temporal, from the things that are not seen, and are eternal.

*　　　　*　　　　*

We lived in the dear old house in Nightingale Lane for many happy
years, and, looking back upon them from this distance of time, I think
they must have been the least shadowed by care and sorrow of all the
years of our married life. We were both young, and full of high spirits.
We had fairly good health, and devoutly loved each other. Our
children grew apace in the sweet country air, and my whole time and
strength were given to advance my dear husband's welfare and
happiness. I deemed it my joy and privilege to be ever at his side,
accompanying him on many of his preaching journeys, nursing him in
his occasional illnesses—his delighted companion during his holiday
trips, always watching over and tending him with the enthusiasm and
sympathy which my great love for him inspired. I mention this, not to
suggest any sort of merit on my part, but simply that I may here record
my heartfelt gratitude to God that, for a period of ten blessed years, I
was permitted to encircle him with all the comforting care and tender
affection which it was in a wife's power to bestow. Afterwards, God
ordered it otherwise. He saw fit to reverse our position to each other;
and for a long, long season, suffering instead of service became my
daily portion, and the care of comforting a sick wife fell upon my
beloved.

I have already said what a great joy the garden was to us. At first,
there was always something fresh and new to interest us; and when,
by degrees, the novelty of its possession wore off, then we loved it all
the better, because we knew more about it. Here my dear husband
enjoyed, not only rest and recreation for the body, but stimulus and
quickening for the mind. Original illustrations for sermons—side-
lights on texts—metaphors and parables, whereby the hearts of
hearers might be moved or impressed—all these Mr. Spurgeon found
ready to his hand in this old pleasance, which ungrudgingly laid its
stores at his feet. It mattered not to him how commonplace was the
figure which could supply a barb or a feather to the arrow which he
designed to send straight home to the heart of a saint or a sinner. He
did not disdain to employ the simplest incidents or similes to further
the important purposes of illustration and instruction.

He himself gives a noble instance of the working of this life-long habit, in one of the lectures to his students, where he says: "If you keep your eyes open, you will not see even a dog following his master, nor a mouse peeping up from his hole, nor will you hear even a gentle scratching behind the wainscot, without getting something to weave into your sermons if your faculties are all on the alert. When you go home to-night, and sit by your fireside, you ought not to be able to take up your domestic cat without finding that which will furnish you with an illustration. How soft are pussy's pads, and yet, in a moment, if she is angered, how sharp will be her claws! How like to temptation, soft and gentle when it first cometh to us, but how deadly, how damnable the wounds it causeth ere long!

I recollect using, with very considerable effect in a sermon in the Tabernacle, an incident that occurred in my own garden. There was a dog which was in the habit of coming through the fence, and scratching in my flower-beds, to the manifest spoiling of the gardener's toil and temper. Walking in the garden, one Saturday afternoon, and preparing my sermon for the following day, I saw the four-footed creature—rather a scurvy specimen, by-the-by—and having a walking-stick in my hand, I threw it at him with all my might, at the same time giving him some good advice about going home. Now, what should my canine friend do but turn round, pick up the stick in his mouth, bring it, and lay it down at my feet, wagging his tail all the while in expectation of my thanks and kind words! Of course, you do not suppose that I kicked him, or threw the stick at him any more. I felt quite ashamed of myself, and told him that he was welcome to stay as long as he liked, and to come as often as he pleased. There was an instance of the power of non-resistance, submission, patience, and trust, in overcoming even righteous anger. I used that illustration in preaching the next day, and I did not feel that I had at all degraded myself by telling the story."

If my memory does not play me false, there used to be sundry crusts, or even bones, secretly conveyed to that mongrel cur after this memorable encounter.

Here, too, the young Pastor could peacefully enjoy all the ordinary sights and sounds of an open space in the country. The song of birds was sweetest music to him, and the commonest flowers gave him joy, because they both revealed to him the love of his Father's heart. "When I go into my garden," he once said, referring to this same old place of which I am writing, "I have a choir around me in the trees. They do not wear surplices, for their song is not artificial and official.

Some of them are clothed in glossy black, but they carol like little angels; they sing the sun up, and wake me at break of day; and they warble on till the last red ray of the sun has departed, still singing out from bush and tree the praises of their God. And all the flowers—the primroses that are almost gone—convey to my heart deep meanings concerning God till the last one shuts his eye. And now the mignonette, and the wallflowers, and the lilac, and the guelder-roses, and a host of sweet beauties are pouring out their incense of perfume as if they said, 'Thank the God that made us! Blessed be His Name! The earth is full of His goodness.' "

"Preach, preach twice a day, I can and will do; but, still, there is a travailing in preparation for it, and even the utterance is not always accompanied with joy and gladness; and God knoweth that, if it were not for the good that we trust is to be accomplished by the preaching of the Word, it is no happiness to a man to be well known. It robs him of all comfort to be from morning to night hunted for labour, to have no rest for the sole of his foot or for his brain—to have people asking, as they do in the country, when they want to get into a cart, 'Will it hold us?' never thinking whether the horse can drag them—so they ask, 'Will you preach at such-and-such a place? You are preaching twice, couldn't you manage to go to the next town or village, and preach again?' "—C. H. S., *in sermon preached at the Music Hall, Royal Surrey Gardens, June* 28, 1857.

"I can say, and God is my witness, that I never yet feared the face of man, be he who or what he may; but I often tremble— yea, I always do—in ascending the pulpit, lest I should not faithfully proclaim the gospel to poor perishing sinners. The anxiety of rightly preparing and delivering a discourse, so that the preacher may fully preach Christ to his hearers, and pray them, in Christ's stead, to be reconciled to God, is such as only he knows who loves the souls of men. It is no child's play to be the occupant of a pulpit; he who finds it to be so may find it to be something more fearful than devil's play when the day of judgment shall come."—C. H. S., *in sermon preached at Belfast, August,* 1858.

Chapter 34

Week-day Services

WHEN the project for the building of the Tabernacle was fairly launched,[1] the Pastor set to work most energetically in gathering the funds needed for the great enterprise. By means of his preaching, speaking, and lecturing, a very large proportion of the required amount was collected. In many cases, half the proceeds were devoted to local objects, and the remainder given to Spurgeon, for his new chapel, but, in other instances, the whole sum was added to the Building Fund. Scarcely a single monthly list of contributions was issued without the inclusion of several of these items. The congregation at the Surrey Gardens Music Hall was of such a special character that it was only on rare occasions that the young minister could be absent on the Lord's-day. Once, when he did spend a Sabbath, as well as some week-days in Scotland, he was able, on his return, to pay into the treasury the sum of £391 as the net result of his visit to Glasgow and Edinburgh. He also continued, as far as he was

[1] The Building Committee for the proposed new Tabernacle was appointed in June 1856, and, at the first public meeting in aid of the new project in New Park Street Chapel on September 29, it was unanimously resolved that a Tabernacle holding 5,000 sittings should be erected. The total cost was estimated at £12,000. By the beginning of March 1861 the building was completed at an ultimate expenditure of £31,000 and the opening services were inaugurated with a great prayer meeting on the morning of Monday, March 18. The spiritual blessing resting upon the congregation of New Park Street is strikingly illustrated by the financial accounts of the church. The total income of the church in 1853 was less than £300. From the commencement of Spurgeon's ministry the figures were as follows:

Year.	Church Receipts.	Ordinance Poor Fund.	Receipts for other purposes.	Separate Services Account.	Building and Enlargement Account.
	£ s. d.	£ s. d.	£ s. d.	£ s. d.	£ s. d.
1854	515 5 5	..	57 14 4	..	..
1855	834 7 9	104 17 6	74 17 3	..	1,359 18 6
1856	868 0 9	140 0 1	125 10 9	479 2 3	229 11 6
1857	1,146 8 8	165 9 10	255 18 2	3,211 4 0	6,100 0 0†
1858	1,090 2 5	216 12 1	213 6 10	1,956 5 9	9,639 3 10†
1859	1,104 16 2	222 16 5	307 3 5	1,298 9 4	16,868 6 2†

† These figures represent the amounts in hand, at the end of each year, towards the cost of the new Tabernacle, and they include a large proportion of the sums received on the Separate Services Account.—P.

able, to preach on behalf of various provincial churches which sought his aid, and it sometimes happened that where the collections had been given one year towards the new Tabernacle, the next year Spurgeon would go again, and raise as large a sum as possible for the funds of those who had previously helped him.

A bare outline of these week-day services, even if it could be made, would occupy far more space than can be spared in this work. There is no need to attempt the task, for that campaign of love is recorded on high, and it is gladly and gratefully remembered in thousands of the cities, and towns, and villages of the United Kingdom; and the story of it has been told, again and again, from sire to son, in almost every part of the land. Eternity alone will reveal how great was the young evangelist's influence upon the religious life of that portion of the nineteenth century, and those who formed a part of his vast audiences may well treasure in their memories, and hand on to their descendants, reminiscences of the notable incidents of those long-past days. Just a few representative instances only can be given, from which may be gathered something of the character of the "labours more abundant" in which the New Park Street Pastor was engaged in addition to his arduous occupation in connection with his ever-growing church and work.

In London, Spurgeon's services were constantly in request every day or hour that was not required to meet the claims of his pastorate, and he was ever the ready and willing advocate of all who were down-trodden and oppressed. In a discourse upon Isaiah lxii. 10, "Gather out the stones", delivered at the Scottish Church, Regent Square, on February 22, 1858, in aid of the Early Closing Association, he gave utterance to sentiments which are as appropriate to the present time as to the occasion when they were first spoken, although "early closing" has made great advances during the intervening period. After trying to remove, out of the way of those who desired to tread the Heavenly road, such "stones" as these—(1) the supposed sacred character of the buildings in which the gospel was preached; (2) the obscure and learned language of many of the preachers; (3) the inconsistencies or gloominess of professors of religion—Spurgeon thus referred to the object for which he had been asked to preach:

"And now, what else have you to say? Perhaps you reply, 'What you say is well and good; no doubt religion is a holy and Heavenly thing; but, sir, there is one more stone in my path—can you take that away? I am so engaged in business that it is utterly impossible for me to attend to the concerns of my soul. From Monday morning to

Saturday night—or, rather, till Sunday morning—it is work, work, work, and I scarcely seem to throw myself upon my bed before I have to rise in the morning, and resume my tasks. You invite me to come to your place of worship on the Sabbath morning; do you wish me to go there to sleep? You ask me to come and listen to the minister; if you fetched an angel from Heaven, and gave him Gabriel's trumpet, with which he could wake the dead, then I might listen; but I require something almost as powerful as that to keep my poor eyelids open. I should be snoring while the saints were singing; why should I come to mar your worship? What is the use of the minister telling me to take the yoke of Christ upon me, because His yoke is easy, and His burden is light? I know not whether Christ's yoke be easy, but I know that the yoke a so-called Christian population puts upon me is not easy. I have to toil as much as if I were a slave, and the Israelites in the brick-kilns of Egypt could hardly have sweated more fearfully under the task-master's lash than I do. Oh, sir, this is the great stone in the midst of my path; and it so impedes me, that it is all in vain for you to talk to me of Christianity while this obstacle is in my way!'

I tell you all, that this barrier is like the great stone that was laid at the door of the sepulchre of the dead Christ. Unless you try to remove it, where is the hope of getting these people under the sound of the Word? It is for this reason that I came, this evening, to preach a sermon on behalf of the Early Closing Movement. I felt that I could not make that matter the staple of my discourse; but that I might bring it in as one of the points to which I would ask your very special attention, and I am endeavouring to do so. I do think, Christian people, that you ought to take this stone out of the path of those who are without; and to do so, you must put a stop to that evil but common custom of visiting shops and houses of business at a late hour. If you make a man work so many hours in the six days—really, it is twelve days in six, for what is it better than that when he has two days' labour crowded into every one?—how can you expect the Sabbath to be kept sacred by him? And even if the man is willing so to keep it, how can you imagine that he can be in a proper frame of devotion when he comes into the house of God? Our Lord Jesus Christ is able to save to the uttermost; were He not, the salvation of poor dressmakers, and young men employed in drapers' and other shops, would be impossible; for it is saving to the uttermost when He saves them notwithstanding their exhaustion, and gives them strength to feel and repent, when they have scarcely physical and mental power enough left for any effort at all. O brethren and sisters, gather out the stones! If you cannot take them all away, do not strew the road more thickly with them by unthinkingly keeping your fellow-creatures at work when they ought to be at rest.

There are many young men and women, who are seeking something higher than the dust and ashes of this world, who might be converted to Christ, and who might be happy, but who are restrained because they have not the time which they desire for seeking the Lord. I say not that it is a valid excuse for them to make—for very little time is needed for the exercise of repentance and faith—but I do say that there are hundreds and thousands who are hindered from coming to Christ, and have their early religious impressions checked and damped, and their convictions stifled, and the first dawn of a better life quenched within them, because of the cruel system of the present state of society. I remember seeing a good farmer stop his chaise, and let his old grey pony stand still while he got down to pick off the road the bottom of a glass bottle, and throw it over the hedge. 'Ah!' he said, 'I remember how my pony cut his foot by stepping on a glass bottle, and I should not like anyone to lame a valuable horse in the same way, so I thought I would get out, and remove the cause of danger.' Let all of us act in the same fashion as that old farmer did, and gather out all stones that may be an occasion of stumbling to any of our brothers and sisters."

*   *   *

It must have been a memorable sight for those who saw the Surrey Gardens Music Hall packed on a week-day morning—April 28, 1858, when Spurgeon preached the annual sermon of the Baptist Missionary Society from Psalm xlvi. 8, 9: "Come, behold the works of the Lord, what desolations He hath made in the earth. He maketh wars to cease unto the end of the earth; He breaketh the bow, and cutteth the spear in sunder; He burneth the chariot in the fire." The discourse is published in *The New Park Street Pulpit*, under the title, "The Desolations of the Lord, the Consolation of His Saints," so it need not be described at length; but it is interesting to note Dr. Campbell's comment on the new era which had dawned in connection with the Society's anniversary:

"The missionary sermon of Mr. Spurgeon, on Wednesday, at the Surrey Music Hall, was a magnificent affair. The immense edifice was crowded to overflowing at the early hour of 11 o'clock in the forenoon. The great preacher was, as usual, completely at home, full of heart, vivacity, and business. Mr. Spurgeon cannot devote weeks, if not months, to the preparation of such a sermon, and then take a fortnight's rest to recruit his strength before the great day. All his days are great, and they come in such rapid succession as to exclude the possibility of finish and elaboration, even if he aspired to it. But, with him, there is no aiming at greatness; exhibition has no place in his thoughts. He scorns it. What the occasion supplies, amid ceaseless toils, past and coming, is all that he seeks, and all that he gives. In the proper sense, he preaches; and preaches, not to the ministers, but to the people; and he has his reward. He has no conception of reading a treatise, by way of a May Meeting sermon, extending to two or three hours! This he would deem a perversion of his office, and an insult to his hearers. His discourse on Wednesday was of the usual length, and of the usual character, only throughout highly missionary. Common sense in this, as in most of Mr. Spurgeon's doings, obtained for once a thorough triumph. The collection amounted to nearly £150."

Two notable week-day sermons were preached by Spurgeon, on Friday, June 11, 1858, on the Grand Stand, Epsom race-course. The text in the afternoon was singularly suitable to such a place: 'So run, that ye may obtain"; in the evening, the discourse was a powerful gospel invitation founded upon Isaiah lv. 1: "Yea, come, buy wine and milk without money and without price." There was a large congregation on each occasion, £60 was contributed towards the funds of a chapel in Epsom, and none who were present were likely to forget the unusual purpose to which "Satan's seat" was that day devoted.

*   *   *

In August, 1858, Spurgeon paid his first visit to IRELAND, and preached four sermons in Belfast. He gave his services freely, in order that the whole of the proceeds might help the Young Men's Intellectual Improvement Association to build new school-rooms. That he was in a very unfit state of health for making such an effort, is evident from his remarks at the Music Hall service on the Sabbath morning after his return. Preaching on the words, "As thy days, so shall thy strength be," he said: "Children of God, cannot you say that this has been true hitherto? I can. It might seem egotistical if I were to talk of the evidence I have received of this during the past week, but, nevertheless, I cannot help recording my praise to God. I left this pulpit, last Sunday, as sick as any man ever left the pulpit; and I left this country, too, as ill as I could be; but no sooner had I set my foot upon the other shore, where I was to preach the gospel, than my wonted strength entirely returned to me. I had no sooner buckled on the harness to go forth to fight my Master's battle, than every ache and pain was gone, and all my sickness fled; and as my day was, so certainly was my strength."

The first sermon was an earnest appeal to the undecided; the text was Mark xii. 34: "And when Jesus saw that he answered discreetly, He said unto him, Thou art not far from the Kingdom of God." Twenty-three years afterwards, Spurgeon received from a missionary the following cheering note:

"Your first sermon in Belfast caused me to decide finally to enter the ministry. Since then, I have given ten years to mission work in Damascus, where I built the first church ever erected for the spiritual worship of the true God in that city. I built two churches on Mount Hermon, and again and again I have preached there your sermons in Arabic; one of them was delivered on the top of Mount Hermon at a picnic given to our different villagers."

The second discourse was upon a subject of which Spurgeon was especially fond. In those early days, if he was preaching several sermons at any place, one of them was almost certain to be founded upon Revelation xiv. 1—3: "And I looked, and, lo, a Lamb stood on the Mount Sion, and with Him an hundred forty and four thousand, having His Father's Name written in their foreheads. And I heard a voice from Heaven, as the voice of many waters, and as the voice of a great thunder: and I heard the voice of harpers harping with their harps: and they sung as it were a new song before the throne, and before the four beasts, and the elders: and no man could learn that song but the hundred and forty and four thousand, which were redeemed from the earth"; and in the course of the sermon, Spurgeon usually introduced a few sentences describing his love for the harp. It was so at Belfast, as the following extract shows:

"John says, 'I heard the voice of harpers harping with their harps.' Surely, of all instruments, the harp is the sweetest. The organ has a swelling grandeur, but the harp has a softness and sweetness about it that might well make it a fit instrument for a royal musician like David. I must confess that a harp has so great a charm for me that I have sometimes found myself standing in the street, listening to some old harper making music on his harp. I have bidden him come into the house and play to me that I might prepare a sermon while he played; and I have found comfort, and my heart has been stirred within me, as I have listened to the thrilling strains. The singing in Heaven has all the tender melody of the harp, while it thunders like the rolling sea. Why is this? Because there are no hypocrites there, and no formalists there, to make a jarring noise, and spoil the harmony. There are—

'No groans to mingle with the songs
Which warble from immortal tongues.'

No pain, nor distress, nor death, nor sin, can ever reach that blessed place; there is no drawback to the happiness of the glorified spirits above. They all sing sweetly there, for they are all perfect; and they sing all the more loudly, because they all owe that perfection to free and sovereign grace."

The text of the third sermon was Matthew xxviii. 5: "The angel answered and said unto the women, Fear not ye: for I know that ye seek Jesus, which was crucified"—and was specially aimed at finding out and comforting true seekers.

The last of the four services was held in the Botanic Gardens, when it was estimated that 7,000 persons heard the discourse delivered from Matthew i. 21: "Thou shalt call His Name J E S U S: for He shall save His people from their sins." Towards the end of the sermon, Spurgeon told the story of Jack the Huckster, whose theology was comprised in the familiar lines—

"I'm a poor sinner, and nothing at all,
But Jesus Christ is my All-in-all."

In closing the service, the preacher said: "I have to thank you all for the kindness with which I have been received, and especially I have to thank the ministers of Belfast. I never was in a town in my life where I met with such a noble body of men who love the good old truth, and I can say that I love every one of them. I thank them for all the kind things they have said to me and concerning me, and I wish them and all my friends a hearty good-bye, and may the day come when we shall all meet in Heaven!"

Spurgeon went to Ireland many times after this, and Irish friends contributed very generously to the building of the Tabernacle. On one of his visits, after the great revival, when preaching in Exeter Hall, from Amos ix. 13, "Behold, the days come, saith the Lord, that the plowman shall overtake the reaper, and the treader of grapes him that soweth seed; and the mountains shall drop sweet wine, and all the hills shall melt," he said:

"Here we are told that 'the mountains shall drop sweet wine'; by which we are to understand that conversions shall take place in unusual quarters. Brethren, this day is this promise literally fulfilled to us. I have this week seen what I never saw before. It has been my lot, these last six years, to preach to crowded congregations, and to have many, many souls brought to Christ; it has been no unusual thing for us to see the greatest and noblest of the land listening to the Word of God; but this week I have seen, I repeat, what mine eyes have never before beheld, used as I am to extraordinary sights. I have seen the people of Dublin, without exception, from the highest to the lowest, crowd in to hear the gospel; and I have known that my congregation has been composed in a considerable measure of Roman Catholics, and I have beheld them listening to the Word with as much attention as though they had been Protestants. I have noticed military men, whose tastes and habits were not like those of the Puritanic minister, but who have nevertheless sat to listen; nay, they have come again, and have made it a point to find the place where they could hear the best, and have submitted to be crowded if they might but hear the Word. I have heard, too, cheering news of men, who could not speak without larding their conversation with oaths, who have come to hear the Word; they have been convinced of sin; and I trust there has been a work done in them which will last throughout eternity.

But the most pleasing thing I have seen is this, and I must tell it to you. Hervey once said, 'Each floating ship, a floating hell.' Of all classes of men, the sailor has been supposed to be the one least likely to be reached by the gospel. In crossing over from Holyhead to Dublin and back—two excessively rough passages—I spent the most pleasant hours that I ever remember. The first vessel that I entered, I found my hand very heartily shaken by the sailors. I thought, 'What can these men know of me?' They began calling me 'Brother'. Of course, I felt that I was their brother; but I did not know how they came to talk to me in that way. It is not usual for sailors to call a minister 'Brother'. They paid me the utmost attention; and when I made the enquiry, 'What makes you so kind?' 'Why!' said one, 'because I love your Master, the Lord Jesus.' I enquired, and found that, out of the whole crew, there were but three unconverted men; and that, though the most of them had been before without God, and without Christ, yet, by a sudden visitation of the Spirit of God, they had nearly all been converted. I talked to many of these men; and more spiritually-minded men, I never saw. They have a prayer-meeting every morning before the boat starts, and another prayer-meeting after she comes into port; and on Sundays, when they lie-to off Kingstown or Holyhead, a minister comes on board, and preaches the gospel. Service is held on deck when it is possible, and an eye-witness said to me, 'The minister preaches very earnestly, but I should like you to hear the men pray; I never heard such pleading before, they pray as only sailors can pray.' My heart was lifted up with joy, to think of a ship being made a floating church—a very Bethel.

When I came back by another steamer, I did not expect to have my previous experience repeated; but it was. The same kind of work had been going on among these sailors; I walked among them, and talked to them. They all knew me. One man took out of his pocket an old leather-covered book in Welsh, and said to me, 'Do you know the likeness of that man in front?' 'Yes,' I replied, 'I think I do; do you read those sermons?' 'Yes, sir,' he answered, 'we have had your sermons on board ship, and I read them aloud as often as I can. If we have a fine passage coming over, I get a few around me, and read them a sermon.' Another man told me the story of a gentleman who stood laughing while a hymn was being sung; so one of the sailors proposed that they should pray for him. They did so, and the man was suddenly smitten down, and on the quay began to cry for mercy, and plead with God for pardon. 'Ah! sir,' said the sailors, 'we have the best proof that there is a God here, for we have seen this crew marvellously brought to a knowledge of the truth; and here we are, joyful and happy men, serving the Lord.'

Now, what shall we say of this blessed work of grace, but that the mountains drop sweet wine? The men who were loudest with their oaths, are now loudest with their songs; those who were the most daring sons of Satan, have become the most earnest advocates of the truth, for, mark you, once get sailors converted, and there is no end to the good they can do. Of all men who can preach well, seamen are the best. The sailor has seen the wonders of God in the deep; the hardy British tar has got a heart that is not made of such cold stuff as many of the hearts of landsmen; and when that heart is once touched, it gives big beats, and sends great pulses of energy right through his whole frame; and with his zeal and energy, what may he not do, God helping him, and blessing him?"

*   *   *

So far as can be ascertained, Spurgeon's first sermons to a WELSH audience were delivered in the ancient village of Castleton, midway between Newport and Cardiff, on Wednesday, July 20, 1859. Pastor T. W. Medhurst, who kindly forwards this information, says:

"This visit is still greatly talked about by the aged people in the district; I have often been delighted to see their glistening eyes as they have related their recollections of this red-letter day in their past experience. Never in the annals of the village, either before or since, has there been anything at all approximating to the scene which was witnessed that day. For some time previously, it had been made known through Monmouthshire and Glamorganshire that the popular preacher, C. H. Spurgeon, would deliver two discourses in the open air at Castleton. The excitement among the people, and especially among the inhabitants of the hill-districts, in anticipation of the services, was immense. The question, 'Are you going to hear Spurgeon?' took the place of the usual remarks about the weather. The various railway companies ran excursion trains, and the result was an enormous gathering of people from all parts.

The first service began at eleven o'clock in the morning, in a field which was admirably adapted for the occasion, as it gradually sloped to a level at the bottom. The seats were arranged in a semi-circular form. Everyone had a full view of the preacher, and his powerful voice was distinctly heard by the nine or ten thousand persons assembled. Before announcing his text Mr. Spurgeon said: 'My dear friends, I most earnestly and humbly entreat your prayers that I may be enabled to preach the gospel with power this day. I do not know that at any time I ever felt my own weakness more than I do now. I recollect to what mighty men of God some of you have sometimes listened, ministers whose names ought to be held in reverence as long as any man's name endures on the face of the earth. I can scarcely hope to tread in the footsteps of many of those preachers whom you have heard. This, however, I can say to you—you may have men in Wales who can preach the gospel *in a better manner* than I can hope to do, but you have no one who can preach A BETTER GOSPEL. It is the same gospel from first to last, and tells of the same Saviour, who is ready to receive the meanest, the feeblest, the most guilty, and the most vile, who come unto God by Him. May the Holy Spirit graciously rest upon us now! I will read my text to you from the Gospel according to Matthew, the twenty-eighth chapter, and the fifth verse, and then Mr. Davies, of Haverfordwest College, will read it to you in Welsh—a feat which I cannot accomplish.'

The sermon was a most powerful discourse, delivered with impassioned earnestness and fire, never surpassed by the most eloquent of the Welsh preachers. The text in the evening was Revelation xiv. 1—3. Every word of the preacher was plainly audible to the whole of the vast audiences at both the services; and at the close of the day it was remarked that his voice was as clear and as vigorous as at the commencement."

Spurgeon preached in the Principality on several occasions afterwards; the service to which he refers on page 366 was probably the one held at Abercarn on Wednesday, May 30, 1860, when it was estimated that 20,000 persons heard the discourse which he delivered in the open air.

* * *

Among all the notable week-day services in his earlier years, few were more memorable to both preacher and people than those held in Paris, on Tuesday, Wednesday, and Thursday, February 7—9, 1860. The record of them is preserved in a pamphlet of thirty-two pages. On the title-page of Spurgeon's own copy is inscribed, in his handwriting: "By Rev. Wm. Blood, who escaped at the burning of the *Amazon*." This gentleman was temporarily officiating as minister of the American Church in Paris, and he thus narrates the circumstances which resulted in Spurgeon's visit:

"I had not been long in Paris, when it occurred to me that a good opportunity presented itself for inviting my friend, the Rev. C. H. Spurgeon, to preach in the French capital; hoping that, thereby, with the blessing of God, a revival might commence in this land of superstition and error. And well knowing that France and the Continent offered a fine field for missionary enterprise, though awfully neglected since the days of the Reformation, I did not see why an attempt should not be made to enkindle the smoking embers of pure religion, which might eventually send forth a flame of light and heat which would spread over the entire country. It was a solitary monk, in his lonely cell, who, discovering the Word of God, read it, and, finding that it cheered his otherwise dismal hours, and gave light and warmth to his heart, determined that others should be made happy by the celestial fire. He snatched the torch of Divine truth, went forth from his darkness, and held it up, that all might see the living light; other hearts were illumined by the same flame, and soon a blaze of Heavenly truth spread all over Germany. Why should there not be another and even a better Luther raised up in beautiful France? Why not many? Why should not the ministry of the Lord's servant, which has been blessed to the conversion of so many souls in Great Britain, be also blessed in this great country?

Still, there were obstacles to encounter. Mr. Spurgeon had engagements made for almost every day for two years to come, and he had refused to go to America, even for a short time, although £20,000 had been offered to help build his chapel in London. I had, it is true, preached for him under peculiar circumstances when he had been seized with severe illness. But would it not be '*uncanonical*' for a clergyman to invite one to preach not 'in holy orders'? But is he not 'in holy orders', God having evidently '*ordered*' him to preach the gospel of peace; for he can already point to thousands of sinners made '*holy*' by his preaching and say, 'The seals of my ministry are ye, in the Lord.' The matter was then decided. I at once applied to my friend, Mr. Curtis—a generous and noble-spirited American, who had originated the erection of the American Chapel—for the use of that building, expressing the desire that, if any collection were made, it might be given to liquidate the debt on the chapel, or for the poor. The Committee met immediately, when the following resolution was agreed to:

'Paris, January 18, 1860.—The Committee have unanimously resolved to give up the American Chapel to the Rev. William Blood, to be disposed of as he thinks proper for the use of his friend, the Rev. C. H. Spurgeon; but they decline the collection for the American Chapel, preferring to give it towards the erection of the chapel for Mr. Spurgeon.'

Application was next made to the *Consistoire* of the Reformed Church of France for the use of a much larger building—the *Église de l'Oratoire*, nearer the centre of Paris. The application was at once responded to by the following resolution:

'The *Consistoire* held a council last night, and decided to lend the *Église de l'Oratoire* to the Rev. W. Blood, for the *prédications* of his friend, the Rev. C. H. Spurgeon.'

This was accompanied by a few lines from one of the venerable Pastors, the Rev. Dr. Grandpierre, in which he said: 'I fervently pray that the Holy Spirit may bless the *prédications* of our brother, Mr. Spurgeon, to the conversion of many souls, and the strengthening of the regenerate in the faith.' "

Spurgeon was then asked if he would go to Paris, and he cheerfully consented to preach three sermons. To the further request that he would deliver two discourses on each of the three days of his visit, he replied:

"My Dear Mr. Blood,

I am willing to preach once on Tuesday, in the evening, wherever you please. Then twice on Wednesday, and twice on Thursday, but I must return the first thing on Friday morning. I thought I was coming over to serve the American Church, but, as the Committee prefer to give the collection for the chapel in London, I am content. Let me stay *in some quiet house*, where I shall not be overwhelmed with visitors. The lionizing is the worst part of my labours. I hope the visit will be blessed by God.

Yours very heartily,

C. H. SPURGEON."

The following account of Spurgeon's preaching in Paris was written by Dr. Grandpierre, and published in the French religious paper, *L'Espérance*:

"The eminent preacher officiated three times at the American Chapel, Rue de Berri, and twice at the Church of the Oratoire. The subject of his first discourse in the American Chapel was, 'Salvation' (Acts xvi. 31); that of the second, 'The Unfathomable Love of Christ' (Ephesians iii. 19); and the third, 'Jesus, the Shepherd of the Faithful' (Psalm xxiii. 1). At the Oratoire, he preached, the first time, on 'Prayer' (Psalm lxxiii. 28), and the second, on 'The New Song of the Redeemed' (Revelation xiv. 1—3).

No one will feel inclined to contradict us when we declare that this celebrated orator fully justified, or even surpassed, the high opinion which the generality of his auditors had conceived of him. Mr. Spurgeon appears of a strong constitution, and nothing in his exterior betrays at first the excellence of the gifts which so particularly distinguish him. As a Christian, he is animated by the warmest piety, and, from his whole person, there seems to shine the sacred fire of the love of souls. One feels that he preaches especially for the salvation of unconverted sinners, and for the strengthening of the faith of those who are regenerate. As a theologian, his doctrine is clear, precise, square—we might say, he is Calvinistic, incontestably—but moderately so. It was, with peculiar satisfaction, that we heard him proclaim, from the pulpit of the Oratoire, with a vigour and a clearness equalled only by his eloquence, the perfect Divinity of the Saviour, and redemption by the expiation of His death, the eternal election of the children of God, and other essential points.

As an orator, he is simple and powerful, clear and abundant. The plans of his sermons are easy to comprehend and to follow; his developments are logical, and his language, always flowing and elegant, never fatigues. One would willingly hear him for hours at a time. Among the requisites to oratory which he possesses in a remarkable degree, three particularly struck us—a prodigious memory, which furnishes him, on the instant, with the comparisons, facts, and images, best calculated to throw light upon his ideas—a full and harmonious voice, which he modulates with peculiar ease, from the lowest to the highest tone—and, lastly, a most fruitful imagination, giving colour to all his thoughts, constantly varying their expression, and painting to the eye of the mind the truths of Christ.

Mr. Spurgeon is in reality a poet. But without having heard him, an idea can scarcely be formed of the richness of his conceptions—never, however, carrying him beyond the simplicity of the Christian pulpit, or the dignity of a minister of Christ. It is affirmed that Mr. Spurgeon has never been to College, and has been in the habit of preaching since the age of seventeen. He is not yet six-and-twenty; but once having heard him is enough to convince us that, in every respect, physically, morally, and spiritually, God has specially qualified him to be an orator—and a Christian orator. He has left, in the hearts and minds of his auditory, the most pleasing, and, let us hope, the most salutary impression. Before and after his preaching, special meetings for private and public prayer took place, in order to beg of God to bless his proclamation of the gospel.

We have no doubt that some souls have been converted. We are certain that all Christians must have felt their activity and inner life invigorated and reanimated. Our dear and honoured brother has received the most fraternal reception from the Christians of every Evangelical denomination in this capital, and he quitted us, apparently touched, grateful, and happy, promising to return, if possible, shortly, to visit us again. For our part, we bless God that the Council of our Reformed Church at Paris has considered it an honour and a privilege to respond to the request of his friend, in opening for him the doors of its great temple, which, during both services, was filled with a compact crowd. In the midst of this vast assemblage, the members of our own church were happily by no means in a minority. Our church has thus once more given proof that she possesses many families who value and appreciate the faithful and living exposition of the doctrine of our Lord and Saviour Jesus Christ."

Even more remarkable was the article in the *Journal des Débats*, from the pen of M. Prevost-Paradol, its principal leader-writer, and one of the most popular and distinguished of the Parisian *littérateurs*; though a Romanist, he wrote in this appreciative strain of Spurgeon and his services:

"Mr. Spurgeon has fulfilled his promise. The indefatigable apostle has spent three days among us, and during his visit he preached five times without our being able to detect the slightest weariness in this gifted man. Yet we do not think that any other orator could put more emphasis into his words, or give himself up more completely to his audience. Without posing, or getting too much excited, Mr. Spurgeon animates his discourse from beginning to end. The subject of his sermon is generally commonplace, and the end of it can be foreseen; but what is neither commonplace nor foreseen, and which is incomprehensible without hearing Mr. Spurgeon, is the persuasive, familiar, and yet forcible way in which he compels his audience to follow him, without fatigue, through the long continuous recitals, full of vivid pictures, exhortations, timely warnings or entreaties, with which he, by so much art, makes up the rich and solid groundwork of his discourses. But why speak of art, when gifts are in question, or rather, we would say, the most inspired oratory we have ever had the pleasure of hearing? Never has a sermon been preached with less apparent preparation, or given to the hearer the idea of a studied discourse; yet where is the audience that has noticed the least weakness, or the slightest hesitation, in his flowing and simple eloquence? One listens with pleasure to his powerful and sympathetic voice, which never rises or falls beyond proper limits, and yet fills the whole church with its sweet cadences.

The man who possesses these gifts, and uses them so generously, is not yet twenty-six years of age. It is impossible to look upon his energetic and loyal face without reading there conviction, courage, and earnest desire to do the right. This orator, who is the most popular preacher in a country where liberty of speech and conscience exercises such potent influence, is not only the most modest, but also the most simple of men. It is true that he has the happiness to address a nation which does not think it necessary to be unjust in its public criticism, but, after all, Mr. Spurgeon owes to himself alone the great and salutary influence which he has acquired, and yet no one could ever rightly accuse him of egotism. It is without affectation that he, unreservedly, ascribes all the glory to God. It seems to us that all disputes concerning religion ought to vanish before such an apostle; and to recognize his power, is but just. As for us, who have seen in this youthful and eloquent preacher one of the most happy examples of what modern Christianity and liberty can produce, we feel that it is an honour to come into contact with such a man as Mr. Spurgeon, and to exchange with him the grasp of friendship."

Mrs. Spurgeon had the great joy of accompanying her husband on this visit. Deacon James Low, who was another of his Pastor's companions on this occasion, gave the following account of an extra service of considerable interest: "By special invitation, Mr. Spurgeon visited the College at Passy, where there were several young men of great promise being educated for the mission field. Mr. Spurgeon received the students with much heartiness, and gave them a very touching and interesting address on the importance and duties of missionary work, especially urging them to preach Christ and Him crucified, as that doctrine would influence their hearers' hearts more than any other theme. The President translated the address into French, and the students appeared very grateful for the visit.

Mr. Spurgeon was very much pressed by the various ministers and others to preach again in Paris as soon as possible. The results of the services were altogether most gratifying. To show the kindly feeling of the friends, collections were made at the American Chapel, amounting to £64, towards the Tabernacle Building Fund. Two collections were also made at the Oratoire for the poor of Paris; they realized £40."

Mr. Blood wrote: "It is gratifying to know that, not only in Paris was there a great wish to hear Mr. Spurgeon, but the same desire existed in different parts of France, in consequence of the articles which had been disseminated by the press. Several came hundreds of miles to attend the services; and amongst others, the ministers of Marseilles and Lyons. After the last service at the Oratoire, Mr. Spurgeon was invited to meet the *Consistoire* at the house of the Pastors. There was a great number of Christian friends present; in fact, the *salons* were crowded. Hymns of joy and praise were heartily sung, and fervent prayers were offered that God might bless the seed which had been sown, and cause it to take deep root in many a heart. Mr. Spurgeon was cordially thanked for his kind help to the Church in France, and he gave a brief farewell address. It was indeed a sweet and solemn time—a little Pentecostal season, not soon to be forgotten. This service was entirely in French."

*   *   *

This chapter may fitly be closed with a brief reference to the week-day services at Whitefield's Tabernacle, Moorfields, which were among the fixed engagements of each year. Dr. John Campbell, who had long stood forth as the friend and advocate of the young Pastor, thus spoke of this annual visit: "Every 365 days, Mr. Spurgeon and his dear companion and the two little Princes Imperial honour my family with their presence for a whole day. We count on it; it is a high day with us. By two sermons, on that occasion, Mr. Spurgeon almost entirely supports our City Mission at the Tabernacle." In the reminiscences, of which mention is made on page 360, Spurgeon referred to this happy compact in the following terms: "It was always a great pleasure to me to have been associated with good old Dr. Campbell, the Editor of *The British Banner*. He was a very dear friend of mine. I used to preach for him every year, and it was understood that, when I went, I must take my dear wife and our two little boys with me. The day before we were to go, that great stern strong man, who had no mercy upon heretics, but would beat them black and blue—I mean in a literary sense, not literally—used to visit a toy-shop, and buy horses and carts or other playthings for the children. One time, when he sent the invitation for us all to go to his house, he wrote: 'Our cat has had some kittens on purpose that the boys may have something fresh to play with.' It showed what a kind heart the old man had when he took such pains to give pleasure to the little ones."

One of the most memorable of these annual visits was paid on Wednesday, March 14, 1860. There had been, near that time, a great many serious accidents and notable sudden deaths. A mill in America had fallen, and buried hundreds of persons in the ruins. A train had left the rails, and great numbers of the passengers were in consequence killed. The captain of the largest vessel then afloat, who had been brought safely through many a storm, had just said farewell to his family when he fell into the water, and was drowned. A judge, after delivering his charge to the grand jury with his usual wisdom, calmness, and deliberation, paused, fell back, and was carried away lifeless. Mr. Corderoy, a well-known generous Christian gentleman, was suddenly called away, leaving a whole denomination mourning for him. Spurgeon's sermon—"Memento Mori"—at Exeter Hall, the following Lord's-day morning, contained a reference to these occurrences, and also to another which more directly affected Dr. Campbell. Preaching from the words, "O that they were wise, that they understood this, that they would consider their latter end!" Spurgeon said:

"It was but last Wednesday that I sat in the house of that mighty servant of God, that great defender of the faith, the Luther of his age— Dr. Campbell; we were talking then about these sudden deaths, little thinking that the like calamity would invade his very family; but, alas! we observed, in the next day's paper, that his second son had been swept overboard while returning from one of his voyages to America.

A bold brave youth has found a liquid grave. So that here, there, everywhere, O Death! I see thy doings. At home, abroad, on the sea, and across the sea, thou art at work. O thou mower! how long ere thy scythe shall be quiet? O thou destroyer of men, wilt thou never rest, wilt thou ne'er be still? O Death! must thy Juggernaut-car go crashing on for ever, and must the skulls and blood of human beings continue to mark thy track? Yes, it must be so till He comes who is the King of life and immortality; then the saints shall die no more, but be as the angels of God."

"When the preacher at the Surrey Music Hall saw his congregation scattered by the uproar of wicked men, and mourned over precious life which was so suddenly sacrificed, there were friends who read in that shocking disaster an omen that the work was not of God, and that the preacher must desist; but the young man did not believe in omens, but in duty; and, therefore, as soon as he could, he reappeared in his pulpit, and as the result of his after-ministry in that place, it is not too much to say that thousands found Christ by his direct teaching, while the preaching of the Word in cathedrals, abbeys, music-halls, and theatres, became a tolerated agency, and even a popular method of evangelization."—C. H. S.

Chapter 35

Later Services at the Music Hall

THE preaching in the Music Hall was resumed in the morning only, so that daylight prevented any further deed of darkness, although the evening would have been a time more favourable for the gathering of large congregations. Our first morning service there was held on November 23, 1856, and our last on December 11, 1859. In the providence of God, the great hall was ready exactly when it was needed, and it was available for use almost as long as it was required. The rent paid for its occupation, during the mornings only, was a respectable item in its accounts, but Sunday takings were preferred to this sure income. The Sabbath before the gardens were opened to the public on the Lord's-day, we cleared out of the place, and with our occupancy, there departed from the company its chief source of revenue. Its downward way to ruin was rapid enough from that hour; both morally and financially it sank hopelessly. We, that is, preacher and people, are bound to commemorate the kind providence which found us such a shelter at a time when we could not otherwise have obtained one for ourselves. All classes—from the Prime Minister downwards—heard the Word there; at no time have so many of the aristocracy made acquaintance with Nonconformist worship. The list of notable persons present on any one Sunday is a long one: statesmen, nobles, divines, great travellers, and all sorts of distinguished persons came to hear the preacher at the Surrey Gardens. Their presence and aid were hopeful signs that the building of our permanent house of prayer would be the provision of a necessity, and that we could accomplish the heavy task. As for the multitude, they were always there in force; and these, not only from the religious section of society, but largely from those who never went to public worship. The reading of newspapers before the commencement of service, though in itself objectionable enough, was the proof that those were present for whom the effort was designed. The best of all is, that God was with us. Conversions were numerous, and some of them were of a very striking kind; they were mainly from that stratum of society which is not touched by ordinary religious services. Though the hall is completely swept away, it will never cease to hold a place in the memory of those to whom it was their spiritual birthplace. All along through the years in which we worshipped in it, there were continual additions to the church, perpetual discoveries of fresh workers, and constant initiations of new enterprises. The College, Orphanage, Colportage, Evangelists, College Missions, and our various branch mission-stations, have all benefited through the advance made by the church during those services. We have seen good brought out of evil; and in our case we have been made to say with the psalmist, "Thou hast caused men to ride over our heads: we went through fire and through water; but Thou broughtest us out into a wealthy place."

When I began to preach at the Surrey Gardens, I had such a diversified congregation as few men have ever had to address from Sabbath to Sabbath. God alone knows what anxiety I experienced in selecting my subjects and arranging my appeals for such a vast fluctuating assembly. There was a time when my brain was all in a whirl at the very thought of ascending that pulpit, while for all the services among my own people I enjoyed the greatest liberty. With the confidence of one who felt his heart at ease amidst the home-circle of his own family, I spoke as if my perfect love to the brotherhood had cast out all fear of missing the mark, or failing in the true work of a Pastor. There was all the difference between preaching in the hall, and in the chapel, that might be expected from the contrast between the neutral ground occupied in the one case and the sacred prestige enjoyed in the other.

*   *   *

[After a time, in addition to the great numbers of strangers who always flocked to the Music Hall, so large a part of the assembly consisted of Spurgeon's regular hearers that he felt almost as much at home there as in New Park Street Chapel, and he adapted his preaching to the altered condition of affairs. In a discourse delivered on Lord's-day morning, February 28, 1858, he said: "When first I preached in this hall, my congregation assumed the appearance of an irregular mass of persons collected from all parts of this city to listen to the Word. I was then simply an evangelist, preaching to many who had not heard the gospel before. By the grace of God, the most blessed change has taken place, and now, instead of having an irregular multitude gathered together, my congregation is as fixed as that of any minister in the whole of London. I can, from this pulpit, observe the countenances of my friends, who have occupied the same places, as nearly as possible, for these many months; and I have the privilege and the pleasure of knowing that a very large proportion, certainly three-fourths of the people who meet together here, are not persons who stray hither from curiosity, but are my regular and constant hearers. And, observe, that my character also has been changed. From being an evangelist, it is now my business to become your Pastor in this place, as well as in the chapel where I labour in the evening. I think, then, it will strike the judgment of every person that, as both the congregation and myself have now changed, the teaching itself should in some measure show a difference. It has been my wont to address you from the simple truths of the gospel; I have very seldom, in this place, attempted to dive into the deep things of God. A text, which I have thought suitable for my congregation in the evening, I should not have made the subject of discussion in this hall in the morning. There are many high and mysterious doctrines which I have often taken the opportunity of handling in my own place, but which I have not felt at liberty to introduce here, regarding you as a company of people casually gathered together to hear the Word. But now, since the circumstances are changed, the teaching will be changed also. I shall not now simply confine myself to the doctrine of faith, or the teaching of believers' baptism; I shall not stay upon the surface of truth, but shall venture, as God shall guide me, to enter into those things that lie at the basis of the religion that we hold so dear. I shall not blush to preach before you the doctrine of God's Divine Sovereignty; I shall not hesitate to proclaim, in the most unreserved and unguarded manner, the doctrine of election. I shall not be afraid to propound the great truth of the final perseverance of the saints; I shall not withhold that undoubted teaching of Scripture, the effectual calling of God's elect; I shall endeavour, as God shall help me, to keep back nothing from you who have become my flock. Seeing that many of you have now 'tasted that the Lord is gracious', we will endeavour to go through the whole system of the doctrines of grace, that saints may be edified and built up in their most holy faith."

The following Sabbath, the Pastor preached on "Human Inability", from our Lord's words, "No man can come to Me, except the Father which hath sent Me draw him." A little later, he discoursed upon "Human Responsibility", taking for his text another of Christ's most weighty sayings: "If I had not come and spoken unto them, they had not had sin: but now they have no cloke for their sin." Not long afterwards, he sought to set forth both sides of Divine truth in a sermon entitled, "Sovereign Grace and Man's Responsibility", in which he avoided the errors of Arminianism on the one hand, and those of Hyper-Calvinism on the other. In course of time, either at the Surrey Gardens or at New Park Street Chapel, Spurgeon had expounded all the doctrines of grace, and one result of that method of teaching the truth was thus described by him:

"Among the many candidates for baptism and church-membership who came forward every month, there were great numbers of young people, and others of riper years who had but recently found the Saviour; and I was delighted to hear them, one after another, not only express themselves clearly upon the great fundamental truth of justification by faith, but also give clear evidence that they were well instructed in the doctrines that cluster around the covenant of grace. I believe that one reason why our church has been, for these many years, so signally blessed of God, is that the great majority of those who have been added to our ranks have been well established in the old-fashioned faith of the Puritans and the Covenanters, and therefore have not been turned aside or drawn away from us. It used to be said, in those early days, that we were taking into the church 'a parcel of girls and boys'. I remember, long afterwards, at one of our great gatherings in the Tabernacle, reminding our friends of this con-temptuous remark, whereat they laughed, and then I added, 'I am happy to have around me, still, those very same girls and boys, they are a good deal older now, and many of *their* sons and daughters have followed their parents' example, while some even of the grandchildren of my early converts are already united with us.''']

*   *   *

So far as the general public was concerned, the Music Hall services were a great evangelistic campaign, in which "the slain of the Lord" were many. I determined that, whether my hearers would receive the gospel, or reject it, they should at least understand it; and therefore I preached it in plain, homely Saxon that a child could comprehend, and with all the earnestness of which I was capable. I recollect a friend saying to me, one Sabbath, as we went down the stairs from the hall, "There are eight thousand people this morning, who will be without excuse at the day of judgment"; and I hope that was the case many another time as the vast multitude dispersed from the Surrey Gardens. I did not please everybody even then; and some found fault who ought to have been my best friends. I recollect great complaint being made against my sermon on the words, "Compel them to come in," in which I was enabled to speak with much tenderness and compassion for souls. The violent, rigid school of Hyper-Calvinists said that the discourse was Arminian and unsound, but it was a small matter to me to be condemned by the judgment of men, for my Master set His seal very clearly upon that message. I think I never preached another sermon by which so many souls were won to God, as our church-meetings long continued to testify; and all over the world, wherever the printed discourse has been scattered, sinners have been saved through its instrumentality; and, therefore, if it be vile to exhort sinners to come to Christ, I purpose to be viler still. I am as firm a believer in the doctrines of grace as any man living, and a true Calvinist after the order of John Calvin himself; and probably I have read more of his works than any one of my accusers ever did; but if it be thought an evil thing to bid sinners "lay hold on eternal life", I will be yet more evil in this respect, and herein imitate not only Calvin, but also my Lord and His apostles, who, though they taught that salvation is of grace, and grace alone, feared not to speak to men as rational beings and responsible agents, and to bid them "strive to enter in at the strait gate", and "labour not for the meat which perisheth, but for that meat which endureth unto everlasting life."

Among the sermons preached in the Music Hall, another which was very greatly blessed was the one entitled, "Looking unto Jesus". It was often mentioned by converts who were brought to the Lord through hearing it delivered; and when it was published, and scattered abroad, I received many testimonies that the reading of it had been attended with a like unction from on high. This fact I do not wonder at, for it is but another proof of the Sovereignty of God, since the discourse is one of the most simple of the series, and would probably be overlooked by those who were seeking for anything original and striking. The Master is in the sermon; and, therefore, it has rejoiced the hearts of His people, when applied by the Holy Spirit. I value a discourse, not by the approbation of men, not by the ability manifest in it, but by the effect produced in comforting the saint, and awakening the sinner. The sermon on "The Shameful Sufferer" was the means of a great blessing to very many. Christ bleeding always makes the heart bleed, and His shame makes men ashamed of sin. Let but the Holy Spirit open the eyes of men to behold a sorrowing Saviour, and they will at once sorrow for sin.

There were many instances of remarkable conversions at the Music Hall; one especially was so singular that I have often related it as a proof that God sometimes guides His servants to say what they would themselves never have thought of uttering, in order that He may bless the hearer for whom the message is personally intended. While preaching in the hall, on one occasion, I deliberately pointed to a man in the midst of the crowd, and said, "There is a man sitting there, who is a shoemaker; he keeps his shop open on Sundays, it was open last Sabbath morning, he took ninepence, and there was fourpence profit out of it; his soul is sold to Satan for fourpence!" A city missionary, when going his rounds, met with this man, and seeing that he was reading one of my sermons, he asked the question, "Do you know Mr. Spurgeon?" "Yes," replied the man, "I have every reason to know him, I have been to hear him; and, under his preaching, by God's grace I have become a new creature in Christ Jesus. Shall I tell you how it happened? I went to the Music Hall, and took my seat in the middle of the place; Mr. Spurgeon looked at me as if he knew me, and in his sermon he pointed to me, and told the congregation that I was a shoemaker, and that I kept my shop open on Sundays; and I did, sir. I should not have minded that, but he also said that I took ninepence the Sunday before, and that there was fourpence profit out of it. I did take ninepence that day, and fourpence was just the profit, but how he should know that, I could not tell. Then it struck me that it was God who had spoken to my soul through him, so I shut up my shop the next Sunday. At first, I was afraid to go again to hear him, lest he should tell the people more about me, but afterwards I went, and the Lord met with me, and saved my soul."

I could tell as many as a dozen similar cases in which I pointed at somebody in the hall without having the slightest knowledge of the person, or any idea that what I said was right, except that I believed I was moved by the Spirit to say it; and so striking has been my description, that the persons have gone away, and said to their friends, "Come, see a man that told me all things that ever I did; beyond a doubt, he must have been sent of God to my soul, or else he could not have described me so exactly." And not only so, but I have known many instances in which the thoughts of men have been revealed from the pulpit. I have sometimes seen persons nudge their neighbours with their elbow, because they had got a smart hit, and they have been heard to say, when they were going out, "The preacher told us just what we said to one another when we went in at the door."

Several persons who joined the church at New Park Street traced their conversion to the ministry in the Surrey Gardens Music Hall, but they said it was not the preaching alone, but another agency co-operating with it that was the means of bringing them to decision. They were fresh from the country, and one of our friends, who is in Heaven now, met them at the gate, spoke to them, said he hoped they had enjoyed what they had heard, asked them if they were coming to the chapel in the evening, and told them he would be glad if they would be at his house to tea; they went, he had a word with them about the Master, and then brought them again to our service. The next Sunday the same thing occurred; and, at last, those whom the sermons had not much impressed, were brought to hear with other ears, till, through the good old man's persuasive words, and the good Lord's gracious work, they were converted to God.

While I was preaching at the Music Hall, an unknown censor, of great ability, used to send me a weekly list of my mispronunciations and other slips of speech. He never signed his name, and that was my only cause of complaint against him, for he left me with a debt which I could not discharge. With genial temper, and an evident desire to benefit me, he marked down most relentlessly everything which he supposed me to have said incorrectly. Concerning some of his criticisms, he was himself in error, but, for the most part, he was right, and his remarks enabled me to perceive many mistakes, and to avoid them in the future. I looked for his weekly memoranda with much interest, and I trust I am all the better for them. If I repeated a sentence which I had used two or three Sundays before, he would write, "See the same expression in such-and-such a sermon," mentioning the number and page. He remarked, on one occasion, that I too often quoted the line—

"Nothing in my hand I bring"—

and he added, "we are sufficiently informed of the vacuity of your hand." Possibly, some young men might have been discouraged, if not irritated, by such severe criticisms; but they would have been very foolish, for, in resenting such correction, they would have been throwing away a valuable aid to progress.

THE FAST-DAY SERVICE AT THE CRYSTAL PALACE.

During the time of our sojourn at the Surrey Gardens, it was my privilege to conduct one service which deserves special mention, for it was the occasion on which I addressed the largest congregation to which I ever preached in any building. This was on Wednesday, October 7, 1857, when 23,654 persons assembled in the Crystal Palace to join in the observance of the day appointed by proclamation "for a solemn fast, humiliation, and prayer before Almighty God: in order to obtain pardon of our sins, and for imploring His blessing and assistance on our arms for the restoration of tranquillity in India". About a month previously, in my sermon at the Music Hall on "India's Ills and England's Sorrows", I had referred at length to the Mutiny, and its terrible consequences to our fellow-countrymen and women in the East. The Fast-day had not been proclaimed, but when it was announced, I was glad to accept the offer of the Crystal Palace directors to hold a service in the centre transept of the building, and to make a collection on behalf of the national fund for the sufferers through the Mutiny.

The Lord set His seal upon the effort even before the great crowd gathered, though I did not know of that instance of blessing until long afterwards. It was arranged that I should use the Surrey Gardens pulpit, so, a day or two before preaching at the Palace, I went to decide where it should be fixed; and, in order to test the acoustic properties of the building, cried in a loud voice, "Behold the Lamb of God, which taketh away the sin of the world." In one of the galleries, a workman, who knew nothing of what was being done, heard the words, and they came like a message from Heaven to his soul. He was smitten with conviction on account of sin, put down his tools, went home, and there, after a season of spiritual struggling, found peace and life by beholding the Lamb of God. Years after, he told this story to one who visited him on his death-bed.

A complete record of the service is preserved in Nos. 154-5 of *The New Park Street Pulpit*, so I need not give details here, but simply mention that the text was, "Hear ye the rod, and who hath appointed it". The collection amounted to nearly £500, to which the Crystal Palace Company added £200, beside contributing £50 to the Tabernacle Building Fund, as I declined to accept any fee for preaching. It was a service that I was not likely ever to forget, and one result upon my physical frame was certainly very remarkable. I was not conscious, at the close of the service, of any extraordinary exhaustion, yet I must have been very weary, for after I went to sleep that Wednesday night, I did not wake again until the Friday morning. All through the Thursday, my dear wife came at intervals to look at me, and every time she found me sleeping peacefully, so she just let me slumber on until—

"Tired nature's sweet restorer, balmy sleep,"

had done its work. I was greatly surprised, on waking, to find that it was Friday morning; but it was the only time in my life that I had such an experience. Eternity alone will reveal the full results of the Fast-day service at the Crystal Palace.[1]

*   *   *

[1] The strain which this momentous gathering imposed upon Spurgeon is also illustrated by an incident that occurred at the beginning of the service, and which was later recalled by a hearer who sat close to Mrs. Spurgeon. For once Spurgeon's equilibrium was apparently unsettled by the sight of his wife who was near the pulpit and whose anxiety was clearly discernible to her husband. Summoning a stout, grey-haired deacon with his finger to the pulpit, the preacher gave a message to him which, after a pause as

[The last service at the Surrey Gardens was held on Lord's-day morning, December 11, 1859. Spurgeon preached, on that occasion, from Paul's farewell to the Ephesian elders: "Wherefore I take you to record this day, that I am pure from the blood of all men; for I have not shunned to declare unto you all the counsel of God." That discourse so well summarizes his three years' ministry in the Music Hall that an extract from it may be appropriately inserted here:

"If any of us would clear our conscience by delivering all the counsel of God, we must take care that we preach, in the first place, *the doctrines of the gospel*. We ought to declare that grand doctrine of the Father's love towards His people from before all worlds. His sovereign choice of them, His covenant purposes concerning them, and His immutable promises to them, must all be uttered with trumpet tongue. Coupled with this, the true evangelist must never fail to set forth the beauties of the person of Christ, the glory of His offices, the completeness of His work, and above all, the efficacy of His blood. Whatever we omit, this must be in the most forcible manner proclaimed again and again. That is no gospel which has not Christ in it; and the modern idea of preaching THE TRUTH instead of Christ, is a wicked device of Satan. Nor is this all, for as there are three Persons in the Godhead, we must be careful that They all have due honour in our ministry. The Holy Spirit's work in regeneration, in sanctification, and in preservation, must be always magnified from our pulpit. Without His power, our ministry is a dead letter, and we cannot expect His arm to be made bare unless we honour Him day by day.

Upon all these matters we are agreed, and I therefore turn to points upon which there is more dispute, and consequently more need of honest avowal, because more temptation to concealment. To proceed then: I question whether we have preached all the counsel of God, unless predestination, with all its solemnity and sureness, be continually declared—unless election be boldly and nakedly taught as being one of the truths revealed of God. It is the minister's duty, beginning from the fountain-head, to trace all the other streams; dwelling on effectual calling, maintaining justification by faith, insisting upon the certain perseverance of the believer, and delighting to proclaim that gracious covenant in which all these things are

---

he limped to Mrs. Spurgeon's seat, was conveyed to her: "Mr. Spurgeon says, please will you change your seat so that he will not be able to see you; it makes him nervous." Mrs. Spurgeon moved immediately to another seat not visible from the preacher's position. (Pike, Vol. II, p. 275).—P.

contained, and which is sure to all the chosen, blood-bought seed. There is a tendency in this age to throw doctrinal truth into the shade. Too many preachers are offended with that stern truth which the Covenanters held, and to which the Puritans testified in the midst of a licentious age. We are told that the times have changed, that we are to modify these old (so-called) Calvinistic doctrines, and bring them down to the tone of the times; that, in fact, they need dilution, that men have become so intelligent that we must pare off the angles of our religion, and make the square into a circle by rounding off the most prominent edges. Any man who does this, so far as my judgment goes, does not declare all the counsel of God. The faithful minister must be plain, simple, pointed, with regard to these doctrines. There must be no dispute about whether he believes them or not. He must so preach them that his hearers will know whether he preaches a scheme of free-will, or a covenant of grace—whether he teaches salvation by works, or salvation by the power and grace of God.

But, beloved, a man might preach all these doctrines to the full, and yet not declare all the counsel of God. It is not enough to preach doctrine; we must preach *duty*, we must faithfully and firmly insist upon *practice*. So long as you will preach nothing but bare doctrine, there is a certain class of men, of perverted intellect, who will admire you; but once begin to preach responsibility—say outright, once for all, that if the sinner perish, it is his own fault, that if any man sinks to hell, his damnation will lie at his own door, and at once there is a cry of 'Inconsistency; how can these two things stand together?' Even good Christian men are found who cannot endure the whole truth, and who will oppose the servant of the Lord who will not be content with a fragment, but will honestly present the whole gospel of Christ. This is one of the troubles that the faithful minister has to endure; but he is not faithful to God—I say it solemnly—I do not believe that any man is even faithful to his own conscience, who can preach simply the doctrine of Sovereignty, and neglect to insist upon the doctrine of responsibility. I do assuredly believe that every man who sinks into hell shall have himself alone to curse for it. The apostle Paul knew how to dare public opinion, and on one hand to preach the duty of man, and on the other the Sovereignty of God. I would borrow the wings of an eagle, and fly to the utmost height of high doctrine when I am preaching Divine Sovereignty. God hath absolute and unlimited power over men to do with them as He pleases, even as the potter doeth with the clay. Let not the creature question the Creator, for He hath given no account of His matters. But when I preach concerning man, and look at the other aspect of truth, I dive to the utmost depth.

I am, if you will so call me, a low doctrine man in that, for as an honest messenger of Christ I must use His own language, and cry, 'He that believeth not is condemned already, because he hath not believed in the Name of the only begotten Son of God.'

Moreover, if a man would declare all the counsel of God, and not shun to do so, he must be very outspoken concerning the crying sins of the times. The honest minister does not merely condemn sin in the mass, he singles out separate sins in his hearers; and without drawing the bow at a venture, he puts an arrow on the string, and the Holy Spirit sends it right home to the individual conscience. He who is true to his God looks to his congregation as separate individuals; and he endeavours to adapt his discourse to men's consciences, so that they will perceive he speaks of them. If there be a vice that you should shun, if there be an error that you should avoid, if there be a duty that you ought to fulfil, if all these things be not mentioned in the discourses from the pulpit, the minister has shunned to declare all the counsel of God. If there be one sin that is rife in the neighbourhood, and especially in the congregation, should the minister avoid that particular vice in order to avoid offending you, he has been untrue to his calling, dishonest to his God.

But, then, let me remark further, the true minister of Christ feels impelled to preach the whole truth, because it and it alone can meet the wants of man. The believer in Christ, if he is to be kept pure, simple, holy, charitable, Christ-like, is only to be kept so by the preaching of the whole truth as it is in Jesus. And as for the salvation of sinners, ah! my hearers, we can never expect God to bless our ministry to the conversion of sinners, unless we preach the gospel as a whole. Let me get but one part of the truth, and always dwell upon it, to the exclusion of every other, and I cannot expect my Master's blessing; but if I preach as He would have me preach, He will certainly own the Word; He will never leave it without His own living witness. But let me imagine that I can improve the gospel, that I can make it consistent, that I can dress it up and make it look finer, I shall find that my Master has departed, and that 'Ichabod' is written on the walls of the sanctuary. How many there are kept in bondage through neglect of gospel invitations! They go up to the house of God, longing to be saved, and there is nothing but predestination for them. On the other hand, what multitudes are kept in darkness through practical preaching! It is, 'Do! Do! Do!' and nothing but 'Do!' and the poor soul comes away, and says, 'Of what use is that command to me? I can do nothing. Oh, that I had the way of salvation pointed out as available for me!'

I must now address to you A VERY FEW EARNEST, SINCERE, AND AFFECTIONATE WORDS BY WAY OF FAREWELL. I wish not to say anything in self-commendation; I will not be my own witness as to my faithfulness, but I appeal to you, I take you to witness this day, that 'I have not shunned to declare unto you all the counsel of God.' Often have I come into this pulpit in great weakness, and I have far more often gone away in great sorrow, because I have not preached to you as earnestly as I desired. I confess to many errors and failings, and more especially to a want of earnestness when engaged in prayer for your souls; but there is one charge of which my conscience acquits me this morning, and I think you will acquit me too, 'for I have not shunned to declare unto you all the counsel of God.' If in anything I have erred, it has been an error of judgment. I may have been mistaken; but, so far as I have learned the truth, I can say that no fear of public opinion, nor of private opinion, has ever turned me aside from that which I hold to be the truth of my Lord and Master. I have preached to you the precious things of the gospel. I have endeavoured, to the utmost of my ability, to preach grace in all its fulness, I know the preciousness of that doctrine in my own experience; God forbid that I should preach any other! If we are not saved by grace, we can never be saved at all. If, from first to last, the work of salvation be not in God's hands, none of us can ever see His face with acceptance. I preach this doctrine, not from choice, but from absolute necessity, for if this doctrine be not true, then are we lost souls; your faith is vain, our preaching is vain, and we are still in our sins, and there we must continue to the end. But, on the other hand, I can also say, I have not shunned to exhort, to invite, to entreat; I have bidden the sinner come to Christ. I have been urged not to do so, but I could not resist it. With bowels yearning over perishing souls, I could not conclude without crying, 'Come to Jesus, sinner, come.' With eyes weeping for sinners, I am compelled to bid them to come to Jesus. It is not possible for me to dwell upon doctrine without invitation. If you come not to Christ, it is not for want of calling, or because I have not wept over your sins, and travailed in birth for the souls of men. The one thing I have to ask of you is this—Bear me witness, my hearers, bear me witness that, in this respect, I am pure from the blood of all men, for I have preached all that I know of the whole counsel of God. Have I known a single sin which I have not rebuked? Has there been a doctrine that I have believed which I have kept back? Has there been a part of the Word, doctrinal or experimental, which I have wilfully concealed? I am very far from perfect, again with weeping I confess my unworthiness, I have not served God as I ought to have done, I have not been so earnest with you as I could have desired to be. Now that my three years' ministry here is over, I could wish that I might begin again, that I might fall on my knees before you, and beseech you to regard the things that make for your peace; but here, again, I do repeat it, that while as to earnestness I plead guilty, yet as to truth and honesty I can challenge the bar of God, I can challenge the elect angels, I can call you all to witness, that I have not shunned to declare unto you all the counsel of God.

In a little time, some of you may be frequenting places where the gospel is not preached, you may embrace another and a false gospel; I only ask this thing of you—Bear me witness that it was not my fault, that I have been faithful, and have not shunned to declare unto you all the counsel of God. Possibly, some here, who have been restrained from evil by the fact of having attended a place of worship, seeing the chosen minister has gone, may not go anywhere else afterwards. You may become careless. Perhaps, next Sabbath-day you may be at home, lolling about, and wasting the day; but there is one thing I should like to say before you make up your mind not to attend the house of God again—Bear me witness that I have been faithful with you. It may be that some here, who have professedly run well for a time while they have been hearing the Word, may go back; some of you may go right into the world again, you may become drunkards, swearers, and the like. God forbid that it should be so! But I charge you, if you plunge into sin, do at least say this one thing for him who desired nothing so much as to see you saved, say I have been honest to you; that I have not shunned to declare unto you all the counsel of God. O my hearers, some of you in a little time will be on your dying beds! When your pulse is feeble, when the terrors of grim death are round about you, if you are still unconverted to Christ, there is one thing I shall want you to add to your last will and testament, it is this—the exclusion of the poor minister, who stands before you this day, from any share in that desperate folly of yours which has led you to neglect your own soul. Have I not implored you to repent? Have I not bidden you look to Christ ere death surprises you? Have I not exhorted you, my hearers, to lay hold upon the hope set before you in the gospel? O sinner, when thou art wading through the black river, cast back no taunt on me as though I was thy murderer, for in this thing I can say, 'I wash my hands in innocency; I am clear of thy blood.' But the day is coming when we shall all meet again; this great assembly shall be merged into a greater one, as the drop loses itself in the ocean; and, in that day, if I have not warned you, if I have been an unfaithful watchman, your blood will be required at my hands; if I have not preached Christ to you, and bidden you flee to Him for refuge, then, though you perish, your soul shall be required of me. I beseech you, if you laugh at me, if you reject my message, if you despise Christ, if you hate His gospel, if you will be damned, yet at least give me an acquittal of your blood. I see some before me who do not often hear me; and yet I can say concerning them that they have been the subject of my private prayers; and often, too, of my tears, when I have seen them going on in their iniquities. Well, I do ask this one thing, and as honest men you cannot deny it me; if you will have your sins, if you will be lost, if you will not come to Christ, at least, amid the thunders of the last great day, acquit me of having helped to destroy your souls.

What can I say more? How shall I plead with you? Had I an angel's tongue, and the heart of the Saviour, then would I plead; but I cannot say more than I have often done. In God's name, I beseech you, flee to Christ for refuge. If all hath not sufficed before, let this suffice thee now. Come, guilty soul, and flee away to Him whose wide-open arms are willing to receive every soul that fleeth to Him in penitence and faith. In a little time, the preacher himself will lie stretched upon his bed. A few more days of solemn meeting, a few more sermons, a few more prayers, and I think I see myself in yon upper chamber, with friends watching around me. He who has preached to thousands now needs consolation for himself; he who has cheered many in the article of death is now passing through the river himself. My hearers, shall there be any of you, whom I shall see upon my death-bed, who shall charge me with being unfaithful? Shall these eyes be haunted with the visions of men whom I have amused, and interested, but into whose hearts I have never sought to convey the truth? Shall I lie there, and shall these mighty congregations pass in dreary panorama before me; and as they subside before my eyes, one after the other, shall each one curse me as being unfaithful? God forbid! I trust you will do me this favour that, when I lie a-dying, you will allow that I am clear of the blood of all men, and have not shunned to declare unto you all the counsel of God. Thunders such as have never been heard before must roll over this poor head, and lightnings more terrific than have ever scathed the fiend shall blast this heart, if I have been unfaithful to you. My position—if I had but once preached the Word to these crowds, not to speak of many hundreds of times—my position were the most awful in the whole universe if I were unfaithful. Oh, may God avert that worst of ills—unfaithfulness—from my head! Now, as here I stand, I make this my last appeal: 'I pray you, in Christ's stead, be ye reconciled to God.' But if ye will not be, I ask you this single favour— and I think you will not deny it me—take the blame of your own ruin, for I am pure from the blood of all men, since I have not shunned to declare unto you all the counsel of God."

On page 527, Spurgeon states that, after the preaching at the Surrey Music Hall was discontinued, "both morally and financially it sank hopelessly." A remarkable confirmation of this assertion came to hand while this volume was in course of preparation. It was contained in a letter written by a Christian man who was baptized in the Metropolitan Tabernacle, in November, 1897, but who had long before been employed at the hall under the circumstances which he describes. In his communication, the names of all the persons mentioned are given in full; he writes:

"Having spent my last sovereign of compensation for the loss of the sight of my right eye while in the 'nigger' business, I was given to understand that Mr. ———, the manager of the Alhambra, Leicester Square, was going to re-open the Music Hall as a theatre with a capital of £63,000; no expense was to be spared to make the venture a brilliant financial speculation. The opera (a burlesque) was entitled *Eurydice*, and was a shameful travesty on Holy Writ, some of the characters portrayed lost souls in hell. Knowing the principal manager, Mr. ———, at Norwood, I applied to him for something to do; he engaged me, and suggested that I should go, under ———, the decorator and property-master, at sixpence an hour, and two shillings for the evening, attending to the female Blondin. When the rehearsals were on, the performers were constantly enquiring, 'What will Spurgeon think about it? What will Spurgeon say about it? What will Spurgeon do about it?' We had not long to wait before we heard what Mr. Spurgeon was doing; it came in this wise. On learning that the tenants of the houses overlooking the Gardens were nearly all members of Mr. Spurgeon's flock, and that they were going to petition against what they considered an intolerable nuisance, Mr. ——— tried to mollify them by sending free passes of admission for themselves and their lodgers. He received the passes back by post, with tracts and letters urging him not to attempt to wage war against Christ; the writers, in many instances, adding these significant words, '*We are praying for you.*' This all leaked out through the manager's confidants when drinking at the theatre bars.

Well, from the opening, everything connected with the venture of converting that place from a temporary hospital to a theatre and pleasure gardens, went wrong. The performers played to paper (admission free by ticket); the money lavished on the speculation to reproduce the gods and goddesses of heathen mythology went out of Mr. ———'s pocket, never to be returned, and failure upon failure came thick and fast. The very elements assisted in keeping the people away, the violent thunderstorms (almost phenomenal while they lasted) caused the visitors to exclaim, 'There is a judgment on this place; it will never pay,' while every fresh financial disaster was met by the usual cynical phrase, '*They're praying again*'—meaning Mr. Spurgeon and his congregation. As I write this true account, it seems but last week that it all happened. Poor ———, who died of a broken heart, always put his failure down to the prayers of C. H. Spurgeon and his flock. We rallied round him, and got what scenery, etc., we could away from the Surrey Gardens, and tried the Satanic venture again at the Royal Amphitheatre, Holborn, but with the same result, nothing but disaster.

Perhaps you wonder why I never mentioned all this to you before; it was because I had gone back to the 'nigger' business, and being a servant of the devil, I did not wish to furnish you with anything in the shape of testimony which would only make you more importunate in urging me to come to the Saviour. But now, being a child of God, through the blood of Jesus, I do what I can to show forth His power over sin and Satan."

After this chapter was in the hands of the printer, the following interesting letter was received. The writer of it was evidently a most appreciative member of the great congregations that assembled at the Music Hall, and it contains such a graphic description of the Surrey Gardens services, that a place is gladly found for it here, with heartiest thanks to the unknown correspondent:

"Dear Mrs. Spurgeon,

As I believe there will shortly be issued a second volume of Mr. Spurgeon's *Autobiography*, I thought I would venture to send you some of the impressions I had concerning him at the Music Hall, Royal Surrey Gardens. I have always been of opinion that his ministry there was the most wonderful and the most romantic that ever fell to the lot of any Christian minister. The vast concourse of people, the almost-dramatic excitement experienced by them when expecting to see the youthful preacher appear, the sudden hush and impressive silence of the great throng (composed of all classes, from the aristocracy to the very humblest) as he was seen to approach the pulpit stairs, the solemn and pale face contrasting with the black hair, and the beautiful voice that charmed every ear as he said, 'Let us commence the worship of God by prayer'—all this, though it occurred forty years ago, is as vivid in my recollection as if it had only happened recently. I am sorry that I cannot recall *the first time* I heard Mr. Spurgeon. I know I had done so before a certain Sunday, in April, 1857, when my father came home full of admiration for the sermon entitled, 'David's Dying Prayer', which, for its matchless preface, and the stirring character of the whole discourse, must have been one of the most notable ever delivered. But the first sermon of which I have a distinct recollection is No. 133, 'Heavenly Rest', preached in the following month. How well I remember enjoying that sermon, and his reference to the 'Stitch, stitch', of the poor needlewoman! I believe Mr. John Ruskin was present on that occasion.

I attended a Sunday-school in Camberwell, but I had such a passionate enthusiasm for C. H. Spurgeon that I obtained permission to leave a few minutes after ten, which enabled me to reach the Gardens in time for service. I only missed one Sunday morning, and that was through ill-health. I remember how solemn was the sermon entitled, 'The Warning Neglected', preached November 29; and how happy he was on December 20, when he preached on 'The First Christmas Carol', and wound up his sermon by wishing all his hearers the happiest Christmas they had ever had in their lives. It made me wonder whether the assembled thousands would not verbally reciprocate the kind wish. Nor can I ever forget the discourse, 'What have I done?' delivered on the last Sabbath of the year 1857. With what burning eloquence he condemned the sin of men who were leading others astray, and warned them that they would have a double hell unless they repented. He seemed to speak like one of the old prophets or apostles, and several persons in the galleries, and other parts of the building where they were not able to see him when seated, rose to look at the preacher who was uttering such wondrous words. In the sermon about Felix trembling, Mr. Spurgeon made some remarks about the workings of the Holy Spirit which received strong censure from a preacher at Kennington. He said that, if the Holy Spirit acted in the way Mr. S. said He did, he would shut up his Bible, and never read it again. I know, however, that, in after years, the same minister had the highest opinion of C. H. S., just as a good many others subsequently gravitated towards him whom they had originally opposed.

During the months of February and March, 1858, I thought he seemed sad. It was about this time that he told his audience that he looked upon them as a fixed congregation, and that he would shape his discourses accordingly. Still, he seemed troubled; and, one Sunday morning, he commenced his sermon by saying that the prophets in the olden times spoke of the message they had to deliver as 'the burden of the Lord'; and I thought to myself, 'You seem to have the burden of the Lord resting upon you also.' I shall never forget the way in which, about this period, he quoted those words of our Lord, 'My God, My God, why hast Thou forsaken Me?' The piercing, wailing, almost shrieking cry, and the sorrowful tones of his voice, must have gone to many another heart as they did to mine. Very enjoyable was it to notice how grateful Mr. Spurgeon was for having escaped a serious accident, mentioned in the discourse entitled, 'Providence'. It was in April, 1858, that he preached from John xvii. 24; and, coming from the hall, I told a friend my opinion of the sermon; and an old man, a stranger to me, hearing what I said, remarked, 'Ah, my lad! does it not make one wish to go to Heaven?' I was very much impressed by the discourse on 'The Wicked Man's Life, Funeral, and Epitaph'; there was something specially solemn about it. In the introduction, the preacher spoke of children playing among the graves in a churchyard, and recalled some of his early memories of Stambourne. But how happy he was when he preached, in the month of August, from that text, 'As thy days, so shall thy strength be.' He had been unwell a few days previously, and I well remember two lines of a hymn we sang then—

> ' 'Tis He that heals thy sicknesses,
>   And makes thee young again.'

In September, the sermon entitled, 'His Name—Wonderful!' was listened to by a lady-relative of mine, who, for years after, whenever I saw her, always referred to it in terms of admiration; and the following month, as you are aware, Mr. Spurgeon was laid aside by severe suffering, which necessitated his being absent from the Music Hall for three Sundays. I recollect his coming back, the first Sabbath after his illness, and being almost carried up the pulpit stairs; the preliminary part of the service was conducted very efficiently by Mr. Probert, of Bristol. The sermon about Samson, delivered in November, I did not hear, as I was unwell; and you may smile when I tell you how I endeavoured to sing to myself, during the Sunday morning, such hymns as 'Grace, 'tis a charming sound', and 'Blow ye the trumpet, blow'—both being great favourites with C. H. S.

On December 19, 1858, the congregation at the Surrey Gardens suddenly dwindled down to very small dimensions; the weather was not bad, but the platform was only half-full, there was scarcely anyone in the third gallery, and the area was only three-parts filled. Mr. Spurgeon preached a delightful discourse on God's love, and I so wondered what effect the reduced audience would have on his mind that I went to New Park Street in the evening. He certainly appeared sad, but his spirits rose as he went on with his sermon. I was rather anxious, during the week, as to how the Music Hall would look on the following Sabbath; and when that day came, and with it rain, I was still more concerned. However, my sister and I walked to the service all in the wet, and I remember that she said, 'Well, there will be two of us present, at any rate.' But I had been only meeting trouble half-way, for, on arriving, I found that the congregation was much larger than on the previous Sunday, and, in a short time, it reverted to its original dimensions. Early in the New Year (1859), it was rumoured that Mr. Spurgeon was going to America, and he confirmed the truth of the report by telling his hearers that he might be away for some time. However, we know he never went there. About this time, he preached a very able sermon, which was entitled, 'Reform', parts of which were aimed at some of the amusements of the people, such as dancing and the theatre. Were any in his audience offended, I wonder?

A month or two later, during the singing of a hymn, he suddenly stopped, and said, 'A little while ago, when I was worshipping in a Jewish synagogue, I kept on my hat in accordance with the custom of the friends meeting there; I notice two gentlemen, probably of the Jewish persuasion, who have their hats on; will they kindly take them off as we do when we meet for worship?' I could not see the parties referred to, but, doubtless, they did as the preacher requested, for, after a moment's pause, the service was resumed. Not many could have conveyed a reproof in such a kind manner to the irreverent individuals who, possibly out of bravado, had kept on their hats after the service had commenced.

On the first Sabbath in July, Mr. Spurgeon delivered a very pathetic sermon from the text, 'Kiss the Son, lest He be angry,' &c. On the following Sunday afternoon, he preached on Clapham Common, under a tree where a man had been killed by lightning a fortnight previously. I shall never forget the sermon on July 17, 1859, 'The Story of God's Mighty Acts'. I believe the Music Hall authorities had proposed to open the place for concerts on Sunday evening, but Mr. S.'s threat to leave prevented them doing so. How he revelled in preaching that morning! It was very hot, and he kept on wiping the perspiration from his forehead; but his discomfort did not affect his discourse, his words flowed on like a torrent of sacred eloquence.

As you are aware, in August was laid the foundation stone of the Tabernacle, the ruins of which can now be regarded with feelings similar to those experienced by the old Jew when he thought of the destruction of the first Temple, for the new Tabernacle can never be quite the same as the old one. I was present at the last service held in the Music Hall, on December 11, 1859. It was very foggy, but the place was crowded, as much indeed as it could be. I had a front seat in the second gallery, and therefore enjoyed a splendid view of the people. Mr. S. preached an earnest sermon on declaring the whole counsel of God. There is always something sad about last things; and, as I came away, I felt that one of the happiest experiences of my youth belonged to the past. So also—in my opinion—passed away the most romantic stage even in Mr. Spurgeon's wonderful life.

The other day, I stood opposite what used to be the entrance to the old Gardens. I could not help thinking of more than forty years since, when the carriages, like a stream, used to roll up and down the neighbourhood with their fashionable occupants, and the thousands of people coming away from the hall when the service was over; also of the number who used to wait to see the young minister take his departure; and when he was seen to approach, with head uncovered, a section of the crowd, kindly and respectfully, would call out, 'Put on your hat, sir; put on your hat, sir.' All is now changed; and where there was once life, excitement, and curiosity, nothing but dulness, and apathy, and lifelessness reign. Were not C. H. Spurgeon in his *youth*, and W. E. Gladstone in his *old age*, the two most wonderful phenomena of the nineteenth century? Both are gone; but I shall always count it a great privilege, as well as a high honour, to have lived under the influence of those good and noble men."

*   *   *

The following testimony from the lips of the great preacher in a sermon on John xiv. 16 at the Metropolitan Tabernacle on October 6th, 1872 is a striking summary of the main lesson to be found in those "early years" and provides a fitting conclusion to this volume:

"At this moment the only vindication of our existence is the presence and work of the Paraclete among us. Is He still working and witnessing for Christ? I fear He is not in some churches, but *here* we behold Him. Look at His workings in this place. Nearly twenty years ago our ministry commenced in this city, under much opposition and hostile criticism, the preacher being condemned on all hands as vulgar, unlearned, and, in fact, a nine days' wonder. Jesus Christ was preached by us in simpler language than men had been accustomed to hear, and every one of our sermons was full of the old-fashioned gospel. Many other pulpits were intellectual, but we were Puritanical. Rhetorical essays were the wares retailed by most of the preachers, but we gave the people the gospel, we brought out before the world the old Reformers' doctrines, Calvinistic truth, Augustinian teaching, and Pauline dogma. We were not ashamed to be the 'echo of an exploded evangelism', as some wiseacre called us. We preached Christ and Him crucified, and by the space of these twenty years have we ever lacked a congregation? When has not this vast hall been thronged? Have we ever lacked conversions? Has a Sabbath passed over us without them? Has not the history of this church from its littleness in Park Street until now been a march of triumph, with the hearts and souls of men as the spoil of the war, of which the standard has been Christ crucified? And it is so everywhere. Only let men come back to the gospel and preach it ardently, not with comeliness of words and affectation of polished speech, but as a burning heart compels them, and as the Spirit of God teaches them to speak it; then will great signs and wonders be seen. We must have signs following, we cannot answer the world else. Let them sneer, let them rave, let them curse, let them lie, God will answer them. It is ours in the power of the Spirit of God to keep on preaching Christ and glorifying the Saviour."

[APPENDIX]

DECLARATION OF FAITH AND PRACTICE OF THE
NEW PARK STREET CONGREGATION

This was drawn up at the time of Dr. John
Gill's ministry when the church met in Carter
Lane. It is not known when the declaration
passed out of use but its theology was clearly
accepted by Spurgeon and taught to the church
in his day. See above pages 397–399.

DECLARATION

OF THE

Faith and *Practice* of the Church of CHRIST, in *Carter-lane Southwark*, under the Pastoral Care of Dr. *John Gill*;

Read and assented to, at the Admission of MEMBERS

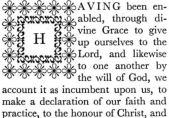

H AVING been enabled, through divine Grace to give up ourselves to the Lord, and likewise to one another by the will of God, we account it as incumbent upon us, to make a declaration of our faith and practice, to the honour of Christ, and the glory of his Name; knowing, that as *with the heart man believeth unto righteousness*, so *with the mouth confession is made unto salvation;* which declaration is as follows, viz.

I. We believe, That the Scriptures of the old and new Testament, are the word of God, and the only rule of faith and practice.

II. We believe, That there is but one only living and true God; that there are three persons in the Godhead, the Father, the Son, and the Holy Ghost, who are equal in nature, power, and glory; and that the Son and the Holy Ghost are as truly and properly God as the Father. These three divine persons are distinguished from each other by peculiar relative properties. The distinguishing character and relative property of the first person is *begetting*; he has begotten a Son of the same nature with him, and who is the express image of his person; and therefore is with great propriety called *the Father*. The distinguishing character and relative property of the second person is that he is *begotten*, and he is called the only begotten of the Father, and his own proper Son; not a Son by creation as angels and men are, nor by adoption as saints are, nor by office

as civil magistrates are, but by nature, by the Father's eternal generation of him in the divine nature; and therefore he is truly called the Son. The distinguishing character and relative property of the third person is to be *breathed* by the Father and the Son, and to proceed from both, and is very properly called the *Spirit* or Breath of both. These three distinct divine persons, we profess to reverence, serve and worship as the one true God.

III. We believe, That before the world began, God did elect a certain number of men unto everlasting salvation; whom he did predestinate to the adoption of children by Jesus Christ of his own free grace, and according to the good pleasure of his will; and that in pursuance of this gracious design, he did contrive and make a covenant of grace and peace with his Son Jesus Christ, on the behalf of those persons; wherein a Saviour was appointed, and all spiritual blessings provided for them; as also that their persons, with all their grace and glory, were put into the hands of Christ, and made his care and charge.

IV. We believe, That God created the first man *Adam*, after his image, and in his likeness, an upright, holy, and innocent creature, capable of serving and glorifying him, but he sinning, all his posterity sinned in him, and came short of the glory of God; the guilt of whose sin is imputed; and a corrupt nature derived to all his offspring descending from him by ordinary and natural generation: that they are by their first birth carnal and unclean; averse to all that is good, uncapable of doing any, and prone to every sin; and are also by nature children of wrath and under a sentence of condemnation; and so are subject, not only to a corporal death, and involved in a moral one, commonly called spiritual, but are also liable to an eternal death, as considered in the first *Adam*, fallen and sinners; from all which there is no deliverance, but by Christ the second *Adam*.

V. We believe, That the Lord Jesus Christ, being set up from everlasting as the mediator of the covenant, and he having engaged to be the surety of his people, did in the fulness of time really assume human nature, and not before neither in whole nor in part; his human soul being a creature, existed not from eternity, but was created and formed in his body by him that formed the spirit of man within him, when that was conceived in the womb of the virgin; and so his human nature consists of a true body and a reasonable soul, both which, together, and at once the Son of God assumed into union with his divine person, when made of a woman and not before, in which nature he really suffered and died as the substitute of his people, in their room and stead; whereby he made all that satisfaction for their sins which the law and justice of God could require, as well as made way for all those blessings which are needful for them both for time and eternity.

VI. We believe, That the eternal Redemption which Christ has obtained by the shedding of his blood is special and particular, that is to say, that it was only intentionally designed for the Elect of God, and Sheep of Christ, who only share the special and peculiar blessings of it.

VII. We believe, That the Justification of God's Elect is only by the righteousness of Christ imputed to them, without the consideration of any works of righteousness done by them; and that the full and free par-

don of all their sins and transgressions, past, present and to come, is only through the blood of Christ according to the riches of his grace.

VIII. We believe, That the work of regeneration, conversion, sanctification and faith is not an act of man's free will and power, but of the mighty, efficacious and irresistible grace of God.

IX. We believe, That all those who are chosen by the Father, redeemed by the Son, and sanctified by the Spirit, shall certainly and finally persevere, so that not one of them shall ever perish but shall have everlasting life.

X. We believe, That there shall be a Resurrection of the dead, both of the just and the unjust; and that Christ will come a second time to judge both quick and dead; when he will take vengeance on the wicked, and introduce his own people into his kingdom and glory, where they shall be for ever with him.

XI. We believe, That Baptism and the Lord's Supper are ordinances of Christ, to be continued until his second coming; and that the former is absolutely requisite to the latter; that is to say, that those only are to be admitted into the communion of the church, and to participate of all ordinances in it, who upon profession of their faith, have been baptized by immersion, in the name of the Father, and of the Son, and of the Holy Ghost.

XII. We also believe, That singing of Psalms, Hymns and Spiritual Songs vocally is an ordinance of the gospel to be performed by believers, but that as to time place and manner everyone ought to be left to their liberty in using it.

Now all and each of these doctrines and ordinances we look upon ourselves under the greatest obligation to embrace, maintain and defend; believing it to be our duty to stand fast in one spirit, with one mind, striving together for the faith of the Gospel.

And whereas we are very sensible that our conversation, both in the world and the church, ought to be as becometh the gospel of Christ, we judge it our incumbent duty, to walk in wisdom toward them that are without, to exercise a conscience void of offence toward God and men, by living soberly, righteously and godly in this present world.

And as to our regards to each other in our church communion, we esteem it our duty to walk with each other in all humility and brotherly love; to watch over each other's conversation; to stir up one another to love and good works; not forsaking the assembling of ourselves together, as we have opportunity, to worship God according to his revealed will; and when the case requires, to warn, rebuke and admonish one another, according to the rules of the Gospel.

Moreover, we think ourselves obliged to sympathize with each other in all conditions, both inward and outward, which God, in his providence, may bring us into; as also to bear with one another's weaknesses, failings and infirmities; and particularly to pray for one another and that the Gospel, and the ordinances thereof, might be blessed to the edification and comfort of each other's souls, and for the gathering in of others to Christ, besides those who are already gathered.

All which duties we desire to be sound in the performance of, through the gracious assistance of the Holy Spirit; whilst we both admire and adore the grace which has given us a place and a name in God's house, better than that of sons and daughters. Isa. 56. 5.

INDEX

Some Other Banner of Truth Trust Titles

The Forgotten Spurgeon

Iain Murray

This book traces the main lines of Spurgeon's spiritual thought in connection with the three great controversies in his ministry – his stand against the diluted Gospel fashionable in the London to which the young preacher came in the 1850's; the famous 'Baptismal Regeneration' debate of 1864; and the lacerating Downgrade controversy of 1887–1892 when Spurgeon sought to awaken Christians to the danger of the Church 'being buried beneath the boiling mud-showers of modern heresy'.

'I am simply thrilled with *The Forgotten Spurgeon*. I think that the emphasis which it brings out is so badly needed today. We have lost all sense of a true and genuine Calvinism in our preaching and for that matter, preaching seems to have lapsed badly. We need to pray that God will raise up men who will preach the sovereign grace of God without fear and without seeking the favour of men, and who will bring forth the grand particularities of the Reformed faith as Spurgeon did so well.'   E. J. Young

Paperback, 272 pp, illus, 40p

An All-Round Ministry

C. H. Spurgeon

In his day Spurgeon was an inspiration to many of his colleagues in
the ministry and through his writings he continues to challenge and
stimulate. This work contains twelve addresses delivered to his
annual ministers' conference. In lucid language enlivened by delightful illustrations and irrepressible humour he supplies exposition,
exhortation, advice and prophetic warning for the greater efficiency
of the Gospel ministry.

'This is a deeply moving book. Spurgeon loved nothing more than
the fraternity of ministers of the Pastors' College he himself had
founded. For more than a quarter of a century he opened his heart
to these men on deep and burning issues. And Spurgeon had a
largeness of heart, a greatness of mind and a balance of truth as
none other had in his day.'

Stanley J. Voke, *Crusade*

'No mincing matters for Spurgeon! These twelve addresses originally delivered to his annual conference of ministers are all gusto and
red-blooded conviction. They are a tonic to any minister who has
begun to doubt his calling or to fear his flock.'

John C. King, *TSF Bulletin*

Paperback, 402 pages, 55p

The Metropolitan Tabernacle Pulpit

C. H. Spurgeon

Spurgeon's sermons provide the most valuable source of material upon the Bible ever gathered into one set. To maintain his ministry for more than thirty years, Spurgeon went deep into the finest expository and devotional works of the whole Christian era – having some 12,000 volumes in his own library. Today the man who does not himself have the resources to possess or the opportunity to read such a wealth of literature, will find its riches ready to hand in the *Metropolitan Tabernacle Pulpit.*

While each volume is complete in itself the purchaser who builds up the whole series will come to have what amounts to a commentary on the whole Bible. By use of the *Textual Index to Spurgeon's Sermons* the possessor of the series has immediate access to the finest pulpit exposition on a very large amount of Scripture. This *Textual Index* is given freely on request with an order for two or more volumes.

Volumes 26 to 37 (1880–1891), approx. 700 pages per volume, £1.50 each.
Volumes 32 to 37 are also available in leather binding.

For free illustrated catalogue write to

THE BANNER OF TRUTH TRUST
3 Murrayfield Road, Edinburgh EH12 6 EL
78b Chiltern Street, London WIM IPS
P.O. Box 652, Carlisle, Pa 17013, U.S.A.

THE OLD CONDUCTOR.